Florida's Politics and Government

Florida's Politics and Government

Second Edition

Manning J. Dauer
General Editor

University Presses of Florida
University of Florida Press
Gainesville

Library of Congress Cataloging in Publication Data

Main entry under title:

Florida's politics and government.

"A University of Florida book."
Includes index.
1. Florida—Politics and government—1951 – .
I. Dauer, Manning Julian, 1909– .
JK4416.F59 1984 320.9759 84–7303
ISBN 0–8130–0797–6

UNIVERSITY PRESSES OF FLORIDA is the central agency for scholarly publishing of the State of Florida's university system, producing books selected for publication by the faculty editorial committees of Florida's nine public universities: Florida A&M University (Tallahassee), Florida Atlantic University (Boca Raton), Florida International University (Miami), Florida State University (Tallahassee), University of Central Florida (Orlando), University of Florida (Gainesville), University of North Florida (Jacksonville), University of South Florida (Tampa), University of West Florida (Pensacola).

ORDERS for books published by all member presses of University Presses of Florida should be addressed to University Presses of Florida, 15 NW 15th Street, Gainesville, FL 32603.

Printed in the U.S.A. on acid-free paper

Contents

List of Contributors

Kern Alexander is professor of educational administration and director of the Institute for Educational Finance, University of Florida. He is author or editor of 15 books, including two commonly used texts, *Public School Law* and *Financing Education*.

Robert Anderson is on the political science faculty at the University of West Florida.

Robert Benedetti teaches urban politics at New College, University of South Florida. His current research explores councils of government and historical examples of citizen participation in cities.

Sanford V. Berg is associate professor of economics at the University of Florida. His field of research and writing is public utilities.

R. Lewis Bowman, professor of political science at the University of South Florida, has written in many policy areas of political science. He is former chairman of the Departments of Political Science at Emory University and the University of South Florida.

James W. Button is associate professor of political science at the University of Florida. He has written a major book, *Black Violence: Political Impact of the 1960s Riots,* and an article in *Social Science Quarterly*. His current research is on the black civil rights movement in Florida.

Joan S. Carver is professor of political science at Jacksonville University. Her publications and research are in metropolitan governance and on women in politics.

James C. Cato is a marine economics specialist with the Florida Sea Grant and Cooperative Extension Service Marine Advisory Program and an associate professor in the Food and Resource Economics Department, University of Florida. He has published widely on the economics of Florida's commercial fishing industry and has led numerous educational workshops for the seafood industry and state and federal fishery resource managers.

H. B. Clark, professor of food and resource economics, University of Florida, is author of numerous studies in agricultural economics. He formerly taught in the field of agricultural engineering.

David R. Colburn is associate professor of history and director of the Institute for the Study of American Culture at the University of Florida. He has published two books and is coauthor with Richard Scher of a forthcoming book, *Florida's Gubernatorial Politics in the Twentieth Century*.

Clayton C. Curtis is associate professor of finance and real estate at the University of Florida. He has been a consultant to the Florida Real Estate Commission and is active in studies in this area.

Manning J. Dauer, distinguished service professor of political science at the University of Florida, is author or coauthor of a number of books and over 50 articles, and he has served as consultant to many government agencies. His writings and research are on political theory and American politics, and among his books is *The Adams Federalists*.

Michael V. Gannon is Ring Professor of Ethics in the University of Florida's Departments of Philosophy and History, assistant dean of the College of Liberal Arts and Sciences, alumnus professor, and author of numerous works on Florida and southern history.

Bill O. Gibson is in administration in state government at the Capitol in Tallahassee.

Frederick O. Goddard is associate professor of economics and director of the Center for Economic Education at the University of Florida. His major fields of research and teaching are economic theory and public finance.

Joel Gottlieb is associate professor of political science at Florida International University, where he has directed the Environmental Studies Program and Urban and Environmental Center. His current research is on landscaping policies and energy conservation.

D. Robert (Bob) Graham, governor of Florida, 1979–, received his B.A. degree majoring in political science, with high honors, in 1959 from the University of Florida, where he belonged to Phi Beta Kappa and to Florida Blue Key. He earned his law degree from Harvard in 1962. He has served in the Florida

Senate and, by appointment of President Carter, as chairman of a Caribbean liaison commission.

Roger B. Handberg is professor of political science at the University of Central Florida. He has written over 50 articles on the criminal justice system, decision making by appellate courts, public opinion, and the political socialization process.

The late Norman G. Keig was associate professor of economics at the University of Florida. His teaching and research were in labor economics and industrial organization.

Ralph Kimbrough is professor of educational administration, University of Florida. He writes frequently in his field and is nationally known for his research on the politics of education.

George J. Miller is in the Department of Political Science at the University of West Florida. He is a member of the Florida Bar and author of numerous articles on Florida law and government.

Carter Osterbind is professor of economics and director of the Institute of Gerontology, University of Florida, and former director of the Bureau of Economic and Business Research at the university.

Douglas G. St. Angelo is professor of government at the Florida State University and has published widely in the area of policy and political behavior.

Richard K. Scher is associate professor of political science at the University of Florida. He has published several articles on southern politics and is coauthor with David Colburn of the forthcoming book *Florida's Gubernatorial Politics in the Twentieth Century*.

Philip L. Smith is associate professor and director of the Social Work Program at the University of South Florida. He has written many articles on human resource planning in social welfare and is coauthor of *Delivering Human Services*.

Mark Stern is associate professor of political science at the University of Central Florida. He has published several journal articles on southern roll-call votes on civil rights in the U.S. Congress and on interparty competition.

Gordon F. Streib is graduate research professor of sociology at the University of Florida. He has written extensively. Some of his best known books are *The Sociology of Aging and the Aged, Social Structure and the Family: Generational Relations,* and *Retirement in American Society*. He has participated in White House Conferences on the Aging.

Christopher L. Warren, assistant professor of political science at Florida International University, has studied the role of Hispanics in Florida politics.

James L. Wattenbarger is director of the Institute of Higher Education at the University of Florida and chairman of the Department of Educational Administration. Recognized as one of the nation's leading experts in the field of higher education coordination and in the development of community colleges, he serves as lecturer, consultant, researcher, and author in areas related to university and college administration and management.

Foreword

by Bob Graham

GOVERNOR OF FLORIDA, 1979–

The most significant lesson that can be learned from the last two decades of American government is the need for greater emphasis on policy development at the state level in our federal system. Attempts by the federal government to fashion national programs to respond to problems of poverty, unemployment, and housing have repeatedly failed to achieve the desired goals.

As the decade of the eighties continues, the federal government's attention and resources are being increasingly oriented toward issues of national security, international relationships, and strategic economic planning. A consequence of this reorientation is likely to be reduced federal initiative on the development of domestic policy. As this void emerges, the timeliness and importance of effective state policy development take on new urgency.

The diversity and complexity of modern American society require the development of distinct public policies responsive to the unique characteristics of the fifty states. A sound energy conservation policy for Florida will differ dramatically from the policies of Vermont and Kansas. The educational programs of states with substantial bilingual populations will not resemble those of states with more homogeneous populations. Economic development strategies to create new jobs must reflect the unique economic structure of each state.

If America is to meet the challenges of the 1980s, strong and innovative policy leadership must be provided by the states. The capacity of state governments to provide this leadership has been strengthened in recent years by improvements in executive management practices and the professionalization of the legislative process.

There remains a continuing need for an intensive focus on the activities of state government. This book on the government of the State of Florida provides a timely response to that need.

The contributors to this volume approach state government from an eclectic perspective. Scientific attention to theory is combined with colorful anecdotes of Florida political history. Detailed descriptions of the constitutional framework are linked to insightful analyses of the processes by which public policy is determined.

Under the skillful editorship of Professor Manning J. Dauer, the chapters coalesce to form a definitive portrait of Florida state government. While the focus is on Florida, the insights into the political process transcend the boundaries of a single state.

A particularly rewarding feature of this book is the use of illustrative examples of political leadership. With a single omission the major political figures of Florida's history are captured in a descriptive style that is all too rare in political literature. The one omission, that of the editor, must be remedied in this foreword.

For more than half a century, Manning Dauer has been a significant influence in Florida politics. A professor by vocation and a lobbyist for the people by avocation, he has helped to shape today's Florida in both direct and subtle fashion.

Twenty years ago I was a student of Manning Dauer's at the University of Florida. His influence on my life was substantial. As a professor, his wise counsel was always available. He challenged each student to develop skills of reason and logic, frequently switching sides in a classroom debate just to keep the argument going. His razor-sharp wit kept his classes lively.

As governor of Florida, I have declared the improvement of the quality of education to be a primary goal of our state in this decade. When all of our teachers can match the standards set by Manning Dauer, we will have achieved it.

Manning Dauer retired from teaching in 1980. But this book, along with his other contributions to the literature of American history and political science, will continue to share his wisdom with the generations of Floridians to come.

Preface

Planning for this book began after the 1976 meeting of the Florida Political Science Association in Sarasota, Florida. Mark Stern (author of chapter 5 in this volume), Bob Benedetti (author of chapters 11, 12, and 13), and I were among others in the motel swimming pool on Sunday morning following the convention. We decided that a book on Florida government was needed and that we should plan one. We corresponded, but the next step was not taken until we had found that the energetic director of the University Presses of Florida, Phillip Martin, was interested in entertaining such a proposal. Thereupon, at the association meeting in May 1978 the three of us talked with Martin at the New College apartment of Dr. Peggy Bates on the campus of the University of South Florida in Sarasota. We decided that the book should be aimed at the lay reader who would be interested in Florida government and also at the Florida college student in introductory level courses in state government or Florida government. We decided further that the book should include more than descriptions of government structure. In addition to chapters on political parties, the state constitution, and the branches of government, there also should be background chapters on the history of Florida and on the social and economic makeup of the state. Furthermore, we decided that a large part of the book should be devoted to governmental functions and policies in areas such as social services, business, labor, agriculture, extractive industries, and taxation and public finance. This scope determined that not all contributors should be political scientists. Many of the chapters would be by authorities in other disciplines—the humanities, the social sciences, business, and other areas. On that basis we began to outline chapter titles and to consider some possible contributors. Letters inviting participation were mailed to twenty-five people. Later, as topics were added—minorities, the environment, and other areas—the contributors grew to the present number.

As editor, I am deeply grateful for the diligence and patience of those who have contributed and who have worked with several revisions of the manuscript. I am also grateful to the University Presses of Florida for extensive editorial help. The complexity of the problems has involved much more than normal editorial work. Thanks are also due to extended critiques by three readers of the entire manuscript: Marion Irish, formerly of Florida State University and American University, now of Scientists' Cliffs in Maryland; Ernest Bartley of the University of Florida; and Robert Huckshorn of Florida Atlantic University. In addition, specialists have given critical readings to specific chapters. We are all grateful to many departments of Florida government which have provided information and photographs. The number of typists who have worked on the volume are legion, as are the number of research assistants or student assistants. I am particularly grateful to Pat Reichert and Hazel Pridgen of the University of Florida Political Science Department; to the department chairman, Alfred Clubok, who arranged typing time and expense support; and to a number of student assistants, including John Svarlien, Charles D. Farris, William Heller, Joanne Pendleton, David Hogan, and Ray Benson.

Special thanks are also due to the University of Florida's vice-president for academic affairs, Robert Bryan, who at an important stage arranged fiscal support, and to the governor of Florida, D. Robert Graham, who, in the midst of a busy schedule, has written the foreword.

Through special arrangements the University Press and its staff made available preliminary typeset copy of a number of chapters of this book for use in the political science class on state government in the summer of 1979. Jeaninne Webb and Wayne Daniel of the University of Florida Division of Instructional Resources and Sam Getzen of the Campus Shop and Bookstore then arranged production of 150 copies of a preliminary edition. This enabled us to have student input for the first edition.

It should be noted that on the part of the contributors this has been a labor of love. All have signed waivers vesting copyright, without compensation, in the University Presses.

It is our hope that we may have contributed to a better understanding of Florida government by citizens and by students of that government.

The first edition of this book appeared in 1980, followed by an updated printing in 1982. It was revised in 1983 for this second edition in 1984. In the second edition, Christopher Warren, writing on Hispanics, was added. Assistants working on the project were Ronald Vogel, Lisa Norman, David B. Haber, Mitchell J. Habib, Wayne Hackett, and Ellen Beidler. The work has received strong support of the staff of University Presses of Florida. The political science secretaries continued to provide expert typing. Many of the original authors have brought materials up to date and have participated in this revision.

Manning J. Dauer

Part One

Introduction

1 Introduction

by Manning J. Dauer

UNIVERSITY OF FLORIDA

Historically and politically, Florida is an interesting state. The phrase "Florida under Five Flags" reflects the varying, sometimes rapid, changes in its history. Ponce de León discovered the land in 1513 and claimed it for Spain. The first permanent Spanish settlement was made in 1565 at St. Augustine, where the Castillo de San Marcos stands, the best-preserved Spanish fort in the United States and a remarkable legacy from the Spanish era. There are also in St. Augustine some exceptional restorations, mostly houses, from that period. The French also had claim to part of Florida, establishing a foothold at Fort Caroline on the St. Johns River in the 1560s just north of present-day Jacksonville, where there has also been restoration from that period. The settlement was wiped out by the Spanish in 1565. In 1763 Spain ceded Florida to England but regained it two decades later. The territory was transferred to the United States in 1821 and admitted to statehood in 1845. At the beginning of the Civil War, Florida followed others out of the Union and into the Confederacy for four years, to be rejoined to the Union by the Constitution of 1868.

But the physical reminders of Florida's past and the areas of North Florida that seem unchanged from the agricultural South of the last century do not explain the characteristics and enigmas of Florida today.

Florida's most important characteristic in the 1980s is its rapid growth, in which it resembles California, New Mexico, and Arizona. Since World War II, the state's population has tripled. In 1983, Florida was the seventh largest state, with over 10 million inhabitants. The growth rate in the 1980s has been 250,000 annually. If it continues, Florida will be the fourth largest state in the union in 1990, surpassed only by California, New York, and Texas. One projection for the year 2020 places Florida's population at 19 million. For income the state depends more on tourism than on manufacturing, and there are many motels, hotels, shops, and other service enterprises. Agriculture has become increasingly corporate and large-scale, as has the mining of phosphate and limerock.

Another vital factor in Florida's makeup is the increasing number of retirees—in 1977 over 17 percent of the population was over age 65, twice the national average percentage. Labor unions are strongest in the public employee sector, the building trades, and transportation. The comparative shortage of manufacturing means that many of the traditional unions do not play the role they do in the industrialized states of the North and the Midwest or in Texas and North Carolina. Racial attitudes were moderate in the 1950s and 1960s and continue so.

The effect of these social and economic factors is that the state lacks an extensive liberal voting bloc, yet at the same time there is interest in modernization and growth. These interests demand the updating of local and state government structures to provide needed social services, even though conservative voters often put such services at the end of the line.

Politics and government in Florida tend to resemble and follow the patterns of rapid-growth states rather than traditional southern states, though, contrary to the record in the other rapid-growth states, the Republican party, while it has grown, has not yet achieved a status approaching that of the Democratic party. The state had a dominant Democratic party when Reconstruction ended in 1876, but that was also true of Texas and North Carolina. Yet those states have developed a more active two-party system, as have the rapid-growth states of Arizona and California. Why not Florida? First, Republicans have not developed grass-roots organizations in county and local governments, with the exception of the Gulf coast communities from Naples north through Ft. Myers, Bradenton, Sarasota, and St. Petersburg. There is fairly large Republican representation in the counties around Orlando—Orange and Seminole—and extending to the east coast from Brevard (the space center area) down to Ft. Lauderdale. These areas include twelve to fifteen counties with fairly well organized Republican groups. Such effective organization is not seen in Dade (Miami), Hillsborough (Tampa), Duval (Jacksonville), or the remainder of the sixty-seven counties.

In most Florida counties, the lack of local Republican candidates causes most voters to register as Democrats in order to participate in elections of local officials. A second limitation on Republican effectiveness is the fact that the Republicans show a tendency to be exclusive and not to include in local party committees and councils representatives of labor, blacks, and other minorities.

Still another factor is that the Republican candidates who won statewide elections, Governor Claude Kirk in 1966 and Senator Ed Gurney in 1968, were tarred with scandals after their elections, which further disrupted the statewide party and alienated independent voters. In contrast, recent Democratic officials like Governors Reubin Askew and Robert Graham and Senator Lawton Chiles have consolidated a moderate position which has strengthened Democrats and attracted independents. The Republicans have not offered legislative candidates in many districts, and their proportion of the legislature has declined from 33 percent in the 1960s to 20 percent in 1982. The Republicans scored in national elections in 1980 when a Republican senator, Paula Hawkins, won in a national and state landslide for Ronald Reagan.

Federalism

State politics is, of course, conducted under a federal system. The U.S. government has the delegated power under the Constitution to conduct foreign policy, provide for defense, control the monetary system (including the Federal Reserve

System for control of credit) and the chartering of national banks, control interstate and foreign commerce, provide for national security and for a system of social security, and administer the three branches of the central government which carry out these activities; it also has several other powers, including the power to tax.

States, so long as they maintain a republican form of government and so long as they do not jeopardize federal functions or equality of rights guaranteed all citizens by the federal government, carry out governmental functions not conducted at the federal level. Activities of state and local governments include, among others, the maintenance of highways and streets, of state institutions such as universities, state hospitals, and the prison system, of state, county, and local police, of school systems, and of services not covered by Social Security. Many of these activities involve uses of federal, state, and local funds.

State governments operate statewide and at regional, county, and municipal levels. The growth of metropolitan areas has caused overlapping of functions at the regional, county, and municipal levels and has led to many problems. The state government has the traditional three branches—legislative, executive, and judicial. From the standpoint of the citizen, state and local governments have more impact on daily activities than does the federal government. Most immediate and visible government functions are under state or local jurisdiction: schools, social services, law enforcement, fire protection, and so on. Moreover, most public employees work for state or local governments as schoolteachers, police, street maintenance workers, garbage collectors, and so on. In Florida 19.2 percent of the total work force is in this category.

Urbanization

The trend toward greater reliance on government is accentuated by the growth of cities. Today 80.5 percent of the U.S. population is urban, and Florida reflects this percentage. At the same time the pressures of urbanization cause Floridians to be concerned with the environment—citizens object to pollution, and they want access to beaches, rivers and lakes—so environmental politics is a factor in Florida's governments.

Who Controls Policies?

There are three contradictory concepts of power and control in Florida politics and government: the Elitist theory, the Pluralist theory, and the Marxist theory.

The Elitist theory.—According to this interpretation, elections are controlled by what C. Wright Mills calls the Power Elite, in his book of that title. U.S. politics, he declares, is controlled by the leaders of the business and agricultural communities, those who own the media, some labor leaders, and leaders of the armed services and defense industries. A few government officials are also included, but most are puppets of the other sectors. Political parties are controlled by the Power Elite. The poor and other minority groups have little impact. Moreover, some theorists argue that the organization of a political community matters little—whether under a dictator or in the freedom of a democracy, the elites still control. Some theorists even argue that this is valid for the Marxian system, as in the Soviet Union.

The Pluralist theory.—Theorists of Pluralism argue that free elections are meaningful, that there is interaction between candidates and voters, that some policies change as the result of elections, that voters can align in coalitions and make their impact felt. Candidates have to adapt to the use of media such as television, but they do present more than a "beauty contest" of aspirants who are controlled by others.

Not all elections are equally significant, but when issues are clear-cut there will be significant results. Primaries serve to control the parties, as do such measures of "direct democracy" as the initiative petition for amending the state constitution, which permits action by the voters when the legislature does not act. Interest groups representing specific blocs form lobbies in Tallahassee, but the general citizens form public interest lobbies like the League of Women Voters and Common Cause. There may be two opposing lobbies, such as labor and Associated Industries, on certain issues.

Pluralists believe that separation of powers among state legislative, executive, and judicial branches provides checks and balances among the levels of government. The three components also provide the citizens with multiple access, which includes the right to organize, to petition, to see one's representative, to form neighborhood groups, to protest, to write letters, and to participate actively in a political party. Some who urge the expansion of pluralism argue for the establishment of quotas, such as for women and minorities; most pluralists agree that there should be access and equal treatment but that quotas would place too many restrictions on true representation. Political scientists call the non-quota version of pluralism a type of representative government, combining group politics and polyarchy, using the last term in the sense it is used by Robert Dahl in his book of that title.

By and large the authors in this book argue that pluralism best explains and describes the functions of the governmental process in democratic countries with a free press, open political parties, and equality before the law and that the U.S. government and Florida's government fall in this caterogy. While every citizen may not have equal impact, access is provided, and there is a commitment to the principle of equality before the law.

The Marxist theory. — Some points of Marxist theory align with the part of the elitist theory that holds that elections are only a facade under the pluralist system. But a different remedy is proposed. Marxists see the holding of private property as the root of social, political, and economic evils. Property must be publicly owned. Only then can access be equal and opportunity guaranteed. In the more orthodox Marxist systems, such as the U.S.S.R. and Cuba, there is only one political party and a dictatorship called the dictatorship of the proletariat. There are less extreme Marxist systems, but the abolition of private property is generally accepted, as is limitation or abolition of freedom of the press and freedom of speech. In Florida politics this system has only a small number of advocates but is a factor to be considered.

The Centrality of Florida Politics

Florida has a type of political system that is moderate in the political spectrum of pluralist politics. Social service functions are funded at a level in the lower range among the fifty states. Florida's educational system is funded at a slightly higher level but below the middle range. Taxes are comparatively low. There is no state income tax. Property taxes are limited to no more than 10 mills (1 cent on each dollar of value) for city and county governments unless special bond millage is approved by the voters. Public schools may not tax more than 8 mills. The state sales tax is in the moderate range—five cents for each dollar of goods purchased, with food and drugs exempt.

Because of the state's rapid growth, there is some experimentation. New techniques are tried at the state level and new systems of government at the local level. Strict fiscal reporting is required of government officials. There is fairly strict regulation of pollution and other controls in the interest of conservation. As the political climate changes, so does the structure of government in response.

In summary, Florida does not fit the label of either liberal or conservative. In fiscal matters a conservative mood prevails, tending to affect the level and extent of social services offered. Yet the state is not conservative in structural innovation at state, regional, and local government levels. In planning for growth and in protection of the environment all levels of government are adopting fairly advanced procedures. In race relations the state has, since World War II, been moderate. This mood of moderation, with emphasis on efficient government management, is characteristic of the type of legislation and programs enacted at all levels of government, of the patterns of presidential voting, and of the voting records of Florida's congressional delegation in Washington.

This book departs from the idea that political science is a self-contained discipline. The authors comprise a variety of specialists: many are political scientists, but also included are economists, writing on government, business, and labor; agricultural economists; education specialists; a lawyer–political scientist, writing on the work of the courts and law; a psychologist, on criminal justice; a sociologist, on the aged; environmental specialists; historians, on the background of Florida's social structure and institutions; a social worker, on social services in Florida; and an administrative specialist. While this book focuses on government, the providing of information on the many disciplines affected by government can best be done by those who have studied the various disciplines most deeply.

Old and new capitol buildings, Tallahassee, Photo courtesy State of Florida Department of Commerce.

At the same time, the book is intended for the lay reader: for the introductory student in state government as well as for Florida citizens seeking to understand their government. We hope it will be of use not only to individual readers but also to study groups. The book is designed to show the interaction between the dynamics of politics and specific acts of government—how these acts originate and how they affect the citizen.

In studying authors from different fields we encounter the question of the extent to which social sciences actually constitute a science. The point of view on this matter will differ from contributor to contributor in this work.

My personal view is comparable to that of many in the field of medicine. There are three levels of differentiation. The first level is that of science; the second is that of best judgment; the third is that of art. Science consists of those areas of a discipline in which there is reasonable predictability. For example, in the field of the physical sciences, Boyle's Law can produce an exact prediction of the increase in pressure as a gas is heated degree by degree. However, even the physical sciences are not always this exact. In the social sciences few such laws exist. An example in economics is the quantity theory of money: if the volume or amount of a product remains constant and demand also is constant, the price will rise as the amount of money and credit in circulation increases. Most of the material discussed in this book exemplifies the second level—that is, best judgment. In each case, the author is well qualified and presents judgments based on his or her knowledge of the subject. This orientation to the social sciences is discussed by Charles Lindbloom and David K. Cohen in *Usable Knowledge* (Yale University Press, 1979).

The third aspect of the social sciences has been referred to as art. Why is a particular type of campaign conducted by a candidate? Why does he think that it should have voter appeal? Scientific findings can be a part of such a decision (public opinion surveys, questionnaires based on a scientific sample, etc.). But the final style of presentation of a speech or media presentation involves, to the greatest degree, best judgment and art. In dealing with these last two areas, the social scientist departs to a considerable degree from the realm of science.

Some critics would argue that a political science book should include only material which is acknowledged to be at the level of science. However, at this stage of the development of the social sciences, such an approach would eliminate many of the topics presented here. This is because most of the social sciences' techniques of exact analysis are applicable only to data collected for microanalysis, i.e., the study of small-scale aspects of societal or individual behavior. To study social problems on a larger scale—macroanalysis—is to greatly increase the proportion of the discussion based on best judgment and art, including discussions of political ethics and about the effects of issues on most societal matters. Thus the reader should remember that when an author advocates a policy, such an evaluation departs from science and rests on the best judgment of the writer.

Eugene J. Meehan has stated in his book *Contemporary Political Thought: A Critical Study* (Dorsey Press, 1967) that there are three levels of social sciences. The simplest level is *description,* which can mean merely the outlining of facts or the discussion of government structure. The second level is *explanation,* which attempts to present material that will give reasons why a change has occurred. For example, we have described Florida as a state with a moderate-conservative attitude. To justify this statement, material has been presented which is based on facts and includes some scientific analysis and other analysis based on best judgment. Meehan's third level is *evaluation*. Is a given policy the right one or the wrong one to achieve a specific desired result? Here we enter the field of values, and many social scientists argue that this is beyond the concern of the social scientist as a scientist.

Meehan warns that when social scientists of a discipline have attempted evaluation, their work has been sharply criticized by others, and no specific procedure for such evaluation has been accepted beyond the specific group of scholars employing it. Despite such strictures, this book does attempt some evaluations (some of them presented in chapter 21), representing the best judgment from the author's point of view. Since the level of science is not attached to such large-scale analysis, the dictates of caution might be to avoid these evaluations; but to do so would deprive the reader of certain perspectives and of the discussion of questions which are of great importance. This book is an attempt to analyze Florida's government. In the first part we consider the concept of self-government and try to pinpoint the forces that have contributed to the particular way in which Florida's governments developed until 1900. There are also chapters on social and economic forces at work in the state's politics since 1900.

Focusing on several trends in a single state demonstrates that some of these trends are also found in other states. But in-depth analysis of other trends in a particular policy raises some doubts about the wisdom of political analysis based on cross-state studies, since such studies may show seemingly contradictory trends. For example, studies in the 1960s and 1970s by Dye, Sharkansky, and Hofferbert (for bibliographical references, see chapter 15) use cross-state expenditures to determine that, after reapportionment, categories of expenditures change but slightly—a method which omits the study of substantive legislation. This study, on the other hand, shows that, following reapportionment, women's rights legislation was adopted through legislative votes from those districts securing the reapportioned seats. Chapter 9 shows that an increase in Republican legislative seats came from these same areas when reapportionment added seats. Chapter 20, on government and social services, shows that proportionate expenditures do not increase after reapportionment, which is also demonstrated by the earlier studies named, and thus would argue against effects of reapportionment. However, upon adopting administrative reorganization, decentralization of services to local areas was established, resulting in sharp reorganization after reapportionment. The same aspect of reorganization was shown in state decentralization of personnel administrative practices with the 1979 Florida Government Reorganization Act (see chapter 8). Moreover, planning legislation, environmental clean air provisions, the water regulation acts of 1972 and 1975, and legislation showing support for purchase of environmentally endangered lands have been supported by those sitting from the reapportioned areas. This is a pattern of information which is useful to the study of Florida but which also challenges some of the conventional wisdom of general political science analysis, which lacks depth in specific empirical phenomena as cited here.

Other trends demonstrate a considerable amount of emphasis in support of pluralism springing from citizen participation groups. Some of this evidence is found in chapter 15 on minorities, which notes that advisory groups of the elderly play increasingly active roles. Here and in the chapter on agriculture, there is considerable evidence of the role of advisory citizens' committees. The efforts of citizens tie in with federal action as well as with local government matters, including urban development. This trend is also illustrated in the chapters on local government (11, 12, 13).

Chapter 18, on agriculture, describes even closer interaction among groups, government, and developers in marketing agreements regarding milk, and notes the tax on the citrus crop goes to finance a national advertising campaign to increase the drinking of orange juice: "It isn't just for breakfast anymore." The labor sections of this chapter also show citizen interaction involving agricultural producers, manufacturing, and labor. The Revised Florida Workmen's Compensation Act of 1979 is a collective product of the state working with business and labor.

Still another set of projects occurs when voluntary citizen's groups interact with federal or local fund-generating agencies, as shown in chapter 21, on arts and leisure. Sometimes symphony orchestras, art galleries, local theaters, and athletic units coordinate both with local facilities and with federal and state subsidies.

The concluding chapter (21) reviews the material developed in this volume and considers such issues as energy and its effect on Florida living and the future of the state. This chapter returns to the subject of pluralism, depicting aspects of leadership under two major headings: the first presents a series of vignettes on issues of corruption; the second appraises the differences between elitism and categories of leadership, characterizing leadership as interaction with followers and thus distinct from elitism.

The total result is an attempt to depict politics as having many facets—to show that these interact in a continual dynamic and are subject to constant change.

Selected References

Dahl, Robert. *A Preface to Democratic Theory*. Chicago: University of Chicago Press, 1956.

Kelso, William. *American Democratic Theory*. Westport, Conn.: Greenwood Press, 1978.

Lockard, Duane. *The Politics of State and Local Government*. 2d ed. New York: Macmillan, 1971.

Lowi, Theodore. *The End of Liberalism*. New York: W. W. Norton, 1969.

2

A History of Florida to 1900

by Michael V. Gannon

UNIVERSITY OF FLORIDA

Florida was Europe's first frontier in North America. Its history of permanent settlement by Europeans goes back over four centuries. One would not know that fact, however, from reading the typical American history textbook, even those used in Florida's own school systems. According to the best-known account, Western civilization arrived in our country with the landing of the Pilgrims at Plymouth Rock in 1620—by which date Florida had long been explored and settled and the city of St. Augustine was already fifty-five years old.

It was Juan Ponce de León, lately governor of Puerto Rico, who first happened onto this peninsula. It was Eastertime of 1513, and he named the place *Pascua florida*—"flowery Easter." In the next fifty years, six expeditions, one of them French, either traversed the land or attempted to settle it. The last of these, directed by Spain's most experienced admiral, Pedro Menéndez de Avilés, succeeded in founding St. Augustine, which today proudly wears the mantle of the first permanent European settlement and oldest city in the United States. The year was 1565.

By the time the Puritans came ashore in the cold waters at Plymouth, St. Augustine was a going enterprise with fort, church, seminary, six-bed hospital, fish market, and about 120 shops and houses. Because *la Florida,* the name Spain gave to all continental territory, stretched north from the Keys to Newfoundland and west to Texas, St. Augustine could claim to be the capital of much of what is now the United States. Though its territorial claims would shrink over the next 200 years, particularly through English colonial encroachments, and though it would never know prosperity or power of the sort that could be found in Mexico and Peru, St. Augustine would nonetheless endure. The Spanish nation called her *la siempre fiel ciudad,* "the ever-faithful city." Except for a twenty-one-year period under British rule, St. Augustine would salute the flag of Spain for two and a half centuries. Not until the year 2055 will the American flag have flown over Florida as long as did the flag of Spain.

Menéndez's success in founding a settlement at St. Augustine came at the end of a long series of unsuccessful similar attempts; and even after St. Augustine was established, things went badly for Spain in this sandy land. Sir Walter Raleigh told the story of the early expeditions in his *History of the World:* "I cannot forbear to commend the patient virtue of the Spaniards. We seldom or never find that any nation hath endured so many misadventures and miseries as the Spaniards have done in their Indian discoveries ... Yea more than one or two have spent their labour, their wealth, and their lives in search of a golden kingdom without getting further notice of it than what they had at their first setting forth, all of which notwithstanding, the third, and fourth, and fifth undertakers have not been disheartened.''

So it was in Florida over the space of fifty-odd years before the final conquest. Failure followed failure as a long succession of Spanish captains, beginning with Florida's discoverer, Ponce de León, carried their proud lances into this wilderness only to see them broken by outrageous fortune. Here there was no sated conqueror resting amid Aztec splendor, no master of Inca wealth and magnificence. What we see instead is Ponce de León at Charlotte Harbor staggering from the Indian arrow that would carry off his life; Pánfilo de Narváez attempting escape from the coast below Tallahassee, his rough-hewn raft awash and the Gulf of Mexico in his lungs; Hernando de Soto, the ''never conquered cavalier,'' dying far away, lonely and impoverished, on the banks of the Great River Mississippi; Fray Luis Cáncer de Barbastro, cruelly slaughtered at Tampa Bay before he could do any more than hold aloft the crucifix before his Indian assassins; Tristán de Luna, a failure in the eyes of both his colonists and his viceroy after two inglorious years at Pensacola Bay.

Even Menéndez failed in most of his purposes. True, he founded a city and he accomplished his immediate military mission, the destruction of Fort Caroline, a French settlement established by René de Laudonnière at the mouth of the St. Johns River. But he discovered no gold or silver; Florida soil never produced great crops under the Spanish hand; St. Augustine was of negligible importance as a protector of the Bahama Channel through which Spain sent its treasure fleets twice each year; and it would be difficult to describe the city as a military stronghold when, for a century and a half, almost any pirate who passed by could sack it with ease, as Francis Drake did in 1586 and Robert Searles in 1668.

La Florida was not conceived by Menéndez in the beginning as a battlefield. Its conquest and settlement were undertaken as a commercial enterprise. Menéndez, an entrepreneur, aspired to be Florida's first great land developer, industrialist, and agribusinessman. Before his death in 1574 some nine Spanish Asturian families, all closely related to the founder by blood and marriage, had joined with him to invest in the adventure. Unhappily, their returns were meager. The reasons were many: no discoveries of precious metals, gems, or minerals; no abundant crops in the infertile coastal soil; the general ineffectiveness of Menéndez's Indian policy; and costly fraud by corrupt minor officials.

Throughout its ''first Spanish period'' (1565–1763), Florida's European population had to depend on an economic subsidy, the *situado* sent each year from Mexico City. This annual allowance of specie (cash), food, and supplies was often pilfered or delayed, with the consequence that in some years the population of Florida lived on the borders of outright starvation. Spanish plans to develop a colonial dyestuffs industry based on cochineal and indigo failed, as did efforts to raise fruit, to smoke fish for export, and to develop the culture of silkworms. Menéndez had not launched a thriving enterprise.

There were occasional successes. Franciscan missionaries instructed the Apalache Indians around present-day Tallahassee in the cultivation of maize, wheat, beans, and pumpkins and of tobacco and cotton, valuable trade crops. In some years when the *situado* was interrupted, the fertile hills of Apalache were an emergency breadbasket. A more permanently successful agriculture might have developed in the region if the frequently oppressive policies of the governors toward the Indians had been more accommodating. In the Alachua prairie, near present-day Gainesville, a thriving cattle industry developed in the seventeenth century. Cattle were driven from La Chua [Alachua], crossing the St. Johns by flatboat, to St. Augustine, where the fresh meat was sold for local consumption and the hides were tanned for shipment overseas. Some cattle, however, were smuggled to Cuba by way of the Suwannee River, thus avoiding export duties. In the first half of the eighteenth century the cattle ranches in Alachua collapsed under pressures from the English and Indian rustlers. By 1763 the interior ranch lands were untended domains of buffalo, deer, wild black cattle, and ungoverned human runaways—Indians, blacks, Englishmen, and others.

Of all the motives that led Menéndez to Florida, the only one that succeeded, beyond the survival of his city, was the Christianization of the aborginal inhabitants, or "Indians." These first residents of Florida were remarkable peoples of rich and diverse cultures. It would be a mistake to think of them as "savages." Still, the Spaniards believed that Spain possessed a higher culture and a superior religion, which they felt compelled to impart to the Indians. Thus began the Florida missions, a century and a half before the better-known missions of California.

Missions

The first mission, Nombre de Dios ("Name of God"), was founded at St. Augustine by the secular priests who accompanied Menéndez in 1565. Jesuit missionaries came to the peninsula the next year, but their work was not successful. It was the Franciscans, arriving first in 1573, who would eventually succeed in building an effective mission system. By the middle of the next century they could count thirty-one missions in the peninsula (and five more to the north along the Georgia coastal islands). Altogether some thirty thousand Christian Indians who lived in and around the missions were learning not only the catechism of the Roman Catholic faith but also the rudiments of European arts and crafts.

The Christianization and Europeanization of these native inhabitants were remarkable accomplishments for the missionaries, even if, in the long run, they succeeded in applying only a thin veneer of Christianity and Western culture over persistent aboriginal customs and beliefs. Mission documents of the period express this worry again and again. Still, the Franciscan friars must be credited with unusual dedication, to their God and to the people whom they served. The records only hint at the hardships voluntarily undertaken by these gallant men in order to administer sacraments under wilderness conditions: the constant hunger, long and exhausting overland treks, sweltering days and mosquito-filled nights, and tribal warfare. Theirs were truly committed lives, completely devoid of ambition for human glory or pleasure. One of them, Fray Francisco Pareja, justly said, "We are the ones who bear the burden and the heat."

The missionaries appear to have had no other purpose than to elevate the mind and spirit of the Indians among whom they dwelled. They did not expropriate their lands or push them back along an ever advancing frontier, as happened later in the Indian lands of the Anglo-American country to the north. To thousands of Indians the missionaries taught farming, cattle raising, carpentry, weaving, and, in many instances, reading and writing. Theirs was a heroic humanitarian effort for the amelioration and spiritual development of Florida's indigenous peoples.

The missions' end was tragic. English Governor James Moore of South Carolina in 1702 led a raiding party that left the coastal missions in ruins. In 1704 and again in 1706, Moore returned with Yamassee Indians and Carolina ruffians to destroy the missions in Apalache and in Timucua, the north-central part of Florida. Most of the mission compounds he burned to the ground or depopulated; the few that survived would be ravaged by other raiding parties in succeeding years. Three Franciscans died martyrs' deaths in Apalache, as did many of the mission Indians. Those Indians who escaped Moore's marauders fled in terror to the woods. Some went to St. Augustine; some were reported to have gone as far west as Mobile. By his own estimate, Moore took several thousand captives whom he sold into slavery or settled in villages among the Yamassee. A great civilizing work of the human spirit was wrecked. The missions would never again achieve their former extent or influence. After Florida was ceded to England in 1763, they would disappear altogether.

Military and Civil Life

At the end of the seventeenth century, Spain established two political and military monuments that last to this day. The first was the town of Pensacola, founded for the second time, and permanently, in 1698. With its wooden Fort San Carlos de Austria, Pensacola would successfully guard the western approaches to Florida against French incursions from the Mississippi Valley and the Gulf of Mexico. Because of the great distance separating them, however, Pensacola and St. Augustine would have closer contacts with Havana than they would have with each other.

The second monument was the extraordinary fortress Castillo de San Marcos

Castillo de San Marcos National Monument, St. Augustine, Florida. Photo courtesy National Park Service.

(Castle of St. Mark), built at St. Augustine and substantially completed, after fifteen years of labor, in 1687. Built entirely of *coquina,* a native shellrock, the fortress twice repulsed massive sieges by the English, the first by Moore of Carolina in 1702, when the entire city was put to the torch, and the second by Governor James Edward Oglethorpe of Georgia in 1740. San Marcos was one of the military bases intended by Spain to string a cordon of fire from Florida to Colombia, through Havana, Vera Cruz, and Darién. It stands today, its dank gray walls brooding over the city it saved.

The governmental structure of Spanish Florida was never complex in theory, since almost total authority in the province was held by the governor. The only other royally appointed officials were the sergeant major and captains of the military garrison and the officials of the royal treasury. Each function of government was authorized by the king operating through his Council of the Indies. Regional superintendence of the Florida province was given to the viceroy of Mexico and the governor general of Cuba, neither of whom relished the responsibility since unproductive Florida was a continual drain on their treasuries. Minor officials in the colony were frequently the products of royal favoritism or the selling of offices; many were guaranteed their offices for life and tended to form an entrenched, even hereditary, bureaucracy. The more venal among them were guilty of such offenses as misappropriation of funds, illicit trade, absenteeism, slipshod judicial practice, and careless accounting. Toward these failings the king and his council were generally indulgent, tolerating in the hardship post of Florida practices that would have brought harsh punishment in Mexico or Peru. Occasionally in the almost 200 years of the first Spanish period the governor would form a temporary advisory council, or junta, composed of the military commander, treasury officials, and pastor of the principal church, but no other Spanish governmental institutions took hold at St. Augustine, not even the town council, or *cabildo,* familiar elsewhere in the Spanish Americas.

Eventually Spain would have to yield on paper what she had never yielded on the field of battle. The reason was that to the north of her, France and England were contending for hegemony over the larger part of the continent: French fur-hunting ranges were pushing eastward from the Mississippi and the Great Lakes, while English farmsteads were moving westward from the Atlantic. The two were bound to collide. In the collision we call the French and Indian War (1754–63), Spain, worried about English dominance over the continent, threw in her lot with France in 1761. It was a disastrous decision, for England quickly and easily seized Havana. In the humiliating peace treaty that followed, Spain had to sacrifice Florida in order to regain her rich Cuban port. France, of course, lost much more—all her North American territories. Louisiana she might have kept, but those lands she gave in gratitude to Spain. Florida was now English, and the treaty provisions placed the western boundary of Florida at the Mississippi River.

Two Decades of British Rule

Florida was so extensive from east to west, in fact, that Britain created out of it two separate colonies: East Florida with a capital at St. Augustine and West Florida with a capital at Pensacola. The Apalachicola River was made the boundary between them. About these fourteenth and fifteenth North American English colonies little is said in the history books, because in the American Revolution they would remain loyal to the British crown. The first civil governor of West Florida, George Johnstone, arrived in Pensacola in October 1764. He found an excellent harbor and an impressive military structure, but little else. Five British governors would preside over West Florida between 1764 and 1783. At the transfer of power in East Florida, the entire Spanish population of 3,046 persons took ship, most for Cuba. The first British governor, James Grant from Scotland, arrived at St. Augustine in August 1764, and took office in the old Spanish governor's residence. From there he and his successors could look out on a shady plaza that ran to the guardhouse on the bay, on small coquina houses with overhanging balconies, and on a bustling population that would do more to develop Florida's land and resources in twenty years than the Spaniards had done in two hundred.

The acquisition of the Floridas was very much to Britain's advantage: the colonies rounded out her possessions from Canada to the Mississippi; an end was made to the Spanish haven for runaway black slaves from Georgia and the Carolinas; an entry could be made into the rich southern fur trade begun by France; and although she did not know it at the time, England would have in the Floridas two loyal refuges for Tories during the American Revolution.

In West Florida the principal industries were the fur trade, barrel staves, and naval stores. Some agriculture, too, was carried on around the old French settlements of Mobile, Biloxi, Natchez, and Baton Rouge. In East Florida the economy turned principally on agriculture. Vast tracts of land were cleared along the St. Johns River and the seacoast, and, aside from St. Augustine, the plantations were the centers of life in the colony. The most elegant country home, Governor John Moultrie's "Bella Vista," was located on the Matanzas River. The large stone mansion surrounded by parkland, gardens, walkways, fish ponds, and bowling green was destroyed by Indians following the departure of the British. The chief crops on the plantations were indigo and rice. Oranges, which had been introduced by the Spaniards, were grown and exported, as was timber. The most famous of the plantations was that of Andrew Turnbull, a Scottish physician, at New Smyrna, which Turnbull named after the birthplace of his Greek wife. To New Smyrna Turnbull brought 300 families from the British-held Mediterranean island of Minorca together with other colonists from Greece and Italy. They came as indentured servants. It was, reported Governor Grant, "the largest importation of white inhabitants that was ever brought into America at a time." The indigo plantation was a failure, however, and the colonists, after nine years of sickness and death, protests and punishment, fled to safety in St. Augustine, where many of the Minorcan families remain today.

Florida had a variegated population during the twenty-one-year British period. Most numerous were blacks, most of whom were slaves. Not only did they till the fields and operate the mills; they also sailed as crew members of naval and merchant ships, where frequently they outnumbered whites. In the last few decades before the Spanish departure, Creek Indians from the Chattahoochee and Flint rivers districts in present-day Georgia and Alabama moved south to Alachua and other areas in Florida where previously the scattered Christian tribes had lived. The British called them "Seminoles" after the Creek word for "runaways" or "separatists." In the towns one could hear a great many languages spoken: English (often with a Scottish burr), Mandingo, Muskogee, Hitchiti, Cherokee, Catalan, Greek, French, German, Spanish, Italian, and Sicilian.

The effect of the Revolutionary War on East Florida was pronounced though indirect. With the major fighting far away and tax monies plentifully supplied by Parliament, Floridians remained loyal to King George III. Thousands of Tory refugees from Savannah, Charleston, and other seaboard points north poured into St. Augustine or settled along the St. Johns, swelling the colony's population from 6,000 persons before the war to over 17,000 at its end. The more talented newcomers produced plays and books and published Florida's first newspaper, the *East Florida Gazette*. Numerous patriot leaders also found their way to St. Augustine as prisoners, including three signers of the Declaration of Independence: Arthur Middleton, Thomas Heyward, and Edward Rutledge.

Although about a tenth of the British army was stationed in the Floridas, the military forces in East Florida did little fighting. Defending the St. Marys border from patriot forays out of Georgia was their principal activity. The southernmost incursions of the patriots, in 1778, was repulsed at Alligator Creek bridge at the headwaters of the Nassau River. In West Florida British military activity was more intense but less successful. Spain entered the war on the patriot side in June 1779, and the governor of Spanish Louisiana, Bernardo de Gálvez, quickly struck at British forces guarding Baton Rouge, Mobile, and Pensacola. By 1781 Spain had recaptured all of West Florida. In the treaty ending the Revolution two years later (1783), East Florida also was returned to Spain.

The Second Spanish Period

Spain's second occupancy of Florida was tenuous at best. From the beginning it was clear that Florida could not long withstand the expansionist ambitions of the infant United States of America. Whereas Spain had earlier attempted to pacify and control the interior through her line of missions (an attempt defeated by the Moore raids of 1702 through 1706), in this second possession she intended to hold the Floridas by trade and immigration. The resulting prosperity, it was hoped, would cause Floridians from the Atlantic to the Mississippi to resist both blandishments and threats from the new nation. To promote trade Spain gave special standing and privileges to an English company, Panton, Leslie and Company, a holdover from the British occupation. Indian alliances originally forged by the British, particuarly that with Alexander McGillivray, half-breed chieftain of the Creek nation, were continued. This part of Spain's two-pronged policy proved successful.

The other part, immigration, proved Spain's undoing in West Florida. The more that land grants were made available, the more Anglo-Americans poured in from the north; and the more local populations became non-Spanish, the more the province became independence-minded. U.S. Secretary of State Thomas Jefferson wrote to President George Washington in 1791: "... I wish 10,000 of our inhabitants would accept the invitation. It would be the means of delivering to us peaceably what must otherwise cost us a war. In the meantime, we may complain of this seduction of our inhabitants just enough to make the Spanish believe it is a very wise policy for them.'' The inevitable happened: in 1810 the Anglo-Americans in Baton Rouge established a government of their own and declared themselves the ''Republic of West Florida.'' President James Madison seized on the event by annexing the lands between the Mississippi and the Pearl rivers; in 1813 the United States annexed the remaining lands of West Florida as far as the Perdido River, the present western boundary of the state of Florida.

In East Florida, meanwhile, there were several independent governments founded by adventurers in and around the town of Fernandina on Amelia Island, where in the last years of Spanish rule one could see the flags of the declared ''Green Cross Republic'' or the ''Republic of Mexico.'' American agents, acting under ill-defined instructions from Washington, were taking advantage of the instability in the province and Spain's inability to defend it. The clearest indications of Spain's weakness came in the War of 1812 and in the First Seminole War.

With the outbreak of war between the United States and Great Britain, British forces seized Pensacola for use as a Gulf Coast base and stirred up trouble with the Creek Indians. Indian fighter General Andrew Jackson and his Tennessee troops descended on the Creek nation, forced the surrender of the British-held fortifications at Pensacola, and then pushed on to spectacular victory over the British at New Orleans. Both British and U.S. forces had moved with impunity through Spanish-claimed Florida. Jackson would return to do the same in 1817, leading a punitive expedition against rebellious Seminole tribes. Seizing the Spanish fort of St. Marks (below Tallahassee), the new U.S. national hero quickly put down the rebellion, executed two British traders whom he accused of fomenting the uprisings, and for good measure marched on Pensacola, where he brashly, and successfully, demanded the surrender of the Spanish forts.

The United States Acquires Florida

Spain had no alternative but to get out of Florida under the best terms she could secure. To that end, on 22 February 1819, her minister to the United States, Don Luis de Onís, and Secretary of State John Quincy Adams signed a treaty of cession by which, in return for Florida, the United States assumed $5 million worth of Spanish debts to American citizens. Other provisions of the treaty required the United States to surrender any claims to Texas. The Senate ratified the treaty two days later, and Spain, after internal political changes, did so two years later. Andrew Jackson thereupon made his third entrance to Florida, this time as the first military governor of the new U.S. possession. Impressive ceremonies including the exchange of flags took place at Pensacola and St. Augustine in the summer of 1821.

Jackson resigned after three months to return to Tennessee, but not before issuing ordinances and establishing precedents that would begin Americanization of Florida. Among his actions were the division of Florida into two counties, Escambia and St. Johns; provision for trial by jury; and establishment of county courts. The possession formally became the Territory of Florida on 4 March 1822, and in the same month Congress provided for a tripartite territorial government with the usual executive, legislative, and judicial branches. The first territorial governor, William P. Duval, was appointed in May of the same year. A native of Virginia, he had spent most of his life in Kentucky. He would remain in office for four terms until 1834.

Territorial Years and Statehood

The first session of Florida's Legislative Council met on 22 July 1822 at Pensacola. The members from St. Augustine had traveled fifty-nine days by water to attend. One result of the first session was the formation of two new counties, Duval (out of St. Johns) and Jackson (out of Escambia). The second legislative session met at St. Augustine in the following year. This time it was the western delegates who had been inconvenienced: shipwrecked in the passage around the peninsula, they had barely escaped death. Not surprisingly, the principal decision made at the second session was to select a half-way or compromise location for a capital that would shorten the sea voyage or the twenty-eight-day overland crossing from St. Augustine to Pensacola.

Two appointed commissioners selected the Indian fields of Tallahassee in the old Apalache land, now occupied by the Creeks. Congress approved the site as the capital, and the third legislative session, in 1824, met there in a rude log capitol, where Indians leaned through the windows to hear the strange goings-on. A stone building would be started two years later. Among the decisions in 1824 were laws to establish ferries over rivers, to incorporate churches and towns, and to authorize construction of roads, highways and canals.

Florida's population in 1821 numbered less than 8,000 persons, including black slaves, but it grew rapidly from immigration, particularly the cotton lands of "middle Florida," where by the 1830s the counties of Jackson, Leon, Gadsden, and Jefferson had not only half the territorial population of 34,530 persons but also the majority of the territory's wealth and culture. There were certain boom towns, too, notably Apalachicola and St. Joseph, twenty-two miles apart, which profited from their positions as Gulf ports for up-country river commerce; a yellow fever epidemic, followed soon afterward by a hurricane, destroyed St. Joseph in 1841. Pensacola grew erratically, a brief boom period shortened by yellow fever. It was joined to St. Augustine in 1826 by the "military road" constructed across the Panhandle under the direction of U.S. Quartermaster Corps Captain Daniel E. Burch and its extension eastward from Tallahassee called the "Bellamy Road" after a rich planter, John Bellamy, who built the greater part of it.

St. Augustine remained the most important city on the east coast. Until 1835, when a prolonged freeze killed all the trees, St. Augustine was the center of the citrus industry. Jacksonville, called Cowford in British times because of the shallowness of the St. Johns at that point, was renamed to honor General Jackson. The first streets were laid out in 1822. Jacksonville stood alongside the first major road in Florida, called King's Road, which the British had built to unite New Smyrna in the south with St. Marys on the Georgia border. Once prominent Fernandina declined in population and importance. Numerous new towns sprang up in the 1820s and 1830s, among them Mayport, Green Cove Springs, Palatka—like Jacksonville a "cow ford"—Alachua, Micanopy, Ocala, and Tampa. South of the headwaters of the St. Johns River there were no settlements of note until one reached Key West, where a U.S. naval station was established and a flourishing salvage industry made it one of the important early towns in Florida.

Two problems vexed Florida's government during territorial days: Spanish land grants and the Seminole Indians. Certain large tracts of interior lands granted by the Spanish monarch to individuals prior to American occupation were in litigation for years during the territorial period. Among these were the Forbes grant of 1,300,000 acres on the lower Apalachicola River and the Arredondo grant of 289,600 acres in the Alachua district. Much more serious were the Indian grants legitimized in a treaty negotiated in 1823 with leaders of the Seminole nation by representatives of the territorial and federal governments. Over 400 Indians attended the treaty negotiations at Moultrie Creek, five miles south of St. Augustine. There the chiefs agreed to remove their people to a protected reservation of 4 million acres north of Charlotte Harbor and south of Ocala but not within twenty miles of either coast. In the years immediately following, the treaty proved unsatisfactory to both Indians and whites. The chiefs complained that the designated lands were too small to support their peoples; the whites, lusting after the rich interior farmlands, proposed a policy of general Indian removal to the trans-Mississippi West. That policy took formal shape at Payne's Landing on the Oklawaha River in 1832, where seven chiefs and eight subchiefs (as against thirty-two signers at Moultrie Creek) signed a treaty pledging that they would remove to Arkansas, provided seven of their number inspected the new lands and approved of them. The latter delegation duly visited the western lands and signed a ratifying document at Fort Gibson, Arkansas. The federal government made plans for Indian removal within three years. A number of Seminole chiefs, however, rejected the treaty.

On 28 December 1835, Indians shot and killed an Indian agent and a lieutenant outside Fort King, near Ocala. On the same day Indians ambushed Major Francis L. Dade and two companies of soldiers, of whom only three survived, near Bushnell. Thus began in Florida the Second Seminole War, the longest and most expensive Indian war in the country's history. For nearly seven years, in a guerrilla campaign unlike any that the U.S. Army had fought before, the Seminoles resisted a massive military effort to drive them from their homes. Leading the U.S. forces were officers who would later go on to distinguish themselves in the war with Mexico and in the Civil War. It would be hard to say that any, with the possible exception of Zachary Taylor, distinguished themselves against the gallant Seminoles. The more durable heroes that emerged from the protracted agony were the chiefs of the tribes, among them Osceola, Micanopy, Jumper, Alligator, Tiger Tail, and Coacoochee, who fought nobly against overwhelming odds. By 1843 a total of 3,824 Indians had been shipped westward. An uncaptured remnant took up arms against the white invaders during the 1850s in what was called the Third Seminole War. At its conclusion the survivors, less than 100 in number, fled into the vastness of the Everglades, ending at last one of the darkest chapters in Florida's long history.

Territorial governors following Duval were John H. Eaton (1834–36), Richard Keith Call, who served two nonconsecutive terms (1836–39 and 1841–44), Robert Raymond Reid (1839–41), and John Branch (1844–45). In addition to subjugating the Indians and encouraging the economic development of the territory, the governors promoted statehood. East Florida, remembering the British and Spanish model of two provinces, was pushing for the establishment of two states; middle Florida wanted one state; and West Florida talked of annexation to Alabama.

The first significant step taken to resolve the issue was the convocation of a territorial constitutional convention at St. Joseph in 1838. A census taken that year revealed a total population of 48,223 persons, of whom 21,132 were slaves and 958 free blacks. Although the total was 8,000 less than required for statehood, the convention, choosing one state over two, boldly drafted a constitution and submitted it to the people, who ratified it by a close vote.

The General Assembly, as the territorial legislature was now called, petitioned Congress for admission as a state. But it was not until 1845, that, thanks to adroit lobbying by Florida's territorial delegate in Congress, David Levy (Yulee), and the support of Governor Branch, Congress finally passed a bill for admission. It was duly signed by President John Tyler on 3 March of that year. Florida became the twenty-seventh state of the American union. The practice of the time was to balance admission of slave and free states in order to keep the number of votes in the Senate equal; accordingly, the admission of Florida was balanced by the admission of Iowa in 1846. In the elections for Florida offices, William D. Moseley, Jefferson County planter and Whig, became the first state governor in a closely fought contest with Democrat Richard Keith Call. The first senators were James D. Westcott, Jr., and David Levy Yulee. The latter, who had changed his surname to his family's honorary Moorish title of *yulee,* became the first Jew in the country's history to hold the office of U.S. senator.

Numerous private schools were established during the territorial period, and after statehood 91,120 acres were set aside for a system of public schools. The General Assembly authorized two seminaries for teacher training in 1851, and two years later the East Florida Seminary, to which the University of Florida traces its origins, opened in Ocala. A West Florida Seminary, from which Florida State University claims descent, opened in Tallahassee in 1858.

The first newspaper of the territorial period was the *Florida Gazette,* published in St. Augustine in 1821. Papers of the time were small, consisting mostly of advertisements. In one year, Tallahassee had eleven such papers, Apalachicola ten, Key West six. Many of the editors held public office or were independently influential in public affairs.

Churches of many denominations took root in the environment of religious liberty first declared here by the British in their occupation and now reaffirmed under American law: Anglicans, or Episcopalians, in St. Augustine in 1821; Methodists in Pensacola in the same year; Baptists in Nassau County in 1821 and in Bethlehem in 1825; and Presbyterians in St. Augustine in 1824. Jews had been in Pensacola since the 1760s and in St. Augustine since the 1780s. Roman Catholics, of course, had lived in the state since the earliest Spanish occupation nearly three centuries before, but in the mid-nineteenth century their numbers were small.

Writers of the period included Daniel G. Brinton and George Fairbanks, who both wrote histories of Florida; Buckingham Smith, who translated Florida-related documents in Spanish archives; Caroline Lee Hentz, novelist of plantation life; Dr. Wentworth Chapman, author of *Flora of the Southern United States;* and Dr. John Gorrie, a frequent contributor to medical journals. Gorrie, of Apalachicola, is best remembered for his invention in 1848 of an ice-making machine, an offshoot of his attempt to cool the hospital rooms of his feverish patients.

Statehood led to rapid economic growth in Florida during the antebellum years. Population grew from 70,000 persons in 1845 to 140,424 in 1860, of whom 40 percent were slaves, which suggests the principal supports of the economy: cotton and forest products. Planters concentrated in middle Florida dominated the life of the state. Cattle raising, Florida's oldest industry, continued in what are now Hillsborough, Manatee, Polk, Hernando, Orange, and—its place of origin—Alachua counties. Railroads became a major interest after 1845, at which date only one line, from Tallahassee to St. Marks, was in operation. Subsequently lines were built from Jacksonville to Alligator (later Lake City) in 1860 and from Fernandina to Cedar Key in 1861.

Secession

By this time Florida had lived under four flags—Spanish, French, British, and U.S. In 1861 she would raise a fifth standard. With Abraham Lincoln's election to the presidency in November 1860, mass meetings took place in many Florida towns to protest the expected Republican assault on the institution of slavery. "We say Resist," declared the Fernandina *East Floridian*. That most Florida whites declared the same was demonstrated the next January when both houses of the General Assembly unanimously passed a bill calling for a constitutional convention. That convention in turn, on 10 January 1861, adopted an Ordinance of Secession by which the independent "nation of Florida" withdrew from the American union, the third state to do so, following South Carolina and Mississippi. The vote, sixty-two to seven, was observed throughout Florida by torchlight processions, bonfires, bellringing, and general celebration. Less than a month later, when a confederacy was formed, Florida would salute the stars and bars of the Confederate States of America.

Military action followed at once. During January state troops seized federal property: the arsenal at Chattahoochee, Fort Clinch on Amelia Island, Fort Marion (San Marcos) at St. Augustine, and the navy yard at Pensacola. In the same month federal troops occupied Fort Taylor at Key West and Fort Jefferson on Garden Key in the Dry Tortugas; both forts would remain in Union possession throughout the war. Another important federal emplacement was at Pensacola Bay, where U.S. forces withdrew from two mainland forts, McRee and Barrancas, to Fort Pickens on Santa Rosa Island, which guarded the bay entrance. Fort Pickens was so weakly garrisoned and armed it might easily have been captured by a rebel attack. Confederate leaders, however, feared that the resulting bloodshed might cause immediate war. By 12 April 1861, when Fort Sumter in South Carolina was fired on, Fort Pickens had been reinforced and a successful attack was no longer possible. Fort Pickens, like Forts Taylor and Jefferson, would remain in Union hands throughout the war and would serve as federal headquarters in Florida. Pensacola was the scene of most of the conflict that occurred during the first year of the war. Raids and artillery bombardments were exchanged between Fort Pickens and mainland Confederate forces until May 1862, when the Confederates withdrew and left the city, by then a ghost town, in federal hands.

During 1862 federal forces began consolidating their control of coastal Florida, seizing Fernandina, Jacksonville, St. Augustine, Tampa, Cedar Key, and Apalachicola. Jacksonville would be invaded four different times and suffer burnings by both federals and Confederates. Control of the coastline enabled federal blockade ships to reduce importation through Florida of foodstuffs, supplies, and munitions desperately needed by the Confederacy. Blockade running continued throughout the war as a variety of rebel vessels made the passage from Havana and the British Bahamas to deposit cargoes in Florida's countless bays, inlets, rivers, and inland waterways. On the return trips the boats would take cotton, turpentine, and tobacco for trade.

Confederate strategy was to hold the interior of Florida, according to plans devised by General Robert E. Lee on two wartime visits to Fernandina. It was critical to the Confederacy that Florida's food-producing farmlands and cattle ranches be protected. At one point cattle were being driven north from the ranchlands at the rate of 600 a week. Some cattlemen in South Florida played both sides, selling to the highest bidder whether it was the Confederacy, the Union garrisons at Fort Myers and Key West, or the Cubans at Havana. Even more precious to the Confederacy was salt, for without it meat could not be preserved. Salt was needed also in the preparation of hides for tanning in the manufacture of leather. The principal salt works, where men boiled sea water in huge kettles and sheet-iron boilers, were located around St. Andrews Bay (near present-day Panama City) and Apalachee Bay in Taylor County. At its height the war-created industry employed 5,000 men, all exempted from military service. Union blockade squadrons sought out and destroyed the salt works from time to time, but the installations were quickly rebuilt.

The main battles of the war in Florida took place in the interior and were occassioned by Union threats to the breadbasket regions. In February 1864 a federal force of 5,500 men marched west out of Jacksonville in the direction of Lake City. Confederate General Joseph Finegan, with a reinforced army of 5,200 men, met the invaders at Olustee, thirteen miles from Lake City, and scored a decisive victory in pitched battle lasting from noon until six o'clock on the evening of 20 February. The federals lost 203 killed, 1,152 wounded, and 506 missing, whereas Finegan counted 93 killed, 847 wounded, and six missing. It was the single major engagement of the war in Florida. The Union defeat and retreat at Olustee were followed soon by federal embarrassments at Gainesville, Cedar Key, and Natural Bridge, which crossed the St. Marks River near Tallahassee. Often young boys and old men in home-guard units were responsible for the Confederate successes, although one such "cradle and grave" company could not prevent the Union's capture of Marianna.

At war's end Tallahassee was the only Confederate capital east of the Mississippi that had not been captured. Florida had given some 15,000 of her sons to Confederate service, about a third of whom lost their lives in combat or from disease. It is estimated that 1,200 white Floridians and, in the last years of the war, an equal number of freed slaves served in the Union army. Numerous Floridians achieved high command and distinction in the conflict, among them Stephen R. Mallory of Key West, successor to David Levy Yulee as U.S. senator before the war, who became secretary of the navy in the cabinet of President Jefferson Davis; General Edmund Kirby-Smith of St. Augustine who ended the war as one of the seven full generals of the army and one of the last to surrender to Union forces; and William Wing Loring, also of St. Augustine, who was senior major general in active field service at the time of Appomattox. Florida's women endured the war heroically: they rolled bandages, made uniforms, nursed the wounded, and in the absence of their men managed the estates and farms. To the surprise of many, loyal black slaves remained to help the women—the slave insurrection that had been expected and feared never happened. On 10 May 1865 Union troops occupied Tallahassee without opposition. Florida's governor throughout most of the conflict, John Milton of Jackson County, was not present to see the invaders march through his defeated capital. Believing that "death would be preferable to reunion," he committed suicide the month before.

Reconstruction

A way of life had ended. For black Floridians, nearly half the state's population, freedom had come at last, but for those who left their masters and mistresses for the towns and federal army camps there were at first no jobs—only promises. Without money or homes, many died from malnutrition, exposure, and lack of medical attention. For white Floridians one representative of the old order described things aptly when he said: "The world is upside down." Farmers struggled to make something of their fields, now untended; merchants scrambled for goods and for capital; and state government stood still in humiliating confusion. Within a short time, however, both blacks and whites would right themselves and Florida, least damaged physically of the southern states, would rebound dramatically to economic and political health. Unfortunately for the blacks, their share in the resurgence would not last for long.

The first meaningful assistance given the free blacks was administered through the Freedmen's Bureau, established by Congress in March 1865 to supply rations, to organize black schools and orphanages, to advise adult freedmen of their rights and duties, to regularize marriages, and to encourage the former slaves to return to work. By January 1866 most blacks were returning to the farms and plantations to begin crop planting. Christian denominations in the north sent both clerical and lay missionaries to teach in black schools and to instruct the black populations, in many places for the first time, in the Christian faith professed by their former masters.

Florida's first postwar state government was not nearly so enlightened and generous toward the blacks as were the Freedmen's Bureau and the northern churches. After the inauguration of Governor David S. Walker in January 1866, the legislature passed harsh and discriminatory laws directed against blacks. Emphasizing such crimes as rape, insurrection, and vagrancy, these so-called Black Codes represented an attempt by the former slaveholders to reinstitute the slave system in fact if not in property law. Similar initiatives were taken in other southern states. They had just the opposite effect from what was intended. Congress in quick reaction extended the life of the Freedmen's Bureau, then passed the Civil Rights Act of 1866 and the very similar Fourteenth Amendment. Because the Congress had as yet no southern members, it replaced the almost pro-South form of Reconstruction proposed by Lincoln and conducted by his successor, President Andrew Johnson, with an earnestly directive congressional Reconstruction designed by radical Republicans to discipline recalcitrant southern state governments.

Radical Republican representatives, in and out of the Freedmen's Bureau, came south to Florida to form secret black societies and to organize black voters, who had suffrage by congressional mandate. Their success was manifest in the results of the 1868 elections when sixteen Republicans but only eight Democrats (the party of the white southern conservatives) were elected to the state senate, and thirty-seven Republicans but only fifteen Democrats were elected to the lower house. Of the fifty-three Republicans, thirteen were "carpetbaggers," northerners who had come south to take advantage of Florida's new opportunities, twenty-one were "scalawags," southerners who had supported the Union, and nineteen were blacks. Among the black legislators was a preacher, Jonathan C. Gibbs, who would become secretary of state in the cabinet of Governor Harrison Reed. Other black leaders of this period and later were Josiah Walls, John Wallace, and H. S. Harmon.

Governor Reed, a native of New Hampshire, was a newcomer to the state. His Republican administration, the first civil authority to replace postwar military rule and martial law, would last five stormy years, during which Reed succeeded in angering both the conservative white Florida natives and the radical Republicans of his own party. In the process he survived four separate attempts at impeachment. His successor in 1873, Ossian B. Hart, was the first native Floridian to be elected to the governorship. He died within a year, however, and was succeeded by Lieutenant Governor Marcellus L. Stearns, a Maine Republican.

The 1876 elections were particularly hard fought. Stearns was nominated by the Republicans; the Democrats, by now resurgent, put forward George L. Drew, a native of New Hampshire but a long-time resident of the state. Black voters were grossly exploited by both sides and the actual balloting was marked by widespread chicanery and fraud, again by both sides. Although Stearns emerged the apparent winner—and Florida's four electoral votes went to Rutherford B. Hayes, giving him the presidency by one electoral vote over Samuel J. Tilden—the Florida Supreme Court, acting on an appeal from Drew, ordered a recount, with the result that Drew was given the governorship by a margin of 195 votes.

With Drew's inauguration in 1877, two-party politics came to an end in Florida. So did the presence of federal troops. Southern white conservatism was now in a position to restore the political and social values that reconstructionists had challenged. Where northern radicals had attempted to build a political base on the votes of blacks and lower-class whites, the new leaders, eager to keep the freedmen "in their place," created an all-white unity that would place Florida squarely in the Democratic Solid South then forming. Though their condition between the years 1868 and 1877 was arguably better than it would be for the next three-quarters of a century, blacks had contributed more to the Republican party than they had received from it. And now, under the Democrats, they would begin to lose the effective exercise of such rights as they had, including that of suffrage. The theory of white supremacy would permeate statutory, even constitutional law. Hooded riders, such as the Ku Klux Klan members, would spread intimidation and violence in black districts. By 1887 a series of "Jim Crow" laws enacted by the legislature would ensure that the state's blacks would be subjugated to a status suggestive of social if not complete legal physical bondage. And by 1890, thanks to poll taxes and multiple ballot boxes, most blacks would no longer vote. The failure of this part of Reconstruction would not be repaired until the second half of the twentieth century.

For the whites Reconstruction would be recalled for several generations as a source of shame and bitterness. Most scorned "Negro rule" and resented it as the apparent northern desire for revenge, while others lamented the political wrangling, the exploitation, and the corruption that plainly abounded. It can be argued, however, that the period overall was one of political advancement. The state constitution of 1868 was an enlightened document, the best that Florida would have in the century. In other respects, too—the criminal code, state services, and public schools—the Reconstruction leaders achieved notable gains. Those leaders were by and large good men, nobly motivated, who, apart from the divisive social issue of racial equality, shared the goals of the native Democrats: economic growth and development. Once the backwater of the rural South, postwar Florida promised to become a boom state, and every white man with or without means, Republicans and Democrats alike, wanted a part of it. Between 1860 and 1880 the population swelled to 269,493, an increase of 90 percent. For everyone but the blacks there were good times ahead.

The Bourbon Era

Governor Drew's inaugural address summarized what would be called Florida's Bourbon era: "That government will be most highly esteemed that gives the greatest protection to individual and industrial enterprises at the least expense to the taxpayer." For the next decades Florida would attract investors and immigrants, allow for unrestricted development and management of the state's resources by private individuals and corporations, keep taxes to the minimum, and maintain limited public services. Social, political, and educational reform would have to give way to coastal and interior land development. For that to happen, however, Florida's new laissez-faire government would have to offer considerable land grants for railroad construction. Yet bondholders, supported by court order, held a mortgage on those public lands that would be suitable and necessary for the railroads.

The problem was solved by Drew's successor in office, William D. Bloxham, who in 1881 arranged for the sale of 4 million acres of swamp and overflowed lands to Philadelphia capitalist Hamilton Disston at twenty-five cents an acre. While Disston engaged in the work of draining and selling his land, Bloxham paid off the state's creditors and opened up millions of acres for railroad construction.

When Bloxham assumed office in 1881 there were 550 miles of railroad in operation. By 1891 there were 2,566 miles and by 1900 there were 3,500 miles. This remarkable growth was supported by the governors of the period, Bloxham

An excursion train on the Jacksonville, St. Augustine and Halifax River Railway in the 1880s. Photo courtesy Florida East Coast Railway and P. K. Yonge Library of Florida History, University of Florida, Gainesville.

(1881–85), Edward A. Perry (1885–89), Francis P. Fleming (1889–93), Henry L. Mitchell (1893–97), and again Bloxham (1897–1901). The accomplishment itself was the work principally of three industrialists: William D. Chipley, Henry B. Plant, and Henry M. Flagler. Chipley, a native of Georgia, was general manager of the Louisville and Nashville Company. By 1882 he constructed 161 miles of rail called the Jacksonville, Pensacola, and Mobile Railroad. He invested heavily in Pensacola and became for a time the city's mayor. As Chipley connected the Panhandle with the rest of developed Florida so Henry B. Plant, a Connecticut Yankee, joined the Atlantic port of Jacksonville with the Gulf port of Tampa. At Tampa, to encourage passenger travel, Plant built the exotic Tampa Bay Hotel (now the University of Tampa). Because his line traversed central Florida, Plant made possible the first development of the now flourishing citrus industry in that part of the state. Three years after Plant's death in 1899 his Florida line would merge with the Atlantic Coast line. John S. Williams, a Virginian, purchased and built 600 miles of rail in Florida, which in 1903 would merge with Seaboard Air Line Railroad.

By far the most celebrated railroad magnate of the period was Henry M. Flagler. A partner of John D. Rockefeller, he had made a great fortune before moving to Florida in the 1880s. In St. Augustine he built a magnificent tourist hotel, the Ponce de Leon (now Flagler College), to accommodate northerners who wished to take advantage of Florida's winters. Completed in 1887, the hotel, first major structure in the country to be built of poured concrete, would become in its first quarter-century a mecca for affluent and important travelers, including four U.S. presidents. Flagler built a railroad, the Florida East Coast, to bring his clientele south from Jacksonville. In 1894 he extended the line to West Palm Beach, where he erected two other resort hotels, the Royal Poinciana and the Breakers (called first the Inn), as well as a $2,500,000 marble mansion for himself to which he gave the name Whitehall.

The winter of 1894–95 brought severely damaging freezes throughout most of Florida, except for the pioneer village of Miami. Flagler had already developed plans to push his railroad south to that city, but he was waiting for two principal landowners, Julia D. Tuttle and William B. Brickell, to deed him half of their property, hers north of the Miami River, his south. The deeds were made and, according to a story (probably true), Mrs. Tuttle sent Flagler an orange blossom cutting on dampened cotton to convince the railroad magnate that the freeze had not touched Miami. In April 1896 some 300 area settlers watched the first train chug into town. Though Flagler expressed his belief that Miami itself would never be more than a "fishing village," he did build there a resort hotel, the Royal Palm. After the turn of the century, in an act that required engineering genius, enormous capital, and personal courage, he would extend his rails across 128 miles of water and keys to Key West.

The railroads dramatically changed Florida's communications, especially along the eastern seaboard. Notably affected were the mails. Prior to the completion of Flagler's line to Miami, mail between that city and Palm Beach and several points in between was carried by barefoot mailmen who walked the beach three days each way. The railroads opened up Florida to numerous new commercial and agricultural opportunities. Along with the pleasure-seekers who crowded the coastal hotels, farmers, laborers, merchants, and professional people poured into Florida's cities and rural areas. Settlement and drainage turned the southern quarter of the peninsula into a thriving agricultural region. The "orange mania" swept the northern central counties until the freeze of 1894–95 caused the citrus industry to focus on land south of the frost line. Ranching expanded, as did logging, which with the railroads was no longer dependent on navigable rivers to move logs to mills. Cigar factories grew rapidly in number at Key West and particularly at Tampa.

In 1898 Tampa's population exploded briefly as 23,000 U.S. troops, including Colonel Theodore Roosevelt and his Rough Riders, made the port city their embarkation point for invasion of Cuba during the Spanish-American War. Other Florida cities, too, were campsites for a time, including Lakeland, Fernandina, Jacksonville, Miami, Key West, and Pensacola. After the one-year war Florida's bullish economy returned to normal, but word spread by returning soldiers about the state's attractions provided valuable national publicity and spurred further immigration.

With the exception of the great freeze, a hurricane in 1896 that destroyed Cedar Key, and two yellow fever epidemics (Key West, Manatee, Tampa, and Plant City in 1887 and Jacksonville in 1888), the Bourbon era counted nothing but successes and good times. As the change of centuries drew near, Floridians took understandable pride in the growth and development that had taken place. It was clear that Florida's economic position was different from that of her sister states from the old Confederacy. Though once an emerging cotton state, after the war Florida had moved away from cotton, and her population, predominantly southern in origin, became engaged in different activities: timber, cattle, citrus, winter vegetables—and tourism. Before the war tourism had been advertised for health reasons, and as

U.S. Army 3d Cavalry, Tampa, May 1898. Only part of the unit sailed for Cuba. Photo courtesy P. K. Yonge Library of Florida History, University of Florida, Gainesville.

one hotel resident at St. Augustine in the 1850s observed, "You hear the funereal cough all over the house, and in the parlor they loll at full length on the sofas and expectorate almost constantly. . . ." In the last decades of the century Florida attracted many more well people than invalids as thousands of northerners came into the state simply for travel, rest, and recreation. Originally called "strangers," the travelers now were called "visitors"; in the twentieth century they would be called "tourists." By both train and ship they arrived to winter in the new seacoast hotels or to explore Florida's rivers, such as the St. Johns, Suwannee, and Oklawaha, in steamboats outfitted with staterooms and salons. Many stayed or returned to build homes.

Tampa was joined on the Gulf coast by the new towns of Clearwater, St. Petersburg, Tarpon Springs, Sarasota, and Fort Myers. Joining Palm Beach and Miami on the south Atlantic were Fort Pierce and Fort Lauderdale. Inland, Orlando was the largest city in central Florida, and the new towns of DeLand, Sanford, Kissimmee, Lakeland, and Bartow were growing fast. By 1900 the general population numbered 528,000, an increase of 42 percent in the decade. Jacksonville was contesting with Key West and Pensacola to become the largest city; ten years later it would have nearly double the population of each of the other two cities. Because of the rapid development of east and south Florida, a movement mounted to move the capital from Tallahassee to a more central location. In a statewide referendum held in 1900, however, 52 percent of those voting favored keeping the capital where it was. And there —despite several later and similar attempts to move it—it has stayed ever since.

References

Gannon, Michael V. *The Cross in the Sand: The Early Catholic Church in Florida*. Gainesville: University of Florida Press, 1965.

Johns, John E. *Florida during the Civil War*. Gainesville: University of Florida Press, 1963.

Lyon, Eugene. *The Enterprise of Florida: Pedro Menéndez de Avilés and the Spanish Conquest of 1565–1568*. Gainesville: University Presses of Florida, 1976.

Shofner, Jerrell H. *Nor Is It Over Yet*. Gainesville: University Presses of Florida, 1974.

Tebeau, Charlton W. *A History of Florida*. Coral Gables: University of Miami Press, 1971.

Florida Politics in the Twentieth Century

3

by David Colburn and Richard Scher

UNIVERSITY OF FLORIDA

Despite the demographic, economic, and political changes Florida experienced in the last decade of the nineteenth century, nearly half the state still remained unsettled and most residents were engaged in agriculture or activities related to agriculture in 1900. Sixty years later Florida had become an urban state and had taken on many of the demographic and economic characteristics of the rapidly growing sunbelt states of the Southwest (California, Arizona, New Mexico, and Texas). Tourism had replaced agriculture as the principal industry, and the state had become cosmopolitan in its social and ethnic composition. Not surprisingly, these changes have profoundly affected state politics in the twentieth century.

Florida in the South

As Florida underwent numerous changes in the twentieth century, observers noted that the Sunshine State was in many ways unlike its southern neighbors. In 1949 V. O. Key, Jr.'s *Southern Politics* showed that though the South could not be considered a homogenous region politically, Florida was even then so eccentric in its politics that it was only remotely like other southern states. More recent analysis has largely confirmed this view.

Even if Florida is "the different state," it nevertheless has some features in common with other southern states of this century. It is farthest south of all the states and in any regional analysis must be accounted for along with its southern neighbors. Until quite recently Florida's economy has been primarily agricultural as have been the economies of most of its neighbors. Since the end of World War II industry has been moving to the South, and into Florida; but the state's rural agrarian heritage remains influential in Florida's politics. Moreover, while Florida's economy has diversified along with the economies of other southern states, its base remains relatively narrow; it rests fundamentally on tourism and related services, agriculture, mining, and a small but growing manufacturing sector.

Florida's most important tie to other southern states is its cultural heritage. Once part of the Confederacy, Florida may not have suffered from the Civil War and Reconstruction as much as other southern states did, but it nevertheless carried scars from these two periods far into the twentieth century. In particular, a caste system was established in law and custom which permeated the entire society. If racial hatred was less virulent in Florida than in some neighboring states, racial prejudice was widespread; Florida has had its share of ugly racial incidents.

Another important aspect of Florida's heritage, which it has in common with the rest of the South and which has shaped the state's politics during the twentieth century, is the traditional political party structure. Since the end of Reconstruction (1877), Florida has been primarily a Democratic state; the Republican party emerged as a significant second party only in the 1960s. Indeed, it is this heritage of one-party (or, perhaps, no-party) politics that most clearly identifies Florida with other southern states. Politics in Florida throughout much of this century can be seen largely as an effort by whites to use the Democratic party to maintain white supremacy and to prevent the rise of a Republican party. The state's significant political contests have been struggles within the Democratic party between traditional, rural (particularly northern) Florida and the growing, more urban, more progressive, generally southern regions. These features are characteristic of politics found throughout the South during most of this century.

Florida in the Twentieth Century

The state's development over the past eighty years can be divided into five major historical periods: populism-progressive, 1900–1916; demagogic populism and postwar economic boom, 1916–25; Florida depression and national depression, 1926–40; postdepression recovery and explosive growth, 1940–73; contemporary Florida, 1974 to date.

In 1900 Florida was a sparsely populated, frontier-like state. Despite a large land area, it had the smallest population in the South—528,000 persons who lived mostly in the counties within fifty miles of the Georgia and Alabama borders. In other parts of the state there were a few small cities such as Daytona Beach, Orlando, Tampa, Palm Beach, and Miami, but the rest of the state was wilderness punctuated by small towns like Sanford, Palatka, and Chiefland. Until 1940 Florida had more open acreage and more frontier characteristics than any other eastern or southern state. Development, the residents thought, was essential; the state's future lay in opening up virgin territory for settlement. Except for cigar making in Tampa, the role of manufacturing was negligible. Over half the population was engaged in agriculture, growing predominantly cotton, tobacco, truck crops, and citrus. Lumbering, naval stores (resin and turpentine), and the mining of limerock and phosphates (the extractive industries) remained important. The small cities had commercial enterprises, some shipping, and the beginnings of a tourism industry. Thus the economy in 1900 was a low-income one. Florida's estimated average annual per capita income of $112 was well below the estimated national average of $202.

During the latter part of the nineteenth century Florida politics were particularly influenced by racial tensions carried over from the Civil War. Throughout the South, Reconstruction had freed and enfranchised former slaves. Military occupation and Republican domination marked the period 1865–77. After 1877, Floridians, like their southern neighbors, attempted to return to their antebellum institutions. Gradually they supressed the freedoms of black Floridians and removed the scalawags of the reconstructionist Republican party. The Democratic party waxed strong and the Republican party was rapidly reduced to minority status. After 1877, the office of governor became inaccessible to Republicans. This Bourbon era (a nickname celebrating the restoration of an older civil order) in Florida politics continued till the turn of the century.

At the end of this period, a progressive-populist movement developed throughout the nation. A peculiarity of this political era in Florida and throughout the South after 1900 was the disfranchisement of blacks, in which the poll tax and literacy tests were employed. The state's politics became one-party, Democratic, and white. The primary system prevented blacks from voting in Democratic contests. Politics became essentially a contest between two factions—the lower-middle-class laboring folk (populist-progressives or "wool hats") and the conservatives or Bourbon ("silk hat") Democrats.

Racism—the conditions arising from the conflict between the concept of white supremacy and the concept of equal opportunity so eloquently described by Gunnar Myrdahl in *An American Dilemma*—was obvious in this period. A reservoir of racial tension filled and stood ready to spill over into violence. During Reconstruction, for example, the Ku Klux Klan was established in the Florida black belt (the northern and western counties). In 1868 there were fifteen murders in four black-belt counties. Seven murders occurred at the end of the year in Jackson County alone. This violence continued. From 1882 to 1936 there were 4,717 lynchings in the United States, and 3,421 of the persons lynched were black. Florida had 281 lynchings during this period; 256 were blacks. Between 1900 and 1920, Florida had the highest lynching rate in the country: 4.5 lynchings for every 10,000 black residents, twice as high as the rate for Mississippi, Georgia, or Louisiana, three times the Alabama rate, and six times the South Carolina rate.

The development of Florida's frontier lands early in the century captured the attention of all Floridians during this period. Even among the reformers of the populist-progressive period, the goal of draining the Everglades to permit settlement of the southern part of the state was fervently pursued. Led by Jennings and Broward, the movement to drain and reclaim the millions of acres of glades in South Florida became the dominant economic program of the state from 1900 till World War I. Florida's governors during this period (William Jennings, Napoleon Broward, Albert Gilchrist, and Park Trammell) strongly supported the segregation of the races; Broward urged a resettlement of Florida's black population in Africa.

The years from 1916 to 1925 were a time of tumultuous growth in the state.

Sidney J. Catts, elected governor in 1916, was swept into office on a wave of prohibitionist, anti-Catholic, racist sentiment. A man of enormous energy, he quickly polarized opinions throughout the state. His four years in office were a period of extreme conflict; his demagogic efforts to establish such populist reforms as initiative and referendum on legislation and recall of public officials were resisted by the Bourbons and others who disliked him and his programs.

Lincoln Road, Miami, looking west from about Meridian, 1905. Photo courtesy State Photographic Archives, Strozier Library, Florida State University, Tallahassee.

After Catts, Florida experienced rapid growth during the early 1920s. A land boom brought millions of dollars into the state (in most instances on a purely speculative basis), and the population began to increase. But the boom, resting on an unsound financial base, began to collapse by the mid-1920s. The economy of the entire state suffered tremendously, and Florida entered a period of prolonged economic decline. All aspects of business declined sharply. The assessed value of real property dropped from $623 million in 1926 to $441 million in 1930. From 1925 to 1926 accounts in Florida's national banks declined by $300 million; forty banks failed. The incomes of the Seaboard and Florida East Coast railroads were cut in half by 1936, and both went into receivership. The collapse of Florida's boom in 1926 thus merged into the national business collapse of 1929–40. The programs of four Florida governors—Doyle Carlton, David Sholtz, Fred Cone, and Spessard Holland—were severely restricted by this economic collapse.

The postdepression period witnessed a substantial economic recovery, but the years 1940–45 did not permit state spending for educational and social programs because of wartime needs. As the war ended, economic growth developed gradually and it accelerated through the 1950s and 1960s. The population leaped from 1,897,414 in 1940 to 6,789,343 in 1970. Florida resembled other southern states less and less. In its rapid (and virtually unregulated) growth, Florida was more like Arizona, Nevada, and California. Per capita income rose to approach the national average. Overt forms of racial segregation and discrimination in the state declined. Florida has emerged as the nation's ninth most populous state.

The period after 1970 began with continued economic expansion, but in the nationwide recession at mid-decade the state's growth slowed once again. A modestly neopopulist leadership appeared in the person of Governor Reubin Askew, who sought a number of governmental, economic, and social reforms. The extremely rapid growth of the state's population alarmed many Floridians, and for the first time planning and even limiting the future development of the state were advocated. High on the list of the objectives of the new planning was the preservation of the environment.

Florida's Demography

The size and diversity as well as the rapid growth of its population have distinguished Florida most from its southern neighbors. Physically, Florida is a very large state, the largest in the Southeast. The road distance from Key West to Pensacola is greater than that from Pensacola to Chicago. Not surprisingly the sheer distance helps explain many of the socioeconomic and political differences within the state. Like its neighbors, Florida has a large white, Anglo-Saxon, Protestant population, especially in the northern and western parts of the state, and a sizable black population. But since 1900 Florida has also received substantial numbers of Greeks, Italians, Poles, Orientals, Jews, and, most recently, Cubans; indeed, there were more than 400,000 Cubans in the Miami area by 1980. This ethnic and religious diversity means a wide range of interests in the state and a more fluid politics than would likely be found in other southern states, which are demographically more homogeneous.

Equally significant in the state's politics has been the rapid immigration from the North. In every decade since 1900 the rate of growth of Florida's population has far exceeded the national average; in 1979 Florida remained the second fastest growing state in the country. Table 3.1 shows the rapid increase in Florida's population between 1880 and 1970. Especially noticeable is the change in the post–World War II period, when Florida easily outstripped its neighbors in population growth. In 1950 the state had nearly 3 million people and ranked twentieth among the states in population. In 1960, the population had increased to nearly 5 million. By 1970, Florida had 6.8 million people, ranking tenth nationally. Florida's population of 9,739,992 in the 1980 census placed it seventh among the states. Its cumulative growth rate since 1950 has been about 175 percent, rivaled only by the growth of Arizona and Nevada (both of which started with much smaller populations).

TABLE 3.1. Population of Florida, Other Southern States, and the United States, Census Years 1880–1970 (*in millions of persons*)

Year	Fla.	Ala.	Ark.	Ga.	Ky.	La.	Miss.	N.C.
1880	0.269	1.262	0.802	1.542	1.648	0.939	1.131	1.399
1890	0.391	1.513	1.128	1.837	1.858	1.118	1.289	1.617
1900	0.528	1.828	1.311	2.216	2.147	1.381	1.551	1.893
1910	0.752	2.138	1.574	2.609	2.289	1.656	1.797	2.206
1920	0.968	2.348	1.752	2.895	2.416	1.798	1.790	2.559
1930	1.468	2.646	1.854	2.908	2.614	2.101	2.009	3.170
1940	1.897	2.832	1.949	3.123	2.845	2.363	2.183	3.571
1950	2.771	3.061	1.909	3.444	2.944	2.683	2.178	4.061
1960	4.951	3.266	1.786	3.943	3.038	3.257	2.178	4.556
1970	6.789	3.444	1.923	4.589	3.218	3.641	2.216	5.082

Year	S.C.	Tenn.	Va.	W. Va.	U.S.
1880	0.995	1.542	1.512	0.618	50.189
1890	1.151	1.767	1.655	0.762	62.979
1900	1.340	2.020	1.854	0.958	76.212
1910	1.515	2.184	2.061	1.221	92.228
1920	1.683	2.337	2.309	1.463	106.021
1930	1.738	2.616	2.421	1.729	123.202
1940	1.899	2.915	2.677	1.901	132.164
1950	2.117	3.291	3.318	2.005	151.325
1960	2.382	3.567	3.966	1.860	179.323
1970	2.590	3.923	4.648	1.744	203.184

Source: U.S. Department of Commerce, Bureau of the Census, *Census of Population 1960*, vol. 1, pt. 2; *1970 Census of Population: General Population Characteristics*, advance report for each state.

Significantly, Florida's overall birth rate has been consistently lower than the national average, though the nonwhite birth rate generally has been higher. The rapid rise of Florida's population, therefore, has not been simply or even primarily a result of fertility among Florida's residents. It has resulted from the arrival of newcomers in massive numbers. The vast majority of Floridians today are not native born; they are immigrants from other parts of the country, especially the Midwest and the urban Northeast. The consequence is a rapidly changing policial environment, with voters having little background in local politics and few local ties.

Shifts in Florida's population have not, however, been uniform. Most of the increase has been concentrated on the state's urban areas. Throughout this century Florida has had a higher percentage of its population living in urban centers than any other southern state (see table 3.2). In 1979, 81 percent of the people lived in urban areas, a figure slightly higher than the national average. Because Florida politicians have had to appeal to a fairly sizable urban and ethnic population, Florida politics has not exhibited the rustic demagogy found in other southern states. Florida's numerous urban centers have probably lessened the role of racial issues in state politics compared to that in other southern states.

TABLE 3.2. Urban and Rural Populations of Florida and the United States, 1890–1970

	Florida				United States	
	Urban		Rural			
Year	Number	Percent	Number	Percent	Percent Urban	Percent Rural
1890	77,359	20	315,065	80	35	65
1900	107,031	20	421,511	80	40	60
1910	219,080	29	533,539	71	46	54
1920	353,575	37	614,955	63	51	49
1930	759,778	52	708,433	48	56	44
1940	1,045,791	55	851,623	45	57	43
1950	1,813,890	65	954,415	35	64	36
1960	3,661,383	74	1,290,177	26	69	31
1970	5,468,737	80	1,321,306	19	80	20

Source: U.S. Department of Commerce, Bureau of the Census, *1970 Census of Population, Characteristics of the Population*, pt. 1, United States Summary, Section 1, 42, 60–61.

Urban Florida has become what one long-time observer of Florida politics calls a "giant suburbia," a continuous belt of cities and towns running up the state's west coast from Fort Myers to Tampa, across central Florida through Orlando and Daytona Beach, and south through Ft. Lauderdale to Miami to Key West. This huge suburbia includes areas of considerable social and political diversity. It is the habitat of a growing Republican party. (Except for Hillsborough County [Tampa] and Dade County [Miami], the urban belt tends to be politically conservative.) To this urban belt have come most of Florida's new manufacturing plants and the immigrant retired population (more than 17 percent of the state's population is over sixty-five years old, compared to about 10 percent nationally). During these two decades of rapid growth Florida's northern urban areas have also increased in size. Fifteen of Florida's 67 counties now account for nearly 80 percent of the state's population.

Florida's Economy

Along with this population explosion, Florida's economy has been transformed from a primarily agrarian to a mixed economy that relies heavily on tourism and services. Agriculture is still important, especially citrus, sugarcane, dairy products, both indoor and outdoor ornamental trees, shrubs, and plants, truck crops, and livestock. Agricultural employment, however, has declined in absolute numbers and in percentage of the work force across this century. In 1920 agricultural workers in Florida numbered 279,000 and comprised 29 percent of the population. By 1960 their number had shrunk to 105,000 (2 percent). Both these figures are by far the lowest in the southeastern United States. This trend shows a significant increase in corporate farming, especially in the areas of citrus and beef cattle. The number of farms has fluctuated since 1900, but by 1974 it had declined to 34,000, about three-fifths the number in 1920.

Developers' tour buses promoting Hialeah, 1921. Photo courtesy State Photographic Archives, Strozier Library, Florida State University, Tallahassee.

Perhaps the most important indicators of the strength of the changing Florida economy are per capita income and nonagricultural employment. Between 1948 and 1974 Florida's per capita income approached that of the United States as a whole, although it still lagged slightly behind. While the state's per capita income has consistently ranked ahead of that of other southeastern states, it has yet to equal the national figure. In 1974 the gap had closed to only $199: $5,235 for Florida, $5,434 for the United States. But the average annual income of Floridians is by no means evenly distributed among the people. Indeed, the average figure is very much skewed upward because of unusually high upper-income categories. The top 15 percent specifically has been very high, while the remainder of the state's population has a rather low income. It is the concentration of wealth at the top that makes Florida's average income figures compare favorably with those for the United States overall.

Relatively little of the available personal wealth in the state is taxed. State and local taxes have traditionally been low. A survey of state taxes in the late 1970s showed Florida's tax effort (expressed as a share of personal income) to be only 10 percent compared to a national average of 12.5 percent, ranking Florida forty-seventh among the states. While Florida's aggregate wealth by southern standards is high, it is highly concentrated among a small minority of residents and is subject to low tax rates. Indeed, proponents of development regularly argue against raising tax rates on the grounds that the low rates attract corporate businesses and persons of wealth to the state.

At the end of the 1970s, manufacturing represented about 16 percent of the Florida economy, agriculture 5 percent, construction 9 percent, and service trades 19 percent. Florida's manufacturing component is quite small compared to that of other states. The state's economy is therefore peculiar: high per-farm income, few farms; low manufacturing income; high proportion of wage earners in service trades; and high earnings in hotels and motels. The value of Florida's mineral production has increased dramatically between 1930 and 1972—by 2,766 percent (in constant dollars), five times the rate of increase for the nation as a whole. Florida's recent wealth has thus been highly dependent on tourism, agriculture, and mineral production.

Increased government revenues and expenditures are an indirect measure of the growth of the state's economy. State government outlays for services are at least partially determined by the relative health of the economy. Tax revenues in this period rose from $205 million in 1951 to $2.9 billion in 1974, an increase of 1,300 percent. Expenditures and disbursements rose from $289 million to $8.2 billion, an increase of 2,700 percent. Total state revenues went from $293 million in 1941 to $8.4 billion in fiscal 1973–74, an increase of 2,900 percent.

The biggest change, of course, has been in federal grants to state and local governments. In 1937 total federal aid to Florida was $2.8 million; by 1974 the figure was $1.2 billion, an increase of 4,300 percent. During this same period, government employment rose very rapidly (not unnoticed by political conservatives in the state). In 1939 there were 59,500 government employees in Florida; by 1970 there were 444,500, an increase of 640 percent. This increase is in part attributable to the impact that federally funded programs have had in Florida, programs that in many cases have followed upon the great increase in Florida's population.

Along with the population explosion have come numerous problems requiring governmental response. But the Florida economy, while growing rapidly, has not been particularly well balanced or stable during this century, and as a result it has been especially prone to suffer from economic dislocations like the depression of the 1930s, the recession of the mid-1970s, and the Arab oil embargo of 1973. Its large service component makes the Florida economy quite dependent upon what happens in other parts of the country. Such an economy has limited the government's effectiveness in meeting the public needs, particularly because the state has refused to tax at rates comparable to tax rates in most of the other states.

Florida's Politics

Not only has the economy heightened differences between Florida and its southern neighbors, the one-party political system traditionally found in Florida has helped to mark it off sharply from other southern states. If Democratic party politics in the South during the twentieth century were lined up along a scale ranging from stable to unstable, Florida would occupy the extreme "unstable" end. Key's *Southern Politics* characterized Florida politics during this century as "every man for himself"; in Florida, "anything can happen in elections, and does." Permanent alliances and a stable party structure were nonexistent. Candidates for office built their own factions and their own campaign organizations; there were virtually no alliances among candidates. Once in office, politicians favored only the loosest attachments with one another, and these tended to be temporary. On election day, candidates with widely different views of appropriate policy might be chosen and then, upon assuming their offices, be forced to work together as well as they could. There was no hierarchy within the system of factions nor were there sharp lines (certainly none of an ideological nature) separating them, features that could be identified in other one-party southern states.

Throughout most of this century, Florida has had an atomized, factional political system. Why this has been the case remains a topic of endless speculation for observers of Florida politics. The large size and stretched-out, boomerang shape of the state have been important. Widely separated population centers and their dissimilar economies and ethnic groupings helped give rise to diverse political cultures. Huge intrastate distances, the lack of rapid communication or transportation systems for most of the century, and the dispersion and differentation among populations nurtured localism, which in turn promoted fragmentation and factionalism in politics. Rare has been the Florida candidate who could attract a large statewide following. Indeed, it has not been unusual in gubernatorial primaries for a candidate to win a convincing majority in his home county and immediately adjacent ones but less than 20 percent of the vote elsewhere.

Rapid immigration has contributed to the fragmentation of Florida politics. The flood of newcomers has apparently brought about a system of politics "without form and without issue." Loyalties have not been established and traditional political behaviors have not had time to develop in much of this new population. It is not unreasonable, Key argues, to expect "a diverse, recently transplanted population" to lead to "an unstable politics." Immigration has accelerated political fragmentation along regional lines. Immigrants from the Northeast have tended to settle around Miami; midwesterners have generally located near St. Petersburg and Tampa and near Orlando; immigrants from the South have preferred job-rich areas.

Urban-rural cleavages and sectional cleavages have been especially important in

Florida's politics. Not always sharp or easy to identify, they have nevertheless been recurrent, although the urban-rural split had been apparent in legislative actions prior to reapportionment of the legislative seats in 1967. A "friends-and-neighbors" kind of localism in which rural legislators sought to reward their sections of the state often at the expense of urban Florida prevailed in Tallahassee. The urban-rural cleavage has been blurred because of the absence of a unifying tie among the cities. Frequently legislators from northern urban areas have allied themselves with rural North Floridians against representatives from South Florida, especially on the issues of roads and public services.

Miami, looking east from top of Fisher Building on Lincoln Road, 1933. Photo courtesy of State Photographic Archives, Strozier Library, Florida State University, Tallahassee.

The urban-rural cleavage has been further blurred by the failure of cities to vote as a bloc in gubernatorial elections. Cities form an essential part of any gubernatorial candidate's constituency, but before 1956 no candidate had ever constructed a coalition that included all of the state's cities. Typically cities have voted sectionally in statewide elections and, in fact, most Democratic gubernatorial candidates have been sectional rather than urban or rural candidates. Only in recent years have gubernatorial candidates such as LeRoy Collins, Reubin Askew, and Bob Graham put together factions that included blocs of urban voters from throughout the state, as well as sizable percentages of rural voters. The elections of Askew and of Graham may well represent the emergence of a true "urban vote" which seeks specific programs in such areas as schools, roads, and social amenities from its candidates.

Sectionalism is much easier to identify in Florida's politics. Splits between the northern and southern parts of the state have been decisive in gubernatorial elections and subsequent administrations. Sectional support for gubernatorial candidates, and for particular issues, can be seen clearly by comparing the location of the counties that voted for particular candidates. A marked clustering effect, which reflects both local and sectional tendencies, can invariably be observed. The traditional north-south sectional division, moreover, has been fraught with subsectional cleavages as well. Northern Florida, for example, has not been politically homogenous during this century (although it more nearly approached that condition earlier in the century), for the western or Panhandle section is frequently at odds with the eastern part of northern Florida. In the south, the eastern "Gold Coast" has often voted differently from either the western "Sun Coast" or the urbanized central region. Some observers of Florida politics identify the central region as an entirely separate political section.

During this century, Florida politics has been generally nonideological and even relatively issue-free. Liberal-conservative splits have been few (when they occur, it is usually in the form of populism versus Bourbonism, or wool hats versus silk hats). In many gubernatorial contests it has been hard to tell which candidates have been the more "liberal" or "conservative." Often they have said much the same thing, and voters have had to tell them apart on the basis of their tone, style, personality, and county of origin rather than by the substance of their proposed programs or their ideologies. Occasionally an ideologue has risen to prominence—Sidney Catts and Sumter Lowry, gubernatorial candidates in 1916 and 1956, were perhaps the most visible—but generally they have not been well received by the voting population. Governors and other Florida politicians who appear to have been most successful during much of the century have ranged in ideology only from conservative to moderately progressive.

Nor have issues played significant roles in the state's electoral politics. A North Florida judge who says that issues "don't have a damn thing to do" with Florida's politics may be overstating—but just barely. The factional structure of political campaigning seems to account for this. Factions have been based fundamentally on personalities. Campaigns for political office have generally been popularity contests among personalities, not clashes of ideologies or disputes over policies or methods. Even in gubernatorial elections in which issues have seemed important, there has usually been as much attention to personalities as to issues of the public weal.

While strong political leaders have emerged, factionalism has made it difficult to translate gubernatorial programs into fully effective and coherent policies. The elected governor has been the head only of a winning faction, and his claim to statewide preeminence usually has had to rest precariously on such factors as his warmth of personality, his stand on particular issues, his ability to use patronage, and the size of his victory in the Democratic primary. Moreover, before 1968 the

Miami Beach, 1954. Photo courtesy State Photographic Archives, Strozier Library, Florida State University, Tallahassee.

governor could not succeed himself. But the cabinet with which he is surrounded comprises a group of competing political executives, who, unlike the governor, are eligible for reelection. The cabinet members have statewide constituencies independent of the governor's and usually more stable and permanent than his faction. The system seems to stand in the way of elective, concerted executive leadership.

The continual turmoil within the Democratic party now jeopardizes the party's control of state government, for the Republican party has grown in influence since the mid-1950s. In 1954 there were about 115,000 registered Republicans in the state, about three times as many as in 1938. By 1964 there were approximately 500,000 Republicans registered in Florida. Ten years later the figure had doubled: Republican registrations passed the one million mark. Though nationally Republican registrations seem to be declining, in Florida they have grown dramatically, although the increase seems to have reached a plateau. In the mid-1970s Republicans comprised about 30 percent of the state's registered voters.

Most of the state's Republicans live in relatively new urban and suburban areas in the southern part of the state. They are concentrated in the coastal regions, both east and west: about 59 percent of them live in these two areas. The urban areas of central Florida surrounding Orlando contain another 40 percent. Rural areas, northern and central, contain only about 1 percent. About 75 percent of Florida's Republicans were born outside the South. Only about a third of the state's population is native born, but it would appear that immigration has had a disproportionately large effect on the number of Republican residents.

These Republicans, however, are by no means all alike. The two regions in which they live are remarkably distinct in terms of certain social and economic characteristics. Republicans living in the central region are on the average about ten years younger than their counterparts living on the coasts. More than 80 percent of those on the coasts were drawn from outside the South; many have apparently moved to Florida to retire. In contrast, nearly half of those in the central region are native southerners who appear to have migrated to Florida at a relatively young age. Perhaps the greatest contrast is in income. Nearly 60 percent of Republicans in the central region earn more than $13,000 per year; fewer than half of those living in the coastal regions are in this income bracket.

The political consequences of this diversity of Republican populations are clear. Socioeconomic differences between the two groups suggest that candidates must face the problem of appealing to two Republican constituencies with differing political backgrounds, interests, and priorities. "For the candidates, success in Florida depends upon their ability to devise a campaign strategy to force a majority out of the state's diverse Republican electorate," according to pollster Paul Cohen. As if this process is not difficult enough, the party must also attract a large bloc of Democratic voters to attain statewide office, for registered Democrats still outnumber registered Republicans in Florida by 2.5 to 1.

Another important change in Florida politics since World War II has been the increase in the numbers of black voters. Throughout this century, the number of blacks in Florida has been less than the number in other southern states, and they have represented a smaller percentage of the state's population (see table 3.3 and fig. 3.1). For that reason race has been less important in Florida's politics than in other southern states. Virtually disfranchised up to 1940, blacks have rejoined the electorate and now constitute about 13.7 percent of the total population, of whom some 500,000 are registered to vote. These new black voters have been influential in Florida's gubernatorial politics. Since 1965 a number of candidates for statewide office have openly courted the black voter (see table 3.4). The vast majority of the state's black voters are Democratic; only about 2 percent of Florida's Republicans are black. The support of the black voters in an election, especially a crowded primary, can spell the difference between victory and defeat. Blacks have also begun to seek public office in Florida. In 1983 there were ten blacks in the Florida House of Representatives and two in the Florida Senate, and blacks are increasingly found on city councils and in other local

TABLE 3.3. Population, By Race, for Florida, Other Specified Southeastern States, and the United States, 1940–80

Year and State	White	Negro
1940		
Florida	1,381,986	514,198
Georgia	2,038,278	1,084,927
Alabama	1,849,097	983,290
Mississippi	1,106,327	1,074,578
Louisiana	1,511,739	849,303
South Carolina	1,084,308	814,164
United States[a]	*118,214,870*	*12,865,518*
1950		
Florida	2,166,051	603,101
Georgia	2,390,577	1,062,762
Alabama	2,079,591	979,617
Mississippi	1,188,632	986,494
Louisiana	1,796,683	882,428
South Carolina	1,293,405	822,077
United States[a]	*134,942,028*	*15,042,286*
1960		
Florida	4,063,881	880,186
Georgia	2,817,223	1,122,596
Alabama	2,283,609	980,271
Mississippi	1,257,546	945,713
Louisiana	2,211,715	1,039,207
South Carolina	1,551,022	829,291
United States[a]	*158,454,956*	*18,860,117*
1970		
Florida	5,711,411	1,049,578
Georgia	3,387,516	1,190,779
Alabama	2,528,983	908,247
Mississippi	1,393,283	815,770
Louisiana	2,539,547	1,088,734
South Carolina	1,794,430	789,041
United States[a]	*177,612,309*	*22,672,570*
1980		
Florida	8,184,513	1,342,478
Georgia	3,947,000	1,465,457
Alabama	2,873,000	995,623
Mississippi	1,615,000	887,206
Louisiana	2,902,000	1,237,263
South Carolina	2,147,000	948,146
United States[a]	*188,372,000*	*26,488,218*

[a]Continental.

Source: *Florida Statistical Abstract, 1967* (Gainesville: University of Florida Press, 1967), p. 16. *Florida Statistical Abstract, 1971*, 5th ed. (Gainesville: University of Florida Press, 1971), p. 20.

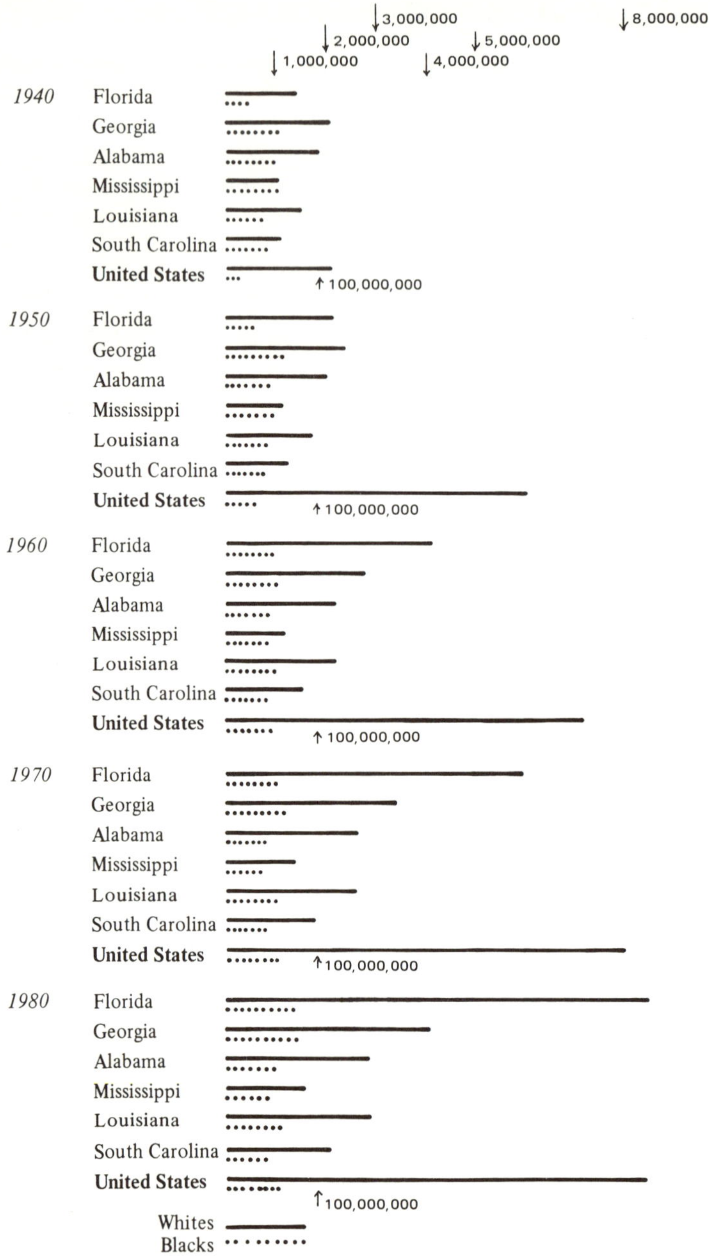

Fig. 3.1. Population, by Race, of Florida, Other Specified Southeastern States, and the United States, 1940-80. Source: table 3.3.

governmental offices. (A more detailed account of recent black officeholders appears in chapter 15.)

Reapportionment has also brought about a significant alteration in the state's politics. Prior to 1967, the Florida legislature was one of the worst-apportioned in the nation. In 1961, for example, less than 13 percent of the state's population could elect a majority of the senate and less than 15 percent a majority of the house. Although the 1885 constitution required that reapportionment be effected every ten years, only minor changes in legislative districts were implemented before 1960. Most governors did not even try to encourage the legislature to act. Without reapportionment after World War II, the state legislature remained in the control of the so-called pork chop gang, a group of northern Florida legislators, most visible in the senate, who flaunted their rural backgrounds and preferences and were remarkably unsympathetic to the needs of Florida's growing urban population. (The pork-choppers were given their name by James Clendinen, an editorial writer of the *Tampa Tribune,* when he wanted to point out that this northern, rural clique was feeding its local interests preferentially.)

TABLE 3.4. Voter Registration by Race in Florida, 1960–80

Year	Number of Blacks Registered	Percent of Black Voting-Age Population Registered	Number of Whites Registered	Percent of White Voting-Age Population Registered
1960	183,080	39.4	1,819,667	69.3
1970	302,000	55.3	2,495,000	65.5
1980	462,392	55.2	4,347,329	68.0

Source: *Florida Statistical Abstract, 1972,* 6th ed. (Gainesville: University of Florida Press, 1972), p. 515; Registration of Voters, Report of Secretary of State, 1980, copy in files of Political Science Department, University of Florida, Gainesville.

In 1967 the U.S. Supreme Court ruled in *Swann* v. *Adams* (385 U.S. 440) that the malapportionment of the Florida legislature was unconstitutional and ordered apportionment based on legislative districts of equal population (see chapter 9). The reapportionment mandated by the Court's decision brought an end to the legislative suzerainty of the porkchoppers. The balance of power in the legislature shifted southward, and urban and especially suburban interests began to be prominently reflected in both the senate and the house. Yet from an ideological point of view, the change has not been as dramatic as some might have expected; Florida remains primarily a conservative state. Most of the new legislators have come from the new, largely suburban areas of the state. Though not uniformly conservative, legislators from these areas tend to lean in that direction, particularly on taxation and spending programs.

While wrestling with reapportionment in the mid-1960s, Floridians saw that the state's constitution was as outmoded as its legislature. Written in 1885 but amended more than 150 times, it was criticized for containing inconsistencies, contradictions, and detailed provisions that belonged in statutes rather than in a constitution. In 1966 a Citizens' Constitutional Revision Commission met and drafted a new constitution, which was presented to the legislature in 1967. After that body altered several of its provisions, the voters overwhelmingly ratified the new constitution in the general election of November 1968 (see chapter 6).

The new constitution strengthened the governor's office by permitting him to succeed himself for a second term and by increasing his administrative authority over certain state agencies and departments. It also made possible the modernization of the legislature, a process that was begun just after reapportionment. By 1969 the legislature had added a large professional staff. It has also created an ongoing, year-round system of committee meetings; presession meetings to deal with prefiled bills; and a computerized system for keeping track of the progress and whereabouts of bills. As a result of these changes, the National Citizens' Conference on State Legislatures in 1971 rated the Florida legislature fourth among the fifty states in overall effectiveness.

The large size and the great diversity of demographic and economic changes that Florida has experienced since the turn of the century have profoundly affected the electoral aspects of Florida's politics. The state's fundamental conservatism remains and has strengthened the Republican party. The Democrats may be unable to defeat an invigorated Republican party, although ironically the party of Lincoln in Florida has so far proved itself to be as disorganized and factionalized as the Democratic party. The Republicans have also been hampered by weak leadership and have yet to fully recover from the administration of Claude Kirk and the questionable practices of Senator Edward Gurney. Kirk's ignorance of state budgetary matters, his use of a private security agency to control crime, and his abortive effort to block school busing in Manatee County all weakened his leadership. Gurney was alleged to have accepted political payoffs.

Republicans in Florida were rejuvenated by the 1980 elections in which they easily carried the state for presidential candidate Ronald Reagan and elected Paula Hawkins as U.S. Senator. Their strength in the legislature was not greatly changed. The 1982 reapportionment, however, promised to transfer legislative seats and to add four new congressional seats to the competitive Republican areas of South and Central Florida.

Politically the state has also been significantly affected by reapportionment. Gone are the days of the pork chop gang, when rural Florida benefited at the expense of the urban areas. The legislature, while still quite conservative on fiscal matters, has been somewhat more supportive of the educational and social needs of the urban residents. Florida has thus abandoned the politics of the past and entered an era of urban progressivism.

Selected References

Cash, William. *History of the Democratic Party in Florida*. Tallahassee, Fla.: n.p., 1936.

Dauer, Manning J. ''Florida: The Different State.'' In *The Changing Politics of the South,* edited by William C. Havard, pp. 94–148. Baton Rouge: Louisiana State University Press, 1972.

Flynt, Wayne. *Sidney J. Catts, Cracker Messiah*. Baton Rouge: Louisiana State University Press, 1978.

Key, V. O., Jr. *Southern Politics*. New York: Vintage Books, 1949.

Pierce, Neal R. *The Deep South States of America,* pp. 435–94. New York: W. W. Norton and Company, Inc., 1974.

Proctor, Samuel. *Napoleon Bonaparte Broward, Fighting Democrat*. Gainesville: University of Florida Press, 1951.

Part Two

Government Structure

Political Action: Elections, Parties, and Lobbies

by Manning J. Dauer
UNIVERSITY OF FLORIDA

and Douglas St. Angelo
FLORIDA STATE UNIVERSITY

4

Political activity in Florida centers around party organizations (including party committees), party primaries, the general election, and the work of lobbies. To participate effectively in the political process, the citizen needs a basic understanding of these agencies and activities.

Campaigns and Elections

Florida, like all other states, requires voters to register. Under the federal Constitution (Amendment 26) they become eligible to register at age 18. About 60 percent of Florida's eligible voters actually register. The voter has a choice of registering as a Democrat, a Republican, or an independent, and the choice is important. In Florida the primaries are the method of selecting the party's candidates that appear on the general election ballot. Moreover, Florida's primaries are "closed," meaning that only registered Democrats can vote in the Democratic primary and only Republicans in the Republican primary. A voter registered as an independent may vote only in a nonpartisan judicial election (held at the time of the second primary) and in the general election—but not in the partisan primary. Thus the voter registered as an independent loses the right to influence the choice of a candidate whose name will appear on the general election ballot.

In presidential election years there are actually three party primaries in Florida. In March there is the presidential preference primary, in which candidates for the Republican and Democratic nominations run to win pledged delegates to the national nominating conventions of the two parties. In September there are the Democratic and Republican party nominating primaries to choose contenders for county, state, and congressional offices. In October there are party run-off primaries for those races in which no candidate received over 50 percent of the votes cast in the September primary. The general election is held in November, with Republicans running against Democrats and, in some cases, independent candidates. Cities set their own election dates, usually in the spring. Most cities have nonpartisan elections to select city council or city commission members and other municipal officers.

Financing campaigns.—The financing of primary campaigns is up to each candidate—the parties do not help. Florida has had for over thirty years a "who gave it, who got it'' law, which requires that each candidate for office name a campaign treasurer. This treasurer records the names of all contributors and the amounts given; the treasurer must also keep track of expenditures. Reports must be filed regularly with county officials in local elections and with the secretary of state in state elections. These reports are open, public records. How much a contributor may give in support of each type of race is limited by law. How much the candidate may spend out of personal funds, however, is unlimited (a U.S. Supreme Court decision established this ''no limit'' rule).

Financing campaigns by soliciting contributions invites the contributors to expect to influence either the campaign behavior or the later performance of a successful candidate. Interest groups and individuals often seek to ensure their access to the official elected by contributing to the campaign of more than one candidate in the same race. Some sentiment has developed for public financing of campaign expenses out of state or county treasuries, but no such legislation has yet been adopted. Newspapers occasionally donate space for candidates to publish their platforms or summaries of their positions on issues. Commercial radio and TV stations and PBS stations allocate time to forums in which all of the candidates are invited to participate, frequently under the auspices of nonpartisan groups such as the League of Women Voters or other civic groups. Still, the candidate must raise funds to meet the incidental expenses of campaigning. Volunteer workers may man the phones and stuff envelopes, but cash to pay the phone bills and postage expenses is indispensable. The 1978 gubernatorial campaign in Florida found the candidates spending over $10 million contributed by their supporters, with the candidates who won nomination also contributing much of their own funds.

Campaign techniques can include imaginative attention-getting activities. In his successful U.S. Senate campaign, Lawton Chiles walked from one end of the state to the other, discussing issues as he went through each community. Governor Bob Graham spent 100 days during his campaign working at various jobs, mostly blue-collar, in different communities around the state. He not only discussed the issues with his fellow workers but asked them for suggestions. Graham's working experiences were broadcast as TV spot announcements, which combined attention-getting with statements on issues. If techniques such as these are seen as ''gimmicks,'' they may alienate many voters; but they can serve both to humanize the candidate and to win attention to the program he or she is presenting. Such procedures supersede the old-fashioned political rally, which in most areas of Florida has become obsolete.

Professionals in the campaign.—A statewide campaign requires the following: (1) a campaign manager knowledgeable in state politics; (2) a professional polling organization to gather survey research data on issues and on the relative standing of candidates; (3) media specialists and an advertising agency to prepare and schedule TV spots and radio and newspaper advertising; (4) staff, frequently volunteers, to analyze issues; (5) a campaign treasurer and finance chairperson; (6) county chairpersons to manage the campaign headquarters personnel; and (7) paid or volunteer workers to give local "meet the candidate" events, including receptions and coffees in residential neighborhoods, and to drive voters to the polls.

But the professionals, including pollsters and media specialists, cannot supply the strategy of the campaign. The theme of the campaign and the candidate's stand on issues are up to the candidate and his or her advisors. The media and polling specialists supply data and help in presenting the candidate's message, but content, style, and position on issues must come from the candidate. Without sufficient money, the candidate cannot hope to employ and coordinate these vital professional services.

The media in politics.—The media play a prominent role in interpreting politics and then in the campaign. Metropolitan Florida newspapers employ staff reporters specializing in local politics and a dozen maintain staff correspondents in the state capitol at Tallahassee. The press services maintain similar Tallahassee headquarters, as do the larger television stations. There are a Florida radio network and a Florida public broadcasting system. All cover regular news, and many of the papers have sufficient staff to assign personnel to in-depth reporting or special feature reporting on such special projects as land purchase problems, tax problems, welfare problems, custodial issues in state prisons, the debate over the death penalty, and the issue of plea bargaining. The *Tallahassee Democrat* devotes considerable space to news from the capitol and the legislature. Other Florida newspapers have regional circulation with special editions for different localities in their area, but they also cover statewide news; they include especially the *St. Petersburg Times, Tampa Morning Tribune, Miami Herald, Today* (Cocoa), *Fort Lauderdale News, Daytona Beach News Journal, Orlando Sentinel,* and *Florida Times-Union* (Jacksonville).

At election time, candidates for important offices will be interviewed by the editorial staff of many newspapers, and editorial endorsement may be forthcoming. Particularly in the larger metropolitan areas with large mobile populations, editorial endorsement in many races can be decisive. This is especially true for Dade County (Miami) when there are many not-well-known candidates in a local race or when in a state race there is no local candidate. For the county at large, some observers place the value of a *Herald* endorsement as high as 30,000 to 40,000 votes.

Generally the Florida press follows an active policy of reporting political news. The press also will often give space to nonpartisan organizations which send questionnaires to candidates on the issues, often publishing the candidates' replies. Television stations also supply free time for candidate debates; this is a common practice of the PBS network. Other coverage, however, is paid for by the party or the candidate, including spot announcements, longer broadcasts, and newspaper advertising.

Who votes?—Voting and registration are highest among middle-class, moderate-income, and higher-income groups who are past the mid-twenties in age. While there are no legal barriers to black registration, the proportion of blacks registered is slightly less than the proportion of blacks of voting age in the population. (The role that blacks and other minorities play in Florida politics is more fully treated in chapter 15.)

Participation in politics.—An individual wishing to be active in politics can be a member of a number of citizens' groups. Nonpartisan organizations include the League of Women Voters, Common Cause, the NAACP, and other statewide and local groups. Labor unions and industry associations support political action committees. In local politics neighborhood associations frequently are influential on matters of planning and zoning that affect the daily lives of residents.

The person who seeks deeper involvement in politics than that offered by a civic group can seek a position on a party committee as a precinct committeeman or committeewoman. This can lead to a position on a state party committee. At the same time the person may wish to volunteer to serve locally on advisory committees to the city and county commissions. Ultimately, the person might offer to stand for election to the city council or county commission or the state legislature. After that, opportunities for higher political office may open up.

Alienation.—Nonvoting is a widespread civic problem. In some cases it is a part of the complete alienation of the individual from the political system. Is political activity worthwhile? Does it make a difference if a person votes? Is the time spent listening to election campaigns worthwhile? If a person answers "no" to these questions, he or she is likely to withdraw from political activity, even from voting. If that same person faces a local land-use zoning problem or finds the public schools unsatisfactory or other governmental services inadequate, he or she should place the blame on the citizen who does not participate in the political system. Not every citizen, to be sure, can have equal political impact; but for all citizens, political participation can be personally satisfying and rewarding.

Corruption in politics.—Corruption is a conspicuous problem, but analysts find that it is no more prevalent in politics than in business or in other areas of American life. Whether in the executive, judicial, or legislative branch, improper and corrupt practices are the work of a small minority. Florida has endured political scandals that have led to the trial of members of the cabinet, of the judiciary, and of the legislature. Such officials, however, have been removed from office when convicted or defeated for reelection. Therefore, while corruption is a continual problem, it is not the prevailing mode of behavior among politicians. In addition to stringent auditing of records of expenditures of public funds, other remedies, such as public financing of election campaigns, are viewed as potentially helpful. Stringent fiscal disclosure provisions for public officers, codes of ethics, and statutes requiring an official to disqualify himself or herself in cases of conflict of interest are other provisions that inhibit corrupt behavior.

An independent Public Ethics Commission has been specified by the Florida Constitution with the same purpose. It requires candidates to report their financial worth and fiscal holdings. The state also has a law requiring public officials to disclose any business interests they may have in the awarding of any government contract. The same provisions also apply to city and county officials.

Combined with Florida's "government in the sunshine" law, which requires all meetings of public officials to be open, the regulations implemented by the Ethics Commission provide a number of safeguards in Florida to inform the public of what transpires in the public domain.

Florida's Sunshine Law.—The Sunshine Law is based on the concept that all government business—except for the personnel records of individuals in public schools and universities and a few other categories of records, such as those of investigations by grand juries—is public business. Based on a model law advocated by Sigma Delta Chi, an honorary journalism organization, it was enacted by the legislature in 1967. It requires that all elected officials, when meeting to transact government business, must admit the public, including, of course, journalists. It opens all public documents and papers to public inspection. The law has brought about more open transaction of the public's business. It has become a model for other states and for recent legislation by the U.S. Congress relating to federal agencies. It is criticized by some officials, but it has strong public support. Its principles have also been applied to the requirement of fiscal disclosure by public officials (a provision added in 1976 to Florida's constitution and discussed in chapter 6).

The purpose of such fiscal disclosure is to increase citizens' confidence in public officials by showing that they do not profit improperly from their political positions. On the other hand, many officials resent disclosing their assets and income, and at least a few have resigned rather than take such a step. There is also argument that, since so many individuals resent public disclosure, the quality of public officials could decline because many would refuse to serve. Conclusive evidence on the total effect of public disclosure is lacking.

"Resign to run" law.—A rare feature of Florida government is a law that requires any state, county, or local officer to resign before the end of his or her term of office if he or she qualifies as a candidate for any other office—federal, state, or local. This law was inspired by the practice of some officeholders who, for example, were elected for a four-year term and then would run at the end of two years for a higher office. If such a person ran successfully, a special election had to be called to fill the vacancy created. There was also criticism that this type of activity prevented the officeholder from concentrating on the duties for which he or she was elected. For example, Governor Claude Kirk (1968–72) was frequently absent

from the state seeking the Republican nomination for the vice-presidency or possibly the presidency. The public reaction against his absences contributed to the enactment of this stringent "resign to run" law. However, the law may have the undesirable effect of preventing an able individual from continuing in office if he or she fails in a try for a higher position.

Party Organization

There are separate Republican and Democratic party committees in each county and each congressional district of Florida and at the state level. The party voters of each precinct may choose at least one committeeman and committeewoman to each party's county committee. If no one files for those positions at the time of the primary, then the county committee may fill the vacancies from precinct lists. The party county committee receives the filing fees from candidates and opens a party headquarters at the time of the general election. The committee meets periodically and can take out advertising on behalf of candidates in the general election. The county committee elects members to the state committee; the state committee supports statewide candidates and spends party funds for them and for the presidential candidate at the general election. Each party periodically holds a party convention, which sets forth the platform of the party. However, the platform of the candidate may receive much more attention than his or her party's platform at the state level. Finally, the state committee choses members to the national party committee.

Some delegates to the national party nominating conventions, which name the party's candidates for president and vice-president every four years, are chosen from among the state committee members and from the state party's representatives to the national committees. Most of the delegates are pledged to the candidate who wins in the presidential primary, which is held in March of presidential election years. The total state delegation is distributed among statewide delegates and congressional district delegates. The delegates ultimately chosen may include some selected in congressional district assemblies, but they must be pledged to the presidential candidate who won in the congressional district. There is a further requirement that the delegate positions be distributed among men and women and among minorities.

Another feature of party structure in Florida is the November party convention in the year before the quadrennial presidential election. The Democrats started this practice in 1975, when party organization members in the county and state committees, wishing to head off George Wallace's 1976 quest for delegates, arranged for a fall 1975 Democratic state convention. Delegates to the state convention would be chosen partly from county caucuses, but there also would be heavy representation from state Democratic officials and state party members. Further to ensure a majority against Wallace, potential national Democratic candidates for the nomination joined—only for the purpose of this convention—to throw delegate votes to Jimmy Carter as the most likely candidate, partly because he was a fellow southerner, to stop Wallace. The strategy worked and the move served to slow the Wallace candidacy. At the same time it helped to project Carter into the national picture and gave his campaign impetus that other national Democratic candidates would envy.

In 1979 the presidential straw vote convention was repeated with the Republicans following the lead of the Democrats and holding a separate convention on the same November weekend as theirs, the Republicans meeting in Orlando and the

Miami precinct, 1976. Photo courtesy *Miami Herald*.

Democrats in St. Petersburg. The Democratic convention brought out a strong Carter effort, while at the same time a draft-Kennedy movement, centered in Dade County (Miami), was also launched. Governor Jerry Brown's forces had no statewide campaign at that point.

On the Republican side the most intensive campaign was launched by the organization for John Connally, along with less vigorous campaigns by Phillip Crane, George Bush, and Howard Baker; the Ronald Reagan forces, though already well organized, did not launch a statewide television drive nor did their candidate appear.

In addition to the prepresidential straw vote, the state still held its 11 March 1980 preferential primary, and only at the time of this primary were choices actually made by the voters that bound delegates at the national nominating convention. For the would-be presidential nominees, the necessity to be preferred twice by Florida's voters taxed their time, energy, and campaign treasuries.

In all of Florida's sixty-seven counties there are active Democratic organizations and Democratic committees. Except in central and southern Florida and in a few of the larger counties, the Republicans do not have very active county committees or substantial county party structures. In many counties no Republican candidates contest for county offices or school board positions or for state legislative positions. The Democratic party in Florida thus has a much better "grass roots" organization than does the Republican party.

The state party committees have full-time staffs. They maintain complete lists of the county committees and computer printouts of all party members. Funds for the party committee are provided by the filing fees which candidates must pay in order to file for the party primary. Fees for candidates for local office are provided by the local county committee, which then approves expenditures for the general election contests of its candidates. The committee may have handbills and leaflets printed, take out newspaper advertising, purchase radio and television time, and rent sound trucks and hold rallies in various parts of the county. Fees for statewide candidates who file in the statewide party primaries are given to the respective state party committees; at the time of the general election, these fees help to pay for the travel of party candidates and committee members, purchase media time, mailouts, and expenses of soliciting for private contributions to increase the party treasury, and operating expenses for the permanent party headquarters, including salaries of full-time headquarters personnel.

Although at the time of the general election, the party committees pay some of the expenses of the party candidate at the state or local level, this is only a minor part of general election campaign expenditures. In local elections, where there are strongly opposed parties and numerous contested positions, each candidate must expect to continue to raise funds and to pay many of his expenditures from his own campaign treasury. At the state level the same holds true. Democratic and Republican candidates for the governorship continue to find it necessary to pay the bulk of campaign expenses from their own treasury. In the case of congressional candidates and national presidential campaigns, the national organizations do the bulk of the financing.

Lobbying

Informal agencies representing the interests of various kinds of groups in our society, which we call political lobbies, play an important role in Florida's politics both during election campaigns and in the quieter intervals between them.

Lobbying has the full protection of the First Amendment to the U.S. Constitution, which guarantees to every citizen the right of free speech. It also guarantees the right to join with others, to petition for redress of grievances, to present this petition to representatives of the people, and fully to criticize those representatives. Thus lobbying cannot and should not be prohibited, and it offers significant opportunities for political activism.

Regulations upon lobbyists can require that they register and state whom they represent, identify their publications, and list their expenditures and the purpose for which monies were spent. But to attempt to prevent their contacting governmental officials or agencies would be to adopt a rule of censure, which is constitutionally prohibited. This does not mean, however, that they should be protected from the full glare of publicity.

Lobbying consists of activities aimed at getting governments to do what individuals and groups want them to do. The name comes from the practice of prowling the halls, chambers, and lobbies of legislative or executive quarters by persons, both paid and unpaid, who are trying to shape government policy. Lobbyists still work the halls and lobbies of legislatures, but their activities now go far beyond the personal contacts they make there.

Though the legislature is most often thought to be the target of lobbyists, they also attempt to influence decisions of the state cabinet, administrative agencies, regulatory commissions, and even the courts. They are interested in all aspects of government. By influencing governmental appointments, they try to secure friendly personnel in key positions. In election campaigns they are often active in trying to elect legislators, commissioners, and cabinet members who will at least listen to their positions and perhaps push for the governmental policy or action that the lobbyists desire.

The popular view that lobbyists are all bad and that their efforts to influence government are evil is incomplete. Like any other group of people lobbyists are not all alike. Some lobbyists work for noble causes while others work for selfish causes. Some are effective, others are not. Some entertain government officials and provide campaign funds and other favors, many do not. Almost all lobbyists agree that the most important activity they do is provide officials with information. Of course they want the information they provide to support their interests, but the most effective of them know that lying to officials is dangerous.

The most positive aspect of lobbying is the provision of information. Executive branch agencies inform legislators about the needs of their programs. A county supervisor of elections can tell how election law changes will affect registration procedure—for instance, how long it takes to update registration rolls and get them to the precincts.

Business lobbyists can supply information about business taxes in other states or about the effect of a tax on a specific enterprise. A Florida developer can present cost data concerning environmental regulations. Then the legislative committee staff concerned with each topic can check the data with agencies in other states.

Another type of lobbying group is the so-called public interest lobby. Common Cause and the League of Women Voters present data about proposed reforms in campaign expenditures. The Audubon Society and the Sierra Club argue for preservation of the environment.

It should be observed, however, that many of the lobbies for particular interests will seek to avoid taxes or will ask for specific benefits. The legislature, the executive agencies, and the staffs of legislative committees must try to sort out these conflicting interests and influences.

Favors.—Legislators and other members of the Florida government can receive favors from lobbyists, many of whom provide—occasionally or regularly—dinners, parties, and other forms of entertainment for officials. Large parties are a regular feature of the opening week of a new legislative session. The families of legislators are most likely to be in the capital that week, and these parties are heavily attended by legislators, their spouses, aides, and friends. For many years the Tallahassee Chamber of Commerce has hosted one of the more lavish of these affairs. The lobbyist for the trucking companies has had a daily free buffet breakfast in a special room of a local hotel for a number of legislative sessions. The lobbyist for the mobile home industry is a regular nightly host to legislators and guests in a club the industry maintains for this purpose in a quiet setting just outside Tallahassee called "The Trailers." The club is just that: it centers on a complex of mobile homes arranged and furnished for the sole purpose of providing food, drink, and entertainment for the legislators. Party nights at "The Trailers" are a topic of hot gossip and get newspaper attention almost every year. Other lobbyists, such as the prestigious and well-heeled Associated Industries of Florida, take a quieter approach to entertainment. Their style is to have their director of lobbying activities provide almost nightly cookouts for selected officials in his backyard; drinks and steak dinners are served in this traditionally American symbolic setting of family solidarity. Many nights during the legislative session there may be as many as four or five functions hosted by lobbyists.

Some lobbying interests go in for bigger affairs. A cruise to the Bahamas for a few key legislative leaders financed and conducted by an association of harbor pilots was an embarrassment when it became the subject of news stories. Legislative appreciation weekends have been a standard lobbying practice; the City of Sarasota has provided one of the most attractive of these. Universities and other governmental agencies have sponsored such weekends. Officials are given special seating at university sporting events and the Florida vs. Florida State football game is an annual fall highlight for government officials. The

Department of Natural Resources has special facilities and employees who provide services to officials. These entertainments by other state government units are all lobbying efforts, although they do not seem as controversial as the gratuities provided by the lobbyists for private interests.

Regulation of lobbyists.—Some lobbyists lobby against lobbying. Common Cause and the Florida League of Women Voters, with other groups, have been successful in efforts to secure lobbyist registration and disclosure of funds spent in behalf of legislative lobbying. Both houses of the legislature now have rules that require the registration of any citizen who goes to the legislature to influence the lawmakers. Casual visitors and one-day lobbyists are exempt. The rules cover both private lobbyists and government employees. At the end of the session registered lobbyists are required to file a form showing how much money they spent on legislative lobbying activities and the categories of their expenditures. In 1973 over $100,000 was reported for wining and dining legislators. This amounted to $10 per day per legislator. The lobbyists are not required to say on whom the money was spent. There is no registration or disclosure legislation for lobbying nongovernment officials. Efforts are underway to pass such legislation.

Bribery and campaign contributions.—Outright bribery of legislators or their key staff members has rarely come to light in Florida. Several conflict-of-interest cases involving cabinet members have resulted in resignations and removal of those involved. It is clear that there are government officials in Florida who are willing to enter into such arrangements, but the legislature has not been accused of this kind of corruption.

Campaign contributions are legal for lobbyists and their organizations, and some people look upon these as legal bribes. The Florida Medical Association has an organization used heavily for the purpose of providing campaign funds to legislative candidates. Most campaign funds come from business interests, but some are provided by unions and educational associations. The lobbyists' interest in making contributions may be to prevent defeat of a friendly legislator, to defeat an unfriendly legislator, or merely to ensure that a legislator knows them so that they will be able to get an audience easily. Reformers see public financing of campaigns as a means of ending this practice, but thus far such reforms have failed in Florida.

Candidates' reports from 1972 indicate that lobbyists gave one of every four contributed dollars reported. Over $600,000 of lobbyists' contributions to legislative candidates could be traced. Another $300,000 came directly from builders, developers, and realtors. Lawyers gave $204,000, financial institutions $112,000, insurance interests $70,000, and auto dealers and agricultural dealers $41,000 each. In the 1980s political action committees, which represent special interests, play an increasingly important role. In the 1982 legislative races in Florida, PACS contributed $2.8 million.

Sometimes lobbyists are almost obliged to make campaign contributions. The president of the senate and the speaker of the house often form committees to have an appreciation dinner held in their honor. Tickets may be sold for a specific price, often $250, and lobbyists can buy as many tickets as they feel are necessary—whether they use them or not. The speaker and the president are very powerful in the legislative process and these dinners are almost always very successful. In 1976 the president of the senate and his dinner took in $46,000 and netted, after expenses, $37,959. That year he had a tough reelection campaign and applied the funds to that successful effort. Had he not needed it for the campaign he could have used it as he liked. Some leaders distribute portions of these funds to favorite members of the house or senate for their campaigns. This largesse serves to strengthen the power of the leadership by further obligating those members to the fund-givers. Under the law the members could actually keep the funds for their personal use.

The 1976 senate president's committee received over 800 checks. The checks came from grocery chains like Winn-Dixie and Publix, from a host of insurance associations and private insurance companies, from banks and bank holding companies, from associations representing five different kinds of doctors, from people who build state highways and those who sell asphalt to the state, from wine, beer, liquor, and horse-racing interests, from international corporations, paper, timber, and phosphate industries, and even from a wildlife association and the Police Benevolent Association. To complete the list, a cemetery association found reason to appreciate the senate president. One lobbyist representing contractors, natural gas interests, and security dealers, among others, was so moved in his devotion that he gave twice, one donation listing his office address and one listing his home address. He thus earned the distinction of giving both at home and at the office.

The lobbyists who engage in the practice of doing favors for officials nearly always maintain that they have to do so. They think it is expected of them by the officials and is an important way for them to get to know those officials. The legislature brings 160 members to Tallahassee each year. At least 30 of these will be new members each session. A good lobbyist wants to be on a first-name basis with as many legislators as possible, wants to be able to get appointments to see them, and wants phone calls returned. Entertainment and campaign support help in accomplishing these goals, although most lobbyists say that they do not often talk about legislation with lawmakers at social functions.

Effective lobbyists, in their day-to-day activities, try to stay in close contact with legislative leaders and legislators in key positions related to their interests. They also hope to maintain close ties with legislative staff members, since these people are important in the legislative process. Gaining access, giving information, and maintaining trust are the tools of the lobbyist. Money and a large group of supportive voters help maintain that access. Prior to reapportionment in the 1960s, with one or two exceptions, the racetracks were so successful that they maintained control over the presidency of the senate. This assured favorable legislation for tracks, limitation of competition, and favorable racing dates.

Roles of the lobbyist.—Effective lobbying is a full-time activity. The lobbyist must be there for committee meetings, floor debates, and informal meetings. Part-time lobbyists are at a disadvantage because of the flow of legislative activity. If they are not there all the time, the things they want may not get moved when they need to be moved and the things they don't want may get moved without their knowledge. For this reason many interests find it vital to have full-time lobbyists in Tallahassee before and during the legislative session. Year-round representation is even better for their cause, since legislative committee meetings take place year-round. As a result, lobbying has become a major occupation in Tallahassee. Some of these people became lobbyists by representing their professions, some through the practice of law, some from former service in the legislature or as legislative staff employees, and others from jobs in various branches of government. There are lobbyists who learned the legislative and governmental ropes as private citizens and journalists. There are lobbyists who went from college to an apprenticeship with established lobbyists. Lobbying is an occupation without formal training or certification. It is largely based upon such attributes as judgment, discretion, and tact. The knowledge needed comes mostly from on-the-job training.

It is obvious from the description of the senate president's dinner that business and professional interests are heavily represented among the ranks of Tallahassee lobbyists. They have a host of policies to pursue, ranging from favorable tax breaks through friendly regulation to little items like permitting the use of nonreturnable soft drink bottles. However, many nonbusiness groups are active in lobbying. Educational lobbyists are a case in point. Among the educational interests besieging the legislature are lobbyists from the State of Florida Department of Education, School Board Association, community college associations, private college associations, the State University System, each separate state university, school superintendents' associations, principals' associations, and unions representing teachers, professors, bus drivers, clerical workers, and many others.

There are a handful of lobbyists for senior citizens; there are associations and government employees lobbying for the physically and mentally handicapped, retarded children, alcoholics, university students, and abused animals.

There are lobbyists representing a whole spectrum of occupational groups.

Doctors and lawyers have very strong lobbies. Bail bondsmen, barbers, innkeepers, nurses, hairdressers, realtors, and migrant farm workers are served by lobbying.

Some of the most effective lobbying is done by former members and staff of the legislature. In 1978 three former senate presidents had active lobbying firms representing a host of interests from state highway patrolmen and automobile travel clubs to the giants of the trucking industry.

The American Civil Liberties Union is represented. Two people represent the two Roman Catholic bishops and one part-time person represents seven Protestant denominations.

Perhaps the strongest lobbying is done by government employees, who represent the interests of their programs, their clients, or themselves. In recent years the legislature has moved to restrict these activities, but they are still intense. Almost four hundred Florida cities are represented by the Florida League of Cities. All sixty-seven counties are represented through the Association of County Commissioners. In addition, some cities and counties have their own lobbyists present.

Demonstrations are a form of lobbying, and in recent years the capitol has seen demonstrations for and against wars, for blacks and migrant workers, and against the Shah of Iran. When Congress proposed the Equal Rights Amendment (ERA), there was an annual mob scene in the capitol's halls as anti-ERA women under male leadership did battle with women supporting the ERA. The congestion was so great that this regularly scheduled match almost halted legislative action until the final vote was taken on the matter each session.

In spite of the seemingly endless list of lobbyists, there are some groups which are not represented. Most notable among these are the least powerful groups in our society. Neither the poor nor the blacks are directly represented. Blue-collar criminals are not represented and white-collar criminals continue to get advantages that are not available to their less wealthy counterparts. Lobbying requires money and resources. Groups without these two necessities are underrepresented and may lose out in the policy-making process.

Informal rules.—Among experienced lobbyists and legislators a set of behaviors is expected if there is to be any chance of being effective at the job. Lobbyists come and go; some of those who have gone have done so because they failed to follow these informal rules.

Foremost among these rules is that one must never lie to a public official. Misleading an official can lead to his or her embarrassment. Any lobbyist who makes an official look bad because of false information is in trouble. The word spreads quickly, and the lobbyist is widely ignored by all who hear it.

Also near the top of the list of things not to do is to threaten an elected official with defeat. Lobbyists with large constituency groups such as teachers or senior citizens may be tempted to tell a legislator that they will defeat him or her in the next election if the legislator does not go along with their program. This approach is certain to anger the legislator and make him or her less cooperative in the future. Secondly, if the group fails to defeat the legislator, that lawmaker will owe the threatening group nothing in future sessions. Perhaps this rule should be stated: never threaten to defeat an official unless you are absolutely certain that you can cause that defeat to take place.

Expressing anger to an official is also bad form. A lobbyist should always be in a position to come back to an official. The effective lobbyist will express sorrow that an official was not with his or her group on one issue but will want to be in a position to request support on the next issue and those that follow. Officials also get upset with masses of identical letters that are duplicated and flood their offices. Impersonal mail is not taken seriously. It clogs the office and takes up valuable staff time.

Personal mail and personal phone calls are considered effective. Phone calls to legislators are more likely to be answered if they are made early or late in the day when the legislature is in session, as committees and regular sessions occupy much of the middle of the day. Visits by constituents are also good.

Other positive actions considered effective include preparation, requiring the ability to answer legislative inquiries as well as questions which the opposition might raise. Lobbyists should not overlook state agencies which make regulations and draft statutes in the lobbyists' area of interest. It is also important that the lobbyist be present for any meeting that might affect his or her group. A lobbyist caught short by missing a crucial decision had better have a good excuse to give to his or her employers. Finally, it is important to make contact with key staff and officials before committee or floor votes. Much of the action that takes place at official meetings is merely window dressing, and the votes on many issues are decided before the formal meetings are held.

Right to lobby.—Some people consider only the negative aspects of lobbying or become upset because it distributes power unfairly or unequally. These aspects are certainly present. On the other hand, lobbying permits the placing of citizens' views before officials and provides some needed information to persons responsible for making public policy. Basically it must be recognized that lobbying is protected in the constitutions of the United States and Florida under provisions for free speech and the right to petition the government. This does not mean that lobbying practices cannot be regulated, but it does mean that lobbyists cannot be denied access to governmental officials.

With increased population, Florida has a growing impact in presidential elections, its 19 electoral votes making it the state with the seventh largest number. It has a greater impact on both national conventions due to the size of its delegation and its early presidential preference primary in election years. In 1984, leading

Democrats Gary Hart, Walter Mondale, Jesse Jackson, and John Glenn all contested for Florida's endorsement in the primary.

We will next consider how the election process actually works. What are the dynamics of Florida politics? How do the parties interact? Who supports them? What types of individuals are active in Florida politics, and what types of social and economic groups support them? Who are the Republicans, who are the Democrats, how many voters are independent? These answers and a view of how the voters and the candidates interacted in a number of recent election contests is called analysis of political behavior.

Selected References

Alexander, Herbert E. *Financing Politics: Money, Elections, and Political Reform*. Washington: Congressional Quarterly Press, 1972.

Dauber, Greg. "Lobbying." *Tallahassee Democrat*, 13 February 1976.

Ezell, Wayne. "Barron Dinner Raises $46,000." *Tallahassee Democrat,* 3 March 1976.

Florida. Legislature. *Journal of the House of Representatives*. Tallahassee, 1845– . (Contains list of lobbyists registered with the house.)

Florida. Legislature. *Journal of the Senate*. Tallahassee, 1845– . (Contains list of lobbyists registered with the senate.)

Giles, Bruce. "Florida Lobbyists Had a Busy Session." *Tallahassee Democrat*, 16 July 1973.

Huckshorn, Robert J. *Party Leadership in the State*. Amherst: University of Massachusetts Press, 1978.

Keefe, William J., and Ogul, Morris S. *The American Legislative Process: Congress and the States*. 4th ed. Englewood Cliffs, N.J.: Prentice-Hall, 1977.

Mansfield, William, and Giles, Bruce. "The Greening of the Legislature." *Miami Herald, St. Petersburg Times,* and *Tallahassee Democrat,* 25–29 March 1973.

Morris, Allen C. *The Florida Handbook*. Tallahassee: Peninsular Publishing Co., 1977.

Roady, Elston E., and Dauer, Manning J. "The Florida Legislature." In *Southeastern State Legislatures,* edited by William G. Cornelius. Atlanta, Ga.: Emory University, 1968.

Zeigler, Harmon. "Interest Groups in the States." In *Politics in the American States,* edited by Herbert Jacob and Kenneth N. Vines. Boston: Little, Brown, 1965.

Florida's Elections

by Mark Stern

UNIVERSITY OF CENTRAL FLORIDA

5

Florida Growth and the Republican Party Base

All across the South the tide of Republican voting was rising in the 1960s. Forecasters saw in the ever improving showings of Republican candidates a permanent shift away from the solidly Democratic South. In Florida the Republican party's major accomplishments were the election of Claude Kirk, Jr., to the governorship (1966) and the election of Edward J. Gurney as United States senator (1968). With Gurney's election, the Republican party had a sitting governor and United States senator from Florida for the first time since Reconstruction.

An era of two-party politics, long awaited and often prophesied, was thought to be at hand, but by the late 1970s the tide of Republicanism had ebbed, leaving "might-have-beens" in some numbers along the high-water mark. In 1979 no statewide elective office in Florida was held by a Republican, and of 15 congressmen, only 3 were Republicans. But in 1980 one U.S. senator was Republican. By 1983 the GOP held only 22.5 percent of senate seats and 30 percent of house seats, down from almost 36 percent in 1973. As others have pointed out, Florida's Democrats may be as factious as ever, but Republicans have not been very successful in taking advantage of the situation.

In 1928, Florida gave Herbert Hoover the highest percentage of the popular vote, almost 57 percent, that he received in any state of the old Confederacy. Florida next went Republican in 1952, for Eisenhower, and subsequently has voted Republican at every presidential general election except in 1964 and 1976. Thirty years ago Key noted that "Florida is Different" in ways that made him believe it would be among the first states of the "solid South" to support a real two-party system.

Florida's per capita income was the second highest of the southern states in 1947 and in 1975. Among southern states in 1940, Florida led in population classified as urban, and in 1975 Florida was still the South's most urban state. In the 1940s only three Florida counties had populations that were 50 percent or more black—a factor, Key felt, that would prevent domination of Florida's politics by the race question and allow competition for the black vote. Parts of the South with large black populations had dominated the area's politics through the one-party system, deemed necessary for eliminating competition for votes of poor whites and blacks. Virulent racism did not prevail in Florida politics after

World War II; 63.8 percent of Florida's eligible black population was registered to vote in 1964, the second highest in the South. Yet, despite the high rate of black registration, only 9.61 percent of the state's registered voters in 1980 were black. The white population has grown rapidly in Florida, and although the total number of blacks has increased in each decade since 1920, the rate of growth of the white population was consistently more than twice that of the black. The proportion of blacks was constantly diminishing in a state that had few large concentrations of blacks except in a few metropolitan centers and in a few rural Panhandle counties.

All of these factors contributed to the development of a two-party system in Florida. In addition, among southern states Florida had one unique advantage for developing of a solid Republican base: a large immigrant population from nonsouthern Republican areas. In 1940 nearly half of Florida's population (48.1 percent) came from outside the state, more than twice the immigration rate of any other southern state. Key noted in 1949 that the "large immigrant Republican population . . . has not been activated by the Republican organization," a comment perhaps even more appropriate today. Florida's growth has been over twice the national average in every decade since 1910. In the 1970s Florida had the largest numerical population gain in the country. These immigrants have usually entered the southern metropolitan areas of the state. A 1974 report indicated that 94 percent of the immigrant population in the period 1950–70 moved into the area of the state below the frostline. H. Douglas Price employed an imaginary boundary line that runs approximately east-west below Ocala to divide Florida north and south, paralleling the frostline, below which is found the citrus-growing area. Figure 5.1 shows the boundaries of Florida's 19 congressional districts, four of which were added after the 1980 census. Twelve are represented by Democrats, seven by Republicans (Democrat Andy Ireland switched to the Republican party in March 1984). All Republican congressmen are from below the frostline.

Table 5.1 shows the ten most populous counties by location above or below the frostline and by percentage of the state's registered Democrats and Republicans in each. Over half (52 percent) of all Floridians live in the most populous 6 of the state's 67 counties, and only one of these (Duval) is above the frostline. The populous southern counties also contain most of the state's registered voters.

Nine of the ten largest counties are located below the frostline, as are most registered Republicans. While five counties (of which only Duval is in the northern part of the state) account for nearly half (49.4 percent) of all registered

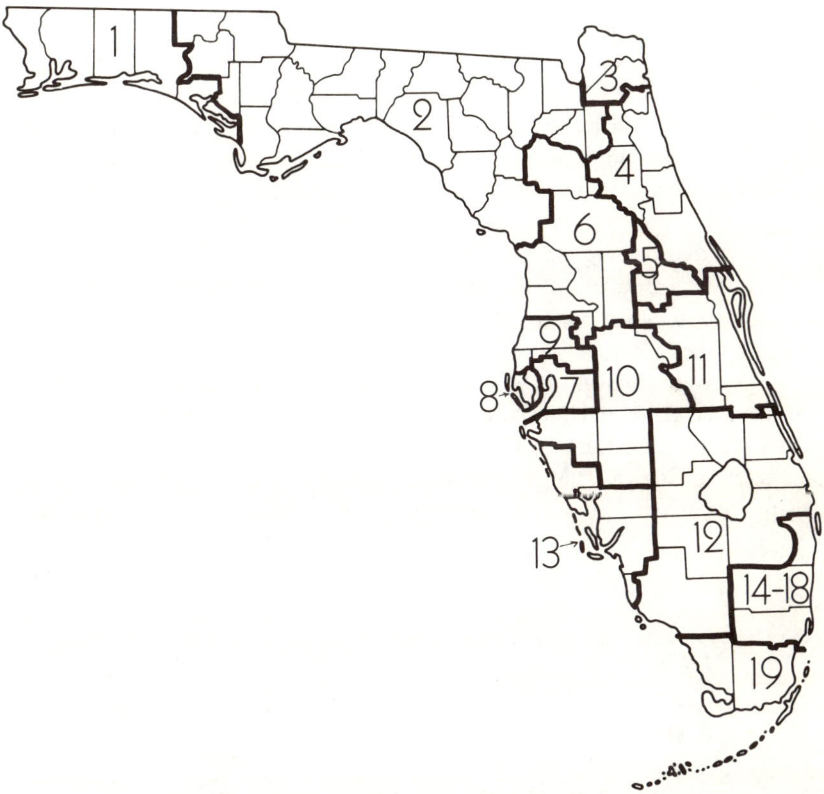

Fig. 5.1. Boundaries of Florida's Congressional Districts after the 1980 Census.

Democrats, four counties (all below the frostline) account for more than half (50.8 percent) of all registered Republicans. Sarasota County, thirteenth in population, ranks sixth in percentage of total registered Republicans in the state. Pinellas County may be considered the birthplace of the "new" Florida Republicanism; it is the home county of William Cramer, the first popularly elected Republican congressman since Reconstruction.

GOP strength in Florida is thus located in the southern portion of the state. The 11 counties with the highest percentage of Republican registration are below the frostline and account for 76 percent of all registered Republicans in the state. Of the 19 congressmen now from Florida, 6 are Republican, all from the Republican horseshoe which starts on the west coast below Sarasota, runs north to include St. Petersburg, crosses the state through Orlando to the east coast, and goes down that coast to include Palm Beach County and Ft. Lauderdale.

The growing areas of the state are those where the Republican base is strongest. This continues a pattern noted in earlier years by Manning J. Dauer in "Florida: The Different State." Florida is a state with a high proportion of recent immigrants, two-thirds of whom are nonsoutherners; of these, 37 percent consider themselves to be Republicans, 31 percent Democrats. Pearson's coefficient of correlation (r), which varies from +1.0 for a perfect positive association between two variables to 0.0 for no association and −1.0 for a perfect negative, or inverse, relationship, shows a +.31 relationship between Republi-

TABLE 5.1. Population and Political Preference of Voters in Florida's 10 Largest Counties, 1980

County	Above (N) or Below (S) Frost Line	Population	Percent of State's Democrats Registered	Percent of State's Republicans Registered
Dade	S	1,625,781	16.3	10.5
Broward	S	1,018,200	10.6	12.4
Pinellas	S	728,531	7.2	14.4
Hillsborough	S	646,960	6.1	4.0
Duval	N	576,863	5.5	8.0
Palm Beach	S	571,000	6.3	2.9
Orange	S	471,016	3.5	4.8
Polk	S	321,652	3.1	2.3
Brevard	S	272,959	2.9	4.0
Escambia	N	258,762	2.6	2.8

Note: Population figures are from the U.S. Census of 1980. Registration figures are from Secretary of State as published in *Florida Statistical Abstract 1982*, p. 545.

can registration in 1976 and county population change in the period 1960–76 and a + .35 relationship between Republican registration and net migration into each county during the period 1960–70. The correlation of Democratic registration with population change and net migration into each county in 1976 is only .13.* The growth of registration and of Florida's population appear to be inseparable, yet while Florida has continued to grow, Republican officeholding in Florida has not progressed much since the 1960s and has, in some respects, slid backward.

Elections in the 1960s and 1970s: Governor and United States Senator

At the time of Key's study, contesting elections was not the major concern of Florida Republicans; control of presidential patronage was the party's goal. Dauer, reviewing the early 1950s, found that this pattern of GOP state leadership had not changed and that electorally "active Republicans were regarded as a nuisance, threatening control of the party machinery and of patronage coming through presidential appointments" (p. 116). The election of Representative William Cramer in 1954 and the election of Governor Claude Kirk in 1966 clearly shifted the focus of Republican concerns in Florida. No matter how much Republican leadership wished to keep the party small and not have to put up with bothersome serious contesting of elections, the influx of new residents combined with changes in the state made public office seeking by potential GOP upstarts too tempting a target to be bypassed.

In the 1940s the Democratic gubernatorial candidates who had opposition, Millard F. Caldwell (1944) and Fuller Warren (1948), received 78.9 percent and 83.4 percent, respectively, of the popular vote. In 1940 Spessard L. Holland faced no opposition for control of the executive mansion. In 1952 Dan McCarty received 74.8 percent of the vote; LeRoy Collins received 80.5 percent of the vote in 1954 and 73.77 percent in 1956. Clearly Republican opposition was not threatening the Democratic gubernatorial candidates of this period. The contested United States Senate elections offer an even sharper picture of Democratic dominance. In 1940 Democrat Charles O. Andrews faced no opposition; Spessard L. Holland in 1952 and George A. Smathers in 1960 received

*Pearson's r, as a measure of association between two variables, is widely used in the social sciences. Often given with the correlation coefficient is the level of statistical significance. Statistical significance means the likelihood of the particular association being a nonrandom event. This is usually expressed as $p<.05$ or $p<.01$, which means there are less than 5 chances in 100 or less than 1 chance in 100 that the particular relationship is just a random occurrence. The .31 and .35 correlations are both $p<.01$. The .13 correlation is not significant.

76.3 percent of the popular vote and in 1958 Holland received 71.2 percent of the vote. Clearly, the 1950s were a continuation of the forties insofar as two-party gubernatorial and U.S. Senate election patterns were concerned.

In the 1960s a different picture emerged for Florida Republicans. In 1960 Democrat Farris Bryant garnered only 59.8 percent of the gubernatorial vote in his run against Republican George C. Peterson. Haydon Burns in 1964 received only 56.1 percent of the vote in his run against Republican Charley R. Holley. In 1966 Robert King High, a moderately liberal mayor of Miami, won only 44.9 percent of the gubernatorial vote to Claude Kirk's 55.1 percent. High had fought a bitter primary contest with Governor Burns to win the Democratic nomination, but in the general election he was able to carry only Dade, Monroe, and Hillsborough counties below the frost line. In addition, the Democratic primary had been so fierce and High had been painted with the liberal brush so effectively in both the primary and general elections that Kirk actually carried eight counties in the heart of the solidly Democratic Panhandle. Kirk, in a U.S. Senate contest in 1964, had been soundly defeated by Spessard Holland, getting only 36 percent of the general election vote. In the 1968 U.S. Senate contest, former Governor Collins was branded an unrepentent liberal and Edward J. Gurney won 55.9 percent of the vote. Collins carried only Dade, Monroe, and Hillsborough counties in the south. In the northern section of the state, the solid Democratic Panhandle became, except for Alachua County, the solid Republican Panhandle. Although the Republican party base was in the south, a Republican candidate demonstrated that the Panhandle could be won.

Throughout the years after 1965, all of Florida's Democratic gubernatorial candidates campaigned on nonsegregationist positions (see Black's study, *Southern Governors and Civil Rights*). While the leading Democratic gubernatorial candidates were clearly moderating their positions on segregation and racial issues, Governor Kirk closed down the Manatee County school system in 1970 rather than observe court-ordered busing of schoolchildren. The governor backed down under threat of a court-imposed penalty, but clearly he had made a point that he felt the conservative Panhandle would not miss.

In 1970, however, a Democratic legislator from the Panhandle region, Reubin Askew, received 56.9 percent of the popular vote in his gubernatorial contest against Governor Kirk. Only two of the ten counties that Kirk carried were above the frost line. A moderate, nonsegregationist Democrat had carried the state and the Panhandle against a conservative Republican. In the same year a Democrat, Lawton Chiles, won 53.9 percent of the popular vote for United States senator against Congressman William Cramer, who carried only eleven counties, all in the south. Cramer had fought a bitter battle against Harrold Carswell to get the Republican nomination. He had spent years building up the

Republican party organization and had given up his state house seat to run for the Senate. Carswell had been nominated for the Supreme Court by President Nixon and had been rejected by the U. S. Senate. Edward Gurney and Claude Kirk had persuaded Carswell to make a run for the Senate seat. The primary election deeply split the Republican party, and the Cramer loyalists were convinced that Gurney and Kirk had pushed Carswell to run against Cramer in order to gain control of the state Republican party organization. The aftermath: Republican chaos and strife.

On the Democratic party side, the 1970 election ushered in a new era for the Democratic party organization and the government of the state. As Bass and DeVries observed in *The Transformation of Southern Politics*, "among the New South governors who emerged in the early 1970s none surpassed Askew either in programmatic achievements or in exercising leadership" (pp. 126–27). Askew had campaigned on a platform advocating a state corporate income tax, environmental protection, financial disclosure, and what has since become one of Florida's trademarks, "government in the sunshine." His achievements, once he won the governorship, were remarkable by almost any standard. Florida's electorate was pleased with Askew, and in 1974 he won 68.8 percent of the vote in a four-way Democratic primary, then went on to take 61.1 percent of the vote in the general election against a former Democrat, Florida Senate President Jerry Thomas. Seventeen of the twenty-one counties Thomas carried were in the northern part of the state. Moderate Askew carried the south almost solidly, while conservative Democrat-turned-Republican Thomas won only the southern counties of Pinellas, Hendry, Lake, and, by less than forty votes, Okeechobee. The large core Republican counties of Palm Beach, Broward, Sarasota, and Orange all went Democratic.

There was also a U.S. Senate seat open in 1974. Jack Eckerd defeated Paula Hawkins in the Republican primary (67.5 percent to 32.5 percent) but lost to Democrat Richard (Dick) Stone in a three-way general election. John Grady, a physician from the south-central town of Belle Glade, ran as the American party candidate and received 15.7 percent of the total vote; Eckerd received 40.9 percent, and Stone won the election with 43.4 percent of the vote. In 1974 eleven candidates ran in the state's first Democratic U.S. Senate primary; Stone's 19.4 percent placed him in a runoff with Representative Bill Gunter of Orlando, who received 28.9 percent of the Democratic primary vote. Stone won the runoff with a 50.8 percent majority vote, amassed primarily in the Dade area and in the Panhandle. In the general election Stone put together a coalition that included most of the northern counties and the big urban counties of the south. He carried Escambia, Leon, Duval, Broward, Palm Beach, and, by a better than two-to-one margin, Dade. The Dade County margin of 90,275 votes exceeded his winning margin over Eckerd (767,291 to 721,013). A Miami-based Jewish candidate with strong Miami backing had brought together the old Democrats of the Panhandle with the big-city Democrats of the south to win the Senate seat.

In 1976, Lawton Chiles successfully won a second term as U.S. senator and in 1982 won a third term. He is minority leader of the U.S. Senate Finance Committee and a leading figure in the tax battles of the Reagan administration. When Richard Stone ran for a second term in the 1980 senatorial race, he was defeated for renomination by a Democratic opponent, State Treasurer William Gunter. But in the Reagan landslide, Gunter was defeated by Republican candidate Paula Hawkins, who won narrowly by heavy majorities in the Republican southern and central counties.

In 1978 both political parties had highly contested gubernatorial primaries. The Republican contest involved a head-on confrontation between Central Florida Congressman Lou Frey and Central-Gulf-coast-based Jack Eckerd, unsuccessful 1974 GOP nominee for the U.S. Senate and successful developer of a cross-state chain of drugstores that bears his name. Eckerd soundly defeated Frey (63.7 percent to 36.3 percent) in the primary, but the contest and its aftermath were both bitter and GOP ranks were never successfully closed. The loser complained of party outsiders buying elections and the winner moved haltingly to heal the breach. The Democrats had seven candidates running in their first gubernatorial primary, including such luminaries as former Republican Governor Kirk; Bruce Smathers, the son of a former U.S. senator and the incumbent secretary of state; Hans Tanzler, mayor of Jacksonville; Jim Williams, the incumbent lieutenant governor; Robert Shevin, the incumbent attorney general; and Bob Graham, a state senator from the Miami area.

Senator Graham conducted a "jobs" campaign that was as effective as Senator Chiles' 1970 "Walking Lawton" campaign. Up and down the state Graham spent one day each in 100 different jobs. He received 25.2 percent of the total vote cast in the first primary and made it into the runoff. His margin included winning a majority or plurality of the votes in seventeen northern counties and eight southern counties. Of the six largest counties in Florida, Pinellas was the only one carried by Graham, with 39.2 percent of the vote. On the other hand, although he did not carry any of the other large counties, almost half (47.3 percent) of Graham's total vote came out of the six largest counties in the state.

Attorney General Shevin, favored by many pundits to become the Democratic nominee, won 34.8 percent of the total votes cast. Shevin was an aggressive and well-known attorney general; he had strong union support and strong intraparty organization support in the Miami area. He carried a majority or plurality of the vote in ten northern counties and seventeen southern counties—Broward with 58.3 percent, Dade with 54.6 percent, Hillsborough with 32.4

percent, and Palm Beach with 46.6 percent. The six largest counties provided 62.7 percent of his total vote. The runoff campaign took on a strident tone as Shevin sharply attacked his opponent's "liberal" legislative voting record. The effort backfired, as Shevin's attack became the center of attention. Liberal record or not, Graham won the primary election, sweeping all but Broward, Dade, Brevard, Lee, Sarasota, Lake, and Sumter counties in the south and losing only Dixie and Escambia in the north. In the general election, Graham carried five of the six largest counties, losing only in Pinellas, where he received 43.5 percent of the vote. Graham lost thirteen other southern counties and carried all but three of the thirty-six northern counties. Except for Martin and St. Johns, Graham carried every county from Monroe to Dade and up the east coast. He swept every county north and east of Citrus, Marion, and Clay. Graham proved to be an effective and popular governor in the mold of Reubin Askew, and in 1982 he won an easy victory over the Republican gubernatorial candidate, U.S. congressman "Skip" Bafalis.

The Panhandle–urban southern county coalition was breached by winning Republican candidates, Kirk (in 1966) and Gurney (in 1968), both of whom carried a majority of the northern counties and a majority of the six largest urban counties. No other Republican candidate for the U.S. Senate or the governor's mansion was to achieve this feat. Palm Beach–based GOP gubernatorial candidate and former Democrat Jerry Thomas won seventeen northern counties and none of the six largest urban counties in 1974. In the same year, south-based candidate Jack Eckerd carried three of the six largest counties but could not tie this to any significant northern county victory. In U.S. Senate and gubernatorial elections the Democratic hegemony based in the Panhandle and the large urban centers continues to dominate the state. Tough primary fights, as in 1978, do not alter this coalition significantly in general elections. The ticket of Graham from Miami and Wayne Mixson from the Panhandle as lieutenant governor personifies this coalition. The coalition has matured as it has extended its embrace to Miami-based candidates, unheard of prior to the 1970s. Radicals surely will not win Florida elections, but even moderately liberal Democrats of Jewish or Miami origin, or both, find winning support in this coalition.

Elections in the 1960s and 1970s: The Presidency

Eisenhower carried Florida for the GOP in 1952 and 1956. In 1952 with 55 percent of the popular vote, he won a majority in all but nine of the southern counties, including every major urban area south of the frost line. The Panhandle remained true to the Democrats, however, and only the six most southeasterly of the north counties went Republican. In 1956 Eisenhower's majority of 57.2 percent exceeded his 1952 vote but the pattern of victory in 1956 was remarkably similar to that of 1952. Except for Duval County switching to the Republican column and Flagler County switching to the Democratic side, Eisenhower won exactly the same northern counties and again won every major urban area in the south, cutting his loss to only seven counties in this region.

In 1960 Florida again went Republican, giving Nixon 51.5 percent of the total vote. Nixon carried only Alachua in the north, but he won twenty-four of the thirty-one southern counties, losing only Hillsborough and Dade among the large centers of population. Beginning in 1964 Florida had a series of presiden-

TABLE 5.2. Correlation Coefficient (Pearson's r) of Florida's County Vote between Democratic Presidential Nominees, 1948–76

Candidate (Year)	Stevenson (1952)	Stevenson (1956)	Kennedy (1960)	Johnson (1964)	Humphrey (1968)	McGovern (1972)	Carter (1976)
Truman (1948)	.92*	.94*	.89*	–.05	–.41*	–.27*	.69*
Stevenson (1952)		.96*	.91*	–.04	–.50*	–.38*	.69*
Stevenson (1956)			.93*	–.01	–.43*	–.31*	.76*
Kennedy (1960)				.10	–.30*	–.21**	.79*
Johnson (1964)					.38*	.31*	.14
Humphrey (1968)						.69*	–.14
McGovern (1972)							.04

*p < .01
**p < .05

tial elections that turned past patterns upside down. As Bernard Cosman points out in *Five States for Goldwater,* historic battle lines that had endured in presidential elections since Reconstruction were disrupted not only in Florida but across the South. Table 5.2 shows the countywide correlation of Democratic presidential votes between consecutive elections in the period 1948–76.

From 1948 through 1960 the county-by-county pattern of Democratic support was extremely consistent. In 1964, 1968, and 1972, elections all appear to have had a very different voting pattern than the presidential elections of 1948 through 1960. The 1964 election pattern is somewhat consistent with those of 1968 and 1972; the 1968 and 1972 county patterns appear to be highly related. The 1976 election appears to have been, for the most part, a return to the pattern of the earlier period—a matter to be discussed.

Another approach to electoral patterns is to assess any continuity in the socioeconomic bases of the vote of each party's candidate. Table 5.3 uses selected county socioeconomic characteristics and shows the correlation between each of these variables and the county-by-county vote received by each Democratic presidential candidate for 1960 through 1976.

While the Kennedy-Carter pattern of socioeconomic bases of support are remarkably consistent, the Johnson, Humphrey, and McGovern bases appear to be distinctly different from those two. The Kennedy vote is from smaller, less changed, less urban, younger, less educated, lower-income areas with higher

TABLE 5.3. Correlation Coefficient (Pearson's r) between Selected Florida County Socioeconomic Variables and County Democratic Presidential Vote, 1960–76

	Candidate (Year)				
Socioeconomic Variable	Kennedy (1960)	Johnson (1964)	Humphrey (1968)	McGovern (1972)	Carter (1976)
Population size, 1970	–.36*	.21**	.51*	.46*	–.28*
Net population change, 1960–70	–.53*	.03	.16	.07	–.46*
Rate of population inmigration, 1960–70	–.56*	.03	.16	.07	–.45*
Percentage of urban population, 1970	–.56*	.18	.46*	.35*	–.68*
Median age of population, 1970	.55*	.05	.17	.08	–.43*
Median education of population, 1970	–.64*	.22**	.41*	.25**	–.74*
Median income of population, 1970	–.41*	.13	.33*	.25**	–.46*
Percent of nonwhite population, 1970	.26*	–.07	.33*	.43*	.37*

*p < .01
**p < .05

concentrations of black populations in the state. Except for Dade and Hillsborough counties, all of the most populous southern counties went Republican in 1960. Except for Alachua, however, Kennedy swept the traditionally Democratic Panhandle, the area of the state that is typified by this socioeconomic description. The 1964 Democratic presidential vote correlates with little except, very moderately, population size, urbanism, and education. Goldwater carried twenty-seven of the thirty-six northern counties and nineteen of the thirty-one southern counties. Of the six largest counties, Dade, Hillsborough, and Pinellas went into the Democratic column, by 64 percent, 58.5 percent, and 55 percent of the vote, respectively. Johnson's Dade County net margin of 91,461 votes was not only more than his total statewide margin of 42,599 votes but also amounted to more votes than the total cast for both candidates in every county except the next five most populous counties. Johnson won 51.1 percent of the votes cast in 1964, and Dade County provided the victory for him in Florida. He lost a majority of the votes across the state, but the overwhelming Dade vote canceled out this deficit.

In 1968 and 1972, elections showed an increasingly important trend: since 1948, the Democratic vote has become concentrated in the more populous counties. Humphrey carried only three counties, Dade, Monroe, and Alachua, receiving 30.9 percent of the total state vote, while Nixon received 40.5 percent and Wallace 28.5 percent. Nixon swept every county in the state in 1972 and won 71.9 percent of the total state vote. McGovern's 40.9 percent in Dade County was the best he did in any of the six most populous counties, yet he did better in the populous areas than he did across the rest of the state. In both 1968 and 1972, 64.3 percent of all votes cast in the Democratic presidential column came out of the six most populous counties in the state. The importance of the contribution of the most populous counties to the Democratic ticket had been increasing consistently since 1948. In 1948 only 49 percent of the total state Democratic vote was cast in the six largest counties, while in 1952 it was 51 percent; in 1956, 53 percent; in 1960 and 1964, 60 percent

In 1976, Jimmy Carter won 51.9 percent of the total state vote, but only 50.3 percent of the Democratic state vote came from the six major counties. Carter carried 32 northern counties and 16 southern counties. With 166,469 votes more than Gerald Ford, Carter's 1976 victory could not be ascribed to Dade County alone, where his winning margin was 91,889. His state margin more than exceeded the overall gain of 153,379 votes that he received by carrying four of the six most populous counties. The large-county vote, while important to Carter, was not as important as it had been in other recent Democratic elections. The 1976 reversion of the relationship between county population size and Democratic vote to a significant negative correlation, after the positive association found in the three prior elections, is a substantial indicator of the shift of voting patterns that occurred.

The correlation coefficients for the relationship between the socioeconomic variables and the 1976 Democratic vote are all similar to those of 1960. Carter's victory was produced with the old combination of the "faintly tropical rebel" Panhandle and the liberal urban south. His loss of only four northern counties paralleled presidential Democratic sweeps in North Florida in 1960 and before. Perhaps 1976 was merely a friendly vote of North Floridians for one of their neighbors. Without North Florida support Carter would not have carried the state. After the voting patterns of the 1960s, perhaps the 1976 pattern indicates a return to a stable coalition which has been seen before in Florida politics.

In 1980, Carter lost Florida by a margin of 600,000 votes, losing all metropolitan counties except Alachua and also losing ten North Florida counties. In presidential races since World War II, Democrats have only carried three elections in the state, Truman in 1948, Johnson in 1964, and Carter in 1976, whereas Republicans have carried six presidential elections. In presidential politics the state has become Republican.

Elections in the 1960s and 1970s: The 1976 Presidential Primaries and the Right-Wing Vote

In the 1968 election George Wallace's Florida vote was proportionately more than twice his national vote. In 1972 Wallace swept the Florida presidential primary with 42 percent of the total vote. Runner-up Hubert Humphrey received only 18 percent of the vote; Henry "Scoop" Jackson placed third with 13 percent and Edmund Muskie ran fourth with 9 percent. Mayor John Lindsay of New York, Congresswoman Shirley Chisholm, and Senator George McGovern were all far down the list of successful vote-getters. The Wallace phenomenon had struck hard and successfully in Florida presidential elections.

The 1976 Democratic presidential primary developed initially as a bruising head-on contest between Wallace of Alabama and Carter of Georgia. Jules Witcover's study of the 1976 presidential election, *Marathon*, points out that

TABLE 5.4. Correlation Coefficient (Pearson's r) of Florida's County Vote between Democratic Presidential Primary Contestants, 1976

	Carter	Jackson	Shapp	Other Democrats
Wallace	–.87	–.80	–.55	–.68
Carter		.45	.44	.54
Jackson			.51	.46
Shapp				.38

Note: For all correlation coefficients, $p < .01$.

Carter was taking on "the anti-Wallace position for his own" (p. 271). Senator Jackson of Washington and Governor Milton Shapp of Pennsylvania joined the scrap with serious efforts as it became evident that Wallace was vulnerable in Florida. Carter received 34.5 percent of the total Democratic primary vote, while Wallace received 30.5 percent, Jackson 23.9 percent and Shapp 2.4 percent. Wallace's county-by-county vote pattern was different from that of the other Democrats. Table 5.4 shows the correlation matrix of the vote for the 1976 Democratic presidential contenders.

Wallace's socioeconomic base of support was different from that of the other major Democratic candidates. Table 5.5 shows the similar socioeconomic bases of support for the other Democrats and the different Wallace pattern.

Carter, Jackson, and Shapp were more likely than Wallace to draw their votes from larger, more urban areas experiencing population growth. Their voters tended to have higher levels of education and income than Wallace voters and were older. Wallace swept the First Congressional District with almost 60 percent of the vote and he carried the Second, Third, and Eighth Districts. Carter carried all of the six major urban counties except Dade. Carter and Wallace placed first or second in every congressional district across the north and center of the state, while Jackson and Carter placed first or second in the southeastern Broward–Dade–Palm Beach area. Carter was the most consistent vote-getter across the state, while the other two top Democrats appear to have been more localized in their vote-drawing powers: Wallace in the more rural counties and Jackson in the urban southeastern counties. Carter appears to have drawn support across the spectrum both geographically and along socioeconomic lines.

TABLE 5.5. Correlation Coefficient (Pearson's r) between Selected Florida County Socioeconomic Variables and County Vote for Leading Democratic Presidential Candidates, 1976 Primary Election

Socioeconomic Variable	Wallace	Carter	Jackson	Shapp
Population size, 1970	–.57	.28	.77	.30
Net population change, 1960–70	–.53	.40	.53	.55
Rate of population inmigration, 1960–70	–.54	.41	.55	.57
Percentage of urban population, 1970	–.62	.40	.66	.42
Median age of population, 1970	–.49	.34	.57	.47
Median education of population, 1970	–.72	.53	.70	.49
Median income of population, 1970	–.53	.37	.53	.33
Percent of nonwhite population, 1970	.13#	.05#	–.34	–.27

NOTE: All correlation coefficients are significant at $p < .01$ except those marked #.

The Republicans also had a sharply contested presidential primary in 1976. Ford carried the state with 52.8 percent, but Ronald Reagan won eight of fifteen congressional districts. Reagan carried the Panhandle and the southeast Miami metropolitan counties, while Ford carried the more usual Republican counties up the east coast through Central Florida and down the west coast. Was Reagan a different kind of Republican than Ford with a different appeal? Table 5.6 shows the socioeconomic correlates of the votes cast for each of the two Republican candidates.

Reagan's sources of primary electoral support appear to have been similar to Wallace's in 1976 (see table 5.5). Both were generally acknowledged to be the right-wing, or very conservative, candidates in their party primaries. The Wallace 1968 general election vote shows a .61 correlation with the 1976 Reagan vote. The Wallace 1972 and 1976 primary results show, respectively, a .56 and .65 correlation with the Reagan vote. The vote for Goldwater, the 1964 conservative Republican candidate, shows only a .26 correlation with the Reagan vote and .22 with the Wallace 1976 vote. The two right-wing 1976 candidates may have drawn their votes from similar sources, but there appears to have been little continuity between their pattern of support and that for earlier presidential candidates of the right. Not only was the Goldwater relationship only mildly positive, but the Thurmond (1948 Dixiecrat)–Wallace (1976) relationship was −.14 and the Thurmond-Reagan relationship was −.16. The Thurmond-Goldwater correlation is only .09, again reflecting a lack of continuity in Florida's right-wing vote prior to Wallace and Reagan. The Wallace-Reagan base of support among the more rural, less affluent, younger, less-growing constituencies may serve other right-wing candidates in the future. This base, however, appeared to be insufficient to carry the state in the 1970s.

TABLE 5.6. Correlation Coefficient (Pearson's r) between Selected Florida County Socioeconomic Variables and County Vote for Ford and Reagan, 1976 Primary Election

Socioeconomic Variable	Ford	Reagan
Population size, 1970	.16	−.17
Net population change, 1960–70	.36*	−.36*
Rate of population inmigration, 1960–70	.39*	−.39*
Percentage of urban population, 1970	.19**	−.21**
Median age of population, 1970	.42*	−.43*
Median education of population, 1970	.39*	−.39*
Median income of population, 1970	.09	−.10
Percent of nonwhite population, 1970	.23**	−.23**

*$p < .01$
**$p < .05$

The pattern of Florida's fifteen United States congressmen's roll-call voting reflects the pattern of conservative-moderate-liberal voting of the electorate. The Americans for Democratic Action (ADA) rates each congressman for "liberal" voting, and the Americans for Constitutional Action (ACA) rates each congressman for "conservative" voting. The higher the congressman's score, the more he or she has voted with the group's position on the issue in question. In addition, the AFL-CIO's Committee on Political Education (COPE) rates each congressman's prolabor position. In 1976, a typical year, the congressmen from the First through the Tenth Congressional Districts, excluding the Seventh District, had a remarkably uniform pattern of roll-call voting. The mean ADA score was only 9.3, the mean ACA score was 86.5, and the COPE score was only 30.5. The highest ADA score was only 25, the highest ACA score was 100, the highest COPE score was only 43. These scores surely represent a pattern of "conservative" roll-call voting in Congress.

On the other hand, congressmen from the populous southern metropolitan districts (with one exception, former Congressman J. Herbert Burke of the

Broward County Twelfth District) exhibit a more moderate to liberal pattern of roll-call voting. Burke's ADA, ACA, and COPE scores of 21, 85, and 22, respectively, are very different from the mean ADA, ACA, and COPE scores of the other five congressmen in the south metropolitan group from the Seventh, Eleventh, Thirteenth, Fourteenth, and Fifteenth Districts: 66, 9.6, and 76.2, respectively. Republican Burke is now out of office, and his replacement, a Democrat, will likely have a more moderate voting record in Congress—a parallel movement, so to speak, with the district population's moderate voting in the elections. Florida's two U.S. senators in 1976 had ADA, ACA, and COPE scores that reflect a moderate position. Lawton Chiles's scores were 45, 48, and 84, respectively, and Richard Stone's were also generally in the middle range, 50, 48, and 75. The higher COPE numbers may reflect a growing labor movement in Florida, but overall the ADA and ACA scores reflect a generally moderate rollcall voting pattern. This one measurement is taken as a reflection of an overall pattern of voter moderation in the whole state. These roll-call scores also reflect, again, the difference between the metropolitan southern areas of the state and the central and northern areas of the state.

Conclusions

Florida's growth and Florida's election results are inseparable. Immigrant population continues to be drawn into the state's southern counties. The base of Florida Republicanism, as indicated by party registration, party representation in the state legislature, and congressional and presidential voting, is most consistently located in the southern counties. Democratic candidates have had to court increasingly the more urban South Florida counties if they want to win their party's nomination and carry the subsequent general election. Yet the northern counties are not politically moribund. With rare exception (the outstanding example of which is the Johnson victory of 1964), for Democrats to carry the state it takes a combination of winning the northern counties and the metropolitan southern counties. Since 1952, Republican presidential candidates, with the exception of Nixon in 1968 and 1972, have carried the state without the major northern counties, but two of the Republican gubernatorial and senatorial victories did include strong support from northern counties.

Manning Dauer aptly described a 1950s and 1960s conservative Republican voting pattern as forming a horseshoe on the map (''Florida: The Different State,'' pp. 124–26). The horseshoe went up the coast from Fort Lauderdale to Daytona Beach, across to Orlando, over to the St. Petersburg area, and down the coast to Fort Myers and Naples. It appears that this base of Republicanism continues to hold, with perhaps additional strength now evident in such upper west coast counties as Pasco, Hernando, and Citrus, and such Central and South Florida counties as Seminole, Lake, Polk, Highlands, and Collier.

Presidential elections from 1948 through 1960 showed a very stable pattern of Democratic and Republican socioeconomic bases of support. The 1964–72 presidential pattern was entirely different, but 1976 appears to have been a return to the earlier pattern. Goldwater, Wallace, and McGovern all had a profound effect on Florida's electoral patterns. Goldwater was the first Republican presidential nominee to win heavily in the Panhandle. Wallace in 1968 carried the Panhandle and did well in traditional Democratic areas elsewhere, as Nixon carried the state. McGovern accomplished a feat previously unknown for a presidential Democrat: he lost every county in the state. Florida rejected Goldwater, Wallace, and McGovern. Carter's 1976 pattern of victory harkens back to the pattern of earlier presidential elections. In 1964–72, Democrats won in counties whose populations were more urban, more immigrant, more highly educated, older, and more metropolitan centered, and had higher income. Carter won in the traditional Democratic Panhandle and the less populous areas, as the Democratic urban strength actually decreased in 1976.

Bartley and Graham's analysis of Florida's elections in the 1950s and 1960s, *Southern Politics and the Second Reconstruction,* concluded that the sectional cleavage of north versus south was the major factor in Florida politics (p. 65). Since 1970, Florida's pattern of gubernatorial and senatorial voting can best be described as an arrangement of loose north-south Democratic coalitions emerging out of factious multicandidate primaries that produced victories for moderates. Askew, Graham, and Chiles faced little primary opposition once they ran for reelection, and their general election victories were very strong. Dauer pointed out that the Democratic coalitions may be based on "personal and programmatic" factors rather than party (p. 117), but what is remarkable is the consistency of the Democratic coalition in senatorial and gubernatorial elections. Askew, Stone, Chiles, and Graham won office with the more urban southern counties voting strongly with the Panhandle.

In the 1970s Florida elected moderates, renominated them with little opposition from within their own party, and reelected them with substantial majorities. Factionalism is still present in Florida's Democratic party and is most evident when an incumbent is not seeking reelection, but the GOP has not been successful in turning this Democratic weakness to its advantage. Republican strength, as indicated by party registration, continues to grow. But Republican strength, as indicated by electoral success, has not. The voter base is there, but the state Republican party organization has yet to take full advantage of its development.

Reagan's 1980 presidential victory and that of Senator Paula Hawkins have revived Republican hopes, which were further buoyed by the fact that population increases in Florida added four more congressional seats in strong Republican areas for the 1982 congressional election. Florida's weight in the electoral college will be increased for the 1984 presidential election, 21 electoral votes compared with 17 in 1980. The 1982 reapportionment of the Florida state house and senate requires transfer of legislative seats to competitive Republican areas in Central and South Florida.

References

Bartley, Numan V., and Graham, Hugh D. *Southern Politics and the Second Reconstruction*. Baltimore: Johns Hopkins University Press, 1975.

Bass, Jack, and DeVries, Walter. *The Transformation of Southern Politics: Social Change and Political Consequence since 1945*. New York: Basic Books, 1976.

Black, Earl. *Southern Governors and Civil Rights: Racial Segregation as a Campaign Issue in the Second Reconstruction*. Cambridge: Harvard University Press, 1976.

Cosman, Bernard. *Five States for Goldwater: Continuity and Change in Southern Voting Patterns, 1920–1964*. University: University of Alabama Press, 1965.

Dauer, Manning J. "Florida: The Different State." In *The Changing Politics of the South,* edited by William C. Havard, pp. 94–148. Baton Rouge: Louisiana State University Press, 1972.

Havard, William C., ed. *The Changing Politics of the South*. Baton Rouge: Louisiana State University Press, 1972.

Key, V. O., Jr. *Southern Politics in State and Nation*. New York: Alfred A. Knopf, 1949.

Morris, Allen, ed. *The Florida Handbook, 1977–78*. Tallahassee: Peninsular Publishing Co., 1977.

Pierce, Neal R. *The Deep South States of America*. New York: W. W. Norton Co., Inc., 1974.

Price, H. Douglas. *The Negro and Southern Politics: A Chapter of Florida History*. Westport, Conn.: Greenwood Press, 1957.

Witcover, Jules. *Marathon: The Pursuit of the Presidency, 1972–1976*. New York: Viking Press, 1977.

6 Florida's Constitution

by Manning Dauer

UNIVERSITY OF FLORIDA

Political scientists consider that a constitution of a political body is more than a single written document. England, for example, does not even have a written constitution. Yet certain fundamental principles exist, some consisting of very important statutes or laws such as the Petition of Rights, others of customs such as the fact that the British monarch may not veto a law. In the United States, on the other hand, the federal government has a written document, executed in Philadelphia in 1787, and the amendments later added to it; but this is not all there is to the constitution. Augmenting the written document and the written amendments are important court decisions, interpretative acts of Congress, and customs. For example, the Fourteenth Amendment, providing every citizen with equal protection of the laws, was added to the U.S. Constitution after the Civil War, but interpretation permitted separate schools for the different races until the Supreme Court decision of *Brown* v. *Topeka, Kansas* (1954).

In similar fashion, a state has a written document as its constitution, and this document also has written amendments. But the fundamental state constitution, like the federal one, also consists of court decisions, certain interpretative statutes passed by the state legislature, and customs.

The Relationship between the Federal System and the States

States in the American system of government are part of a federal system. At the national level we have the U.S. Constitution, the fundamental law for the country. It establishes the powers of the central government, sets up the legislative, executive, and judicial branches of that central government, and provides that the federal government is supreme when operating within its delegated powers. It also provides that, subject to certain limitations, the state governments have all other governmental powers. The states must provide citizens with a republican form of government, and certain guarantees for each citizen (provided for in the federal Bill of Rights and later amendments to the original Constitution) limit the authority of the states. Each state must provide equal protection of the laws and due process. There may be no discrimination because of race or color. Religious freedom is guaranteed. These and other provisions are enforced by the U.S. Supreme Court.

The U.S. Constitution and its amendments are confined to fundamental provisions. The original Constitution prints out to some fifteen pages. The amendments each run from a sentence to a paragraph in length and add altogether another ten pages. Because its provisions are so general, the U.S. Constitution does not require frequent amendment, and the basic document survives as it was written in 1787. Yet the broad nature of its provisions permits change. This change is accomplished by laws enacted by Congress, by court interpretation, or by executive action.

The State Constitution

The federal Constitution is brief because it contains only basic law. Congress enacts more specific provisions in what is called statute law. State constitutions are much longer. In addition to fundamental provisions, they contain many detailed, specific provisions. The longest state constitution, that of Louisiana, contains 350,000 words and prints out at over 600 pages.

What fundamental provisions properly belong in a state constitution? Basically they consist of the following types: (1) provisions for popular control of the state and local governments through elections; (2) provisions for the structure of the government (the legislative, executive, and judicial branches); (3) provisions for separation of powers and for checks and balances among the lawmaking, administrative, and adjudicative functions; (4) provisions for local government (the structure of county and city government); (5) provisions guaranteeing the rights of individual citizens (a Bill of Rights placing limits on the agencies and powers of government); and (6) provisions for amendment and revision of the fundamental law, the constitution itself.

What details are included that cause state constitutions to be so long? Florida's Constitution is only about a fifth as long as Louisiana's, but it still prints out at over a hundred pages. It contains detailed provisions for the governmental structure of Dade County (Miami) and for other exceptions to the regular arrangements of local government. It also provides for many specific taxes and other elements of state finance. The judiciary article lists many details concerning the levels of judges. Such details have been included because of the popular wish of the citizens to require their vote of approval before a law is changed; a popular vote is necessary to change the constitution itself. The state constitution thus limits the legislature's power to change or make law, as well as the power of the executive and of the courts. Changing a law included in the constitution requires a constitutional amendment or revision of the constitution.

Florida has had six state constitutions. A seventh version was offered to the voters in 1978 but was rejected by the people in the November general elections. The current state constitution was adopted in 1968 and has been changed by over 30 amendments since then. The first Florida Constitution was adopted to permit admission to the Union as a state in 1845. The second, in 1861, was the constitution of the Confederate state. A new constitution, to be used as a basis for readmission to the Union, was attempted after 1865, but readmission was refused. The Reconstruction constitution of 1868 was followed by the revision of 1885, marking the end of Reconstruction. The 1968 constitution, prepared by a Constitution Revision Commission, superseded the 1885 version.

Constitutional Revision after World War II

Florida's Constitution of 1885 was much criticized after World War II. The document itself was long and detailed and contained many obsolete provisions. Three major trends in favor of constitutional revision developed. One trend was simply to eliminate obsolete language and redraft the document; for this purpose a new draft was prepared by a committee of the Florida Bar. A second trend encouraged general reorganization in the interest of modernizing the administrative structure of the state, in changing provisions for local government, and in making a number of other substantive changes. This movement crystallized in the 1950s and 1960s in the establishment of a nonprofit citizen's group called the Citizens' Constitution Commission. Prominent in the leadership of the organization were members of the League of Women Voters and several members of the legislature. A third trend was a movement toward reapportionment, engendered by the continual failure of the Florida legislature to enact meaningful reapportionment measures that would establish new legislative districts in accord with changes in population.

In 1954, State Senator LeRoy Collins won election to the governorship, and one of his platform planks called for a constitutional revision. The legislature established a Constitutional Revision Commission, which then reported back to the legislature; the legislature in turn placed a draft of the new document on the ballot as a series of amendments. The amendment series was linked together by a "daisy-chain" provision which sought to link each article to others. The Florida Supreme Court declared that this method of proposed revision violated the 1885 constitutional procedure for amending the state constitution. Therefore, the daisy-chain constitution was ruled off the ballot.

Next, in 1962, the U.S. Supreme Court in the case of *Baker* v. *Carr* ruled out apportionment provisions of state constitutions which did not conform to the principle of "one man, one vote." Under this precedent the case of *Swann* v. *Adams* declared the apportionment provisions of the Florida Constitution of 1885 to be null and void. This decision served to remove one of the principal issues that had delayed earlier constitutional revision. At the same time, more and more pressure developed for other reforms. The 1885 constitution contained provisions which did not conform to new rulings affecting the treatment of blacks and other issues of civil rights. By the mid-1960s it had been amended over 150 times. The administrative structure of the executive branch was chaotic and included over 200 agencies.

Thus in 1965 a new Constitution Revision Commission was created as an advisory body to the state legislature. This commission was headed by Chesterfield Smith, a Lakeland and Bartow lawyer, who later was president of the American Bar Association. The commission also contained a number of lay members and members of the Florida House and Senate. Just as the commission's report was laid before the legislature in a special session in January 1967, a final decision in *Swann* v. *Adams* ordered new elections in new districts for the legislature. Thus when the legislature finally assembled later in 1967 it contained many new members, and the domination of rural legislators was ended. The outcome was a favorable reception of the basic work of the Constitution Revision Commission, whose new document, with some changes by the legislature, was placed on the ballot in 1968 as a new constitution. The voters approved it, and the state at last received an updated constitution.

It is interesting to contrast this work with the next proposed revision of 1978. The 1968 constitution provided for a Constitutional Revision Commission ten years after that constitution and every twenty years thereafter. For the 1978 revision, there was an important difference in procedure. The commission which prepared the 1968 constitution reported back to the legislature, and the legislature changed some of the provisions before the finished product was put on the ballot. But the commission that prepared the 1978 proposed revision did not have to return it to the legislature for approval. The individuals comprising the commission included a mix of gubernatorial appointments and some members from each chamber of the legislature and from the supreme court.

The proposed document that was placed before the voters in 1978 was quite complex. There were eight propositions to be voted upon, many of them containing a grouping of a number of changes. An omnibus Proposition 1 contained some fifty-seven proposed changes. Controversy attended a ninth proposal on the ballot, which was presented independently of the Constitution Revision Commission; it provided for the legalization of casino gambling in Miami Beach and part of Fort Lauderdale. Voters opposed all eight revision proposals (one of which would have eliminated the six elected cabinet members and provided for their gubernatorial appointment). There was also an overwhelming rejection of casino gambling.

The 1978 Constitution Revision Commission did not report its work to the legislature. Moreover, some legislators who served on the commission acted as "spoilers" by including proposals that were so sweeping that the majority of the legislature opposed the new document when it was considered for adoption in the 1978 general election. Thereupon, the 1979 legislature proposed a constitutional amendment to remove the provision for a revision commission from the constitution. The voters defeated this amendment in the 1980 general election, leaving the next such revision commission to propose a new constitution or amendments in 1998. Meanwhile, the legislature could still establish an advisory commission that would report back through the legislature itself, and it still continues to initiate constitutional amendments when it wants. The voters also can initiate constitutional amendments through initiative petition. Any amendments initiated by either the legislature or by initiative petition still require voter approval at a general election.

Structure of Florida's Constitution

Article I of the Florida Constitution is the Bill of Rights, which includes freedom of speech, freedom of the press, equal protection of the laws, right of trial by jury, freedom of the home from search and seizure except when a proper search warrant is issued, freedom of worship, and other civil liberties traditional in the United States. One section of the Bill of Rights guarantees "freedom of choice" in labor contracts; this means that labor unions may organize but cannot require all employees to be union members (i.e., no "closed shop"). Thus Florida's constitution includes a "right-to-work" provision. This amendment is common in southern states. It provides that any business enterprise must be open to employ nonunion members. If a union contract be adopted, then only union members can provide for check-off of dues. Further, if there is a strike the nonunion members individually decide whether to strike or not.

Organized labor is sharply opposed to right-to-work provisions, arguing that the very term is misused and that the provision should therefore be repealed. Business and industry, of course, are anxious to see the open shop maintained; the movement of business and industry from the North and mid-Atlantic states to the South is partly stimulated by right-to-work provisions. But labor leaders point out that southern labor has lower wages and not as much protection regarding conditions of work such as health and safety measures, vacations, and pensions. Another provision of the Bill of Rights guarantees the right of public employees to unionize but prohibits them from striking, important provisions in view of the state's large number of public employees.

Article II, a general article, sets forth such matters as the state boundaries. Section 7 of this article provides that the legislature shall enact laws to protect natural resources, to provide against air contamination, and to prohibit water pollution. Only six other states have such provisions in their constitutions. Section 8, added in 1976, provides for fiscal disclosure by public officials.

The next several articles establish the structure of state government. Article III provides for a bicameral legislature, with house members elected for two-year terms and senators for four years. Article IV on the executive branch provides that the governor be elected for a four-year term and that he may run for only one additional consecutive term. It makes the governor the chief executive, but his power is shared with six other officers, known collectively as the cabinet, all also chosen by the voters for four-year terms but all eligible for re-election to any number of consecutive terms. These officials are secretary of state, attorney general, comptroller, treasurer and insurance commissioner, commissioner of education, and commissioner of agriculture. Each of these officers heads an executive department and may have important additional duties as provided by statute law. For example, the state comptroller is the banking commissioner of the state, and the state treasurer is the insurance commissioner. Furthermore, the governor and the six cabinet members collectively may be assigned duties. They constitute, among others, the State Pardon Board and the State Board of Education.

Some critics argue that the present cabinet system weakens the governor and so divides the executive authority of the state that it is difficult for the executive branch to act effectively or for the citizens to pinpoint responsibility. The issue of divided executive authority embodied in Florida's cabinet system was considered by the Constitution Revision Commission of 1978. One proposal before the commission was to end most of the collective aspects of cabinet authority and to reduce the number of cabinet officers to only two (in addition to the governor and lieutenant governor). The secretary of state and the attorney general would be retained as elective officers; the other four officers would be appointed by the governor. Sensing that a majority of the commissioners favored changing the system, defenders of the cabinet system joined with the extreme proponents of revision to change the proposal so that the election of all six cabinet officers would be abolished. This proposal was placed on the ballot, and a strong and successful campaign was mounted to defeat all of the constitutional revisions proposed to the electorate in 1978. Seventy percent of the voters voted against the proposal to eliminate the election of six cabinet officers and to change the cabinet system.

Thus Florida remains among those states having numerous elective executive officials. This arrangement contrasts with the executive authority in the federal government, which centers executive responsibility in the president. Moreover, the plural executive in the state establishes a system of checks and balances within the executive branch itself. The argument for retaining a plural executive system is that the cabinet transacts its business in public, subject to the watchful public eye; that cabinet members develop much expertise since they are eligible for perennial reelection; and that they constitute a check, one against the others, on possible abuses of executive powers.

Article V provides for the judiciary by establishing four levels of courts. Judges at the top two levels—the state supreme court and the courts of appeals—are appointed for six-year terms by the governor from a list of qualified persons screened by a judicial nominating commission. At the end of a term a judge then runs simply against his or her record. The ballot reads, ''Should Judge —— be continued for another term of six years, yes —— or no ——.'' There is no opposition candidate. This plan, adopted from the State of Missouri, is based on the idea that a judgeship should not be the spoils of a partisan election but should be held by a person of legal competence and personal probity, that the election of judges should not be a contest of personalities but a system for the public review of a judge's performance or record. The 1978 constitutional revision proposed to extend this Missouri plan to the trial courts (the circuit and county courts). This proposal was defeated, though narrowly, in the generally negative response to all the revisions proposed in 1978. (Because it was only narrowly defeated, the Missouri plan for selection of trial judges will probably be presented again to the voters for adoption.) So circuit and county judges continue to run for office in opposed elections, but their names appear on the ballot without party designation. This so-called nonpartisan judicial election is held at the same time as the Florida primary elections in the fall of even-numbered years.

Other features of the judiciary set out in Article V show modern trends for improvement of the judges and of the system of civil and criminal justice. (1) There is provision for a judicial nominating commission to screen candidates for appointments to judgeships by the governor. (2) As an alternative to impeachment, there is provision for a judicial qualification commission, which is empowered to investigate complaints against judges and to make recommendations to dismiss the complaint or to discipline or remove the judge. (3) The chief justice is given authority to assign judges to areas of the state where there might be case overloads and to recommend the creation of additional judgeships. (4) Justice of the peace courts, municipal courts, traffic courts, and all special courts have been eliminated. There are only four levels of courts in Florida (supreme court, courts of appeals, circuit courts, and county courts). (5) Except for a few county court judges who were "grandfathered" in, all judges, whether elected or appointed, must be lawyers.

Article VI pertains to suffrage and elections: discrimination in either activity because of race or sex is prohibited. An obsolete provision remains that sets the voting age at twenty-one; it has been superseded by the federal constitutional amendment granting the vote to eighteen-year-olds.

Article VII pertains to finance and places certain fiscal limitations on the legislature and on local governments. All taxes and appropriations must be provided by the legislature. Except for revenue bonds (for example, for building a toll road or bridge whose revenues can pay off the bonds), no Florida governmental unit may borrow money by issuing bonds without approval by the voters who would be taxed to pay them off. Limits are placed on the taxing authority of local government, including the ten-mill property tax limit on each local government unit.

The prohibition against borrowing by the central state government is found in a number of state constitutions. A comparable proposal for the U.S. Constitution is now being circulated, and the argument is being advanced that because such a prohibition works for a state it also could be effective at the federal level. The federal government, however, in order to "provide for the common defense" and to "promote the general welfare," has to meet many emergency situations such as defense expenditures, war, and economic depressions. Whereas state government, unable to borrow without voter consent, can struggle along in emergencies like war or depression perhaps by curtailing some services that do not threaten the nation's survival, the federal government cannot meet its constitutional responsibilities without the power to borrow.

The constitution prohibits any state income tax and limits the amount of the inheritance tax to match the federal tax rate. Thus the federal tax is offset and the individual charged pays only one tax, to the state. Homeowners are entitled to an exemption of the first $25,000 valuation of their real property homestead. In the 1980 elections, voters increased the exemption, scaling the increase by years until it reached $25,000. This change has caused a fiscal crisis for county, city, and school budgets. Even though Florida's state and local taxes are in the lowest 10 percent per capita among all states, an initiative petition for a constitutional amendment had sufficient signatures to place a rollback provision on the 1984 general election ballot. Despite the great annual growth of the state, this amendment would roll back taxes to the 1980 level except for local assessments on new construction plus up to 5 percent on an inflation index. Further discussion of this amendment is found in chapter 17.

Article VIII provides for local government. The units of local government are creatures of the state. Counties and cities have only the powers and system of government provided by the state constitution, by general law enacted by the legislature, or by special law. The special constitutional amendments provide for systems of consolidated county-city government for Duval County (Jacksonville) and Dade County (Miami). The constitution provides that there may be locally adopted laws for cities or specially approved local charters for counties. General or special law provides that cities may draft their own charters, but those charters may also be made or amended by special statute laws applying only to a specific city. Such local city laws must be advertised in advance of their local adoption or be ratified by local referendum. The traditional structure of county government is found in all counties except those governed under local charters. County officials must include county commissioners, plus a separately elected county clerk, sheriff, tax appraiser, tax collector, and supervisor of elections. This traditional American form of the dispersal of authority creates administrative problems for urbanized counties. The 1968 constitution does provide, however, that government units may contract with one another for consolidation of services, and this provision has been much utilized.

Article IX provides the means to change the constitution itself.

(1) Ordinary amendments are proposed by a resolution adopted jointly by both houses of the Florida legislature and by a three-fifths vote of each house. Since the governor does not receive a joint resolution, he does not have to sign it and has no opportunity to veto it. The amendment goes directly to the voters at the next general election. It becomes a part of the constitution if it is approved by a majority of the votes cast on the amendment.

(2) The second method of change is by a joint resolution approved by a three-fourths vote of each chamber of the legislature, followed by the calling of a special election before the next general election. Again, a majority vote for the amendment will add it to the constitution.

(3) A third method of amendment is by initiative petition. The amendment is framed—that is, written out in the exact form in which it would be added to the constitution. Then it is placed at the head of a petition asking that it be added to the ballot of the next general election, and many copies are printed and circulated for signatures of registered voters. To get the amendment on the general election ballot, the voters' signatures on the petition must equal 8 percent of the number who voted in the previous presidential election in the state, and these signatures must be so distributed as to equal 8 percent of the voters in at least half of the U.S. congressional districts. If this number of signatures is secured at least 90 days before the general election, the signatures are verified against

the registration lists by county supervisors of elections and the amendment is placed on the ballot. To be added to the constitution, the amendment must win a majority of the votes cast on the amendment.

Since the petition procedure was added to the constitution in 1968, a number of initiative petitions have been launched. To succeed, this procedure requires a statewide organization. The most successful such campaign was launched in 1976 to add to the constitution a stringent requirement that full-time public officials, whether elected or appointed, disclose all their assets and income. Governor Reubin Askew had recommended such a measure to the legislature, which had rejected it. The governor and the attorney general then drafted the measure in cooperation with the statewide League of Women Voters. The league and other citizens' groups circulated the petition and secured the necessary signatures, and the measure went on the ballot. The campaign to win voter approval for the amendment was led by the governor. In opposition were state senate leaders, arguing that the disclosure requirement invaded their privacy and would therefore discourage many citizens from seeking public office. Over 70 percent of the voters nevertheless approved the amendment in the 1976 general election. While the amendment provides for its own enforcement by a state ethics commission, full compliance was resisted by several state senate leaders, who challenged the measure as unconstitutional. The U.S. Supreme Court refused to hear their case. A technical question of the effective date of the amendment was rejected by the state supreme court, and the amendment was validated in 1977. Furthermore the recalcitrant senators have fought against legislation that would establish penalties for noncompliance in addition to the forfeiture of office, which is prescribed in the amendment itself.

A second method of securing signatures was employed in 1978. Miami Beach hotels and casino gambling interests framed amendments to legalize casino gambling in Miami Beach and Fort Lauderdale. The groups advocating the amendment raised $2.5 million and paid the solicitors of petition signatures for their work. After the necessary number of signatures had been secured, an intensive contest ensued. Governor Reubin Askew headed the opposition and was joined by most of the candidates, Republican and Democrat, who sought to succeed him. Seventy percent of the voters rejected the proposal. Another initiative petition amendment, calling for a rollback of state taxes to the 1980 level (with exceptions as noted), had sufficient signatures to place it on the general election ballot for 1984.

(4) A fourth method of changing the state constitution is by constitutional revision, discussed earlier in this chapter. Thomas Jefferson advocated that all political institutions should be reappraised every generation. Heeding this ad-

vice, the 1968 constitution provided that in 1978 and every twenty years thereafter there should be established a Constitution Revision Commission, whose thirty-seven members are to be appointed by the governor (fifteen members), the speaker of the house (nine), the president of the senate (nine), and the chief justice of the state supreme court (three); one of the members must be the attorney general. The commission comes into being a year before its recommendations are to be placed on the general election ballot. It holds hearings around the state, deliberates, holds more hearings, and finally certifies the changes, if any, it recommends to the general election ballot. This revision procedure differs from the one employed in 1967 in that the work of the commission does not go back to the legislature but goes directly onto the ballot instead. The 1978 Constitution Revision Commission rewrote the entire state constitution, and the ballot presented the voter with eight yes-or-no choices, with many of the eight items proposing a large number of constitutional changes. Provision 1, for example, contained fifty-seven changes, all of which the voters had to approve or disapprove in a single package. The ballot also carried highly controversial changes such as a proposed state-level Equal Rights Amendment and a separate proposal to abolish the elected cabinet and retain only the governor and lieutenant governor as elected officers. Amid considerable public confusion about the significance of proposed changes and the negative momentum created by the presence of the casino gambling proposal, all provisions were defeated in the general election, some by a fairly close vote.

(5) The final method of changing the constitution in Florida is by constitutional convention, which is launched by a petition from the voters. The petition for the calling of such convention must be signed by at least 15 percent of the number voting in the preceding presidential election in the state, including 15 percent of the number voting in half of the congressional districts. Each signer of the petition must be a registered voter. The voters' names are checked, and the proposition that a convention should be called is placed on the ballot of the next general election.

If the issue carries in that election, then candidates for the convention seats announce in each district of the house of representatives and are elected at the next general election. Thereafter, the delegates meet in convention and present their proposals for revisions to be placed on the ballot at the next general election. To be adopted, each such proposal must be approved by a majority of those voting on it. Since general elections are two years apart, it would require six years for this process to be completed. The last such convention produced the constitution of 1885.

All five of these procedures for changing the constitution have been used. On the average each general election ballot carries at least six proposed amendments to be approved or rejected by the voters. Ordinarily, these proposals originate in the legislature.

Article X provides for education. School districts in Florida have been consolidated for over thirty years, so there is only one school district per county. In each such district there is a school board with jurisdiction over schools from kindergarten through the twelfth grade. There is also a county superintendent who may be elected or appointed. The supervision of the schools is under the State Board of Education, composed of the governor and his cabinet. The administrator is the elected state commissioner of education.

Summary

Florida's constitution has been updated by the 1968 revision. Compared with other state constitutions its length is about average, but it still is subject to frequent amendment because it contains so many detailed and specific provisions.

Aside from excessive length, and too much detail in certain provisions, the 1968 Florida Constitution stands as a document which has facilitated modernization of the state's governmental processes. It has updated the Bill of Rights to guarantee equal treatment before the law to all people, regardless of race, color, or previous condition of servitude. It has modernized the state machinery in regard to apportionment, thus helping to move the center of political power to the urban areas of the state. Following this transfer, much legislation has been adopted to update state practices in such areas as planning, protection of the environment, and control of water resources. The structure of the executive branch has been reorganized, as have the courts. Provisions for local government introduce the possibility of reorganizing the structure of county government and of coordinating use of the state's water supply by regional governments. New requirements have been adopted for public reporting of financial standing by public officials. The machinery of the constitution for engineering change now incorporates constitutional amendment initiation by petition.

The result is a series of measures which have demonstrated the wide scope and comprehensiveness of Florida's basic document of government. Many of the newer types of governmental problems find recognition in procedures outlined in this 1968 document. No written constitution can guarantee good government, but a bad constitution can restrict and prevent adequate solutions. Ultimate results depend on the alertness of voters and the caliber of public officials, and these can be improved by adequate government machinery and constitutional amendments.

References

Dauer, Manning J. *Proposed 1978 Florida Constitution Revision and Proposal on Casino Gambling*. Civic Information Series, no. 61. Gainesville, Fla.: Public Administration Clearing Service, 1978.

Dishman, Robert B. *State Constitutions: The State of the Document*. New York: National Municipal League, 1960.

Florida Constitution Revision Commission. *Revised Constitution of the State of Florida*. Tallahassee, 1978.

Havard, William C., and Dauer, Manning J. *The Florida State Constitution of 1885*. Gainesville, Fla.: Public Administration Clearing Service, 1955.

Livingston, William. *Federalism and Constitutional Change*. London: Oxford University Press, 1956.

Secretary of State of Florida. *Constitution of the State of Florida* (as revised and amended in 1968). Tallahassee, 1977.

Sturm, Albert L. *Methods of State Constitutional Reform*. Ann Arbor: University of Michigan Press, 1954.

Wildavsky, Aaron, ed. *American Federalism in Perspective*. Boston: Little, Brown & Co., 1967.

The Governor and His Office

7

by Richard K. Scher and David Colburn

UNIVERSITY OF FLORIDA

Becoming governor of Florida means traveling a long and arduous route. Even when the goal has been reached the successful candidate's tasks have scarcely begun. Because there are enormous problems in carrying out the tasks of office, it is a wonder that so many persons seek to become governor of Florida: the chances for electoral success are often slight, the duties overwhelming, and the rewards few.

Who Are Florida's Governors?

There have been twenty-one governors of Florida in this century. While each has had unique characteristics, their background and political experiences exhibit some general patterns. Most have come from North Florida and the Panhandle, where the state's population and political power were concentrated during much of the century. To be elected governor a candidate had to have a strong organization based in rural areas. If some of this strength was based on the candidate's own rural background, so much the better. It was not until 1956 that a governor of Florida from rural North Florida, LeRoy Collins (1955–61), won office through the support of urban, South Florida voters. Even today rural voters are powerful in Florida politics, and their votes, though not always the decisive factor in gubernatorial elections, are influential in shaping the behavior and alliances of the candidates.

While most of Florida's governors have been well-educated men (the majority have been lawyers), few have come from affluent backgrounds. In fact, many have come from families of modest, almost penurious circumstances. For some, politics generally, and the governor's office in particular, has been a way up from poverty to the middle class. Quite a few governors of Florida upon leaving office have taken positions in the law or in business, thus acquiring more affluent life styles.

All but two governors of Florida, Fuller Warren (1949–53) and Claude Kirk (1967–71), had substantial political experience prior to their election to office. Most had served in the state legislature; a few had had only local experience. Only one governor, Millard Caldwell (1945–49), served in the U. S. House of Representatives before becoming the state's chief executive. Several governors had previously held positions of prominence at the state level: Park Trammell (1913–17) had been attorney general and several others had been speaker of the house or president of the senate. Contrary to popular myth, most successful candidates did not have to run for the office twice. The traditional view–that one ran the first time to acquaint the public with his name and the second time to win the election–proved not to be correct: while there have been many two-time candidates for office, only two of the twenty-one who were ultimately successful had to run more than once.

Gubernatorial Elections

The greatest problem for a would-be governor has been overcoming the state's fragmented political party system. "Every man for himself," as V. O. Key described Florida politics, has required every candidate to assemble out of little or nothing an effective political organization in a state where continuity and stability in politics are rare. A minimum lead time of two or three years seems to have been needed to put together a reasonably well organized campaign. During this interval a candidate had to raise funds and recruit lieutenants in various parts of the state who would identify and mobilize voters and remain loyal to the organization during the campaign. All of this, of course, took place within the Democratic party. For most of the century the Republicans did not present a real electoral threat, so winning the Democratic nomination meant winning the election.

An important consequence for the wide-open gubernatorial elections in Florida has been that numerous candidates have usually entered the Democratic primary. With the Democratic party split into factions and the state's politics without a well-defined center of gravity, almost anyone felt free to file as a candidate for governor and many did. In 1936 there were fourteen candidates in the first primary, in 1960 ten; as recently as 1978 there were at one time more than a dozen, although the number shrank by the date of the primary. Such elections are circuses in which it is nearly impossible for citizens to sort out the candidates.

In part because Florida's political parties are severely divided into factions and in part because of the large number of candidates for office, localism in gubernatorial elections has been common. Candidates usually receive more than a majority of the total vote in their home county and adjoining counties, but coming even close to a majority statewide is difficult. Polls on name recognition have only recently become available; it is likely that before there was heavy use of media in campaigns, a candidate would scarcely be known outside his own part of the state.

In addition to localism, one also found the effects of regions heavily reflected in gubernatorial elections. The most persistent cleavage seems to have been between North and South Florida, and it was not unusual for candidates to play deliberately on the voters' regional loyalties by announcing that they were "North Florida" or "Panhandle" candidates. Mapping out county voting patterns over time shows substantial consistency of regional voting in gubernatorial primaries.

Perhaps also as a result of the extraordinary fragmentation in the state's politics, issues have not been crucial in determining the outcome of elections. A few issues seem to have become commonplace in the rhetoric of the candidates: fiscal conservatism, economy in government, low taxes, improvement of education, attracting tourists, old-age assistance. But these issues have been more like articles of faith shared by all candidates than principles distinguishing one candidate from another. Issues often became blurred; the voting population sorted out candidates more on the basis of personality and locale than on their stance on issues. In recent years, with the heavy reliance on media, the importance of issues in elections has increased; but they still seem not to be decisive. In 1978 in the most heavily media-oriented gubernatorial campaign in the state's history, the outcome seemed determined more by differences in the candidates' style than by their positions on issues.

With the field so crowded, runoffs in gubernatorial campaigns have been common. LeRoy Collins in 1956 was the first governor to win without a second primary; his performance was not repeated until 1974, when Reubin Askew (1971–79), running as an incumbent as had Collins in 1956, also won on the first try. But in 1978 Bob Graham had to come from far behind to defeat Robert Shevin in two primaries. The effect of this need for runoffs has been to increase campaign costs enormously. Indeed, it is estimated that in 1978 over $10 million had been spent by all Democratic candidates by the time of the general election. Also, of course, the runoff system forces a great deal of jockeying and dealing for support between those getting into the second primary and those who have had to drop out.

For most of this century political campaigns for the governorship have been limited to the Democratic party. While the Republicans usually put forward a candidate in the general election, until 1960 they seldom ran a vigorous race. Often the Democratic nominee ran only a perfunctory campaign for the November election, since victory had been assured in the primaries. Claude Kirk's victory in 1966 changed that. Democrats realized they could no longer expect to win without making a good-faith campaign effort. Moreover, the Republican gubernatorial primary began to be contested in the seventies, in contests that have resembled in rancor (if not in the numbers voting in them) the Democratic primaries. Florida still is not fully a two-party state, but it seems likely that the general election will become more vital in the ultimate choice of governor than it has been in the past.

Being Governor

What happens once a successful candidate emerges from the electoral process? Preparations begin immediately for the new administration, since there is not much time between the November election and the January inauguration. Because there is not a systematic and well-articulated mechanism of transition from one administration to the next, there is a great deal of scurrying about to set up the new administration and to determine the direction of its policies and programs.

What immediately impresses the governor-elect is the number of his duties and tasks. Governors are called upon at once to make appointments to state offices, to start shaping the budget, and to prepare a legislative program. In a more general sense, the governor has to come to grips with the vast set of the public's expectations of him. Immediately he becomes leader of the state, solver of problems, the person to whom the population looks to move the state in new directions. He is chief of state, symbolic leader of all the people, and the polity's principal citizen; he is chief executive, the state's principal administrator responsible for ensuring the smooth operation of state machinery; he is chief proposer of legislation, principal architect of the state's budget and new programs and policies; he is chief diplomat, representing the state to such communities and populations as Washington, other states, foreign countries, and business and labor; he is not party chief, as are the governors of some other states, but he does have some party responsibilities; and, very important, he is the state's chief moral leader and formulator of public opinion, with heavy responsibilities in outlining the state's moral and policy directions and in establishing an agenda of state problems and a priority list for dealing with them.

This set of expectations is awesome and, along with the specific duties and responsibilities it encompasses, creates an enormous burden on a new governor. Indeed it is an open and debatable question whether citizens might really expect too much of their governor, especially in view of the severe constraints on him. What happens, of course, is that while responsibilities are great, powers, by comparison, are relatively few.

An examination of the governor's two most important functions, his executive and legislative duties, shows the disparity between what the governor is expected to do and what he can reasonably expect to accomplish. These two functions form the basis for the governor's scorecard, the record he makes for himself in office.

The Chief Executive

The governor's administrative functions are among his most important. These functions are not always widely recognized and are often largely invisible, particularly in Florida, where the executive's power is fragmented by a unique cabinet system and the governor has great difficulty in controlling his administration. The governor's lack of total control helps keep down his visibility as an administrator. In situations of executive fragmentation and decentralization there is little accountability of bureaus and agencies, and they have considerable latitude to operate quietly and away from the public eye. Moreover, as long as state services are provided in a reasonably effective manner, the public pays little attention to most of the governor's work, except for his decisions concerning schools. Only if governmental machinery breaks down or there is a public scandal do citizens take notice. Thus in the politics of the executive branch there is a paradox for the governor: Although how he carries out his executive functions is important to his overall rating, his effectiveness is least noticed when he is running the state's machinery smoothly. Deficiencies attract attention, but it is the kind of attention that is likely to alienate and antagonize citizens. On the other hand, the cumulative effect of a job well done can achieve for the governor the reward of an excellent reputation. A good example of this achievement is the gubernatorial career of Reubin Askew, who, at the end of his first four-year term, was renominated in the first Democratic primary and was easily elected for a second term. Even at the end of his administration his influence continued to be felt at a special session of the legislature just prior to the end of his term. In January 1979 he left office with a considerable national reputation.

To aid the governor in carrying out his duties, many departments and agencies have been created, charged with the day-to-day operation of government. Obviously the governor cannot operate all, or even some, programs by himself; therefore a bureaucracy has developed, which acts theoretically as an extension of the governor's office. In addition there are other executive offices, in Florida called the Cabinet and Little Cabinet, that share some of the state's executive power. Whether the bureaucracy actually functions as an arm of the governor to do his bidding, and whether other executive officers form a true partnership with the governor in carrying out administrative functions, are open questions. The important issue is that even though the governor does not hold all executive authority, he does as the chief administrative officer bear the responsibility for it. The public never ceases to remind him that he carries this burden.

The cabinet in Florida is an institution made up of seven elected executive officials: governor, secretary of state, attorney general, comptroller, treasurer, commissioner of agriculture, and commissioner of education. The existence of a group of separately elected state executive officials does not make Florida unique, for other states have even more of these officials. Florida's uniqueness stems, rather, from the fact that the cabinet serves as a collegial decision- and policy-making unit, acting as the governing board for several state agencies and functions (see figure 7.1). Several administrative anomalies can be seen in this arrangement. There are agencies directly under individual cabinet members, some of which are not related to the title of the cabinet position. There are agencies administered by the cabinet as a collegial body. There are the collegial functions of the governor and cabinet as boards or commissions, such as the Board of Pardons and the State Board of Education. Moreover, the cabinet and governing board system have bred decentralization of authority, dispersion of responsibility, and an incoherent administrative structure. Until recently, for example, the system was responsible for an anomaly

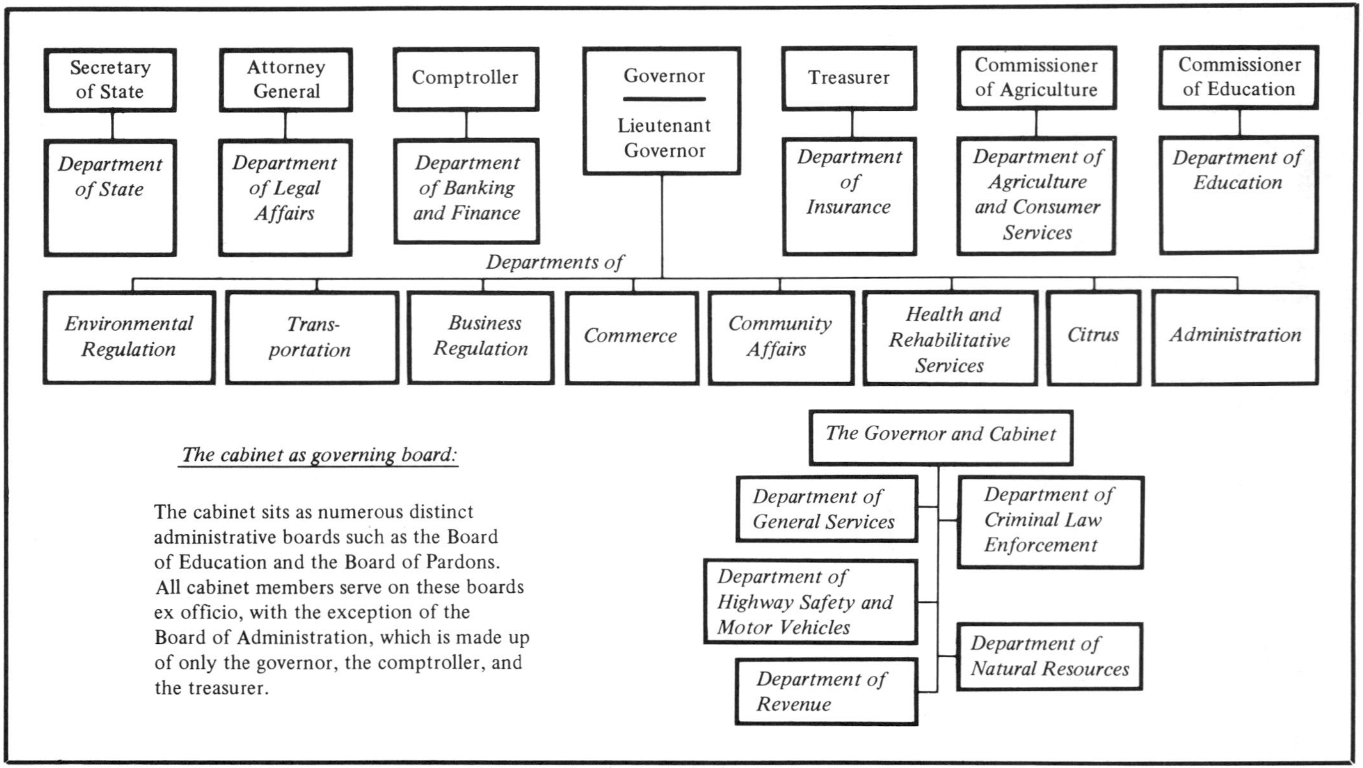

Fig. 7.1. Florida's Divided Executive Branch. For complete list of agencies, see fig. 8.1.

in which the state prison system became part of the Department of Agriculture, headed by the commissioner of agriculture, while prison camps were located in the old Road Department, under a board appointed by the governor.

In contrast to popular myth, governors and their cabinets have worked in reasonable harmony, for the most part. Cabinet members have remained quiescent in the face of gubernatorial initiative. Traditionally, cabinet officials seem to have taken the view that if the governor advanced a new policy that did not affect them or their departments, they would not oppose him. Governors, as Haydon Burns (1965–67) pointed out, would frequently tailor their demands to suit the cabinet, to adopt programs that they felt cabinet members would accept. Undoubtedly governors recognize the structural and political independence of cabinet officers, and they respect it. Disagreements between governors and cabinets are usually worked out privately, although open conflicts have occurred. Thus, agreement between governors and other cabinet members comes as a result of a desire to cooperate and a mutual understanding that "territorial boundaries" will normally be respected. It is unquestionably this cooperation, overlooked by most observers of Florida politics, that has enabled such a fragmented executive structure to function at all. On the other hand, this respect for territory and the willingness of governors and cabinet officials not to invade each other's areas has circumscribed gubernatorial initiative. The governor is not free to act in any policy area he chooses, or even necessarily one that might be of importance to the state; he cannot dictate to cabinet members in their areas. He knows, rather, that they will cooperate with him only if he does not interfere in what they do; this represents a serious constraint on the potential range of gubernatorial policy-making.

Although they may not have always agreed with their cabinets, most Florida governors have publicly and privately supported the cabinet system. In fact, of course, they had little choice: They might complain about it, but they knew they had to live with it. Too much public criticism would antagonize not only other cabinet members but legislators and citizens as well, all of whom have consistently supported the system. Indeed, most governors have realized they had to come to terms with the cabinet if they were to be at all successful.

A comparative rating of executive branches of the fifty states places Florida in forty-seventh place, considering the organization of the executive branch in terms of administrative responsibility. The five criteria considered, and Florida's ranking on a scale from 5 = top to 1 = bottom, are as follows: tenure in position, 3; appointive power, 2; budget power, 1; veto power, 3; cumulative total, 9. (This analysis is from James A. Schlesinger, "The Politics of the Executive.") Some changes have been made since this analysis, but many problems continue. It also should be noted that the comparison is on the basis of formal organization of the executive branch. A skillful and dynamic governor can have greater impact in leadership. But this shows that the structure of the executive in Florida does not help the governor.

Two governors of Florida have suggested that the time has come to change the system. LeRoy Collins argued that the cabinet no longer assisted the governor, as it once had; on the contrary, the growth of cabinet departments and budgets, the acquisition of new functions, and the addition of public-relations staffs have created a system of "little governors," each of whom places his own interests above those of the state. The cabinet, he felt, had diluted executive authority far beyond what had been originally intended and far beyond what was good for the state.

Reubin Askew also advocated dropping the cabinet system in favor of governor-appointed executive officers. He regarded the system as an unnecessary obstacle to effective governing and an impediment to progress. A plan embodying his ideas was proposed by the Constitution Revision Commission in January 1978 but was voted down later that year. While the reasons for the rejection of the proposed constitution were manifold, one of the most important seems to have been the voters' desire to maintain a decentralized collegial executive.

Following the rejection of the 1978 constitution with its proposal to abolish the elected cabinet system, incoming governor Robert Graham moved in the direction of making Florida's collegial executive work. Under his leadership, the cabinet has studied long-range problems such as education, environmental issues, and the acquisition by the state of endangered lands and adopted long-range policies for legislative implementation. This approach has resulted in governor and cabinet members working together on a number of coordinated programs and mobilizing public support for legislative implementation.

Controlling the Administration: Patronage

An important device that governors have at their disposal for controlling their administrations is the dispensing or withholding of patronage. Governors are very much aware of its usefulness in administrative affairs. For example, Governor Sidney Catts (1917 – 21) once said, in referring to political patronage, "It is a mighty poor cat that won't look out for its kittens" (*Tampa Morning Tribune,* 11 April, 1923). It seems safe to say that every governor of Florida in this century would agree, regardless of his ideology. It should be realized that patronage can be used in positive and negative ways, to reward friends and to punish enemies. Every governor of Florida in this century has used patronage, in its positive and negative manifestations, as a means of trying to control his administration and of influencing both legislators and local officials.

Patronage covers a broad range of behaviors and activities. Every day the governor is besieged with pleas for reduction of prison sentences or pardons, requests for building or improving roads, solicitations for jobs or state business, and petitions for removal of various officials. All of these can be considered part of the patronage system because they involve the granting or withholding of favors.

One of the most important patronage mechanisms has been the granting of state contracts to private business firms. Governors have had considerable discretion in letting contracts. Centralized purchasing did not exist in any systematic way until LeRoy Collins's administration, although prior to that time there had been laws on the books that provided in some measure for such methods of keeping costs down and avoiding waste. (Central purchasing is a system whereby governmental contracts are let on bids and the lowest responsible bidder receives the contract; the system of competitive bids limits favoritism.) The absence of such purchasing meant that governors could influence the letting of contracts to any companies they wished. The absence of central purchasing allowed numerous opportunities for patronage, and many executive departments' contracts did not have to be let on the basis of competitive bidding. Thus governors were in a very strong position to use contracts to reward friends and supporters. For some agencies, especially the Road Department, contracts were at least as important as appointments and the actual selection of rights-of-way as mechanisms of patronage.

In using contracts as a form of patronage, most early governors employed a style that might be called a spoils system. This term refers to a deliberate effort to reward friendly companies and supporters including friendly legislators, if necessary at the expense of the state's economy or budget. To what extent is the spoils system functional or dysfunctional in terms of the governor's administrative control? The answer seems to be that as long as scandal is avoided, the use of the spoils system did not hurt the governor and could actually help him. The public seems to expect and tolerate a certain amount of reward and punishment in politics. Only when there is evidence of conflict of interest, corruption, or extreme heavy-handedness in the use of contracts does the public take notice and cause the governor political embarrassment.

As important as contracts have been in the politics of the executive branch in Florida, they still take second place to appointments. A governor may appoint as many as four thousand or five thousand persons to positions during his administration. Not all of these appointments are overtly partisan, and many are to relatively minor positions. Yet the fact remains that through appointments the governor can try to place in key administrative posts persons who, he hopes, will cooperate with him and respond to his definition of problems and his priorities. It is therefore an important mechanism that the governor uses in trying to control the executive branch despite its divided authority.

Governors themselves have pointed out most of the significant difficulties in making appointments. Ideological agreement or similarity of views is desirable but not always possible. For political reasons governors sometimes have to

Governor and Mrs. Spessard L. Holland and Governor-elect and Mrs. Millard F. Caldwell leaving governor's mansion for the capitol, January 1945. Photo courtesy State Photographic Archives, Strozier Library, Florida State University, Tallahassee.

yield to certain demands in order to gain other advantages. For example, LeRoy Collins fired his state prison director, Richard Culver, and appointed in his place H. G. Cochran, who was acceptable to Senator Charley Johns; he, in turn, agreed to cooperate (not for very long, as it turned out) with Collins on reapportionment. In a state as large as Florida, geographical balance is important in making appointments. Various regions of the state must be recognized, and a balance has to be struck between some of the traditional divisions, such as north and south, urban and rural. Since World War II various minority groups have had to be recognized. Fuller Warren was widely applauded for appointing the first woman, Mrs. Jessie Ball DuPont, to a high-level state agency, the State Board of Control (later the Board of Regents) in the early fifties. Fred Cone

(1937 – 41) had appointed the first woman sheriff. On the other hand, LeRoy Collins got considerable criticism when he appointed black members to his racial advisory board. He argued, however, that since matters directly affecting the black community would be discussed, blacks should be included on the board. Reubin Askew deliberately set about to appoint blacks and women to a range of public offices; Joseph Hatchett, a black man he appointed to an unexpired term on the Florida Supreme Court, later was elected to the justiceship (and more recently still was appointed to the federal bench).

In appointing loyal and responsive persons to office, governors face something of a paradox. If they surround themselves with "yes men," there is danger of a decline in the quality of leadership and an isolation from large issues facing the state. But appointing persons who are too independent compounds the governor's problem of trying to control an already divided and unwieldy administrative authority. A governor must try to find persons who strike the right balance between loyalty and independence, those who merit appointment but also are supporters of the governor. This issue has troubled most Florida governors, and on occasion they have gone to considerable lengths to find the right person for a particular assignment. Both Spessard Holland (1941 – 45) and Millard Caldwell, for example, established an elaborate network of trusted friends and advisors across the state to help locate capable, loyal persons to hold appointed posts.

The use of patronage in appointments is further limited by the establishment of judicial nominating commissions, which give the governor a panel of names of acceptable judicial appointees from whom to choose. This procedure, used for appointments to all levels of state courts, is aimed at fostering the appointment of qualified judges.

In summary, the appointment powers of the governor have been strictly limited since World War II by the placement of more positions under the merit system and by the use of nonpartisan nominating commissions. The governor, however, retains control of high policy positions even though appointees to some high positions must be approved by the Florida senate before they can take office. Appointees to some positions must be confirmed by a majority of the cabinet.

The conflict between the "professional" or "merit system" style of gubernatorial appointments and the spoils system is nowhere better seen than in the tremendous furor that arose in the brief administration of Charley Johns (1953 – 55). Almost immediately upon assuming the office following the untimely death of Gov. Dan McCarty in 1953, Johns requested and then demanded the resignation of a substantial number of McCarty's little cabinet appointees. When they refused to cooperate, Johns suspended seventeen of them. Many of these individuals were widely respected throughout the state, and charges of cronyism were leveled at Johns. The outcry from other public officials, the press, and the general public was so great that Johns's actions became a campaign issue in the 1954 special gubernatorial election. Additional fuel was poured on the fire when it became known that Johns was using several agencies, especially the Road Department, to reward his friends and punish his enemies through patronage. Governor-elect LeRoy Collins was so incensed that he called for public hearings to investigate Johns's suspensions of officials and his use of patronage in the little cabinet.

Johns refused to attend the hearings. The ousted officials accused him of smear tactics and alleged that political considerations had been his primary motivation. They said that the current suspicion surrounding the Road Board resulted from "dishonorable" requests made by Johns, giving as examples his demands for a supplemental agreement to a contract with a road builder who said he was not making enough money on his work for the state, a reevaluation of a piece of land owned by a friend of Johns on the Jacksonville Expressway right-of-way, and the granting of an engineering contract to a firm he favored whose bid was $100,000 more than the losing bid.

Collins declared at the end of the hearings that there had been no grounds for Johns's suspension of the seventeen officials and that he would reinstate them. Johns retired from the governorship under a cloud, returning to the senate for the rest of his active political career. Throughout this episode, Floridians let it be known that the use of patronage was acceptable but not when the governor was heavy-handed or blatantly one-sided in its use.

Budgeting

The budget process begins when the governor prepares the executive budget, which contains recommendations for expenditures for the entire state government for the coming year or biennium. In a few states the legislature actually works with the governor in preparing budget proposals but not in Florida. Rather, the legislature has its committees review the proposed budget as the basis for its appropriations. In Florida the governor can veto the whole budget or can veto an item in the appropriation act. Then the legislature has a chance to pass the budget or item over his veto.

After the appropriation act is passed, it becomes the administrative budget, which the governor must implement. The state may not borrow money; so if tax revenues do not equal appropriations, the governor is empowered to withhold budgeted funds so that monthly expenditures do not exceed the money in the state treasury. During the economic recession of 1974, and again in 1982, for example, expected tax revenues fell short; the governor withheld 5 percent of each state agency's funds to avoid monthly deficits.

The concept applied to budget preparation by the governor is that ''budgeting is a tool of management.'' This means that there is a limited amount of money to fund state and local government programs without increasing taxes. The question is where to put the available money: on roads? on welfare? on programs for the elderly? on tax relief? These budget recommendations are among the most vital decisions the governor makes.

Unless there is a strong push by the governor to change budgeted funds from one program to another, most allotments are based on the previous year's budget for a function or service and held there for the coming year, unless there is an increase for salary raises and/or costs of supplies. This method is called *incrementalism,* and a number of studies show this to be the usual approach to budgeting in Florida and in many other states.

An alternative method that allows direct control of decision-making is called zero sum budgeting. Instead of starting from last year's base, each department presenting a budget is required to show the accomplishments of each of its programs, to reassess each program and recommend it for continuation or termination, and to show how this decision will affect services rendered.

Much of a state budget is designated by state or federal law for specific purposes, and the actual budgetary transfer of funds to other purposes is difficult. Certain tax sources are earmarked for specific purposes; for example, the gasoline tax in Florida is used for building or maintaining state or local roads.

Florida's Budget System

Florida, unlike other states, has always used an executive budget in this century, but with an important qualification. The governor did not have to share budget-making with the legislature, but he did have to share it with the cabinet. One of the cabinet's most important functions was to sit as the State Budget Commission, which prepared a budget every two years and sent it to the legislature for approval. The governor chaired and sat as a member of the commission. He established a system of legislative and program priorities, and, as noted, so long as he did not interfere with the interests of the cabinet members, his budget was generally accepted. The governor's campaign promises, though not binding, combined with this system of priorities, helped to establish boundaries within which budget discussions occurred. But even within these constraints imposed by the governor, the State Budget Commission had considerable room to make changes. While the governor was undoubtedly influential in the budget process, he certainly did not dominate it. In 1968 the governor was finally given exclusive control of the budget, and the old State Budget Commission was abolished.

The mechanics and politics of the State Budget Commission and the governor's relatively modest role can be easily described. The commission convened about the middle of January in odd-numbered years. When a new governor had just taken office, this meeting took place only a few weeks after his inauguration. He knew little about the state agencies and their programs on which he was asked to make budgetary decisions. Meetings lasted several hours, usually daily, for four to six weeks. Legislators and representatives of executive agencies and interest groups attended the meetings to make formal budget requests. The commission, after meeting in executive session, decided on the allocation for each agency and department; the budget was printed and delivered to legislators several weeks before the new session began.

The entire budget process under this system was political. As one recent governor said, it was nothing but logrolling and mutual accommodation. Each cabinet official protected the allocation for his department and acted as an advocate for increases in his programs. He confined his interest to his own department and rarely questioned the use of funds or allocations for other departments. Thus the cabinet served as both judge and jury. Often cabinet members had attended these sessions for years, as a result of long tenure, and had established fairly clear sets of mutual expectations and methods of operating which were seldom, if ever, violated. The governor could ask questions, but he knew relatively little about the inner workings of the departments. By his third year he had learned a good deal about state operations, but by then he was a lame duck.

Under this system there was no possibility for a complete "root and branch" budget review or for the governor to use the budget as an instrument of policy determination or executive control. From his perspective it was hardly even "muddling through," for he had relatively little to say about budget allocations. It is fair to say that between 1900 and 1968 the budget process in Florida served to fragment, not to strengthen, the executive and administrative capacity of the governor's office. It was only through the item veto that the governor exercised any independent, direct control over the budget process.

One important development in moving toward a more systematic budget process was the creation in 1945 of a position for a professional budget director. Very early in his administration, Governor Caldwell, along with the comptroller, state auditor, Budget Commission secretary, and several members of the legislature, had advocated a position for a full-time budget director. It was felt that such a post was needed to create a uniform system of budgeting (until then each department had its own system) and accounting for state funds. Caldwell in particular had stressed the need for uniform budgets and for someone to keep a constant check on state spending. But the presence of the budget director, while a big step in making the budget a more comprehensible and integrated document, did not fundamentally alter the politics of the budgetary process.

It should also be noted that throughout most of this century legislators have complained about the budget process. They have felt, not without justification, that they lacked sufficient information to deal intelligently with the budget when it was delivered to them by the governor's office. Trying to improve this situation, even in a small way, Governor McCarty invited legislators to the hearings of the Budget Commission so they could listen, ask questions, and acquire needed information. Governor Collins continued the practice, but ultimately it was abandoned: Senators Charley Johns and Doyle Carlton both com-

Governor LeRoy Collins signing junior college law, with members of the 1955 legislature. Photo courtesy State Photographic Archives, Strozier Library, Florida State University, Tallahassee.

plained that they were wasting their time. They argued that the rapid-fire presentation of budget requests — in one meeting fifty-six agency requests were examined and approved in less than four hours — and the limited information available contributed little to their ability to handle the budget. It is noteworthy that even with the addition of large permanent staffs for house and senate appropriations committees, many legislators say that they still feel unprepared to deal with the governor's budget.

The 1968 constitution contained a provision giving greater budget powers to the governor. No longer is he subordinated to other members of the cabinet in making out the budget.

The full impact of this change in the budget system is not yet known, but it is clear that it remains an intensely political process. Substantial lobbying, trading, and bargaining still go on inside the governor's office as the budget is prepared. Available evidence suggests that last year's budget provides the principal guidelines for this year's budget. There is still little overall analysis of the total budget. The legislature can still make whatever changes it wishes in the governor's budget. The governor can lobby legislators to follow his wishes in the event they disagree with him, but his choices are only to accept their changes or to use his item veto.

There are some differences from the older pattern. The governor maintains much closer control over the design of the budget, and if bargains are struck and accommodations made he is instrumental in creating them. In his second administration Askew used his lieutenant governor, Jim Williams, as his chief budget aide, thus placing an executive official in full-time oversight of the budget process. At the same time the legislature has reintroduced the cabinet into the process of supervising any transfer of major items within the budget after appropriations are made. It also has sought to have appropriations committee chairpersons supervise certain expenditures within departments based on what is called "legislative intent" and, on occasion, supervisory authority over expenditures by committee chairpersons during the fiscal year has been written into appropriation acts. The governor has challenged such authority over expenditures, and his own authority has generally been upheld by the state supreme court. However, a general law was enacted by the 1983 legislature to institutionalize legislative supervision in certain instances. Thus, the governor's authority over annual expenditures continues to be challenged.

The Governor and the Legislature

Florida's governor has become influential in the legislature partly by design and partly by default. The enormous growth of the state during the century, especially since World War II, has made it necessary for the governor to become active in forming appropriate solutions to resulting problems. The legislature, for the most part, has been unable to respond to these urban and suburban problems rapidly or creatively and has fallen behind the governor in policy development. Until recently, power in the legislature was divided among many offices and members in many small parcels. The legislature met only for a short term in odd-numbered years; it lacked a professional staff; it was dominated by rural conservatives who were not anxious to recognize the problems of a growing populace. Indeed, during much of this century the legislature would not and could not act until the governor presented it with a program; legislators, for example, complained about the lack of leadership shown by ultraconservative Gov. Fred Cone in the late 1930s when he refused to make recommendations on legislation.

The situation has been changed considerably by the increase in professional staff assistance to the legislature, by annual legislative sessions and ongoing committee operations, and by reapportionment. Nonetheless, the governor is still expected to address the legislature at the beginning of each session and to present a series of proposals and programs for the state. He is expected to follow up these early recommendations during the legislative session with specific recommendations for legislative enactment. He thereby becomes a chief contributor to the state's legislated policies and programs.

But the problems the governor must overcome to satisfy these expectations are great. Although an unwieldy body, the legislature maintains its independence. It does not meekly follow the governor's lead, even though it expects him to make specific recommendations for enactment. The governor can wheedle and cajole legislators one by one, but ultimately, as a body, the legislature can delay action on or modify his proposals or even defeat his purposes altogether. Another related problem is that cabinet members have their own contact with the legislature and can thus influence measures, not only in their own specific areas but also on other topics.

The governor's traditionally brief term of office has been a major problem in his quest for legislative cooperation. When the governor was limited to only four years in office, and when the legislators assembled only in alternate years, the governor's chances for legislative victories were comparatively slim. It was usually the case that if he did not gain passage of most of his program during the first legislative session of his term, he would not achieve it at all. By the governor's third year (and the second legislative session of his term), he was already a lame duck. Legislators jockeying for personal power, some of them perhaps with their eyes on the governorship, paid little attention to the incumbent governor's recommendations. With the change to annual sessions of the legislature and with the possibility of the governor winning election to a second four-year term, legislators must give more attention to the governor's recommendations in every legislative session. One may doubt, however, that these changes have made the governor's tasks in securing legislation significantly easier.

In seeking legislative cooperation, the governor has available a number of strategies and tactics, but none guarantees success. The civic goals presented in the "state of the state" annual address can be perceived either as inadequate or as overly ambitious (the latter perception is the more common, given the traditionally conservative fiscal attitudes of the legislature). The governor may seek to influence the selection of legislative leaders, but if "his" candidates lose he can expect little cooperation from the winners. His attempts to influence the outcome of legislative leadership contests is likely to be resented, and the governor is well advised not to become embroiled in them. The governor's use of publicity, press conferences, public speeches, and other such efforts to bring public pressure on the legislature in support of his programs may also be resented by legislators; and legislators from "safe" districts, where the governor's wishes are a matter of voter indifference, will resist his programs with impunity. Meeting with legislators individually and in small groups both before and during the legislative session, the governor will employ the carrot and stick in the form of patronage and of bargaining to grant or withhold support for programs desired by the legislators in order to win their votes for his proposed legislation.

But these stratagems guarantee nothing since patronage for one side may provoke the antagonism of the other — and, if blatant, may incite public mistrust of the governor and his programs generally. The governor can threaten to veto legislative acts he disapproves of, and he may in fact veto them; he can threaten to call special legislative sessions (disliked by legislators who must earn their living in part from the private sector). But the veto and special sessions are the governor's "ultimate weapons" and must be used only occasionally and judiciously if he is to succeed in winning the support of a recalcitrant legislature for his programs.

Both Askew and Graham have found their legislative strength to be greatest at the start of their second terms. In 1983, Governor Graham used three procedures to push through his legislative program. First, he formed a coalition with the speaker of the house and the president of the senate, to help his programs in the legislature. Second, he used his line-item veto to eliminate projects in the districts of critical legislators. Third, he staged meetings around the state to stimulate public support for his programs. These measures proved effective when he combined them with calling special sessions for a single or a few issues. By 1983 he had fine-tuned his methods, and his legislative program had been successfully implemented.

In dealing with the legislature, the governor of Florida is most severely handicapped by the lack of a permanent base of support for his programs. The factionalism of Florida's party politics is reflected in factionalism in the legislature. Without party unity among legislators, the governor must continually form coalitions of his own and other factions. The memberships of factions shift frequently; few are ongoing. The governor's supporters on one issue become his opponents on another. Only in recent years have urban coalitions given rise to reasonably stable support for gubernatorial initiatives in such areas as urban aid and some social welfare programs. But even Florida's cities have no permanent system of alliances, and it is not unusual to see urban, even suburban, legislators from different regions of the state opposed to one another on matters pertaining to urban affairs. The effect for the governor, of course, is to create one more difficulty in building a stable base of legislative support.

Conclusion

The governor of Florida faces an enormously difficult series of tasks in carrying out the duties of his office. While the populace has high expectations that the governor will lead the state forward, he is hemmed in by structural and political forces that prevent his meeting all the demands placed on him. He lacks the power to control even his own executive branch of state government. The techniques and devices available to him for dealing with the legislature, even under the best of circumstances, yield uncertain results. Without real power, the governor must rely on his personality and political skill and must be fortunate in the circumstances of the state if he is to achieve his goals in office. Because it is so difficult a job, it is no wonder that many governors of Florida have been relieved to see their terms of office end. Yet the governorship is a position in which the officeholder has many opportunities for satisfaction in successful work of enduring importance to the state.

Selected References

Beyle, Thad, and Williams, J. Oliver, eds. *The American Governor in Behavioral Perspective*. New York: Harper and Row, 1972.

Black, Earl. *Southern Governors and Civil Rights*. Cambridge: Harvard University Press, 1976.

Colburn, David R., and Scher, Richard K. *Florida Gubernatorial Politics in the Twentieth Century*. Gainesville: University Presses of Florida, forthcoming.

Kallenback, Joseph. *The American Chief Executive*. New York: Harper and Row, 1966.

Schlesinger, James A. "The Politics of the Executive." *In Politics in the American States,* edited by Herbert Jacob and Kenneth Vines. Boston: Little, Brown, 1971.

Administrative and Functional Agencies

by Douglas St. Angelo

FLORIDA STATE UNIVERSITY

with Bill O. Gibson

PUBLIC SERVICE COMMISSION

8

This chapter is concerned with administrative departments and divisions of departments that encompass most of the operating agencies in the executive branch of Florida's government, including the agencies responsible for budgeting, planning, purchasing, personnel, and other support services.

Two major changes in the functions of these agencies have come about in the 1970s. The first has been a trend toward centralization of the budgeting, planning, purchasing, and personnel functions; agencies that in the past performed such services for themselves have seen them more and more entrusted to one of a small number of central agencies specifically responsible for regulation and coordination of these services among many state departments. The second change has been a strong tendency to place greater administrative control under the governor and his staff.

The state constitution, and the laws enacted under it, that controlled Florida from 1885 through 1968 mandated and encouraged a highly decentralized administration. They restricted the powers of the governor much more than did the laws in other states and much more than federal law limits the administrative powers of the president of the United States.

The constitution of 1885 circumscribed the powers of the governor by providing for other elected officers to head executive departments. This constitutional provision allowed the legislature to create a cabinet system in which the administrative power commonly granted to the governor in other states is shared among the elected department heads. The cabinet thus consists of six executive officials elected statewide — the secretary of state, attorney general, treasurer, comptroller, commissioner of agriculture, and commissioner of education — together with the governor.

Governments of this cabinet type were common in the last century. They conformed to the populist tradition established by President Andrew Jackson that established protection against official misfeasance through the election of a number of public officials among whom executive power was dispersed. That tradition remained strong in rural and southern areas well into the twentieth century.

In recent decades, however, the populist tradition of dispersal of power and decentralization of services has been increasingly replaced by management views that encourage centralization under a single elected official. In state government that official is the governor. The trend toward centralization is demonstrated by the widely noted model state constitution, drafted under the auspices of the National Civic League, which places all executive agencies under the control of the governor and the governor's staff and makes the governor and supreme court justices the only public officials elected in statewide contests.

With the constitution adopted in 1968, Florida began to expand the governor's administrative powers and to centralize executive administrative authority in fewer agencies. These changes were accomplished in two ways. First, the constitution removed some administrative powers from the cabinet and gave the office of the governor independent control over those areas. These powers included preparation of the state budget for submission to the legislature, statewide planning functions, and regulation of state personnel practices. The constitution also required that the legislature consolidate over 200 agencies that it had created under the old constitution into no more than 25. These consolidated agencies, with only a few specific exceptions, had to report to the governor or to the governor and cabinet acting jointly. The legislature met these constitutional requirements by the Executive Reorganization Act of 1969, which reduced the 200-plus agencies to 22.

The Legislative Reorganization Act of 1969 was a compromise measure: it left the cabinet with some administrative powers, but it greatly reduced them. The cabinet system—or the cabinet officers—still had strong friends in the legislature; the people of Florida signaled their trust in the election of executive department heads by defeating a proposed constitutional amendment in 1978 that would have empowered the governor to appoint the heads of executive departments and would have abolished the cabinet. Even so, there may yet be more centralization and consolidation of executive responsibility and authority in the office of the governor at the expense of the elected department heads' powers.

Figure 8.1 shows the present organization of the executive branch of Florida's government. There are three categories of agencies: those under the executive office of the governor, those under elected cabinet officers, and those under the governor and cabinet acting jointly. In addition to departments with employees the chart also lists some boards, such as the executive clemency board which consists of the governor and cabinet and which grants pardons and paroles. The addition of these boards creates a greater number of agencies than the list of operating departments previously discussed.

In this chapter not all the departments and agencies on this chart will be examined; later chapters treat education, agriculture, arts, recreation, and so on. This chapter will center on those departments concerned with overall management.

Before taking up the departments with general jurisdiction, we consider the executive office of the governor, to which were transferred some functions from the Department of Administration. Now directly under the governor's office are the Office of Budget and Planning, and the State Energy Office.

Fig. 8.1. Florida's Administrative Agencies

Voters

Agencies under elected department heads (cabinet)

→ Attorney General
Department of Legal Affairs
- Division of Cabinet Affairs
- Division of Opinions
- Division of Criminal Appeals
- Division of General Legal Services

→ Commissioner of Agriculture
Department of Agriculture and Consumer Services
- Division of Animal Industry
- Division of Chemistry
- Division of Consumer Services
- Division of Dairy Industry
- Division of Forestry
- Division of Inspection
- Division of Marketing
- Division of Standards
- Division of Fruit and Vegetable Inspection

→ Commissioner of Education
Department of Education
- Division of Blind Services
- Division of Community Colleges
- Division of Public Schools
- Division of Universities
- Division of Vocational Education

→ Comptroller
Department of Banking and Finance
- Division of Accounting and Auditing
- Division of Banking
- Division of Finance
- Division of Securities

→ Secretary of State
Department of State
- Division of Archives, History, and Records Management
- Division of Corporations
- Division of Cultural Affairs
- Division of Elections
- Division of Library Services
- Division of Licensing

→ State Treasurer and Insurance Commissioner
Department of Insurance and Treasurer
- Division of Insurance Company Regulation
- Division of Insurance Consumer Services
- Division of Rehabilitation and Liquidation
- Division of Risk Management
- Division of State Fire Marshall
- Division of the Treasury

Voters

Agencies under the governor

→ Governor
Executive Office of the Governor
- Inspector General
- Office of Budget and Planning
- State Energy Office

***Department of Administration**
- Division of Administrative Hearings
- Division of Personnel
- Division of Retirement
- Division of Human Resource Management

***Department of Business Regulation**
- Division of Alcoholic Beverages and Tobacco
- Division of Florida Land Sales and Condominiums
- Division of Hotels and Restaurants

***Department of Commerce**
- Division of Economic Development
- Division of Tourism

***Department of Community Affairs**
- Florida Housing Finance Agency
- Division of Public Safety Planning and Assistance
- Division of Local Resource Management

***Department of Corrections**

---

*Director appointed by the governor and confirmed by the senate.

Fig. 8.1. (continued)

***Department of Environmental Regulation**
Division of Environmental Permitting
Division of Environmental Programs

***Department of Health and Rehabilitative Services**

***Department of Labor and Employment Security**
Division of Employment Security
Division of Labor
Division of Workmen's Compensation

***Department of Military Affairs**

***Department of Transportation**
Division of Transportation Planning
Division of Public Transportation Operations
Division of Road Operations
Division of Preconstruction and Design

***Department of Professional and Occupational Regulation**
Division of Regulation
Division of Professions
Division of Real Estate

Voters

Agencies under the cabinet

Department of General Services
Division of Bond Finance
Division of Building Construction and Property Management
Division of Communications
Division of Electronic Data Processing
Division of Motor Pool
Division of Purchasing
Division of Security
Division of Surplus Property

Department of Highway Safety and Motor Vehicles
Division of Driver Licenses
Division of Florida Highway Patrol
Division of Motor Vehicles

Department of Law Enforcement
Division of Criminal Investigations
Division of Criminal Justice Information Systems
Division of Staff Services
Division of Standards and Training

Department of Natural Resources
Division of Law Enforcement
Division of Marine Resources
Division of Recreation and Parks
Division of Resource Management
Canal Authority
Division of State Lands
Division of Beaches and Shores

Department of Revenue
Division of Audits
Division of Collection and Enforcement
Division of Valorem Tax
Division of Information Systems

Office of Executive Clemency

Parole and Probation Commission
(Commissioners are appointed by the governor and cabinet from nominees named by the Board of Examiners for the Parole Commission)

Independent agencies

Department of Citrus
(Members are appointed by the governor and approved by the senate)

Public Service Commission
(Members are appointed by the governor from nominees named by the Qualifications Commission)

Game and Fresh Water Fish Commission
(Five members are appointed by the governor and confirmed by the senate)

Ethics Commission
(Five members appointed by the governor, two by the president of the senate, and two by the speaker of the house)

State Board of Administration
Governor
Treasurer
Comptroller

Office of Budget and Planning: Budget Function

Budgeting is a process that expresses itself in numbers. Since those numbers allocate the cash resources of state government, however, the budget represents the basic document of the state's public policies. Money and manpower make programs go, and the budget decides how much, how far.

Florida's budget is a detailed plan for the spending of the available revenue dollars for one year or for two years. It specifies program by program the amounts that can be spent during the period and sets a maximum on the number of personnel that can be employed by state agencies in each area. To the extent that program decisions involve dollars — and there are few truly noneconomic decisions — the budget is the approved plan of operations. Although it is not widely recognized, it is impossible to separate budget decisions and program decisions.

The budgeting process in Florida has been affected to some extent by national trends, such as the Planning-Program-Budgeting System (PPBS) and zero base budgeting. In little more than a decade the state has gone from a biennial to an annual and back to a biennial budgeting process. The ability to influence the final budgeted allocations by shaping the budget recommendations to the legislature has shifted from the governor and cabinet acting jointly to the governor solely. But the budgeting process has otherwise remained essentially unchanged.

Possibly the biggest recent change came about after the reapportionment battles of the late 1960s when a more urban legislature reorganized all three branches of Florida's government. The legislature had had few permanent employees. It had previously borrowed budgeting staff personnel from the executive branch in preparation for its biennial sessions. It changed to annual sessions in 1969 and provided itself with the staff it needed to allow lawmakers to exercise fully their policy-making role. It also reorganized the executive branch, making the governor the chief budget officer and, with minor exceptions, giving him exclusively the budgetary powers he had previously shared with the cabinet. These reorganizations, of course, affected not just budgeting but all the state's executive administrative procedures.

Budgets also have been affected by rapid population growth, inflation, and wide swings in tax revenues, which have either built up huge surpluses or forced spending curtailments in the middle of the budget year. That the changes in the budgeting process itself have been relatively small is probably due in part to the stability of the budget staff from administration to administration for almost two decades.

How the budget is assembled. — The budgeting process in Florida begins months before the legislative session. Key people in each agency decide what amounts they need to have in order to operate their programs in ways that program managers believe are appropriate. Their requests are not limited by any arithmetical constraints, and the amounts requested may be significantly higher than the amounts included in the current budget. The asking budgets go to the department level, where the department head trims and fits them into an agency request that he or she believes can be defended or justified to the governor and the legislature.

When the budget requests of the various agencies are received by the governor, they are viewed from a different perspective. Instead of recommending the amounts that each agency wants for its programs, the governor must measure the cash requirements of these several programs against the amount of revenue that will be available. Because of inflation and rapid population growth, the amount of revenue available and the total budget authorized have set new record highs in almost every recent year. But the growth in revenue is offset substantially by higher costs, and the total cash available is far less than the amounts requested by the various agencies.

Florida law requires the governor to submit a balanced budget for legislative enactment. If he wants to spend more than anticipated revenue will cover, he must recommend the new taxes required to raise the additional revenue. Even when a governor decides to recommend new taxes, substantial reductions in agency requests are necessary to make the total balance with the revenue that will be available. Agencies that do not get their full request recommended often complain of budget cuts even if the amount recommended by the governor represents an increase over their current spending level.

When given the choice of cutting programs, raising taxes, or borrowing money, politicians will favor borrowing almost every time: the U. S. Congress, for example, routinely adds to the national debt by appropriating more than taxes will produce.

The option of deficit financing for the operations of government is not available in Florida because the constitution prohibits borrowing except for a limited amount of citizen-approved bonding. With only the alternatives of taxing or trimming, governors are usually reluctant to recommend new taxes if the budget possibly can be balanced by reducing program requests. Even when a governor determines that he must recommend an unpopular tax increase, it is not always approved by the legislature.

A governor's budget recommendations are effective only to the extent that they are accepted by the lawmakers. Essentially the governor provides a starting point for the legislature by proposing an overall budget developed from the many departmental budget requests. Issues are addressed and policies are established by the governor working through the staff of the Office of Budget, which was transferred in 1979 from the Department of Administration to the Office of the Governor.

Legislative appropriation. — Getting a program included in the governor's recommendations does not assure an agency of a legislative appropriation. It does, however, lend a certain amount of credibility to the budget request during the legislative process. For one thing, a member of the governor's budget staff attends every meeting of the appropriations committees of the house and senate to explain and defend the amounts recommended. All agencies directly under the governor's supervision also are expected to support the governor's recommendations. Other agencies and many special interest groups must each decide whether to accept and support the amounts recommended by the governor for their programs or to try for more (never less). Teachers' groups, for example, usually actively seek more money than the governor recommends for public schools.

The legislature does not have to rely wholly upon the recommendations of the governor and the arguments of pressure groups for information on the needs and services of programs. Each agency gives its asking budget to the legislative appropriations committees at the same time that it presents its asking budget to the Office of Budget for gubernatorial review. Agencies provide additional information on request to the legislative committees, which routinely hold their own budget hearings, calling agencies in to present and defend proposals. The legislature can make any changes in the governor's recommendations, and there are always pet projects or additional amounts that influential legislators want to see included. Since the legislature also is required to keep the budget in balance, however, every dollar added must be offset by a reduction unless the lawmakers want to initiate a tax increase.

The legislature includes its final budgetary decisions in the General Appropriations Act, which lists each organization of state government and provides appropriations by fund categories such as salaries, expenses, and operating capital outlay. (A major exception to the partitioning of appropriated amounts into fund categories is the State University System, which receives a lump-sum appropriation for the Florida Board of Regents to distribute to the system's nine universities for further allocation by the university presidents.) Program descriptions and plans are not included in the act. But each appropriation represents the original agency request as modified by the governor's recommendations and then changed or approved by the legislature. If the final figure is different from that recommended by the governor, the law requires the chairman of the house and senate appropriations committees to issue a letter of intent, which specifically identifies the reductions or additions that were made. The letter itself does not have the force of law, but the changes that it identifies traditionally have been enforced by the budget staff in its monitoring role to see that agencies conform to legislative intent. Since appropriations generally are released quarterly, agency operations are subject to periodic review by the budget staff.

The constitution provides that the legislature may use the appropriations act to write restrictions and limitations on how the money will be spent but it may not use the appropriations act to make new laws. Each item in the appropriations act also is subject to the governor's veto, which can eliminate the funds provided for in the item along with any legislative stipulations on the spending of those funds. The governor's item veto power, restricted to use on the appropriations act, is subject to the same affirmation or override by the legislature as any other veto.

The limitations on the legislature and the governor in this part of the process are not well defined. Twice in recent years the courts have been called upon to define where allowable restrictions stop and the writing of substantive law begins. Florida's courts also were asked to determine if a governor can veto an unconstitutional or illegal provision without eliminating all the money appropriated in the same item. The courts have not provided the requested clarification of these and related questions. In each case, the annual budget expired before a final decision was reached, and the issue was declared moot. Since Florida has returned to biennial budgets, however, the questions may come up again.

The agencies' operating budgets.—The detailed asking budgets of the agencies, as modified in the governor's recommendation and then changed by the legislature in the appropriations act and signed into law by the governor, go back to the agencies as their specific operating budgets for the new fiscal period. Any change that an agency requires during the fiscal period must be approved through the Office of Budget and Planning. After review by the budget staff, many types of changes can be approved by this office. Larger changes, such as the proposed transfer of appropriations within an agency or the initiation of programs, must be approved by the Administration Commission, which is composed of the governor and the cabinet. This power to approve major allocation changes within limits authorized by law is the main budget function left to the commission since governmental reorganization shifted most budgetary authority to the governor. Even in this process the governor's role is decisive. Unless the action involves a single cabinet agency, authorizations by the Administration Commission of changes in allocations require majority approval, the governor to be included in the majority. This process created by the Florida legislature amounts to veto power for the governor over changes in budgeted allocations.

Estimating revenue. — The other side of the budget is revenue, primarily the income that is anticipated from current taxes. Since spending cannot exceed revenue, an accurate estimate of revenue agreed to by all parties is extremely important to the successful functioning of the budgeting process. Florida, however, has no formal revenue estimating process prescribed by law. Instead, revenue estimates are agreed upon by an ad hoc group, which includes fiscal officials of the legislature and of agencies involved in the financial matters of the state. This process was devised to prevent the state's several fiscal officials from coming up with differing estimates of revenue. The informal group usually meets around the beginning of the calendar year before the governor makes his budget recommendations to the legislature. This early estimate is later reviewed by the group and revised, if necessary, before the legislature makes its final budget decision in the spring. No other state's budgeting system is exactly like Florida's. Whether in theory it is considered to be a good or a bad system, good people can make any system work; and Florida's system works relatively well.

The Planning Function

The job of public planners is difficult. They are charged with resolving political differences with rational answers. Good planners know that the future is not so much planned as negotiated. Planning success depends more on getting politicians, citizens, and business interests to come together on a good answer than on finding the theoretically best answer. Sometimes Florida's planners are able to manage this well, but sometimes the political realities seem beyond management.

Upon assuming the governorship in 1979, Bob Graham proposed moving the budget and planning functions out of the Department of Administration. This proposal gave rise to many new schemes for the organization of the Division of State Planning. The governor's office presented proposals; so did the division, which had been working on modifications. Comprehensive planning was assigned to the executive office of the governor and the old Planning Division transferred out of the Department of Administration. The planning office's intergovernmental relation function was transferred to the state Department of Community Affairs.

State Energy Office

The third agency under the executive office of the governor is the State Energy Office, created after the Arab oil embargo of 1974–75. Its function is to recommend state policy in relation to energy. The energy crisis became less acute, but it continued at a slower pace until 1978–79. By then it had become clear that there was a permanent energy shortage and that Florida, dependent on tourism, needs to concern itself with problems of transportation and conservation of energy. The governor appointed a new energy director in 1979. One function of the agency is to coordinate state programs with existing federal programs. Other state agencies, especially those concerned with air quality, are affected by the programs of the energy office because the shortage of low-pollutant fuels creates additional problems. This office can be expected to assume increasing importance.

The Personnel Function

The Department of Administration has some divisions which set policies for all departments of state government. One of these is the Division of Personnel.

The Division of Personnel is charged with the responsibility of creating and maintaining a uniform personnel system for the state, to cover approximately 70,000 state career service employees. Exemptions to this coverage can be made by law. Elected officials and their personal aides are exempted as are high-level state administrators, employees of the courts, and nonclerical employees of the university system and the Public Service Commission. The great majority of state employees, however, are under the Career Service System and subject to its rules and protections.

The personnel system was first established in 1937 so that the state could receive federal funds. At that time it covered only state agencies receiving federal funds. The system was extended in 1957 under the leadership of Governor LeRoy Collins, but most state employees were not covered until the passage of a career service act in

1967. That program was directed by the cabinet-level State Personnel Board. The functions of that board were transferred to the Department of Administration in the 1969 reorganization.

Public personnel systems are generally designed to protect employees from capricious supervisors and political pressures while attempting to secure high-quality performance from the employees. Central personnel agencies, such as Florida has, are charged with the responsibility of achieving these goals. The division, working through four bureaus, is required to establish job qualifications, test job applicants, classify jobs, provide employee training programs, maintain a pay system that disburses equal pay for equal work and an equitable promotion system, and create merit rewards for good service.

Florida's system, because it is heavily centralized, is not highly regarded by specialists in personnel administration. A recent report on state personnel practices, "Improving Florida Personnel Practice: An Agenda for Action," implies in very diplomatic language that Florida's system has not been successful in attracting highly qualified executives and trainees. This report suggests that the system does not recruit well and that it discriminates against nonwhites, women, and the disabled. Experience requirements are seen as a screen used to eliminate such minority group members along with recent graduates of colleges and universities. Recruitment and job listing processes are described in a manner that leads one to believe that the new positions are not visible, that job seekers are able to get information on professional-level vacancies only through the help of friends even though job announcements have been required since 1976. To help fulfill program efforts (rather than to create barriers), personnel procedures are said to require streamlining. Disputes are said to cause costly and frustrating delays in processing job appointments. The merit system is criticized for tending to reward years of service rather than good work, and the classification and pay systems are seen as outmoded, discriminatory, and counterproductive. The report did not find any emphasis upon career development and training. The authors acknowledge that their report did not comment upon the "great bulk of the personnel process that is working well."

Because of criticisms of the Division of Personnel, some restructuring was attempted in 1979. First, some of the functions have been reassigned to operating personnel sections of functional departments of state government. Second, recruitment arrangements have been improved. The general effort under Governor Graham is further to upgrade state government personnel practices.

Division of Administrative Hearings

For many years prior to the enactment of the controversial current law in 1974, Florida had an administrative procedures act. Under the old act, legislators and some affected parties complained that state agency rules were made or changed without public notice and often without a hearing. Some lawmakers also believed that agencies often wrote rules that went beyond the limits of the law.

The Administrative Procedures Act of 1974 was designed to solve these problems by giving citizens the right to be heard before new rules were adopted. Critics called the law a "lawyers' relief act," and some administrators predicted that it would bring government to a halt.

The process initiated by the new act did not bring the bureaucracy to its knees, but neither did it merely provide an uncomplicated procedure for hearing citizens' complaints. It established, in effect, an administrative court system to hear petitions and legal objections from interested people or organizations. Although a lawyer has not been strictly required, hearings presided over by the hearing officers of the Division of Administrative Hearings have taken the place of trials on administrative determinations previously held in circuit courts.

Of possibly greater effect, however, were the changes that the Administrative Procedures Act made in the rule-making process. It requires agencies to establish rules on how laws within an agency's oversight responsibilities will be enforced. Agencies also have to publish information concerning their organization, responsibilities, and procedures. Before adopting a rule, an agency is required to give notice citing legal authority and including information on the purpose and economic impact of the proposal. The notice is also required to include the time and place for a public hearing to be held if any citizen requests the right to be heard. The Joint Administrative Procedures Committee of the legislature was given the authority to challenge any rule that goes beyond the boundaries of the law, and the hearing officers are given the power to set aside any rule that does not meet requirements of the adoption procedure or that is determined to be beyond the powers granted by the legislature.

The legislature gave the Division of Administrative Hearings ten hearing officers plus clerical support. During the first four years of operation, the number of hearing officers grew to twelve, including the division's director and assistant director, who also conduct hearings.

To assure the independence of the small agency, the legislature provided career service system protection for the hearing officers and created a unique process, which requires the division director to be appointed by the governor and cabinet acting jointly and confirmed by the senate. Since senate confirmation normally is required for gubernatorial appointments, not for those made by the governor and cabinet acting jointly, there is no set length for the term of the division director.

Department of General Services

The Department of General Services (DGS) is probably best understood as the agency assigned the housekeeping functions of state government. It was created by the Executive Reorganization Act of 1969. At its creation some existing agencies were transferred to the new department, some new agencies were established, and some functions of other agencies were assigned to it.

General Services is one of five departments controlled by the governor and cabinet acting jointly. It represents one of the compromises that the pro-cabinet forces won in the Executive Reorganization Act. The executive director, the chief officer of DGS, is appointed by a majority vote of the governor and the cabinet and may be fired by them at any time.

The responsibilities of DGS are great. It oversees the spending of hundreds of millions of state dollars and has often been the center of controversy having to do with its efficiency and integrity. In the past, the agency's rental of private buildings for state government use has been repeatedly questioned in the news media. Other state agencies have often quarreled with DGS over purchasing decisions and the design and construction of state buildings. Management of this department is a difficult job, and its officers can always expect to be under fire.

The Department of General Services is organized in eight divisions. All are headquartered in Tallahassee, but some have branch and district offices elsewhere in Florida.

The *Division of Bond Finance* arranges for loans to the state for construction or purchase of buildings, facilities, toll roads, bridges, and tunnels. This is normally done by issuing bonds against the tax revenues of the state. The interest on these bonds is not taxed by the federal government so they are very attractive investments to wealthy persons and large institutions such as banks, trusts, and insurance companies. Loans to the state are sometimes arranged by issuing bonds whose principal and interest are paid from revenues derived, for example, from tolls; these are called revenue bonds, and they are obligations only against the specific revenue source whose creation they fund. They are not general obligation bonds and are therefore not obligations against state tax revenue. Such revenue bonds do not require approval by the voters, but under the constitution general obligation bonds do. By good timing of bond sales and by maintaining a good credit rating, the state can save a great deal of money in the course of issuing bonds.

The sensitive areas of building construction and rental of space for state agency use is under the direction of the *Division of Building Construction and Property Management*. This division is charged with the planning of net state construction, including the choice of architects. This responsibility entails not only engineering and aesthetic problems but significant political ones as well. Among its duties are awarding bids and supervising the construction of state facilities. This agency also arranges for state rentals, approves leases, and supervises rental agreements. The state rents acres of space in buildings in Tallahassee and throughout Florida. Charges of political and economic favoritism have raged around all of these responsibilities. This division also maintains most state-owned property, performing renovations and repairs of state buildings and the landscape maintenance of their grounds.

The *Division of Communications* is relatively new in state government. This division was assigned the large responsibility of planning, coordinating, and managing a communication system for all state agencies and local governments. While its work is not complete, this agency's efforts are a success for centralized state administration. It has developed a state-operated long-distance telephone network called SUNCOM, which ties into most of Florida's private telephone systems and provides the state government with long-distance rates that are less than commercial rates.

The *Division of Electronic Data Processing,* another new division, supervises computer and computer-related operations for state government. It maintains three large computer centers in Tallahassee. Unlike SUNCOM for long-distance phone service, the state's computers do not constitute a statewide system, and many state units continue to operate their own computing services. These operations represent a mixture of centralized and decentralized activities.

A *Motor Pool Division* controls the inventory, use, and maintenance of over 12,000 road vehicles, watercraft, and airplanes. Its regulations affect every state agency except the State Highway Patrol. This division also contracts with a rental car agency for statewide car leasing. This contract both enables and requires state agencies to lease rental cars at rates below normal commercial rates.

Commodities purchased by state agencies fall under the direction of the *Division of Purchasing,* which negotiates purchase agreements and contracts. The division determines standards, specifications, and prices for a staggering variety of materials bought by state agencies. This practice permits the state to take advantage of quantity discounts. It also locks state agencies into the statewide contracts. Occasionally agencies find that some products can be bought less expensively than provided for in state contracts; permission to purchase items competitive with those contracted for is possible, but to get it entails effort and time-consuming delays. Centralization of services thus seems to create both advantages and disadvantages. Florida's local governments also are authorized to use the services of the Division of Purchasing.

This department has two more divisions. The *Division of Surplus Property* manages the disbursement of surplus state and federal materials to eligible health and educational institutions, and it sells usable goods the state has removed from service. Policing and security for most state-owned or -leased property is provided by the *Division of Security.*

Other Departments under the Governor or Cabinet

State roads in Florida are managed by the *Department of Transportation,* which has a secretary appointed by the governor with approval of the senate. It builds and maintains state roads and turnpikes and supervises maintenance.

Pardons and paroles are under the jurisdiction of the cabinet. A *parole board* supervises parole officers and makes recommendations to the entire cabinet.

Another important agency is *Health and Rehabilitative Services* (see chapter 20). The *Department of Military Affairs* is under the governor. He appoints, with approval of the senate, the state adjutant general, who heads the department. This department contains the National Guard, which can be called into state service by the governor and into federal active duty by the president.

The *Department of Law Enforcement* is under the governor and the cabinet. It investigates large-scale criminal activities and disburses federal funds to local law enforcement agencies. The Florida Highway Patrol is in the *Department of Highway Safety and Motor Vehicles,* which also licenses motor vehicles. This department is under the governor and cabinet.

Two executive agencies that regulate business are the *Department of Business Regulation* and the *Department of Professional and Operational Licensing*. The Department of Business Regulation supervises specialized subagencies, such as the Florida Hotel Commission, which inspects and licenses hotels, motels, and restaurants. Another subagency regulates sale of securities and marketing of real estate subdivision lots, seeking to protect investors and purchasers and prevent illegitimate practices or fraud that would hurt legitimate developers as well as consumers. Still another subagency of this department licenses horse and dog racetracks and jai alai frontons, sets racing dates, and seeks to limit betting to on-track operators. This department also regulates licensing of liquor stores and mobile home parks.

The Department of Professional and Operational Licensing is an umbrella central department over 25 boards, which license lawyers, doctors, accountants, barbers, real estate brokers and agents, and so on. The respective boards have the functions of admitting to practice, setting standards, hearing complaints, and disciplining those licensed. There is a constant tug of war over the power of the central department and that of the operating boards, lest the boards become captives of the profession or occupation. To relieve part of this fear, lay members are being added to the boards, and the accounting for fees collected is being tightened.

Continuation of these boards depends on the Florida Sunset Law, which specifies that such boards may not be continued unless reviewed by the legislature every five years. This review process places a considerable burden on the legislative staffs and committee members who must carry it out.

Another important executive agency, the *State Department of Revenue,* headed by an executive director, is under the cabinet. It collects state taxes and also has the function of supervising tax assessment rates in each of the 67 counties.

Consequences of Reorganization

The decade that began with the creation of the Department of Administration has been one of great change in Florida government and politics. The change started with a high turnover in the membership of the legislature, reapportionment having produced a younger, more critical legislature. With its enlarged professional staff, the legislature took a much more aggressive approach to influencing and monitoring administrative agencies. Social services and administration were the two areas most affected by this surge of legislative attention.

Those early changes produced pressures and information that have recently given rise to a current wave of reaction. As a result not much is stable in the Department of Administration. The location and performance of the function of budget and of the function of state planning have been changed by 1979 law from the Department of Administration to the Executive Office of the Governor. The Division of Personnel is a recent new target for persons demanding modifications of state practices.

Obviously the turmoil caused by the reorganization activity flowing out of the Executive Reorganization Act of 1969 has not pleased all current policy-makers or interested private parties. The entire nation faces significant new problems arising from technological advances, problems that may be even greater in rapidly growing and ecologically fragile states like Florida. As a result, it may be a long time before the developmental nature of the activities included in the current Department of Administration will finally settle into place.

References

Burns, James M.; Peltason, J. W.; and Cronin, Thomas E. *State and Local Politics*. 2d ed. Englewood Cliffs, N.J.: Prentice-Hall, 1968.

Booz, Allen, and Hamilton. *Organization Study of the Executive Branch of State Government*. Tallahassee: Florida House of Representatives, 1969.

Florida State University, Institute of Science and Public Affairs. "Improving Florida Personnel Practice: An Agenda for Action." November 1978.

Grant, Donald R., and Nixon, H. C. *State and Local Government in America*. 2d ed. Boston: Allyn and Bacon, 1968.

Levine, E. Lester. "The 1969 Florida Legislature: A New Constitution and New Procedures." *Governmental Research Bulletin* no. 3 (May 1969). Tallahassee: Institute for Social Research, Florida State University.

Morris, Allen. *The Florida Handbook, 1977–1978*. Tallahassee: Peninsular Publishing Co., 1977.

Parker (-Flory), Daisy. "The Florida Executive and Constitutional Revision." *Governmental Research Bulletin* no. 2 (March 1967). Tallahassee: Institute for Social Research, Florida State University.

______. "The Executive Department." In Allen Morris, *The Florida Handbook, 1971–72*. Tallahassee: Peninsular Publishing Co., 1971.

Pettigrew, Richard A. "Executive Reorganization: Uniformity with Responsibility." In Allen Morris, *The Florida Handbook, 1971–72*. Tallahassee: Peninsular Publishing Co., 1971.

Florida's Legislature

by Manning J. Dauer

UNIVERSITY OF FLORIDA

9

Composition of Florida's Legislature

In every state the legislature is the law-making body of the state government. Its functions are comparable to those of Congress for the U. S. government. But there are differences in the composition of the lawmaking bodies at the two levels. Members of Congress have a full-time job and are paid accordingly. But the state legislator's job, except in the largest states, is a part-time job for a part-time salary. An examination of the Florida legislature shows that its members are paid $12,000 annually; they also receive travel and per diem allowances.

With but few exceptions, Florida's legislators have other jobs. Lawyers are the most numerous professionals in the legislature, and there are many proprietors of businesses, especially insurance and real estate agencies. In addition, there are usually some farmers, a few teachers or employees of other government agencies, and one or two housewives. Most legislators are white males, but in the 1983 legislature there were 28 women, 12 blacks, and 4 Hispanics.

Regular sessions of the Florida legislature last 60 days, and there are often special sessions, each lasting only a few days. Committees of the legislature, however, operate year-round. Bills may be introduced at any time and are mailed out to members by the full-time staff. In addition to committee hearings on proposed legislation there are local hearings on bills affecting specific local matters. Locally held hearings enable legislators to evaluate popular sentiment on general legislation that applies to the whole state as well as on local issues. Legislators also spend time in inspection visits to state institutions and facilities such as prisons, hospitals, and universities, and they attend civic club or labor meetings and appear on radio and TV programs, partly to keep in touch with as many citizens as possible. Legislators put in about two-thirds of their working time on legislative matters, and their average work week is not 40 hours but 55 or 60.

The public is informed of legislative work through the state capitol press and broadcast media corps, through local media reports, and through Public Broadcasting System programs. Florida's PBS stations carry a 60-minute program daily on the work of the legislature while it is in session and less frequent but regularly scheduled programs on the work of state government at other times.

Legislative Structure

It is often argued that state legislatures should consist of only one house, not two. Yet only one American state, Nebraska, has a unicameral legislature. The argument for a single chamber is that it simplifies matters for both the legislator and the voter. The public, it is claimed, could follow the work of a single house more readily. The opposing — and prevailing — argument is that harmful legislation might be enacted more quickly if there were only one chamber. The delay provided by the requirement that two houses must act separately on legislation gives a better chance for the public to be alerted and to react.

In Florida the 120 house members serve two-year terms. Until the 1982 reapportionment, some Florida house members were elected from single-member, some from multimember districts. In Florida the 40 senate members serve four-year terms, half of them elected every two years. Like members of the house, some senators were elected from single-member districts and some from multimember districts until 1982.

It is argued that multimember districts are unfair or inequitable. Minorities—Cuban-Americans, blacks, Republicans—all favor single-member districts. In large districts that elect more than one representative, minority voters find even their combined vote overwhelmed by the votes of the majority residents. A proposal to eliminate multimember districts almost became a constitutional requirement in 1978. The governor in 1979 and his immediate predecessor both endorsed single-member districts.

One can argue against single-member districts that the viewpoint of a representative from a small part of a metropolitan area is likely to be too parochial. In local government, for example, such parochialism can easily lead to "ward politics." It can produce legislators who become so engrossed in cultivating a small constituency that they lose sight of broader issues. Furthermore, in multimember districts, minorities such as blacks and Cubans can and do influence the legislative behavior of all the representatives of the districts, not just one. Individuals, even members of minorities, can enter politics, become known, and ultimately win election, so in this respect multimember districts do not deprive minorities of representation. After the 1980 census, extensive hearings were held by the Florida House Committee on Reapportionment; single-member districts were overwhelmingly endorsed by such organizations as the NAACP and the state Republican party. The 1982 reapportionment created single-member districts for all 120 house and all 40 senate seats. Thus black and Hispanic representation was greatly increased, but the Republican party actually lost ground in the 1982 election, keeping only 30 percent of the seats in the house and 22.5 percent in the senate.

Apportionment and Reapportionment

Throughout the U.S. urbanization has made necessary new state programs to serve the needs of city inhabitants. Historically America has been an agricultural country, but by World War I city problems had become acute. The structure of state legislatures made it very difficult for city dwellers to secure representation in proportion to their numbers. In every state the legislature had full power to reapportion itself, and in many instances reapportionment required amendment of a state constitution. But to enact reapportionment, whether by law or by constitutional amendment, meant not only that sitting legislators might vote themselves out of office but also that they might take legislative districts permanently from their own communities and constituents. Thus reapportionment rarely occurred. Unless the U.S. Supreme Court intervened, there was a deadlock between legislatures and urban voters. Cases arguing that city dwellers were deprived of the Fourteenth Amendment guarantee of "equal protection of the laws" were taken before the Supreme Court by urban dwellers from a number of states. At first the Court refused to act: in 1946 it refused to take jurisdiction in *Colegrove* v. *Green*. But at last, in 1962, in *Baker* v. *Carr,* the Supreme Court finally intervened, declaring that the Fourteenth Amemdment guaranteed equality of representation on the principle of "one man, one vote."

Despite this precedent the Florida legislature refused to enact a reapportionment that gave proper numerical representation to the urban population. From 1946 until the matter was settled by the U.S. Supreme Court in the case of *Swann* v. *Adams,* reapportionment of the legislature was a major issue. After the legislature failed to reapportion representation satisfactorily in accordance with population, a three-judge federal court implemented the Supreme Court decision by ordering, in 1967, a plan for apportionment in which new districts would be equal in population. This plan was drawn up and presented to the federal district court by Manning Dauer. Prior to that reapportionment both houses of the legislature were dominated by representatives of the state's rural areas. Less that 13 percent of the state's population elected a majority of the legislators. This clique of rural senators and representatives, called the "pork chop gang," staunchly resisted efforts to reapportion. Following the 1967 reapportionment this domination by rural interests was overturned when the legislature had a strong influx of new members from urban areas. And because of this a number of changes occurred.

(1) The Republicans gained members, their numbers growing to just over one-third in each house (see tables 9.1 and 9.2). This happened because the newly created districts gave more representation to the "new growth" Central and South Florida regions where Republican strength was greatest. Although their numbers were not as great, more blacks and women were elected from these same new urban areas.

(2) The Democratic leadership changed. In 1970 for the first time a representative from Miami, Richard A Pettigrew, was chosen as speaker of the house.

(3) Under the new leadership the legislature modernized its operations. Electronic voting machines, computer indexing of bills, and computer service in framing the calendar helped streamline the work of the legislature. Additional staff were employed, and traditional alliances with old-line lobbyists were broken.

(4) New types of substantive legislation followed. The 1968 constitutional revision was considered and a provision was adopted requiring consolidation of executive departments into no more than 25. Thereupon governmental reorganization acts were adopted, and the structure of the executive branch was modernized in many respects. The cabinet system was retained, but budget authority was placed solely under the governor.

TABLE 9.1. Republicans and Democrats in the Florida Legislature before and after Reapportionment

Year	Actual districts		Republican percentage
	Democrat	Republican	
1961 Senate	37	1	3
1961 House	88	7	7
1963 Senate	43	2	4
1963 House	109	16	3
1965 Senate	42	2	5
1965 House	102	10	9
1967 Senate	28	20	42
1967 House	80	39	33
1969 Senate	32	16	30
1969 House	78	41	35
1971 Senate	32	16	30
1971 House	79	38	32

(5) The legislature revised laws of many different types. While the level of funding for various budget areas did not change greatly (social services, for example, still received the same percentage of the total budget), there was a shift in geographic areas affected. For example, more road monies were transferred to South Florida, and more custodial institutions were allocated to the urban centers. There were especially important qualitative changes in legislation. Women's rights, including property rights, were increased. General planning legislation was introduced. Water conservation districts were established or additional regulatory powers were enacted. Planning legislation was launched and regional planning authorities were created. Bonds were authorized for purchase of environmentally endangered lands.

(6) In an analysis made in 1971 by the National Citizens Conference on State Legislatures, the Florida legislature, because of these forward-looking actions, was ranked

fourth in the nation. Some of this momentum for innovation has since diminished with the reestablishment of older types of leadership, but the new legislation remains on the statute books, and some additional conservation acts have been adopted. An evaluation of all 50 state legislatures was made in 1971 by the Citizens' Conference on State Legislatures. Florida's average ranking among the 50 was fourth and in the other categories, functional ability, fifth; accountability, eighth; well-informed, fourth; independence, first; representativeness, tenth. Florida was the only southern state with high ranking.

Reapportionment System

Each ten years, after the federal census, the legislature must reapportion the house and senate seats. In a rapidly growing state this means that there will be considerable

TABLE 9.2. Election Returns (1967) for Legislature Applied to Florida Legislative District for Earlier Years

	Constructed district		Republican percentage
	Democrat	Republican	
1961 districts			
Senate	27	11	29
House	71	24	25
1963 districts			
Senate	30	15	33
House	90	35	28
1965 districts			
Senate	29	15	34
House	81	31	28
Actual 1967 districts			
Senate	28	20	42
House	80	39	33
Actual 1969 districts			
Senate	32	16	30
House	78	41	35

change in districts. In 1971, acting under the 1968 constitution, the legislature successfully redistributed both house and senate seats on a one-man, one-vote basis. The house and senate reapportionment committees drew up the districts for their chambers, and the bill passed into law. The 1968 constitution provides for review of the apportionment plan by the state supreme court if the bill should be challenged. In 1971 no unconstitutional violation of court-prescribed guidelines was found by either the state or the federal courts that reviewed the apportionment. The 1982 Florida legislative reapportionment act was approved by the U.S. attorney general who reviewed it under the provisions of the 1965 Federal

Voting Rights Act (updated in 1982). The reapportionment was also approved by the Florida Supreme Court, with one judicially ordered change requiring all senators to run in the new districts. The 1968 constitution provides that had the state supreme court review been negative, the legislature would have had one more chance; but if that also had been disapproved, the state supreme court would itself have made the final reapportionment.

The proposed 1978 constitutional revision included provision for a bipartisan commission to take over apportionment duties from the legislature, but this change was rejected by the voters. Federal courts have the responsibility to review the results of apportionment work; if both branches of the state government, legislative and judicial, should fail to enact proper legislative districting, a federal court could order corrections.

The Work of the Legislature

In the Florida legislature there is considerable turnover of elected members — approximately 31 percent in the house every two years and 45 percent in the senate every four, a turnover rate similar to that of many other states. Many legislators cannot afford a job that occupies 60 percent or more of their time but pays only $12,000 annually (plus some travel and expense reimbursement). Some house members move to the senate, where they become still more upwardly mobile. Reubin Askew and Bob Graham started in the house, then went to the senate and to the governorship. Others have followed this route from the legislature to the U.S. Senate, still others to the Florida cabinet. But most legislators, after a few terms, return to their business or to their profession.

Legislative Business

Florida has two primaries, followed by the general election. The primaries are closed, that is, only registered Democrats vote for Democratic candidates, and only registered Republicans vote in the Republican primaries. Candidates for the party nominations must, therefore, form their own organizations to support them in the primary campaign and raise their own campaign funds. Florida requires that a campaign treasurer be named and that all funds received and all expenditures be reported. In metropolitan areas campaign costs are high because radio, TV, and newspaper advertising rates are based on coverage of the entire area even though a candidate's district may be only a part of that area. When there are opposing candidates, campaign costs can run from $20,000 for a house seat to $70,000 or more for a senate seat. Some free time is provided by the broadcast media and some free space by newspaper reporting. There may also be volunteer workers, but cash is still required to pay many expenses. In the general election the party will help with costs, but not in the primaries. Before the formal campaign most candidates will seek public exposure by participating as prominently as possible in civic affairs and in appearances before civic groups and clubs.

Once the candidate is elected he affiliates with the caucus of the other members of his party who have been elected. The constitution provides that there be an organizational meeting of each house shortly after the November election. Here newly elected members will find that the majority party has already chosen the leadership of each house: the speaker of the house, the president of the senate, and so forth. The custom in Florida is that a new speaker of the house and new president of the senate are chosen every two years, but this choice is made by the members of the old legislature. The senate caucus to choose the 1981 president of the senate was held in January 1979. Members newly elected in 1980 obviously do not participate in that choice. The speaker of the house for 1979 was chosen by the Democratic caucus in 1978, during the session of that year and before the primaries or the general election. Thus only members who had already been elected participated.

Both the speaker of the house and the senate president occupy strong positions. Each presiding officer appoints all committee members and places himself on all committees in accord with the rules. Each presiding officer also names the chairman of each committee. He may change committee membership during the session should he find a committee recalcitrant in carrying out its duties. Each party in each house has its own caucus, and its leadership determines the appointment of members on each committee. The number of minority party members on a committee is proportional to their number in the total chamber.

The work of the legislature is continuous. From the time of the November organizational meetings, bills are introduced in each house, printed, and referred to committees by the presiding officer. Committees work year-round. Hearings are held and the committees may take formal votes. The house requires bills to be introduced before the formal session begins in April each year, though there may be exceptions. The senate requires bills to be introduced no later than the opening weeks of the formal session. Unless reported out by the committee and placed on the calendar by the Rules Committee, a bill has little chance of passage.

There are sixteen senate committees and twenty-three house committees. In each chamber the majority party leadership—the presiding officer, the chairman of the rules committee, two or three other important chairpersons, and the majority leader—determines much policy and the fate of most bills. The most important committees are Rules (which sets the calendar, in consultation with the leadership), Finance and Taxation, Appropriations, Health and Welfare, Education (public schools), Higher Education, Agriculture, Natural Resources, Transportation, Government Operations, and Criminal Justice.

Committees are grouped so their meetings do not overlap. Each house member has a secretary or aide, each senate member has both. Each committee also employs a permanent professional staff, which helps in preparing bills and amendments to bills. Interested executive departments and lobbyists are eager to offer their help as well.

The work of committees needs examination. An average committee in either chamber has a dozen members. When a bill reaches a committee it has already been printed and sent to all members of that chamber, including, of course, members of the committee and its staff. The staff is instructed by the chairman to study the bill. Rules of each chamber require that if the bill has any "fiscal impact" it must also be studied by the staff of the appropriate fiscal committee and have dual reference to that fiscal committee — i.e., Appropriations in the house and Ways and Means in the senate. Such information is then incorporated by the staff in its report on the bill and must accompany the bill in any report by the committee.

If the committee chairman and members decide that it is desirable, a public hearing is listed in the calendar, giving due notice to all interested parties, including the press, of time and place for the hearing. The committee chairman presides; at most committee hearings there are a number of lobbyists, representatives of the general public, and representatives of the media. The legislator introducing the bill presents testimony and is subject to questions by committee members. Let us consider, for example, a bill that proposes a property tax reduction for new industry locating in the state, such reduction to be for a period of ten years. Officials from the State Department of Commerce present figures comparing such a tax break with legislation in other southern states. Spokesmen from the State Chamber of Commerce urge passage of the bill as a means of attracting industry. A spokesman for labor supports the bill as a means to create additional jobs.

In opposition, businessmen with established enterprises point out that they are already paying full taxes, so the bill will discriminate against them. The same argument is presented by homeowners and by representatives of "citizens' lobbies" such as the League of Women Voters and Common Cause. Schoolteachers' organizations, fearing a decline in the local tax base, and older citizens, fearing an increase in the tax rate on their homes, also oppose the bill.

The committee, possessing information on the amount by which tax rolls in counties and cities will be reduced, must decide if the possibility of bringing in new enterprises and increasing jobs justifies the proposed tax break. The chairman will call for a vote; if proponents of the bill have a majority, the bill will be reported out favorably with the recommendation that it be scheduled on the calendar. If its opponents have more votes, the bill dies in committee.

The fate of much legislation can be determined by the selection of committee members by the chamber's presiding officer. For this reason many lobbies are interested not only in the election of the chamber's presiding officer but also in his appointments of committee members.

For a bill to be passed in one house requires three readings, the first simply by reference to a committee without floor action except for report in the journal. Most bills are reported to the floor with committee amendments. On the floor the bill may be further amended. If it passes one house it goes to the other. There it may have already been introduced as a companion bill; any bill also may have several co-introducers.

In the other chamber the bill may be further amended. If it is, it goes back to the chamber where it originated to be voted on again. Ultimately the bill must pass both houses in exactly the same form before it goes to the governor. If the two houses fail to agree, a conference committee appointed by the presiding officers tries to arrive at a version acceptable to both the house and the senate. The work of this committee then must go back to both chambers. Once a bill is passed in the same form by both the house and the senate, it goes to the governor for his signature; if he signs the bill it becomes law. If he vetoes the bill, it returns to the legislature. To be passed into law over the governor's veto, a bill must receive a two-thirds vote in both the house and the senate.

The governor of Florida has the item veto only over appropriations bills. This permits him to veto a part of an appropriations bill rather than the entire bill. If the legislature has adjourned, a veto, whether of an appropriations item or of an entire bill of another sort, causes the bill to be referred to the next session of the legislature.

Many members of the Florida legislature and many citizens are critical of the extensive powers of the majority party leadership. Most state legislatures provide that committee appointment recommendations be made by a committee on committees and that those recommendations be approved by the respective party caucuses. This system has been proposed for the Florida legislature, but all attempts to change the rules to alter the committee appointment system have failed.

The Sunset Law was enacted by the legislature in 1976. There are in Florida some 27 licensing boards, which provide for the regulation of certain trades and professions, including medicine, law, undertaking, and so on. There is an umbrella administrative agency, but the boards have typically been composed of members of the same trade or profession whose members they are to examine, license, and discipline. The closed aspect of this process has caused both public and legislative criticism.

In addition, throughout the state government there are over 100 other regulatory and advisory boards, some with statutory power, others of merely advisory nature, such as park or local historical commissions or economic councils.

The Sunset Law provides a calendar for periodic reviewing of the continuation of the boards. A six-year maximum was established for the life of any board. Two years before expiration date, a legislative committee must begin to consider abolition, consolidation, or modification of the board and its powers. The boards are divided into categories so that a certain number are reviewed each legislative session.

The general objective of the Sunset Law review provision was to force the legislature to consider the issue of government regulation. Is it in the public interest to provide for licensing of a specific trade or profession? If so, is the determination of admission to practice, standards, and enforcement of discipline solely a matter of the trade or profession, or should there be public members of such regulatory boards? Is the general public being served by the boards or just the members of the trade or profession? What is the role of government in such matters? The Sunset Law, requiring periodic review, seeks to have these issues studied by legislative committee and then have the legislature arrive at decisions concerning them.

One interesting outcome of consideration of these issues has been the addition of public members to many of the boards and a review of their licensing and disciplinary practices. There has been some increase in the authority of the central department to establish an investigative staff to consider public complaints, with hearings before the board to determine disposition of cases. This is an interesting example of a procedure seeking to review what government agencies actually do.

About 1,200 general bills are introduced in the senate and about 1,800 in the house each year. In 1977 there were 476 general laws adopted by the legislature, and 190 special or local bills. In 1978, 447 general laws and 277 special or local acts were adopted. The state constitution requires that special bills pertaining to a single locality be either advertised in advance or be subject to local referendum in the area affected. Such bills receive automatic passage if the legislative delegation from the area in the chamber considering such a bill is united in favor of its passage. These bills are not debated but are simply placed on the calendar for passage. Otherwise, the leadership or a committee may determine the fate of local bills.

Consideration of local bills focuses choice between home rule for cities and counties and the power of the local legislative delegation to make decisions on city, county, and regional matters for governments within their districts. For example, Florida has a difficult procedure for allowing a city to annex territory outside its limits. (This issue will be explored further in chapters 11, 12, and 13 on local government.) Here we should also consider the problem from the legislature's standpoint. The existing state law requires that in order for annexation to take place, there must be an affirmative vote by both voters within the corporate limits of the city and voters in the geographic area to be annexed. Because of fear of additional taxes, few voters in areas to be annexed support the proposed change in their status. Yet there is demand in these areas for city services, and residents use the city library, recreational facilities, and so on. Thereupon, the city officers seek a special annexation bill from the local legislative delegation; or the county commission seeks authority to create a special urban service tax district and itself gets into the business of providing urban services such as water, sewers, and fire protection. The 1968 constitution sought to limit the number of local bills and to permit such procedures as local charter provisions or contract agreements between local units, thus relieving the legislature of such matters. The argument for such home rule control is that legislators should focus on state issues, while locally elected officials should be responsible for other problems. But the complexity of local governmental problems makes this application of home rule difficult to achieve in practice. The outcome is a fairly large number of local bills, as noted.

Legislative sessions and committee hearings are open to the public, whose testimony is often sought at hearings. The last two weeks of the formal legislative session are hectic, with the leadership and the rules committees in even greater control of the proceedings. Normally, the legislature completes its work in the 60-day session. One change made in 1979 was the return to biennial rather than annual budgeting. The basic idea is to provide for better long-range planning, both by the legislature and by the executive agencies. The governor

Opening day of the 1978 legislature. Photo courtesy State of Florida Department of Commerce.

presents his budget in February, the fiscal committees consider it, and the legislature receives the recommendations of its committees.

In addition to the permanent staff of the fiscal committees the legislature has information from the reports of the state auditor. This officer, appointed by the legislature, audits all past expenditures of state agencies and of the counties. His work provides information on past performances and operations. The governor proposes the future budget, but it is the legislature that enacts both taxes and appropriations.

The Florida legislature also has the power of impeachment and removal of state executive and judicial officers. To impeach an officeholder—that is, to bring the accused official to trial on charges of misfeasance, malfeasance, or nonfeasance—requires a two-thirds vote of the house. The trial is conducted before the senate. After the trial, to remove an officeholder from his office, two-thirds of the senators must vote for his removal. This impeachment power has been used against both executive and judicial officials.

The senate has the special power of approving certain gubernatorial appointments. If the governor suspends a county official for impropriety, for example, the senate must hold a hearing and vote to remove or to reinstate the officer.

The work of legislative committees is quite important, as is the work of individual legislators who specialize in certain issues requiring legislation. While the leadership controls many crucial decisions, the groundwork of the committees is indispensable for sound drafting of legislation and for sensitive response to public needs. In the face of new issues, such as environmental protection and the restructuring of state and local executive government to adapt to the state's rapid growth, the Florida legislature has been able to make accommodative changes.

Summary

In 1946, at the end of World War II, members of the Florida legislature simply had desks on the floor of the house or senate. Except for hearing rooms and an office for the presiding officer, there were few facilities, little technical help, and little secretarial help, although limited assistance could be secured from the state attorney general's office for bill drafting. Then a legislative reference bureau was established with a staff director and some experts in public finance, taxation, and so on. Next, the legislative reference service was dissolved and the staff assigned to the legislative committees. Additional technical and secretarial staff was added, the committees acquired permanent offices in the capitol, and members secured private offices and an aide or secretary for house members and both for senate members. Moreover, provision was made for each legislator to rent office space in his or her home district.

Much technical assistance was added, including computer indexing of bills, which was tied into the calendar of committee hearings, and the daily calendar while the legislature was in session. The introduction of bills and the committees' work became year-round procedures.

There has been a great strengthening of legislative influence compared to that of other branches of state government. On many types of legislation the initiative has passed from the departments in the executive branch to the legislature. Currently, for example, much of the regulation of public school matters originates in house and senate committees, for instance, the requirement that high school graduates pass a functional literacy test in the use of English and basic mathematics. The legislature initiated teacher competence exams in both subject matter and class procedures before licensing.

In another area, expenditures by departments, even after enactment of appropriations, are surveyed by legislative appropriations and other committee staffs to decide if executive departments are following "legislative intent." Such a procedure almost leads to dual administration.

In still another area the legislature has sought to limit the power of departments to enact administrative rules that govern action of the department over the general citizenry. In 1976, there was a proposed constitutional amendment that would have permitted legislative committees to suspend administrative rules while the legislature was not in session. Since a citizen affected by such a rule already had the right to appeal for court review to determine if administrative rules conform to powers conferred by law, such committee power would have duplicated court review. Fortunately, this amendment was rejected by the voters on the grounds indicated. This is, of course, an extreme example of attempted extension of legislative power, but it indicates the extent to which the legislature has become an innovative force in Florida government.

From the 1930s to the 1960s, political scientists generally spoke of the decline in legislative authority and the transfer of power to the executive. But in Florida, at least since 1969, this tendency has been reversed. The rising authority of the legislature is reinforced by the fact that executive power in Florida is distributed among seven elected executive officials, the governor and the cabinet. Thus the executive branch does not speak with one voice, and some cabinet members, who can be reelected indefinitely, develop close ties with legislative leaders, especially with senior senate members. The outcome is an interrelationship between part of the executive branch and part of the legislature that creates a special axis of power.

References

Citizens Conference on State Legislatures: The Sometime Governments. New York: Bantam Books, 1971.

Florida Legislature. *Journal of the Florida House* and *Journal of the Florida Senate,* both annual.

Keefe, William J., and Ogul, A. Morris. *The American Legislative Process: Congress and States*. 4th ed. Englewood Cliffs, N.J.: Prentice-Hall, 1977.

Morris, Allen C. *The Florida Handbook*. Tallahassee: Peninsular Press, 1977.

Roady, Elston E., and Dauer, Manning J. "The Florida Legislature." In *Southeastern State Legislatures,* edited by William G. Cornelius. Atlanta: Emory, 1968.

Zeigler, Harmon. "Interest Groups in the States." In *Politics in American States,* edited by Herbert Jacobs and Kenneth N. Vines. Boston: Little Brown, 1965.

Law and the Courts

by Robert L. Anderson

and George John Miller

UNIVERSITY OF WEST FLORIDA

10A

In this chapter we sketch that portion of the process of interpreting, making, and administering Florida law that the Florida constitution assigns to the judicial branch of the state government. We include in the process those active participants who are not judges but nevertheless function in close relation to the judiciary. Reorganization of the state court structure in 1972 created a four-level arrangement and eliminated all courts below or at the county level except the county court. The system of electing, nominating, and disciplining judges was also revised. These changes and others update to a considerable degree the judicial system of the state.

One of the most basic terms used here is *jurisdiction,* meaning the authority granted and assigned by a political society to a certain governmental branch or agency to state the law officially within the limits legally set by the society in its constitution and statutes. Within Florida the federal courts exist and operate along with the state courts. Federal law is declared in the federal constitution to be the supreme law of the land, and the federal law prevails if a conflict arises between federal law and state law. The operation of the federal judiciary is beyond our scope here, and in any event most court proceedings are handled by state courts.

What may be called ranks of law exist within each of the state and federal systems. Within the Florida system the *supreme law* (also called the *organic or basic law*) is set forth in the state constitution. Second in rank are valid *statutes*, which are enactments by the state legislature. Third are the *judgments and decisions of the judiciary* interpreting these statutes. Fourth are valid *administrative regulations or rules* made by various state executive agencies.

If the validity of a statute is questioned, the issue is decided by the judiciary; but only in such a situation does a decision declaring a statute invalid under the constitution outrank the statutory provision. Even then the legislature can enact another statute within the constitutional limitations set by the judiciary. Furthermore, even a decision of the supreme court construing a provision of the constitution can be changed by amendment to the constitution; and, although this process occurs infrequently, the fact remains that the ultimate authority to formulate law rests with the citizens. If the validity of a statute is not challenged, or if it is challenged and the statute is upheld as valid, the legislature can nevertheless change the law by changing the statute, regardless of what the judiciary may have declared the older statute to mean.

In summary, this ranking of constitution, statute, judicial decision, and administrative regulation exists in both Florida law and federal law. But conflict between any valid provision of federal law and any valid state law is resolved by the federal judiciary, and the federal law prevails over *any* conflicting provision of Florida law.

Jurisdiction is always limited to some extent by the subject matter that may be considered. It is also limited by the geographical area to which it applies and in relation to the nature of the function authorized, that is, whether the authority to state the law in a given instance is assigned by the constitution to the legislature, the executive, or the judiciary. We emphasize here the jurisdiction of the Florida judiciary in formulating Florida law.

Jurisdiction is also differentiated on the basis of whether it is *original* or *review*. Broadly speaking, *original jurisdiction* pertains to the commencement of the legal proceeding; *review jurisdiction* refers to examination by a higher court of the initial judgment or order. Review jurisdiction is in turn further classified as *mandatory* or *discretionary*. If *mandatory,* it is called an *appeal*; in these cases the higher court must, upon request, consider and decide the case on the merits. If *discretionary*, the losing party normally files a request for review by the higher court of a lower court decision, known as a petition for a *writ of certiorari*, which the higher court may grant or deny. In practice most of these petitions are denied, and the judgment or order of the lower court remains in force. On review, whether mandatory or discretionary, the higher court does not retry the matter itself; rather, it examines the trial on the basis of the lower court record, in order to correct errors of law, either substantive or procedural, to preserve consistency of the law throughout the jurisdiction involved, to furnish a more thorough examination of the issues (in most instances by three or more judges), to provide reasoned, written opinions on new issues for the guidance of the lower courts and for attorneys in counseling clients, and to assure a losing party at the trial level that his contentions will receive more detailed consideration if he chooses to request review.

The usual rule in Florida is to allow only one review. In a few instances the matter goes directly to the supreme court, but usually it goes to the appropriate district court of appeal for final disposition. The reasons that justify one review do not necessarily justify two. If they did, they would also justify three, or ten, or a hundred; and certainty of determination as to what the law is in a given instance requires that there be an end to the litigation at the earliest stage commensurate with due consideration of the issue or issues involved.

Another distinction is made between *substantive law* and *procedural law*. Speaking very broadly, *substantive law* deals with *what*, and procedural law deals with *how*; substantive law expresses what the parties have a right to, while procedural law tells them how to obtain enforcement of this substantive right. Another way of expressing this point is that *substantive law deals with rights*, whereas *procedural law deals with remedies*. The layman tends to underrate the practical importance of procedural law. As in playing football or driving in traffic, rules of procedure are essential to the process. The rights of the individual are declared for the most part as general rules by the constitution, by statutes, by judicial decisions, and by authorized administrative regulations; but the rules for enforcing them are assigned to the judiciary, which with the active assistance of the bar is continually improving them to meet the changing needs of the society. One of the most important recent provisions in the state constitution is Article V, subsection 2(a), which directs that

> The supreme court shall adopt rules for the practice and procedure in all courts including the time for seeking appellate review, the administrative supervision of all courts, the transfer to the court having jurisdiction of any proceeding when the jurisdiction of another court has been improvidently invoked, and a requirement that no cause shall be dismissed because an improper remedy has been sought. These rules may be repealed by general law enacted by two-thirds of the membership of each house of the legislature.

The historic distinction between *law* and *equity* is still important in some respects. Examples of equity matters are dissolution of marriage, foreclosure, state homestead law, suit for accounting, and demand for specific performance of a contract. There is no jury; the judge decides the disputed questions of fact as well as the issues of law; and the judgment takes the form of an order to the defendant, usually called an injunction, which forbids or commands him to perform a certain act. If he disobeys he is liable to imprisonment, fine, or both, for contempt of court.

Another distinction exists between *criminal law* and *civil law*. Although both types ultimately rely for enforcement on the use of compulsion by the law enforcement officers authorized by the political society, *criminal conduct* is an *act or failure to act that the society deems important to the welfare of all its members*. Violation of these rules of conduct is punished by fine, imprisonment, or both, even when nobody is damaged by the particular instance of disobedience. *Civil law* deals primarily with *disputes between two or more persons about their respective rights* in relation to each other as individuals. Whether the winner chooses to enforce his rights, once these have been determined, is up to him; and the society prescribes by law the further steps that he may or may not take in attempting to enforce them through law enforcement officers.

Finally, we come to the familiar question as to whether the judiciary interprets the law or makes the law. The answer is that judges do both. If a constitutional provision, a statute, or a valid administrative regulation exists with regard to the matter in question, the duty of the judiciary is to find and interpret the appropriate legal provision and apply it to the facts established as relevant before the court or, stated in another way, to find in these facts an illustration of the appropriate principle in action. Instances arise, however, in which no general rule has been expressed, yet the court is expected to do something with the problem presented. In these instances the judge makes law, but he is not free to do as he pleases in this process. He is expected to observe what is known as the *doctrine of precedent*; that is, he reasons by analogy and attempts to find a similar factual situation to which the appropriate principle has been applied in a previous case. This principle, to the extent illustrated by the particular case, is binding upon the lower courts to the extent that its application was necessary to reach a decision on the issue presented by those facts, and it is usually followed in future cases by the court that formulated it. In this limited signification, it constitutes what is known as a *precedent*. The common law has been gradually built by this process, decision by decision, over the centuries. The process is slow, since it leaves room for variation if any of the relevant facts in a later case are different; but it has the merit of reducing substantially those errors on a broad scale that are admittedly made rather frequently by the legislature in statutes, or by an administrative agency in regulations, in laying down a general rule for the future.

State Court Jurisdiction

Article V of the state constitution begins:

> The judicial power shall be vested in a supreme court, district courts of appeal, circuit courts and county courts. No other courts may be established by the state, any political subdivision or any municipality. The legislature shall, by general law, divide the state into appellate court districts and judicial circuits following county lines. Commissions established by law, or administrative officers or bodies may be granted quasi-judicial power in matters connected with the functions of their offices.

The constitution specifically states that all judicial officers shall be conservators of the peace; but beyond this provision the respective jurisdictions of the four types of courts are specified in detail by the constitution or by general law authorized by it. Stated broadly *circuit courts* and *county courts* constitute the *trial tier* of courts, while the *supreme court* and *district courts of appeal* constitute the *appellate tier*. No Florida court has authority to handle both original and review matters at all levels. A *trial court* can best be understood as *the court in which the legal proceeding starts*; it is also called at times the *court of first instance*.

County court. — Within the trial tier of courts, the lower level is the county court. It is called lower because the law assigns to it those numerous civil disputes that involve small amounts of money or other personal property and, on the criminal side, those many failures to comply with the law that our political societies in Florida regard as relatively minor and therefore punishable by a small fine or a local and short period of imprisonment or sometimes both. The county court has no appellate jurisdiction; all of its jurisdiction is original. Most Florida cases start in county courts and go no farther.

The county court has civil jurisdiction over actions at law in which the matter in controversy does not exceed $2,500, exclusive of interest and costs, except those types of actions assigned exclusively to the circuit court regardless of the amount involved. The county court also has jurisdiction over delayed birth certificates and matters previously handled by the numerous types of local trial courts, recently abolished—the municipal court, the small claims court, and the justice of the peace court. Their abolition in 1972, effective even for the last few remaining municipal courts by the beginning of 1977, was prompted by the confusion engendered by a proliferation of types of local courts and by a lack of qualified judges and the resultant public criticism. Reform of this sort has been advocated, with varying success, in other states; its achievement places Florida in the forefront of modern court structure and procedure. The workload remained, however, and the bulk of it fell on the county court. (Probate and guardianship matters formerly handled by the now defunct county judge's court are assigned to the circuit court.) Furthermore, of all the county court matters, approximately 80 percent pertain to traffic infractions (explained later), about 60 percent civil and 20 percent criminal. The other 20 percent of county court matters are divided about equally between civil and criminal.

The important categories of civil matters other than traffic infractions relate to collection of money allegedly owed, tenant evictions, and repossession of items either sold on credit and not paid for as agreed or borrowed and not returned. Summary procedure is heavily used when the matter in controversy amounts to $1,500 or less. Legal counsel is rarely employed by the defendant or in many instances even by the plaintiff; the procedure is fast and simple; and filing fees are nominal. For example, in 1979 the basic service charge was $6 for claims less than $100; for claims between $100 and $1,000 it was $15; and for claims between $1,000 and $1,500 it was $20. Each of these basic service charges may be increased by county ordinance or by special or local law to provide for a legal aid program or to provide and maintain facilities, including a law library, for the use of the county court in the county collecting the fee. Accordingly the total service charge for each claim bracket varies from county to county; the office of the county court clerk in each county is readily available for information and instructions.

The criminal jurisdiction of the county court embraces misdemeanors (other than those arising out of the same circumstances in which a felony is also charged) and violations of county and municipal ordinances. County judges also serve as coroners and as committing magistrates. The function of *coroner* is to conduct inquests into the probable cause of death under suspicious circumstances indicating the possibility of foul play. The function of *committing magistrate* is to determine promptly, on preliminary examination following an arrest, whether an offense was committed and whether there is probable cause for believing that the person arrested committed it. If probable cause is not found, the magistrate orders a discharge then and there. If probable cause is found and the offense charged is within the county court jurisdiction, the magistrate commits him to custody or admits him to bail. For most offenses he can arrange release on bail right after arrest in an amount already set by a schedule of amounts according to the nature of the offense charged; and he may have taken this step even before his commitment appearance. He is then assigned a date on which to appear and enter his plea; and at that time he is sentenced, or, if he pleads not guilty, he is assigned a trial date.

If probable cause is found but the offense charged is within circuit court jurisdiction, the procedure normally involves an additional appearance. The committing magistrate commits the person arrested to custody or sets an early time for his first appearance in circuit court to arrange bail and receive full instructions as to his rights. At this circuit court appearance he is also assigned a date on which to appear and enter his plea. On plea day he is assigned a date for sentencing if he enters a plea of guilty or of *nolo contendere*, which means that he is unwilling to offer any defense but does not admit guilt. If he pleads not guilty the matter is set down for trial at a later date. County judges handle almost all the commitments; but in some circuits the circuit judges and the county judges share this function on weekends, serving in rotation.

By way of explanation of the important distinction between a *felony* (a matter for the circuit court) and a *misdemeanor*, Article X, section 10, of the constitution defines a felony as "any criminal offense that is punishable under the laws of this state, or that would be punishable if committed in this state, by death or by imprisonment in the state penitentiary." As a practical matter this sentence is for more than one year. Examples of felonies include murder, kidnapping, arson, rape, grand larceny (which means "big theft" and relates to theft of property of $100 or more), armed robbery, burglary, passing a worthless check of $50 or more in certain instances, resisting arrest, perjury, forgery, and possession of more than 20 grams of marijuana, including stems and leaves. Lesser crimes are known as misdemeanors. Examples include driving while intoxicated, petit larceny (which means "little theft" and relates to theft of property worth less than $100), disorderly conduct, passing a worthless check of under $50, reckless driving, driving without a license, leaving the scene of an accident in which no one is injured, trespassing, prowling, and possession by a first offender of not more than 20 grams of marijuana. These lesser crimes are punishable by fine, imprisonment in the local jail, normally for not more than one year, or both. Within each of the two major categories of felony and misdemeanor there are, as might be expected, many degrees and gradations of severity.

A recent statutory change of practical importance is the Florida "speedy trial rule," designed to meet growing complaints of delay in being brought to trial. It requires that the person charged be brought to trial, without demand, within 90 days for a misdemeanor and within 180 days for a felony. Each period commences when the person is taken into custody for allegedly committing the crime charged and ends when the jury panel is sworn for examination or, upon waiver of jury trial, when the trial proceedings begin before the judge. But if the person charged files a demand for earlier trial with the court and serves a copy of it on the prosecuting attorney, he must be brought to trial within 60 days. In either event, if he is not brought to trial within the required period he must be forever discharged of the crime charged if he files a motion for discharge and the court determines that he has been continuously available for trial during the applicable period. Some allowance for extending the period under certain exceptional circumstances is detailed in the rule.

Violations of traffic laws have recently been further subdivided by statute into civil and criminal infractions. Civil infractions, being violations of law, may logically appear to the layman as crimes; but legally they are not, and the penalty is a relatively small fine or perhaps an order to complete an official course in defensive driving. Examples of infractions are speeding or running a stop sign or a red light without causing an accident and, of course, illegal parking.

Circuit court. — The circuit court has exclusive original *civil jurisdiction* in all actions at law in which the matter in controversy exceeds $2,500, exclusive of interest and costs; in all matters of equity regardless of the dollar amount involved; in matters relating to juveniles (persons under 18 years of age), except traffic infractions; in proceedings relating to settlement of estates of decedents and minors; in matters of guardianship; in matters of involuntary hospitalization and determinations of incompetency; in matters of probate of a will, meaning establishment of its validity, and the granting of letters testamentary and letters of administration in the absence of a valid will; in determinations of the legality of a tax assessment or toll; in actions involving title, boundaries, or right of possession of real property, including the action of ejectment; in the issuance of injunctions; and in authorizing a county judge to order emergency hospitalizations and to issue other orders and temporary injunctions relating thereto.

The criminal jurisdiction of the circuit court embraces all felonies and those misdemeanors that arise out of the same circumstances as those giving rise to a felony that is also charged.

The circuit court also has the power to issue what are known in Florida as the five extraordinary writs: habeas corpus, certiorari, mandamus, quo warranto, and prohibition, as well as all other writs necessary or proper to the complete exercise of its jurisdiction.

The *appellate jurisdiction* of the circuit court, which in practice involves review proceedings constituting less than 1 percent of its total workload, is confined to appeals from judgments of the county courts.

Although each of the four types of Florida courts has some original jurisdiction, and each type except the county court has some appellate jurisdiction, the bulk of the appellate work is handled by the five district courts of appeal and in a few instances by the supreme court.

District court of appeal. — The jurisdiction of the district courts of appeal is concisely stated in Article V, subsection 4(b):

> (1) District courts of appeal shall have jurisdiction to hear appeals, that may be taken as a matter of right, from final judgments or orders of trial courts, including those entered on review of administrative action, not directly appealable to the supreme court or a circuit court... .
>
> (2) District courts of appeal shall have power of direct review of administrative action, as prescribed by general law.
>
> (3) A district court of appeal or any judge thereof may issue writs of habeas corpus returnable before the court or any judge thereof or before any circuit judge within the territorial jurisdiction of the court. A district court of appeal may issue writs of mandamus, certiorari, prohibition, quo warranto, and other writs necessary to the complete exercise of its jurisdiction. To the extent necessary to dispose of all issues in a cause properly before it, a district court of appeal may exercise any of the appellate jurisdiction of the circuit courts.

Most appeals and also most reviews of administrative action, whether by statutorily authorized appeal or by writ of certiorari, are disposed of with finality by a district court of appeal.

Supreme Court. — Article V of the constitution and the authorized statutes set the jurisdiction of the Florida Supreme Court. The thrust of the recent constitutional amendment, ratified in the 1980 special election is to reduce the mandatory review jurisdiction of the state supreme court and to render the bulk of its review jurisdiction discretionary. Accordingly it can now concentrate on those matters certified by a district court of appeal to be of great public importance, as well as on determining with finality the law of Florida in the relatively few instances of express and direct conflict, on the same question of law, of a decision of a district court of appeal with a decision of another district court or of the supreme court. The supreme court may also review any decision of a

Members of the Florida Supreme Court, 1980. Left to right: Justices Joseph W. Hatchett, Ben F. Overton, James C. Adkins, Chief Justice Arthur J. England, Jr., Justices Joseph A. Boyd, Jr., Alan C. Sundberg, James E. Alderman.

district court of appeal that expressly declares valid a state statute, or that expressly construes a provision of the state or federal constitution, or that expressly affects a class of constitutional or state officers. It may review a question of law certified by the federal Supreme Court or a federal court of appeals which is determinative of the cause in the federal court and for which there is no controlling precedent of the Florida Supreme Court. It retains its discretionary original jurisdiction by writ in a few instances, including the issuance of habeas corpus by the court or by any justice thereof.

The mandatory jurisdiction of the state supreme court is now limited by the constitution to appeals from final judgments of trial courts imposing the death penalty and from district court of appeal decisions declaring invalid a state statute or a provision of the state constitution. The constitution also requires it, when so provided by general law, to hear appeals from final judgments in proceedings for the validation of bonds or certificates of indebtedness, as well as to review actions of statewide agencies relating to rates or service of utilities providing electric, gas, or telephone service.

An unusual feature of the Florida constitution is Article IV, subsection 1(c), which authorizes the governor to request in writing an advisory opinion of the supreme court justices as to the interpretation of any portion of the Florida constitution upon any question affecting his executive powers and duties. If four justices concur that the question itself is not within the purview of the authorization they so notify him; otherwise they may call upon persons whose substantial interests may be affected to present briefs, oral argument, or both, and thereafter the opinion written by the justice assigned to this task is sent to the governor. The justices do not act as a court in these instances but rather as individual justices giving the advice requested.

In addition to all of the foregoing duties the supreme court is charged with the function of adopting rules of practice and procedure for all state courts, as already noted, as well as exclusive jurisdiction to regulate the admission of persons to the practice of law and the discipline of persons admitted. It must also review recommendations of the state Judicial Qualifications Commission. It has delegated the bar admission and discipline functions, for initial performance, to the Florida bar and to some extent to the judges individually, but the supreme court retains final authority to determine these matters.

State Court Organization and Administration

The present statewide court structure consists of the supreme court, with 7 justices; 5 district courts of appeal; 20 circuit courts; and 67 county courts. The number of judges below the supreme court depends on caseloads and is set by the legislature each two years. Between 1972 and 1982, the caseload of trial courts doubled, from 250,000 per year to 500,000, and of appellate courts almost tripled, from 5,300 to 14,000 per year. Figure 10.1 shows the boundaries of each court of appeal district, circuit, and county. On the recommendation of the supreme court the legislature in its regular session of 1979 created by statute a fifth district court of appeal to meet the growing caseload. It abolished the Industrial Relations Commission and transferred its review jurisdiction to the First District Court of Appeal and increased the number of judges at the district court of appeal and trial levels.

The constitution directs the supreme court to establish by rule, for all other Florida courts and all their judges, uniform criteria for determining the need to increase or decrease the number of judges. It is also charged with recommending increases, decreases, or changes in the boundaries of appellate districts and judicial circuits. It certifies from time to time its findings and recommendations

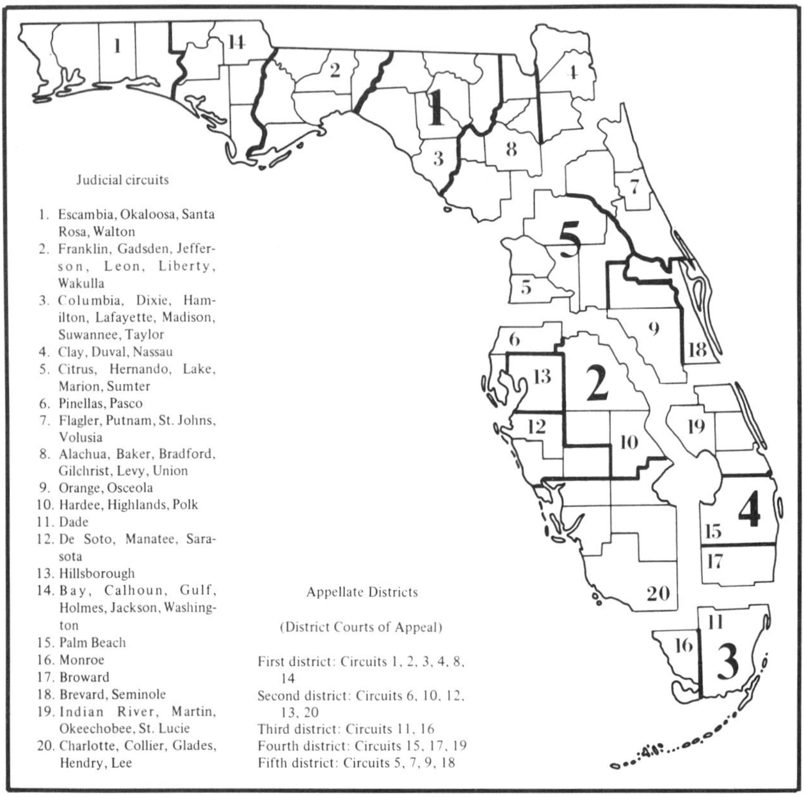

Fig. 10.1. Jurisdictional Boundaries of Florida's Courts: Supreme, Appellate, Circuit, County. Small numbers are judicial circuits and large numbers are appellate districts. Florida Supreme Court jurisdiction is statewide.

on these matters to the legislature for rejection or implementation by law in whole or in part. To create more judicial offices than the supreme court recommends, or to decrease these by more than it recommends, the legislature must find, by a two-thirds vote of the entire membership of each house, that such a need exists.

All courts except the supreme court may sit in divisions, as may be established by general law. The divisions of the district courts of appeal do not specialize by type of case, although the first district court may do so for industrial claims appeals. In some circuits the circuit and county judges specialize by subject matter; in others they do not. In either event they sit individually rather than in groups.

Supreme Court. — The Florida Supreme Court sits in Tallahassee and has statewide jurisdiction. The constitution sets the number of justices at seven, among whom there must be at least one from each court of appeal district who resided in it when originally appointed or elected to the supreme court. A majority of the justices elect one of their members as chief justice to serve as the chief administrative officer of the entire state judicial system. Traditionally they elect, for a term of two years beginning in July of even-numbered years, the most senior justice in point of service on the court who has not already served as chief justice. For most matters five justices constitute a quorum, but all seven sit on appeals from judgments imposing the death penalty, as well as some reviews of major civil proceedings. In every instance the concurrence of four justices is necessary to a decision.

The court's internal administration is through numerous committees of its members, who are assigned to these by the chief justice. Each justice other than the chief justice is entitled to two research aides and one secretary; the chief justice is entitled to an executive assistant, an administrative assistant, a research aide, an internal auditor, and two secretaries. The court appoints a clerk/supreme court administrator, who serves at its pleasure as the chief nonjudicial officer of the court under the direction of the chief justice, and also a marshal and a librarian. The clerk's major functions include case-flow management, comprehensive keeping of records of all documents and of minutes of all executive sessions and conferences of the court, management of finances, including initial preparation of the annual budget for the court, and supervision of space and equipment requirements. Under the direction of the court and chief justice the clerk also handles personnel matters relating to the nonjudicial staff and acts as chief planning and evaluating officer with regard to performance of nonjudicial functions.

The marshal is empowered to execute the process of the court throughout Florida, and in any county he may deputize the sheriff or a deputy sheriff for this purpose. He is also custodian of the supreme court building and of its furnishings and grounds.

In 1972 the supreme court created the office of state courts administrator to assist the chief justice in performing his extensive administrative duties. Today a large majority of the circuits also have a local circuit court administrator. In addition to collecting and analyzing valuable statistical data utilized by judicial planning agencies this office renders substantial assistance in case-flow management, especially at the trial level, financial management and budgeting, jury management, in-service training and continuing special education for judicial personnel, space assignment and utilization, and other basic, practical projects.

District courts of appeal.—In each of the five district courts of appeal, the judges elect one of their members by majority vote to serve as chief judge for two years. These judges sit in divisions of three and decide by concurrence of two. Each court appoints a clerk and a marshal, who serve at its pleasure.

Circuit and county courts.—The constitution requires a circuit court in each circuit and a county court in each county. Each judge sits individually, and its judgment or order is that of the respective circuit or county.

Each circuit's judges choose one of their members to serve as chief judge of that circuit for two years and he may be reselected if willing to serve. He is responsible for the administrative supervision of the circuit court and all county courts in his circuit; and in some circuits he designates, for the larger counties, one of the circuit judges and one of the county judges as administrative judges to assist him with court administration in that county.

Trial court clerk. — The constitution requires a clerk of the circuit court in each county, elected by the electors of the county for a term of four years, along with a sheriff, tax collector, property appraiser, and supervisor of elections. A different method of choosing any of these officers may be provided by county charter or special law approved by vote of the county electors but unless otherwise so provided, the clerk of the circuit court is also ex officio clerk of the board of county commissioners, auditor, recorder, and custodian of all county funds. Several counties have in recent years split these enumerated duties between a clerk of court and another clerk who performs the other functions.

State attorney and public defender. — The constitution prescribes for each judicial circuit a state attorney and a public defender, each elected for a term of four years. Each must be a Florida elector, must reside within the territorial jurisdiction of the circuit, and must have been a member of the Florida bar for the preceding five years. Each is directed to appoint assistants authorized by law. A state attorney must devote full time to his official duties and must not engage in private practice. He serves as the prosecuting officer of all trial courts in the circuit. The former offices of county solicitor and prosecuting attorney have been abolished, and their duties are now performed by assistant state attorneys.

The state attorney decides whether to prosecute in criminal cases. He may also permit a person charged to plead guilty to a particular offense. Since the vast majority of cases are decided before trial, this officer largely determines the matter of *plea bargaining*, whereby he may accept a plea of guilty on a lesser charge and then send the accused directly for sentencing, if he and the defense can agree, with final concurrence of the judge. He may conclude that the available admissible evidence does not support a conviction for a more serious crime. He also advises the grand jury, which can indict a person if it finds probable cause for believing that he committed a crime, whereupon he has to stand trial. It can also render criticism and make recommendations, as well as indict a public official.

The position of public defender has been created to provide counsel for those charged in criminal cases who cannot afford to employ an attorney and who take oath to that effect. Formerly such individuals were dependent on an attorney assigned to a case by the judge to act as defense counsel; the attorney was paid a reasonable fee by the county for his services on the case. Public defenders are usually overloaded with cases, as are many of the state attorneys at times; but the advent of this dual system creates more equitable conditions for defense.

Justices and Judges: Eligibility, Restrictions, Salaries, and Terms

Every justice or judge must be an elector of the state and must reside within the territorial jurisdiction of his court. He cannot serve after age 70 except upon temporary assignment or to complete a term of which he has already served half. He must devote full time to the duties of his office; he is compensated solely by state salary fixed by general law and can neither practice law nor hold office in any political party. Table 10.1 lists the annual salaries at the different levels (including the percentage raises effective in January 1980), the minimum number of required years of Florida bar membership preceding appointment or election to the judicial office and the number of years in a full term.

Judicial nominating commissions and retention elections. — Involving the public in the selection of judges presents a dilemma. Raising campaign funds puts a judicial candidate in an awkward situation. If he runs with a party label he may not be considered on his individual merits. The nature of his function rarely attracts public attention to the caliber of his performance. In some areas, there may be many judicial candidates on the ballot, possibly over 50 in Dade

County. Yet the voters have traditionally wanted some say in this matter — in particular they want to be able to remove an unsatisfactory incumbent.

Florida has accordingly instituted two systems designed to secure for the bench those applicants best qualified. At the circuit and county levels judicial candidates run against opponents but on a nonpartisan ballot. At the appellate levels a special nominating commission screens applicants and recommends a certain number and the governor appoints one of these applicants. After a trial period in office of at least one year the appointee runs against himself, so to speak, on the issue of continuing in office. This type of system is known as the "Missouri Plan" because it originated there in the 1940s and has served effectively. The two systems offered in Florida present a practicable method for selecting and retaining judges of high caliber while still utilizing voter input. In addition Florida has created a Judicial Qualifications Commission to deal specifically with those few incumbent judges allegedly dishonest or incompetent.

TABLE 10.1 Florida Justices' and Judges' Salaries, 1980

Judicial Office	Yearly Salary	Minimum Required Years of Bar Membership	Number of Years in Term
Supreme court justice	$51,921	10	6
District court of appeal judge	$49,287	10	6
Circuit judge	$46,769	5	6
County court judge	$44,000	a	4

a. A county court judge must now be a Florida Bar member prior to qualification for election or submission of his name to the Judicial Nominating Commission. If not, he may stand for election if on the first day of the qualification period he is already serving as county judge and is not under suspension or disqualification, or if, in a county with a population of 40,000 or less, he served as county judge in such a county prior to July 1, 1978, and has completed a three-year law training program approved by the supreme court for county court judges who are not bar members.

By a 1976 constitutional amendment the governor is directed to fill each vacancy on the supreme court and district court of appeal by appointing one of three persons nominated by the appropriate judicial nominating commission. The appointive term ends on the first Tuesday after the first Monday in January of the year following the next general election occurring at least one year after the date of appointment. Unless then ineligible the appointee can qualify for retention in that general election, the sole question on the ballot being whether or not he shall "be retained in office." If a majority of the electors voting within the territorial jurisdiction of the court on which he is serving vote to retain him, his new term runs for six years from the end of his appointive term. A negative vote or his ineligibility or failure to qualify for retention creates a vacancy, in which event the nominating process begins again.

In 1978 the voters emphatically rejected, along with all the other amendments proposed, an attempt to extend this version of the "Missouri Plan" to trial judges. As a result each circuit judge and county judge is still elected by vote of the qualified electors within the territorial jurisdiction of his respective court. He runs in a nonpartisan election against any eligible opponents who qualify for election. The timing of this election poses the problem of insulating the nonpartisan general election of judges from the normal general election, in which each candidate is the official nominee of a political party, without requiring the voters to make a separate trip to the polls for the sole purpose of electing judges. There may be more than one candidate for some of the trial court judgeships, yet each is running as an individual without party designation.

The general election of judges is now scheduled at the time of the primary elections of party nominees for other offices. Presumably most registered party voters will be at the polls anyhow; but the registered independents, who can vote in general elections only, have to make a special trip at this time. Voter apathy remains a problem, yet it does not necessarily indicate dissatisfaction; on the contrary, it may signify general satisfaction with the performance of the state judiciary. The system is new, and even the party voters appear to be confused by retention elections for appellate judges. They incorrectly assume that a failure to vote on the question of retention amounts to approval, thereby enabling a small but energetic minority to secure a negative majority of the few votes cast. Voter education may eliminate this problem. Meanwhile it is as yet too early to determine the full efficacy of the two new systems.

Even at the trial level an initial screening process takes place, as a practical matter. If a vacancy in office, as defined in Article X, section 3, of the constitution, occurs before the end of the regular term of a circuit or county judge (as it frequently does), the appropriate circuit nominating commission promptly presents to the governor at least three nominees for each vacancy, from which he must appoint one as the judge. The appointive term ends on the first Tuesday after the first Monday of the year following the next primary and general election and the winner in that election serves from then to the end of that regular term. Normally the incumbent appointee has an advantage over opponents, if there are any, and wins the election.

The constitution prescribes separate judicial nominating commissions for the supreme court, for each district court of appeal, and for each circuit for all trial courts therein. Each commission consists of nine members serving for four-year staggered terms and follows substantially the same procedures. Three Florida Bar members actively engaged in law practice with offices within the territorial jurisdiction of the affected court, district, or circuit are appointed by the Florida Bar's board of governors; three electors residing within the territorial jurisdiction of the court or circuit, who may or may not be members of the bar, are appointed by the governor; and three electors who reside within the territorial jurisdiction of the court or circuit and are not Florida bar members are selected and appointed by majority vote of the other six. No commission member can be a justice or judge or be appointed to state judicial office while a member or for two years thereafter. All commission acts require concurrence of a majority of its members.

Florida Judicial Qualifications Commission

For decades the state constitution has provided for impeachment (formal accusation by the house of representatives) and trial by the senate of supreme court justices and judges of district courts of appeal and circuit courts. Judges below these levels (meaning today the county judges) have been subject to suspension from office by the governor and removal by the senate. These two disciplinary methods are still available, in addition to any civil or criminal responsibilities of the judge as an individual, but conviction by trial on impeachment has proved cumbersome and largely ineffective. The only one in Florida history resulted in the conviction of Circuit Judge Samuel S. Smith on September 15, 1978.

Accordingly, by 1972 amendment, a more practicable alternative or additional method of disciplining judges was created: the Florida Judicial Qualifications Commission. The procedure begins with a confidential investigation of a complaint. If the commission finds probable cause and files formal charges against a judge with the supreme court clerk, the proceedings become public. Upon recommendation by two-thirds of the commission members the supreme court may order reprimand or removal of a justice or judge from office without pay for "willful or persistent failure to perform his duties or for other conduct unbecoming a member of the judiciary demonstrating a present unfitness to hold office." It may order involuntary retirement of a justice or judge who has a permanent disability that "seriously" interferes with performance of judicial duties, and may suspend a justice or judge with or without compensation pending final determination in a particular inquiry.

The commission's results since its beginning in 1973 have been significant. Its 140 formal investigations include twelve proceedings in public, three private reprimands, four public reprimands, and six removals from office or resignations from office prompted by the charges and the evidence.

Of the thirteen members of the commission six are judges: two each from district courts of appeal, circuit courts and county courts. They are selected by the judges of their respective courts. The Florida Bar board of governors also selects two members of the bar. The governor selects the remaining five, none of whom can be a bar member or have held judicial office. Commissioners serve staggered terms not to exceed six years and are barred from holding office in a political party. Judicial members may participate in their own campaigns for the bench; but with this exception no member may hold judicial office while a commissioner or for two years thereafter, nor may he participate in a political campaign or hold public office.

Judicial Branch: Cost, Caseload, Types of Cases, and Disposition

Cost.—The Florida judicial branch expenditures for the state fiscal year 1977–78 amounted to slightly under $85 million, approximately 1.5 percent of total state expenditures of over $5.4 billion. These judicial branch expenditures are split about equally between the court system itself and the official salaried counsel. The trial courts, as might be expected, require the bulk of the court half, while the other half is split approximately two to one between the offices of the state attorney and the public defender. The counties provide local facilities and some nonjudicial personnel for the trial courts, as well as space and utilities for official counsel, but by far most of the funding comes from state general revenue funds.

Caseload. — Table 10.2 shows statewide figures for 1977 by level of court for the number of cases disposed of annually, the number of courts at each level, the number of judges for each court, the average annual caseload per trial judge, and the daily average number of cases disposed of by each trial judge. Caseload per judge is left blank at the appellate level, since the judges work primarily as groups in rotating panels or as a full court. (Individual responsibility for writing the first draft of a proposed opinion is discussed later.) Each proceeding handled is called a case, although it may not be an adversary proceeding; in any event it is usually disposed of before reaching a hearing or a trial. An approximate figure of 230 normal working days per year, used for the computation in the final column, is reached by subtracting from 365 an annual vacation of one month, all official legal holidays, and Saturdays and Sundays.

Judges are able to perform effectively at this speed for several reasons. Almost all of them are highly competent. At all levels they work far more than a normal number of hours per week. Most cases are disposed of at the trial level, especially in county court, without reaching a final hearing in civil proceedings or a trial in criminal proceedings. If civil, the case is dealt with by summary procedure or is settled; if criminal, the accused may plead guilty or *nolo contendere* ("I am unwilling to plead"), resulting in uncontested conviction without admission of guilt. In the circuit court only 3.6 percent of criminal cases and 1.6 percent of civil cases are disposed of by jury trial, a procedure that requires far more time per case. In the county court the corresponding figures are 0.9 percent for criminal, 0.3 percent for civil, and 0.3 percent for criminal traffic infractions. The relatively infrequent resort to trial by jury does not, of course, diminish the importance of this historic, constitutionally guaranteed institution; its availability when requested is important to the citizen as a safeguard against encroachment on his rights by a dictatorial government whenever one develops.

In the appellate tier of courts, the supreme court disposes of two-thirds of its cases by a short order disposing of the request for review, often in the form of a denial of the petition for a writ of *certiorari*. Even so it produced 199 detailed written opinions in 1977 and 145 *per curiam* opinions, a very condensed form

TABLE 10.2 Judges' Caseloads, 1977

Court	Annual Caseload	No. of Courts	No. of Judges[a]	Caseload per Judge	
				Annual	Daily
Supreme	2,623	1	7	–	–
District court of appeal	10,647	4	28	–	–
Circuit	398,328	20	292	1,333	5.80
County	2,214,943	67	190	11,658	50.69

a. Or supreme court justices

of written opinion "by the court" with no indication of the individual draftsman. In practice, each justice produces about one opinion every week. In addition, he must consider and vote on most of those drafted by the others and he spends a substantial portion of his time hearing oral arguments, along with at least four of his colleagues, and in conferences with justices on cases heard but not yet decided. Furthermore, each justice serves on several court committees, the continuing work of which consumes many hours.

In each district court of appeal the workload is much the same, although the committee work is somewhat less while the writing of opinions takes a larger portion of judges' time. Each district court produced on average 380 detailed written opinions and 361 *per curiam* opinions, or two per judge per week.

Types of cases.—Over half the cases disposed of by the supreme court reached it by petition for *certiorari* until appeals by this writ were drastically limited by a 1980 constitutional amendment. The bulk of these requests were for discretionary review of district court of appeal judgments on the basis of their alleged conflict with the law as established by precedents. In recent years the supreme court has granted fewer than 54 percent of these requests. It disposes of most matters by a short order without opinion, but it must first examine each request and decide whether to grant or deny it. There is a large amount of detailed work to be done on the cases it decides to review at greater length. "Easy" cases do not reach the appellate courts, especially the supreme court; the issues involved at these levels are usually complicated, and final answers to them require intensive consideration and often a conference among all the justices or judges.

Each district court of appeal receives most of its cases by appeal, as might be expected. Although approximately 25 percent of all cases are decided *per curiam* without opinion, over 28 percent are decided with either a concise, *per curiam,* written opinion or with a detailed opinion drafted and signed by one of the judges and concurred in by all or a majority of the others involved in the case.

The statewide averages for the circuit courts show that all civil cases exceed all criminal cases by three to one. The largest group of cases is the general civil group, followed quantitatively by juvenile and probate. In the general civil group, dissolution and annulment of marriage is the leading category by far, followed by contract and indebtedness cases, negligence actions, and real property matters, including mortgage foreclosures. Approximately 22 percent of all cases are criminal, the largest single category being crimes against property, followed by crimes against persons and by drug cases. The judge deals with most cases, civil as well as criminal, without a jury. He disposes of the bulk of the criminal cases before trial, in many instances on the recommendation of the state attorney. He also disposes of over one-fourth of the civil cases before hearing.

Of all the cases handled by Florida courts in 1977 the county court disposed of approximately 85 percent, and in almost every instance its disposition was final. Over 80 percent of all county court cases are traffic infractions. Of these almost 1.4 million, or 77 percent, are civil; the judge disposes of most of these by summary procedure before hearing. He also disposes of most of the criminal infractions, over half of these resulting in conviction before trial after a plea of guilty or *nolo contendere*. Similarly, he disposes of the approximately 10 percent of total cases that are civil and 10 percent that are criminal. In fact he disposes of one-third of the civil cases before hearing and over half of the criminal cases before trial as convictions after plea. These statistics, which demonstrate that the vast majority of the cases do not go beyond the trial court, emphasize the vital importance of filling the circuit and county court benches and the offices of state attorney and public defender with people of integrity, competence, and skill in dealing efficiently with numerous cases at high speed.

Disposition.—Despite the steady annual increase in number of cases filed at each level, a condition that should be expected in a rapidly growing state like Florida, the courts are performing ably. The trial courts are disposing of most of the cases filed, and the legislature can periodically increase the number of judges to meet increasing caseloads. There are, however, indications of continuing problems with appellate caseloads in the future, especially in the revised second appellate district and possibly in the revised first, with its recently added caseload of all industrial claims appeals. The very nature of the appellate process does not permit disposition of a case within a month from the time of filing the appeal. In any month recently filed cases are pending, that is, filed, progressing procedurally, and receiving consideration, but not yet decided. When filings consistently exceed dispositions in a year, a court gets further and further behind. The number of cases that have been pending for more than a year in appellate courts is increasing at a substantial rate, and it may soon reach intolerable proportions. In 1978, when the supreme court asked the legislature to propose a constitutional amendment to reduce its mandatory review jurisdiction, the court was trying to handle approximately 3,000 cases per year but was about 1,500 cases behind.

The present constitution authorizes periodic statutory change by the legislature, on the recommendation of the supreme court, in number and boundaries of appellate districts and judicial circuits and in number of judges per court at all levels below the supreme court. The legislature also has constitutional authority to alter by general law the jurisdiction of the trial courts and also much of the jurisdiction of the district courts of appeal, as well as the provisions relating to sitting in divisions and to judicial salaries. The rules of practice and procedure in all courts, already placed in the hands of the supreme court, are being revised constantly.

The Florida Bar

Development, organization, and function. —Early in the fourteenth century in England a square of logs was constructed to bar the crowd of spectators from that portion of the commons or field within which the king's traveling justices and persons who were part of the court or parties to the argument were conducting legal business. The term "admission to the bar" became synonymous with practicing law, and the bar has come to mean the organized group practicing law in a particular area. Recorded history of the bar in Florida goes back to 1889, when the state's population was under 400,000. In 1907 the Florida State Bar Association was organized as a small voluntary group concentrating on publication of a legal journal, drafting court procedures, and presenting an occasional educational course. Fewer than two-thirds of Florida's attorneys were members. Then, in the summer of 1949, the supreme court authorized this association to form a bar with compulsory membership. In 1950 the Florida State Bar Association shortened its name to "The Florida Bar," and the 3,758 attorneys then practicing in Florida automatically became members of the new integrated bar.

Today it has approximately 25,000 members (half under age 36), with new headquarters, financed entirely by bar members, on a two-acre site three blocks from the state capitol. Its governing body, the board of governors, consists of the president and president-elect, the president and president-elect of the young lawyers' section, and 34 others elected by members of the bar from the 20 judicial circuits in Florida in accordance with a formula according at least one board member to each circuit and slightly larger representation to the circuits with more attorneys. In addition to the Tallahassee headquarters and small branch offices in Fort Lauderdale, Miami, Orlando, and Tampa, there are over 70 voluntary local bar associations throughout Florida. The Florida Bar staff is headed by a salaried executive director, chosen by and responsible to the board of governors, and a staff of over 100. The work of the bar is also carried on, at its expense, through 13 sections and over 60 committees composed of individual members of the bar. In addition to paying dues they donate their time, office overhead, and expertise and in practice they pay their own travel expenses in most instances.

A few selected activities of the Florida Bar serve to exemplify the range of its works. The bar works closely with the bench in the continuing process of improving procedure and judicial administration in order to offer better remedies for achieving the ever changing rights of individuals and of society as a whole. It suggests to the legislature many needed amendments to statutes and regulations that conflict with each other or are ambiguous or inconsistent. It conducts an extensive program in continuing legal education throughout the state in the form of published materials and lectures at numerous institutes. It publishes a journal monthly and the *News* twice monthly. It maintains a clients' security fund, completely supported by Florida lawyers with an appropriation from their annual dues, to repay those few clients suffering financial loss through misuse of clients' funds by Florida Bar members. It maintains a lawyer referral service and legal aid and group legal service programs. It strongly supports the law schools in the state, and publishes numerous pamphlets for the information of the public.

The Florida Bar is now the fourth largest in the United States. It consistently receives national recognition in the American Bar Association's annual competition for state and local bars. In 1977, for example, the Florida Bar won top honors for overall excellence, as well as for single-project excellence on the computerized records system in its grievance department.

Discipline. — The discipline of members of the bar is assigned by the constitution to the supreme court, which has delegated initial action in this arduous task to the Florida Bar, and to some extent to the bench, subject to the supervision and final authority of the supreme court. Most of the investigation and the trial work is carried out by over 300 volunteer attorneys, appointed by the board of governors and serving on 50 grievance committees within the circuits, together with counsel and volunteer referees, the latter selected from a panel of attorneys certified annually by the supreme court. The discipline process begins with an investigation of complaints received by the Florida Bar, primarily from clients, running in recent years at an annual average of approximately 1,600. Some 90 percent of these letters either are on their face not valid complaints or are found to result from misunderstandings, which the bar resolves. Investigation of the remainder leads to a hearing before a local grievance committee, which may find no probable cause for believing that misconduct occurred, in which event the case is closed. In some instances the committee may admonish the attorney as to his future conduct. If it finds probable cause a formal proceeding follows, with volunteer counsel and trial by referee. His findings and recommendations are reviewed by the grievance committee and are subject to further review by the board of governors. For minor misconduct the committee or the board may issue a private reprimand. Further review by the supreme court is required if the referee recommends public reprimand, suspension, or disbarment, or if either the respondent attorney or the board petitions the supreme court for review of the referee's findings or recommendations. The bar currently devotes approximately half of its dues income to disciplinary proceedings. For the year July1, 1977, through June 30, 1978, there were 9 disbarments, 23 suspensions, 11 public reprimands, and 4 resignations from the bar, in addition to a somewhat larger number of private reprimands and admonitions. The fact remains that over the years those attorneys who are found after careful investigation to have engaged in misconduct and are accordingly penalized have amounted to only a small fraction of 1 percent of the state's legal profession.

The notion that the Florida bar is the professional counterpart of a labor union is unfounded, for the supreme court retains final authority and its justices are elected by all the voters of Florida rather than by just the bar members. Any disciplinary penalties on an attorney are imposed in addition to whatever criminal and civil liability he may have as a citizen. The added penalty of being removed from one's profession is justified by the demand for high standards of ethics required by the legal profession and scrupulously observed by the vast majority of attorneys. A bench is rarely any stronger than its bar, and the few bar members requiring discipline are dealt with thoroughly and, when necessary, sternly by the bar and the courts.

Some laymen have criticized the bar for allegedly engaging in too much litigation. Such criticisms, however, prove on analysis to be complaints against the adversary type of proceeding rather than against the bar. In essence they constitute disapproval of the statutes enacted by the legislature, which are binding on judges and attorneys as well as on laymen. For example, the recent provisions for what is known as no-fault divorce mark an overdue recognition of the fact that in modern American society many couples mutually desire to end their marriage even though formerly the law required an adversary proceeding and evidence by the plaintiff of conduct by the defendant proving at least one of certain specified grounds for divorce, of which mutual consent was not one. Most attorneys welcomed the statutory change that finally remedied this deficiency.

Another example is found in the statutes and regulations governing workmen's compensation. Florida's employers, numbering over 100,000, were complaining about the high cost of compensation insurance premiums, which were approaching $900 million per year. The drastic revision of the law that had been in effect for almost half a century achieved a mandatory 15% reduction in rates, with perhaps further reductions later; but it renders most of the injured workers ineligible to receive impairment benefits, which are now limited to major injuries, such as loss of sight, amputation, or serious disfigurement.

Still another example is the hodge-podge version of so-called no-fault insurance adopted by Florida with regard to motor vehicle operation. The coverage is decidedly reduced, but the predicted substantial reduction in premiums has not appeared as yet. The financially responsible driver and the car owner still need the original type of third-party insurance for accidents causing major injuries, medical expenses, and property damage, as well as uninsured motorist coverage for such instances. Whether in the long run these changes will benefit the motorists, as distinct from the insurance carriers, remains to be seen.

Appointing laymen to serve as members of the recently created judicial nominating commissions and the Judicial Qualifications Commission is a move strongly supported, not opposed, by the bar and bench. This lay participation has proved itself very valuable. Our point is that, while the bar, like all the vocations and the other professions, is not and never has been above criticism, it has been singled out by some as responsible for changes that it did not produce and that in any event are of doubtful efficacy, as well as for allegedly opposing changes that it in fact recommended or welcomed.

In summary, most legal problems are handled entirely by attorneys in their capacity as legal counselors. These matters are not publicized and do not get to a court; misunderstandings are avoided by legal counseling and careful drafting as a matter of preventive law in the first place. When accidents occur or disputes do arise, most of them are settled out of court, or in any event before trial or final hearing. Indeed, without a competent bar the judicial process could not function without having thousands of judges and inordinate expense.

Florida Board of Bar Examiners. — The state Board of Bar Examiners is assigned the task of determining initially which applicants shall be admitted to membership in the Florida Bar. It conducts a rigorous investigation into the applicant's character and integrity. It also examines applicants, after graduation from an accredited law school, on knowledge of the law and competence in using this knowledge. The examination has three parts: the so-called multistate examination on general law subjects, administered by a national service organization; a special essay section emphasizing Florida law in specified major fields; and a section on knowledge of legal ethics. The board may use experts to draft questions and trained, expert readers to grade, but it must go over all questions submitted and all examination papers. To avoid the possibility of favoritism each examinee is assigned a number, and he is identified solely by this number. Only a grade of pass or fail is used; and at present approximately three-fourths of the candidates pass.

The board consists of 12 examiners appointed for staggered terms of five years. They receive no pay, and their compensation is limited to reimbursement for reasonable travel and subsistence expenses. In other words, each examiner donates his time and normally incurs expenses that exceed his reimbursement. Whenever a term expires or a vacancy in the membership occurs, the board of governors of the Florida Bar recommends to the supreme court three names for each vacancy; it appoints one of the three. The 12 members elect annually one of their number to serve as vice-chairman for one year, and he automatically becomes chairman for the following year. All proceedings and results are subject to review by the supreme court, which maintains supervision over the entire process. Requests for review are rare, as might be expected, but they do occur.

Related Commissions and Agencies

Judicial Council of Florida. — The Judicial Council of Florida, established in 1953, has 17 members appointed by the governor for three-year terms: one justice or retired justice of the supreme court (who serves as chairman), one circuit judge, one county judge, the Florida attorney general or assistant attorney general, four members of the Florida Bar, and nine laymen. Its major functions are (1) to continually survey and study the organization, procedure, practice, rules, administration, and operation of each Florida court; (2) to collect, compile, analyze, and publish statistics showing the work of the courts; (3) to receive, consider, and in its discretion investigate criticisms and suggestions pertaining to the administration of justice; and (4) to recommend from time to time to the legislature any changes requiring legislative action exclusively and to recommend to the courts any changes in rules, practice, and administration of judicial business designed to improve the administration of justice. Its statistical mandate has been largely performed since the beginning of 1973 by the state courts administrator and staff, but the judicial council remains important in planning and recommending legislative and administrative changes.

Judicial Administrative Commission. — The Judicial Administrative Commission has six members serving two-year terms. The chief justice or a justice designated by him usually serves as chairman; the president or chairman of each statewide judicial conference selects one judge from each level of courts; and the chairman of the Florida Prosecuting Attorneys Association and president of the Public Defenders Association each appoint one from their respective groups. The commission employs an executive director at its Tallahassee headquarters.

The several courts and officials from which members of this commission are appointed, as well as the official court reporters, are required by statute to submit budgets, vouchers, and various other reports to the commission, which records these documents and submits them to the proper state officer. When requested, the commission assists these courts and the other officials in preparing budgets and other documents, or it may prepare them entirely itself.

Judges of industrial claims. — The governor is authorized by statute to appoint as many judges of industrial claims as may be necessary to dispose of workmen's compensation proceedings for injury and workmen's unemployment proceedings. They serve full time for a four-year term. They cannot engage in law practice while serving, but each must have practiced law within the state for three years prior to his nomination for appointment. The appellate district judicial nominating commission for the district in which the judge will primarily hold hearings nominates at least three persons, and the governor is required to appoint one from this list. Prior to the expiration of his term his conduct is reviewed by the nominating commission, which no later than six months before the expiration of his term determines and reports to the governor whether the judge should be retained. A negative report prevents reappointment; a favorable vote results in reappointment by the governor for another term.

With the abolition of the Industrial Relations Commission (effective October 1, 1979), all appeals from judgments of industrial claims judges throughout Florida go to the first district court of appeal. A ninth judge has been added to that court to help handle this substantial extra caseload. The court's decisions will be final except in the very rare instances of supreme court review by discretionary certiorari.

Florida Public Service Commission. — The Florida Public Service Commission regulates public utilities operating within the state: railroads, other common carriers, telegraph and telephone companies, and gas and electric companies. The commission, formerly an elective body of three members, was changed by 1978 statute to an appointed body of five members. A Public Service Nominating Council of nine members was created at the same time to recommend to the governor at least three persons for each commission vacancy; he must appoint from this list. If he fails to do so within the time alloted by statute, the council is authorized to appoint a person by majority vote from those recommended. All appointments are subject to senate confirmation. The law provides that the council shall not recommend any person unless satisfied that he is "competent and knowledgeable" in the law, energy, public affairs, or another area closely related to the work of the commission.

The change from an elective to an appointive commission was made because of problems with a long ballot and with the lack of voter information on candidates and their qualifications. In state elections voters must choose a governor and six members of the state cabinet, plus members of the house and senate. Former governor Reubin Askew, believing that the public service commissioners do not have sufficient visibility for the voters to be well informed about their qualifications, recommended the change to an appointive commission, and the legislature agreed. The voters disagreed when they rejected shortly thereafter a proposed amendment that would have anchored this system in the constitution. Meanwhile, however, the statute remains in force, since its provisions are not constitutionally forbidden.

Administrative hearing officers. — In 1974 a Division of Administrative Hearings was created within the Department of Administration for the purpose of conducting hearings on disputed matters after a complainant has exhausted his administrative remedies. An administrative commission (composed of the governor and cabinet) appoints, subject to senate confirmation, a division director, who in turn is instructed to employ full-time hearing officers from among Florida Bar members in good standing for the five years preceding appointment and to establish procedures for their assignment.

When the division is unable to furnish a hearing officer promptly, the division director may designate a full-time, qualified employee of an agency other than the one requesting a hearing officer to conduct the hearing. He is also authorized to designate qualified lay persons to conduct hearings, provided he assigns a hearing officer to assist them in conducting the hearing and to rule upon procedural matters, including questions involving evidence.

References

American Judicature Society. *Judicature*. Periodical on state judicial systems and proposals for changing them. (Available from the society, 200 W. Monroe St., Suite 1606, Chicago, IL 60606)

England, Arthur (chief justice of the Florida Supreme Court). Address, Nova Law Conference, November 17, 1979, reported in the *Florida Times Union*, November 18, 1979, sec. B, p. 11.

Florida Appellate Practice. Tallahassee: The Florida Bar, 1978.

Florida Appellate Procedure Rules. Tallahassee: The Florida Bar, 1978.

The Florida Bar Journal Directory Issue 20–121, 566–631. Tallahassee: The Florida Bar, 1978.

The Florida Bar Pamphlets. Various short pamphlets on practical legal matters, designed for the layman and distributed from time to time as a public service by way of current information and general advice. Tallahassee.

Florida Constitution. Tallahassee: Office of the Secretary of State, 1980.

Florida Judicial System Statistical Report 1977. Tallahassee: Office of the State Courts Administrator, Supreme Court of Florida, 1978.

Florida Rules of Criminal Procedure, R. 3.191. St. Paul, MN: West Publishing Co., 1978.

Florida Statutes Annotated. Chapters 25–44 and sections 20.17, 97.041, 120.65, 440.45, 775.08, 812.021, 832.05, 893.13. St. Paul, MN: West Publishing Co., 1978.

1979 Report on the Florida Judiciary. 53 *The Florida Bar Journal* 296–305. Submitted by Chief Justice Arthur J. England, Jr., to the Florida Legislature, April 1979.

Rules Relating to Admission to the Florida Bar. Tallahassee: Florida Board of Bar Examiners, 1976.

The Criminal Justice System in Florida

10B

by Roger Handberg

UNIVERSITY OF CENTRAL FLORIDA

Florida, like most other states, has a rising crime rate. The problems of crime in Florida are intensified by two environmental factors, climate and geography. The mild climate supports Florida's tourist industry but also makes the state attractive to transients. Their growing numbers have been accompanied by a steady increase in the rates of street crimes and violent crimes, especially in tourist areas, and the cities in those areas have had to increase police services to maintain their attractiveness to tourists.

Florida's nearness to the Caribbean islands and to Central America has made it an important entry point for smugglers of drugs and of people from other countries. The long coastline and the sparsely inhabited rural expanses in the center of the state make their apprehension difficult. State, local, and federal law enforcement agencies maintain numerous task forces whose efforts result in spectacular drug seizures, but their impact on the total drug traffic is minimal.

Figure 10.2 plots the incidence of crime in Florida against the aggregate number of crimes and against the rate per 100,000 population. The crime rate traditionally follows the level of economic prosperity: A dip in the mid-to-late seventies reflected an improving national economic picture, but around 1980 the crime rate surged, reflecting the impact of the latest Mariel boatlift refugees from Cuba and the decline in the national economy. Florida's absolute level of crime has risen, but that rise is partially a reflection of the state's increasing population. The greatest increase has been in property crimes.

These figures do not reflect the total picture because organized crime activities are not fully reported or even known. The state has long been concerned with the problem of organized crime, especially in southeastern Florida and in the metropolitan Tampa area. Law enforcement efforts have been sporadic and relatively ineffectual, in part because of fragmentation within the law enforcement system. There is some evidence that the presence of organized crime is increasing the drug traffic—it is lucrative, and the apprehension rate is low. Most law enforcement systems are more effective in dealing with the street criminal than with the organized crime operative.

Law Enforcement in Florida

The law enforcement component of the Florida criminal justice system is relatively simple. The basic parts in the system are the 66 sheriffs' departments with almost 15,000 employees and 269 municipal police departments with over 16,000 employees (*Crime in Florida,* 1982). For most purposes, these are the frontline agencies in the struggle against crime. These local efforts are supplemented at the state level by officers from the Division of Alcoholic Beverages and Tobacco (in the Department of Business Regulation), the Division of Florida Highway Patrol (in the Department of Highway Safety and Motor Vehicles), the Department of Law Enforcement, the Florida Marine Patrol (an agency of the Division of Law Enforcement, Department of Natural Resources), and the Game and Fresh Water Fish Commission.

As their names indicate, these agencies generally have much more limited jurisdictions than the general purpose police or sheriffs' departments. The exception is the Department of Law Enforcement, which has attempted to model itself on the Federal Bureau of Investigation. It has been plagued by leadership problems and political difficulties, but with the appointment of James York in 1979, an attempt was launched to revitalize the department. The success of that effort will help determine Florida's success in combating organized crime. No other agency, state or local, has the necessary jurisdiction or potential resources to conduct such a statewide effort.

Historically, the dominant local law enforcement agency has been the sheriff's department. In fact, the sheriff as a matter of law is the chief law enforcement official in the county. Municipal police departments operate within their jurisdictions. Usually the sheriff's deputies operate only in the unincorporated areas of the county.

The sheriff's office is unique in that the sheriff is an elected law enforcement officer. Law enforcement officers such as police chiefs are usually appointed by the executive branch of local governments—by city councils or commissions or by city mayors. In contrast, the county sheriff is elected for a four-year term with the possibility of reelection. In southern folklore and fact, the sheriff has the power to be an important, even dominant, figure in local politics, especially in rural areas. The sheriff's deputies provide a ready-made campaign organization. The political position of sheriffs, represented as a group by the Florida Sheriffs Association, has remained basically intact, although efforts by criminal justice reformers have eroded some of their independence.

In most counties, the sheriff's department operates the local jail facility. (Since the abolishment of the municipal court system in January 1977, many municipal police departments forward their prisoners to the county facility because prosecution is handled by the state attorney's office.) The sheriff's office is often responsible for furnishing a bailiff staff for the courts. These functions have the effect of increasing departmental size while not increasing the number of deputies on patrol.

The municipal police departments range in size from one person to nearly a thousand policement. This size disparity has required the state to provide supplemental resources to smaller departments. For example, the state operates a number of crime labs (under the Department of Law Enforcement) to provide forensic science services to departments lacking such facilities.

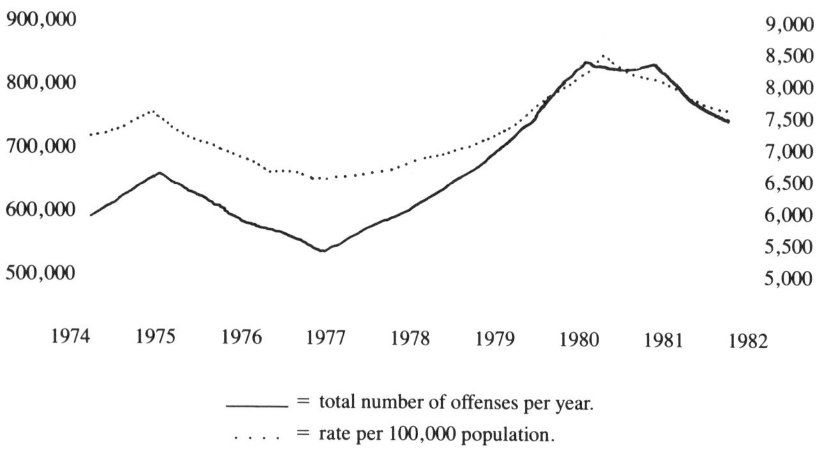

Fig. 10.2. Numbers of Crimes and Crime Rates in Florida, 1974–82. Source: *Crime in Florida, 1974–82.*

Corrections in Florida

The Florida Department of Corrections is the governmental bureau that oversees the statutory punishment of convicted persons and, later, their reintroduction into the community. It is organized both by program function and by geographical area. Over 9,000 departmental employees work in 80 correctional facilities and 82 probation and parole offices. Types of facilities include major institutions (primarily for incarcerated adult males), road prisons, community correctional centers, women's adjustment centers, vocational centers, and probation and restitution centers. The department is organized geographically into five service regions, which, it says, allows greater flexibility in each region and close community ties, which facilitate rehabilitation.

The department's role is not restricted to incarcerating convicts. Judges' sentencing decisions can be influenced through pre-sentence investigations that are made by the department's probation and parole officers. Consequently, some individuals can remain outside prison under the department's supervision, which can consist merely of scheduled visits with the local probation and parole officer or, more intensively, of residence in a halfway facility such as a probation and restitution center. The goal in any situation is to maintain the individual's links to the community and to ensure development of a life style that reduces the likelihood of further crimes.

According to national statistics, Florida has 27,000 individuals in its correctional facilities and another 56,000 under supervision in its communities. Florida ranks fourth in the total number incarcerated, behind Texas, California, and New York, and third per capita. These rankings reflect Florida's punitive attitude toward criminal behavior. The high incarceration rate has severely strained available resources. Occupancy is often at or above capacity, and facility staff turnover is high. In frequent federal court suits, inmates claim that imprisonment in Florida's facilities constitutes cruel and unusual punishment. Such challenges along with high costs of maintaining prisons have stimulated debate over the extent to which supervision in the community should be substituted for incarceration.

Because of the costs of additional prisons, the 1983 legislature put a cap on the number of prisoners and directed early release for less dangerous prisoners when that cap was reached. The Correctional Reform Act of 1983 specified a population limit of 275 prisoners per 100,000 population through 1988 and a reduction to 250 per 100,000 by 1993. It also set out sentencing guidelines and delineated more clearly the use of probation and parole as alternatives to incarceration. Consideration is also to be given to other alternatives, such as work supervision for first-time offenders.

The cost savings of nonincarceration are clear. In 1982, it cost on average \$21.94 per day to handle an incarcerated offender but only \$1.51 per day for supervision in the community, a daily saving of \$20.43 per offender. The cost of constructing a secure correctional facility is over \$17,500 per bed. Given the obvious savings, potential and actual, the important question becomes what goal the criminal justice system is attempting to maximize through punishment.

Crime and Punishment in Florida

A variety of goals can be pursued by the Florida criminal justice system, either independently or together. Three broad categories of goals have been identified over the years: rehabilitation, retribution, and deterrence. By the term rehabilitation we refer to efforts to reform the offender so that he will not repeat his offense and will emerge from punishment a better person than before. This goal has not been abandoned in Florida, but it has come to have less emphasis in debates over what is to be done about crime in Florida.

The last two goals have been much more widely accepted and, in fact, constitute the theoretical basis for several legislative initiatives in recent years. "Retributionism asserts that a person who is guilty of an offense deserves to be punished in proportion to the seriousness of his offense'' (Cederblom and Blizek, 1977, p. 4). Such a view of punishment underlies legislative attempts to establish a policy of determinate sentencing. That is, convicted individuals will receive fixed sentences for certain crimes with no hope of parole before a specified minimum term has been served. Presently, convicts serve indefinite sentences; their early release is contingent upon evidence of remorse or rehabilitation or both. In contrast, under fixed-term sentencing, criminals are confronted by the certainty of the term of punishment rather than an indeterminate sentence. The state is extracting retribution from the offender not only in terms of prison time but, increasingly, in the form of financial compensation as well. Offenders are expected to contribute to the cost of their probation and parole supervision and, in certain circumstances, to make restitution to their victims. Such efforts, while not unique, have been pushed farther in Florida than in most other states.

The third goal, deterrence, has been much more controversial, largely because it involves the continuing debate over capital punishment. Franklin E. Zinning and Gordon J. Hawkins (1973, p. 71) define deterrence as "applying only to cases where a threat of punishment causes individuals who would have committed the threatened behavior to refrain from doing so." Translated into criminal justice policy, the threat of severe and certain punishment for specified crimes can reduce the incidence of those crimes. The punisher hopes to deter two groups: those punished, who will not repeat the same criminal offense, and outsiders, who, observing another's punishment, will not commit that criminal offense at the high risk of severe punishment. An analogy is often made between criminals and children. Children obey not only because they are taught to do good (some say they are "socialized into moral behavior") but also because they are aware that they will be punished if they fail to obey. Criminals, it is reasoned, are subject to the same disincentives. In theory, if a person knows that he or she will be severely punished for committing a robbery, that potential offender will not commit the crime. The would-be criminal is assumed to conduct a rational cost-benefit analysis before committing a crime. Such assumptions underlie recent Florida legislation like the minimum three-year sentence for persons convicted of using a firearm in the commission of a felony.

The difficulty with the deterrence approach is that several key conditions are not normally satisfied. First, most criminal penalties are unknown to most of the populace, including arrested persons. Most people do not have deterrent information except in the most general sense. The firearms law, however, was widely publicized, and thereafter reports of armed robberies declined, although the decline could have been purely a function of changes in crime reporting practices. Second, the deterrence approach has to rely on certainty of punishment to be effective. But no police department solves every crime. Most crimes, in fact, are unreported (only about 25 percent of all crimes are reported) or, if reported, are unsolved (only 19 percent of reported nonviolent crimes are solved). Therefore, most criminals escape punishment. Third, and more damaging to the deterrence model, is the length of time that elapses between the crime and the punishment (if any), which is so great as to destroy the deterrence value of the mandatory sentencing law. The exceptional individuals who are quickly caught and punished are seen not as the victims of an inescapable system but as poor wretches who were too stupid to avoid being caught. The lesson of the likelihood of punishment that is fundamental to successful deterrence of criminal acts seldom comes across.

Capital Punishment in Florida

Capital punishment and its justifications have been significant in the problems of crime and punishment in Florida. The main debate over capital punishment in Florida has been among adherents of the death penalty, who are split over whether capital punishment is justified because it deters criminal acts generally or merely because it is society's right to punish extreme transgressors to the ultimate degree. Advocates of the abolition of the death penalty, while legally and vocally prominent, have been relatively insignificant politically.

Public opinion has consistently supported capital punishment probably some 60 percent of the populace favors it. Candidates in favor of the death penalty are frequently elected, and jurors are frequently willing to recommend the death penalty. Florida, as a result, had the largest death row population in the United States in June 1979—over 130—and was the first state to execute an involuntary individual since the U.S. Supreme Court upheld the constitutionality of the death penalty in 1976. Given the state's large death row population and Governor Bob Graham's apparent willingness to sign death warrants, Florida should be the state with the most executions in the 1980s.

The death penalty is imposed by a fairly straightforward procedure. In a capital case the jury first decides the guilt or innocence of the accused. If it convicts, the jury then makes a separate recommendation of life imprisonment or death. The trial court judge is not bound by the jury's recommendation but must state the factors that guide the decision to impose the death penalty. Upon appeal of the conviction, appellate judges in the District Court of Appeals or the state Supreme Court must examine the fairness of the trial and the sentence. The sentence is compared to sentences imposed in other parts of the state. If all appeals are unsuccessful, the condemned person then appeals to the executive branch for clemency.

Clemency is reviewed by the governor and cabinet sitting as the Executive Clemency Board. Members of this board, like judges, are sworn to uphold the law. They do not simply vote on whether they like or do not like capital punishment. Rather, in the specific case before them they consider the severity of the crime and whether it meets the statutory criteria that justify imposing the death penalty. Files prepared by officials of the Florida Pardon and Parole Board contain the facts of the crime, the evidence, and the condemned person's record. Attorneys for the condemned person also present information and arguments to the board. The board then acts either to uphold or reduce the punishment. If the board upholds the sentence, the governor can sign the death warrant that actually authorizes the execution. If such a warrant is signed, the condemned person's attorneys appeal to various courts in an effort to delay or prevent the execution. The consequence of this procedure is that executions come long after the crime. John Spenkelink was on death row for a number of years before his execution on 25 May 1979, the first execution in Florida since the early 1960s.

Why is Florida apparently so willing to use this particularly harsh punishment? One major reason relates to the social conservatism of the South generally and of Florida specifically. This conservatism is buttressed by a religious fundamentalism that emphasizes retribution of the sort endorsed in the Biblical maxim "an eye for an eye, a tooth for a tooth." Another explanation focuses upon the fact that many of the death row inmates are members of minorities. Some observers allege that racial prejudice motivates the use of the death penalty in Florida. Before 1972, racist attitudes were not uncommon, especially in the more rural areas of the state. Other observers point out that many of the death row inmates are transients, individuals who lack ties to the local community and are, therefore, vulnerable to community vengeance.

One additional argument, not yet proved or disproved, is that capital punishment deters crime. Unfortunately for deterrence theory, most murders are "crimes of passion"; in those crimes the rationality of behavior that deterrence theory assumes is not to be expected. Furthermore, whether the death penalty is imposed or carried out appears to be unrelated to changes in the crime rate. Whatever the civic reasons for the sentences handed down by Florida's criminal courts, including the death penalty, Florida has clearly stamped itself as the state with the harshest punishment of crime and criminals.

Selected References

Cederblom, J. B., and Blizek, William L., eds. *Justice and Punishment*. Philadelphia: Ballinger, 1977.

Federal Bureau of Investigation. *FBI Report* (annual). Washington. (Reports on crime in America)

Florida. Department of Corrections. *Annual Report*. Tallahassee. (Information on the operations of the Florida corrections and probation and parole systems)

Florida. Department of Law Enforcement. *Crime in Florida* (annual). Tallahassee. (Information on crime rates, arrest rates, and law enforcement patterns)

Sheriff's Star. Tallahassee. (Official publication of the Florida Sheriffs' Association)

Zinning, Franklin E., and Hawkins, Gordon J. *Deterrence*. Chicago: University of Chicago Press, 1973.

10C Conclusion

by Manning J. Dauer
UNIVERSITY OF FLORIDA

The treatment in this chapter of law, the courts, and criminal justice reflects the concerns of American society and the social attitudes particular to Florida. Although many authors in this book take the position that Florida is a moderately conservative state with concern for adaptation to growth, in the area of law and the courts there is considerable innovation. Within a decade the state has abandoned the partisan election system for judges and adopted, for the upper tier of courts, the Missouri Plan of merit selection and merit retention. For the lower courts, Florida now has nonpartisan election of judges. At the same time, the whole system of courts has been consolidated into four articulated levels. Modern methods of keeping up with caseloads have been introduced, and the state has adopted the use of nominating commissions to pass on qualifications for lawyers considered for judgeships. Concurrently, the state adopted a Judicial Qualifications Commission to review charges against judges and the make recommendations on possible disciplinary action.

A considerable number of procedural and structural reforms of the courts have occurred in Florida. By statute and by procedural rules adopted by the Florida Supreme Court, rules of both civil and criminal procedures have been simplified. On other issues, however, there are tensions between the organized Florida Bar and the Florida Supreme Court, for example, over the matter of what should be done about certifying the competence of lawyers. The bar has proposed that certification of lawyers should include various specialities, such as tax law and trial practice. (Certification simply means approved designation of a specialty and is distinct from licensing, which means admission to practice.) This proposal was rejected by the supreme court, although it is, of course, still concerned with this matter of competence and revised rules are still being considered for certification. In the quest for simplifying legal procedures, a system of magistrate hearings has been adopted for small claims, and the state supreme court and the bar are investigating the possibility of administrative rather than full legal processes for such matters as divorce proceedings and the probating of estates where the amount involved is small. The divorce issue was triggered by the case of a legal stenographer who was offering a $50 package of legal forms to be filed by individuals without the employment of an attorney. While the state supreme court upheld a suit by the bar on this issue, it has ordered a further investigation into simplifying such legal proceedings into administrative hearings without full court procedures. Some other states have developed such procedures, and this issue will occupy considerable attention in Florida.

Early in 1980 the University of Florida Holland Law Center for Governmental responsibility made a lengthy report on the problems raised by the Supreme Court and the bar in regard to costs of litigation. It found that legal processes are becoming increasingly complex, with costs that are beyond the capacity of much of the population. The exceptions, those who can afford such costs, are the wealthy and the indigent, who can qualify for public counsel. The report recommends changes to be considered by the bar and by the legislature, including the adoption of simplified administrative procedures, as in many divorce cases and in the settlement of small estates.

In the area of criminal justice the action of the legislature reflects the concern that poor members of society receive adequate counsel, so public defenders have been instituted to provide paid counsel for the poor. In regard to the treatment of offenders there is a strong trend toward law and order. The state prison population is constantly increasing and for certain cases the mandating of minimum sentences has been established by the legislature. Capital punishment also has been reintroduced. Thus the pattern reflects the outlook of Floridians as moderate conservatives who are willing to adopt certain changes but who also are concerned with any threat, as they see it, to their society.

11

Local Government in Florida: An Introduction

by Robert Benedetti

NEW COLLEGE, UNIVERSITY OF SOUTH FLORIDA

The first principles of local government in the United States are contradictory. In legal theory and state constitutional practice, cities, counties, and most of the newer regional authorities are creatures of the states. They are established by acts of state legislatures and state constitutional provisions, which define their powers and the administrative procedures they employ. But what a state government provides, it may take away. It is not unknown in Florida and in other states for a city to lose its corporate powers by legislative act. Thus the "federal analogy" does not hold. Congress cannot abolish the states; they are sovereign. The states, however, can abolish their cities, counties, and regional authorities; they are districts for administrative convenience.

On the other hand, with the legal primacy of state government stands the custom of home rule. Cities, counties, and regional authorities are not simply administrative bureaus. Typically they are led by independently elected officials possessing substantial legislative power, including the power to tax. Further, they are often guaranteed by a corporate charter from the state, providing many services for local citizens with limited supervision by the state. Informally, at least, cities, counties, and often regional organizations are understood to be as dependent on the will of local citizens as on the will of state governments. Moreover, constitutions like that adopted in Florida in 1968 provide legal recognition of city and county home rule, though the extent of such protection continues to be in dispute.

Local governments thus serve two masters, which theoretically can contradict each other. State and local leaders do respond to different constituencies. Yet in practice, the two perspectives have coexisted. Local government in Florida functions to serve both state policy and local initiatives.

One reason for this coexistence may be a consensus between the state and the locality concerning the scope of government. Both appear to accept the maxim that that government is best that governs least. Therefore neither risks the sweeping legislative program that might challenge directly the prerogatives of the other. Each regulates little, and with limited policy comes little conflict.

Furthermore, the support of the state for efficient administrative procedure and of the locality for truly representative institutions can complement one another. The implementation of a state program becomes sensitive to local conditions and hence more precisely targeted when local institutions provide rapid feedback concerning the impact of a program. On the other hand, efficient administrative procedures guarantee local citizens that benefits they vote themselves will be provided with a minimum of overhead and bureaucratic distortion. Thus, home rule institutions can help the state improve the effectiveness of its policies, while state procedures can assure efficient government to localities.

Whatever the mechanisms by which these contradictory principles have been held in tension in the past, the rapid urbanization of Florida continues to challenge them. The local governments of Florida are being reshaped. Migrations from the North are changing the nature of urban problems. Renewed interest in local administration by federal and state authorities is providing new solutions. This is a time of ferment, and local institutions cannot emerge unscathed. The city hall and the county courthouse are the targets for new citizens demanding new services and for government bureaucrats promulgating new guidelines.

In general, Florida cities and counties appear to be better prepared for their position within a web of intergovernmental bureaucracies than for their role in the resolution of conflict between local citizen groups. Their past includes a traditionally close tie with state government and dependence on professional staff for much urban decision making. The manager form of government, widespread among Florida cities and growing among counties, provides efficient, businesslike management with a minimum of internal conflict. State and federal agencies are particularly cooperative with such governments because they are able to comply with strict bureaucratic regulations.

On the other hand, local governments which put a premium on efficiency and the maintenance of professional standards may, of necessity, limit citizen participation. Nonprofessionals often introduce amateur ideas, if not senseless conflict and even corruption, into government. Throughout much of Florida, the absence of partisan elections, ward systems of representation, and elected executive officials is an attempt to remove such threats to good government.

However, such reforms restrict the access of citizens to their government and therefore the ability of local people to hold their officials accountable for their actions. To be sure, private citizens do forge political action groups in reaction to specific problems, and these groups do influence local decisions in crisis situations. But organizations and procedures capable of sustaining citizen involvement over the long run are underdeveloped in Florida. The role of the average citizen in monitoring his government and determining its future direction remains small in Florida cities and counties.

This emphasis on professional competence rather than on citizen involvement may result in increased dependence on other governmental authorities beyond the city boundaries. When citizens find local governments unresponsive and seek other, more receptive channels among state legislators and federal bureaucrats, cities and counties will serve less and less as the people's spokesmen to higher authorities. Rather, they will become simply the lowest rung in a governmental bureaucracy. Communications from Tallahassee and Washington will naturally proceed from "top down" rather than from "bottom up."

Further, as local professionals find their success tied to the success of programs initiated at higher levels, their perspective will become increasingly broad and less focused on local affairs. It will become more important for a particular project to succeed in a locality than for the problems of that locality to be solved. Winning grant moneys from higher sources can quickly become an end in itself, particularly where no additional tax revenues can be expected from a disillusioned local citizenry.

Similar trends can be seen in the development of the new governmental forms that are challenging the local monopoly of cities and counties: special districts, metro governments, councils of governments, regional regulatory bodies, and federally funded public advocates. These organizations often have larger boundaries but substantially less autonomy than do the traditional city and county units. They serve only a limited number of functions and their relationship to local constituents is usually indirect. However, most have professional executive directors and highly qualified staff organizations. Thus here too professional norms and modern bureaucratic structures have succeeded, but the role of popular participants has remained ill defined and underdeveloped.

In general, as Florida's cities, counties, and the newer regional governments become increasingly professional, they risk becoming isolated from their citizens. They are better prepared to carry out the will of higher authorities than to aggregate the will of local citizens. Increasing state and federal involvement in local government will require change, but the structures to accommodate such changes are in place. On the other hand, local representative institutions may require serious repair to recapture the hearts, minds, and energies of local residents.

Still generalizations can be misleading, particularly when they involve the future. It is therefore important to analyze in some detail present city, county, and regional practices, the growing demands of citizens, and the evolution of urban policy at the state and federal level. In the subtle interplay of all three lies the new face of local government in Florida.

Traditional Forms of Local Government: Cities and Counties

In Florida, cities and counties hold constitutional status, and Miami/Dade County, Jacksonville/Duval County, Tampa/Hillsborough County, and Key West/Monroe County each has special constitutional provisions. Article 8 of the Florida Constitution assigns local governmental powers under three categories: noncharter counties, charter counties, and municipalities. Noncharter counties "shall have such power of self-government as is provided by general or special law," while charter counties "shall have all powers of local self-government not inconsistent with general law or with special law approved by a vote of the electors.'' That is, charter counties can do anything not prohibited by law, while noncharter counties can act only where existing law provides authorization. With a charter, then, comes a great measure of home rule. All municipalities share with charter counties this expansive grant of power, though the phraseology is slightly different: ''Municipalities shall have governmental, corporate and proprietary powers to enable them to conduct municipal government, perform municipal functions and render municipal services, and may exercise any power for municipal purposes except as otherwise provided by law.''

Provisions for home rule have been interpreted to mean different things in different states, but their basic thrust is to free cities and charter counties of the necessity of checking all but major policy initiatives with the state. Without home rule rights, local governments tend to be governed by their legislative delegations, who decide whether a particular policy is worthy of passage as a local bill in the legislature.

Florida local governments were extended home rule rights in the Constitution of 1968. Prior to that time all cities and counties were subject to Dillon's Law, a nineteenth-century legal principle whereby no creature of the state could act in ways not previously authorized in specific terms by state statutes. Today, however, only the noncharter counties are affected by this rule, and even they are only restricted from independent action when it challenges the authority of constitutionally mandated county officers.

In addition, the Constitution of 1968 allowed charter governments to change their charters by referendum without legislative approval and limited the powers of the legislature in passing laws directed at a particular charter government. Subsequent statutes have strengthened these aspects of home rule. Another result has been the growth of local charter review boards who sit, as local legislative delegations once did, to determine what changes in charters are desirable. Such bodies at times conflict with other elected officials, but it is too early to assess their impact on local politics.

Writing in 1974, six years after the passage of the new constitution, Steven Sparkman concluded: ''It appears from . . . continuing resistance to home rule as now provided by the constitution and statutes that the attempt at a legal re-ordering of legislative power relationships has not fully succeeded in the face of lingering influence of old philosophies.'' What kindled Sparkman's pessimism was a series of court rulings and attorney general opinions that limited the scope of home rule. Specifically, it has been argued that there are certain areas of law-making authority which the constitution inherently reserved for the legislature and which no local entities can preempt even in the absence of state law. Therefore, in reality, cities and charter counties cannot act in all areas left unspecified by state statutes but only in areas of ''municipal purposes'' or ''local self-government'' narrowly construed.

Further, at least one interpreter sees a clear distinction between the home rule power available to counties and those available to cities: "It seems somewhat incongruous that counties in Florida, which have never had charter powers (except those given in the Constitution such as to Dade and Duval), be now given more autonomy than municipalities who have always exercised charter authority." Until the courts completely settle the law in this area, the precise extent of home rule will remain uncertain.

Whatever the courts decide, other forces are also at work to limit local autonomy. The Constitution of 1968 did allow the legislative enactment of special or local laws to continue, provided that there be timely advanced notice of the proposed special or local law or that legislative passage be followed by a referendum within the city or county. Though it entails a cumbersome process, this provision affords the legislative delegation a way to take initiative for local reform away from local officials. More typically, however, the delegation may continue to play a role in identifying local problems through hearings and investigations in search of proposals for future statutes. The number of local bills enacted by the legislature is large, and the fact that the legislative delegation can take control makes the delegation members a focus for discontent in communities where local elected officials are weak or divided.

More threatening to home rule, however, is the fact that the Florida legislature and executive agencies have become increasingly interested in making uniform such local functions as planning and public employee relations. The Comprehensive Planning Act of 1975 required every city and county to submit a comprehensive plan to the state before July 1, 1979. The state has preempted public employee commissions at the local level by creating a single statewide agency. Together with statutes such as these, which spell out procedures for local governments or preempt previously local functions, other laws prescribe intergovernmental cooperation on certain issues as, for example, controlling pollution.

The Department of Community Affairs has the statutory power to assess the impact of local services and has review authority, through its division of planning, over city, county, and regional master plans. The very creation of such a department appears to signal an increasing interest by the legislature in controlling local government. It may be that the home rule provisions of the Florida Constitution limited legislation directed toward specific cities but stimulated general legislation aimed at standardizing local practice. Such legislation includes state supervision of water resources, of provision of adequate sewer systems, and of control over coastlines, wetlands, pollution, and waste disposal (see chapter 14).

Though many legislative initiatives have the virtue of increasing efficiency and coordination, their requirements often interrupt the agenda of local governments and preempt time or resources for state purposes. Cities and counties may, in fact, have home rule over only those matters which as yet cannot be standardized. As such uniform procedures are developed, the State of Florida seems ready and willing to implement them even over local objections.

County Government

Though cities and counties in Florida share a measure of autonomy from the state as recognized in the state constitution, they have traditionally differed in the services they provide to local areas. Counties, for example, are mandated to establish a sheriff, a tax collector, a property appraiser, a supervisor of elections, and a clerk of the circuit court. In addition, statutory provisions assign to counties large responsibilities in road construction and maintenance, public health and welfare, and agricultural extension services.

More overtly than cities, counties function as administrative arms of the state. Their duties are prescribed with greater specificity, and state supervision is more comprehensive. Florida is divided into 67 counties, making it possible for the state to reach all its citizens through county government. In fact, Florida counties, until challenged by the courts in the 1960s, were the electoral districts for both the house and the state senate. As Marando and Thomas put it: "Counties . . . have always operated as administrative subdivisions of the state. Thus much of what counties do is directly affected by what the state requires them to do. More than cities, counties have historical and substantive links to state government. Counties (except for chartered counties) more than cities must look to the states for organizational policy and administrative guidance." This direct tie with the state is the heritage of earlier times when the county embraced the whole of state bureaucracy in the local area. However, with the growth of state services, bureaucratic structures have developed which tie clients in local areas directly to Tallahassee. Also, as will be discussed later, the newer forms of regional government are now competing with counties to be the local representatives of state policies.

Though the reorganization of state bureaucracies has affected county government, basic changes have also occurred in response to the increasing demand of local citizens for new services. Traditionally, counties were units providing services to rural areas, and their officials were part-time, receiving fees for services; for example, the sheriff was a farmer who received fees when he served a writ or when he made an arrest. Today the urban spread necessitates urban services for many parts of the county; the officials work full-time. In the past, county-elected officials sat as executive boards to expedite state directives; these boards have been transformed into legislative councils providing ordinances expressing local problems and local solutions. In fact, county government is increasingly difficult to distinguish from city government.

To be sure, counties usually are the sole providers of the election, court, and tax services recognized in the Florida Constitution. However, counties now sell municipal services (water, fire, police, sanitation, etc.) to rural and suburban districts if not to the entire county, since incorporated areas often wish to benefit from the county's expanded purchasing power. The lack of clarity regarding the functions of county government symbolizes the transition this unit of government is undergoing. Cities and counties are in the process of sorting out municipal functions in an attempt to decide which services are more equitably and efficiently provided by each unit. The critical variable is, of course, size. Services easily standardized, which are technical in nature and decline in cost when purchased in large quantity, are properly county functions. The determination of such services, however, seems destined to be a trial-and-error process. The opportunity to transfer functions is specifically recognized in the Florida Constitution.

The process of "trading" functions is complicated by special districts and consolidation. In some cases, a function may be removed from both city and county jurisdiction and placed under its own "special" administrative district. Similarly, it is possible that all city functions be transferred to a county, making municipal institutions obsolete. This is commonly called consolidation; the Jacksonville–Duval County experiment is an example of this form in Florida.

The creation of special districts, then, sidesteps the assignment of a complex function to either traditional local unit. Consolidation eliminates the question altogether by asserting the primacy of the county. That the first solution, creating special districts, has been so widely utilized indicates the difficulty inherent in making a reasonable division between city and county functions.

In sum, the very definition of county government is currently in flux. Historically the county was the local arm of state authority. With the development of a strong, centralized state bureaucracy and new regional authorities, the county was forced to share this role with others. Yet, as it has declined as an arm of the state, it has grown in its ability to provide municipal services to rural and urbanized areas alike. Out of this competition with state bureaucracy on the one hand and cities on the other, counties are forging a new identity.

Cities

In contrast to county governments, which appear on the verge of shedding state administrative functions while gaining municipal ones, cities are moving in precisely the opposite direction. Cities are increasingly webbed into state bureaucratic structures through growing regulatory procedures, while hard-pressed to defend traditional service functions against the claims of the counties and other regional authorities. Still, the definition of the city as a corporation, managed for the mutual benefit of its members and catering to their wishes, stands.

The monopoly of cities over municipal services stems from the early nineteenth century, when American cities transformed themselves from medieval regulators of commerce to modern purveyors of public services. Since, it was argued, urban services were of use only to those in the city and the costs were borne by urban dwellers themselves, the city was the logical authority to control these self-sufficient operations. However, over time both of these assumptions have eroded.

Urban services are now enjoyed by the many suburbanites who live just beyond the city limits. Cities can no longer tax all who benefit from their services, because users live outside their jurisdiction. Such facilities as roads, public transportation systems, libraries, and parks are obvious examples of the diverse services which benefit suburbanites at little or no cost to them. Furthermore, cities have become so interdependent with their surroundings that most changes in urban policy quickly affect those who have no direct voice in city politics. Air pollution, water pollution, traffic patterns, and crime are city problems which spill over into other jurisdictions. If the city does not solve them responsibly, the suburbs are unnecessarily burdened. In sum, the city of today cannot collect for all the services it renders nor is it accountable to all the people who are affected by its policies.

One response to this change has been the regulation of city functions in order to prevent excessive costs on nonusers of city services. Hence, regional and state authorities have increased their surveillance of city decisions, particularly in the areas of land use and environmental planning. However, increased regulation does not address the first issue – the inability of cities to collect from all users, or the so-called problem of urban sprawl.

As implied above, counties increasingly see themselves as a solution to this problem. With the growing urbanized fringe around Florida cities draining off resources without returning tax monies, it makes economic sense to "internalize the externalities" by having the larger unit, the county, tax and thereafter provide many municipal services. Despite this logic, Florida's cities stand with much of the rest of the nation in resisting centralization at the county level, or consolidation. With the notable exception of the experiments in Miami and Jacksonville, Florida's cities have fought back attempts to transfer wholesale their municipal functions to county government. Moreover, the Florida League of Cities opposed successfully a recent constitutional amendment which was interpreted as easing the procedure for consolidating city and county functions.

The Florida Constitution of 1968 actively promoted the increased role of the county by allowing county charters to include provisions whereby county ordinances would supersede city law as well as providing for the transfer of powers and consolidation. However, cities in charter counties such as Sarasota successfully blocked the inclusion of such optional clauses, thereby preserving their autonomy. Cities across the state have aggressively and successfully pressed dual taxation suits against their counties, asserting that the growing role of counties in municipal services should be limited to unincorporated areas and paid for by those areas alone.

Instead of county-city consolidation, cities prefer their own solution: annexation. They argue that expansion of the city, not transfer of powers to the county, would provide the best solution to the drain on their resources. Melvin Reese, city manager of Miami, has written: "As a community ages and develops, its existing boundary lines are often obsolete because, with the community's growth, corresponding satellite growth develops which should become part of the core city in order to establish a more realistic political sub-division of an overall area."

State laws have made annexation difficult in two ways. First, until recently, it was relatively easy for an unincorporated area to gain a city charter. Though statutory procedure exists by which a handful of property owners can create a municipality, most cities were created by special legislative act. In the 1950s and 1960s, before the legislature voted to regulate the creation of municipalities, the number of incorporated areas increased by a third. Almost any area threatened with annexation could incorporate and avoid paying its share of the services provided by the primary city. However, in the seventies the legislature has restrained itself and the growth of new municipalities has ceased. The number of municipalities in 1976 was 390, the same as in 1972; by 1978 the number was but 394.

On the other hand, the second legal problem still remains. Most statutory provisions concerning annexation in Florida require the approval of the majority of voters in the city and the majority in the area to be annexed. Thus the group to be incorporated must see a clear advantage or the annexation vote will fail. Under such circumstances, annexation is often proposed as a special legislative act rather than a statute, resulting in a political test of strength between incorporated and unincorporated areas. At this writing, the legislature is considering enacting annexation procedures which, if adopted, could make the task of cities much easier; significantly, the bill is opposed by county governments. In 1974, the Commission on Local Government suggested an alternative: the creation of a statewide boundary commission which would settle such disputes. Should such a commission ever be created, the balance between city and county representatives would obviously be critical.

In summary, Florida cities are laboring under increased regulation, but they are resisting the transfer of traditional municipal powers to county government. They continue to maintain their historical identity even as their ability to provide services efficiently is challenged. They offer annexation as a solution to their problems — an option which would not only preserve but extend their powers.

Thus, battle lines are drawn between the traditional forms of local government. If the future promotes annexations, the cities will retain their vitality; if consolidated, the counties will flourish. The piecemeal transfers of powers and the continued creation of special districts would not signal a clear victory for either form but would be a logical compromise unless the state takes a more definite hand. The city possesses an identity it would preserve; the county is searching for a new personality; both face an uncertain tomorrow.

Federal Presence or Federal Absence

Federal government entered the local picture heavily after World War II through federal grants to states. Originally, the grants were specific or categorical—for such things as urban renewal, airport construction, or sewage treatment plants. The Reagan administration sought to cut off many such grants and to establish instead a program called the "New Federalism." It would define more specifically limits on programs belonging to states, counties, and cities. Pending a more sweeping solution, such as the transfer of all welfare grants to state and local governments, the administration sought to limit specific grants and instead to turn over "block grants" to states. These grants would decrease over time, and states and localities would decide whether to continue such local programs as welfare and transportation. Combined with the recession of the early 1980s, this move expanded existing fiscal problems for state and local governments. In a rapid-growth state such as Florida the recession has not been so severe, but the general costs of providing services for a growing population have caused a budgetary strain.

City Forms of Government

The traditional form of city government in the United States was known as the *weak mayor-council type*. Under this the mayor was the chief executive and the council was the legislature, but the council also made the budget, so the mayor had little fiscal control.

With the twentieth century this form changed to the *strong-mayor type* in which the mayor prepares the budget, but the council passes on it and can change it (fig. 11.1). The council also votes taxes. The mayor then administers the budget and also is chief executive over all city departments. This form exists, for example, in Tampa, and in the consolidated system of Greater Jacksonville, which also embraces Duval County.

The third type of city government is the *commission plan*, adopted in Galveston, Texas, at the turn of the century (fig. 11.2). This model has five commissioners, each having a separate executive department. Typically, the mayor is commissioner of public safety, over fire and police departments. There also is an elected commissioner of finance, an elected commissioner of public works, and two others who may preside over parks and recreation or some other function. The commissioners sit together as the city legislative body to enact city ordinances, and they make the budget and levy taxes.

The problems with the commission type are threefold. First, there is no guarantee that the elected commissioners will be sufficiently experienced to handle daily administration of specialized departments, such as police, fire, finance, or engineering. Second, there is no central coordinator over all the executive departments. Finally, there is no separation between the legislative and executive functions — although the desirability of such separation for local government is debatable. In any event, this system has fallen into disfavor.

The fourth city type is the *commission-manager form* (fig. 11.3). Originating just after 1910, it has been widely followed in Florida in medium-sized cities and is also found in Miami and, at the county level, in Metro–Dade County. Under this system the commission is elected but is part-time. It is the legislative body, enacting city ordinances, approving the budget, and levying city taxes. It also establishes policies for the executive function. But administration is executed by a full-time city manager selected by the commission. This official is supposed to be a professional and may be selected from individuals who have been managers or assistant managers in small cities. The manager is general executive over all city departments, appointing and supervising the chief of police, chief of fire department, city engineer, and city finance director. The manager brings policy questions to the commission, which gives directives. If the manager loses support, a majority of the commission can discharge him or her.

One of the problems of this system is that it is not easy to separate policy from administration. It becomes difficult for issues on policy to be focused for the voters in elections. Partly for this reason, larger cities with more complex issues often adopt the strong-mayor type.

County Forms of Government

There are three major types of county government. The traditional form is characterized by *dispersed authority* (fig. 11.4). The voters elect the county commission, which is the county legislative and executive body over certain functions. It sets the tax rates, enacts county ordinances, and administers some functions of county government, such as roads. But the voters also elect other county administrators who are then independent of the commission; in Florida, they include the sheriff, the county clerk (who also keeps county finances and is clerk of the court and record keeper for the commission), the county tax appraiser, the tax collector, and the supervisor of elections. The school system, it should be noted, is under a separate county school board and the superintendent of schools. This *disintegrative system* of administration was designed for a rural America and is difficult to adapt for the provision of urban services for an urbanized county.

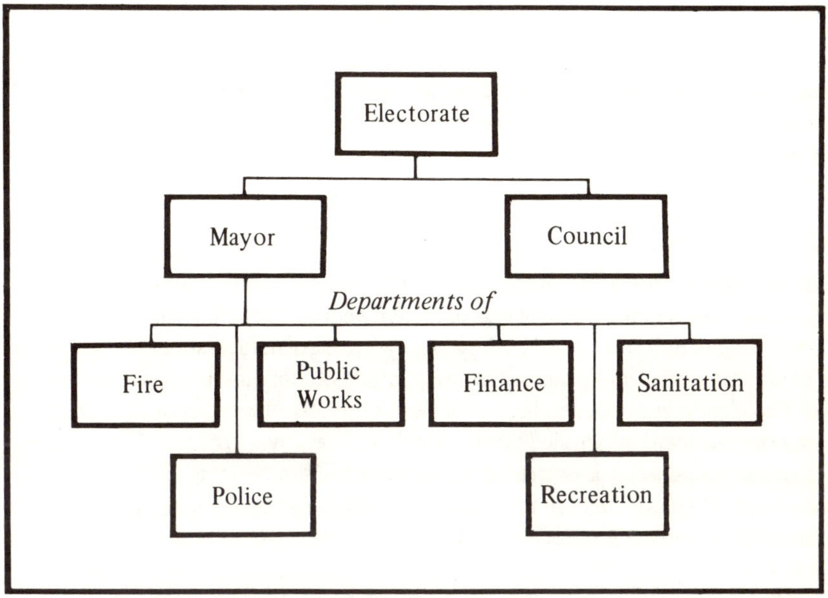

Fig. 11.1. Mayor-Council Type of City Government

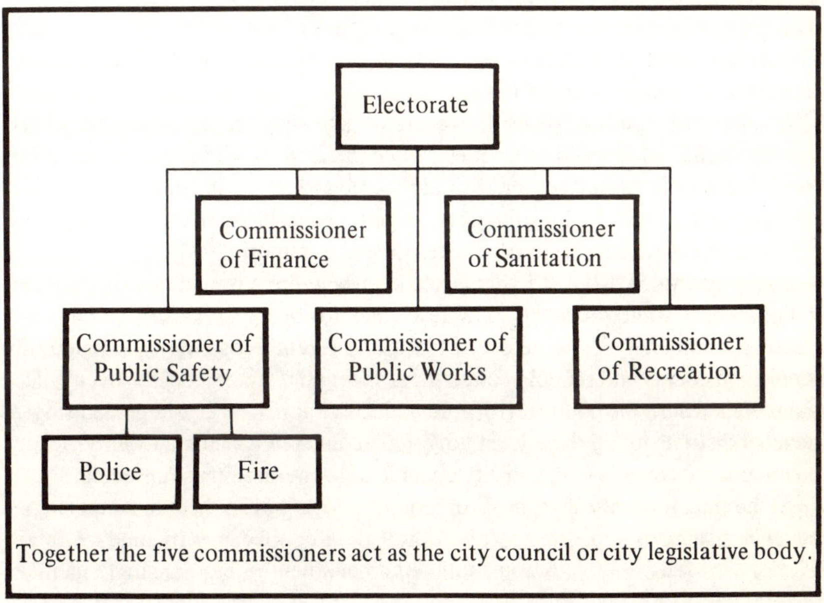

Fig. 11.2. City Commission Government

Consequently, two other forms have emerged in Florida. The *commission-manager form* is modeled after the commission-manager form of city government; it is employed in the Dade–Metro system. The other is the Jacksonville–Duval County type, which has the *strong-mayor* format, but for a county.

Local Elections

Single-member versus at-large election of councilmen and commissioners. — An issue of considerable debate in regard to members of city and county commissions and in regard to county school boards is how election districts should be drawn up. To put this matter into perspective, we should note that in the nineteenth century city commission or council members were generally elected from districts of the city known as wards. This led to what was known as "ward politics." Each council member bargained, for example, for a number of street lights for his ward, and there would be no attention to an overall system of street lighting. Each councilman had a narrow point of view. This method led to a reform movement after 1900.

Under the reform, members of city councils or commissions were elected at large, though candidates for these offices have typically been required to reside in specific districts. The aim was to promote the election of commissioners with a broader point of view and to encourage a larger view of city and county programs. The at-large election is typical of the commission-manager type of government. Florida has had at-large election of county commissioners and school board members since it became a state in 1845.

In some other southern states, however, at-large elections have been associated with the denial of seats to minorities. Since the U.S. Civil Rights Act of 1965, many federal courts have ordered single-member districts in southern cities and counties where there had been recent adoption of at-large elections, and where city, county, or school services had been denied to minorities.

It may be argued that districting is needed where there is evidence of polarized voting, where white precincts show few votes for black candidates and at-large elections continually show defeat of blacks. A recent Pensacola case found this problem in county and school board at-large elections, and to a degree in city elections. As a result, the court in 1978 ordered a combination of at-large and single-member districts for all three local government units in Escambia County: school board, county commission, and city council and commission in Pensacola.

At the state level, the argument for requiring local government to adopt single-member districts is supported by the NAACP, the Republican Party, and Common Cause, a citizens' lobby. A constitutional amendment to require single-member districts has been proposed.

On the other hand, at-large elections in cities such as Jacksonville and Gaines-

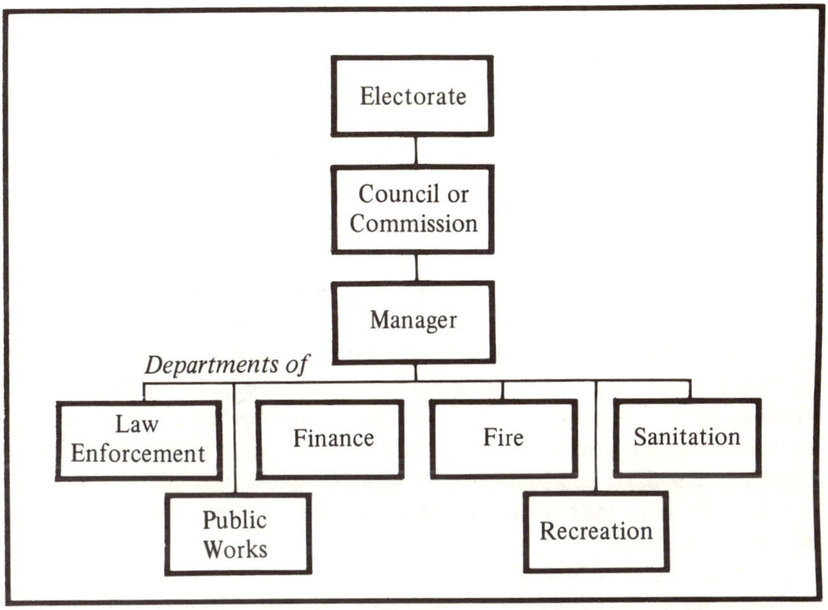

Fig. 11.3 Commission/Council-Manager Type of City Government (also County Manager Type)

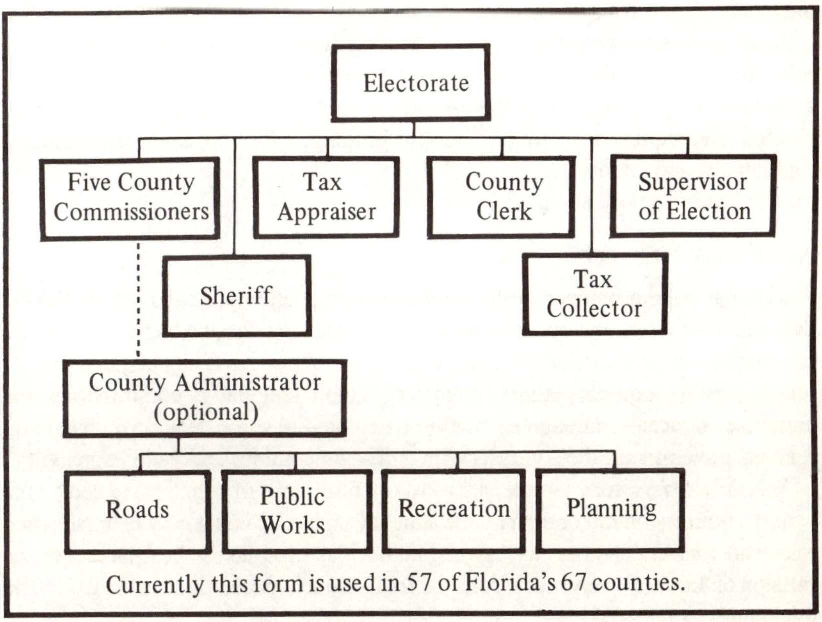

Fig. 11.4. Traditional Form of County Government

ville do result in the choice of minority members for city councils, school boards, and county commissions. Also such elections permit minorities to influence the choices of more than a single individual, because they vote for more than one candidate. The result may be that there is more impact on the total number of those serving on a council.

Thus there is argument for both single-member districts and at-large elections. A combination such as that in Jacksonville and in Pensacola could be the answer.

Nonpartisan or party elections. — At the local government level most Florida cities hold city elections at a different time from the state and federal elections, often in the spring. This is to permit voters to focus on city or county issues. Also, most city elections are by nonpartisan ballot, i.e.,the candidate's political party is not listed. This is to assure a choice of qualified candidates and to encourage attention to local issues. An unfortunate result is that turnout in city elections, on the average, is only 20 to 30 percent of the registered voters.

County elections and school board elections in Florida are held at the time of the regular fall elections.

Local referenda. — At the time of the city elections there may be local issues on the ballot, such as proposals for fair housing ordinances, antismoking provisions, planning and zoning procedures, environmental protection and limits to growth, and so on. A local ordinance may be proposed, to become effective if approved by the voters.

Local government reform issues. — Among other issues that arise in local government are the establishment of a merit system for employment; provision for classifying employees to provide uniform pay scales; provision for central purchasing; and requirements for competitive bidding. All of these are reform issues for both city and county.

New Forms: Regional Governments

Florida has been a pioneer in the establishment of alternatives to the traditional dominance of cities and counties in local governance. These experiments can be summarized in five categories: special districts, metro governments, councils of government (or regional planning councils), regional regulatory commissions, and corporate advocates. Though each will be explored in some detail in a chapter on regional government, the contrasts with cities and counties are readily apparent.

Special districts, for example, are most often subunits of counties created by the county commission rather than by the state legislature. Thus it may be misleading to consider special districts as regional authorities, despite the fact that the Commission on Local Government found 28 multicounty special districts in 1974. The total number of special districts in Florida is 1,200.

There are two major types of such districts. The first type are dependent districts, usually multipurpose, such as urban service districts, which are administered by the county commission itself yet exist in only part of the county's area. The second type are independent special districts, which exist usually for a single purpose and have a specially elected managerial board.

An independent special district, as the name implies, deals with narrowly prescribed functions: navigation and flood control, soil conservation, utilities, and fire. Generally these districts provide a single service for which they have the right to tax. They are usually governed by a district board elected from the appropriate population and by professional staffs. Special districts furnish a mechanism by which unincorporated areas can gain services specific to their needs without becoming municipalities. They also provide a way to cut across the traditional boundaries of cities and counties in cases where a specially designed unit can handle a problem more effectively.

The proliferation of special districts can, of course, cause fragmentation of government, making coordination policy and public control difficult. With a host of small boards to be elected to service the same area, voters may act without having the least knowledge of the candidates. Districts are not, as a rule, carefully monitored by the citizenry and are therefore easily dominated by self-interest cliques.

Metro government is in some ways at the opposite extreme from special districts; it is an attempt to centralize and coordinate all governmental activity in a given region. There are two such experiments in Florida: Miami–Dade County and Jacksonville–Duval County. Though neither has completely abolished cities and special districts, each has established a central governmental authority for the entire region. The Miami–Dade County venture is perhaps the less radical, since it continues the traditional two levels of government — the cities and Dade County — while attempting to rationalize the functions each carries out. One author has called the Miami structure a "comprehensive urban plan." The traditional governments are organized by charter to work closely together. The county, renamed Metro, emphasizes the role of local coordinator, rather than state functionary or service provider for unincorporated areas.

Jacksonville–Duval County, on the other hand, has attempted to eliminate city governments as well as the traditional county machinery and autonomous special districts. One metro government forms a consolidation of powers originally diffused throughout the Duval County area. Because of this radical recentralization, Jacksonville has adopted a commission and elected-executive form of government (also called the strong-mayor type), thereby giving the electorate a direct check on both legislators and the executive. Miami has selected the commission-manager plan instead, reasoning that the continued existence of cities already provides the check of federalism in their system. Jacksonville also adopted a mixture of the at-large and the district electoral system for its council.

Metro government, then, is an attempt to wed city, county, and special district powers as well as to join their boundaries toward a single multifunctional body capable of encapsulating urban sprawl. Much like its alternative, annexation, the metro system is an attempt to put the socioeconomic city back under a single political jurisdiction. However, unlike annexation, the metro government co-opts the powers of the county and special districts as well as of the municipality to tame a megalopolis. Thus metros usually result in a revitalization of county government under a different name, whereas annexation reenforces the autonomy of traditional municipal units.

Metros and special districts share with cities and counties a direct relationship to the electorate as well as a measure of autonomy from state control. The remaining forms of regional governance in Florida are only indirectly tied to the electorate and have less autonomy from state and national authorities. Councils of government — generally called regional planning councils in Florida — are the result of cooperative agreements between cities and counties under strong pressure from state and federal agencies. Councils of government are not part of a state bureaucracy, nor are they incorporated under a state charter. Their legal status is defined by one of two state statutes (FS 160 or FS 163), which differ primarily in the representational formula they provide. The charter of these organizations is simply the agreement between the member governments, though the councils must function under state procedures.

In most cases these councils were formed to respond to the demands of state and federal agencies for regional coordination of government grant applications and later to review land uses that would have a regional impact. These purposes are mirrored in the heavy funding of these councils from state sources. However, the councils are governed by boards composed of representatives appointed by member cities and counties. The council reacts to policies brought by an executive director and his staff, much as the members of the United Nations might react to the secretary-general. There are few conflicts. If the executive director can get a grant to fund a project, the board will not stand in the way.

Thus, in addition to grant clearance, these councils produce a variety of planning studies with grant moneys and occasionally become administrators of regionally focused federal or state programs on a contractual basis. Councils of government have no powers to tax or to enforce their policies save through appeals to member governments or their state sponsors. Regional planning councils, organized under chapter 160, Florida Statutes, must report their plans to the State Department of Community Affairs for approval. Developments of regional impact must also be reviewed through this channel. Planning councils have limited powers to act.

State regional regulatory commissions, on the other hand, may have substantial power, even the power to tax. Like special districts, these commissions serve a limited number of functions. For example, the five state water districts possess wide-ranging powers but focus on water usage and the protection of existing supplies. State authorities like the water districts have the power to permit water use as well as to purchase land and to raise taxes.

Corporate advocates also share most of the structural alternatives of the regional regulatory commission, with the exception that they have greater autonomy. They are independent corporations that are tied to state and federal bureaucracies only because they are dependent on grant aid from these bureaucracies. Like councils of government and regulatory commissions, they plan and approve grant requests. On occasion, they may administer federal or state programs; however, while other regional bodies act as advisors to or regulators of local government, corporate advocates may take a more assertive stance. They are essentially government-supported interest groups expected to produce community change.

For example, health systems agencies and mental health agencies advocate as well as plan health care facilities. Community action agencies press for local poverty relief as well as poverty programs. Corporate status allows these agencies to claim the standing of an independent local group. Guidelines from higher levels of government also set the structure of their governing boards and of their staffs.

Summary. — Regional governments are more responsive to state and federal controls and less connected to local constituencies than cities and counties are. Some, like regional regulatory agencies, are part of a hierarchical bureaucratic structure but are granted a degree of autonomy from that structure so that they may respond better to local problems. Others, like corporate advocates and councils of government, are regulated by funding rather than by legal constraints. Only special districts and metro governments have any power that even resembles the freedom and local control of traditional local governments.

If the new regional authorities are compared in terms of power rather than of automony, however, a different ranking emerges. Metro governments have the most power, both in the functions they can provide and in their ability to enforce policy directives. Councils of government are also multifunctional, but they do not have similar enforcement powers. Special districts and regional regulatory commissions are narrow in focus but possess sanctions to work their wills: the corporate advocates, equally narrow, have basically the powers to persuade.

What all regional governments do share is the desire to centralize decisions that have lacked coordination under traditional city and county government. They are responses to the fragmentation of government authority in the face of urban sprawl, yet their very number contributes to that fragmentation. The Commission on Local Government, therefore, made a significant suggestion when it proposed multicounty planning commissions in an attempt to reduce the number of regional units. The problem faced by such commissions, however, is which boundary lines to select. The very reason for the multiplicity is the failure of any single district arrangement to encapsulate the growing city.

Conclusion

This chapter has been full of contradictory definitions and categorizations. Local government, at its core, is divided between two masters. Cities, counties, and regional authorities are all creatures of the state with responsibilities to local populations. To be sure, they differ in their organization, assignment of functions, and autonomy, but each has a different strategy for mixing local opinion and state purpose.

The proliferation of forms of local government in recent years is a response to the growth of cities beyond their legal borders and to the realization that different problems are best addressed by units with different boundaries. The trend is toward larger units with greater functional specialization. The problems that urban growth and these new forms of government pose for the implementation of state policy and the continued self-determination of local citizens will be investigated in the next two chapters. Change is very much in Florida's future, and local government will bear a heavy burden as the state meets this challenge.

Note: Information in this introductory chapter is amplified in the bibliographical references in chapters 12 and 13.

12 Cities and Counties

by Robert Benedetti

NEW COLLEGE, UNIVERSITY OF SOUTH FLORIDA

and Manning Dauer

UNIVERSITY OF FLORIDA

A knowledge of the legal relationships that define local governments is indispensable to an understanding of local politics in Florida. But in addition to their powers and responsibilities formally spelled out in statutes, cities and counties make informal or extralegal adaptations to help resolve the issues facing them. A theory of local politics thus includes at least three components: the legal powers of local governments, the social problems they are expected to solve, and the informal arrangements, or customs, that evolve to meet pressing local needs.

We have seen in the preceding chapter that cities and counties are creatures of the state but that their customary autonomy and overlapping jurisdictions lead them to the brink of conflict. The rise of regional governments and, behind them, a new activism on the part of state and federal authorities, have further complicated the effective conduct of local governance. Cities and counties in Florida are prepared to cope with the complexity of intergovernmental relations that recent laws have prescribed for them. Compliance with state and federal regulations, however, may compel local governments to be less responsive to the needs of local citizens.

To neglect demands from below invites conflict, for those demands are increasing and citizens view present responses to them as inadequate. The demographic characteristics of Florida's cities and counties and the inadequacy of services presently provided by those cities explain why demands on local governments are increasing. To the extent that social cleavages divide the communities served by local governments, and to the degree that governments fail to provide expected services, citizens are provoked to insist on more and better. Moreover, cities and counties have developed only rudimentary methods for ascertaining what issues their local citizens deem most pressing. Citizen concerns, therefore, have less impact than they would if the structures and procedures for citizen participation were more adequate. The development of party machinery at the local level or of neighborhood and civic group networks could stimulate citizen input. Thus in Florida conflicts between groups may go un-

Note: The introductory section and the parts of this chapter on city government were written by Robert Benedetti. Manning Dauer wrote the sections on county government.

heard and their call for services may go unrecorded as long as opportunities for the public to voice its concerns are limited.

A Demographic Portrait of Florida's Cities and Counties

Florida's communities are meccas for persons who would begin a new life. Between 1970 and 1975, 90 percent of Florida's largest cities grew faster than the national average. The growth rates of 53 percent for the counties and more than 37 percent for the larger cities were above the growth rate of the state as a whole. Of the ten metropolitan areas in the United States that reported a population increase between 1970 and 1974, six were in Florida. In 1970 the Office of Management and Budget, an administrative agency of the federal executive branch, listed only nine regions as Standard Metropolitan Statistical Areas (SMSAs) in Florida. Since then the number has risen to sixteen. As the Office of Management and Budget reserves this designation for metropolitan areas of significant size and complexity, the increase in their number in Florida indicates that the state is fast becoming a major urban state. The SMSAs designated are:

Bradenton*
Daytona Beach*
Ft. Lauderdale–Hollywood
Ft. Myers*
Gainesville
Jacksonville
Lakeland–Winter Haven*
Melbourne–Titusville–Cocoa*
Miami
Orlando
Panama City*
Pensacola
Sarasota*
Tallahassee
Tampa–St. Petersburg
West Palm Beach–Boca Raton

*Since 1970.

The exceptional migration into Florida has been going on for over 25 years. Typically, large central cities experienced their greatest growth in the period 1950–60 (as did the state as a whole). Inmigration has continued at a lessening pace, dipping between 1960 and 1970 but rebounding since 1970 in most areas. (Of the 87 cities of over 10,000 population, only six reported declines in the period 1970–75; between 1970 and 1974 only one county, Gadsden, declined in population.) Thus Florida's local governments have been constantly under pressure not only to provide basic services (police, fire protection, highways, etc.) for growing numbers of residents but also to create a sense of community identity for a burgeoning immigrant population. The settlement patterns of the immigrants and their social characteristics further complicated the local governments' problems. For governments that fell behind in their responsibilities, there have been few chances to catch up.

This quarter century of rapid population growth has affected all of Florida's cities and counties, but the degree of impact has varied greatly. At present the pressures of inmigration are easing in the Miami-Dade, Tampa-Hillsborough, and Jacksonville-Duval areas, but these are increasing in Sarasota, Bradenton-Manatee, and Ft. Myers–Lee. Overcrowding has been a more serious problem for some counties than for others: Pinellas County, for example, has almost three times as many persons per square mile as Duval County or Dade County, so additional inmigrants are of particular concern there.

The metropolitan areas surrounding major cities have grown at a particularly fast pace. Between 1960 and 1970, the City of Miami grew at a rate of 14.8 percent — but the metropolitan area surrounding the city grew at a rate of 35.6 percent. The creation of the Dade County Metro government extended services to the newly populous areas around the central city. But around Orlando, Tampa, West Palm Beach, or Pensacola, where similar growth patterns occurred, no metropolitan government was available. Since 1970 the nonmetropolitan and unincorporated areas have been growing faster than the cities. Outside the cities' legal borders a population explosion is taking place. These satellite communities want to share the resources of the cities, but they resist full incorporation into them. Recent innovations in regional governments, annexation, and consolidation, therefore, have come none too soon.

Florida's local governments must now respond not only to urban dwellers just outside their borders, but they must also serve a diverse set of subcommunities that have grown up within the city proper. In 1970 over 75 percent of Florida's counties had more black residents than the national average. Of Florida's larger cities 60 percent have black communities larger than the national average, and 20 percent of these cities are one-quarter or more black. Ft. Pierce, a city of over 25,000, is approaching a black majority, and two smaller cities, Belle Glade and Riviera Beach, now have black majorities. Few blacks are recent inmigrants; rather they are long-time residents whose needs have until recently been largely neglected. Long excluded from political participation, they are now voicing their demands for governmental services. Local governments must therefore right old wrongs and at the same time discover ways to meet the needs of new residents.

One might expect that the new residents would be easily absorbed, but this is not always the case. Persons arriving from foreign countries and cultures need specialized social services and may face discrimination in some Florida communities. In the early 1980s, 36 percent of Dade County's population was Hispanic, as was over half of the cities of Miami and Hialeah. There are sizable Hispanic communities in Tampa, Miami Beach, and Coral Gables. More than half of Florida's large cities had a greater percentage of foreign-born residents in 1970 than the national average. Sarasota, Palm Beach, Pinellas, Monroe, and Broward counties all have about 20 percent foreign-born residents. Forty percent of Dade County's population in 1970 was foreign born; just over half of that group were from Latin American countries. In recent years, Canadians, Germans, Britons, Italians, and even Russians have come to Florida in significant numbers. These immigrants are all alien to the social and political institutions of the United States, and many of them require the help of local government in one form or another. Florida's cities and counties, therefore, must socialize as well as provide services for cosmopolitan communities.

Florida has at the same time become the retirement capital of the United States (if not of the world), with 17.3 percent of the state population sixty-five or older in 1980. Twenty-one of Florida's 67 counties are at or above this average. Miami Beach's population over sixty-five is 51 percent although the average for Dade County is only 15 percent. Counties with large populations over age sixty-five include Palm Beach, 23 percent; Collier (Naples), 19.1 percent; Lee (Ft. Myers), 22 percent; Sarasota, 30 percent; Pinellas (St. Petersburg), 28 percent; Broward (Ft. Lauderdale), 22 percent; Volusia (Daytona Beach), 22 percent; Manatee (Bradenton), 27 percent; Hernando (Brooksville), 24.4 percent; Pasco (New Port Richey), 30.7 percent. These counties include entire retirement communities. Retired people bring both their wealth and their experience to Florida, but they also demand a complex variety of services, which cities are just beginning to recognize. More significantly, they are often on fixed incomes and are particularly sensitive to changes in utility rate or tax structures. With time on their hands, the need for services on their minds, and a built-in sensitivity to tax increases, senior citizens are emerging as a powerful force in local politics. The Gray Panthers and the American Association of Retired Persons are active in Florida, and retired persons also voice their wishes through a growing number of homeowners groups. Since the package of taxes and services acceptable to a retired community may not be acceptable to younger segments of the society, groups of retired persons are more and more often pressed into battle in local politics.

Local governments thus face rifts between newcomers and long-time residents, between black or other ethnic minorities and a white majority, and between old and young over the preservation of different life styles and competing needs for govermental support. These groups require not only a mediator for their differences but a benefactor for their needs. When government can afford to benefit all, local pluralism can be maintained; but when resources are scarce, policies benefiting one group rather than another may be unavoidable. The array of services provided by cities and counties illustrates that local governments have sometimes had to make hard choices. The advent of some 600,000 Cuban and Hispanic residents in Dade County raised ethnic tensions not only between whites and Hispanics but also blacks and Hispanics. The acute pressure for minimum-wage jobs gave rise to serious racial outbreaks in two black ghetto areas of Miami.

City Services

In Florida's cities old and young, black and white, new arrival and long-time resident all face problems that require governmental attention. City governments, however, have neither the legal powers nor the financial resources to address each and every issue that local residents may raise. The functions of municipal government in Florida are in fact less diversified than in many other states. Virtually all U.S. cities provide for public safety (police and fire departments) and highway or transportation maintenance. As table 12.1 indicates, however, other functions are not universally provided.

Florida's cities do not supply judicial, educational, and welfare services. Education is a county function, managed by county school districts and their boards, which are increasingly the objects of state regulations. Welfare and judicial functions are largely discharged by the state. But the problems that involve education and welfare have a heavy impact on the quality of life in the cities.

The average percentage of black pupils is higher in half of Florida's cities than it is in the state as a whole or nationally. Efforts toward school desegregation can create community frictions that may require municipal services — police intervention, the formation of human rights boards, specialized employment opportunities. However, even in Jacksonville and Miami, where municipal governments span the county, schools are separately administered, limiting the opportunity for coordination between municipal offerings and educational planning. Thus the cities must deal with the results of embattled educational systems over which they have no direct control.

Similarly, poverty is a problem that municipal governments approach only tangentially. Half of Florida's largest cities have a larger percentage of people below the poverty level than the average nationally. This number is particularly startling in light of the number of large cities, 65 percent, which have a per capita income figure above the national average. The very rich and the very poor rarely coexist in the same town, despite examples like Miami Beach where

13 percent of the families were at the poverty level, and 11 percent earned over $25,000 annually in 1975. More typical is Boca Raton with many very rich (15.5 percent) and few poor (4.6 percent) or Bradenton with many poor (17.8 percent) and few very rich (1.8 percent). Nationally, 20.6 percent of all families made $15,000 annually in 1975; of Florida's 13 large cities with a higher percentage than the national average, only four (Sarasota, Tallahassee, Delray Beach, and Miami Beach) had more families below the poverty level than the average figure for the nation. Given the fact that the rich and the poor are located in different cities, it is understandable that welfare policy is a state function. Poverty creates an increased demand for local services, but the cities are denied a direct role in alleviating this problem. In recognition of the burden that the disadvantaged place on cities, the Commission on Local Government proposed in 1974 a grant program of $7 million annually to help municipalities develop services for the poor.

Yet, despite the existence of problems whose solutions lie with other authorities, Florida cities do exercise considerable control over their physical and human environments. To appreciate the functions cities can provide in Florida, it

TABLE 12.1. Functions Provided by City Governments

	Percentage Providing Service Nationally	Percentage Providing Service in Florida
Judicial	12	0
Education	22	0
Welfare	24	0
Hospital	13	9
Health	70	55
Sewers	60	68
Sanitation	72	91
Parks and recreation	89	100

SOURCE: Liebert, 1976, pp. 22, 201.

is important to review briefly the areas of housing, public safety, transportation, health care, environmental protection, and land use planning. In all of these, cities play more than just a supporting role, but in none can a city be entirely free from the need for intergovernmental cooperation.

Housing. — The quality of housing is often measured by the percentage of homes that are without plumbing or in which there is overcrowding (more than

1.01 persons per room). Only 12.5 percent of Florida's cities have more homes without plumbing than the national average. If we measure overcrowding, 27.5 percent of Florida's larger cities have more homes overcrowded than the national average. To whatever extent governmental policy is responsible for keeping most Florida cities at or below the national average for housing blight, municipal governments must receive credit, for housing is their responsibility. Cities enforce building codes, prepare and administer development plans and zoning ordinances, and have the right to organize urban renewal projects. It is difficult to measure the success of local governments in holding builders and homeowners to codes, comprehensive plans, and zoning ordinances. Some idea of urban renewal activity can be found in the number of federal grant requests originating in the state. In 1975 Florida stood eleventh among all states in funds received for low-income public housing and eighteenth for other urban renewal projects. So some Florida cities are actively pursuing a better housing mix. Yet, as Florida ranked eighth in population in the country in 1974, the state may not yet be active enough to gain its full share of federal funds.

Public safety. — Public safety presents a great challenge to the cities. The crime rate in 90 percent of Florida's larger cities is above the national average. But given the transient society of many of Florida's tourist cities, as well as the wealth represented within them, it is not surprising that crime is a major problem. What is surprising, considering the nature of much of the state's building, is the number of "points of deficiency" given the cities for fire safety. On a scale of 1 to 10, where 1 indicates the fewest deficiencies, 62 percent of Florida cities reporting had 6 points or above. In response to the threats of crime and fire, Florida has employed the eighth largest public safety force (police and fire) in the nation. But the number of public safety personnel per capita was less than the national average in 1975.

Transportation. — Florida's cities have a better record in transportation than in other areas. They share the responsibility for highway construction with state and county governments. Though it is difficult to determine if the cities are bearing their full share of the burden, 57.5 percent of the larger cities do allocate a greater percentage of their budgets to highways than do similar cities nationally. But mass transit has yet to be developed in Florida beyond city and county bus systems. These systems often run in the red, a fact which provoked the Commission on Local Government to propose in 1974 that the state share some of the costs of running them. To the extent that the issue has been addressed in a more sophisticated fashion it has been on a regional basis. The ill-fated Tampa Bay Area Rapid Transit project (TBART) is illustrative. It used federal aid to undertake extensive transportation planning; but its proposals were never accepted by member communities, and TBART has since folded. As more senior citizens, many dependent on public transportation, enter the political arena, the debate over mass transit may intensify. In the early eighties, when federal funds for transportation were sharply reduced and a complete curtailment proposed, the state raised the gasoline tax and authorized additional county gasoline taxes to support road construction and give some financial assistance to local public transportation systems.

Airports also have been treated as regional concerns. In some instances, Tampa, for example, the mayor serves on the airport authority along with county representatives. In other cases airports are run by independently elected boards. In Jacksonville the Port and Airport Authority is appointed partly by the mayor and partly by the governor. In Miami-Dade the Metro Council sits as the Port Authority and can appoint its director. Generally airports have operated as self-contained units, though rising concern over environmental quality may earn them increasing municipal attention.

Health. — A problem of particular interest to retirees is the level of availability of health care. One indicator of available care is the number of hospital beds per 100,000 population. In 1974, the national figure was 720 beds per 100,000 people; Florida's was 658 per 100,000. However, none of the nine Florida SMSAs reporting approached even the state average, much less the national figure. The number of beds available is further complicated by the fact that beds are not evenly distributed within SMSAs; some hospitals have excess capacity, others substantially less than is needed. Florida's inadequate supply and distribution of hospital beds cannot be laid wholly at the door of municipalities. In a survey of urban services, reported in table 12.1, only two of Florida's cities of over 25,000 population claimed responsibility for hospitals. Furthermore, only 55 percent of these larger cities even mentioned health as one of their responsibilities. Thus, health care is a shared function that appears to be falling between the cracks. The Commission on Local Government suspected that the state had some responsibility for this confusion: "The Commission has noted not only a substantial lack of data at the state level [on health services] but also conflicting policy decisions at the state level resulting in the blurring of local responsibilities." The role of municipalities in health care needs more precise definition before improvement can be expected. Unfortunately, the health systems agencies organized with federal funds to plan for local health care do not follow municipal lines, nor do they necessarily include representatives from local governments.

Environment. — Florida's cities have traditionally had a major responsibility in the protection of the environment through proper sewer construction, waste disposal, parks maintenance, water provision, and many other services. In the survey reported in table 12.1, 68 percent of the larger cities reported that they provided sewers, 91 percent that they provided for sanitation, and 100 percent that they oversaw park and recreation facilities. But given the delicate nature of Florida's environment, future activities will require careful regional coordination. Cities may continue to play a vital role in collecting waste, maintaining parks, and selling potable water, but the disposal of waste, the designation of parks, and the production of potable water may become the responsibilities of higher levels of government. (More will be said about the import of environmental concerns on urban areas in the discussion of regional governments in chapter 13.)

Land use planning. — Planning and zoning, near and dear to the hearts of city governments, allow a city to control the life style of the citizens within its confines. Cities violently oppose surrendering these powers to other levels of government. The continuing argument in Sarasota County over the right of North Port, a "developer's town," to plan and zone without county oversight is a good example. Though the other cities in Sarasota County objected to the lack of environmental concern traditionally shown by North Port in its approval of housing developments, they have taken North Port's side in the controversy for fear that the county may in the future attempt to strip them of their powers of defining land use.

Land use controls in a city are often inadequate to preserve a style of life; developments across municipal borders may influence air and water quality, traffic on city streets, the type of people who use local facilities, and so on. Thus the need to locate some planning power beyond the locality increases as cities become interdependent with their environs. City zoning and planning are critical defenses but are seldom sufficient to guarantee the character of a community in times of rapid growth. In Florida, developments of regional impact are reviewed not only by regional planning councils but also by state agencies whose input is coordinated through the state Department of Community Affairs. Cities and counties are required to produce a regional master plan, which is subject to advisory review by regional planning councils and the Department of Community Affairs. The issue of enforcement authority over such plans is still sharply debated by the legislature. Cities and counties have maintained control of land use but have little say in how planning of other local governments may influence their communities. The time when local governments alone decided how to distribute the right to develop is quickly passing. Florida's cities do have responsibilities in housing, public safety, transportation, environmental planning, and land-use control. There are ample problems and issues in these areas, but in seeking solutions, cities face a growing need to coordinate with higher authorities.

City Administration

Whatever their functions, cities continually risk making their own administration a public issue. Though accusations of corruption are not widespread, the management strategies of Florida's cities may be questioned, specifically the ways in which cities collect revenue and hire personnel. Local taxpayers' associations are increasingly concerned about rising tax rates, new assessments, fewer grants-in-aid from state and federal sources, and increasing demands from local employees.

In light of the passage of Proposition 13 in California, it is useful to note that the per capita revenue raised by property taxes in California in 1975 was more than twice the comparable figure for Florida. Based on 1975 figures, Florida is tied with Pennsylvania and Idaho for thirty-second place in amount of per capita property tax revenue collected by cities. Cities depend on property taxes for only 22.0 percent of their total revenue. Thus, Florida cities, in part because of the homestead exemption, have had to find alternate sources of revenue to the property tax. In 1974, states picked up 19.8 percent of local budgets, while Florida underwrote only 18.1 percent. The state does rebate to cities from cigarette taxes collected in their limits, but this provides only limited funds. The 1980 constitutional amendment increasing homestead exemption for local property taxes to $25,000 has resulted in a serious increase in city millage on the smaller remaining tax base. This change, combined with the 1981 budget cuts in federal revenues for cities, has placed a serious burden on Florida's cities. The problem is compounded by loss of federal subsidies for expansion of sanitary sewer facilities, espcially serious in rapid growth areas. As a result there has been pressure on the state legislature, beginning in 1982, to earmark all or part of an additional one cent sales tax to replace revenue lost to cities, counties, and school boards.

The bond market is not convinced that cities are fiscally reliable. Of Florida's 87 cities over 10,000 population in 1975, Moody's Bond Record listed the status of 36 cities as A(1), 25 percent; A, 30 percent; Baa(1), 13.9 percent; Baa, 27.8 percent; Ba, 2.8 percent. None was accorded the top designation (Aaa or Aa); rather, all were rated as "medium grade," though the code number "1" means that 38 percent had strong investment attributes. The lower rating for Florida's cities than for other areas is presumably because of the state's municipal bankruptcies of the 1920s and 1930s.

Another problem is the organization of public employees. As of 1975, 40 percent of Florida's municipal employees were members of an employee collective bargaining organization as allowed by the state constitution. Among public employees only the schoolteachers are better organized. Such organization suggests that cities will no longer have firm control of their labor forces and may be constrained to improve wages or working conditions beyond their current desires. Further, the demands of such groups as the Police Benevolent Association and the firefighters' unions may influence public policy. To decide by labor agreement the type of police patrol or fire equipment wanted gives public employees special influence on issues that have previously been open to wider public discussion. In any case, city officials are beginning to see that labor negotiating is an art well worth learning. At the same time, they must cope with growing requirements for affirmative action, which further complicate personnel policy.

A review of the problems that face local governments leaves the impression that no citizen could be satisfied with the present state of affairs. But, recent surveys find that most Floridians are satisfied with the range of services local governments are providing. When asked if state and local services should be maintained or reduced, 55.2 percent of a statewide sample supported the current service level and 35.9 percent wanted it reduced further to save money. On the other hand, when asked about the most important problems facing Florida, community services were mentioned third, after inflation and taxes. Thus, Florida citizens may be communicating the same message as others across the nation: they do not mind paying the bill for many services if they feel they are getting the best management possible. Unfortunately, it is not always apparent to them that this is the case.

Formal and Informal City Structures

It has long been recognized that Florida is a leader in local government reform. The municipal reform movement in America dates from the early years of the century and is credited with the introduction of council-manager government, nonpartisan and at-large elections (in which the city votes as a whole), and, at a later date, metropolitan-wide governance. Though initially developed to combat boss politics, fiscal inefficiencies, and urban sprawl in northern cities, these reforms have been widely adopted in the South and West. As these areas were becoming urban at the time the reforms were proffered, it was only natural that these new ideas would be proposed to start off new towns.

The council-manager plan promised to eliminate the evils of patronage and fiscal waste. A trained, professional manager appointed by the elected city council was to be the executive officer of the city. He would bring efficiency but would remain under the watchful eye of the councilmen, who could remove him at will. The manager would insure that a professional bureaucracy replaced a staff of cronies and that equity replaced favoritism. In short, the principles of corporate management were to be transferred from business to government with the appointment of this official.

Florida had early converts to the council-manager idea, and the number has grown steadily: "The first council-manager charter was adopted in 1913 in Largo, and in 1920 there were five other cities — Lakeland, Ocala, St. Augustine, Tallahassee, and West Palm Beach — that had chosen this form of government. But the great increase in council-manager adoptions in the state came in the decade of great urban growth, the fifties, as the number of council-manager cities increased from 57 to 107, almost doubling. This jump in adoptions put Florida, in this respect, far ahead of all other states in the Southeast" (Kammerer et al., 1962). Enthusiasm for council-manager government continues to the present despite its abandonment by some towns — Cocoa Beach, Fort Myers, St. Cloud, and Tampa — and the prevalence of many new mayor-council towns in Broward and Seminole counties.

The dominance of this model is most evident in large cities. Though it is often assumed that elected executives usually run large cities, it is not so in Florida. Of the 8 cities of over 100,000 population in 1976, only half have city managers:

Jacksonville	550,801	mayor-council
Miami	343,977	council-manager
Tampa	278,829	mayor-council
St. Petersburg	236,923	council-manager
Fort Lauderdale	152,791	council-manager
Hialeah	126,125	mayor-council
Hollywood	118,872	council-manager
Orlando	118,661	mayor-council

Looking instead at cities of 10,000 population, 76 percent (66) have adopted council-manager plans and 24 percent (21) maintain mayor-council charters, compared to a nationwide distribution of 48 percent council-manager and 43 percent mayor-council governments. Clearly Florida is leading, not following, the rest of the nation in this reform.

Still, that the governmental form has been adopted widely does not necessarily mean the towns are utilizing it in the spirit in which it was intended. A majority of Florida's larger council-manager cities continue to elect mayors rather than provide that they be chosen from the councilmen after the election. This electoral independence empowers mayors to challenge the executive authority of the city manager. Kammerer found that the tenure of city managers is shorter in Florida towns that do elect mayors than in those that designate them after the election. One of her case studies details such a circumstance: "(Mayor) Smith did not hesitate to declare that he could run Orange Point better than any city manager. There is little doubt that Smith was a 'working boss.' He was up at six o'clock every morning to see the garbage trucks start out. Without question he knew more about the physical plant of the city than any city manager could possibly absorb before Smith decided it was time for the manager to leave city employment. Smith dominated city hall, and his normal procedure was to fire managers before their six months' probationary period was over."

Often the city managers who have succeeded in keeping their jobs for a considerable period have done so because of personal ties to a particular community rather than by their managerial skills. There is hope that the criteria for evaluating managers will become more stringent as city populations grow and become more diverse. Kammerer's findings suggest that when several groups are competing for political power, the city council will be unable to agree on criteria for judging a city manager's professional competence. Though it is unclear how many Florida towns are now able to set such criteria, the influx of population from many different places will stimulate the political diversity necessary to assure the enforcement of professional standards on city managers. Thus, the city manager form of government should continue to be perfected.

It is possible, however, that this increasing professionalization will come at the expense of citizen control. The city manager in Florida's past was often the puppet of community leaders, but in the future he may be in a position to play competing groups against one another, reserving for himself the initiative to execute policy as he sees fit. Florida's urban areas may be moving from the control of power elites to that of professional elites.

A challenge to this new type of elite, as well as to the old, should come from the voters as they elect councilmen. However, two traditional stimuli for citizens' participation — political parties and ward elections — have been avoided in Florida. Through the legacy of reform, the same logic that developed council-manager government suggests that parties and geographic representatives breed corruption. Parties pressure for patronage, and geographic units ignore the interest of the city as a whole. Therefore, in the name of a merit civil service and a citywide perspective, nonpartisan and at-large elections were packaged by reformers with the council-manager plan.

Florida's cities accepted nonpartisanship and at-large elections even when they avoided council-manager reform. Of the 21 Florida cities of over 10,000 population that have a mayor-council rather than a council-manager government, only two claim to use national party labels in local elections (Jacksonville and Fort Myers), though an additional two (Cocoa and Panama City) comment that they have local political parties. While 24 percent of Florida's larger cities (over 10,000 population) have council-manager government, only 4.6 percent have partisan elections. Though a similar phenomenon can be observed nationally, the gap is not as large. Thus nonpartisanship has penetrated even where other reforms have not.

Similarly, only 6 of the 87 cities of over 10,000 population in Florida elect any councilmen by wards; 4 are council-manager cities (Lake Worth, Ormond Beach, Pensacola, and St. Petersburg Beach), and the others have mayor-council governments (Jacksonville and Key West). The remaining 94 percent elect their councilmen at large, that is, from the city voting as a whole. Thus it is safe to conclude that neighborhood "machines" or voting blocs do not form as a rallying point for citizen participation. Wards run by bosses and their ward heelers are avoided but at the cost of a meaningful geographic representation.

In place of ward or party organizations, 18 of the larger cities report that organized citizens' groups do participate in electoral politics. Some of these are organizations like the League of Women Voters or the Municipal Leagues, which evaluate the qualifications of candidates or simply give them the opportunity to debate. For example, the Sarasota Civic League, a group of interested citizens several of whom have held elective office, interviews all candidates and publishes a rating (not qualified, qualified, well qualified, and exceptionally well qualified) in the local newspaper prior to the election. The impact of such groups is unclear, but they do not substitute for campaign organizations in mobilizing voters. In all probability such exercises clarify the thinking of those who vote regularly rather than stimulate new participants in the voting process.

Slightly different substitutes for party and ward organizations have been taxpayers' groups and unions' political action groups, both increasing in numbers. These move beyond civic or good government organizations in that they endorse candidates. Nonpartisan politics in Florida is fought largely in the newspapers. Political action groups and good government groups buy ads along with the candidates. Editors publish their selections on the editorial pages. The conscientious voter can survey claims and counterclaims before casting his ballot, but the reliance on press coverage disregards the nonsubscriber and the less interested voter. In towns with ordinances restricting the posting of signs, one would hardly know it was election time in Florida if it were not for the local paper.

A third category of organization has the potential to play a larger role in local electoral politics but has traditionally restricted its attention to lobbying between elections, often bypassing local officials altogether. Collectively this group could be labeled residential associations, but there are three diverse types: neighborhood, condominium, and mobile home park. All three have organized countywide and state coalitions to support particular legislative purposes. At the state level, all three focus on problems of land tenure, particularly in regard to tax rates, insurance policies, and tenants' rights.

On the other hand, their distinctive characteristics determine their role in local politics. Neighborhood associations in Florida were often formed as part of a subdivision or development. Only in a few large cities like Miami are neighborhood groups characterized by ethnic or religious solidarity. Generally neighbors may have been consigned to an association with the purchase of a particular home because some common element — lake, pool, country club, tennis court — required their attention after the developer had sold out his interest in the tract.

Such associations peak in the early years of the subdivision. They serve to mobilize the residents against a developer who has additional units to construct or a local government which fails to extend full city services to the subdivision. And because subdivision residents are often new to their town and to Florida the association provides a social setting in which to meet new people.

When the developer has gone, the city has provided its services satisfactorily, and newcomers have become familiar with the community, these organizations decline unless and until a particular crisis revitalizes them. They re-enter the political arena only when, for example, a new road threatens their peace or an airport their tranquility. In such cases they may move beyond lobbying incumbent politicians and attempt to place one of their own in political office as a guarantor of their interests.

Condominium associations differ from neighborhood associations in several ways. They are mandated by law, and every condominium resident must remain a member. As city services are usually arranged prior to the sale to the resident, these associations focus inward, toward internal maintenance rather than toward municipal decisionmaking. However, because of homogeneity of lifestyle and density of population, condominiums represent a potentially organized bloc of voters for a candidate who has the right issue to interest them. In other words, though condominium associations have as yet participated only tangentially in local politics, they have the potential to play a critical role as they collect and sort significant numbers of people who could thereafter be delivered easily to a candidate. As the upper middle class, which tends to buy condominiums, is generally predisposed to vote in elections, it is not difficult to imagine a candidate who appealed to condominium owners gaining the vote of every resident.

Mobile home parks, though in some cases administered as condominiums, have a more limited political potential. First, membership in these groups is often a requirement for purchase or rental in a given park, but the group itself may continue to be dominated by the owner/developer. Second, the association usually has a social rather than a political purpose; divisive political discussion is avoided. Finally, residents of mobile homes are often from the middle and lower-middle classes, a group less predisposed toward politics. Like neighborhood associations, their political interest may be aroused only in crisis situations.

While the tendency toward electoral participation differs among these groups, as yet none has come to dominate local politics by taking over the role of parties and ward machinery. They seldom try to aggregate citizen interests and to present issues to the political system. It can be argued that citizen groups need not participate directly in the electoral process for their ideas to be represented. Individual councilmen may aggregate the public's interest and represent any number of citizens' groups.

Unfortunately, the study of councilmen in Florida's politics has been neglected; but the councils seem less able to sample public opinion than councils elsewhere because of small size and overlapping terms of office. If a council is to take seriously its function as a representative of popular opinion, greater membership is required to assure that the diversity of the community is reflected in the council chamber.

A comparison of the size of city councils in Florida's larger cities with those of the rest of the nation implies that Florida does not value such diversity. The average size of councils in cities of over 10,000 population is 5.7; the comparable national figure is 6.6. Moreover, the average is misleading, because the overwhelming majority of cities (72 percent) contained councils of five members.

A second structural indication of the limitations of councilmen as barometers of popular opinion is the presence of overlapping terms of office. In 85 percent of Florida's larger cities, staggered terms of office prevent the voter from "cleaning house" by removing the entire council at once. Here again Florida follows the logic of the reform movement at the expense of encouraging popular input. As Robert Boynton explains this logic in the *Municipal Yearbook*

1976, "The election process is not considered the primary method by which the latest political mood of the community is transmitted to the council. Therefore no premium is placed on concurrent council terms. On the contrary, overlapping terms are thought of as providing for stability and continuity in decision-making."

To conclude, Florida cities have heavily subscribed to a reform model of government in which a professional manager serves a city council elected to minimize partisan and factional fighting. Such a system of government minimizes citizen input, particularly in the electoral process, in the name of efficient government. Though this tendency has been checked somewhat by competition between elected mayors and the manager and by the role of various citizens' groups in campaign politics, Florida's cities have yet to develop the structures necessary to aggregate and refine popular opinion. In fact, innovation in local government in Florida has moved to increase still further the distance between the local governing unit and its popular base. The state has become a leader in the development of metropolitan, areawide governments.

History of County Government

Traditionally, the unit of rural government in the United States has been the county. During America's first 150 years, county government only needed to provide limited local services to a primarily agricultural community. Individual farming families ran their own businesses, provided their own labor, and grew most of their own food. The crop was hauled to market, and there were occasionally other visits to town. Most roads were not paved. Water came from the farm well. There was little crime. This agricultural life style made few demands on government.

With this kind of community to govern, local officials served only part-time and were elected from among fellow farmers. They received fees, rather than a salary, for whatever services were performed. The governing body of the county, the commission, met once a month to supervise road repair and let a contract now and then. Law was enforced in the whole county by the sheriff, who was paid a fee for each arrest, for serving legal papers, and for attending court. He was elected independently of the county commission. For minor legal matters the county was divided into justice of the peace districts. Each such district had a constable to enforce the law. Other county officials, also part-time, paid by fees, and elected directly by the voters, included the county judge, the county clerk, and some others.

This simple structure for county government prevailed in most of America during the eighteenth, nineteenth, and early twentieth centuries. Then the advent of the automobile sparked the expansion of suburbia. Manufacturing and industry expanded to areas outside city limits. Housing developments and shopping centers sprang up to change the nature of much of the landscape. At the time of the 1980 census, 73.7 percent of America and 84.3 percent of Florida was urban. But "urban" was no longer neatly confined within city limits; it overflowed into county-governed regions. The traditional county governmental structure was not suitable for urban needs.

County Government in Florida

Present Florida county government, in most cases, remains typical of traditional county government, with one exception: the justice of the peace and constable districts have been abolished. Since the paving of roads, it is most convenient to concentrate county business at the county seat. However, in over 60 of Florida's 67 counties the rest of the structure of county government remains.

It can be noted here that this description of county government does not include schools. Each county is also a school district, with its elected county school board to manage the public schools, kindergarten through high school. The school board system is described in chapter 19.

Florida's system of county government (fig. 11.4) is built around a number of independently elected officials. (The concept goes back to the time when voters knew the capabilities of their neighbors and elected a specifically qualified person to do a particular job.) In a typical county the five commissioners, elected at large, comprise the county commission. They supervise and let contracts for the building of county roads and typically employ the county engineer, who supervises maintenance and has a work force for this purpose.

Other elected officials include the sheriff, no longer a part-time person, who employs deputies; the supervisor of elections, who maintains the voter registration rolls and employs part-time individuals to man the polling places on election day; and the county tax appraiser, who evaluates real property and sets up the tax rolls, from which the commission sets the tax rate. The tax collector receives the taxes and turns the funds over to the county clerk, who maintains the books and pays bills on approval of the commissioners. The county clerk is also clerk of the county court and maintains titles and other legal records. Each county is guaranteed all these officials under the Florida Constitution in Article 8, Section 1 (d). This same article, as interpreted by the Florida Supreme Court, guarantees each such officer independence from the county commission. The commission has jurisdiction only over its own functions and employees. It cannot set up a personnel or merit system that applies to the sheriff and his employees, or to the tax collector and his. The commission cannot provide for central purchasing, and without the clerk's cooperation it cannot use the system of accounts as a tool of management. It cannot set the budget for internal expenditures of the other county officers or their functions. Such a system of government and administration is called disintegrated.

There are checks on all independent county officials. First, they must stand for reelection every four years. Second, they are required to undergo an annual audit by an outside auditor. Third, for misfeasance, malfeasance, or nonfeasance, they may be suspended by the governor and removed from office, after a hearing, if the state senate so votes. Also they are subject to inquiry by the county grand jury and can be indicted and tried for violation of criminal law. But no coordination is provided in either the constitution or the statutes, and in the face of increasing demands for services in urban counties, this lack is a serious flaw.

The County as State Agency

In the past, the county essentially served as a state agency in several of its capacities. For instance, it maintained state and local roads. State departments which operate directly and not through the counties have been created: the Department of Transportation, which directly contracts for the building of state roads; the Department of State Revenue, which collects state taxes; and the Department of Health and Rehabilitative Services. Finally, the state has taken over the administration of the court system.

Other County Functions

Along with the new urban-suburban sprawl, county responsibilities have vastly increased. However, the Florida Supreme Court has handed down decisions that prohibit the taxing of city residents for operations primarily benefiting the county area and at the same time prohibit county residents from being taxed for services provided to a more specific area. This has led to the enactment of Chapter 125 of the Florida Statutes, providing for the establishment of "urban service districts" (Municipal Service Taxing Units) under the county commission. Such a district is an urbanized area of the county, usually just outside central city limits. In this area, any one of many urban services may be established: fire protection, street paving and maintenance, police patrol, trash collection, planning, and sewer facilities. The urban service district then becomes a special tax area, with a millage tax rate for that area only, which is set by the county commission. In separate ordinances, the county commission can set another millage rate for the rural portions of the county and a third rate for taxes levied on incorporated city areas.

As it happens, the traditional structure of county government as outlined in figure 11.4 is not too well suited for the provision of these extra services to separately designated areas. For instance, the sheriff, who may be expected to provide deputies for patrolling an urban service district, is not under the control of the county commission, since he is independently elected. The question arises of coordinating fire protection between city and urban service district fire departments. The same question applies to the coordination of water and sewer services and to trash and garbage collection.

The outcome is often a jerry-built governmental structure. Faced with a multitude of new responsibilities as one or more cities in the county continue to grow, the county commission can employ a county administrator, who then establishes departments for those services that the county will directly maintain. For example, a county already had an engineer; now, in addition to supervising county roads, his forces also pave and maintain streets in the urban service district. Such an administrator is hampered in several ways. Since the fiscal books for the county are kept by the county clerk, the county administrator lacks complete control of this tool of management. Also the commission may require him to have a centralized system of purchasing and an employee merit classification plan, but these cannot be made to apply to employees under the sheriff, the county clerk, the tax collector, or the appraiser. Elected officials can also be inconvenienced under the present system. If the sheriff does not like the budget assigned to him out of general revenue by the commission, he can appeal its decision to the state cabinet. In general, if there are jurisdictional disputes among the county officers, they can, and in many counties do, sue each other all the way to the state supreme court.

Recognizing this awkward situation, those who drew up the 1968 Florida Constitution provided for establishment of a county charter, if the voters of a county want a new system of government. The charter is to be written by a local charter commission, and, if approved by the voters of the county, it can supersede the county organization specified in Article 8, Section 1(d), outlined in figure 11.4. The locally elected charter commission can propose that all independently elected officials except the commission be eliminated. Usually such restructuring has not gone this far, but it does give the commission authority over budget, fiscal controls, and the establishment of central purchasing and a uniform employee classification system. Volusia County (Daytona Beach), Broward County (Ft. Lauderdale), and Sarasota County have established charter county governments.

It also should be noted that the comprehensive Planning Act of 1972 gives the county commission general planning authority, and the 1968 constitution and other statutes increase the power of counties so that the commission may enact ordinances for any local actions not prohibited by state law. This virtually reverses Dillon's Rule (discussed in chap. 11) that a local government unit can carry out only specific functions.

Solving Problems of Coordination

Looking closely at this modernization of county government machinery, one can see that it does not solve the problem of coordination between the county and its city or cities. There may be a county planning department separate from the city's planning department, separate personnel departments, separate central purchasing departments, and so on. Would not consolidated personnel departments and purchasing departments be more effective? Several solutions to these problems have been adopted and tried in various areas of Florida.

Contracts between units of local government. — For some time the tax assessing and collecting by all units of government within a county have been centralized in the offices of the county appraiser and the county tax collector. First, the tax rolls are made by the appraiser. Then the city commission and the county commission each sets its rate. The county tax collector sends out a single bill, and the incoming taxes are distributed to the accounts of the appropriate government units. The office expenses of appraising and collecting are charged to the taxes collected. Another example of this solution to the coordination difficulties is for the county commission to contract with the city for services in the urban service district, such as water mains or fire protection.

Annexation. — The solution preferred by many cities is to simply annex urbanized areas adjacent to the city limits. This solution leaves to the county its traditional function of providing rural services. The problem here is that, under Florida law, annexation is difficult, requiring a favorable vote by both city inhabitants and the inhabitants of the geographical area to be annexed.

Urban service districts. — An urban service district is preferred by both county officials and suburbanites, who enjoy in such a district a tax rate lower than the city tax rate.

Consolidation. — Two Florida counties, Duval (Jacksonville) and Dade (Miami), have followed different models of consolidating city and county governments. Those who designed the Jacksonville-Duval model completely eliminated the separate governments of these two areas and simply set up one government. Incidentally, they chose, among alternatives, an organization that provides a strong mayor-council type of government. Certain towns in the eastern and western parts of the county still continue to function semi-autonomously. The Dade-Miami plan establishes a federal system, with certain functions assigned to the county-wide Dade-Metro authority, organized under the commission-manager plan. The more than twenty cities in the county — including Miami, Miami Beach, Hialeah, and Coral Gables — still continue, but they have more limited functions than those of an ordinary city.

From a purely organizational standpoint, one or the other of the consolidation governments is more coherent than the traditional county vs. city structure. However, many voters are committed to having better access to their governmental officials, so consolidation proposals have been defeated by voters in many areas of the state, among them attempts to amalgamate the governments of Hillsborough County with Tampa, Alachua County with Gainesville, and Leon County with Tallahassee.

Fiscal Problems

Before Proposition 13 was adopted in California in 1978, Florida, by constitution and by statutes, placed limitations on the taxing powers of local governments. The 1885 and 1968 constitutions both prohibited local governments, whether city or county, from borrowing money through general obligation bonds unless such bond issues were approved by the voters. Local government units could float revenue bonds without such vote (e.g., a toll bridge, a marina, or other capital structure with costs paid by tolls, ticket sales, or rental fees). The 1968 constitution also places tax limits of no more than ten mills each on city governments, county governments, and school districts.

The legislature has, in return for the granting of state funds, placed even stricter limits on the taxing authority of school boards. The 1979 legislature placed a 5 percent limit on the annual increase permitted in local government budgets (not including revenue from new construction), unless additional millage is approved by the voters. The Florida Constitution exempts from taxation the first $25,000 of assessed value of an owner-occupied residence. This increase, combined with the Reagan administration's budget cuts, caused grave local millage increases by 1982. One result has been pressure that resulted in the enactment of an additional one cent sales tax to provide funds for counties and cities. A constitutional amendment allows the homestead exemption to be extended to renters who are permanent residents, but legislation on this topic has not been enacted. And the legislature may increase the homestead exemption by a rate tied to inflation. Thus local officials find their fiscal sources increasingly limited by the state.

Another complaint comes from county and other local officials, who often find the state mandating certain functions, for instance, requiring comprehensive local planning without providing additional funds for carrying it out. Standards for local jail facilities, regulated both by the state and by court decisions, may require additional incarceration services, but no additional funds are provided. County and other local officials thus often complain that they are asked to "make bricks without straw."

Assigned Government Functions

Florida does have fairly rational outlines for what should be done by cities, by counties, and by the school boards. Common school education is completely assigned to the school board, while welfare responsibilities and hospital services are county or state functions. Cities rarely have welfare or medical activities. A great hole in the structure is the matter of who should provide mass transportation facilities: city residents are the heaviest users of mass transit, but the system should extend into the county.

Summary

Relationships between the city and the county are in a state of flux. The classic distinction between the city as the unit of urban government and the county as both an arm of the state and the unit of rural government is no longer valid. In addition, the state is taking an increasingly direct role in administration of roads, welfare, and other areas formerly county-controlled. Four systems of adjustment between the city and the county hold out varying degrees of promise in clarifying roles. Clarification of the role of the state in local and regional affairs occurs in succeeding chapters, for example, chapter 13. Immediately, however, we turn to our chapter on regional government, including a survey of state-administered regional units, special districts, and cooperative councils, adding these agencies and their spheres of influence to the already complex mixture of governmental units holding authority over the citizens of Florida.

References

Bollens, John C., et al. *American County Government*. Los Angeles: Sage, 1969.

Commission on Local Government. *Final Report on Legislative Action*. Tallahassee, 1974.

———. *Special Report on Municipal Home Rule*. Tallahassee, 1973.

Grouby, Barbara, and Schellinger, Mary A. "Profiles of Individual Cities." In *Municipal Yearbook, 1978*. Washington: ICMA, 1978.

Kammerer, Gladys M., et al. *City Managers in Politics: An Analysis of Manager Tenure and Termination*. University of Florida Monographs, Social Sciences no. 13. Gainesville: University of Florida Press, 1962.

———. *The Urban Political Community*. Boston: Houghton, Mifflin, 1963.

Liebert, Roland J. *Disintegration and Political Action: The Changing Functions of City Governments in America*. New York: Academic Press, 1976.

Lockard, Duane. *The Politics of State and Local Government*. 2d ed. New York: Macmillan, 1974.

Marando, Vincent L., and Thomas, Robert D. *The Forgotten Governments: County Commissioners as Policy Makers*. Gainesville: University Presses of Florida, 1977.

Piven, Frances F., and Cloward, Richard A. *Regulating the Poor: The Functions of Public Relief*. New York: Random House, 1972.

Shank, Alan, and Conant, Ralph W. *Urban Perspectives, Politics and Policies*. Boston: Holbrook Press, 1975.

Sparkman, Steven L. "The History and Status of Local Government Powers in Florida." *University of Florida Law Review* 25 (1973).

Torrence, Susan Walker. *Grass Roots Government: The County in American Politics*. Washington: Robert B. Luce, 1974.

University of Florida, Bureau of Economic and Business Research. *Florida Statistical Abstract, 1978*. Gainesville: University Presses of Florida, 1978.

13

Regional Governments

by Robert R. Benedetti and Manning J. Dauer

Between 1950 and 1970, the urban population of Florida increased by more than 200 percent. Faced with a great demand for governmental services caused by this growth, the state has been torn between two contending strategies of development. Proponents of the first strategy argue that new residents deserve new grass-roots institutions. The right of every citizen to a close relationship with a local government of reasonable size is considered and the number of municipalities increased to preserve traditional ratios between citizens and local authorities. And, since new populations require differing mixes of services, the special district — a government limited in the functions it performs — has been pressed into service.

In compliance with this strategy, Florida's municipalities increased by a third between 1952 and 1972 (from 294 to 390). Similarly, there had been 1,200 special districts created by 1979, according to a joint legislative committee and Department of Community Affairs report of that year. There has been parallel growth in several other populous states: California has 407 municipalities and over 2,200 special districts; Pennsylvania has 1,012 municipalities and 1,707 special districts.

Simultaneously Florida has also followed a second development strategy, one based on the realization that growth increases the interdependence of population groups; thus, the correct governmental response should be fewer governments, or at least more centralized ones. Such governments should coordinate, even promote, the cooperation among citizens that the increased density requires. In one of its special reports to the governor and the legislature of Florida, the Commission on Local Government in 1972 put the argument for centralization clearly:

> Fragmentation of government is not in itself a problem if they are separated geographically, socially and economically. But in a very real sense, most areas in Florida have become, or are rapidly becoming, highly interdependent units whose boundaries transcend existing local government structures devised when the state was basically rural and developed on an ad hoc basis over the previous century. The tangle of local government units leads to poor coordination, conflicts of authority, diffused responsibility, duplicated or inadequate services, lack of comprehensive planning, and fiscal inequities. Within this framework, it is hardly surprising to find endless sources of imitation, suspicion and misunderstanding. In a

time of rapidly increasing state aid, the apparent inefficiencies of this arrangement are also extremely disturbing.

This argument for centralization is basically economic: little governments are inefficient. They waste resources and fail to recognize common interests. Such a state of affairs might have been tolerated in an earlier time, but not in a day of rapid urbanization and state and federal funding. Suburbanites have created urban sprawl beyond municipal borders; these areas are often without adequate services, and their residents are not charged equitably for the services they do receive. The web of special districts and municipal governments that inevitably rise to ameliorate this condition lacks coordination. Thus when federal and state agencies seek assurances that funds parceled out to these multiple sources will not be used at cross purposes, the fragmentation of authority prevents a convincing response. In other words, advocates of this strategy argue that the new citizens at the city's edge are not getting or giving their fair share and that governmental agencies can get no accurate account of their investments.

Supporters of this strategy offer three reforms as alternative means for ending fragmented government in areas of growth: *annexation* of smaller jurisdictions by larger ones; two variations called *metro* (either *consolidation,* as in Jacksonville/Duval County, or a *federal system,* as in Dade County, where the cities retain certain duties and transfer others to the metro form of county government —see figs. 13.1 and 13.2); establishment of *voluntary councils of government, regional regulatory agencies,* or *corporate advocates,* which will goad local governments into cooperative polities and the resolution of their conflicts. As noted in chapter 11, cities have generally favored annexation while counties support a transfer of services toward areawide consolidation. In general, it has been state and federal authorities that have pressed for the third alternative.

Florida has experienced all three alternatives, though the use of annexation may have been held back by legal restraints. State law requires that parcels annexed be in need of the services a municipality can provide and that they be geographically compact in relation to the city. In addition, both those annexed and the municipality annexing must approve the transaction by referendum unless it is accomplished by legislative act. These requirements attempt to limit "strip" annexations, utilized by towns like Ocala in order to become contiguous with valuable properties miles from the city center. They also protect rural citizens from the type of "imperialism" practiced by Texas cities.

Despite such legal requirements, Tampa, West Palm Beach, and Gainesville did annex to increase their sizes by more than 200 percent. Many of these annexations were not achieved through the general law outlined above but instead by special legislative acts authorizing an annexation vote by a majority of those voting in the city and the district to be annexed, such vote not requiring a majority in each separate jurisdiction. Between 1970 and 1976, 155 annexations were

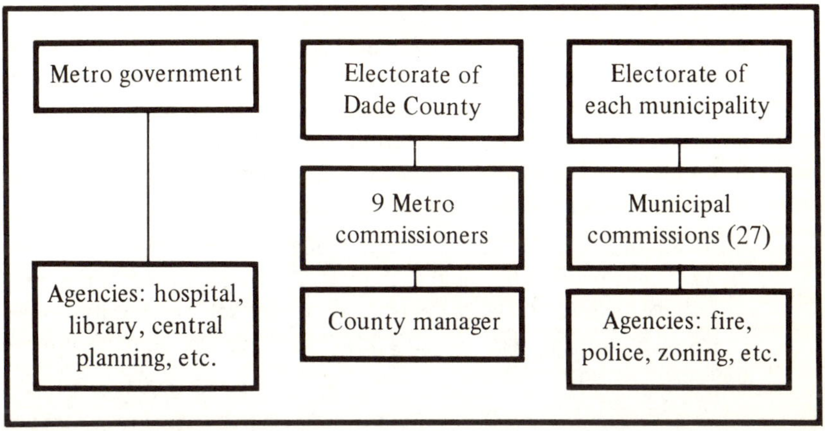

Fig. 13.1. Miami-Dade Metro.

*Not every one of the 27 municipalities has all such agencies. Some of them contract with each other or with the county to provide some services.

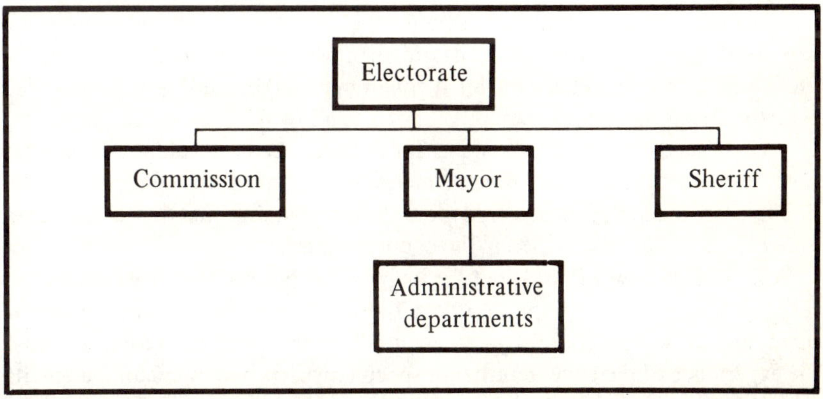

Fig. 13.2 Jacksonville-Duval Consolidation. All functions of former county and city governments, such as fire and police protection, roads, and health, are under the jurisdiction of the commission.

Notes: Four towns—Jacksonville Beach, Neptune Beach, Atlantic Beach, and Baldwin—remain outside the consolidated area. Auxiliary agencies, such as the Jacksonville Electric Authority and the Jacksonville Port Authority, are outside the jurisdiction of the elected commission. Most agency board members are appointed by the governor.

consummated; half of the larger transactions (those involving over 1,000 residents) occurred in cities under 25,000 population. Thus Florida cities, large and small, have used annexation to check urban sprawl and to prevent the multiplication of new jurisdictions.

On the other hand, it may be that the willingness of Florida cities to use annexation has led to defensive incorporations on the part of residents in unincorporated areas. As the *Florida Almanac* notes:

> Throughout Florida unincorporated subdivisions or areas would find the nearest city growing by annexation and getting closer and closer to their community. Many of these cities had large bonded indebtedness, bonds floated to finance sewers, water systems, municipal buildings and street construction. *Ad valorem* or property taxes are usually pledged to repay these bonds, and the only way a city could meet payment and continue to provide normal city services was to continue to grow.
>
> Residents of the unincorporated area would feel they represent a ripe "plum," just waiting for the city to pick. They resent the fact that they might have to have their taxes raised to pay for the debts of the city, so as a means of protection, they would ask the local legislative delegation to grant them a charter . . . .

Such reactions coupled with the difficulty a city may have in obtaining an annexation under state law have often prevented use of this strategy as a satisfactory weapon against the fragmentation of government.

Another partial solution to the problems raised by the second strategy of development is the piecemeal transfer of services between cities and counties by interlocal agreement. Though such agreements have traditionally been negotiated on an ad hoc basis between local governments, they must now be recorded with the Department of Community Affairs to allow for some evaluation of the services traded. Another agreement formula has been developed in charter counties where the charter reflects functions transferred from the cities to the county. For example, in Broward County, the planning function is now executed countywide as specified in the county charter.

Still, Florida is most noted not for its partial solutions but for its attempt to respond with pioneering spirit to both those who recommend more governments and those who counsel greater centralization. In the following sections, the experience of the state in utilizing special districts and in creating councils of government, regional regulatory authorities, and corporate advocates will be reviewed. Each structure has been a response to the phenomenal growth occurring in Florida, but each has its particular cost and benefit for citizens of the state. Whatever the final assessment of these experiences, it cannot be said that local government failed to respond to the challenge of growth.

Special Districts

There are four major types of special districts in Florida, as well as the special Reedy Creek Improvement District that makes provision for Disney World and its adjacent area. In all there are some 1,200 special districts.

Two types are called dependent districts; one is single-purpose, the other multipurpose. Their governing authority and budget authority are under the jurisdiction of a larger governmental unit, but they perform a special function in an area of that unit. A single-purpose dependent district, such as a hospital district, is administered by a county commission. An urban service district (also called the Municipal Service Taxing District) is also under a county commission, but it provides multiple services in the urbanized area of the county outside city limits: fire protection, trash collection, additional sheriff's patrols, street paving, drainage and sewer services. There are about 650 dependent districts.

The other two types of special districts function autonomously of a larger governmental authority. In the third category is the independent special district, numbering about 550; an example is a fire protection district in a specific area with an independently elected administrative and fiscal board, probably with some taxing authority. The fourth type is a development district, a subcategory of the independent special district. The product of a development company that establishes a subdivision, this district has bond obligations for payment of improvements, such as streets and gutters; these obligations, in addition to the purchase price of the lot, must be paid by the lot purchaser.

Urban service districts. — These districts are single-purpose and thus under the jurisdiction of a county commission. Such a district is established by general law (Florida Statutes, Chapter 125) or by county charter to provide any of the following services under the administration of the county commission: fire protection, police service (which may mean special patrol by deputy sheriffs under the sheriff), garbage collection, sanitary sewers, storm sewers, and street pavement, including curb and gutter. A typical urban service district operates under the county administrator, who is appointed by the county commission. It encompasses the built-up suburban area just outside the limit of the central city. The inhabitants of this area probably resist annexation to the central city, but they want and need certain city services. An urban service district is established, and only in that area the commission levies a special tax millage to fund the urban services needed. A lesser tax rate is established for the rural areas of the county.

Under the county administrator the county engineering department will maintain rural roads and will also maintain the streets in the urban service district. But, while the county will pay to pave streets and establish water lines using urban service district funds, the fire station and firemen serving the urban district may be under administration of the central city fire department. In such a case the county commission signs an annual or term contract with the central city and pays the cost of fire protection from the urban service district funds. So part of the services rendered to residents of the urban service district are provided by the county and part by contract with adjacent governmental units.

While this type of arrangement is often favored by suburban residents and by county officials, the adjacent central city has a different attitude. Suburban residents may still drive into the city to use its library and recreational facilities, but they do not pay city taxes. Consequently, there is a sharp conflict between Florida counties and cities on this matter.

Independent special service districts. — Independent special service districts have been established in many areas of Florida, usually to provide a single service. For example, residents of an area outside city limits may wish to establish a volunteer fire department but need revenue to buy equipment. To help them obtain this revenue, a special tax district is established in a defined geographic area, by a special act. This act provides for election in this area of special district commissioners and sets a limitation on the amount of tax that can be levied without the voted approval of the citizens of the district. Land is purchased; a fire station is built; provisions are made for telephone reporting of fire calls and for notification of the firemen. Fire hydrants may be provided if there is a central water system; otherwise, a tanker truck is needed.

While there are a number of special districts in Florida, there are as many in several other states. There are problems associated with such districts. The existence of a special district is often unknown to many of its residents, and election turnout may be meager. There may also be a problem of coordination with city and county authorities.

Development districts. — When real estate developers in Florida offer land for sale, there may be, in addition to the cost of the lot, charges to cover development district bonds which have been floated to provide such capital improvements as central water supply, street paving, and central sewer services. In the past, many purchasers of lots or homes have later found that they also have special bonds chargeable against their lots. Now, in most cases, federal and state land sale regulations require notification to the purchaser whenever there are special bonds and charges.

Special district regulations: 1979. — Because of problems with the management and finances of special districts, the 1979 Florida legislature enacted laws requiring that all special districts provide an annual budget, to be filed with state officials in Tallahassee and with local county officials. There must also be appropriate legal notice of the meetings of boards that comprise the officers of such districts, and the boards must maintain open files for local examination and file copies of their actions with state and county officials.

Comments on special districts. — Many students of government consider special districts to be difficult to administer and lacking in expertise. Generally they recommend that the districts either be united with the county (with consolidation of district and county government) or that there be annexation to an adjacent city. The joint legislative and Department of Community Affairs report in 1979 on the 550 independent local districts in Florida raises a variety of issues for legislative concern.

How should the districts be created? At present, this may be done by special act of the legislature or by ordinance adopted by the local county commission. Some of the provisions in old statutes for such creation of districts conflict with each other and need to be resolved.

The problem of adequate notice involving election of officers who control independent special districts is so great that many believe the officers should simply be placed under the authority of the elected county commission.

Fiscal responsibility is also a problem. Some districts have gone bankrupt. Many do not report their fiscal affairs and are not properly audited. Are the 1979 reporting requirements sufficient? Many, including the task force report and the state comptroller, feel that further supervision is necessary. In summary, the problems attendant upon the 550 independent special districts are so great that there is a danger that Florida is creating a jungle of uncontrolled governmental units.

The special case of Disney World. — In the 1950s Walt Disney Enterprises, operating through a number of purchasers, consolidated large landholdings in Central Florida just west of Orlando. The late Walt Disney desired to achieve three objectives: sufficient land to create an eastern version of California's Disneyland; a buffer zone around Disney World in which he could control the planning; and cooperation with state and local governments so that he could establish a special governmental unit to enable the corporation to control planning for the land he had already bought and for the area adjacent to the amusement facilities (eventually to be his land also), on which he wished to create a model city with housing, international exhibits by foreign countries, and other facilities.

Disney secured the cooperation of then Governor LeRoy Collins, of Farris Bryant when he was governor, of legislative leadership, and of adjacent county authorities. After he purchased the land, the legislature passed one act establishing the Reedy Creek Improvement District and other special acts placing control in Walt Disney Enterprises. First Disney World itself and the town of Buena Vista were built; after Disney's death, Disney Enterprises in the late 1970s developed EPCOT (Experimental Prototype Community of Tomorrow) as an example of a model community.

Metro Governments

Florida is the only state in the union which can claim two major experiments in metropolitan government: Miami–Dade County and Jacksonville–Duval County. At various times Tampa, Key West, Pensacola, Tallahassee, Gainesville, and Fort Pierce have shown interest in similar arrangements, but thus far they have not been developed. However, if the Miami and Jacksonville experiences are typical, it takes several attempts for a metro to be successfully formed.

Miami–Dade County. — Three consolidation plans for this area were defeated during the late forties and early fifties before the present plan was adopted in 1957 (see fig. 13.1). Under the 1957 charter, Metropolitan Dade County (Metro) can set certain service standards for the entire county, including Miami and twenty-seven other cities. However, it provides services only in those areas where there is no existing municipality (that is, in unincorporated areas) or where cities have specifically granted the county the power to service their occupants. Thus, Metro is actually a federal system, picking up functions when and where municipalities agree to consolidate. Zoning, parks and recreation, and police protection have for the most part remained in the hands of the municipalities; planning authority in some areas is transferred to Metro, but in others, as in Miami, it remains with the city; health and welfare, pollution control, traffic control, libraries, and fire protection increasingly have become Metro duties. Metro has the power to tax the entire county for the services it provides.

Structurally, Metro government is a variant of council-manager government. Following Florida tradition, councilmen at the county level are called commissioners. There are nine commissioners: one representative from each of eight electoral brackets, plus the mayor. All are elected at-large in nonpartisan elections. The executive functions of Metro belong to an appointed county manager rather than to the mayor, who simply presides at commission meetings.

The governmental structure was designed to minimize political conflict. For example, though tension has existed between several of the larger cities and Metro, the initial charter allowed only the three largest cities to be represented as entities on the commission; the 1962 reform, which produced the present structure, did away with city representation altogether. Of course, the same structure that prevents the commission from dividing along traditional municipal lines also prevents it from playing a vital role in resolving conflict with the cities.

In fact, most problems in Metro have not been resolved at the commission level but by the professional staff. The acceptance of manager government predates the emergence of Metro, and therefore the parties concerned seem satisfied to let administrators resolve political problems: "Given the predominance of the manager form of government at the city level in Dade County, most controversies have been resolved at the administrative rather than the political level. County managers (with the exception of the present manager) have been city managers before coming to Dade and a professional relationship preexisted which, in spite of battling at the political level, often resulted in compromise and consensus being reached at a professional level'' (DeGrove, p. 113).

That the municipalities have allowed administrative solutions to political problems is not just evidence of their professionalism. It is a fact that city leaders need not put up strong resistance to Metro to satisfy constituents because strong loyalties to particular cities have not developed in South Florida. The most plausible explanation for this is the recent nature of migration to Miami, where residents are more loyal to New York, Chicago, or Havana than to Miami Beach, Bal Harbour, or Hialeah. They read the *Miami Herald* and feel more a part of the region as a whole than of a particular municipality. The *Miami Herald* first promoted the Metro system and for twenty years has strongly supported it, opposing efforts to weaken its powers.

Significant challenges to Metro's authority in the future, then, may not be from the cities but from racial, ethnic, and retirement communities whose support often cuts across municipal boundaries. As Longbrake and Nichols put it, ''issues are currently shifting from Metro versus the cities to Metro versus the people.'' A charter amendment to provide a district or ward election for some of the commissioners was unsuccessfully proposed in 1972; however, such structural reforms may not be adequate to satisfy popular demands, because politically salient communities are often geographically diffuse. Blacks, for example, do not live in a single cluster, nor is the retired community geographically focused.

If, in fact, the issues that Metro faces generate conflict between social groups, and if neither the cities nor the Metro structure provides access for spokesmen from such groups, the stage would appear to be set for citizen frustration and unrest. Such access as does exist has come primarily from federally mandated programs for citizen participation. DeGrove assesses the situation:

> Citizen participation *(not including Community Action and Model City programs)* is of a fairly traditional nature, generally consisting of participation in public hearings before the County Commission and service on numerous advisory boards appointed by the Commission. However, steps have been taken in recent years to facilitate citizen business with the county government. The Building and Zoning Department for the past decade has had sub-offices, and early in 1972 was opened in South Dade to serve the population center furthest from downtown. More recently a citizens' information and referral service has been established with four neighborhood offices. Dade County has not generally addressed itself to the question of decentralizing resources and policy-making *except through the Community Action Agency and the Model City Organization;*

> both of which function as divisions of the County Manager's Office (DeGrove, p. 113; emphasis added).

DeGrove makes clear in this statement that, for Dade County, decentralization means primarily decentralized services rather than decentralized decision-making. In fact, in another section, he notes that federal programs that encourage decentralized decision-making in an effort to involve local people can threaten Metro's authority. It would appear that structures for citizen involvement, which could generate the political leadership Miami lacks, necessarily compromise the unified approach Metro advocates despite its ultimate dependence on an informed citizenry.

To be sure, Metro has made substantial contributions toward tax and service equity in the region. The goals of reform, carried forward by a professional staff, are being realized, but often with limited involvement of local citizens. Such a situation is stable where the population neglects its responsibility to govern or where the issues to be resolved are not critical. But as more migrants from the North and from Latin America make Miami their home, and as fiscal considerations present hard choices concerning public services, the unresolved problem of citizen action may require further attention.

Jacksonville–Duval County. — Florida's second experiment in metropolitan government began in 1967 (see fig. 13.2). Consolidation of the services provided by Duval County and her cities into a single governing authority had been discussed by local reformers since 1918. However, the peculiar coincidence of marked growth and governmental incompetence and corruption in the late 1960s persuaded the county to implement such a plan. Facing the loss of accreditation at local high schools, the soaring of service rates (300 percent in fifteen years), nearly a majority of local officials under indictment, and a suspect system of tax assessment, 64.7 percent of the voters approved adoption of a consolidated government.

Unlike the format in Miami-Dade, the charter adopted in Jacksonville-Duval abolished the existing county government and all but four small municipalities (Jacksonville Beach, Atlantic Beach, Neptune Beach, and Baldwin), which were given the option to maintain autonomy over municipal services. In their place, the consolidated government offered an elected council of nineteen, fourteen to be elected by separate electoral districts and five at-large. The executive of the consolidated government is an elected mayor. The elections are partisan.

The mayor's powers are limited by the continuing existence of an elected sheriff and other minor administrators as well as a number of quasi-independent authorities: an electric authority, two hospital authorities, a port authority, a civil service board, a planning board, and a transportation authority. One estimate is that these agencies spend roughly two-thirds of the budget of the consolidated government of the City of Jacksonville. To be sure, the mayor has budgetary control over the total amount spent by these authorities, and there is a charter provision that places them under the consolidated government's personnel, purchasing, and legal services. However, as the members of some of these boards are elective or are appointed by the governor, the mayor cannot easily control policy. Moreover, there is some indication that he acquiesces to the decisions of all these boards in deference to the elite or constituent groups that their members represent. Such behavior, of course, may change as mayors less receptive to elites are elected.

On the other hand, the council of the consolidated government has shown itself to be quite vigorous. In the short history of the new charter the mayor has not had a clear-cut majority and has been forced to generate support for each item represented. Further, the fact that the council has a staff research arm and an auditor to provide staff support has allowed the council to initiate policy. Finally, the major ethnic minority in Jacksonville, black Americans, has found the council a useful form for the needs of their community. DeGrove makes this point in his summary of an interview with black leaders:

> A black leader–council member who opposed consolidation on the grounds that its central purpose was to dilute the power of blacks in the old city now feels that it has not had that effect. She feels that "blacks have more political power than ever before under consolidation." She noted, as did others, black and white, the sharp increase in jobs for blacks under consolidation. Blacks have been added to the fire department for the first time, and more blacks have been recruited in the law enforcement area. All leaders interviewed stressed the great success in drawing blacks into the political system by appointing at least one black to every advisory board (DeGrove, p. 103).

Blacks are not the only group to benefit from the new structures of the consolidated government. Unlike Miami-Dade, where the entire metropolitan area is charged for services whether they benefit or not, the consolidated government has designated two levels of service, general and urban. General services are provided for the entire area, and the entire area is so taxed; however, urban service districts alone pay for and receive the additional services they require.

Such careful attention to equity and citizen participation does not appear to have compromised the goal of efficiency in Jacksonville, though much of the fiscal success there and in Miami may be tied to federal grants. According to

DeGrove, costs of services did go up after consolidation, but there was also a substantial increase in quality and quantity of services provided. The future of consolidated government is tied to the soaring costs of energy, but the development of political lines of communication with the diverse communities of Duval County should help the new government through any crisis.

The political development of structures for citizen participation appears to be more advanced in Jacksonville-Duval than in Miami-Dade, and it would be unfair to argue that metropolitan reform per se stifles citizen access. In fact, a study by Daniel Grant indicates that a majority of the community leaders interviewed in 1966 felt that the Miami-Dade experiment had improved access to local government, or at least had not made it more difficult. They thought that this was particularly valid in the black community.

However, Grant also found that the consolidation most like Jacksonville's — that in Nashville, Tennessee — had promoted substantially higher confidence in citizens' ease of access to government. The lesson to be learned is that when metropolitan government is not tied to a professional manager and at-large/nonpartisan elections, it is particularly open to citizen participation. Still, should a citizen be forced to choose between traditional government and a reformed metropolitan government, the latter may provide better opportunities for the public to be heard. It is less likely to be dominated by a small clique. Several of Grant's respondents noted, "The old county commission's meetings . . . [were] 'star chamber' proceedings . . . a 'closed-group kind of situation,' with only monthly meetings, no formal agenda, and public hearings discouraged. The metro commission has nine members, meets every two weeks with a formal agenda, and . . . [has] frequent public hearings."

Of course, as only two Florida cities have adopted consolidated government, any generalizations are limited. Still, the very existence of these experiments is consistent with Florida's impulses toward urban reform. As experiences in both Jacksonville and Miami prove, reform can lead to professional and efficient governance. However, special care must be taken that these goals not conflict with the development of avenues for popular participation. Jacksonville appears to have taken a positive step in this regard. The fact that citizens may have more demands to make on Florida's cities in the future could make the Jacksonville way even more attractive.

Even smaller counties are considering adopting the Jacksonville consolidation plan: Okeechobee County and the city of Kissimmee voted on such a move but turned it down. Another factor increasing pressures for consolidation is the recent Florida Supreme Court decisions that have prohibited county taxes in geographic areas that do not receive county services. An alternative to consolidation in such an area is the formation of a tax district.

With the advent of nearly 600,000 Hispanics in Dade County, triracial tension developed among Hispanics, whites, and blacks in the late 1970s and early 1980s, resulting in rioting and other racial disturbances in two black ghettos. While some positive steps have been taken, adequate leadership to bridge the gap between blacks and government officials is lacking.

Councils of Governments (Regional Planning Councils)

By the mid-1960s two trends were becoming clear across the nation: urban problems were no longer within the scope of a single city or county jurisdiction; and the traditional remedies of special districts, annexation, and metro government could not stem the tide. Special districts, in fact, only served to fragment governmental authority still further. Annexations, consolidations, and metros remained plausible alternatives, but few cities, counties, and state legislative authorities were willing to experiment with them. Into this breach came the council of governments.

As the name implies, a council of governments (COG) is a voluntary organization of interested governments within a given area. Advocates argue that the council is an attractive alternative because it does not threaten the autonomy of existing governments. Rather than consolidate many jurisdictions into one, the COG *coordinates* them and leaves their powers untouched. In Florida, membership has included only cities and counties, but special districts and even state or federal agencies are part of COGs in other states.

Governments benefit from a council in two ways. First, a council helps members plan together for the future, thereby eliminating duplication of facilities and coordinating the provision of services (e.g., the building of transportation systems). Second, councils foster the improvement of relations between an area's cities and counties. Conflicts can be intercepted early or quickly resolved. Once a conference table is established at which governments meet, the negative aspects of urbanization seem less formidable. Members, once aware of the costs of inaction, will pull together to solve common problems.

However, few governments voluntarily took the step to form such councils. First attempted in the Detroit area in 1954, only a handful of councils were in operation by 1965. In Florida, only the Tampa Bay Regional Planning Council and the East-Central Regional Planning Council (Winter Park) date from this early period. The fact that today the state is divided among eleven councils is the result of federal and state inducements in the late 1960s (see fig. 13.3).

Federal legislation in 1965 allowed councils to apply for grants to undertake housing and land use planning. In 1967 the federal Model Cities program required that all applications for its funds be approved by a regional council. By

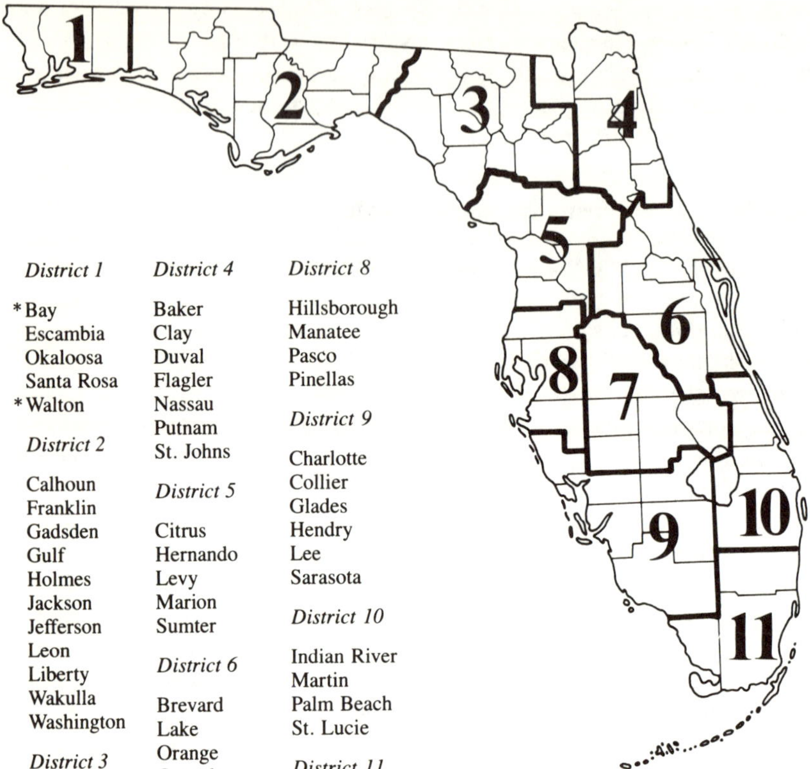

District 1

* Bay
Escambia
Okaloosa
Santa Rosa
* Walton

District 2

Calhoun
Franklin
Gadsden
Gulf
Holmes
Jackson
Jefferson
Leon
Liberty
Wakulla
Washington

District 3

Alachua
Bradford
Columbia
Dixie
Gilchrist
Hamilton
Lafayette
Madison
Suwannee
Taylor
Union

District 4

Baker
Clay
Duval
Flagler
Nassau
Putnam
St. Johns

District 5

Citrus
Hernando
Levy
Marion
Sumter

District 6

Brevard
Lake
Orange
Osceola
Seminole
Volusia

District 7

De Soto
Hardee
Highlands
Okeechobee
Polk

District 8

Hillsborough
Manatee
Pasco
Pinellas

District 9

Charlotte
Collier
Glades
Hendry
Lee
Sarasota

District 10

Indian River
Martin
Palm Beach
St. Lucie

District 11

Broward
Dade
Monroe

*Moved from District 2 to District 1, effective August, 1979.

Fig. 13.3 Councils of Government/Regional Planning Council Boundaries, 1976. Source: Department of Administration, Division of State Planning (now in Department of Community Affairs).

1969 the Office of Management and Budget insisted that all applications for federal money be so screened. In 1972 Florida assigned regional authorities the task of reviewing land use proposals that have a regional impact. In 1974 Florida authorized regional authorities to assist state agencies in coastal management strategies. Finally, the comprehensive planning act of 1975 stipulated that regional authorities were to be part of the review process for local land use plans.

State and federal authorities let it be known that, should local governments not form the regional organizations necessary to carry out the prescribed functions, such organizations would be imposed on them. In fact, in 1972 the state Department of Administration drew up approved boundaries for regional organizations but then allowed the governments in question to form the organizations themselves. The South Florida and the North-Central Florida regional planning councils appear to be the result of federal pressure in the late 1960s. But the Southwest Florida, Central Florida, Withlacoochee, West Florida, and Northeast Florida regional planning councils are clearly products of state stimulants. The Apalachee and Treasure Coast regional planning councils are the most recent additions, the former replacing the Northwest Florida Planning and Advisory Council (which went bankrupt), and the latter being a splinter organization from the South Florida Regional Planning Council (but one approved by the state Department of Administration).

As the councils were formed at different times and under the pressure of different federal and state mandates, it is not surprising that their boundaries do not show any clear justification. For example, the number of counties included in the councils range from ten in the Apalachee Regional Planning Council to three in the South Florida and the West Florida councils. The Withlacoochee Regional Planning Council, the smallest in population (209,000), has less than a tenth of the people in the largest, South Florida (2,426,000). Apalachee, the largest regional planning council, is three times as large in land mass (9,047 square miles) as Tampa Bay (2,915) or West Florida (2,912), the two smallest. The number of cities desiring membership also varies widely.

In 1980 the Florida legislature set up a uniform law for the creation of regional planning councils, the term preferred in Florida to that of councils of government. Chapter 163 of the Florida statutes, permitting voluntary structures, was replaced. Revised Chapter 160 specifies that the boundaries of a district council are set by the executive office of the governor but that the councils report to the Department of Community Affairs. In a regional council district, counties must be represented and cities may be. At least two-thirds of a council's governing body must be elected officials of the constituent counties or cities and serve ex officio on the council's governing board;

citizens appointed by the governor make up the other third. The council's duties include coordination of local government plans, review of proposed private or public ventures called "developments of regional impact," and coordination of ecological plans with water management districts.

Councils differ in form but share a council-executive director form of governance, in which the director serves at the pleasure of the council. None of the councils in Florida has popularly elected representatives: members are designated by participating governments and usually are elected officials of those governments. Only the Apalachee and the Central Florida regional planning councils insist on having some lay or nonelected representatives. Thus councils share the trend toward professional management evident in more traditional governments but are, as a result, only indirectly representative of the people. One might say that they are a "United Nations" of area governments.

The differences among councils arise from their treatment of municipal representatives, their weighing of voting by population, and their use of executive committees. Only four have invited all the cities in their jurisdictions to sit on the council; the other seven either select the cities to be allowed representation or provide a system by which cities rotate on the council. This reluctance to encourage municipal participation may stem from a desire on the part of county members to control council policy. In any case, less than half are structured to serve as open forums for discussions among all cities and counties in the designated area.

Three of the four councils that allow municipalities to participate have adopted a system of representation based on population. For example, West Florida allows each member government two representatives plus an additional representative for each 25,000 people. Such a formula automatically favors the counties as the larger governmental entities. Even the Tampa Bay Regional Planning Council, which invites municipal representation without regard to population, utilizes a voting system weighted according to population. Thus, even when access to COGs (RPCs) is not limited, cities still find that their power within the council is constrained. Smaller counties may also be constricted by representation by population, but only one council, South Florida, has apportioned representation according to population in such a way that the difference between counties is clearly the target.

It might be expected that the executive committees or boards of directors of these councils would be dominated by county representatives. At least four of the eleven councils have clearly defined executive committees including more members than their top officers: West Florida, Apalachee, North-Central and East-Central. From a review of the literature published by these councils in

1978–79, only Apalachee and North-Central take a majority of the executive committee from county government. The East-Central Florida Board of Directors is equally divided between city and county personnel, and West Florida is predominantly municipal. Thus, it is not impossible for municipalities to rise to positions of power or even control in COGs (RPCs), despite the fact that the structure is mobilized against them. For example, the past chairman of the Tampa Bay Council was a city commissioner from Sarasota.

While both cities and counties are anxious that councils of governments remain under their control, they have not moved to expand their functions much beyond those encouraged by state and federal agencies. Councils in Florida have three basic tasks: regional planning, regional administration of state or federal programs, and technical assistance to local governments (see fig. 13.4). Planning is by far the greatest part of the councils' work. One executive director estimated that over 60 percent of staff time was focused in this area. A majority of the councils received federal funds to undertake planning related to water quality and transportation. Five councils accepted state funds for energy planning, and eight assisted the state in coastal zone management. All the councils were charged in connection with the Comprehensive Planning Act of 1975 to review and comment upon local plans completed within their jurisdictions.

Planning is a broad term and covers a multitude of activities. Basically, the councils see themselves as think tanks for local government. Though dependent on federal and state grant money, they collect information about local areas, project local growth trends, and suggest alternate local solutions for present and future problems.

The research undertaken is of vital use to state and federal decision-makers as they seek to extend their influence into local areas. Not only do these governments control the nature of the research through their control of the funds, but at the state level the activities of the councils and their documents are monitored through the Division of State Planning in the Florida Department of Community Affairs.

The interest of the state and federal governments is even more apparent in the administration of programs. A council has a right to accept or decline administrative activities, but, once a program is accepted, the rules of the state or federal agency apply. For example, the acceptance of certain kinds of responsibilities could require that the governing board include consumer, professional, or minority members. To be eligible for federal funding, Apalachee has added municipal and minority representation in accordance with guidelines from the federal Economic Development Administration. Even more likely, the administration of federal programs may require the appointment of citizen advisory

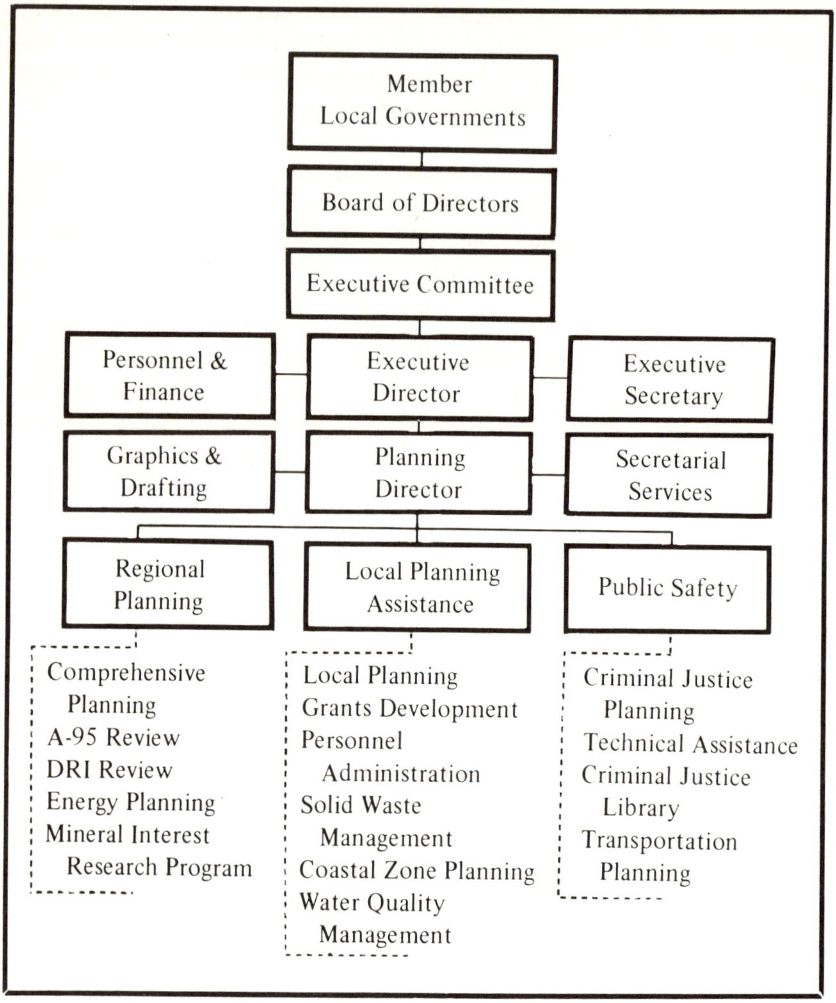

Fig. 13.4. Council of Government/Regional Planning Council Organization of Staff and Functions. Example: Withlacoochee Regional Planning Council. Source: Withlacoochee Regional Planning Council.

boards tailored to the particular state or federal statute. When the Tampa Bay Regional Planning Council accepted the responsibility to distribute federal funds to the elderly, it appointed three such boards: two citizens' boards from Manatee/Hillsborough and Pinellas/Pasco counties, respectively, and a third to coordinate the directors of all programs funded. In other words, the councils, where they accept administrative responsibility, have to be prepared to restructure their organizations to meet legal requirements. Flexibility, up to and including the nature of representation on the governing council, is a necessity.

The major administrative responsibility delegated to the councils by state government is the clearance of developments of regional impact (DRIs). The Environmental Land and Water Management Act of 1972 (Florida Statutes, Chapter 380) required the designation of "appropriate regional agencies" to review land use proposals that may have regional impacts. This review is advisory to local governments, which remain in control of the final decision. However, should that decision go against the recommendation of the regional agency, the agency may ask that the state cabinet consider an appeal on the issue. In other words, the regional agencies have the power to persuade and to appeal but not to veto local land use decisions.

It was not a requirement of Chapter 380 that the regional planning councils be designated the "appropriate regional agency." In fact, there has been continuing debate since 1972 on the feasibility of transferring this land use responsibility to the water management districts, which appear to have more political power and are more clearly an agent of the state. To date no such change in designation has been attempted.

Theoretically this designation should have operated to increase the political and fiscal power of the councils. However, each council of the eleven in the state receives only $45,000 annually to process DRIs, without regard to the number reviewed. This distribution sounds unfair and the sum small until it is recognized that the number of DRIs filed has dropped drastically since the beginning of the review. Only 11 DRIs were filed in 1976–77 and 22 in 1977–78. In most cases the councils approve the request with suggested modifications. Thus the councils are not having a large impact on land use, nor are they receiving much state support for their role. Whatever the original hope, the Environmental Land and Water Management Act was not the salvation of regional planning councils.

A more demanding task for the councils has been their federal responsibility to clear grant requests from governments under their jurisdiction. Following the A-95 circular by the federal Office of Management and Budget in 1969, regional organizations designated by the state were mandated to review grant applications in order to prevent duplication and spillover effects. For example, while the Withlacoochee Regional Planning Council considered only one de-

Structure S-27, a two-gated spillway on the Little River Canal in Miami. The structure controls release of water from the north section of Miami to the bay. Photo courtesy South Florida Water Management District.

velopment of regional impact in 1978, it reviewed 103 federal grant proposals. West Florida reviewed 116 and Tampa Bay passed on 374. As federal grant programs decreased after 1981, so have the number of grant requests reviewed. The review appears to be a professional rather than a political process.

Councils differ greatly in the degree to which they serve the third function: assistance to member governments. For example, Tampa Bay claims only 8 percent of its budget in 1978 was expended for technical assistance, while Withlacoochee put 37.9 percent of its budget in this category. The variable appears to be the size and sophistication of the local governments served. Councils can and do provide comprehensive planning assistance, grant development, personnel administration, and even the writing of technical reports, but many local governments have staffs able to carry out these functions. Councils have acted as consultants to cities and counties in the preparation of the comprehensive plans mandated by the state in 1975. Such contract work does create a possible conflict of interest, because the councils also must critically evaluate these plans for the state.

This dilemma highlights a more general difficulty which runs through all tasks that COGs (RPCs) undertake. It is unclear who is their boss: the state and federal agencies who grant fiscal support and administrative authority or the local governments who formed the councils and are represented on their boards. Regional planning councils have no power to tax and are dependent on funding from local government units or from state or federal grants. Contributions from the state increased and those from the federal government decreased in the 1980s.

The total pie divided among the 11 councils is hardly a large one. In 1977–78, the total of their combined budgets was under $7 million. In 1982–83, total budgets had decreased to $6.1 million. Only two, Tampa Bay and East-Central, spent over a million dollars. Compared to most counties, many cities, and even some special districts, the expenditure is small. In fact, it only buys a small staff and much of a council's budget is expended on salary. In 1977–78 less than 100 full-time employees were involved in all 11 councils. The largest staff was 35 (Tampa Bay), the smallest 5 (Treasure Coast). Staffs include planners with a variety of expertise, administrators, librarians, public relations experts, draftsmen, and a complement of secretaries. One executive director commented that a high turnover of council personnel is expected because projects on grant funds are of limited duration and most jobs are tied to specific projects rather than to ongoing activities. Thus, few seasoned staff people exist; staffs are young professionals just learning their trades. The executive director puts together a new team to accomplish each specific task.

While such fluidity allows the council to respond to a variety of funding opportunities, it also puts constant pressure on the executive director and staff to invent new projects. They must innovate to survive. This, in turn, requires a close connection with the state and federal agencies that fund councils as well as with those agencies involved in allied administrative activities. In hope of hearing an important tip as well as coordinating policy implementation, the staffs attempt to master intergovernmental relations.

The dependency of councils on other governments breeds insecurity. They fear cutbacks even in such stable programs as the Environmental Land and Water Management Act of 1972. Until 1976–77, councils were funded on a per capita basis, receiving a total of $790,500 from the state treasury. In that year, the allocation was cut to $500,000, apportioned equally among the eleven districts.

Designation as the appropriate regional agency is a constant problem under federal programs as well. Assignments as A-95 clearinghouses for federal grants are relatively stable. However, the designation as a ''metropolitan planning organization'' for the Department of Transportation has fluctuated between divisions of the state Department of Transportation, regional planning councils, and county governments. Yet even when the council does not receive the designation as the planning or administrative unit to manage a particular grant, it can recoup by participating as a consultant if the designated agency agrees.

The regional planning councils thus struggle constantly for designation as the appropriate agency and for stabilization of funding. In some cases, like transportation or criminal justice, competition comes from the county planning departments. In water quality and environmental planning, competition comes from the water districts or ad hoc organizations like the Apalachicola Resource Management and Planning Program, which have larger jurisdictions. Even state agencies or private organizations like the United Fund may strive to become regional designates. This competition is particularly difficult because it must be continuously waged, grant after grant, agency after agency. Moreover, the groups who are competitors must become part of a coordinated effort once one or another is awarded the grant.

In their fight for survival, the councils have found it beneficial to develop constituencies in their regions beyond the governments which sit on their boards. Sometimes for their own legitimacy and sometimes to fulfill a grant requirement, COGs (RPCs) generate a host of citizen and technical advisory committees. Tampa Bay in 1977–78 listed 13 such bodies, North Central Florida 6, and Withlacoochee 5. These committees act as sounding boards for council staffs but also, quoting a report from Tampa Bay, "verify the results of council research, in the development of regional and council goals and objectives and in the formulation of plans, policies, and recommendations." As a sizable number of citizens participate on such committees (over 550 in Tampa Bay), the significance of their participation is a topic worthy of further study.

By offering such opportunities to participate and publishing reports and documents (the average number per council for 1977–78 was thirteen), COGs attempt to root themselves in citizen consciousness. Tampa Bay also organized a campaign in which it agreed to serve as an intermediary between the legislature and local citizens through the publication of issue papers written by local residents. Councils are acutely aware that they lack a direct representative base, but they aspire to become even more representative than elected officials. Such rapport with citizens of the regions bolsters their position in the ongoing struggle for authority and security.

Florida is often thought by reformers from other states to have an exemplary regional council system. To be sure, the entire state is served by one regional council or another, and state and local support exceeds the national averages. But support has been unstable; COGs have to struggle for each dollar and administrative prerogative. Further, the councils have, on the whole, been dominated by county representatives, though recent initiatives in the area of citizen participation suggest a trend toward popular representation. Finally, the COGs have yet to attain any real power in local politics; they advise, plan, and administer noncontroversial federal or state programs. Their role in decisions concerning developments of regional impact is a bellwether of their overall strength. They can suggest land use policy to local governments or force a state level review of such policy, but they cannot make their decisions stand without the cooperation of others. Florida has been willing to experiment with COGs but unwilling to give them significant state or local powers. Apparently, their best hope to obtain such authority lies with the commitment of a growing number of citizen participants and the possibilities for mergers with the other regional governments. We now turn to a brief consideration of these organizations.

Regional Regulatory Authorities

The regional regulatory authorities set up under the auspices of the State of Florida tend to be autonomous and are less the creatures of local government. In the case of transportation planning, the initiative for such regulatory authorities was left to local governments. However, the use of such regional transportation organizations has been slowed if not stopped by the legal requirement that they include representatives of the governor as well as of local governments on the boards. Where transportation planning councils have been organized, as among Orange, Seminole, and Osceola counties, they have been satisfied to use as their legal touchstone the same chapter used by councils of governments (RPCs) —Florida Statute 163, Part 1. This legal form does not assure regulatory power or funding from the state, but it does avoid the presence of the governor's representatives.

A more significant example of state involvement in regional regulation, however, is the operation of the five water management districts (see fig. 13.5). These districts were created by the same legislature that designed the review of land use planning under the Environmental Land and Water Act of 1972. While the regional regulation of land use was delegated to COGs (RPCs), a second act, the Florida Water Resources Act of 1972, gave power over water resources to water management districts. Under the general guidance of the state Department of Environmental Regulations, the five districts were charged with developing a permanent system for water usage, regulating dams for water storage, promoting recreational use of water resources, and generally fostering conservation of this scarce resource. In undertaking this task, the districts received financial support from general state revenues, federal grants, the leasing of state property related to water control, permit fees, and most important, ad valorem taxes, which the districts have the right to levy on their own authority (within specified legal limits). Each district is governed by a district board appointed by the governor. In some districts, basin boards have been authorized to deal with water management issues which do not affect the entire district. These boards have taxing power as well as follow the same governance pattern.

In addition to executive directors, the districts employ a healthy complement of technical personnel to undertake water research and manage extensive flood control and water resource facilities. The South Florida Water Management District, for example, employs over 900 people. This is clearly the largest operation of the five, but Southwest Florida employs over 200 and St. Johns River 133. The annual budgets of the five ranged from $750,000 to over $7,500,000 in 1977–78. The value of the property held is phenomenal; for example, the assessed valuation of South Florida's holdings in 1977 was $52,326,230,000.

Water management districts may also use their taxing power to purchase environmentally endangered headwater areas that serve as collectors for aquifers or swamps feeding streams and rivers. For example, drainage of swamplands has threatened the flow of waters in the St. Johns River and has led to land purchases by the area water management district.

Needless to say, with the power to tax and the power to refuse water usage, not to mention the control of extensive landholdings, these are powerful bureaucratic organizations. Though they are administratively under the jurisdiction of the Department of Environmental Regulation which must pass on their budgets, the appointment of their boards by the governor and their extensive resources give them substantial independence from normal administrative channels. It is notable that the appointees to these boards are people of political and economic stature in the state, including one former Environmental Protection Agency official who is rumored to be interested in the governor's chair.

Water management districts are thus particularly responsive to state political currents. They are not simply a portion of state bureaucracy, nor are they necessarily representative of local government interests. To the extent that the governor and his cabinet wish to promote regional regulations, this structure is clearly their best tool.

On the other hand, despite staff goodwill among the water management districts, other regional organizations, and local governments, the perspectives of the units differ. The large view taken by a water management district because of its size can be offensive to smaller governments. For example, a recent attempt by the Southwest Florida Water Management District to collect information for a proposed regional water plan was thwarted by a local government, which ordered its personnel not to respond to the requests. Should a governor attempt to move more power to these districts, local forces might revolt and force the legislature to reconsider the utility of these regional governments.

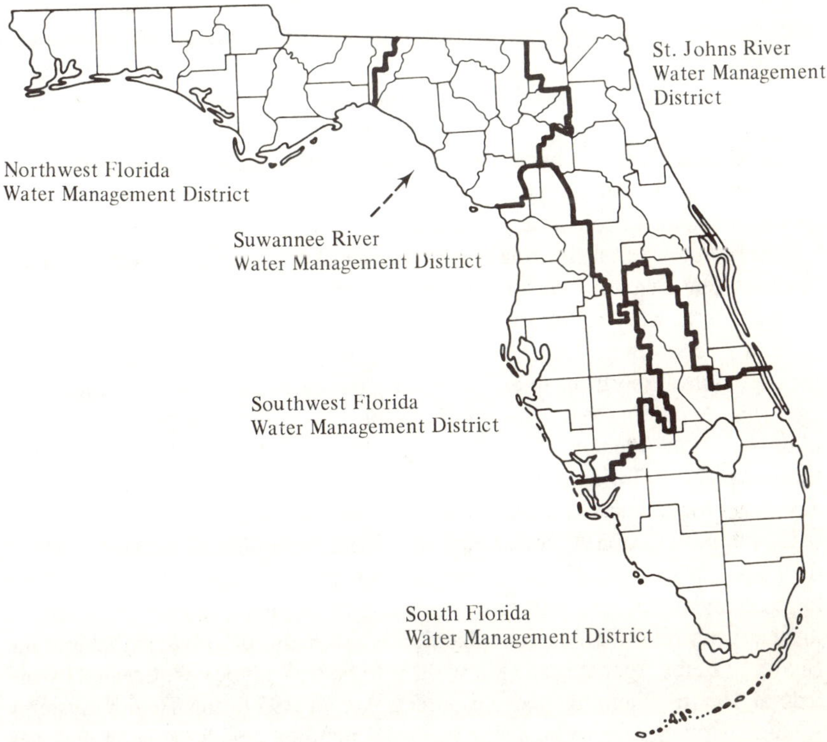

Fig. 13.5. Water Management Districts, 1978. Source: South Florida Water Management District.

Corporate Advocates

Regional regulatory authorities receive citizen input into their proceedings through open hearings and through the political currents that influence their boards. Their role is in some ways quasijudicial, judging the adequacy of competing grant proposals, transit systems, or water uses. Therefore greater openness to public pressure might be unseemly.

Exactly opposite is the case of corporate advocates. They take the role of defense attorney for clients of government. Unlike the other governmental units discussed, the corporate advocates are legally in the private sector. They are incorporated under the laws of the state as nonprofit corporations. However, the financial support they receive is mostly from governmental sources.

Both the state and the federal government have enacted legislation creating such advocates. Local mental health boards are an example of state experimentation with this form, though the funding for these boards is shared by state and county governments. However, the federal government has the most extensive experience with the corporate advocate model. For example, Community Action Agencies (CAA) have been created to articulate the needs of the poor community and Health Systems Agencies to advocate improvements in health care in the name of consumers.

Community Action Agencies are a remnant of the War on Poverty begun under President Lyndon Johnson's administration. The agencies apparently perceived their task to be administration rather than advocacy or planning. They do attempt to coordinate their programs with other local and state agencies, but they are not on the front lines, promoting the cause of the poor before these agencies. According to the Manatee Opportunity Council, the purpose of Community Action Agencies is "extending a helping hand, comfort, and aid to those in need." Florida's CAAs are administrators of relief programs, first, and advocates for new and extended support to the poor, second.

Community Action Agencies may emphasize their administrative role above their advocacy potential because they lack power over local governments. They have no review responsibilities over local grant requests, nor do they approve local poverty relief. On the other hand, it is precisely such powers that arm the Health Systems Agencies and allow them to be true advocates. Created by the federal Health Planning and Resources Act of 1974, the Health Systems Agency network was to be a step toward a national health program and was empowered accordingly.

The purposes of Health Systems Agencies (HSAs) are threefold: to plan for the health needs of an area, to review all applications from public and private health-care providers for changes in health care facilities, and to mobilize community resources to improve existing facilities. Unlike the CAAs, these agencies have not become administrative units for federal programs but attempt only to coordinate the activities of others. However, should any health-related facility need to expand, the support of the local Health Systems Agency is essential. An adverse decision by the local agency can be appealed to a state board within the Florida Department of Health and Rehabilitative Services and to the federal Department of Health, Education, and Welfare. These higher authorities weigh heavily the opinion of the HSA on the scene, and, should the health care provider ignore the agency's opinion once confirmed by an appeal, Medicare and Medicaid funds can be withheld. Local HSAs are also the gateways to federal grant funds for local institutions. Thus, these agencies possess both the carrot and the stick necessary to work their will. They help those who would support their health care planning with advice on available grants and move effectively to deny grant support and even Medicare/Medicaid payment to any who do not conform.

A review of the Florida Gulf Health Systems Agency, Inc., for 1976–77 shows that of the 31 requests for changes in health care facilities submitted, nine — nearly a third — were denied. During the same period, Florida Gulf HSA undertook 55 grant reviews in cooperation with the Tampa Bay Regional Planning Council. The annual report of Florida Gulf also notes a variety of "informal working meetings" with health-related groups and agencies to implement health care plans drafted by the HSA. Such indications of activity are difficult to assess fully, but the willingness to deny requests for facilities and the eagerness to cooperate with other regional agencies are significant. Yet to be revealed is the extent to which this pattern reflects the true voice of local consumers rather than the preferences of staff and existing health care providers.

Corporate advocates, then, vary greatly in strength, but their success in giving voice to local citizens and their problems is in question. Administrative responsibility in the case of the Community Action Agencies and technical complexity in the case of the Health Systems Agencies have served to mute, if not still, the voices of clients and consumers. The potential for mobilizing public opinion remains within these groups, which do appear to promote citizen participation. Possibly this participation will, with time, move them toward significant advocacy concerning issues of regional importance.

Conclusions

As stated previously, regional governments are a response to the failure of cities and counties in the face of urban growth. Special districts serve newcomers who hope to avoid the full tax burden of nearby cities but desire more services than counties provide. Metros and councils of governments (regional planning councils) find support among reformers as well as among state and federal officials who are concerned about the fiscal responsibility of local units. Metros and COGs, as they have developed in Florida, are particularly supportive of county ambitions. Regional regulatory authorities, on the other hand, function more directly for the convenience of state and federal authorities; they are watchdogs, by their very presence challenging the traditional autonomy of local governments. Finally, corporate advocates find favor among client and consumer groups as well as among state and federal agencies, as they attempt to press local government from within.

The overall result of these experiments is a complex, fragmented amalgam of local governmental authorities of doubtful efficiency. The various jurisdictions are confusing and overlapping. The Commission on Local Government, recognizing this problem, suggested that all existing regional governments be reorganized into multicounty planning and areawide service delivery commissions, roughly along the boundaries of the present councils of government (regional planning councils). The idea is logical but may not take into account the subtle political compromises (among citizens, municipalities, counties, the state, and the federal government) that the present patchwork represents. Another problem is that certain functions of regional agencies do not match other functions. For example, the water management districts follow the lines of major drainage contour lines—in some cases whole rivers or a large lake and swamp area such as the Everglades. Such geographic contour lines often do not match existing political boundaries or the needs of metropolitan areas as represented by regional planning councils (compare figs. 13.3 and 13.5). Were Florida to rationalize regional government, a new center of power would be created, and the participants might lose present prerogatives.

References

Commission on Local Government. *Special Report on Local Government Formation*. Tallahassee, 1973.

———. *Special Report on Multi-County and Areawide Service Delivery*. Tallahassee, 1973.

DeGrove, John. "Southern Regionalism." In *The Regionalist Papers,* edited by Kent Mathewson. 2d ed. Southfield, Mich.: Metropolitan Fund, 1978.

Florida Department of Administration, Division of State Planning. *Annual Report on State and Regional Planning 1977–78.* Tallahassee, 1978.

Florida House of Representatives, Committee on Community Affairs. *Special District Report.* Tallahassee, 1979.

Heim, C. J.; Keys, Joyce; and Robbins, G. M. *Regional Governmental Arrangements in Metropolitan Areas: Nine Case Studies.* Washington: Government Printing Office, 1974.

Horan, James F., and Taylor, G. Thomas, Jr. *Experiments in Metropolitan Government.* New York: Praeger, 1977.

Joint Center for Environmental and Urban Problems. *Growth Management in South Florida: A Guide to Public Involvement.* Miami: Florida Atlantic University and Florida International University, 1977.

Longbrake, David B., and Nichols, Woodrow W., Jr. *Miami: Sunshine and Shadows.* Cambridge, Mass.: Ballinger, 1976.

Martin, Richard. *Consolidation: Jacksonville Duval County.* Jacksonville: Crawford, 1968.

Murphy, Thomas P., and Warren, Charles R. *Organizing Public Services in Metropolitan America.* Lexington, Mass.: D. C. Heath, 1974.

Sofen, Edward. *The Miami Metropolitan Experiment.* Bloomington: Indiana University Press, 1962.

Part Three

Government Functions

Florida's Environmental Politics

14

by Joel Gottlieb

FLORIDA INTERNATIONAL UNIVERSITY

There is a new environmental politics in Florida, directed at establishing a public trust for the state's natural heritage. The need for systematic guardianship of that heritage has been made apparent by the pressures of rapid population expansion, urbanization, and economic growth.

The state's recent response to unchecked growth has been a series of environmental initiatives unmatched in Florida's earlier history:

- passage of landmark environmental legislation
- establishment of comprehensive planning functions at the state, regional, and local levels of government
- formation of citizens' interest groups and coalitions of groups around specific environmental issues
- postponement or abandonment of construction on major projects that would adversely affect the fragile ecology of Florida's wetlands

Florida continues to grow rapidly; it is projected to be the fourth largest state by 1990 and the third largest by 2000. Growth management must be a top priority of the state's government in the 1980s.

Although many reforms have been instituted, one should not underestimate the magnitude of change required to reverse the legacy of centuries of environmental exploitation. It often takes twenty to twenty-five years—a generation or more—for a society to make basic changes in its institutional behaviors and individual life-styles. The governmental agencies charged with environmental regulation and management, by their inevitably bureaucratic character, contribute to the length of the lead time necessary for fundamental change. These agencies suffer from the classic problems of underachievement of legislated goals, bureaucratic delay, and excessive costs.

With these reservations in mind to temper our optimism for the future of the natural environment in Florida, we can examine Florida's environmental politics, beginning in 1968 with the adoption of a new state constitution. That constitution modernized state government and created the machinery needed to cope with the demands of urban growth and a developing economy. It inaugurated a decade of significant advances in governmental protection of the environment.

As Florida emerged from the pork chop era of political dominance by northern and rural economic interests, voters accepted in the new constitution of 1968 (Article II, Section 7) a recognition of the state's obligation "to conserve and protect its natural resources and scenic beauty. Adequate provision shall be made for laws for the abatement of air and water pollution and of excessive and unnecessary noise." Although the language of the constitution is essentially hortative, adding nothing to the police powers of the state, it symbolizes a new civic recognition of threats to the environment.

Action to protect the environment followed soon after the constitutional provision of 1968. Between 1970 and 1972, an activist environmental movement matured in Florida. New groups formed to advocate environmental interests; coalitions of these groups appeared (Conservation 1970s was such a coalition). In 1970 the Florida legislature responded by enacting the State Wilderness System Act and the Oil Spill and Pollution Control Act. The Environmental Protection Act and the Florida Litter Law followed in 1971. Riding the crest of national and international enthusiasm and spurred by a drought crisis in 1971, Florida's environmentalists virtually remade the fundamental rules of environmental decision making.

The 1972 legislature assembled in economic good times, and legislative reapportionment had resulted in the election of more liberal politicans from urban districts. Their interests and leadership led to the adoption of several pieces of landmark legislation: the Florida Environmental Land and Water Management Act, the Water Resources Act, and the State Comprehensive Planning Act. Later the same year, the voters of the state approved a $200 million bond issue to underwrite the purchase of environmentally endangered lands. That vote, necessary to fulfill the legal requirement that the state pay just compensation for private property used for public purposes, amounted to a popular referendum approving the legislature's environmental actions.

The Florida Environmental Reorganization Act passed by the 1975 legislature extended and consolidated the gains of the environmental movement. In 1983, Florida's second reapportioned legislature added landmark legislation, the Water Quality Assurance Act, to protect groundwater supplies from pollutants and toxic wastes. These major legislative acts, together with federal approval in 1981 of the Florida Coastal Zone Management program and the earlier power-plant siting act of 1973, provide the framework for environmental decision-making in Florida.

Major Actors

The principal actors in environmental decision making are the governor, the cabinet, the state bureaucracy, the legislature, city and county officials, citizens' groups, commercial and industrial development interests, the press, and higher education. The motives of these actors are seldom identical, and the working out of their differences constitutes Florida's environmental politics.

The governor and the other elected cabinet officers share and compete for political and administrative control over the state's agencies having environmental responsibilities. The present configuration of constitutional, statutory, and political accountability (see fig. 14.1) reflects a number of compromises that have been made between the old and the new Florida politics. The cabinet system, created by laws passed under the constitution of 1885 and continued by the constitution of 1968, has traditionally been dominated by agricultural and rural interests from North Florida and the Panhandle; it has served as a check on the powers of the governor, who has had to depend increasingly since World War II on electoral support from urban areas.

The newer environmental goals of controlling pollution and development arise from urban experience. During his two terms in office (1971–79), Governor Askew actively supported efforts to control pollution and development, as did Governor Graham during his terms. Graham, a leader in the environmental legislation of 1972, initiated a number of comprehensive programs for the state's rivers and coastal areas and for the Everglades. The emphasis on wetlands is especially significant since 80 percent of new development is in coastal counties.

The proper conservation and use of natural resources raise more traditional environmental questions whose answers are less dependent on urban experience. Natural resources are of special concern to economic interests such as the timber and the pulp and paper industries, commercial fisheries, agriculture, oil and gas developers, phosphate mining companies, and sportsmen. Environmental issues pertaining to natural resources are often divisive, for the regulation of the use of natural resources is in part the responsibility of the cabinet.

The controversy that arose in 1973 over the appointment of Harmon Shields as director of the Department of Natural Resources (DNR), the largest state environmental agency, revealed the political division between the governor and the cabinet over who was to control environmental decision making. Shields talked of himself as a "poor country boy," who played Florida politics in the old way. Reports by the state auditor general had disclosed that Shields frequently assigned employees of the understaffed marine patrol to cook at fish fries for civic clubs and politicians (*Miami Herald,* 12 November 1973).

More significant than his qualifications or his conduct in office was Shields' representation of the older "good ole boy" mode of governance under Florida's cabinet system. The debate over his appointment pitted the new environmentalists, led by the governor, against the traditional development-oriented proponents, such as the Southeastern Fisheries Association (the commercial fishing lobby) and the Florida Wildlife Federation (the hunters' and sport fishermen's lobby). The governor lost this particular battle, and Shields won the appointment. However, in January 1979 Shields and the DNR once again became a subject of political controversy regarding alleged illegalities in state land transactions. Shields voluntarily suspended himself (with pay) and eventually resigned.

Newly elected Governor Bob Graham used the opportunity to replace Shields temporarily with Jay Landers, head of the Department of Environmental Regulation, a governor-controlled executive department with a strong urban constituency. Six months later the cabinet still had two department heads on the payroll. After some lobbying by Senator Dempsey Barron, a powerful supporter of Shields, the cabinet decided to have Shields assume a lower position in

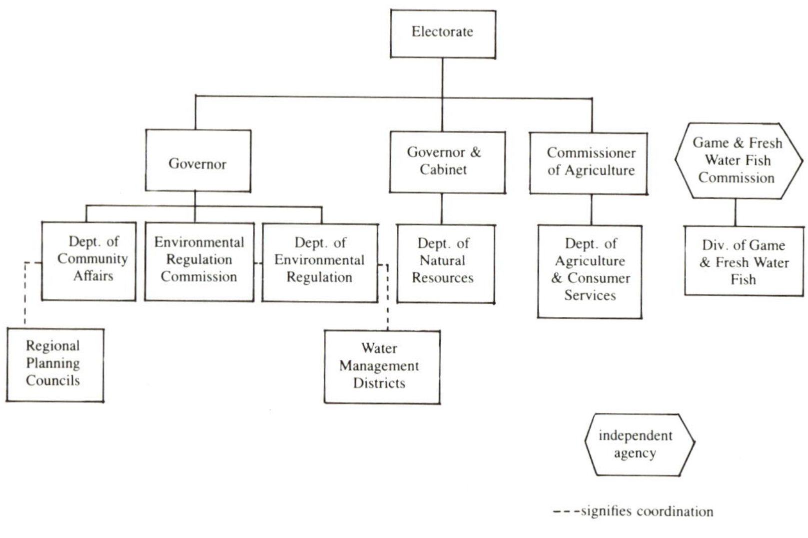

Fig. 14.1. State of Florida Environmental Agencies

DNR pending the outcome of an FBI investigation. This episode is a legacy of the horse trading between the governor and the cabinet, each responsible for one of the two major agencies making conservation and environmental decisions. Shields resigned, after qualifying for a retirement pension.

The Department of Environmental Regulation (DER) is charged with implementing state programs regulating air and water quality (but not quantity), managing coastal zones, and controlling noise and solid waste disposal. These activities are carried out in conjunction with federal programs administered by the U.S. Environmental Protection Agency, the department's federal counterpart, which has a regional office in Atlanta. Water quantity programs are administered by the water management districts, which are not under the DER's administrative control. The DER is responsible for "coordinating" water management programs with the state's water management districts and for approving power plant siting. The DER is emerging as the leading environmental agency and is showing signs of increasing its administrative authority. It recently took over the important coastal zone management program from the Department of Natural Resources and shows signs of becoming a highly professional administrative agency.

Acting under the federal Environmental Protection Agency, Florida's Department of Environmental Regulation coordinates action on contaminated sites that are selected to be cleaned up under the federal "superfund." The location of such sites is shown in figure 14.2.

One of the key mechanisms adopted for the protection of the environment is the requirement of permits for development projects. Permits and certificates, issued at regional offices throughout the state, are required for dredge-and-fill operations, air-polluting installations, water quality, potable water supplies, complex source pollution, industrial wastes, domestic wastes, and landfill operations. The processes of issuing these permits or certificates have often been major points of contention betwen environmentalists and developers.

Acting in conjunction with the DER, a seven-member Environmental Regulation Commission appointed by the governor has the authority to set environmental standards for the state and the responsibility to act as an adjudicatory body on appeals for reversal of administrative actions taken by DER. Normally the commission membership includes one or two persons who have been nominated by environmental interest groups.

The Department of Natural Resources, which reports to the governor and cabinet sitting as head of the agency, operates programs in marine resources (commercial fishing, offshore oil leasing), marine patrol and safety, parks and recreation, management of state lands, and aquatic weed control.

The Game and Fresh Water Fish Commission (GFWFC) is a unique conservation agency. It has had state constitutional status since 1943 and therefore can-

Fig. 14.2. Florida's "Superfund" Hazardous Waste Sites. Source: Florida Department of Environmental Regulation, *Florida's Environmental News*, October, 1983.

not be modified by legislative action; change in its status or duties requires a constitutional amendment approved by the voters. The legislature prescribes the appropriation for the commission. The commission became a constitutional agency through the powerful influence of Florida's sportsmen, who successfully lobbied for its constitutional status in order to insulate it from partisan politics, a protection common in other states as well. The agency and its clientele of hunters and fishermen represented by the Florida Wildlife Federation (which has over 150 affiliated sportsmen's clubs) has a long-term interest in conservation of fish and wildlife habitats as well as in protecting the privileges of hunters and fishermen.

The GFWFC is governed by a five-member commission, appointed by the governor and serving without compensation. The agency combines the functions of law enforcement and biological investigation. Its uniformed law enforcement officers patrol the land, woods, and inland waters with power to arrest persons violating laws relating to hunting, fishing, and littering, and to the sale, use, possession, and importation of wild animals and fish. The commission's law enforcement division even conducts a small undercover operation to apprehend illegal wildlife profiteers. Programs in fisheries and wildlife research and management are operated to provide a supply of game by restocking lakes, streams, and ponds and by managing wildlife habitats through controlled hunting. As part of its wildlife management responsibilities, the commission also administers the Florida Endangered and Threatened Species Act of 1977 and coordinates efforts with the United States Fish and Wildlife Service, which is responsible for similar national programs. The 1983 legislature also gave to the GFWFC responsibility for protection of an additional endangered species, the Florida panther, the official state animal.

Although agencies are often required by law to coordinate their activities, environmental politics is also bureaucratic politics: agencies jealously guard their own "territory," competing with rival bureaus to mobilize public support for their programs. The conflict in the past few years between the Game and Fresh Water Fish Commission and the Department of Natural Resources over the administration of a multimillion dollar aquatic weed control program illustrates the competitive friction between agencies that is characteristic of environmental politics. The proliferation of aquatic weeds—water hyacinth, hydrilla, Eurasian watermilfoil, and alligator weed—threatens inland waterways and lakes with oxygen starvation (eutrophication); what was once just a nuisance now imperils a basic resource of the state.

The Department of Natural Resources and the Game and Fresh Water Fish Commission were publicly feuding over aquatic weed control; each agency had its own program. At issue was DNR's introduction of a fish known as the Chinese grass carp, which consumes its body weight in aquatic vegetation each day. The

GRWFC objected, fearing that the new species would become dominant and be detrimental to desirable game fish. After several years of conflict, in which the legislature was forced to intervene, a special American Assembly Congress conference on aquatic weed management was convened. It recommended that the GFWFC turn over its weed control program to DNR; in return DNR agreed not to interfere in decisions concerning fish. The compromise was signed into agreement and the bureaucratic dispute ended. The GFWFC permits private stocking of sterile hybrid grass carp which has been moderately successful in waters of limited size.

Although the DER, DNR, and GFWFC are the main environmental and conservation bureaucracies, several other agencies have environmental functions. With the transfer of the state planning office, the Department of Community Affairs is the principal planning agency overseeing regional planning, administering "areas of critical state concern," and reviewing power plant siting for conformity with state law.

Several other state agencies have specialized environmental jurisdictions. The Department of Agriculture and Consumer Services administers over 306,000 acres of state forests and the permitting of pesticide use. The 1983 legislature changed the agency's pesticide review committee into the interagency council bringing pesticide use decisions under systematic environmental review. Other agencies with specialized environmental programs are the Department of Transportation's scenic highways system and various bicycle programs and the Department of State's program on historic sites.

No discussion of environmental agencies would be complete without reference to the federal agencies that play a major role in Florida's environmental politics: the Army Corps of Engineers, the U.S. Department of Agriculture, the Environmental Protection Agency, and the Department of the Interior. Each of the national agencies has a continuing relationship with its counterpart state agency as part of the federal system. Similarly, the state legislature must share power with Congress on many of Florida's environmental issues.

The Florida legislature, operating through a system of committees, provides the statutory direction for environmental policies and oversees the state's environmental agencies. The role of the legislative committees is subject to the great combined power of the president of the senate and speaker of the house. Both these officers (the practice varying with the person) can exercise many sanctions, both positive and negative, on their fellow legislators, including assistance in raising campaign funds, appointment of committee members and chairpersons, channeling of enrolled bills to friendly or hostile committees, and appointments to conference committees. The two leaders, often enforcing a strict code of personal political loyalty, play a predominant role in state legislation (in contrast to the U.S. Congress, where legislative committees like the late

Henry Jackson's U.S. Senate Committee on the Interior had control of most of the action and in many respects became a fiefdom).

The key committees that make recommendations on environmental legislation in Florida are the house Natural Resources Committee and the senate Committee on Natural Resources and Conservation. The committee staffs and subcommittees are the centers for preparation of environmental legislation. The senate committee, for instance, has subcommittees on living resource management, energy, environmental protection and the issuing of permits, and land and water management. Other committees, such as the senate Committee on Government Operations, have been responsible for environmental reorganization of state agencies. From time to time, the legislature sets up ad hoc committees to study complex issues and recommend legislation. The creation of a temporary House Select Committee on Growth Management highlights the leadership's intent to place environmental planning high on the agenda for the 1980s. The actions of these committees affect land development and capital expenditures in cities and counties.

Not surprisingly, city and county officials stand on the "front line" of many environmental issues raised by population growth and land development. The Florida League of Cities, representing virtually all of the state's nearly 300 municipalities, and the State Association of County Commissioners, representing all 67 counties, employ professional staffs to lobby on local issues, including environmental quality. Their annual policy positions favor managing growth. But they also vigorously support local decision making, even though it may be at odds with ecological ideals. The Monroe County Commission has resisted regulation of the Florida Keys, and the Polk County Commission has recommended deregulating the environmentally endangered and ecologically valuable Green Swamp. Such policy positions reflect the power of development interests at the local level of government.

At the state level, development interests often organize in coalitions to lobby the legislature and the agencies of the executive branch alike. Land development interests are big business in Florida—real estate, construction, finance, planning, and engineering, all of which are growth oriented. In addition, the agricultural lobby with groups such as the Florida Sugar Cane League and the South Florida Growers' Association have a large stake in land-use and water-management policies. Concentrated in large corporations, these interests have long been successful lobbies in Tallahassee.

Extensive tract subdivision activity in Florida, an indicator of the importance of land development, is reported in *Subdividing Rural America,* a study by the President's Council on Environmental Quality. Florida accounts for 27 percent of all U.S. acreage that has been subdivided into lots. Large companies such as General Development, GAC, Deltona, AMREP, and ITT Community Development are in the business of creating new communities, often on land adjacent to ecologically valuable coastal or inland waters.

Industrial interests play a more local role and are associated with special environmental problems such as water pollution resulting from pulp and paper industries or land and groundwater damage resulting from surface mining operations associated with the nation's largest phosphate industry. Specifically, with regard to air pollution, industrial emissions through smokestacks are a problem in nine of Florida's counties; plans for meeting federal air quality standards were submitted early in 1979. The contribution of power plants to air pollution has been a source of political conflict, since conversion to coal-powered plants means deteriorating air quality and poses problems in meeting federal minimum safeguards. The public utilities, led by Florida Power and Light, are a major lobby.

Counterbalancing the development and industrial lobbies are the environmental and conservation lobbies, made up of diverse groups, often with specialized interests such as sport fishing, half-track racing, wilderness recreation, natural history, population control, environmental health, and land-use planning. Participation in environmental interest groups is voluntary; few groups, if any, have salaried staff. Table 14.1 lists the major groups active in Florida. In addition, there are local environmental groups, such as the Collier County Conservancy and the Sanibel-Captiva Conservation Foundation, and ad hoc coalitions such as Save Our Bay, Save Sand Key, and the Conchshell Alliance.

Coalition activity has tended to form around specific issues such as the proposed South Florida jetport, the cross-Florida barge canal, and the Dade County Masterplan. New coalitions have formed around current issues: the Florida Toxics Campaign, the Clean Air Coalition, the Everglades Protection Association, and the Kissimmee River Restoration Coalition. For the most part, the coalitions dissolve after the unifying issue is resolved.

Two environmental groups are forming statewide coalitions of environmental activists. The Environmental Service Center, affiliated with the Florida Defenders of the Environment, acts as a clearinghouse for environmental groups, using an extensive phone network and a newsletter. It is unique among environmental interest groups: Its efforts are focused exclusively on monitoring the bureaucracy and marshaling expertise from volunteer scientists and professionals for use in dealing with environmental agencies. The second coalition is a reinvigorated Florida chapter of the League of Conservation Voters, with board members from all of the leading environmental groups. The league is organized as a public interest political action committee (PAC) to elect environmentalists to public office. It publishes an environmental report card for Florida's elected representatives. The emergence of these broad-based coalitions indicates the political sophistication of the new environmental politics—a politics that relies increasingly on scientific knowledge and political know-how and less upon "save the baby seals" kind of emotional appeal.

It would be a mistake to view environmental interests as homogeneous, for they exhibit a great range of concerns: from local to global, from short-term to centuries-long. Environmentalists seeking controlled growth may oppose all growth: upper-middle-income homeowners use extreme arguments for environmental preservation to obscure their real objections to proposed higher-density, low-income housing projects. Nor are all developers greedily unconcerned with protection of the environment. Some developments are being constructed that are environmentally accommodating as well as profitable. Developers do complain, however, of the problem of getting answers from various governmental agencies to questions of how regulations apply to a particular project and how long agencies will take to make decisions and issue required permits. Unfortunately the images of environmentalists and developers have tended toward exaggerated stereotypes. What we know with confidence about environmentalists as a class is largely a result of survey research.

TABLE 14.1. Major Florida Environmental Interest Groups

Environmental Service Center, Tallahassee
Florida Audubon Society
Florida Conservation Foundation/Environmental Information Center
Florida Defenders of the Environment
Florida Federation of Garden Clubs
Florida Forestry Association
Florida Trail Association
Florida Lung Association, Committee on Air Quality
Florida Wildlife Federation
Florida Wildlife Sanctuary
Florida Zero Population Growth
Friends of the Everglades/Environmental Information Service, Miami
Izaak Walton League–Florida Division
League of Women Voters of Florida
Nature Conservancy–Florida
Sierra Club–Florida Chapter

Public opinion survey research has had limited success in explaining the general public's environmental concern. Persons who are worried about the environment are likely to be young, well-educated, and liberal. But these demographic factors explain only 10–15 percent of the public's environmental concern. Support for environmental issues is a widespread phenomenon and cuts across all major groupings of society.

Activist members of citizens' environmental groups have a narrower socioeconomic base of support. Volunteers are almost exclusively white, of middle-to upper-middle socioeconomic status, and predominantly between twenty and forty-five years of age. The core activists are dedicated. To mobilize broad support for specific positions, environmental activists exploit scientific and legal arguments along with emotionally charged issues that generate the free publicity of media news reporting.

The press in Florida has become an educational forum on environmental problems; often it has been an aid to environmental advocacy by providing an arena where environmental groups can focus and mobilize public opinion. Newspapers such as the *St. Petersburg Times* and the *Miami Herald* have been journalistically and editorially aggressive in support of environmental reforms.

Citizens' environmental groups have had some successes through the courts. A principal deficiency of the judicial process for environmental protection is that it requires the plaintiff to have legal standing in order to bring suit. The Florida Environmental Protection Act of 1971 attempted to broaden the base for legal actions by citizens aimed at protecting the environment. The legislation intended to give citizens—and thereby citizens' interest groups such as the Sierra Club and the Florida Audubon Society—the right to bring legal actions in Florida courts. Such statutory reforms were necessary because there were many legal obstacles to the effective use by environmentalist groups of the common law remedies of nuisance, trespass, negligence, and the public trust doctrine. But Florida's courts have narrowly interpreted the provisions of the act and have negated its legislative intent. The courts have retained the strict common law requirement of "special injury" and have prevented environmental groups from filing suit by declaring that such groups were not "citizens" under the act.

The League of Conservation Voters is campaigning for a state constitutional amendment guaranteeing citizens the right to sue on behalf of their environment. Patterned after constitutional provisions in Pennsylvania and Illinois, the initiative proposal creates a right to a healthful environment and a right of workers to know about the use of toxic substances in the workplace, an issue that is likely to gain labor union support for the proposal. The amendment would give substantial legal powers to organized environmental interests and is likely to encounter strong opposition from business interests. It reads:

> (a) Each person has a right to a healthful environment and duty to provide and to maintain a healthful environment for the benefit of this and future generations. Each person has a right to know and the duty to give notice shall be provided by law if a healthful environment has been or may be endangered by toxic or other potentially hazardous substances.
>
> (b) The natural waters, air, and wildlife in the state are public resources that shall be managed as a public trust for the use and benefit of all of the people of this and future generations and for the maintenance

of the natural ecosystems. Each person as beneficiary of this trust has a right to leave the trust purposes fulfilled.

(c) Each person, governmental or private, shall have standing to enforce the rights granted by this section against all other persons through legal proceedings.

The universities constitute the last major actor in Florida's environmental movement. Many university researchers volunteer their services as individuals or through organizations such as the Florida Defenders of the Environment. As centers of research, universities provide data and expert testimony to state agencies and legislative committees. The Institute of Food and Agricultural Sciences (IFAS) at the University of Florida must be considered a powerful lobby in its own right. In addition, the legislature, through the State University System, has funded applied research institutes such as the Florida Solar Energy Center at Cape Canaveral, the Florida Atlantic University–Florida International University Joint Center for Environmental and Urban Problems, the Florida Water Resources Research Center, the Center for Wetlands Research in Gainesville, and the Drinking Water Quality Research Center in Miami. The university system's Service through Application of Research (STAR) program encourages state agencies to make known their research needs and to solicit matching research proposals from university faculties.

Long-term Political Issues

One dimension of Florida's environmental politics encompasses specific issues such as the cross-Florida barge canal, the South Florida jetport, the Everglades National Park, the Big Cypress Swamp, protecting the manatee, power plant sitings, regulation of phosphate mining, air quality standards, drinking-water quality, and so forth. The issues are not only important in themselves but have often catalyzed the improvements in environmental decision making.

From a long-term point of view, such specific issues recede in importance. What matters is improving the quality of environmental decision making. Florida's environmental politics has been involved in restructuring coercive authority through governmental reorganization and in establishing a state and regional planning presence.

The Politics of Environmental Reorganization

Above and beyond the publicly recited reasons for governmental reorganization—the elimination of red tape, inefficiencies, and waste; unnecessary duplication and overlapping of governmental functions; and lack of public accountability—environmental reorganization is a political contest in Florida.

In the early 1970s, environmentalists reasoned that the extensive fragmentation of governmental authority on environmental protection matters was seriously hindering their objectives. Proposals circulated in the legislature to establish a Department of the Environment under which the many environmental activities of the Game and Fresh Water Fish Commission, the Department of Agriculture, the Department of Pollution Control, the Internal Improvement Fund, the Department of Natural Resources, and the Department of Health and Rehabilitative Services would be consolidated under a single director appointed by the governor. Such a reorganization would raise the functions of environmental regulation to full department status, serve as a symbol of the state's intent, and provide a powerful bureaucratic base for advancing environmental protection. Not incidentally, it would substantially increase the power of the governor at the expense of other cabinet officers. Conservative and development-oriented interests saw such a department as a threat; it would create a powerful bureau whose mission was to inhibit economic growth. As a result, environmental reorganization was stalemated until 1975. By the time, economic conditions had caused a virtual reversal in political positions of developers and environmentalists on the matter of reorganization. Environmentalists came to realize that the fragmentation and duplication of governmental authority—the multiple decision points for issuing permits and for policy making—made it difficult for developers to get their projects approved. Since time delays add to construction costs, the strategy of delaying approval appeared to be effective in stopping large projects. Developers, feeling the pressures of slowdown in the economy, objected to the additional costs imposed by the multiple permits and multiple decision points that had evolved haphazardly. Now it was the turn of the development interests to advocate environmental reorganization with the purpose of eliminating unnecessary regulation and simplifying the processes of approving development projects and issuing permits for them.

In 1975, a compromise reorganization was hammered out. There would be two major environmental agencies: a Department of Natural Resources and a Department of Environmental Regulation. The Department of Natural Resources, a conservation- and resource-oriented department involved with firms interested in developing the state's resources, would report to the cabinet. The Department of Environmental Regulation, a pollution-control-oriented agency responding to urban environmental problems and interests, would report to the governor. The Game and Fresh Water Fish Commission, constitutionally established, would retain its autonomy with no proposals for changes in its functions that would antagonize the largest conservation constituency, the hunters and anglers.

The reorganization compromise represents the pattern that has emerged in other states and at the federal level, where there is an Environmental Protection Agency charged with pollution abatement and a Department of the Interior concerned with the conservation of natural resources. The new structure for environmental decision making, along with a one-step simplified process of issuing permits, makes Florida's governmental machinery compatible with federal agencies and practices, enabling cooperative administrative relationships to develop regarding regulations and standards as well as federal grants for conservation programs. Only experience will tell if the reorganization compromise can bring about the needed multilevel coordination.

The division between conservation of natural resources and environmental regulation and protection separates the old conservation movement from the new environmental movement. The legacy of conservation—its emphasis on the efficient development of resources over the long term ("sustained yield")—has contributed much to the protection of our natural heritage: state parks, forests, wilderness areas, wildlife habitat protection, restocking of fresh water streams and lakes. At the same time, natural resource administration involves large profits for private companies engaged in mining, forestry, oil and gas, and commercial fishing. The private development of public resources has periodically been the subject of scandal, corruption, and fraud regarding land and resource transactions. The new environmental politics is a different type of politics, dependent upon large federal grants and scientific setting of standards.

No reorganization can resolve the increasing need for coordination. Unfortunately, there is no magical procedure or technique to achieve coordination of diverse public agency functions and a plurality of private perspectives. No technique of coordination can overcome the political reality that some individuals and organizations often have more to gain by refusing to coordinate. In spite of well-founded doubts that coordination will become the rule, there is no doubt that such efforts will continually be made when only mutually acceptable solutions will suffice.

Coordination is likely to involve representatives from both public and private groups addressing specific problems. One such effort is the Kissimmee River Restoration Act of 1976, which created a broadly representative coordinating council. The process of reaching agreement has been long and drawn out with tendencies toward stalemate. Pressure from the governor, who has made saving the Everglades a high priority, and aggressive support from a Repair the Everglades Coalition and the press created conditions for compromise. Nine years later, the Kissimmee River Coordinating Council decided to restore partially four miles of river as an experiment. Its action sets in motion the first restoration of a major river ecosystem. Coordination of the project will test the technical and political capacity of the system.

Coordination of bureaucratic efforts is also influenced by the workings of the federal system. Most environmental issues require more than one level of government action for a solution. In many environmental areas—air and water pollution, endangered and threatened species, funding for construction of sewage treatment plants, and coastal zone management—the federal government is the senior partner in the federal-state effort to mitigate environmental damage. It not only provides a major portion of the money through grants-in-aid but also establishes and enforces national standards and requires environmental impact statements on all major projects involving significant federal participation. The trend is toward more intergovernmental involvement and therefore more federal participation in Florida's environmental politics.

Politics of Regionalism

To manage the growth issues facing the state, especially with regard to land and water, the state has chosen a middle path. Historically, state governments have left land use and zoning decisions to local governments. To manage growth, the state could assume land-use management functions or develop a three-tier model: state, regional, and local government. Florida has made the regional variation primary.

The Florida Environmental Land Management Act of 1972 created a regional planning process, with ten regional planning agencies (later expanded to eleven because of political divisions in South Florida; see fig. 3, p. 248). The regional planning councils, made up of locally elected officials, review "developments of regional impact" (airports, hospitals, shopping centers, large residential developments, etc.) and make recommendations to respective local governments, which issue a "development order" and appropriate permits. The regional planning councils are intermediaries between local governments and the state cabinet. On developments of regional impact, there may be review by the governor and cabinet if the regional council so advises.

With regard to the five regional water management districts created by the Water Reserve Act of 1972, a subsequent constitutional amendment granted the water management districts (WMD) the power to levy a limited ad valorem tax to finance projects. Determining the WMD boundaries was one of those rare instances in which ecological criteria were used as a primary basis for drawing a legal-administrative boundary. Each district corresponds to a regional watershed and can be managed as an ecosystem (see fig. 13.5, p. 259) except that water quality issues are managed by the Department of Environmental Regulation. The administrative separation of water quantity management from water quality management necessitates additional coordination between administrative agencies that are often at odds due to different responsibilities and sources of support.

The basic political difficulty for regional environmental management is the lack of a regional constituency. Individuals and groups identify with a neighborhood, a city, a county, or a state and may vote for representatives at several of these levels. The regions cut across political jurisdictions and do not command the allegiance of regionally defined groups of citizens. The success of regional planning efforts, therefore, lies in gaining voluntary cooperation from local governmental agencies and political support from the governor and the cabinet on decisions that are appealed.

An Environmental Agenda

In the 1980s, the state will probably assume a greater role in environmental planning and management while simultaneously encouraging local and regional initiative. At the same time, federal aid and support will shrink. Without an aggressive federal presence and a steady flow of federal dollars, reversing generations of environmental abuse will challenge the state's political resolve.

The reapportioned legislatures of 1972 and 1982 responded with landmark environmental legislation. Reflecting an urban anxiety with growth and pollution problems, the state's political leadership has taken preliminary steps for building a consensus around growth management.

Recent decisions point to the high priority of growth management in state politics of the 1980s. Task forces have been formed, special legislative committees created, workshops held around the state, conferences convened to study the issues and generate political support for new policies, and environmentalists appointed to key political and administrative posts. Governor Graham has led the way: he appointed the state's second Environmental Land Management Commission; he selected Dr. John DeGrove, a respected academic advocate of growth management, to head the Department of Community Affairs; and he set up three major policy initiatives, Save Our Rivers, Save Our Coasts, and Save Our Everglades. The Florida House of Representatives has a Select Committee on Growth Management and a water management task force, and the leadership of the legislature's Natural Resource Committees is supporting growth management initiatives.

Moderate environmentalists and moderate business interests are more likely to agree on growth management policies that are flexible and allow for compromise. The middle ground of growth management isolates both no-growth and anti-environmental forces, enabling environmental, business, and governmental interests to work out policies for balancing development and environment. Thus Florida's political agenda is once again directed at managing the environmental consequences of growth.

Selected References

Carter, Luther J. *The Florida Experience: Land and Water Policy in a Growth State*. Baltimore: Johns Hopkins University Press, 1974.

ENFO Newsletter. (Bimonthly publication of the Environmental Information Center of the Florida Conservation Foundation, Inc.)

Florida Environmental and Urban Issues. (Bimonthly publication of the Florida Atlantic University–Florida International University Joint Center for Environmental and Urban Problems.)

Florida Naturalist, The. (Bimonthly publication of the Florida Audubon Society.)

Florida Out-of-Doors. (Bimonthly publication of the Florida Wildlife Federation.)

Florida's Environmental News. (Monthly publication of the Florida Department of Environmental Regulation.)

Florida Wildlife. (Bimonthly publication of the Florida Game and Fresh Water Fish Commission.)

Growth Management in South Florida: A Guide for Public Involvement. Florida Atlantic University–Florida International University Joint Center for Environmental and Urban Problems, 1977.

Harrell, Martha L. "A Proposal for Revision of the Florida Constitution: Environmental Rights for Florida Citizens." *Florida State University Law Review* 5, no. 4 (Fall 1977): 809–28.

Henning, Daniel H. *Environmental Policy and Administration*. New York: Elsevier, 1974.

Maggiotto, Michael A., and Bowman, Ann. "Policy Orientations and Environmental Regulation: A Case Study of Florida's Legislators." *Environment and Behavior* (March 1982):155–70.

Ophuls, William. *Ecology and the Politics of Scarcity*. San Francisco: Witt, Freeman & Co., 1977.

Pelican Papers, The. (Bimonthly publication of the Sierra Club, Florida Chapter.)

Rosenbaum, Walter A. *The Politics of Environmental Concern*. 2d ed. New York: Praeger Publishers, 1977.

Van Liere, Kent D., and Dunlap, Riley. "The Social Bases of Environmental Concern: A Review of Hypotheses, Explanations, and Empirical Evidence." *Public Opinion Quarterly* (Summer 1980):181–97.

15 Minorities in Florida Politics

Events of the 1960s and early 1970s, especially the black civil rights movement, raised anew the issue of equality for disadvantaged minorities in both Florida and the nation at large. These recent minority challenges to the political system underscored once again the importance of these groups in the political process. This chapter will explore the political role played in Florida by four different minority groups — blacks, women, the aged, and Hispanics.

A minority should be thought of as a group of people who, because of distinguishing physical or cultural characteristics, are singled out from the dominant group (white males) and have received unequal treatment. White males control a disproportionate share of political and economic power and are afforded higher social status than minority groups, which are excluded (both formally and informally) from full participation in the quest for power. Thus minority status is not necessarily a matter of numbers — if it were, women would be classified as a majority, not a minority — but a matter of group discrimination and lack of proportional political and economic influence.

Although a variety of minority groups have performed significant roles in Florida's recent political history, four groups in particular deserve special attention because of their relative influence. Blacks have been important in Florida since slavery times, and no other minority group recently has so actively asserted its demands for equality. Women, too, have begun to challenge their relegation to second-class citizenship. Hispanics, especially Cuban-Americans, and the aged (those persons over sixty years of age) are more recent arrivals on Florida's political scene, yet they are beginning to organize their considerable numbers for political action. Other minority groups, such as the Seminole Indians and various white ethnics, have also been important in Florida's politics at certain times, but none of these groups has exerted the consistent recent influence of any of the other four groups.

Blacks

by James Button

UNIVERSITY OF FLORIDA

15A

Blacks are the single largest racial minority in Florida, numbering 1,342,955 persons in 1980, or 13.6 percent of Florida's population. At the time of the Civil War, however, blacks (including slaves and a few freedmen) comprised almost 50 percent of Florida's population. No other minority has influenced Florida's political past as much as have its blacks. Black political history has been divided into two phases—the post–Civil War period of almost complete economic, social, and political subjugation of blacks, and the recent period of black political progress. The latter period dates only from the famous *Brown* decision of the U.S. Supreme Court in 1954; since then blacks have actively sought and gained a much greater share of political and economic power in Florida, but the quest for equality for blacks has been a struggle. In a southern state where slaves were perceived as property at least until the time of the Civil War, and where even after that war blacks were assumed to be inferior to whites in almost every respect, blacks have found it difficult to gain greater political voice and economic resources.

Post–Civil War Era

Lacking education and economic skills, newly freed blacks became pawns in the struggle between the radical Republicans and Democrats following the Civil War. Legally freed by the Thirteenth Amendment to the U.S. Constitution and enfranchised by the Fifteenth Amendment, blacks in Florida not only voted in large numbers after the Civil War but also frequently held office. For example, there were nineteen Negroes among the seventy-six members of the first legislature elected under the new Florida constitution of 1868. Several blacks were also elected to the U.S. Congress during this period.

With the end of the period of Reconstruction in 1876, however, Florida's Democrats increasingly attempted to check Negro political advancement. Using violence, threats, and economic coercion, they controlled Negro voting to a great extent. Since a majority of blacks were illiterate and of low economic status, they were especially vulnerable to intimidation by whites.

In the constitutional convention of 1885, Democrats sought to establish formal impediments to black voting. Although the convention voted to restore county self-government, it allowed the governor to retain the power to appoint county commissioners, who controlled local election machinery, and to suspend many locally elected officials. This allowed the chief executive of Florida to control local government and to dilute the power of a local black vote.

By 1889 the Florida legislature had enacted a poll tax and a multiple-ballot-box law. These two legal impediments struck hard at blacks (and the Republican party): poor blacks were unable to pay a poll tax, and multiple ballot boxes and separate ballots for each office tended to confuse the illiterate black voter. The effects of these formal impediments were soon apparent. In 1888, the Republican candidate for governor received more than 26,000 votes, but two years later a Republican candidate for controller, also a statewide office, garnered less than 5,000 votes.

Of all the disenfranchising techniques, however, perhaps the most effectively restrictive was the white primary. By 1902, the Democratic party in Florida was able to set up primary elections that were open only to whites, an arrangement that ultimately applied to state, county, and local elections. This action virtually completed the process of disfranchising Florida's black citizens.

In addition to legal obstacles that limited black political participation, the Florida legislature had also enacted in the period after the Civil War the infamous "black codes." The black codes, a series of laws that limited black involvement in the state's economy and society, institutionalized or legitimated the feelings of a dominant white class that perceived blacks as mentally inferior and incompetent. First enacted in 1856 and 1866, the laws were to be applied specifically to blacks in the areas of crime, vagrancy, apprenticeship, marriage, taxation, labor contracts, and the legal system. For example, the death penalty was to be imposed for the crime of inciting insurrection, raping a white female, or administering poison, and Negroes were denied the right to carry firearms, knives, or various weapons without a license from a local judge. This latter law obviously reflected the anxiety among whites in Florida about the possibility of black insurrections and acts of vengeance against whites for previous injustices. Marriages between blacks and whites were, of course, prohibited. As far as the legal system was concerned, Negroes could only testify in court cases involving blacks, and juries were made up of white men only.

The intervention of the federal government in the South during Reconstruction served to alleviate the effects of these black codes; but once federal pressure was removed, Florida, like most other southern states, returned to restricting blacks in almost every aspect of life. By the late 1880s, the Florida legislature had passed a series of "Jim Crow" laws, which enforced in the state a segregation that already existed by custom. These new laws went beyond the black codes of the earlier period and made racial segregation in Florida even more absolute than it had been at the end of the Civil War. For example, an 1895 statute prohibited school attendance under circumstances in which whites and blacks would attend the same classes, and a 1905 act required that the races be separated on streetcars and other forms of transportation. In addition to legal codes, private violence by whites against blacks increased in the late 1800s. Brutal lynchings were not unusual, especially in the rural counties of North Florida, and were a means by which whites maintained their supremacy over blacks.

Race relations in Florida thus reached a low point in the early twentieth century. They were similar to the relations that existed between whites and blacks in other southern states and were generally supported by racist rhetoric and social science writings that promulgated the theory of racial inferiority. Politics in Florida reflected these developments. There was even a movement to lessen racial problems by sending blacks to Africa, and Governor Napoleon Broward proposed in a message to the legislature in 1907 a mass removal of blacks from the U.S.

In the early 1940s, black politics in Florida were little different than at the turn of the century. Except for the repeal of the state poll tax by the state legislature in 1937, most of the disfranchising provisions were still in effect. The poll tax repeal did have a slight effect upon black voter registration, especially in Duval County (which includes Jacksonville), but for the most part black registration increased only slightly. Blacks still registered primarily as Republicans or as independents. Although registration figures broken down by race were not available prior to 1946, the best estimates were that Negro registration accounted for at least half of the state's Republican party registration. By 1946, however, blacks, attracted primarily by President Franklin Roosevelt and the New Deal, were beginning to register in relatively large numbers as Democrats.

Still there were major barriers to effective black political participation in Florida. The acceptance of the all-white primary rule was still overwhelming and had not yet been overturned judicially in Florida. In 1944, however, the U.S. Supreme Court invalidated the all-white primary in the case of *Smith* v. *Allwright,* bringing an immediate response in the South. Several proposals were introduced in the 1945 session of the Florida legislature to "preserve the purity of the ballot," but these ultimately failed and black voter registration began to increase. Thus the collapse of the Democratic white primary as a legal impediment to voting marked a major change in the political rules. For example, in 1944 it was estimated that approximately 20,000 Negroes were registered as Republicans in the state while almost none were registered as Democrats. These registered voters approximated 5.5 percent of the adult Negro population. By 1948 the number had increased to approximately 64,000 Negro registrants, or almost 17 percent of the voting-age black population; by

1950 the registration figure had jumped to almost 32 percent of age-eligible blacks, more than 90 percent of them registered as Democrats.

The *Brown* Decision and Afterward

Although the decline of the white primary was important, the *Brown* decision of 1954 forbidding separate public schools for blacks and whites marked the major turning point in race relations in Florida. Reaction to the *Brown* decision in Florida was moderate compared to that in other Deep South states; yet most white Floridians prepared themselves to resist. Florida was one of only four states in the country that had no school integration in 1954, and the state had a wide range of laws requiring segregation in various other aspects of society. Not long after the decision, the state legislature enacted legislation providing for the closing of public schools if the federal government should use force to integrate them. It also passed a resolution calling on the governor of Florida to interpose the claimed sovereign authority of the state to protect its citizens from any effort of the national government to enforce the *Brown* decision.

The idea that the state could block federal action was called interposition. Southern states had long defied federal intervention in their activities (especially in matters of race relations), arguing that the states were preeminent in the federal structure except for the few powers specifically delegated by the Constitution to the national government. This theory of states' rights, however, was rejected both by presidential actions and by federal court decisions in the twentieth century.

Not all white Floridians reacted so defiantly. State Attorney General Richard Ervin, for example, had filed a brief in the *Brown* case that accepted integration but urged gradualism in compliance. Gradual racial change did begin to occur. By 1950 Florida's black population, 21.8 percent, was a relatively small percentage compared with those of other southern states and with earlier periods in its own past. This situation served to lessen the fear felt by Florida's whites of increased black demands. Furthermore, the growing migration into Florida from the Northeast and Midwest and the resulting urbanization of the southern region of the state tended to moderate racial strife. Thus with pressure from the courts, black civil rights groups, liberal whites, and later the U.S. president and Congress, the barriers of segregation began to fall.

The statesmanship of Governor LeRoy Collins during this period was crucial, for he emphasized to Floridians that racial integration was coming and that it was now, or would soon be, the law of the land. In addition, several civil rights groups began to push for integration on a number of fronts. The National Association for the Advancement of Colored People (NAACP) filed suits to integrate schools, while the Congress of Racial Equality (CORE) went to great lengths to attack discrimination in public accommodations. Inspired by bus boycotts in Montgomery, Alabama, CORE began direct-action campaigns in Tallahassee in 1956–57 to integrate buses and stores. By the late 1950s and early 1960s, CORE had extended its activities to Miami, St. Petersburg, and other sizable cities in the state.

In voter registration, progress was somewhat slower. The *Brown* case had made many whites more sensitive to actions that promoted black equality, and opposition to black voter registration seemed to increase immediately following the desegregation ruling. For example, black voter registration totaled 35 percent of the age-eligible blacks in 1954 but by 1960 had increased to only 39 percent. This small increase was due partly to the lack of experienced black political leaders and organizations to carry out registration drives, but it was also due to black fears of physical violence and economic intimidation by whites. The memory was still vivid of the 1951 brutal slaying of Harry T. Moore, the black state chairman of the NAACP, who had been active in Negro voter registration. The rejuvenation of white supremacy organizations, such as the Ku Klux Klan, local citizens' councils, and the Federation for Constitutional Government, also frightened many blacks. In addition, state legislative committees had been set up to investigate the activities of various civil rights groups in Florida, especially the NAACP, and the attempt was often made to discredit these organizations by linking them with unpopular or subversive causes.

Nevertheless by the early 1960s, due to a more liberal climate nationally and increased pressure from local civil rights groups, blacks began to register to vote in larger numbers. With increased activity from the Florida Progressive Voters League, CORE, NAACP, and the Voter Education Project, black voter registration increased dramatically in Florida between 1960 and 1964. Voter registration efforts proved to be quite successful in major cities like Miami, Tallahassee, and Jacksonville but were much less successful in the rural counties of North Florida. It was in the North Florida counties, which were cultural and political extensions of the Deep South and which contained ten of Florida's eleven counties with high black populations, that voter registration efforts met the greatest resistance. Yet even in these areas progress was made, and by 1964 fully 64 percent of voting-age blacks were registered. Among southern states only Tennessee and Texas could claim similar success by this period. By 1966, after passage of the national Civil Rights acts and with a large majority of adult blacks registered to vote in the state, major gubernatorial candidates began to solicit the black vote; in 1970, for the first time since the *Brown* decision, all major Democratic candidates for governor campaigned as nonsegregationists.

A clear indication of the extent of change in race relations in Florida was the election of Reubin Askew as governor in 1970. Elected on a reform platform,

Askew supported busing to achieve racial integration of schools despite the fact that a 1972 antibusing resolution was supported by Floridians three to one in a statewide referendum. Askew also established an affirmative action program to correct the underrepresentation of blacks in state government, and by 1972 the number of blacks in state employment had doubled. In 1975, the governor appointed Joseph Hatchett to fill an unexpired term on the Florida Supreme Court, making him the first black to sit on that court; Hatchett subsequently was elected to the court and in 1979 was appointed to the federal bench. In 1978

Mr. and Mrs. Charles Chestnut III being congratulated by opponent Judy Ott on his election to the Alachua County School Board in 1976. Photo courtesy *Gainesville Sun*.

Jessie McCrary was appointed to fill an unexpired term as secretary of state and thus became the first black man in modern times to be a member of the Florida cabinet; McCrary did not run for election at the end of his appointed term.

The most dramatic indication of marked progress in black politics was the tremendous increase in the number of black elected officials in Florida. From less than half a dozen in 1965, the number of blacks elected to office had increased to 118 by 1982. Seventy-one of these officials served as municipal officeholders, and there was evidence that these local elected officials benefited their black constituents. A survey of black municipal officeholders, for example, suggested that they were able to provide improved public services for blacks, especially streets, water and sewage, and recreation facilities. These services were considered to be some of the most pressing problems in most black areas. Federal grants and revenue-sharing funds were often important in helping to improve city services such as public works, streets, housing, and employment. Moreover, the affirmative action requirements that accompanied federal funds served to increase municipal employment of blacks. Perhaps of greatest importance, however, were the more symbolic kinds of benefits that these black officials believed they provided. These benefits included securing black appointments to local boards or committees, encouraging other blacks to run for elective office, breaking down racial stereotypes, and educating blacks on how to become more politically effective.

Nevertheless, black political progress in the 1970s was uneven at best. A Voter Education Project report cited 1974 voter registration statistics showing that for Florida 50.8 percent of black adults were registered to vote, a lower figure than in most other southern states and more than 10 percent less than the comparable figure for white registrants. The reasons for the relatively low black voter registration in Florida seemed to be both institutional and noninstitutional in character. Noninstitutional barriers included black apathy, fear of economic reprisal from whites, and the lingering feeling that politics was "white man's business." Institutional impediments consisted of "purges" of the voter rolls, which resulted in the disproportionate removal of blacks from these rolls, problems of transportation to the polls, and inconvenient registration hours. Furthermore, most city elections in Florida were at-large, making it difficult for blacks to win since their supporters' votes were diluted by a large white vote. Relatively few blacks were elected to positions of any real political authority, like county commissions. By 1982, however, there were 12 black members of the Florida House and two black senators, an increase resulting from adoption of single-member districts in the 1982 reapportionment.

Even among local black officeholders, several factors tended to impede their efforts. Most of these city officials had as many white constituents as black, thus making it difficult for them to respond to the needs of blacks. In addition the impoverished conditions of various communities, especially the predominantly black and rural communities, made it difficult to gain the necessary funds to improve services and to attract industrial and commercial growth. Although intransigent whites were seen as resistant to the goals of many black officeholders, most of these black officials felt that the lack of cooperation and support from their black constituents was at least as important a barrier. Feelings of jealousy and resentment, competition for office, lack of understanding of the political process, and vastly increased black expectations for improvements that went unmet were all suggested as explanations for the lack of black cooperation.

Despite these difficulties, blacks in Florida have made tremendous strides in the decades of the 1960s and 1970s toward improving their political and economic circumstances. Although blacks have not gained socioeconomic equality with whites in Florida, they have improved their living conditions substantially and have done so to a great extent through securing more and better public resources. Yet it may be that the greatest benefits in the long run of the black political movement will be a new black pride and a greater feeling of control over their own destiny. In the words of one local black official, "Being in office made me more aware of government and want to know more about government. ...and my kids are going to know more about government when they grow up. I now realize that government can work for people. ...I didn't use to believe this, but my attitude has changed."

The unrest that arose in Miami in the 1980s showed that although there had been progress in racial relations, there continued to be underlying tensions that could erupt.

Selected References

Black, Earl. *Southern Governors and Civil Rights: Racial Segregation as a Campaign Issue in the Second Reconstruction*. Cambridge: Harvard University Press, 1976.

Button, James. "Impact of Black Elected Municipal Officials: A Descriptive Analysis." Paper presented at the annual meeting of the Southern Political Science Association, Atlanta, Georgia, 10 November 1978.

Colburn, David R., and Scher, Richard K. "Race Relations and Florida Gubernatorial Politics since the *Brown* Decision." *Florida Historical Quarterly* (October 1976): 153–69.

Lawson, Steven F. *Black Ballots: Voting Rights in the South, 1944–1969*. New York: Columbia University Press, 1976.

Matthews, David R., and Prothro, James W. *Negroes and the New Southern Politics*. New York: Harcourt, Brace, and World, 1966.

Meier, August, and Rudwick, Elliott. *CORE: A Study in the Civil Rights Movement, 1942–1968*. Urbana: University of Illinois Press, 1975.

Price, Hugh Douglas. *The Negro and Southern Politics: A Chapter of Florida History*. Westport, Conn.: Greenwood Press, 1957.

Shofner, Jerrell H. "Custom, Law, and History: The Enduring Influence of Florida's 'Black Code.' " *Florida Historical Quarterly* (January 1977): 277–98.

15B Women in Florida

by Joan Carver

JACKSONVILLE UNIVERSITY

In 1970, even though women constituted a majority (52 percent) of Florida's population, their status was that of a minority. On the periphery of power in Florida, women were, and remain, second-class citizens economically and politically. Histories of the state give only bare mention of the activities of women; census data reveal the weakness of women's economic position; lists of elected officials include few women. This situation is hardly unique to Florida. Opportunities for women, in no state equal to opportunities for men, have been particularly limited in the South, where, as Anne Firor Scott points out in *The Southern Lady from Pedestal to Politics,* the myth of the southern lady has served as a golden cord binding women to traditional roles. The southern states were the most resistant to granting women the right to vote, and more recently they have been the most opposed to ratifying the Equal Rights Amendment.

In Florida the traditional attitudes that have limited women's options are being challenged. The movement to Florida of large numbers of nonsoutherners, especially after World War II, has made Florida somewhat different from its sister states of the South: it is a state in the South but not quite *of* the South. The influx of newcomers has resulted in the formation of two cultures with respect to women: a conservative culture in the northern part of the state, where native southerners are most numerous and old attitudes strongest, and a culture more receptive to change in the central and southern parts of the state, which have taken the lead in opening opportunites for women.

Women's involvement in the political life of the state quickened around 1960. Earlier years had seen them acquire the franchise and laboriously build up the foundations of their political power. Since 1960 women have made dramatic progress toward full equality, their progress facilitated by a shift of political power away from the northern part of the state.

Years of Awakening: 1890–1960

The period from 1890 to 1920 was marked by the political awakening of women in Florida. Women's organizations developed; women began to work for the vote and, at both state and local levels, to push for changes in public policy. Their concerns ranged from increasing their own access to political participation and improving public education to getting cows out of the city streets. (The largest and most active of the early women's organizations was the Florida Federation of Women's Clubs; the breadth of its interests is described in Lucy Worthington Blackman's history of the organization's early years.)

The issue of woman suffrage, however, was of prime importance, for only the vote could provide women with an independent base of power. In Florida the suffrage struggle began late and was modest in scale: not until 1912, some fifty years after woman suffrage efforts began in the North, was a continuous campaign for the vote undertaken in Florida. In that year the Florida Equal Franchise League was organized in Jacksonville, and in the following year the Florida Equal Suffrage Association, which was to become the leading suffrage organization, was formed in Orlando. These organizations, never larger than about a thousand members each, were subsequently joined by other groups, the most important of which was the Florida Federation of Women's Clubs, the largest women's organization in the state. While the number of women active in the suffrage effort remained small, the most conspicuous of them were women of education and stature, whose leadership in a variety of community organizations brought respectability to the suffrage movement. (The history of the suffrage movement in Florida is described in detail by Kenneth Johnson in his doctoral dissertation. See also the articles by Johnson and by A. Elizabeth Taylor in *Florida Historical Quarterly*.)

In Florida the suffragists concentrated, first, on persuading Florida's legislators to propose to the voters a state constitutional amendment extending suffrage to women and, second, on winning support for the federal constitutional amendment. Neither of these goals was realized. The Florida suffragists' only successes came at the local level: between 1915 and 1920 twenty-three municipalities granted women the right to vote.

In the southern and central parts of the state a pattern of greater support for women's rights appeared during the suffrage struggle; that pattern would be repeated in later contests on women's issues. Suffrage organizations were concentrated in these regions, as were the twenty-three municipalities that granted women the right to vote. Of Florida's four federal congressmen and two senators, the two who voted for the Nineteenth Amendment to the federal Constitution were the congressmen serving primarily the southern and central sectors of the state. The lowest level of support in the state legislature for the extension of suffrage to women was found among the representatives from the northern counties. For example, in 1913 support for women's suffrage ranged from 27 percent among northern county representatives to 100 percent among those from South Florida.

The Florida suffrage proposals failed to win approval — even though there was no organized opposition to them — for several reasons. First, there was a strong desire to preserve the role of the traditional submissive southern lady;

said one Florida congressman, "Let us then leave woman where she is — the loveliest of all creation, queen of the household." Some envisioned horrible consequences resulting from giving women the vote, such as the destruction of the home, the degradation of woman, and the jeopardy of the public weal through the irrationality of female voting. As in other parts of the South, political considerations were an important source of opposition; the specter was raised of large numbers of black women voting, thereby adding to the political power of blacks and of Republicans. In fact, the immediate impact of the vote, when it was finally achieved in 1920 by the Nineteenth Amendment, was dismayingly small.

Winning the vote transformed neither women's position in society nor policies affecting women. From 1920 to 1960 little was achieved politically by women. Despite the enactment in 1935 of a state law requiring equal representation of men and women on the executive committees at every level of party organization, women were involved for the most part only at the lower echelons. (The background of the mandating of the fifty-fifty rule is described by James McGovern in "Helen Hunt West, Florida's Pioneer for E.R.A.") Few women ran for office; fewer were elected. Those chosen tended to win election by extraordinary strength of personality or by the more usual "widow's route." Florida's only federal congresswoman during these years, Ruth Bryan Owen (Rohde), was an assertive, dynamic person. The daughter of William Jennings Bryan, Ruth Owen crossed Florida's political skies like a meteor. Elected to the house in 1928, less than a decade after moving to Florida, she was defeated after two terms in office, apparently because she voted against the repeal of Prohibition. On her defeat, she chose to remain in Washington; she was later appointed minister to Denmark and never returned to Florida. The only woman elected to statewide office during these years was Mamie Eaton Green, who succeeded her husband to the post of railroad commissioner in 1927 and was twice elected on her own merits.

Women's legislative successes in this period were not impressive. The Legislative Council, set up in 1921 under the auspices of the League of Women Voters and the Florida Federation of Women's Clubs for the purpose of coordinating the lobbying efforts of women's organizations, was active only in the twenties and early thirties. The strength of the council and of the various women's clubs fluctuated sharply over the years; the depression took a heavy toll of women's club memberships, which reduced their financial base and that of the council. The goals of the council and of most of the women's groups were quite conservative, focusing on such long-standing concerns of club women as conservation, public education, and good government. Proposals directly related to the status of women were few in number, modest in scope — and seldom enacted into law. Like their counterparts elsewhere, the major women's

Left: Demonstrating in favor of the Equal Rights Amendment, the capitol building, Tallahassee, 1973. Below: May Mann (Mrs. W. S.) Jennings, 1901. Photos courtesy State Photographic Archives, Strozier Library, Florida State University, Tallahassee.

groups in Florida opposed the Equal Rights Amendment as a threat to hard-won protective legislation for women. Ironically, in Florida women had had little success in getting such protective legislation enacted.

The outstanding figure in the legislative efforts of Florida women was May Mann Jennings, a leader in the Florida Federation of Women's Clubs, the Democratic party, and the League of Women Voters. As the first and only president of the Legislative Council, she shaped its priorities and tactics. From early in the century through the 1930s, May Jennings organized the women of the state and lobbied tirelessly for a variety of causes, including woman suffrage, stricter enforcement of Prohibition, and a variety of conservation measures. But once the vote was won, her attention shifted from women's issues; and her position on many other matters was typically conservative. She was, for example, a strong opponent of the Equal Rights Amendment. Her papers provided a wealth of insight into the interests of women of the time.

Years of Change: 1960 – 1978

Dramatic changes in the political and legal position of women occurred in the 1960s and 1970s. Suddenly Florida led the South in the progress made by women. Some particularly significant factors brought about this transformation.

First, women entered the work force, in Florida and throughout the nation, in increasing numbers. According to the U.S. Census, only 31 percent of the nation's women over sixteen were in the labor force in 1950; by 1975 the Bureau of Labor Statistics reported that this figure had reached 53 percent.

Second, more women attended the state's colleges and universities, where they acquired the training essential for more successful economic and political involvement. In 1950 Florida's universities enrolled 11,605 women, 31 percent of total enrollment. By 1970 women students totaled 94,375, or 40 percent of the enrollment, and 187,470, or 50 percent, by 1978. Especially important was the sharp increase in women law students in the decade of the 1970s: in 1966 there were only 16 women in Florida's two state law schools, or 2 percent of the total number of law students; by 1978 there were 418 women students, or 37 percent.

Women's political influence increased also through higher numbers voting (by the end of the 1960s registered women voters outnumbered registered male voters in the major counties in the state) and through greater activity by feminist groups. In the early 1970s there were state organizations of the National Organization of Women (concerned primarily with lobbying for issues affecting women) and the Women's Political Caucus (which encouraged and supported women candidates and candidates favorable to women's issues). The older and more conventional League of Women Voters shifted leftward to lead the drive for ratification by Florida of the Equal Rights Amendment (which in earlier years it had opposed).

A larger number of women were elected to political office at both the state and local levels in these years. Before 1960 only five women had served in the state legislature; none had served more than three terms. As a result of the 1963 reapportionment of the Florida legislature, three women were elected to the Florida house, and for the first time in Florida history a woman, Beth Johnson, was elected to the senate. All were elected from metropolitan areas whose representation had increased with reapportionment.

A surge in women members of the legislature came in the early 1970s as the political consciousness of women increased nationwide. The Center for the American Woman and Politics reports that the national percentage of state legislators who were women was 4 percent in 1969; by 1979 it had reached 9 percent. In Florida in 1974 twelve women were elected to the Florida house and one to the senate; two years later the numbers were sixteen and two. From 1920 to 1978 a total of thirty women had been elected to the Florida legislature, twenty-five of them after 1962 and only two from the northern tier of counties. These were in many ways not the average Florida woman; only a third of them were born in Florida, over two-thirds were college graduates, and all had been active in party or community organizations (see table 15.1). In 1983, 28 of the 160 Florida legislators (17.5 percent) were women. While these women legislators have not confined their attention merely to women's issues, much of the recent legislation enacted to improve the status of women has been sponsored or strongly supported by them. Their presence may contribute, as one suggested, to a heightened male consciousness of women's needs.

Women got themselves elected more frequently at the local level as well as at the state level. In 1950 only 2 of 335 county commissioners in the state were women. There were no women mayors, and in 180 incorporated communities only 16 women were council members. By 1978 there were 18 county commissioners, 19 mayors, and 204 council members who were women. There were more women holding positions on school boards (one of the earliest objectives of the Florida Federation of Women's Clubs), 26 in 1950 and 83 in 1978, and in county administrative posts. Yet most of the cities in which women held office were small, and the county positions they held most often had little responsibility for policy. Their success in getting elected was greatest in the central and southern regions of the state.

At the end of the 1970s, Florida ranked among the leading states in the South in the number of women on the bench, in the proportion of state legislators who were women, and in the number of local officials who were women. The importance of resident nonsoutherners to the public acceptance of a nontraditional

TABLE 15.1. Characteristics of Florida's Women Legislators, 1918–78

Time Span	No. Elected[a]	Section of Fla.[b]			Party[c]			Race[d]		Place of Birth[e]			Education[f]			Occupation[g]				Age when Elected[h]				No. of Chairs[i]
		N	C	S	D	R	I	W	B	FL	S	OS	HS	CD	GD	Law	BS	HW	0	-30	30–45	45+	U	
1918–62	5	1	3	1	5			5	0	3		2	1	3	1	1	2	2		1	1	3		4
1963–72	10	1	5	4	5	4	1	8	2	2	2	6	5	3	2	2	2	5	1		6	3	1	2
1973–78	15	0	8	7	11	4		15	0	4	2	9	3	9	3	2	4	3	6	2	7	2	4	
Total	30	2	16	12	21	8	1	28	2	9	4	17	9	15	6	5	8	10	7	3	14	8	5	6

a. Women legislators whose terms cut across two time spans are included in the time period within which their date of initial election would fall.
b. Section of Florida: N, northern; C, central; S, southern. See fig. 15.1 for exact line of division.
c. Party: D, Democratic; R, Republican; I, Independent.
d. Race: W, white; B, black.
e. Place of birth: FL, Florida; S, South; OS, outside the eleven states of the South.
f. Education: HS, at least a high school degree; CD, college degree; GD, graduate or law degree. With only two exceptions every person listed under HS had at least some college work and several of those under CD had some advanced work.
g. Occupation: BS, business; HW, housewife; O, other. These are occupations as listed by the legislators. Not all candidates were active in the occupations at the time of their election to the legislature.
h. Age at the time of first election: -30, under 30; 45+, over 45; U, unlisted.
i. No. of chairs: the number of women who held committee chairmanships at some point in their legislative career.

SOURCES: Biographical materials on women legislators since 1957 are readily available. Materials about the first four are more difficult to come by. The four were Edna Giles Fuller (Orange County), elected in 1928 and 1930; Mary Lou Baker (Pinellas), elected in 1942 and in 1944; Edna Pearce (Highlands), elected in 1948, 1950, and 1952; and Mrs. Bryant Patton, elected in 1954 and 1956.

role for women is suggested, first, by the concentration of women officials in the parts of the state least southern in character and, second, by the clear contrast in the origins of Florida's population compared to that of the other southern states. According to the U.S. Census, in 1970 in every other southern state more than 80 percent of the population were born in the South; in Florida only 61 percent have southern origins (see table 15.2). The percentage of the population born in the South was higher in the northern part of the state than in the southern, for example, 77 percent in Jacksonville but 37 percent in Hollywood. Reapportionment had shifted power southward to those sections of the state least southern in character and traditionally most sympathetic to the cause of women's rights.

As late as 1978 Florida still had had only one U.S. congresswoman, Ruth Bryan Owen, and two women elected to statewide office, Mrs. Mamie Eaton Green, who served on the Railroad Commission from 1927 to 1934, and Republican Paula Hawkins, who was elected to the Public Service Commission in 1972 and 1976 and resigned to run for lieutenant governor in 1978. A turning point in the acceptance of women for political office may have been reached in that year. Three of the eight major gubernatorial contenders chose women for running mates, each of whom was clearly chosen not as a token but for the vote-getting strength she brought to the ticket. In that same year, 13 of the 16 women incumbents in the Florida house were reelected. The other three ran for senate seats and two won. In 1980, Paula Hawkins became the first woman from Florida in the U.S. Senate.

The 1960s and 1970s brought marked changes not only in women's political position in the state but also in their legal status. Like other southern states Florida was slow to advance from the legal doctrines that considered a wife to be a dependent of her husband and from statutory distinctions and limitations based on sex. Formerly women were accorded, at law, a status comparable to a child's. For example, until 1970 a wife was prohibited from handling her own property unless she went into court to prove her competency in order to obtain the right to be a "free dealer." Too, the right of women to serve on a jury, an early goal of women's groups, was denied in Florida until 1949, and it was another eighteen years before women would be called for jury duty without registering specifically for that purpose.

Substantial changes neutralized sex discrimination in many of Florida's laws and placed the state among the most progressive states in the nation in this area. The impact of reapportionment in facilitating changes in government personnel and in the substance of legislation affecting women seems to have been far greater than earlier studies of reapportionment predicted. Symbolic of the direction in which Florida was moving was the change of language regarding equality under the law in the 1885 and the 1968 state constitutions. The earlier

TABLE 15.2. A Comparison of Geographic Origins, Office Holding, and the Legal Status of Women in the Eleven States of the South, 1977

State	% of Population Born in South[a]	Officeholding[b] % Women State Legislators	Number of Women State Judges	State Exec.	Local Mayors	Local Council	Sex Neutrality of Laws in Selected Areas[c] Domestic Relations A	B	C	D	E	F	Criminal Law G	H	I	Benefits/Discrim. J	K	L
Fla	60.6	11	10	1	19	238	+		+	+	+	0	+	+	+	+	+	+
Ala.	91.3	2	1	5	14	174	0	+	0		0	0	0	0	+	+	+	
Ark.	85.5	2	1	2	23	136	0		0	+	0	0	+	+	+	0	+	
Ga.	88.3	5	1	0	15	105	0	0	0	0		0	0	0	+	0	0	
La.	89.9	1	0	3	12	74	0	0	0			0	+	0	0	+	+	+
Miss.	91.8	1	1	1	10	116	0		0	+		0	0	0	+	0	0	
N.C.	89.9	14	2	2	16	171	0	+	+	+		+	0	0	+	0	0	
S.C.	89.3	6	0	2	7	71	0	0	0	+	0	0	0	0		0	0	
Tenn.	86.5	2	1	2	10	50	0	0	0	0	0	+	0	0	+	0		
Tex.	84.3	7	1	0	29	322	0		0	0		+	0	0	+	0	+	+
Va.	80.8	6	0	1	11	114	0	+	+	+		+	0	0	+	+	+	+

TABLE 15.2—*continued*

KEY TO COLUMN HEADINGS

A. No-fault as the sole or primary grounds for divorce. (Alabama, Georgia, Tennessee, and Texas have added no-fault to the list of grounds for divorce, while Louisiana, North Carolina, and Virginia allow a voluntary separation ground.)
B. Spousal support upon legal separation.
C. Spousal support upon divorce.
D. Child support upon divorce.
E. Treatment of widows and widowers with respect to elective shares of dower and curtesy.
F. Age of marriage.
G. Statutory rape.
H. Forcible rape.
I. Prostitution.
J. State dependency standards.
K. State laws protecting against sex discrimination in credit.
L. State laws protecting against sex discrimination in real estate transactions and/or housing finance.

a. SOURCE: U.S. Bureau of the Census, *Census of Population: 1970, Characteristics of the Population*. See individual volume for each state listed.
b. SOURCE: Center for the American Woman and Politics, *Women in Public Office: A Biographical Directory and Statistical Analysis*.
c. Plus (+) indicates legislation has been sex-neutralized or that prohibitions have been enacted against discrimination. Zero (0) indicates legislation that maintains a distinction between the sexes or does not protect against discrimination on the basis of sex. A blank space indicates no directly applicable legislation.

SOURCES: Brown et al., *Women's Rights and the Law*, pp. 48–51, 68–73, 130–33, 152–55, 185–86, 256–59, 273–77, 280–85, 357. Supplementary material from *The World Almanac and Book of Facts: 1979* (New York: Newspaper Enterprise Association, Inc., 1979), pp. 963–64.

constitution read, "All men are equal before the law"; eighty-three years later the constitution read, "Natural persons are equal before the law." Sex distinction has been eliminated in matters of divorce, alimony, child support and custody, domicile, rape, and prostitution. In 1971 Florida adopted a no-fault divorce law and in 1978 set out guidelines for granting alimony that included consideration of services rendered in "homemaking, child care, education and career building of the other party." The male advantage in the determination of domicile was eliminated; rape became sexual battery; and, under legislation passed in 1965, prostitution covers activities by both men and women. By the end of the 1970s, Florida's statutes made few distinctions based on sex. (*Women's Rights and the Law,* by Barbara Brown et al., provides data on laws affecting women in all the states, making it possible to place Florida in comparative perspective; see table 15.2.)

The step beyond sex-neutralizing legislation is to ensure actual equality of treatment for women in the face of a history of discrimination. Florida has taken some steps in this direction as well. Discrimination in home financing and granting of credit is forbidden. A human rights bill, passed in 1977, adds marital status to the various characteristics against which discrimination is barred. Spouse abuse and displaced homemaker acts passed in 1977 and 1978 mandate programs to aid women in these positions.

In view of Florida's progress in equalizing the treatment of women at law, it is paradoxical that neither the national Equal Rights Amendment nor a state constitutional prohibition against discrimination based on sex has been able to win voter approval in the state.

The Twenty-seventh Amendment (ERA) came before the Florida House of Representatives only two days after its passage by Congress. With the momentum of national passage still at its peak and opposition not yet mobilized, the Florida house overwhelmingly ratified the amendment. But the resolution of ratification died in the senate without even reaching a vote. Over the next nine years the amendment came before the house on five more occasions, winning approval in four cases, though by smaller margins than in the original vote; on each of six occasions when it reached the senate floor, it was narrowly defeated. Opposition to the amendment has been strongest among Republican legislators and those from the northern part of the state (see table 15.3). The final defeat of the ERA amendment in Florida came from the senate in the spring of 1982. In the 1982 fall elections, however, a number of the opposing senators were defeated so that the senate had a pro-ERA majority for the first time—but too late: the time for ratification of the amendment had expired.

The pattern for and opposition to the ERA in the legislature was apparent in the statewide referendum held in 1978 on the so-called mini-ERA, a state constitutional amendment that would have prohibited discrimination on the basis of sex. This amendment to the state constitution did suffer from the general

TABLE 15.3. Voting in the Florida Legislature on the Equal Rights Amendment, 1972–79

Year of Vote	House of Representatives: Total Vote	% Yes	% Yes by Party: Dem.	Rep.	% by Geog. Area[a]: N.	Cent.	S.	Senate: Total Vote	% Yes	% Yes by Party: Dem.	Rep.	% Yes by Geog. Area[b]: N.	Cent.	S.
1972[c]	91–4	95.8	100	84.6	100	91.4	97.4							
1973[d]	54–64	45.8	50	38.1	35.7	46.3	51.0							
1974[e]								19–21	47.5	64.0	14.3	44.4	42.8	52.9
1975[f]	61–58	51.3	60	29.4	32.1	45.2	67.3	17–21	44.7	57.7	9.1	22.2	50	53.3
1977[g]								19–21	47.5	60	0	44.4	50	47
1979[h]	66–54	55.0	65.2	25.8	28.6	45.2	78.0	19–21	47.5	58.6	18.2	33.3	50	52.9

NOTE: The percentages are calculated on the basis of members voting and paired rather than on the basis of total members of the house and senate.

a. In the house seats 1–28 are in North Florida, 29–70 in Central Florida, and 71–120 in South Florida.
b. In the senate seats 1–9 are in North Florida, seats 10–23 in Central Florida, and 24–40 in South Florida.
c. The 1972 vote was taken 24 March 1972. The party division of those voting: 69 Democrats, 26 Republicans.
d. The 1973 vote was taken 17 April 1973. The party division of those voting: 76 Democrats, 42 Republicans.
e. The 1974 senate vote was taken 10 April 1974. The party division of those voting: 25 Democrats, 14 Republicans, 1 Independent.
f. The 1975 house vote was taken 10 April 1975; the party division of those voting: 85 Democrats, 34 Republicans. The 1975 senate vote was taken 25 April 1975; the party division of those voting: 26 Democrats, 11 Republicans, 1 Independent.
g. The 1977 senate vote was taken 15 April 1977. The party division of those voting: 30 Democrats, 9 Republicans, 1 Independent.
h. The 1979 house vote was taken 17 May 1979 (the Equal Rights Amendment was attached to senate Bill 267); the party division of those voting and paired: 89 Democrats, 31 Republicans. The 1979 senate vote was taken 24 May 1979; the party division of those voting: 29 Democrats, 11 Republicans

Sources: Compiled by the author from the *Journal* of the Florida house and senate.

voter disenchantment that led to the rejection of all eight proposed groups of revisions that appeared on the general election ballot; but it was also opposed in a vitriolic campaign by the same anti-ERA coalition that had vigorously lobbied against legislative ratification of the Twenty-seventh Amendment. The coalition, led by the euphemistically titled Women for Responsible Political Action, included in its ranks the Florida Federation of Women's Clubs, the largest women's organization in the state, and a number of women from the

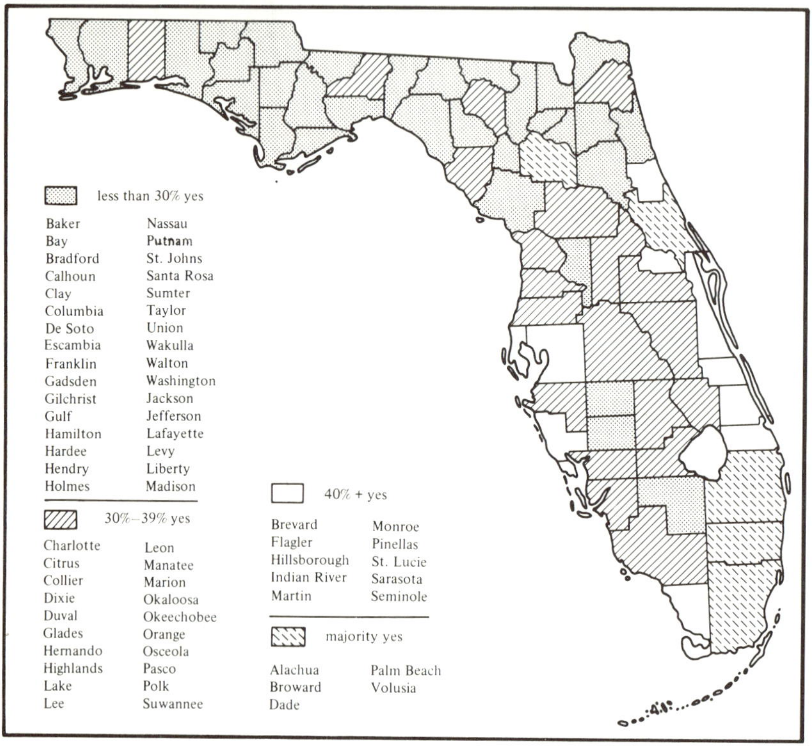

Fig. 15.1. Florida's Vote on Proposition 2 (Prohibiting Discrimination Because of Sex), 1978.

more fundamentalist religious denominations. The pro-ERA coalition, led by the League of Women Voters, spent nearly half a million dollars in the campaign, much of this sum raised outside the state; yet it was able to win majority support for the amendment in only five of the state's sixty-seven counties: Alachua (the locale of the University of Florida), Broward, Dade, Palm Beach, and Volusia. The northern and rural counties supported the amendment least, southern and urban counties most (see fig. 15.1).

The events of the two decades since 1960 suggest, on the one hand, that old attitudes and patterns of political action persist and remain as barriers to the establishment of fully equal status for women in Florida, and, on the other, that in-migration of northerners into southern Florida, and political reform movements such as reapportionment, are strengthening the forces of change in the state and benefiting women's rights in the process.

NOTE: Some of the material in this chapter was taken from Joan Carver, "Women in Florida," *Journal of Politics* 41, no. 3 (August 1979): 941–55. Reprinted by permission.

References

Blackman, Lucy Worthington. *The Florida Federation of Women's Clubs: 1895 – 1939*. Jacksonville: Southern Historical Publishing, 1939.

Brown, Barbara; Freedman, Ann; Katz, Harriet; and Price, Alice. *Women's Rights and the Law*. New York: Praeger Publishers, 1977.

Center for the American Woman and Politics. *Women in Public Office: A Biographical and Statistical Analysis*. 2d ed. Metuchen, N.J.: The Scarecrow Press, Inc., 1978.

Dye, Thomas. "Malapportionment and Public Policy in the States." *Journal of Politics* 27 (1965):586–601.

Jennings, May Mann. Papers. P. K. Yonge Library, University of Florida.

Johnson, Kenneth R. "The Woman Suffrage Movement in Florida." Ph.D. dissertation, Florida State University, 1966.

______. "Florida Women Get the Vote." *Florida Historical Quarterly* 48 (1970):299–312.

McGovern, James. "Helen Hunt West: Florida's Pioneer for E.R.A." *Florida Historical Quarterly* 57 (1978):39–53.

Scott, Anne Firor. *The Southern Lady from Pedestal to Politics*. Chicago: University of Chicago Press, 1970.

Taylor, A. Elizabeth. "The Woman Suffrage Movement in Florida." *Florida Historical Quarterly* 36 (1957):42–60.

U.S. Bureau of the Census. *Census of Population: 1950, Characteristics of the Population*. Florida. Washington, 1953.

______. *Census of Population: 1970, Characteristics of the Population*. Vol. 1, pt. 2. Florida. Washington, 1973.

U.S. Bureau of Labor Statistics. *State Profile of Employment and Unemployment, 1977*. Report 539. Washington, 1979.

Vance, Linda. "May Mann Jennings and Royal Palm State Park." *Florida Historical Quarterly* 55 (1976):1–17.

Williams, Roger M. "Women against Women — The Clamor over Equal Rights." *Saturday Review* 4 (1977):7–13, 46.

The Aged

by Gordon F. Streib

UNIVERSITY OF FLORIDA

15C

For the student of modern state government, Florida's demographic structure offers an intriguing situation. Florida, with 17.3 percent of its population over sixty-five, has the largest percentage of elderly persons of any state, followed by Arkansas (13.7 percent), Rhode Island (13.4 percent), and Iowa (13.3 percent). Only two other states, California and New York, have a larger number of older citizens. Moreover, the percentage of persons over sixty years of age was 23.1 percent—2.25 million out of a population of nearly 10 million. More than elsewhere, Florida's older persons have come to the state from other places after their retirement. Over 600,000 persons over age sixty-five moved to Florida between 1970 and 1980.

Students of Florida's government must also have an awareness of the distribution of Florida's older population and its characteristics. There are certain parts of the state that have heavy concentrations of the elderly, such as the areas around Miami and St. Petersburg. In 1980 there were 17 counties in which the elderly constituted over 25 percent of the population—and in two counties over 40 percent of the population was over age sixty. In Charlotte County, over 45.4 percent of the population was over sixty, a level unmatched in any other county in the United States. In absolute numbers, the elderly in Florida constitute a highly concentrated population, for in Dade County alone there were 335,872 persons aged sixty and over in 1980. This number of elderly in a single county was greater than the number of elderly in any of 17 different states.

Government Structure and the Aged

How is Florida's government organized to deal with this large number of people? The major state agency that handles matters concerning the elderly is the Aging and Adult Services Program Office—one of eight program offices in the Department of Health and Rehabilitative Services (DHRS) (see chapter 20). In 1979 there were 30 professional employees in this state unit on aging. In 1977 Florida ranked fourteenth among the states in terms of the total number of professional employees in aging-services offices.

The Department of Health and Rehabilitative Services is organized adminis-

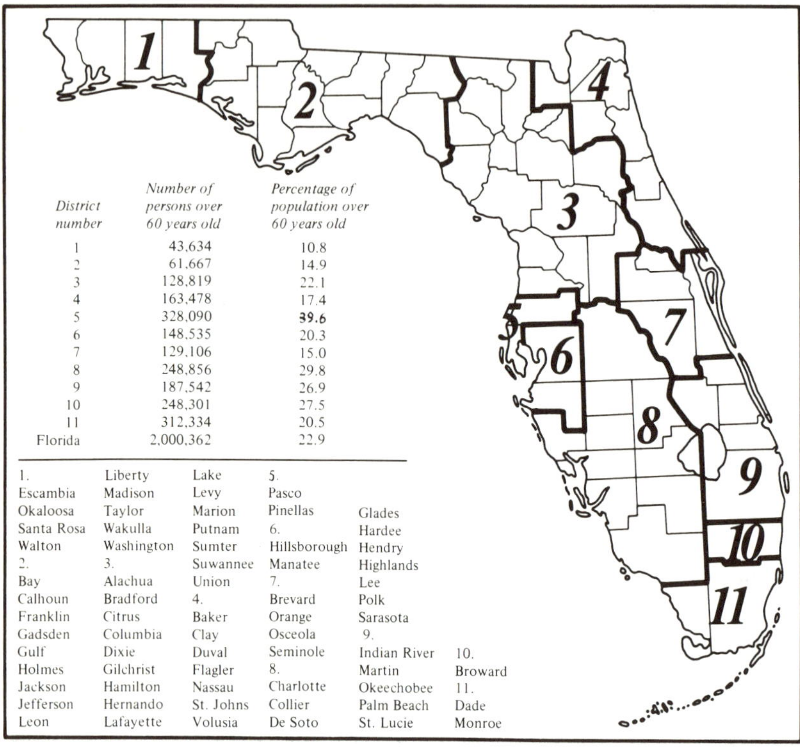

District number	Number of persons over 60 years old	Percentage of population over 60 years old
1	43,634	10.8
2	61,667	14.9
3	128,819	22.1
4	163,478	17.4
5	328,090	39.6
6	148,535	20.3
7	129,106	15.0
8	248,856	29.8
9	187,542	26.9
10	248,301	27.5
11	312,334	20.5
Florida	2,000,362	22.9

1.
Escambia
Okaloosa
Santa Rosa
Walton

2.
Bay
Calhoun
Franklin
Gadsden
Gulf
Holmes
Jackson
Jefferson
Leon
Liberty
Madison
Taylor
Wakulla
Washington

3.
Alachua
Bradford
Citrus
Columbia
Dixie
Gilchrist
Hamilton
Hernando
Lafayette
Lake
Levy
Marion
Putnam
Sumter
Suwannee
Union

4.
Baker
Clay
Duval
Flagler
Nassau
St. Johns
Volusia

5.
Pasco
Pinellas

6.
Hillsborough
Manatee

7.
Brevard
Orange
Osceola
Seminole

8.
Charlotte
Collier
De Soto
Glades
Hardee
Hendry
Highlands
Lee
Polk
Sarasota

9.
Indian River
Martin
Okeechobee
Palm Beach
St. Lucie

10.
Broward

11.
Dade
Monroe

Fig. 15.2. Department of Health and Rehabilitative Services Districts: Counties and Population over 60 Years Old in Each District. Estimates for 1977 are based on *Older People in Florida: A Statistical Abstract*, table 1.46.

Note: In 1979, changes were made in the configurations of Districts 6 and 8. District 6 now consists of Hardee, Highlands, Hillsborough, Manatee, and Polk counties, and District 8 of Charlotte, Collier, DeSoto, Glades, Hendry, Lee, and Sarasota counties.

tratively on a geographical basis into 11 service districts (see fig. 15.2). Each district has an administrator, appointed by the department secretary, who has the authority over all department programs in that district, including Aging and Adult Services. Each service district may establish an Area Agency on Aging to administer funds from the Older Americans Act, and indeed all have done so.

Within each DHRS district, there is a District Advisory Council, which assists in the coordination and integration of the department's programs. This non-salaried council has 12 members and must include a licensed physician, a member of a Board of County Commissioners, a member of a district school board, a practicing attorney, five local representatives of public and private agencies which provide health, social, rehabilitative, or legal services within the district, and two persons who are or have been clients of the department within the district. It is designed for citizen input on departmental policy. Each year three members of this council must consult with the secretary of DHRS on the department's budget request, on the recommendations to the legislature, and on an analysis of clients' needs in their district.

The passage of the Older Americans Act in 1965 had a profound effect on government and delivery of services to older Americans, for it required each state to designate a single organization in its government to administer the programs funded under the act. The governmental unit in which the organization is located varies from state to state; Florida's, as stated, is a program office in HRS.

The major function of the Program Office on Aging and Adult Services is to administer monies derived primarily from two sources—those allocated under the Older Americans Act and those appropriated by the state legislature. In fiscal 1983, the Florida program office administered a budget of $94 million, the third largest amount among the states (New York expended $105 million and Oregon $103 million). Sixty-six percent of the $94 million is derived from federal funds and 34 percent from state funds. Many of Florida's older citizens came from other states, and if state benefits were raised to a higher level, there would probably be even more aged people who would move to the state, increasing costs of services still more.

An emerging function of government in recent years has been that of advocacy, defined here as interceding on behalf of the elderly in order to secure benefits for them. The Older Americans Act requires pooling and coordination of services and programs for the elderly. In Florida, the Aging and Adult Services Program Office performs this function through the monitoring and analysis of legislation affecting older Floridians and through the attempt to increase public awareness about the needs and contributions of the elderly.

The primary responsibility for advocacy resides with the Aging and Adult Services Advisory Council, an unpaid group of 14 voting members, including one member from each of the 11 districts, three appointed at large, and 15 ex officio service providers. It meets at least four times a year; its broad duties are to develop and implement the State Plan on Aging, conduct public hearings, represent the interests of older Floridians, and participate as a statewide advocacy body to improve services for the elderly.

In October 1975 the State of Florida initiated a Nursing Home Ombudsman Project under the sponsorship of DHRS and financed by a model project grant from the Administration on Aging. The project's broad purpose is to improve conditions for Florida's nursing home residents, almost all of whom are elderly. There are a state committee and 11 district committees, composed of volunteers appointed by the governor, who receive, investigate, and resolve nursing home complaints. In 1983, there were 394 licensed nursing homes in Florida, with 43,481 beds, and an estimated 1,045 adult congregate living facilities (ACLF), of which 950 were licensed.

Service Programs and the Older Americans Act

One of the complicating aspects of the relation of government to older people is the way in which different levels of government are interlocked in an intricate network of legislation, funding, planning, and evaluating. At the federal level, the Older Americans Act, as passed in 1965 and amended nine times since, has set the broad framework for services for the elderly. Throughout most of its development, the Administration on Aging has been the agency through which large amounts of federal funds pass to the states, which in turn have the responsibility of allocating these funds according to local priorities. Both state and local bodies must adhere to the guidelines and rules laid down by the federal government. Many programs require some kind of matching funds—in most instances about 15 percent.

In order to understand the multilevel structure of government operations in relation to older Americans, one must understand the titles in the Older Americans Act and then see how sections of the federal law become operating programs in the lives of older persons. A title is a part of the law specifying areas of purpose, operation, and funding. The Older Americans Act as amended in 1978 lists six titles, covering these broad areas:

Title I Declaration of Objectives: Definitions
Title II Administration on Aging
Title III Grants for State and Community Programs on Aging
Part A—General provisions (includes authorization of appropriations, uses of funds, federal share, state agency, area plans, payments)

Part B—Social services (includes health, continuing education, welfare, informational, recreational, homemaker, counseling, referral, transportation)
Part C—Nutrition services (includes congregate and home-delivered services)

Title IV Training, Research, Discretionary Projects and Programs
(includes training, research, and development projects, demonstration projects, comprehensive long-term care projects, demonstration projects of legal services, national impact demonstrations, mortgage insurance and interest grants for multipurpose senior centers)

Title V Community Service Employment for Older Americans

Title VI Grants for Indian Tribes

Examining Health and Rehabilitative District 3 of Florida will illustrate the way such funding operates. This agency administers 16 counties with a population of over 686,000 people inhabiting an area of over 11,000 square miles, almost as large as the states of Massachusetts and Connecticut combined. The area is largely rural, containing only four cities with populations of 10,000. Gainesville is the largest of the four and the headquarters for HRS District 3, and it has one of the most effective programs for older citizens in the state.

It is essential to understand these levels of government because various funds administered by the State Program Office on Aging and Adult Services are turned over to the Area Agency on Aging (AAA) or its equivalent unit, and the AAA then must reallocate the funds to local units of government and local voluntary agencies which deliver services or provide programs. We will discuss briefly Title III and its implementation in District 3.

The broad language of the federal law states that Title III is "to encourage and assist State and local agencies to concentrate resources in order to develop greater capacity and foster the development of comprehensive and coordinate service systems to serve older individuals by entering into new cooperative arrangements in each State with State and local agencies." District 3 received over $3 million under Title III in fiscal year 1983. These monies provide a broad array of social services relating to health, education, information, welfare, legal problems, jobs, recreation, homemaking, counseling, and referral. Moreover, the act enables agencies to provide transportation and to develop means for encouraging the use of the services and facilities that are provided. Under Title III, 90 percent of the monies for social services is provided by the federal government and 10 percent by local sources.

Title III, Part C, which is concerned with nutrition, brings the largest amount of federal funds from the Older Americans Act into District 3—almost $1 million plus other resources such as surplus commodities. Again, 10 percent must be provided by local governmental units. The program provides a hot meal five days a week or more to assure a minimum of one-third of the recommended dietary allowance of nutrients. The meals must be provided in a setting which includes recreational activities, health and welfare counseling, and referral services. There are to be special menus for dietary needs and ethnic backgrounds. In Alachua County, where Gainesville is located, over 360 hot lunches are served five times a week in congregate settings, and over 120 elderly receive home-delivered hot lunches five days a week.

Multipurpose senior centers are designed to provide community support facilities with a broad spectrum of services, including health, social, educational, and recreational programs. For example, the Alachua County Older Americans Council provides such services as blood pressure screening, legal aid, craft and hobby classes, defensive driving classes, help with Medicare, exercise classes, and the like. Each county council determines its direction independently of other counties.

Meals-on-Wheels Program for the elderly homebound. Photo courtesy Alachua County Older Americans Council.

Other Programs for Older Floridians

There are other programs dealing with the elderly that are under the jurisdiction of the U.S. Departments of Agriculture, Labor, and Housing and Urban Development and independent executive agencies such as Action. This last agency funds four programs, including the Foster Grandparents Program, which pays older low-income persons a minimum wage to serve as surrogate grandparents for children, many of whom are mentally retarded. The program is designed to bring older persons together in a one-to-one relationship with children who have special needs. In 1983–84, the program involved the expenditure of almost $403,000 in District 3, of which 27 percent was from local funds.

The Retired Senior Volunteer Program (RSVP), also directed by Action, provides volunteer services to community agencies and nonprofit organizations. The volunteers receive fringe benefits of a hot meal, insurance, and transporation costs, altogether calculated to cost about 90 cents an hour. Over 525 senior volunteers participate in the Alachua County program, which had a budget of approximately $220,000 in 1983—44 percent provided by the federal government and 56 percent, which may be in kind, from local sources.

The Service Corps of Retired Executives (SCORE) is funded by the Small Business Administration. In this program, retired executives provide free consulting services for small businesses. The volunteers are reimbursed for out-of-pocket expenses.

Green Thumb is a program funded by the Department of Labor in which older rural residents (men and women) are paid to perform community services to improve the physical environment—planting shrubs, assisting in the upkeep of parks, playgrounds, and public areas, and miscellaneous work such as driving vans and providing homemaker services.

The Senior Community Service Employment Program has been developed under Title V of the Older Americans Act. This $17.5 million program in Florida is administered by seven national contractors and involves over 3,000 persons who are fifty-five and over.

This discussion is too brief to describe the details of many other state and federal programs and sources of funds provided for elderly Floridians as a subpopulation. In Alachua County some of these are the Social Security Office, Veterans' Administration, Workmen's Compensation, Human Resource Center, Florida State Employment Service, Community Mental Health, Regional Transit System, Santa Fe Community College, University of Florida, and Social and Economic Services.

The complexity and breadth of government concern for older citizens is illustrated in the research and demonstration projects carried out by universities, community colleges, and private organizations. They are funded by grant and contract and deal with many activities—health, counseling, nursing homes, transportation, and mental health. For example, a Community Care Project initiated by the state supports 61 lead agencies in all 11 DHRS districts at an annual cost to the state of $18,592,000.

The federal funds provided under the Older Americans Act are only a partial percentage of the total amount of federal dollars that contribute to Florida's economy. The presence of a large number of older citizens means that huge amounts of federal money in the form of Social Security payments, veterans' benefits, and other pensions are flowing into the state annually. In 1981, payments to Floridians exceeded $700 million monthly under Old Age, Survivors, Disability, and Health Insurance programs. In 1982 1.4 million retired persons in Florida received payments under the Social Security retirement benefit scheme. In addition, there are millions of dollars coming into Florida from retirees' private pensions and savings. The full extent of the stimulation to the economy in housing, food and restaurant sales, and hospital and medical care is not known, but it is a large amount. Furthermore, these funds are relatively constant and are not affected by cyclical changes in the economy, thus having a stabilizing effect on the state's general economic climate.

Some people, in considering the effect of the high proportion of older people in Florida, speak only of the potential expenditures of funds on services and special needs of the elderly, without acknowledging the economic benefits to the state's economy generally or the fact that the funds for services come largely from federal sources.

Retired Senior Volunteer Program member cleaning a schoolyard. Photo courtesy Alachua County Older Americans Council.

Conclusions

The multiple layers of government and the complexity of law and regulation covering programs for the aged mean that there is a considerable amount of bureaucratic structure: filling out forms, complying with guidelines, meeting deadlines. From the standpoint of the local service delivery personnel, these requirements may become onerous and time-consuming. However, one must acknowledge that without federal initiative and federal funding, most states would supply only minimal services to the elderly.

The functioning of government in regard to aging services involves numerous citizen and consumer groups which consult with officials, advise them, and monitor the programs they administer. The efficiency of these citizens' councils and committees depends, of course, on the quality and commitment of the citizens who contribute their expertise and time. The large number of the elderly themselves and the organizations of which they are members constitute important interest and pressure groups on behalf of older citizens, having both direct and subtle influences on policy and administration.

In conclusion, four aspects of programs for the aged should be emphasized:

1. These programs illustrate how goverment has proliferated and grown at all levels—local, state, and federal. Many of the programs under the Older Americans Act have been in operation for only ten years.

2. Federal tax dollars are returned to local communities via these programs, and these monies provide direct services to persons at all levels and create jobs for local citizens. Such funds add to the health and vitality of the local economy.

3. An analysis of aging in relation to government indicates how essential it is for state and local agencies to take the initiative in organizing programs and securing matching funds and services to keep the programs functioning. Although the matching money is often only a small percentage of the total budget, local administrators must convince taxpayers, city and county commissioners, and state legislators of the importance of continuing their programs. These programs, unlike Social Security, require continual evaluation and justification to ensure continuity of service. Another component of this process is the attempt to recruit individual citizens and voluntary organizations to assist in initiating and executing the programs.

4. Finally, the observer may ask why government has become so involved in this multiplicity of programs and services relating to the elderly. The answer is that a slow sociological transition has occurred in which functions that were formerly considered a responsibility of the family are now considered a responsibility of government. This transfer of functions started in the 1930s with the passage of the Social Security Act, which provided a regular source of income to the elderly. The acceptance of this transfer of payments by almost all Americans has been accompanied by an increase of other government programs to provide services that cover what were formerly thought to be private or family matters and to attempt to deal with the autonomous living arrangements and financial independence which most older people and their relatives desire.

The unique situation of Florida as a place where there is a large concentration of older citizens offers provocative research opportunities for the student of political economy. Florida has the largest percentage of persons sixty-five and older of any state in the union, and in absolute numbers only three states have more older citizens. A large percentage of these citizens are migrants, mainly from northeastern and north-central parts of the country. Older migrants differ from natives in that they tend to have higher incomes (often from government and private pensions and private savings), more education, and better health.

Thus, Florida has been enriched by a select group of older residents who contribute positively to the political and economic life of the state.

Many older Floridians take an active part in the political and civic life of their communities, serving on the staffs of local hospitals, community agencies, United Way, service clubs, and religious organizations. They are also active in a wide range of volunteer work which benefits all segments of the community. Older Floridians, like older persons elsewhere, do require more medical and hospital services. However, these demands contribute to the growth of a large health industry, which is an asset rather than a liability to the local economy because so many of the costs of health and hospital insurance for the elderly are paid by third-party insurance carriers or by federal sources. Needless to say, some federal taxpayers—including the elderly—must pay the taxes by which the services are supported.

The creation of an extensive health industry has meant that there are a large number of job opportunities for physicians, nurses, technicians, therapists, podiatrists, and other professionals, who are mainly younger persons and whose livelihood depends in part upon the payments of older Floridians. There is also an enormous bureaucracy operating Blue Cross—again composed mainly of younger persons who process the bills, forms, and checks to operate the health industry. To date, no one has made a careful cost estimate of how the payment system affects the total economy, but a strong case can be made that it is a positive economic benefit to the state and to local areas.

The heavy concentration of the aged in Florida is of further interest because of its effects upon the social life of the state and local communities. It should be emphasized that the concentration of older persons in the state and in retirement communities is a voluntary matter, the result of choices made by better-educated, more affluent Americans. Research indicates that older residents enjoy living in communities that are segregated by age. They like the security, the facilities, and the climate, and, in general, such communities foster friendships, social interaction, and help patterns more than do age-integrated communities.

In 1978, a new event occurred in Florida's political life, the Silver-Haired Legislature, an assembly of older Floridians, elected democratically by their peers on the basis of standard election districts. It convened in Tallahassee and operated as a legislative body by meeting in the capitol and adhering to parliamentary procedures. Its deliberations were marked by a strong sense of responsibility and information. The resolutions passed during the first summer were brought to the attention of the legislature, and some have been enacted into law. Its second year (1979) was marked by considerable interest from other parts of the United States; eight states sent observers, including the lieutenant governor of neighboring Georgia.

Thus, Florida's older citizens are making significant contributions to the vitality of the economic and political life of the state. With the trend toward longer life and a larger proportion of elderly in the population occurring throughout the United States, other states can look to Florida to determine what happens when the demographic equation changes to reflect an older population.

Suggestions for Further Reading

Atchley, Robert. *The Social Forces in Later Life*. 3d ed. Belmont, CA: Wadsworth, 1980. An introduction to social gerontology.

Binstock, Robert H., and Shanas, Ethel. *Handbook of Aging and the Social Sciences*. New York: Van Nostrand-Reinhold, 1976. A general compendium which organizes and interprets data, concepts, theories, and issues from the perspective of various social sciences.

Kraft, John, and Carter C. Osterbind, eds. *Older People in Florida: A Statistical Abstract*. Gainesville: University Presses of Florida, 1981. A valuable source book of facts.

Streib, Gordon F. (ed.). *Programs for Older Americans*. Gainesville: University Presses of Florida, 1981. Through case studies, the authors describe step-by-step ways in which objectives are met in providing services for older Americans.

Organizations Related to Aging and the Aged

Individual Memberships

American Association of Retired Persons (AARP)
1909 K Street, N.W.
Washington, DC 20006

AARP Florida
Florida Information Center
6580 34th Street, North
Pinellas Park, FL 33710
(813) 522-9461

National Council of Senior Citizens
925 15th Street, N.W.
Washington, DC 20005
(202) 347-8800

Gerontological Society of America
1411 K Street, N.W.
Washington, DC 20005
(202) 393-1411

Individual or Organizational Memberships

Florida Council on Aging
P.O. Box 1046
Tallahassee, FL 32302

Southern Gerontological Society
Dr. John Lovitt, Treasurer
Mississippi State University
P.O. Box 5406
Mississippi State, MS 39762
(601) 325-3084

The National Council on the Aging
600 Maryland Avenue, S.W.
Washington, DC 20024

Hispanics

15D

Christopher L. Warren

FLORIDA INTERNATIONAL UNIVERSITY

It is a historical irony that Hispanics are considered a minority group in Florida, since for three centuries Florida's social, political, and economic development was primarily shaped by people of Spanish origin. However, after Florida became a U.S. possession in 1821, Spanish influence quickly waned. By the end of the nineteenth century there was little vestige of the Hispanic contribution to the region's early development, and only a small but steady trickle of Spanish-speaking people immigrated to Florida.

Until the late 1950s, the continued Hispanic presence in Florida was often narrowly measured in terms of the "quaintness" of historic cities like St. Augustine which retained some of their Spanish flavor. The preservation of Spanish architecture and other monuments to the state's Spanish history became a key element in the promotion of tourism. Less visible was the ongoing Hispanic contribution to the state's economic development. For instance, in 1869, Cuban cigar manufacturers settled in Key West and converted that island community into an important center for the manufacture of tobacco products. By 1873, Cubans constituted a majority of Key West's population. This new industry became so vital that Tampa's political leadership lured these Cuban entrepreneurs to Hillsborough County through promises of assistance in the construction of larger and more modern facilities. Today, Tampa remains the site of one of the state's oldest and most established Hispanic communities. Despite this and similar contributions made by Hispanics to Florida's development, it was not until the late 1950s that changing patterns of Hispanic immigration irrevocably altered the state's politics, economy, and culture.

The Changing Demography of Hispanics

It is incorrect to think of those people broadly referred to as Hispanic as a cohesive ethnic group. The Hispanic classification encompasses many people who share little more than Spanish as a native language and who differ in such important matters as national origin, race, and political, economic, and social background. In fact, different governmental institutions have applied varying definitions of the term "Hispanic" as they determine which individuals fall under this designation.

Unfortunately, the U.S. Census Bureau has not always been an accurate source of information on the number of Hispanics living in the United States. Not only has its definition of the Hispanic category changed from census to census, but most social scientists believe that its estimates of the number of Hispanics are at least 10 to 15 percent below the actual numbers. The large number of illegal Hispanic entrants who struggle to remain anonymous and the bureau's history of underestimating the size of urban area minority populations are two factors contributing to this situation. Despite these shortcomings, these statistics remain our best comprehensive estimate of the size and character of the Hispanic population.

According to the 1980 census, at least 14.5 million Hispanics reside in the United States, about 6.7 percent of the total population and an increase of slightly more than 5 million "Latin" residents over the 1970 count. Florida's Hispanic population was conservatively estimated at about 860,000 people, or 8.8 percent of the state's population at the time the 1980 census was taken. The Hispanic population of Florida has increased by at least 400,000 people since 1970. Of the three main Hispanic groups recognized by the census—Cubans, Puerto Ricans, and Mexicans—the Cuban population is the one that has grown the most in Florida. The census indicated that the 470,000 Cubans in Florida in 1980 made up 55 percent of the Hispanic population in the state. It is important to keep in mind, however, that the 1980 census did not count the approximately 130,000 refugees who were boatlifted from the Cuban port of Mariel to Florida between April and September of that year. It is estimated that 100,000 of these more recent Cuban entrants have remained in Florida.

Thus, once the Mariel refugees, the census undercount, and the ongoing influx of Spanish-speaking people into Florida are taken into account, it can be more accurately estimated that over one million Hispanics now live in Florida, of whom a large majority are of Cuban extraction. Puerto Ricans, the second largest group of Hispanics in Florida, numbered about 95,000 in 1980, and Mexicans ranked third, totaling close to 76,000. In the category of "other Hispanics," which includes people from Spain as well as several Central and South American countries, approximately 217,000 were counted in Florida.

In the process of understanding the diversity of the state's Hispanic population, one must further distinguish those Hispanics whose families came to Florida before 1900 from more recent arrivals. In areas such as Tampa–St. Petersburg where the Hispanic population has been an important part of the community for generations, the Latin population is generally assimilated in neighborhoods and professions. There is thus no evident Hispanic enclave in such communities, and so-called Latin issues such as bilingualism are not as readily given priority on the political agenda. Statewide, there is little reason to expect that strong coalitions could be formed between Hispanics recently arrived and those whose families have experienced a high degree of assimilation over several decades. This is not to suggest that no semblance of Hispanic identity or community remains in the more established Latin areas. Rather, in such cities, Latin ethnicity is neither particularly visible nor as likely to exacerbate political cleavages as in those areas where the Hispanic population has only recently arrived.

Most of Florida's recently arrived Hispanic population has settled in the Miami–Dade County area. While the Census Bureau's 1980 count put Dade County's Hispanic population at 581,000, some local sources estimate that the total may have been almost 800,000 in 1983. This high concentration in only one of Florida's 67 counties means that Hispanic influence is profound on almost all aspects of political-economic life in Dade County while it remains virtually invisible in many other parts of the state. While Cuban immigrants comprise the great majority of Dade's Hispanics, there are substantial numbers of Puerto Ricans, Colombians, Venezuelans, and Mexicans and smaller groups from other Latin American nations. Political upheaval in Central America has resulted in the immigration of 20,000 to 30,000 Nicaraguans and El Salvadorans to that area.

The Mariel Boatlift

The rapid growth of Florida's Hispanic population since the late 1950s is one of the most striking aspects of the state's recent history. Florida has been the point of entry for hundreds of thousands of Hispanic refugees who fled their countries in the midst of dramatic events, bringing national attention to Florida's Hispanic population. This publicity was particularly pertinent to the arrival of the Mariel refugees in 1980, since they differed from earlier Cuban migrants in many respects.

During the late 1950s and early 1960s, only some of the Cuban refugees were successful in transferring financial assets to the United States, but many arrived with considerable entrepreneurial experience, marketable skills, and a high degree of formal education. The early Cuban immigrants were more likely than later migrants to have come from an urban area and an upper-middle-class background and were more apt to be white than was Cuba's population as a whole.

In the late 1960s and 1970s, as more of Cuba's working class began to leave the island, the socioeconomic makeup of the emigrés began to change. But it was not until the influx of the Mariel refugees in 1980 that Florida's Cuban population came to be fully stratified along class and racial lines. National, state, and local agencies that have studied the Mariel boatlift observed that the refugees were more likely to be nonwhite, unskilled, and without blood ties to other Cuban-Americans than were previous groups of Cuban entrants. A small number of the Mariel refugees were criminals, mixed by the Cuban government into the mainstream of those leaving the island. The resultant rise in Dade County's violent crime rate created much notoriety for South Florida. Largely ignored, however, was the fact that many of the Mariel refugees demonstrated a remarkable ability to adapt to their new environment. Some took to the streets as peddlers and vendors. Others found housing and employment in several of the predominantly Hispanic neighborhoods in Dade County.

The more established elements of Dade's Cuban community have been torn between support and rejection of these more recent migrants. Bound by nationalism, mutual antipathy toward the Castro government, and a pertinacious determination to succeed in a new country, the Mariel refugees have often found sympathy and support from other Cuban-Americans. At the same time, class and racial divisions, as well as a sense of resentment over the bad publicity Cuban immigrants received in the wake of Mariel, have continued to test the strength of nationalistic and ethnic ties.

Economic Impact

The upper-middle-class background of many Cuban immigrants eased their long-term integration into Florida's economy. Stories abound of the economic triumphs of Cubans who came to this country with little or no money. Yet, while the mythology of the self-made man constitutes an important part of the Latin economic success story, it is inadequate to explain the magnitude of upward mobility among many Hispanics. The Cuban immigrants of the 1960s were not poor, dispossessed peasants but accomplished professionals who, through federal assistance, good fortune, and much personal initiative, readily adapted and contributed to Florida's economy.

Between 1960 and 1980, Cubans founded more than 18,000 businesses in Dade County alone. Their entrepreneurial skills resulted in the creation of companies involved in such diverse activities as real estate, construction, and boat building. Greater Miami boasts 16 Cuban-American bank presidents and about 250 vice-presidents. Hispanics have come to dominate much of Dade County's successful garment industry.

The radically changing demographic and economic character of Dade County in the wake of Hispanic immigration has been described as a process of Latinization—suggesting both the breadth and depth of the Cuban impact. The process affects not only Greater Miami's other Hispanic groups but non-Hispanic whites and blacks as well. For Dade's economic establishment, especially the banking community, real estate interests, and retail stores, the economic growth of the Cuban community has been nothing short of a much-needed miracle. The Latinization of South Florida has provided metropolitan Miami with the crucial international linkages and capital which brought about the spectacular economic growth of the 1970s.

Hispanics and Local Politics

The Latinization of Dade County is evident not only in the economic realm but also in the political. The gradual emergence of a politically potent Cuban-American voting bloc, which has demonstrated significant, if incomplete, cohesion in local elections, serves as the foundation of this transformation. Specifically, the area's traditional racial setting of blacks and whites has been transformed into a more complex tri-ethnic political setting that has challenged the viability and adaptability of many local political institutions.

As late as 1965, not many of the Hispanics in Dade County were citizens, and probably fewer than 5,000 voted. As of June 1983, however, there were approximately 140,000 registered Latin voters in Dade, constituting about 20 percent of the total. Yet even these figures seriously underestimate the actual number of registered Hispanics: the Dade County Department of Elections considers as Latin only those people born in Spanish-speaking countries, thus excluding people born in the United States of Latin parentage.

An important factor shaping Hispanic participation in Dade County politics is the jurisdiction's unique two-tiered governmental structure, which combines a strong county government with 27 separate municipalities. Residential patterns have produced Hispanic voting majorities (or nearly so) in several of these municipalities—Miami, Hialeah, West Miami, and Sweetwater—though Hispanics make up a smaller proportion of the whole county's electorate. In both municipal and county elections, the growing number of Hispanic voters has increasingly translated into electoral success for Latin, especially Cuban-American, candidates. While these successes fall short of the "Cuban takeover" so often prophesied, they are nonetheless significant. Most important, Cuban-Americans hold two out of five seats on the City of Miami Commission as well as the mayor's office and several city council seats in both Hialeah and Sweetwater. The mayor of the City of Miami, Maurice Ferre, a Puerto Rican, has drawn formidable Cuban-American opposition in his last two campaigns.

Voting patterns in City of Miami elections indicate that there is a rather strong tendency for Cuban-American voters to support fellow Cuban-Americans. It is less certain that any similar prediliction exists for support of non-Cuban Hispanic candidates. Only in the last few years have Cuban-American candidates been able to put together coalitions of Hispanic, black, and non-Hispanic white support that enabled them to win in countywide races for the county commission and school board. One Cuban-American sat on each of these bodies in 1983. Thus while ethnicity has proven to be a significant factor in shaping voter response in Dade County, there are a growing number of electoral contests in which Hispanic candidates are attracting substantial support from blacks and non-Hispanic whites.

A second demonstration of the influence of Cuban-Americans on Dade County politics is the injection of several "Latin issues" into the political environment. Several referenda and straw votes placed on the Dade County and City of Miami ballots reflect the ongoing conflict over bilingualism and the emergence of anti-Communism as a significant local issue. In November 1980, Dade County voters passed an "antibilingualism" measure by a substantial margin, in response to a controversial county ordinance passed several years before that had made the county officially bilingual. Yet for much of Dade's non-Hispanic citizenry, the bilingual ordinance represented a symbolic affirmation of their fear of the expanding Latin presence. The petition drive and resultant referendum on a new antibilingual measure turned into a public name-calling contest between the Hispanic and non-Hispanic communities.

The emergence of Latin anti-Communism as an important issue in South Florida's local politics is also increasingly evident. The conducting of nonbinding straw votes and the passage of resolutions by city councils on how best to fight Communism provide the most notable examples of this phenomenon. In November 1982, for instance, the Miami City Commission unanimously decided to place before the voters a nonbinding question on whether city funds should be used to finance any local conventions that were to be attended by representatives of Communist countries. The vote was a symbolic offering to those Latin constituents who had expressed strong opposition to the holding of a travel agents' convention in Miami which was to be attended by representatives from Cuba and other Communist nations.

On numerous occasions, the Sweetwater City Commission has passed resolutions condemning Communism in all of its forms while calling for stronger federal policies to combat its spread in Central America. Similar sentiments have been apparent in local campaign rhetoric and in the emphasis placed on such nonlocal issues as the establishment of Radio Martí, a federally supported anti-Communist radio station which would broadcast to Cuba. Indeed, Dade County is likely the only locality in the United States where anti-Communism is such a significant municipal issue.

Yet within the realm of local Cuban politics there are a number of distinct factions. While capable of demonstrating some cohesion in elections and on certain issues, internally the Cuban political community is fragmented. Factions organize along old divisions transplanted from Cuba and around flamboyant personalities. Political violence between militant factions has been recurrent. This lack of unity has worked against the emergence of strong local Hispanic leadership with broad support. That a vast number of Greater Miami's local elections are nonpartisan has also meant that the political parties have not been an effective base for cultivating Latin political leaders. It is this intra-ethnic conflict that prevents Hispanic influence on local politics from being even more significant. Thus does a certain "internationalism" come to Dade politics. It is a community in which a plurality of the residents have a self-identity that seesaws between U.S. citizen and Hispanic immigrant, exiled expatriate and American nationalist. This uncertainty has not contributed to Hispanic control of local politics but has meant further Latinization of the political environment.

Enhanced Role in State and National Politics

One of the most important factors in the emergence of Hispanics in state politics was the 1982 Florida legislature's adoption of a reapportionment plan which set up single-member districts for the legislature. Redrawing district lines in South Florida created a number of districts with high concentrations of Latin voters. Subsequently, in the November 1982 elections, three Cuban-born candidates were elected to the Florida House of Representatives from disticts in Dade County, a fourth losing by a narrow margin after the absentee ballots were counted. While not the first Cubans to serve in the Florida legislature (Fernando Figueredo of Key West represented Monroe County in the house during the 1885 session), it is likely that Cuban-American legislators have now become a permanent fixture in Florida politics.

As Hispanic candidates have become more numerous in the last several elections, they have run for state office on both Republican and Democratic tickets. The three Cubans elected to the legislature in 1982 were all Republicans, but the state's Democratic party has also shown itself to be a useful springboard for Hispanic politicians—the most important Alfredo Duran, who rose through Democratic ranks to become state party chairperson in the late 1970s.

There is a prevalent but mistaken notion that Cuban-Americans are overwhelmingly Republican and share highly conservative views on most issues, but over the last several years, registered Cuban voters have shown a slight tendency to favor the Democratic party. As of 1980, about 49 percent of the registered Cubans in Dade County were Democrats, 40 percent were Republicans, and 11 percent were independents. It is true that Cubans have registered as Republicans in greater proportion than has the Florida population as a whole, and there seem to be two widely accepted explanations of this. Nationally, the Republican party has attracted much support for its fervent anti-Communist Latin American foreign policy. In state politics, the historic weakness of the Republican party made it easier for prospective Latin candidates to run as Republicans than as Democrats. This tendency to split along party lines also reflects the diversity of the Hispanic political community.

Nevertheless, candidates for statewide and national office have been devoting more time and attention to attracting the Hispanic vote. The Reagan administration has been particularly active in trying to cultivate broad Hispanic support, an attempt that may be in fact the clearest indicator of the growing perception among some candidates of the importance of Hispanics in electoral politics. What is less certain is whether Hispanics in general can be effectively organized behind particular candidates or parties in the same way that many black Americans have been. In fact, Hispanic voting patterns in South Florida in national elections have not usually been significantly different from that of the state's electorate as a whole. Of the 61 Dade County precincts with Latin majorities in

In commemoration of the Day of the Guaimaro Constitution on April 11, Mayor Maurice A. Ferre of the City of Miami delivered a proclamation recognizing the day to Donato Torres, treasurer of the town of Guaimaro in exile, during a city council session. Left to right: Commissioners Rose Gordon and Rev. Theodore R. Gibson, Mayor Ferre, Mr. Torres, Commissioner Manolo Reboso, and Vice-Mayor J. L. Plummer, Jr. Photo courtesy Miami-Metro Department of Publicity and Tourism.

1980, the greatest number of them supported both Ronald Reagan and Paula Hawkins in the presidental and U.S. Senate races. However, the support these candidates received from the Hispanic precincts was not disproportionate from what they received from many precincts with few Hispanics. In short, for Hispanics to have a significant impact on the outcome of any statewide election, there would probably have to be a close race in which a cohesive Latin bloc acted to swing the election toward a particular candidate.

Problems and Prospects

What may be most revealing about the massive immigration of any group to another country is the dramatic impact on the host society. The influence Hispanics are having on South Florida is pervasive but difficult to measure. One can point to their entrance into different neighborhoods, certain sectors of the economy, and state and local politics yet still not have an accurate picture of the extent to which communities have been transformed through this influx. We can identify several divergent and often contradictory phenomena.

Many of the recent Hispanic entrants have been quick to adapt to the language, values, and culture of their new environment; others have been more committed to the building and perpetuation of a distinct Latin subculture. Many of the adult refugees have sought to instill in their children a respect for the values and customs of their homeland, but there is a high incidence of young Cubans marrying non-Hispanics, a tendency that could erode adherence to such traditions. Many of the young have difficulty contemplating a return to a homeland they remember vaguely at best—but a dream that remains important to many of the older exiles. Non-Hispanics, both black and white, have felt under siege in the face of Latin immigration, yet a number of them benefit from Hispanic contributions to the economy and enjoy the cultural and culinary advantages of living in an international city.

Above all, the Hispanic presence and the tri-ethnic character of the South Florida area have served to politicize a community which had long behaved and been governed like a small town. In the process, many of the area's latent and long-ignored problems have been brought into focus. For instance, in the face of tremendous economic growth in South Florida, due at least partly to the infusion of Latin capital, the City of Miami remains sixth among all cities in the nation in the number of families living below the poverty line. As a result of the Mariel boatlift, a larger number of Miami's poor are Hispanic. Furthermore, rioting has occurred in some of Dade County's poorest black neighborhoods, and thousands of destitute Haitians have also settled in Greater Miami. Thus as Dade County becomes more aware of its ethnic differences, its class divisions are also becoming increasingly visible.

All of these factors and others suggest the extent to which Florida has been irrevocably changed through recent patterns of Hispanic immigration. Yet due to the very divergent and often contradictory nature of these changes, it is unlikely that we can predict the long-term influence Hispanics will have on Florida and vice versa.

Selected References

Balseiro, Jose Agustin, ed. *The Hispanic Presence in Florida*. Miami: Seeman Publishing, 1976.

Burkholz, Herbert. "The Latinization of Miami." *New York Times Magazine,* September 21, 1980.

Jaffe, A. J.; Cullen, Ruth M.; and Boswell, Thomas D. *The Changing Demography of Spanish Americans*. New York: Academic Press, 1980.

Jorge, Antonio, and Moncarz, Raul. "Cubans in South Florida: A Social Science Approach." *Metas* 1, 3 (Fall 1980): 37–87.

Metropolitan Dade County. "Social and Economic Problems among Cuban and Haitian Entrant Groups in Dade County, Florida: Trends and Indications." Office of the County Manager, 1981.

Mohl, Raymond. "Race, Ethnicity, and Urban Politics in the Miami Metropolitan Area." *Florida Environmental and Urban Issues* 9 (April 1982): 1–6, 23–25.

Rogg, Eleanor Meyer. *The Assimilation of Cuban Exiles: The Role of Community and Class*. New York: Aberdeen Press, 1974.

Sofen, Edward. *The Miami Metropolitan Experiment*. 2d ed. Garden City, N.Y.: Doubleday Anchor, 1966.

Government, Business, Labor

16A

Introduction

by Carter C. Osterbind

UNIVERSITY OF FLORIDA

Cultural, social, environmental, and economic factors have operated in combination to influence the attitudes of governmental leaders in Florida toward business and labor. The factors that have exerted the greatest influence on governmental policy have been tourism, population growth, changing economic conditions, the pattern of industrial activity, the location of Florida relative to major consuming markets, and the characteristics of the labor force. This introduction considers these factors and their impact on and governmental regulation of real estate and utilities and on the development of labor unions.

At the Fourth Annual Growth Policy Conference held in Gainesville in 1976, then Governor Reubin Askew expressed a view common among Florida's political leaders: "There can be little wonder that those of us who live here often think of Florida as a paradise [referring to the state's climate and topography]. It somehow seems unlikely that the paradise could be part of the confusion and indecision of a benighted land. But, as we learned once before and long ago, it is difficult to live in the Garden of Eden. Paradise is not easily preserved, and it has not been easy for the people of Florida to preserve the paradise God gave them" (*Selected Conference Papers of the Fourth Annual University of Florida Conference on Florida Growth Policy,* edited by Richard H. Schneider, University of Florida College of Architecture, 1976). Askew showed greater concern than earlier governors over the impact of a greatly increased population on the amenities of the state's natural resources. He later declared the state's need for policies and programs for the management and direction of growth in order to protect the environment, the water supplies, and other natural resources.

The usefulness of the state's mild climate and natural attractions for promoting the state's economic development has long been recognized by political leaders and governmental agencies alike. For many years the Florida Development Commission and, more recently, the Department of Commerce have worked closely with the state's communities to publicize Florida as a paradise for residents and visitors. Rapid population growth and the annual influx of millions of tourists attest the success of such publicity.

Recognizing the attractions of Florida for large numbers of tourists each year, state leaders have advocated governmental policies and programs that will stimulate tourism and, by increasing it, benefit the state. The sales tax, for example, derives significant revenue for the state from the vast numbers of visitors. The Department of Commerce and other agencies seeking to stimulate industrial development have made it known that, while it wants new industry, Florida does not want damage to the environment that is so important to tourism through industrial pollution of air or water. State leaders have also sought to attract capital for the expansion of tourist and recreational facilities. The state government has pursued a policy of low business taxes as a means of encouraging development of hotels, motels, specialized recreational facilities, and parks.

The state government has also adopted policies to attract new residents to the state. Most of the large net increase in Florida's population in recent years has been due to in-migration. In 1920 Florida's population was less than one million persons, but by 1980 it was almost ten million. During much of this period, state government leaders held the view that all growth was good. The pressures of increasing population, however, have led to a different view: growth is inevitable in Florida, and, if properly directed, it can work to the economic benefit of the state. This view has led state government to take action to meet the concerns expressed in Governor Askew's statement quoted above.

In 1972 the Florida Legislature adopted the Environmental Land and Water Management Bill, the Land Conservation Bill, the Water Resources Bill, and the Florida State Comprehensive Planning Bill (discussed in chapter 14). These bills were signed into law by the governor. The purpose of these laws is to create a desirable community environment for Florida's increasing numbers of residents. The planning bill, for example, provides that "those communities with a population of 50,000 or more must develop a mass transit plan, air and water port plans, vehicular safety, off-street parking and public facilities. In addition, future public buildings, hospitals, fire stations, schools, and similar improvements must be located. Also required are a community design element, a redevelopment element for slums and blighted areas, a public safety element, a historical and scenic preservation element, and an economic element setting forth principles and guidelines for commercial and industrial development, employment and manpower utilization" (Earl M. Starns, "Florida's Local Government Comprehensive Planning Act—An Overview," *Business and Economic Dimensions* 14:1–4). As the scope of this bill implies, leaders in state government accept the fact that there is little that they can do to prevent growth, but through zoning and land use controls they hope to manage it.

Changing economic conditions have influenced the relationship of Florida's state government to the business community. The market collapse in 1929, the ensuing depression of the 1930s, and the more recent recession of 1974 have caused leaders in state government to examine what the state might do to lessen or offset depressed business activity locally that results from depressed conditions in the national economy. The state has sought, for example, to minimize unethical and unsound real estate promotion and development, and it has considered the repeal of usury laws and the removal of legal interest rate ceilings. The dependency of the state's economy on tourism has led governmental leaders to take strong positions on national fuel conservation measures. Changing economic conditions in recent years have also influenced policies regulating public utilities, financial institutions, and insurance companies.

The structure of Florida's economy, shown by the sources of personal income listed in table 16.1, is quite different from the economic structure of the nation or of other large states. For example, manufacturing accounts for 13.7 percent

TABLE 16.1. Distribution of Personal Income by Major Industrial Source in Florida, 1982

Source	Percent of Income
Farming	2.6
Manufacturing	13.7
Mining	0.4
Construction	7.8
Wholesale trade	7.1
Retail trade	12.9
Finance, insurance, and real estate	7.4
Transportation, communications, and public utilities	8.8
Services	21.7
Other industries	1.0
Government	16.6

Source: Calculated from *Florida Statistical Abstract, 1982* (Gainesville: Bureau of Economic and Business Research, College of Business Administration, University of Florida, 1983).

of industrial income in Florida, whereas in Michigan it is 40.2 percent, in Indiana 39.2 percent, in California 22.2 percent, and nationally 25.8 percent. On the other hand, the percentage of income from retail trade and service industries is considerably higher in Florida than in those states or nationally. Even other southern states have a higher proportion of personal income from manufacturing and a lower proportion from service industries than Florida.

The relatively small amount of income from manufacturing in Florida has caused the state government to appropriate funds for programs designed to attract industry to the state, with the proviso that the type or location of the industry should not harm Florida's tourist industry by damage to the environment.

The effort to lure new industrial concerns to the state, however, has been stymied by Florida's remoteness from large consuming markets. Thus the focus has been on attracting manufacturing that has relatively low transportation costs. But as population grows in Florida and other southern states, Florida grows less remote from the consumers.

The relatively high level of service activities in Florida's economy has permitted utilization of a large supply of unskilled labor; the large work force of unskilled labor has kept wages lower in Florida than in more industrialized states. This lower level of wages in Florida and in other southern states has been used to entice manufacturers to open plants in Florida. Government leaders in Florida have emphasized the advantages of lower wage scales not only in attracting industry but also in expanding activities related to tourism. To retain the cost advantage of low levels of wages, governmental and business leaders in Florida have opposed or discouraged the organization of workers by unions.

Government Regulation of Real Estate

16B

by Clayton C. Curtis

UNIVERSITY OF FLORIDA

The real estate industry in Florida is an extremely important part of the total state economy. In 1978 the construction industry employed about 190,000 people with a payroll in excess of $2.5 billion. The real estate brokerage industry has about 150,000 licensees, and real estate sales in 1978 were about $30 billion. If one included people employed by the various mortgage lending institutions, insurance firms, and other activities related to real estate, the industry's importance is seen to be substantial.

Government regulation of the real estate industry in Florida falls into four categories: the Florida Real Estate Commission (called the Board of Real Estate since 1979), which oversees the brokerage sector of the industry; local planning authorities to oversee regional impact; state authority to designate large areas of critical state concern; and the authority of the Florida State Division of Land Sales and Condominiums, as well as federal authority over the offerings of lots by developers to prospective purchasers.

Regulation of Real Estate Brokerage

State regulation of the real estate industry in Florida has a short history compared to that of other professional fields. In 1923 the legislature passed the first statute relating to real estate brokerage, modeled after a California law passed in 1919. No regulatory agency was created, but the act defined forms of misconduct that the courts were to treat as misdemeanors. The power to revoke or suspend real estate licenses was left to the county courts.

In 1925 the legislature created the Florida Real Estate Commission, to receive and investigate complaints against license holders. License revocation or suspension, however, still could be attained only by the commission taking action before a county judge. A special legislative session in the same year gave the new commission the power to grant or deny a license but left suspension or revocation with the county courts. In 1927 this power was transferred to the circuit courts. In 1941 the act was designated as Chapter 475, Florida Statutes; it remains today the chapter pertaining to the real estate brokerage industry in Florida.

In 1947 the act was amended to give the commission the power to grant, deny, revoke or suspend a license, with the holder or applicant having the right to appeal to the circuit court and beyond. Since 1947 the commission has held the main power in the regulation and control of organized real estate brokerage in Florida. The commission controls, as defined in Chapter 475, those who perform "covered functions"; thus anyone who, for any kind of compensation, assists another in buying, selling, auctioning, renting, leasing, or appraising real property is covered by the license law and required to obtain a real estate license.

Historically, the commission had three members, appointed by the governor, each serving a three-year term. Traditionally they came from the professional leadership of the Florida Association of Realtors. Realtors in Florida, as in other states, were and are still the main force in establishing regulation and, in more recent years, in pushing for extensions and improvements in regulation. In the 1969 Reorganization Act, the Real Estate Commission was placed, along with other professional licensing boards, in the Florida Department of Professional and Occupational Regulation. The commission remained relatively autonomous: it hired its own people and made most of the substantive decisions. In 1978 the legislature added a lay member to the commission, as it did to most state regulatory boards.

In 1979 the commission was reviewed under the Sunset Law, and after a bitter legislative battle several changes were made. The commission was renamed the Board of Real Estate, bringing it in line with the consistent renaming of most state regulatory boards. Its membership increased to seven, two of whom are lay members, all appointed by the governor with the consent of the senate. The Department of Professional and Occupational Regulation was to reorganize into the Department of Professional Regulation. The power of the Department of Professional Regulation over the Board of Real Estate was extended, with all personnel of the board becoming employees of the department. Most of the changes in the 1979 act were administrative and procedural rather than substantive; the board retained the real power involved in granting, suspending, and revoking licenses. In 1982, the autonomy of the board and its control over investigations were increased.

The duties and powers of the Board of Real Estate (BRE) can be separated into four areas: executive, quasijudicial, quasilegislative, and ministerial. Under its executive power it investigates all complaints against license holders, using broad subpoena powers in the process. It then sits as a quasijudicial body to hear the evidence, following strict rules in the process, and to render a decision. The decision can range from public reprimand through suspensions for up to ten years to the most severe, revocation of the license.

Under its legislative function the board issues rules and regulations to spell out and implement in specific ways the powers given it by legislative acts. For example, the legislature gave it the power to require successful completion of an educational requirement to become a salesman or broker but left it to the commission to define the details through rules and regulations.

These rules and regulations passed by the board or any other regulatory agency have the effect of law until changed by the legislature or overruled by the courts. The legislature came to believe that many boards adopted rules going far beyond what the legislature had meant in passing certain acts. Under the new law the secretary of the Department of Professional Regulation can challenge any rule or regulation of the Board of Real Estate or any of the other boards when he feels that the rules exceed legislative authority or that a rule or regulation might inhibit entry to the field or competition in the field.

Over the years the Florida Real Estate Commission (now the Board of Real Estate), along with similar agencies in California and Ohio, has been a leader in progressive regulation. Its educational programs have won national attention and awards. The board, with the assistance of the Florida Association of Realtors, continues to seek for its over 150,000 licensees more educational requirements and a higher degree of professionalism in the industry. It will be interesting to see if the movement into the Department of Professional Regulation means better regulation for this substantial industry.

Development of Regional Impact

In 1972 the Florida legislature passed the Environmental Land and Water Management Act, to bring under review and control those developments that local government could not handle because of geographically constrained planning and zoning jurisdictions. According to Chapter 380.06 of the Florida Statutes, this was "any development which, because of its character, magnitude, or location, would have substantial effect upon the health, safety, or welfare of citizens of more than one county."

The act delineates twelve types of development that may require review by Development of Regional Impact (DRI): airports, attractions and recreational facilities, electrical generating facilities and transmission lines, hospitals, industrial plants and industrial parks, mining operations, office parks, petroleum storage facilities, port facilities, residential developments, schools, and shopping centers.

To make operative the rather vague definition, the act provides specific and usually numerical guides that determine whether one of these types of development would be classified as a DRI and therefore subject to the review process. For example, any residential development, whether an apartment complex, a single-family subdivision, or mobile-home park, will be subject to review depending on the population of the county it is in and the number of dwelling units contemplated. Thus in the smallest counties a development of 250 or more units would be a DRI while in the largest counties such as Dade the development would have to contain 3,000 or more units to come under the DRI legislation. A shopping center covering more than 40 acres or providing parking for more than 2,500 cars would be a DRI. Generating plants producing more than 100 megawatts, mines disturbing more than 100 acres annually, and a college having more than 3,000 students also come under this designation.

When numbers are included in legislation, developers get around the act by staying below them. If a shopping center developer wished to avoid DRI review he has only to develop 39 acres instead of 40. How extensive this kind of dodging has been is not known, and to determine it would require a rather complicated and expensive study. To date there have been over 200 applications, and the residential applications alone would provide, if built, about 2 million dwelling units.

Once it has been determined by the application of the numerical criteria that a development comes under the DRI process, the developer has a series of things that he must do. He must make an application to the unit of local government, i.e., city or county, under whose jurisdiction his project will come. Frequently zoning regulations are involved and must be considered alongside the development order which the DRI requires from local government if the project is approved.

In addition to the city or county involved, the developer must apply for a review by the regional planning council having jurisdiction in the area where his project is located. All counties are included within the boundaries of one of the eleven state-defined regional areas with a corresponding regional planning council. By law the council is required to review the impact of the proposed development on a series of factors, including the local economy, the environment, availability of housing, and traffic. It then will make a recommendation to the local government unit at the public hearing on the request.

The local government unit can approve, deny, or modify the proposal. Unless denial is the outcome, an order of development is issued by the local unit. If such an order is issued and it is contrary to the recommendations of the regional council, the council may appeal the order to the state cabinet; it makes the final decision unless recourse to the courts is used. Originally, the Division of State Planning (then a part of the Department of Administration), after reviewing the order of development, could appeal to the cabinet for a change or reversal. The 1979 legislature transferred some sections of the Division of State Planning to the executive office of the governor. That part of the division concerned with DRIs and areas of critical state concern was transferred into the Department of

Community Affairs. If the developer is turned down or the conditions placed on him are too onerous, he also may follow the same appeal route.

The simple preparation of the initial application can cost between \$3,000 and \$10,000, but the background work on drainage and other problems may cost the developer hundreds of thousands of dollars. More important to most developers, who would have eventually done the work anyway, is the time it may take before any decision is reached on an application: up to two years or even longer, during which time the developer may be paying interest on millions in borrowed money as well as losing interest on his own front money. He may also have to watch the market around his project change to his detriment.

Since the first two years of the DRI legislation the number of applications has steadily declined. It is difficult to say whether this drop is due to developers' electing to take avenues to avoid DRIs or to other factors. Most applications have been for large residential developments, and the demise of the popularity of the "new towns" approach to such development may have accounted for some of the dwindling number of applications. The sheer number of acres and future dwelling units involved in the first wave of applications may have reduced the need, for some time, for new developments. A gubernatorial commission is currently studying the DRI to make recommendations on its legislative future.

Areas of Critical State Concern

At the time the legislature established the developments of regional impact, it also set up legislation for areas of critical state concern. The state cabinet may designate, anywhere in the state, land of critical state concern if at least one of three criteria is met: areas that have an important impact on environmental, historical, natural, or archeological resources of regional or statewide importance; areas that are to be affected in a major way by a proposed major public facility, such as the jetport outside Miami; areas of major new development affecting the region or state, such as a huge new city.

Actual studies to determine whether an area meets one or more of these criteria were to be done by the Division of State Planning, now in the Department of Community Affairs. Because of the enormous technical problems involved and the relatively small state planning staff, few areas have been so designated; but if one is, the state establishes rules and regulations for its development. Local government is given a limited amount of time to make its own ordinances come into conformance with the state rules; if they fail to do so, state rules supersede local development laws. Even if local government does adjust its laws to conform to state rules, state planners will carefully supervise the administration of the local laws.

Local governments have objected strongly to this legislation, since it means that many decisions that can and should be made locally are made in Tallahassee. Developers have also objected, partly because of a well-grounded fear that the state rules will be much tougher, and hence more expensive to follow, than local rules and partly out of a similar fear that getting decisions from the state will require more work and more time than getting them from local government.

Land Sales Controls

In the 1950s the proliferation of large firms selling lots in new areas became a problem, especially in Florida, Arizona, and California. Many sales were to out-of-state buyers who frequently had not seen what they had purchased. Frequent abuses occurred in advertising claims and, more important, in improvements such as roads, drainage systems, and sewer systems that were promised but never built. The Florida legislature responded in the late fifties by giving some weak controls to the Florida Real Estate Commission, and later a land sales board was created, dominated by members of the land sales industry. Since then the mechanism for control has gone through many changes. Today the industry is regulated by the Division of Land Sales and Condominiums of the Department of Business Regulation, which has an advisory council composed of seven members, three from the development industry and four representing the consuming public.

Today a new subdivision containing 50 or more lots must register with the division, although there are numerous technical exceptions to this requirement. Control is exercised in two ways, by requiring full disclosure in advertising and by requiring that promised improvements are either in place or bonds guaranteeing their completion are posted. In many, if not all cases, developers who must register with the state also must register with the Office of Interstate Land Sales in the federal government's Department of Housing and Urban Development.

From the standpoint of the industry the land sales controls represent another set of rules and regulations with which they must comply, which costs them money. The increase in their costs is, of course, normally passed on to buyers. A series of recent studies done at various universities on the costs of regulation come to widely different conclusions on the magnitude of regulatory costs in the development field, but in all cases the costs are very substantial. It is doubtful that controls in Florida have reduced output in the industry, but there is little doubt that it has raised costs.

References

Florida Real Estate Commission. *Handbook*, 1978 rev.

Florida Statutes, Chaps. 475, 478, 380.06.

Healy, Robert G. *Land Use and the States*. Baltimore: The Johns Hopkins Press for Resources for the Future, 1976.

Seidel, Stephen R. *Housing Costs and Government Regulation*. New Brunswick, N.J.: Center for Urban Policy Research, 1978.

Utility Regulation in Florida

by Sanford V. Berg

UNIVERSITY OF FLORIDA

16C

Every citizen is affected by state regulation of public utilities and of the transportation industry. Electricity, telephone, and gas bills are determined by how regulators analyze and alter the economic conditions facing firms and investors. In addition, to the extent that their activities are within the state, transportation industries are under the control of the state's regulatory commission rather than the Interstate Commerce Commission. The economic importance of these regulated industries is partly seen in table 16.2. The value of the gross plant in service, which represents the capital investment still in use, was nearly $14 billion for the three major utility industries in 1978. Investments in trucking and airlines would not be of this order of magnitude, yet these industries too are part of the Florida infrastructure—basic industries which are necessary to serve other industries. The operating revenues (sales) of the two largest industries amounted to almost $5.5 billion in 1978, and these services extend to virtually the entire population. Note that while municipally owned electric utilities are not included in the table, they represent, along with rural electric cooperatives, about 15 percent of statewide output of electricity and are partially regulated at the state level.

Such capital-intensive industries affect statewide investment cycles and represent a substantial source of property taxes. The growth of these industries is sensitive to population growth in the state; demands must be projected for five to ten years so that firms will have the capacity to service new demands (a requirement imposed by regulation). Thus, the economic health of these industries is an important factor in the state's economy.

The responsibility for regulation rests with the Florida Public Service Commission, which was organized in 1887 but did not acquire jurisdiction over gas and electric utilities until 1951. Regulation resembles a situation in which there is an open contract between consumers and producers, with a group of public officials serving as umpires who can alter the rules when it is deemed "in the public interest." Price, profitability, service quality, and exit/entry decisions are all dependent upon how regulators set the continually changing contract which binds together utility consumers and producers. In Florida, the Public Service Commission (PSC) monitors and changes the terms of the contract, allowing producers the opportunity to earn returns on investment similar to those available in comparable investments and ensuring that the prices paid by consumers meet the costs of serving them. The range for disagreement is substantial—but it can be narrowed through the analysis and evaluation of technical information. Although regulation is not a simple task, and will not become easier in the future, Florida has a regulatory environment conducive to incorporating research results and new knowledge into PSC policies.

In this brief review of regulatory policies, the difficulty of the issues involved is self-evident. The task assigned the PSC is to simulate competitive outcomes in markets where competition has been deemed inappropriate or inadequate. Telecommunications, energy, and transportation are examples of industries currently regulated by the PSC. In the case of a natural monopoly, the cost per unit of output falls as output increases. These economies of scale are so substantial, relative to the size of the market, that a single producer can provide the output most efficiently. In the past, the local telephone exchange has illustrated this argument. To prevent monopoly profits, regulators traditionally set limits on rates of return. Maintaining incentives for efficient management and investment strategies in such an environment is a challenge. Competitive markets reward makers of good decisions, innovators who develop new products, and managers who produce at minimum costs and penalize makers of bad decisions. Regulation circumvents this penalty and reward structure, in order to avoid excess profits. The development of procedures which restore strong incentives is a key problem facing the PSC.

Two other market conditions which have brought about regulation of industries are destructive competition and discriminatory pricing behavior. The first situation is where market entry may be easy, but overentry (too many firms) results in quality reduction (sometimes thus reducing public safety), economic losses, bankruptcies, and delayed exit from the industry. The resulting high prices and high profits after some firms exit is sometimes viewed as a market failure. Of course, the extent to which any particular industry, such as trucking,

TABLE 16.2. Utilities under the Florida PSC Jurisdiction, 1978

Industry	Gross Plant in Service ($)	Operating Revenues ($)	Number of Customers
Electricity[a]	7,209,038,970	3,035,149,226	3,260,932
Telephones	6,553,224,654	2,422,186,255	4,342,441
Natural gas	197,461,453	152,843,325	305,736
Airlines[b]			

a. Excludes municipally owned electric utilities.
b. Not available.
Source: Florida Public Service Commission

is susceptible to the destructive competition syndrome is an empirical question. Similarly, some industry conditions allow producers to charge different prices to different consumer groups, even when the cost of service is the same for the two groups. Equity considerations have been invoked for regulation to limit the ability of firms to charge higher prices to customers who have few (or no) substitutes for products or service. Such intervention is unnecessary where competition forces the price to reflect the cost of service.

Regulated industries are important factors in Florida's economy, providing the infrastructure for many economic activities. In the first half of the eighties, utilities will invest $10 billion in Florida, nearly as much as has been invested in the past 50 years. These investments will be occurring during a period of continued general price level inflation and of a rising relative cost of energy. The energy crisis has led to the formation of a federal Department of Energy and state energy offices. Also, telecommunications and transportation seem to have entered new eras as rapid technological changes have increased competitive pressures in both industries. Clearly, regulation must be responsive to these changes if Florida is to continue to have a strong economy.

Regulation has tended to focus either on the ratio of total cost to total revenue or on rates of return to determine whether prices were appropriate. By legislative action, truck rates are no longer regulated by the PSC. The best index of profitability is return on invested capital—the item that regulators tend to emphasize in electric and telecommunication utilities. That rate of return is determined by revenues minus operating expenses, all divided by the rate base (depreciable assets). In recent years, the PSC has adopted a number of rules for dealing with these components. Average rate base rather than year-end rate base is used; on the cost side, advertising expenditures are restricted, charitable contributions are not counted as expenses, and full normalization is used in the accounting treatment of taxes. The PSC has also addressed a number of other economic and financial issues, including treatment of construction work in progress. Thus, the process by which revenue requirements are determined has evolved in response to changing business conditions.

One response in Florida to general public pressure for regulatory reform was the change in 1978 from a three-member elective commission to a five-member appointive one. Perhaps the governor and the legislature viewed the expansion of the commission as a way of incorporating a more diverse set of backgrounds into the regulatory process. Another argument for the change is that the regulatory problems of the 1980s will require technical skills which would more likely be secured under an appointive than an elective system. Nonetheless, the elective system has served Florida reasonably well. Outside evaluations of the PSC have given it high marks in the areas of accountability, financial decisions, and responsiveness to innovative rate designs. In 1972, Common Cause published a report on 20 key questions (out of 102) regarding the openness and accessibility of state regulatory commissions and precautions taken against conflicts of interest and lobbying pressures. Florida was among the 29 states which "passed" the accountability test. These results are a credit to the laws and procedures under which the PSC operates. On the financial front, investment firms, such as Solomon Brothers, have given the Florida PSC high marks in terms of accounting procedures and responsiveness to rate change requests (absence of regulatory lags).

National Economic Research Associates, Inc., conducted in 1977 a survey of regulatory pricing policies. The states showed a remarkable amount of activity in the area of rate design—reflecting interest in seasonal rates, time-of-day pricing, and electricity load management. Florida in particular appeared to have a relatively innovative commission—discouraging master metering (to encourage conservation), and encouraging pricing experiments so that the cost-effectiveness of alternative rate designs can be determined. Other current pricing issues include conservation rates (approved for Florida Power and Light), the fuel adjustment clause, and the possible implementation of prices that varied with the costs of production.

The 1978 Public Utility Regulatory Policies Act inserted the federal government more deeply into state regulation than had been the case. Passed as part of the new energy program, these federal initiatives require state agencies to adapt to a host of new regulations—including standards for rate-making, additional data collection, and forecasting. We can expect major institutional changes within the regulatory process as the PSC and two recent additions to the regulatory scene, the State Energy Office and the Public Counsel, jockey for position in this new world of regulation. For example, on the federal scene, $50 million has been authorized (but not yet appropriated) for financial assistance to regulators; a new National Regulatory Research Institute has been established; grants to consumer advocates (and procedures for compensating intervenors) are being instituted; and millions of research dollars are going to utility pricing experiments. The next decade will find state regulators in the center of a policy battleground, with old weapons unavailable and new weapons untried. Flexibility may well be the posture for the decade ahead in the area of energy policy.

Lest one see the battles as only about pricing and identifying which customer groups pay certain categories of costs, other key issues should be briefly noted, including nuclear waste, environmental protection, and the estimation of a utility's cost of financial capital. As policies in these areas are established or further evolve, regulated firms will respond by altering investments, the quality (and reliability) of service, and proposed prices. Clearly, the regulatory process is not going to get any less complicated in the coming years, given the issues ahead. For example, the Grid Bill, passed several years ago, gave the PSC control over the price structure, but not the price level, of municipal utilities (which, with the rural electrical cooperatives, generate about 15 percent of the electricity in the state). This area has barely been touched by the PSC.

Recent technical studies have already had impacts on some aspects of the electric utility industry. In early 1976, the PSC asked for a general investigation to resolve problems between the Grid Bill, the Florida Electric Power Plant Site Act, and the commission's rate-making. In 1977, the resulting Peninsular Florida Generation Expansion Planning Study was released. It examined several scenarios for plant siting under alternative assumptions about fuel prices and the type of planning, whether joint or independent, that had occurred. Over this same period, at the behest of the Department of Environmental Regulation, the industry funded an independent $2 million study to determine whether air quality standards for sulfur dioxide should be tightened. In both cases, very complicated issues were tackled by seeking new scientific and engineering information. It is likely that future issues will involve similar task force approaches, rather than adversary hearings—given the complexity and site-specificity of the problems. For example, a power pooling prototype experiment has been under way for a year to determine the gains associated with an expansion of current contractual arrangements.

The areas of telecommunications, transportation, and natural gas raise similar complicated issues. In telecommunications, charging for information, pricing by usage (instead of a monthly flat fee), system reliability, and attachments have all received attention in recent years. In addition, ICC initiatives to deregulate some sectors of transportation have affected Florida's citizens and firms operating in the state. Rate regulation of trucking was abolished by the legislature in 1981. Finally, pipeline and gas distribution regulation will be affected by the 1978 energy acts. The right-of-way issues surrounding potential coal slurries further complicate regulatory decision-making in this area. It is too early to tell whether current issues will require major shifts in regulatory policies or a continued evolution of existing practices.

Although this brief overview provides only a partial catalogue of the types of issues addressed by Florida regulators, it illustrates the scope of the problems and the techniques used to resolve conflicts. More than ever before, the research community is participating in the regulatory process to assist in identifying complex interdependencies and in setting reasonable bounds on decisions that will be acceptable to both producers and consumers.

NOTE: A presentation on this topic by Lewis Petteway at the Public Utility Research Center Conference (February 1979) was very useful in providing some historical perspective on these issues.

16D

Public Policy Toward Labor in Florida

by Norman Keig

UNIVERSITY OF FLORIDA

According to a 1943 act of the Florida Legislature, a labor union is "an organization of employees . . . organized for the purpose of dealing with employers concerning hours of employment, rate of pay, working conditions, or grievance of any kind relating to employment." This act was the first law enacted by the Florida Legislature to express public policy toward labor unions and their activities. Public policy itself determines the legal status and powers of trade unions, the procedures for union-management bargaining (and even the permissible content of collective agreements), and the degree to which such weapons as strikes and picketing can be used in labor disputes. Furthermore, public policy may even prescribe the methods to be used to effect settlements when the parties themselves cannot agree on the terms.

In Florida, as in the nation as a whole, public policy prior to the 1940s was relatively vague, to be found in judicial decisions revolving around conflicts between the property rights of employers, including the right to do business, and the freedom of individuals to band together to protect their self-interest and to exercise the freedom of expression guaranteed by the Constitution. If either the goals of a labor organization or the means used to achieve these goals were illegal, then the labor organization was illegal. The judiciary had to pass judgment on both the goals and the means. Today, in Florida, public policy toward labor unions and their activities is expressed in judicial decisions, the Florida Constitution, laws such as Chapter 447 of the Florida Statutes, entitled "Labor Organizations," and administrative rules such as those prescribed by the Florida Public Employees Relations Commission.

This analysis of public policy toward labor organizations in Florida deals with (1) a survey of the current status of labor organizations in Florida, (2) an analysis of statutes covering unions in the private enterprise sector, and (3) an analysis of statutes regulating public employee unions.

The Status of Labor Organizations in Florida

This section is primarily concerned with labor unions and how the state legislature affects them. There are state and federal regulations governing safety in industry, state laws for workmen's compensation in case of injury, provisions for unemployment insurance, and provisions for minimum wage, but these topics are not covered. The chapter on public education (chapter 19) includes certain provisions about vocational training, which vitally affect employment and the training of workers for new skills.

Characteristic of labor conditions in Florida, in common with other southern states, is the low level of wages paid. The relative unimportance of manufacturing in the state decreases the total number of skilled workers. At the same time, wages in such service industries as tourism are likely to be low and their work forces unorganized. In areas such as service trades, however, increased technology has raised wage levels, and the same effect has occurred in government employment. As a result, there has been a decrease of 4 percent in Florida's population at or below the poverty level in the last decade.

Although Florida ranked eighth in population in 1974, it ranked only sixteenth in number of employees in labor organizations and forty-sixth in percentage of nonagricultural employees organized in labor unions and employee associations. (Associations are organizations of state, county, and municipal employees that are not affiliated with the AFL–CIO and professional organizations, such as the National Education Association, which are engaged in collective bargaining.) Only 15 percent of nonagricultural employees belonged to labor organizations in contrast to 30 percent in the nation; among southern states, only Mississippi, South Carolina, and North Carolina rank lower than Florida in this category. In absolute numbers, however, Florida had more than four times the number of members as Mississippi (the lowest number of members) and about a third more than Tennessee (the second highest number of members).

Another distinguishing mark of labor organizations in Florida is the distribution of members between the traditional labor unions and employee associations. Whereas in the United States approximately 88 percent of all members of unions and associations belong to labor unions, in Florida 85 percent belong to labor unions and 15 percent to associations. Among southern states, only in Alabama and North Carolina is the membership in associations a larger percentage of total membership than is the case in Florida.

The growth in union and association memberships in Florida differs from that which occurred nationally. Between 1970 and 1974, total membership increased about 20 percent in Florida and 7 percent nationally, and the percentage increase in union membership was more than four times the national increase. Although the percentage increase in membership associations in Florida was smaller than that nationally, still the percentage increase in such organizations was greater than that for union membership. This appears to be a national trend.

The growth in total membership has continued in Florida, particularly among public employees. In 1975, only 530 full-time state government employees belonged to labor organizations in contrast to 5,794 a year later (*Labor-Management Relations in State and Local Government, 1976*). In 1976, more than a third of all full-time employees of local governments had joined either a labor union or an association for bargaining purposes. The most heavily organized of local government employees in 1976 were the firefighters (70 percent of all full-time firefighters), followed by public school teachers (54 percent). At the state level, 72 percent of all full-time teachers employed by the state and 23 percent of all full-time state police protection workers were members of unions and associations. This growth in membership by state and local public employees reflects the developments in public policy toward the organization of such employees that occurred in the 1970s.

Labor organization membership in Florida covers a wide range of occupations, industries, and geographical areas. Although data on membership by these categories are not available, the distribution of membership within each category may be inferred from the names, number, and location of local unions found in the *Register of Reporting Labor Organizations 1977*. The more than 1,000 locals registered in 1977 include such diverse occupations as physicians and dentists, nurses, practical nurses, teachers, insurance workers, bricklayers, plumbers, musicians, steelworkers, auto workers, postal clerks, airline employees, railway clerks, traffic controllers, railway porters, longshoremen, machinists, laborers, and rural mail carriers. Members of labor organizations can be found in mining, the construction industries, durable and nondurable manufacturing industries, transportation industries, wholesale and retail trade, finance, services, and federal, state, and local governments. Although geographically, membership may be concentrated in the population centers of the state, such as the southeastern coastal region and Hillsborough and Pinellas counties, there are important industrial concentrations of members in the Panhandle and in the northeastern and north-central areas of the state. The letter carriers have 117 locals, one wherever there is a U. S. Post Office in Florida.

Distribution by occupation and industry of the local unions in Florida shows a high level of concentration. Building trades accounted for more than 22 percent of all registered locals in Florida. Carpenters and electrical workers each had more than 50 locals. Among the so-called industrial unions, the steelworkers, machinists, communication workers, chemical workers, and paperworkers each had at least 25 locals, and together with the independent auto workers and teamsters they accounted for 20 percent of all locals. Other national unions with large numbers of locals, although not necessarily large memberships, were letter carriers representing employees in the airline industry. And although the trade and service industries provide proportionately more jobs in Florida than in the nation, the retail, wholesale, and department store union had only 11 locals in Florida and the hotel and restaurant employees, the meat cutters, and the retail clerks only three each.

Locals that are affiliated with national unions which, in turn, are members of the AFL-CIO belong to the Florida AFL-CIO. In 1974 the membership in such locals constituted 76 percent of the total union and association membership in Florida and 90 percent of union membership alone. The state AFL-CIO serves to coordinate many noncollective bargaining activities of its members and to lend at least moral support to members during important work stoppages. It focuses attention on political action by endorsing candidates for public office, raising funds for political campaigns, lobbying in Tallahassee both for and against legislation that affects the welfare of employees, and serving as a watchdog over regulatory agencies whose decisions affect the welfare of workers as producers and as consumers.

Much of the status of labor in Florida can best be understood by examining the Florida State Constitution of 1968, which provided in Article 1, Section 6, that "the right of persons to work shall not be denied or abridged on account of membership or non-membership in any labor union or labor organization. The right of employees, by and through a labor organization, to bargain collectively shall not be denied or abridged. Public employees shall not have the right to strike."

This constitutional provision assured labor both gains and losses. The "right-to-work" clause guaranteed that every enterprise, public or private, could have both union and nonunion employees. This provision prohibits the check-off, or payment of union dues by employees who choose not to join a union; it is strongly opposed by labor unions. On the other hand, the section guarantees the right of collective bargaining to public employees when a majority in any category of work in government vote for a union. But collective bargaining by public employees' unions may not include the right to strike. With this prodding of the new constitution, the Florida legislature in the 1970s enacted legislation to establish public employees' unions, when employees vote for it, at state, local, and county government levels.

Labor's political success may be measured by the fact that Florida is one of 19 states still prohibiting compulsory union membership, and by its unsuccessful campaign in the 1979 legislative session against the repeal of a 40-year-old state law that required builders to pay the prevailing (union) wage on state construction projects.

Although political action by labor organizations is necessary just to protect their legal status, their major purpose is to have a voice in determining the rules for members pertaining to wages, hours, and working conditions. The phrase working conditions has been interpreted broadly enough to include anything and everything that affects the welfare of the worker. Both the negotiation of agreements establishing the rules of the game and the daily employer-employee relationships fall under the heading collective bargaining. Work stoppages may occur with the breakdown of negotiations, and even during the duration of an agreement, when either party becomes impatient with the legal procedure for reconciling disagreements.

In October 1976 there were four labor-management agreements in Florida covering 6,970 state employees and 255 agreements covering 124,625 local government employees (BLS, *Handbook of Labor Statistics, 1977: Work Stoppages*). Agreements at the level of local government involved 19 of the 67 counties in Florida, 149 of 390 municipalities, and 83 of 94 school districts included in the study. Similar data are not available for the private sector.

Work stoppages are indicative of the degree of harmony between labor and management. The number of such stoppages in Florida declined from 130 in 1970 to 55 in 1976. The percentage of private nonfarm working time lost due to such stoppages during a year has ranged from a high of 0.14 percent (1970) to a low of 0.04 percent (1976). The number of workers involved in such stoppages has been relatively small, ranging from a high of 45,900 (1974) to a low of 15,000 (1972). And although public employees do not have the right to strike in Florida, from October 1975 to October 1976 there were four work stoppages that involved more than 1,000 public employees.

In summary, although labor organizations are not as strong in Florida as they are in the nation, an increasing proportion of the labor force in Florida is becoming organized. Much of the growth in recent years has been among public employees. Further growth may take place in manufacturing, which is of lesser importance in the Florida economy than it is nationally. A revival of the construction industry also may bring gains in membership; the building trades unions suffered drastic losses in membership as a result of the severe slump in the construction industry that occurred in the second half of the 1970s. But for labor organizations to increase their economic and political strength in Florida, they will have to organize the trade, service, and finance industries as well as agricultural workers — the dominant industries in Florida.

Regulation of Labor Organizations in the Private Sector

Employees and employers in Florida come under a number of different laws when their activities involve collective bargaining. Public employees and employers of the state, counties, and municipalities are governed by Part II, Public Employees, of Chapter 447, Labor Organizations. Private employees and employers engaged in intrastate commerce fall under Part I, Federal Provisions, of the same statute. Railway and airline employee-employer relationships are governed by the Railway Labor Act of 1926 as amended. Federal employees and employers including those in Florida have their bargaining relationships prescribed by Executive Order 10988 issued by President Kennedy on January 17, 1962, Executive Order 11491 issued by President Nixon on October 29, 1969, and the Federal Pay Comparability Act of 1970. Private employees and employers engaged in interstate commerce are regulated by the Labor-Management Relations Act of 1947 (commonly known as the Taft-Hartley Act) and the Labor-Management Reporting and Disclosure Act (popularly known as the Landrum-Griffin Act) of 1959, and to a certain extent by the laws of Florida. Public utility workers in Florida engaged in intrastate commerce are governed by both Part I of Chapter 447 and Chapter 453, the Public Utility Arbitration Law. Thus, it is obvious that there is no single law that prescribes a uniform public policy toward labor organizations and collective bargaining pertaining to employees and employers within the State of Florida. The major concern here, however, is public policy toward labor organizations and collective bargaining as expressed in the laws of Florida, judicial decisions, and administrative rules.

State and federal legislation. — In principle, the federal government has only the right to regulate activities affecting interstate commerce, leaving to the states the regulation of intrastate commerce. The distinction between interstate and intrastate commerce has not been easy to make. Since the passage by the U.S. Congress of the National Labor Relations Act of 1935 (known as the "Wagner Act") and the Taft-Hartley Act of 1947, the Supreme Court has given a very broad interpretation of the definition of interstate commerce and the phrase "affecting commerce" employed in both acts. Once Congress had passed legislation pertaining to collective bargaining, state regulation either through state court decisions or state laws became inoperative. A no-man's land developed in the general area of industrial relations when the National Labor Relations Board, either by design or lack of funds, failed to exercise fully its statutory jurisdiction over all labor disputes affecting interstate commerce. The Supreme Court, however, ruled that a state may exercise jurisdiction over conduct involving violence and threats of violence in a labor dispute even though the dispute itself affected interstate commerce.

The United States Congress also gave to the states some control over labor activities even though they affected interstate commerce. The Taft-Hartley Act bans the closed shop, wherein a person has to be a union member in good standing when he is hired, and permits the union shop, wherein as a condition of employment a person has to join the union within a specified period after being hired. Section 14(b) of the act, however, permits state laws to determine the legality of a union shop provision in any labor agreement. Thus in Florida, which has a constitutional prohibition as well as laws against compulsory union membership, state regulations prevail. Second, included in the provisions of the Landrum-Griffin Act of 1959 are amendments to the Taft-Hartley Act. These amendments specifically give the states jurisdiction over any labor dispute that does not fall within the jurisdictional standards of the National Labor Relations Board as provided on August 1, 1959, and which the board feels should still be left to the states today.

Thus, under limited circumstances the State of Florida exercises some control over labor activities that affect interstate commerce. These circumstances involve violence and the threat of violence in strikes and picketing and other activities of a criminal nature and cases in which the National Labor Relations Board declines to exercise its jurisdiction. In addition, Florida can police agreements involving parties engaged in interstate commerce to see that they do not violate state laws against compulsory union membership.

General provisions. — Part I of Chapter 447 of the Florida Statutes defines the rights of employees and specifies the regulations under which labor organizations are free to operate. Basic to the rights defined by the provisions of this statute is Section 6, Article 1 of the 1968 Revised Constitution of the State of Florida. This so-called right-to-work amendment was first adopted in 1944. The provisions of Section 6, Article 1 have been quoted above. The statutes add specificity to its provisions.

Section 447.03 sets forth the rights of employees as defined in that constitutional provision. Employees have the right to join or not to join organizations of their own choosing. They cannot be compelled to join a labor organization either as a condition to being hired or as a requirement after being hired. Compulsory union membership is unlawful. But it is the stated policy of the state that workers are free to bargain collectively through representatives of their own choosing and to engage in concerted activities for the purpose of collective bargaining or other mutual aid or protection.

Section 447.09 of the statute recognizes the right of franchise of any member of a labor organization. It is unlawful for anyone, employer or labor organization official or member, to interfere with an employee's exercise of this right —

to make a complaint, file charges, give information or testimony concerning the violations of the law, petition his union regarding any grievance he may have concerning his membership or employment, or make known facts concerning such grievance or violations of law to any public officials. Furthermore, the right of franchise includes the rights of free petition, lawful assemblage, and free speech.

Implicit in these last three rights is an employee's right to solicit membership in a labor organization. He has the right to induce others to join his labor organization, but he must use peaceful methods — persuasion rather than coercion, intimidation, or fraud in the solicitation of members. Furthermore, only persons authorized by a particular labor organization can solicit membership in it or represent it in other activities. Finally, no one can prohibit or prevent the election of the officers of a labor organization.

Basically, the general provisions of the statute impose regulations on the activities of labor organizations. These provisions are restrictive in nature as if the intent were to protect the individual members of a labor organization and employers from the abuse of power by labor organization officials. Labor organizations are required to register with the Department of Labor, giving the name of the organization, the location of its office, and the name and address of its officers, including business agents. An annual fee of $1 must be paid at the time the annual report is filed. The labor organization must keep accurate account books, itemizing all receipts and expenditures, and make these accounts available for inspection by any member. Labor organizations cannot charge an initiation fee in excess of $15 unless a higher fee were in effect on January 1, 1940. All other dues and fees levied by a labor organization must be in accord with the provisions of the organization's constitution or bylaws. No one can solicit advertising in the name of the labor organization without its written permission. No one can claim endorsement by a labor organization without written authority.

The statute, however, imposes qualifications on paid officials of labor organizations. Such officials, termed "business agents" by the law, include anyone who issues membership or authorization cards — work permits — in the name of a labor organization or solicits from any employer any right or privilege for employees. Such a business agent must be a citizen of the United States, have had his civil rights restored if he had been convicted of a felony in the past, and be of good moral character.

A person cannot act as a business agent unless he has obtained a license from the state, and the law imposes a duty on the employer to deal only with qualified union officials. To qualify, a person must file an application under oath with the

Department of Labor. The application must be accompanied by a fee of $25 and a full set of the applicant's fingerprints taken by a law enforcement agency. A statement signed by the president and the secretary of the labor organizations for which the applicant proposes to act as agent must be included.

The Department of Labor may conduct an independent investigation of an applicant. It can deny and revoke licenses. Grounds for denial, suspension, or revocation include making false statements in the application and violating other provisions of the statute. Any persons denied a license or having had his license revoked is entitled to a hearing by the division conducted in accordance with Chapter 120 of the Florida Statutes.

Work stoppages and picketing. — Although the law preserves the right to strike, there are restrictions upon the exercise of this right. It is unlawful to participate in any strike, walkout, or cessation of work if the stoppage has not been authorized in a secret ballot by the majority of the employees involved in the employment relationship. It is also unlawful to seize or occupy property during the existence of a labor dispute. This provision, first enacted in 1943, was Florida's legislative response to the sit-down strikes that occurred particularly in the automotive industry during the late 1930s. Here workers occupied plants in order to gain recognition by their employer for their organization.

Work stoppages that result because of a conflict between two or more labor organizations are also unlawful. Such a dispute represents an attempt to force an employer to assign work to members of the striking union rather than to members of the competing unions. It, too, is partly the product of the bitter disputes that erupted in the late 1930s between those unions affiliated with the AFL and those affiliated with the CIO. Such jurisdictional disputes are prohibited by the Taft-Hartley Act.

Picketing also is subject to restrictions under Part I. It is unlawful to picket beyond the area of the industry or employment within which a labor dispute arises. The purpose of this provision is to reduce the amount of inconvenience the public suffers as a result of a strike and to prevent labor organizations from bringing pressure on other employers to force them to act against the struck employer. It is unlawful to coerce or intimidate any elected or appointed public official, or to intimidate the family, picket the domicile, or injure the person or property of such employee or public official, or his family. And, in brief, picketing must be peaceful and done in a reasonable manner, and it must not prevent ingress and egress on any premises.

In summary, Part I of Chapter 447 is known as a union regulation law. It does not represent an attempt by the state to establish orderly procedures for the settlement of employer-employee disputes. It recognizes the rights of employees to form labor organizations of their own choosing but does not require employers to recognize such organizations or to bargain in good faith. Furthermore, the law does not establish machinery for deciding whether a particular group of employees wishes to form a labor organization or determining which employees belong in the bargaining unit. The law not only regulates labor organizations and their officials; it is also a law that is restrictive. Federal legislation — the Wagner Act and the Taft-Hartley Act — have supplementary provisions for businesses that operate in interstate commerce. Such provisions include the requirement that employers bargain in good faith.

Collective Bargaining in the Public Sector

Part II of Chapter 447 of the Florida Statutes sets forth standards and guidelines for collective bargaining by state and local government employers and employees. It implements the right of public employees to form labor organizations of their own choosing as guaranteed in Section 6, Article 1, revised Florida Constitution.

In 1969 the Florida Supreme Court in *Dade County Classroom Teachers' Association* v. *Ryan* ruled that "with the exception of the right to strike, public employees have the same rights of collective bargaining as are granted private employees [by the state constitution]." This decision replaced earlier decisions which had denied such rights to public employees. The court further said that "it is requisite that the legislature enact appropriate legislation setting out standards and guidelines and otherwise regulate the subject within the limits of said Section 6."

When the legislature failed to act in 1973, the court appointed an eight-member study commission as amici curiae and charged it with the responsibility of recommending guidelines for collective bargaining by public employees. Just prior to the 1974 legislative session, the commission filed with the court a comprehensive set of procedural guidelines which it recommended by adoption in the absence of executive or legislative action. This stimulated the adoption by the 1974 legislature of what is known as Part II of Chapter 447, amended in 1977.

The provisions of Part II extend the power of the state over the employer-employee relationship. They regulate the activities of public employers, public employees, and labor organizations to a far greater degree than the provisions of Part I as they pertain to the employer-employee relationship in the private sector. The provisions create a state agency — the Florida Public Employees Relations Commission (PERC) — to administer the law. The law spells out the rights and obligations of public employers, public employees, and labor organizations, the procedure for determining whether or not public employees wish to form a labor organization, and the methods to be followed for settling disputes between management and labor.

PERC is an independent agency not controlled by any department in Florida government. It is composed of three full-time members, and one part-time alternate, appointed by the governor and subject to confirmation by the senate for staggered four-year terms.

The most important function of PERC is "to assist in resolving disputes between public employees and public employers." Specifically, it (1) registers employee organizations and maintains copies of their annual reports, (2) determines or approves the composition of proposed bargaining units, (3) conducts representation elections to determine majority status of an employee organization, (4) certifies the winner of such elections as the exclusive bargaining agent for all the employees in the bargaining unit, (5) investigates charges and determines whether or not either labor or management has, in fact, engaged in unfair labor practices and provides remedies to redress such unfair labor practices, (6) maintains a list of persons qualified to provide mediation services to resolve impasses reached during collective bargaining negotiations, (7) provides panels of special masters to help resolve impasses which are not settled by the process of mediation, (8) seeks the aid of the courts in enforcing its orders, and (9) enforces certain strike penalty provisions of the law.

With the exception of the right to strike, public employees have the same rights of collective bargaining as employees in the private sector. Public employees have the right to join or not to join labor organizations of their own choosing, to engage in collective bargaining or other forms of concerted activities, and to be free from interference by any person in the exercise of these rights. They cannot be required to join a labor organization and they cannot be coerced, intimidated, or fraudulently persuaded in making their decisions. They have the right to negotiate a written collective bargaining agreement with their employer covering wages, hours, and working conditions, with the exception of retirement provisions. Finally, public employees have the right to be represented in the determination of grievances during the duration of an agreement or to refrain from exercising the right to be represented.

Excluded from coverage under the act, however, are certain groups of employees. These include gubernatorial appointees, elected officials, agency heads, and members of boards and commissions, persons in the organized state militia, negotiating representatives for employers, managerial or confidential employees, and persons employed by the Florida Legislature. Inmates in state prisons also are excluded.

Managerial and confidential employees are excluded because of their more than routine involvement in establishing and carrying out collective bargaining and personnel policies of the public employer. They represent the interests of the employer on a day-to-day basis. Supervisory employees, those whose duties often are of a routine nature, may bargain collectively.

Public employees also have rights under the law. A public employer has the right to (1) determine unilaterally the purpose of each of its constituent agencies, (2) set standards of services to be offered to the public, (3) exercise control and discretion over its organization and operations, (4) direct his employees, (5) take disciplinary action for proper cause, and (6) lay off employees for lack of work or for other legitimate reasons. In exercising these rights, the employer must be careful not to violate the terms and conditions of any collective bargaining agreement in force or any civil or career service regulation.

In addition to specifying the rights of public employers, the act also lists a number of unfair labor practices. Public employers or their agents are prohibited from (1) interfering with public employees in the exercise of any rights guaranteed them under this act, (2) encouraging or discouraging membership in any employee organization by discrimination in regard to hiring, tenure, or other conditions of employment, (3) refusing to bargain collectively, failing to bargain in good faith, or refusing to sign a final agreement agreed upon with the certified bargaining agent for the public employees in the bargaining unit, (4) dominating, interfering with, or assisting in the formation, existence, or administration of any employee organization or contributing financial support to such an organization, and (5) refusing to discuss grievances in good faith with either the certified bargaining agent for the public employee or the employee involved.

In summary, Chapter 447 of the Florida Statutes establishes standards and guidelines for collective bargaining in the public sector. In a real sense, its coverage is similar to that of the Taft-Hartley and Landrum-Griffin acts over collective bargaining that affects interstate commerce. The law establishes the rights and obligations of the parties, machinery for the administration of the law, and penalties for noncompliance. At the same time the law leaves to the state and local legislative bodies final authority to fund the terms of any agreement.

Summary

There are other state laws of a more limited scope that regulate and prohibit certain practices of labor organizations. It is unlawful, for example, to counterfeit a union label — a label that tells the buyer that the product has been made by organized labor — and to penalize any trucking firm for attempting to move truck-trailers on railroad cars, a practice that the Teamsters Union had followed. The 1947 Public Utility Arbitration Law prohibits work stoppages in public utilities and prescribes compulsory arbitration of disputes. But in 1953, the Florida Supreme Court held that the act was unconstitutional as applied to employees of a local transit company because the operations of the company affected interstate commerce. This placed the labor dispute under federal, not state, jurisdiction. It is doubtful that there are any public utilities in Florida whose operations do not affect interstate commerce. The law stands as a pious expression for an easy answer to a complex problem.

To conclude, labor organizations appear to be more extensive in the public sector of the Florida economy than in the private sector. The vast majority of employees in the private sector for the most part are subject to federal laws. To a limited extent, particularly in the case of compulsory union membership and violence in work stoppages, their activities are subject to some state control.

Public policy toward labor organizations in the private sector that is subject to state control is one of protecting the rights of individual employees by regulating the activities of labor organizations. The most commonly known feature of this policy is the right-to-work provision in the state constitution and Chapter 447 of the Florida Statutes.

The state policy toward labor organizations in the public sector is far more detailed and broader than in the private sector. The major problem will be the resolution of impasses in this sector. In 1977, the Florida legislature rejected the recommendations of the special master who had been appointed to resolve a dispute between the faculty personnel of the State University System and the Board of Regents. The legislature refused to fund the salary increases in the agreement signed by both parties. In the end, the legislature made its will felt by providing salary increases less than those received by other state employees. The issue remains: how to resolve such disputes?

References

Florida, Department of Community Affairs, Division of Technical Assistance. *Collective Bargaining in Florida*. Tallahassee, 1978.

Florida, House of Representatives, Subcommittee on Collective Bargaining in Public Employment. *A Study Report of the Committee on Labor & Industry*. Tallahassee, 1970.

Smith, David N. "History of Florida Public Employee Collective Bargaining Laws." Unpublished paper.

U. S. Department of Commerce, Bureau of the Census, and Department of Labor, Labor-Management Services Administration. *Labor-Management Relations in State and Local Governments, 1976*. State and Local Government Special Studies No. 88. Washington: Government Printing Office, 1978.

U. S. Department of Labor, Bureau of Labor Statistics. *Directory of National Unions and Employee Associations, 1975*. Washington: Government Printing Office, 1977.

———. *Handbook of Labor Statistics, 1977: Work Stoppages*. Washington: Government Printing Office, 1977.

U. S. Department of Labor, Labor-Management Services Administration. *Register of Reporting Labor Organizations, 1977*. Washington: Government Printing Office, 1978.

Public Finance

17

by Frederick O. Goddard

UNIVERSITY OF FLORIDA

With a 1980 population of 9,746,324—the seventh largest state in the nation—the State of Florida has a large annual budget. In fiscal year 1980–81 total state budget expenditures for all purposes were $15 billion and total revenues $15.07 billion. But Florida ranks low among the fifty states in total taxes per capita and in taxes as a percent of average personal income. In 1981 Florida's average annual per capita personal income ($10,165) ranked it twenty-eighth among the states. During this period total state and local government taxes in Florida were $1,221 per capita, or $101.8 per thousand dollars of personal income, ranking Florida thirty-seventh in taxes per capita and forty-second in taxes as a percent of personal income. We will examine here the major categories of expenditures in the budget of the State of Florida and the major sources of revenue to finance these expenditures.

Government Expenditures

Florida's total disbursements for all purposes for fiscal year 1981–82 were $19 billion. Over $10.5 billion was for nonoperating expenditures, such as investments for various trust funds (employee retirement, highway construction, and the like), debt service, refunds, and distributions of revenue collected for the U.S. Treasury. The services supplied or supported by state government cost $8.6 billion, $5.2 billion in state operating disbursements and $2.8 billion in disbursements in aid of local government (see table 17.1).

By far the largest share of the State of Florida's expenditures in 1981–82 went to education. Over 39 percent of the $8.6 billion total of state operating disbursements plus aid to local governments went directly to education through the state's university system (over 12 percent) and through county governments to public school and community college programs (over 26 percent).

The second largest category of expenditures was for public welfare. Over $1.3 billion, 15 percent of the $8.6 billion total of state operating disbursements plus aid to local governments, was spent for public welfare. Apart from aid to counties, public welfare is the largest category of programs conducted directly by the state government. Other large functional categories of expenditures, ranging from about 9 percent to 3 percent of the total budget, are highways;

TABLE 17.1. State of Florida Budget: Disbursement by Function (1 July 1981–30 June 1982)

Disbursements by Function	Amount	Percent of Total of Operating Plus Aid to Local Government
OPERATING DISBURSEMENTS		
General Government	$ 630,041,146.39	7.28
Protection to persons and property	173,473,157.32	2.00
Hospitals, health, and sanitation	633,222,608.59	7.32
Development and conservation of natural resources	289,916,016.57	3.36
Highways	806,045,591.01	9.32
Public welfare		
Unemployment compensation benefits	266,773,583.74	3.08
Aids and administration	1,104,902,912.69	12.77
Education		
State universities	723,835,211.99	8.36
Other	393,203,132.71	4.54
Parks, monuments, and memorials	36,568,965.31	0.43
Correctional institutions	356,038,525.86	4.11
Retirements, pensions, and relief acts	288,962,029.32	3.34
Total operating disbursements	5,702,982,881.50	65.91
AID TO LOCAL GOVERNMENT		
Aid to cities	252,521,078.37	2.92
Aid to counties (noneducational)	424,961,270.29	4.91
Aid to counties (educational)	2,272,113,643.83	26.26
Total aid to local government	2,949,595,992.49	34.09
Total operating disbursements plus aid to local government	8,652,578,873.99	100.00
OTHER NONOPERATING DISBURSEMENTS		
Investments	3,956,973,689.82	
County and other debt service	27,831,747.51	
Distributions to U.S. Treasury	1,057,949,826.24	
Refunds, interfund transfers, and other	5,495,762,525.81	
Total other nonoperating disbursements	10,538,517,789.38	
TOTAL DISBURSEMENTS	$19,191,096,663.37	

Source: State of Florida, *Annual Report of the Comptroller, Fiscal Year 1981–82*, pp. 12–13.

educational aid to cities and counties; general government; hospitals, health, and sanitation; correctional institutions; and development and conservation of natural resources.

Most educational expenditures in Florida are administered at the county level—and at the local level education is the largest category of expenditure. In addition to the more than $2 billion distributed to local school districts by the state, these districts raised $1.3 billion from local property taxes and received $353 million in federal aid. Altogether for fiscal year 1981–82, Florida counties had revenue of more than $3.2 billion for public school programs.

Local government expenditures in Florida are also important in financing roads and streets, health and welfare, and fire, police, and sanitation services. The property tax revenues of $3.16 billion in the state for fiscal year 1981–82 were allocated as follows: $1.13 billion for schools, $1.27 billion for other county services, and $586 million for municipal services. Noneducational aid to counties and cities amounted to $1.62 billion, and municipal utilities taxes yielded $287 million. Altogether, Florida's local governments received over $5 billion for expenditures in noneducational programs.

Combined expenditures for state and local governments in Florida in fiscal year 1981–82, including state nonoperating disbursements, were over $13.8 billion ($1,355 per capita). State government direct operating expenditures were almost $5.7 billion ($560 per capita). Total local government expenditures on public schools were $5 billion ($491 per capita). Total local government expenditures for noneducational programs were more than $5 billion ($491 per capita). State government expenditures for health and public welfare were over $2 billion ($196 per capita).

Government Revenues

Total revenues of the State of Florida for fiscal year 1981–82 were over $20 billion. State taxes were the major source of direct revenues (see table 17.2). Of the $5.9 billion in tax revenues, more than $4.4 billion (75 percent) went into the general revenue fund. The remaining $1.5 billion of tax revenue was earmarked for various trust funds.

U.S. government grants-in-aid in 1982 accounted for 21 percent of Florida's total direct revenue. In 1978 Florida ranked tenth among the states in the amount of federal aid received by state and local governments, but it ranked only forty-eighth in federal dollars per capita received. Some states, Florida among them, have chosen not to participate fully in federally aided programs (such as highway construction or public assistance) that require matching state

TABLE 17.2. State of Florida Revenues (July 1, 1981–June 30, 1982)

Revenue Source	Amount	Percent of Total Direct Revenue
DIRECT REVENUE		
State taxes		
Total state taxes	$ 5,921,461,667.31	69.63
Aids and donations		
U.S. Government	1,833,342,519.51	21.56
Other	95,152,233.80	1.12
Total aids and donations	1,928,494,753.31	22.68
Other direct revenue		
Earnings on investments and deposits	282,223,339.22	3.32
Miscellaneous	372,187,258.63	4.38
Total other direct revenue	654,410,597.85	7.69
Total direct revenue	8,504,367,018.47	100.00
NONOPERATING REVENUE		
Retirement and Social Security contributions	1,542,454,233.49	
Nonrecurring revenue	7,118,898,300.50	
Refunds and interfund transfers	2,867,188,125.18	
Total nonoperating revenue	11,532,927,726.38	
TOTAL REVENUE	$20,037,294,744.85	

Source: State of Florida, *Annual Report of the Comptroller, Fiscal Year 1981–1982*.

funds. Since Florida was forty-seventh in state and local taxes per thousand dollars of personal income, it should not be surprising that the state ranked so low in per capita federal aid received.

Thus the key determinants of the level of government expenditure for social services are state and local tax revenues. These tax revenues account for over 69 percent of the total direct revenues; the remainder, including the amounts received through federal aid, is closely dependent upon the level of tax revenues. If Florida is to maintain or increase the level of real per capita expenditure for social services in the 1980s, it must rely primarily upon its own tax revenues. It is an important question, therefore, whether Florida's tax system has the potential to generate adequate revenues for programs that the people of the state are going to expect in the future.

Florida's Tax System

The State of Florida collected $5.9 billion in taxes during fiscal year 1981–82, and county and municipal governments collected an additional $4 billion. Proposals for tax relief or tax limits are increasingly popular around the nation, and Florida's tax system must be carefully examined. The major sources of the state's revenue, the adequacy of the tax system for financing present and projected spending levels, whether the taxes in use place equitable burdens on the various segments of the state's population, whether the tax system encourages efficiency in production and the use of natural resources—these are the perennial issues before the people of Florida and their legislators. To evaluate Florida's tax system, we will consider each major tax with respect to (1) the adequacy of revenues it provides, (2) the fairness of the burdens it imposes, and (3) its impact on economic efficiency.

Adequacy of revenues.—A good tax system, we assume, will automatically and without changes in tax rules or rate schedules provide additional revenues over time to keep up with inflation and to cover increasing costs of serving a growing population. If a tax meets this criterion it can be said to meet the test of generating adequate revenue. If the taxes that make up a tax system fail to generate adequate revenues without being altered, the state must either permit social services to fall off as a result of inflation or population growth or it must constantly legislate new taxes or rate increases to make up for the inadequate revenues generated. Both alternatives are undesirable.

Looked at the other way, taxes that generate adequate revenues permit the state to maintain a constant level of real per capita social services. But if the state wishes to increase the level of social services, even though its taxes generate adequate revenues, new taxes or higher rates for existing taxes will have to be legislated. It is probably politically desirable that new programs of social services should have to be paid for through new tax legislation: the public debate over the new taxes will certainly cause the new programs to be examined closely. What the public and legislature should wish to avoid is a need for new tax legislation to finance accepted, established social service programs at a constant real per capita level.

Fairness.—While a common standard for judging the fairness of a tax may be impossible to achieve, a factual determination important to that judgment of fairness can be made, namely, who actually bears the burden of a particular tax. Although legislation may prescribe who shall pay over the revenues to the government, the economic laws of supply and demand determine where the burden ultimately falls. Changes in prices, wages, or interest rates can and do effectively shift the burden represented by most taxes from the initial payer of the tax to some other person or group.

Two broad principles of taxation are commonly applied in making judgments (admittedly not scientific ones) about the fairness of a tax: the principle of the *benefits received* and the principle of the *ability to pay*. A tax can be considered fair and equitable if its burden falls upon members of the community in proportion to the benefits they receive from the spending program supported by the tax. This principle of the benefits received sees taxes working in much the same way that prices work in the marketplace: each individual pays fully for the goods and services he or she consumes; persons who do not consume any of these goods and services are not asked to bear any of the costs. Under this principle, the costs of game and fish management would properly be borne only by hunters and fishermen (perhaps through license fees). While many governmental services can be implemented by application of the principle of benefits received, many more cannot. Government activities such as general administration or environmental protection provide benefits too indirectly or distribute them too widely throughout the population for any direct assessment of their costs to be made. For other programs, although they may benefit particular, identifiable persons, it would be impractical or impossible to finance them on the principle of benefits received. For example, education at the lower levels benefits children, who cannot be expected to pay the costs of their education; nor can the recipients of public welfare or the physically or mentally handicapped pay the costs of the benefits they receive under state social service programs. For such programs, some other standard for determining the fairness of the means used to meet their costs must be applied, and the one suggested most often is the principle of ability to pay.

There are unfortunately no agreed-upon methods to measure ability to pay. Over their lifetimes, individuals can be ranked for ability to pay about as well either by their consumption or their income or their wealth. But over a shorter interval, say a year, these three measures can give quite different results. A person with a large amount of wealth in real property or other assets that cannot be turned easily into cash might be hard pressed to pay even a small tax amount at any specific time. Nor is income always a clear-cut measure of an ability to pay taxes. Does a doubling of income mean a doubling of ability to pay? Or does the ability to pay taxes go up more slowly (or more rapidly) than income itself ?

While almost every tax takes a greater amount of money from persons with higher incomes than from persons with lower incomes, taxes are commonly characterized as *proportional* or *progressive* or *regressive* depending upon the extent to which they increase the tax burden upon those with higher incomes. A tax is said to be proportional if the *percentage* of income paid in taxes is the same for those with higher incomes and for those with lower incomes. (The familiar biblical concept of the tithe, a tenth part or ten percent of one's income, is an example of a proportional tax.) A tax is said to be progressive if persons in higher income brackets pay a higher percentage of their income than do persons in lower income brackets. A tax is said to be regressive if persons in higher income brackets (while paying a larger absolute amount), pay a smaller percentage of their income than do persons in lower income brackets.

Since it is not possible to measure objectively a person's ability to pay taxes, there can be no universal agreement on whether a particular tax or tax system should be proportional, progressive, or regressive on the basis of ability to pay. Nevertheless, there is broad popular sentiment for the idea that a higher income reflects a more than proportionate increase in ability to pay taxes over a lower income and that a progressive tax is therefore often desirable.

While neither the principle of benefits received nor the principle of ability to pay requires that taxes be progressive, there may be good reasons for preferring that at least some taxes in the system be progressive. One of the more important functions of government is the redistribution of wealth, which in our society is usually accomplished through governmental programs that increase the well-being of the lower income groups and are financed by taxes levied against the higher income groups. We commonly look upon such programs as "progressive" *because* they benefit the poor at the expense of the more wealthy segments of society. But such a redistributive program, one that is progressive in its total net impact, need not be financed only by a progressive tax. A regressive tax, in fact, might be administratively so much more efficient that its proceeds, invested in progressive programs, accomplish the redistribution of wealth most economically for the society. Nevertheless, it is widely felt that progressive taxes are usually the most efficient way to finance social welfare programs.

Governmental programs that aim at benefiting the less well off groups of our society, and thereby in fact aim at a redistribution of wealth, are best carried out by the federal government or, if by the states, as part of a common nationwide program. The abilities of state and local governments to implement redistributive programs are quite limited, for such programs can and do provide incentives for taxpayers to emigrate to states where taxes are lower and for welfare recipients to migrate to states where benefits are higher.

Economic efficiency.—The economic behavior of those individuals who bear the burden of a tax is likely to be changed by the imposition of that tax. Any tax may affect the system of incentives (prices, wages, profits, and so on) that influences economic behavior. The impact of a tax may be desirable or undesirable depending on whether it promotes or discourages efficiency or other economic goals. In general, if a tax is designed in accordance with the principle of benefits received, it will promote economic efficiency: such taxes provoke the taxpayer to consider the full costs of his or her actions, including the costs of the social services consumed. Economists therefore favor taxes based on the principle of benefits received.

Taxes designed in accordance with the principle of the ability to pay, and taxes designed overtly for the purpose of redistribution of wealth from more well off persons to less well off persons, do not promote economic efficiency. Instead they tend to introduce inefficiencies into the economy by distorting patterns of production or consumption of goods. Thus an unavoidable cost of programs designed to increase equity of income distribution is some loss of efficiency and a smaller total output. If no tax can be completely neutral in its effects on economic incentives, government can nevertheless design a tax program that seeks to minimize the adverse effects of taxes on economic efficiency. This is most easily done by using as often as possible taxes based on the principle of benefits received. Whenever that is not possible, broad-based taxes that do not discriminate for or against any particular economic activity should be selected and effective tax rates should be kept as low as possible.

Overview of State Taxes

The State of Florida collects 31 different types of taxes and fees from its citizens, not counting the property and utility taxes collected by counties and municipalities (see table 17.3). Seventeen of these taxes can be considered minor: each provides well under 1 percent of the state's total tax revenues, and together they account for only 3.79 percent of the total. These minor taxes are special purpose taxes that collect amounts approximately equal to the costs of the programs they are intended to support; they represent fairly successful applications of the principle of benefits received. Citrus tax receipts, for example, are earmarked for the citrus advertising fund; hunting and fishing license fees are earmarked for the State Game Trust Fund and Fish Management Trust Fund; and workmen's compensation taxes go into the workmen's compensation and disability trust funds. Each of these minor taxes and fees generally meets economic standards of fairness and efficiency in that the tax burdens fall mainly on the groups that benefit from the particular programs associated with the tax and the monies collected pay only the actual costs of the programs. If in the future the rates of these minor taxes are adjusted to keep up with costs of the governmental programs associated with them, then these taxes will continue to be adequate, fair, and efficient.

TABLE 17.3. State of Florida Tax Revenues

Tax	Estimated Revenues Fiscal Year 1983–84 (in millions $)	Percent of Total Tax Revenue
Auto title and lien fees	13.3	0.17
Beverage licenses	17.3	0.22
Beverage tax *	406.2	5.17
Cigarette tax *	290.6	3.70
Citrus taxes	53.9	0.69
Corporation charter tax	4.1	0.05
Corporation income tax *	592.5	7.54
Corporation report filing fee	2.1	0.03
Documentary stamp taxes *	256.5	3.27
Driver education fee	4.4	0.06
Driver license examination fees	10.8	0.14
Driver license fees	14.9	0.19
Estate tax *	92.0	1.17
Gross receipts utilities tax *	151.5	1.93
Hotel and restaurant licenses	3.3	0.04
Hunting and fishing licenses	9.3	0.12
Inspection licenses and fees	26.4	0.34
Insurance licenses	6.9	0.09
Insurance premium tax *	118.4	1.51
Intangibles tax *	207.6	2.64
Motor fuel taxes *	277.1	3.53
Motor vehicle and motor home licenses *	275.8	3.51
Motorboat licenses	4.3	0.05
Oil and gas production tax	28.1	0.35
Profession and occupational licensing fees	17.0	0.22
Racing tax *	107.0	1.36
Sales tax *	4,550.1	57.93
Securities fees	2.7	0.03
Solid minerals severance tax	57.7	0.73
Unemployment compensation tax *	232.0	2.95
Workers' compensation tax	21.0	0.27
Total	$7,854.8	100.00

Source: *Florida Tax Handbook, 1982*.

* Indicates major taxes collecting 1 percent or more of total tax revenues in a typical year.

Each of the 13 major taxes used by the State of Florida will be examined in turn. Two of these major taxes represent the application of the principle of benefits received and generally meet economic criteria for fairness and efficiency: the *motor fuels tax* (revenues used mostly for state and county roads) and the *unemployment compensation tax* (all revenues go to the unemployment compensation benefit trust fund). Politically it is often tempting to divert revenues from these taxes to the general revenue fund, but if that should happen these taxes would no longer conform to the principle of benefits received, and their fairness and efficiency would be in question.

Motor fuel tax.—Until 1983 Florida had an 8¢ per gallon gasoline tax which, because it was applied against physical units (gallons) instead of value, was inadequate for maintenance of state and local roads. The 1983 legislature retained a 4¢ tax per gallon of gasoline but added an ad valorem tax of 5.7 percent. Until 1985 this tax is to be computed on the basis of an average of $1.14 per gallon, but it will be recalculated then. In addition, a county may adopt an additional per gallon tax of up to 4¢ to meet costs of local roads and public transportation.

These changes will provide motor fuel tax revenues that are more adequate to meet growing needs for highway funds brought on by inflation and population increases. More use of small cars and other fuel-saving behavior will, however, hold motor fuel tax revenues at a less-than-adequate level.

The *estate tax* is unique among Florida's taxes in that it imposes no net burden upon Florida residents. By constitutional amendment (1924), Florida prohibited inheritance and income taxes. In 1926 the Congress enacted a federal estate tax that grants a credit for estate taxes paid to states; thereafter the Florida constitution was again amended to make the Florida estate tax equal to the amount of the federal credit but only so long as the credit remains a part of the federal tax. The estates of Florida resident decedents are thus taxed only in the amount allowable as a credit against federal estate taxes (minus amounts paid to other states). Since the amount of the federal tax is reduced by exactly the amount collected by the State of Florida, no net burden is imposed on the estates by the Florida tax.

Of the remaining ten major taxes, seven are principally on consumption and three are principally on ownership of capital or land.

Consumption taxes.—Three of the consumption taxes—the *alcoholic beverage tax*, the *cigarette tax*, and the *motor vehicle license tax* (tags)—are especially regressive because low-income families do not consume less of the taxed items than do high-income families. Ironically, these taxes, Florida's most regressive, enjoy broad popular support: all fifty states impose cigarette and vehicle license taxes, and every state in the nation either taxes alcoholic beverages or operates state-owned monopoly liquor stores at a profit.

The *alcoholic beverage tax* could be made somewhat less regressive if the value rather than the quantity of alcohol purchased were taxed. People with higher incomes do not tend to drink more alcoholic beverages than those with low incomes, but they do tend to buy more expensive brands. Thus a tax based on the market value or the selling price of the beverage (an ad valorem tax) would fall more heavily on higher income groups. Such a change would not only improve the fairness of the beverage tax; it could also increase its revenue, which, if adequate now, cannot continue to be . Since the tax is currently based upon quantity purchased rather than value, revenue collections will tend to keep pace with population growth but not with inflation. A change to base the alcoholic beverage tax on the price of the beverage purchased would link its revenue production to inflation as well as to population growth.

For the *cigarette tax,* on the other hand, adopting an ad valorem base would not improve the fairness of the tax or make it any less regressive. True, an ad valorem base would make the tax more responsive to inflation and therefore would tend to ensure that it will produce adequate revenue, but since there are no significant differences between the prices of different brands of cigarettes, an ad valorem tax base will not cause the more well off smokers to pay more taxes than less well off smokers.

Administratively, it would be very difficult to apply ad valorem rates to *motor vehicle licenses,* and such a move is inadvisable. While all three of these taxes introduce some distortion and inefficiency into consumption patterns, the size of the distortion is small enough to be generally acceptable. All three taxes involve a relatively small part of an individual's personal income, and they are imposed on activities that are relatively unresponsive to price changes. Furthermore, there is broad popular support, apparently satisfied in its motives by the present arrangements, for the idea that smoking and the consumption of alcohol are socially undesirable activities that should be discouraged through high tax rates.

The four other taxes that fall primarily upon consumption perform much better with respect to their fairness and the adequacy of revenue that they generate.

The *gross receipts utilities tax* is levied on all electric, gas, telephone, and telegraph companies, including municipal corporations, at the rate of 1.5 percent of their gross receipts (except that gross receipts from the sale of natural gas as fuel for use in generation of electricity are exempt). It seems likely (there has not been a definitive study of how the burden of this tax is distributed) that the overall impact of this tax is proportional or at worst mildly regressive with respect to income.

Because this tax is levied on the value of the services provided, it will keep up with inflation and with population growth and will therefore meet the criterion of adequacy of revenue.

A special tax in one form or another on utilities is common to most states, and the gross receipts tax is the most common form. Part of the revenue generated by this tax can be viewed as an offset to the costs of regulating utility companies. Rates in other states vary from 1 percent to 8 percent, making Florida's tax rate of 1.5 percent comparatively low. Since the rate of the tax on the gross receipts of utilities is low, no serious inefficiencies should arise from it.

The *insurance premium tax* is levied against collections of premiums; the rate of tax is 2 percent for companies with home offices outside Florida, 1 percent for those with home offices inside Florida. The burden of this tax falls, ultimately, on the purchasers of the insurance; it is probably proportional, perhaps mildly progressive, in its overall impact. In recent years this tax, again an ad valorem tax, has proved to be more than adequate in the revenues it generates. In the period 1973–78, the combined effects of inflation and population growth required about a 60 percent increase in revenues to maintain a constant per capita level of real expenditure. During this period, insurance premium tax revenues almost doubled.

Every state levies one or more types of tax on insurance premiums; the average rate falls in the 1 percent to 2 percent range. Florida's tax rate, close to the national average and relatively low, should cause this tax to produce no serious inefficiencies.

Florida's *racing tax* can be considered a tax on legal gambling. It was first introduced in 1931 with the legalization of parimutuel betting and extended to jai alai frontons when parimutuel betting was authorized there in 1935. Currently a complicated set of rate schedules applies slightly different tax rates to the various forms of racing and to jai alai. There have been no studies to determine whether this tax is progressive or regressive; most observers assume that it is an approximately proportional tax. Many Floridians support this tax because they believe that gambling is socially undesirable and may appropriately be discouraged by being taxed. Others favor the racing tax because it undoubtedly falls disproportionately on tourists, who make up a large part of the attendance at racing tracks and frontons. Any tax burden shifted to tourists and other nonresidents reduces the amount of taxes that Florida residents must pay. The racing tax undoubtedly discourages participation in track and fronton activities, but reducing participation in gambling is widely looked upon as a desirable effect of the tax. The racing tax is imposed on the monies wagered, thus on an ad valorem basis, and might be expected to yield adequate revenue continuously. But these revenues have not kept up with inflation and population growth in the period 1973–78. While a 60 percent increase has been necessary to offset inflation and population growth during this period, racing tax revenues have increased by only about half that, 30 percent. The shortfall in racing tax revenue, not yet systematically explained by economists, probably reflects changing characteristics of the resident population and of Florida's tourists.

Florida's *sales tax* is by far the most important source of revenue for the state government, accounting for 58 percent of total state tax revenues. Florida first adopted a sales tax, at a rate of 3 percent, in 1949; the rate was raised to 4 percent in 1968 and to 5 percent in 1982. The sales tax base has been broadened in almost every legislative session since the tax was first enacted. The items taxed include most tangible personal property, admissions charges, transient lodgings, commercial rentals, motor vehicles, motor and aviation fuels, and ships and commercial fishing equipment. (Farm equipment is taxed at a rate of 3 percent.) Florida's sales tax base differs from that of most states in that food and medical purchases are exempt.

(General sales taxes are a major revenue source in 45 states. Nationally, general sales taxes vary from 2 to 7 percent; 4 percent is the most common rate. In 32 states this tax is the largest single source of tax revenues.)

General sales taxes have the reputation of being socially regressive insofar as they burden the low-income groups least able to pay them. They may be regressive—by the technical definition given above—if they require a higher percentage of the income of low-income groups than of high-income groups. It was once widely believed that sales taxes were regressive because high-income groups tended to save larger proportions of their income than low-income groups; but more recent analysis does not support this view for two reasons. First, saving just defers expenditure to some future date, thus postponing sales taxes but not avoiding them. Second, empirical studies of long-term economic behavior do not confirm that high-income groups save larger proportions of their income than do low-income groups.

Most general sales taxes are still considered regressive, however, for yet another reason. Sales tax laws tend to exempt intangible services from taxation because they are difficult to tax. Tangible items sold, therefore, bear the brunt of the tax burden (simply because it is administratively easier to collect the taxes imposed on them). Low-income groups tend to spend a larger proportion of their income on tangible items (which are taxed) and a smaller proportion on intangible services (which tend to be tax exempt) than do high-income groups. By this comparison, most state sales taxes tend to be regressive. Exempting food and medicine from the general sales tax, however, as Florida's law does, tends to make the sales tax less regressive inasmuch as low-income groups spend a much higher proportion of their income on these items than do high-income groups.

Economists are uncertain whether Florida's sales tax is mildly progressive, proportional, or mildly regressive. The results of several studies of the tax are inconclusive. It is clear, nevertheless, that the sales tax could be made more progressive by extending the list of items taxed to include more sales of services such as auto repairs, barber and beautician services, and the professional services of lawyers and accountants (but not of health care providers).

Progressive taxes are preferred to other types because they lessen the tax burden falling on low-income groups. Florida's sales tax has been systematically designed to accomplish the same thing by passing on a significant portion of the tax burden to tourists. While food purchased for home consumption is tax exempt, restaurant meals are taxed; household utilities and residential rentals are tax exempt, but motel room charges are taxed. Thus as much as 20 percent of Florida's sales tax is paid by nonresidents. Florida's use of the sales tax as the state's major source of revenue is made more attractive because it passes on such a significant portion of the total tax burden to nonresidents. If Florida substituted the income tax for the sales tax as its major source of revenue, this shifting of 20 percent of the tax burden to nonresidents would not be possible.

Since the sales tax is levied against the price of things sold (and is therefore an ad valorem tax), it might be expected to generate adequate revenues indefinitely. It did so until the 1970s. During that decade, however, sales tax revenues failed to grow as fast as the combined effects of inflation and population growth, in part because personal income in Florida was more adversely affected by the 1973–75 recession than it was in the nation as a whole. This inadequacy of sales tax revenue in the late 1970s was an especially serious problem because the sales tax was expected to supply over 40 percent of the state's total tax revenue and over 60 percent of the general revenue fund.

Several years of strong economic recovery in the late 1970s overcame some of the lag in revenues generated by the sales tax; but a significant gap remained between the total growth of sales tax receipts and the combined effect of inflation and population growth in the period 1973–78. To adjust fully for the shortfall, Florida would have had to increase its sales tax rate to about 4.3 percent from the 4 percent rate current in 1979. In 1982 the tax was raised from 4 to 5 percent, and a portion (10 percent) of its revenues was earmarked for distribution to eligible local governments.

The falloff in sales tax revenues can probably be explained by shifts in consumption patterns toward services and away from tangible goods. That trend is likely to continue. With services tending to be exempt from the sales tax, sales tax revenues could continue to be inadequate to maintain per capita real expenditures for social services. Broadening the sales tax base to include more intangible services would improve the adequacy of sales tax revenues and at the same time make the sales tax more progressive.

The sales tax does promote some economic inefficiencies by encouraging consumers to substitute untaxed goods and services for taxed ones. Broadening the sales tax base to include more sales of services would tend to reduce this effect.

Taxes on ownership of capital or land.—The remaining three major taxes all fall mostly upon the owners of capital and land and are thus progressive taxes.

The *corporation income tax* was enacted in 1971 following a referendum approving amendment of the Florida Constitution to permit imposition of such a tax. (Florida's constitution still prohibits any personal income tax.) The corporation income tax is imposed at a rate of 5 percent on corporation net income in excess of $5,900. Income of corporations that operate also in other states or nations is taxed according to a formula that apportions part of their total income to their Florida operation. Florida uses a worldwide unitary approach in determining apportionable income, using weighted factors of sales, property, and payroll that are located in Florida. All but four states had corporation income taxes in 1979; most impose a flat rate ranging from 2.35 percent to 12 percent (after exempting some amount of income).

Who really pays the corporation income tax is not completely understood by economists. The prevailing view is that the burden of this tax is in part shifted forward to consumers and in part backward to all owners of financial assets. The portion of the tax burden that is shifted backward to capital falls not only on the owners of the corporate stock but passes through the entire financial system to all investors in every type of financial asset. Thus everyone with a bank savings account bears some part of the burden of the nation's various corporation income taxes. Most analysts believe that the portion of the corporation income tax that is shifted forward to consumers is either proportional or mildly regressive; they also believe that the portion shifted backward to the owners of financial assets is a progressive tax. The overall impact of the tax, considering both forward and backward shifting, is generally felt to be progressive, though perhaps only mildly so. A feature of the corporation income tax that makes it attractive to states is that a considerable portion of the burden may be shifted to nonresident consumers and nonresident owners of financial assets.

Over the long term, Florida's corporation income tax will continue to generate adequate revenue even though in the short term it is quite sensitive to the business cycle. Corporation income tax revenues drop sharply during recessions and rise rapidly during economic recoveries. Insofar as the corporation income tax discourages corporate activity in the state, the tax imposes an additional burden upon the state's economy. Decisions to locate corporate operations in Florida rather than in some other state or to expand operations already in Florida are undoubtedly affected by the existence of this tax, which may lead to some loss of jobs and of economic development.

The *documentary tax stamp* is levied on all recorded deeds and other documents relating to realty at a rate of 30 cents per $100 and upon recorded documents relating to corporate shares, bonds, promissory loans, retail charge accounts, and so forth, at a rate of 15 cents per $100. Documentary stamps of some kind are levied by thirty-six states, although the majority of these apply only to real estate transfers. Over half of Florida's documentary stamp revenues are collected from the recording of deeds. The burden of this portion of the tax falls upon the owners of property and is undoubtedly progressive. The burden of that portion of the stamp tax derived from promissory notes and retail credit falls mainly upon the borrower and may be somewhat regressive. The overall impact of the tax in these terms is not clear. The documentary stamp tax has little to recommend it except tradition; it is tolerable because of its relatively low rates.

The *intangible* tax is levied on the ownership of intangible wealth such as stocks, bonds, notes, and the like, at a rate of 0.1 mill annually, with an exemption of $20,000 of intangible wealth to each taxpayer and his or her spouse. Ownership of mortgages is taxed differently than other intangible wealth, at 2 mills of recorded value at the time of recording with no recurring tax obligation. Only nine states have some form of intangible tax. Since the tax is levied upon ownership of intangible wealth (with a $20,000 exemption), it is probably quite progressive in its impact. The documentary stamp tax and intangibles tax are both sensitive to the business cycle in the short term.

Local Government Taxes

Local governments in Florida rely primarily upon two sources for tax revenues: the ad valorem property tax and the municipal utilities tax. The property tax is by far the more important. County and municipal governments collected over $3.4 billion in property taxes in 1981. If we put state and local taxes together, the property tax is the largest single revenue source in the state.

Millage rates vary among local governments but are subject to both constitutional and statutory limits. All local general-purpose governments are subject to a constitutional limit of 10 mills for operating purposes. In addition, school districts are currently subject to an 8-mill statutory limit to be eligible to participate in the state public school funding program. Special tax districts (such as regional water management districts) are limited by the law creating each district. Voters, by referendum, may authorize additional mills to be levied above these limits for debt service. Counties providing municipal services may also levy additional mills above the limit to finance these services.

In 1981 total taxable value of property statewide was over $200 billion, and total property taxes collected were over $3.4 billion, indicating a statewide average of 17 mills for all purposes. Actual millage rates, however, vary considerably from this average, in part because of large differences in taxable values within each county. Part of the reason for differences in taxable values is that counties and municipalities vary in both size and level of economic development. But another reason is that counties are affected differently by constitutional and statutory provisions for exemption of some property value from the taxable value rolls. The most significant of these exemptions are (1) the homestead exemption of $25,000 of assessed value for owner-occupied homes, (2) reduction of agricultural land assessment from fair market value, and (3) exemption of government property. Altogether these three provisions reduced total taxable values in Florida in 1981 by over $76 billion, or 38 percent of total "just value" for property in the state. The agricultural land and government exemptions are not evenly distributed among counties, and some counties are particularly hard hit by these reductions in taxable value.

Just how the burden of the property tax is distributed is an unsettled question: it is agreed that the burden of taxes on land and mineral value is completely borne by the owners of the land or mineral rights and is not shifted to others, but taxes on the value of buildings and other improvements on land are thought to be shifted. The results of this shifting are debated by economists: many feel that property taxes on buildings and improvements are in part shifted forward to consumers and in part backward to all owners of capital and financial assets. In this view, the burden of the property tax closely resembles that of the corporation income tax. But other economists feel that almost all of the property tax on buildings and improvements is shifted backward to all owners of capital and financial assets. If this view is correct, the property tax is clearly progressive.

Whether the property tax is fair raises two main problems. First, taxable property values are not distributed in proportion to the population of the state's counties. This fact requires counties with lesser land values to tax at higher millage rates—while adjacent counties offering the same levels of governmental service may have significantly lower rates. Differences in millage rates among counties could be reduced somewhat if state government assumed a larger role in financing public schools and other state-mandated programs. Second, the fairness of the property tax is questioned by some homeowners, particularly the elderly, whose limited current cash incomes make the property tax on their homes especially burdensome. A $5,000 homestead exemption was introduced in the 1930s (increased in 1980 to $25,000) to relieve this problem. It has been criticized for discrimination against renters: owners of rental property, who have no homestead exemption on the property because they do not occupy it themselves, shift the burden of the tax on the first $25,000 valuation onto the renters.

Although it is sensitive to swings in the business cycle, the property tax performs well in providing continuously adequate revenue. It does not perform well in terms of economic efficiency. A property tax of 20 mills, the common top rate in 1980, is generally equivalent to a 50 percent sales tax on the rental value of the property (assuming a normal return to investment). Such a high tax rate will discourage construction and development. Even small differences in the millage rates of different counties can strongly influence a business firm's decision on where to locate a new plant or office building.

Florida's municipalities may levy a *municipal utilities tax* of up to 10 percent on purchases within the municipality of electricity, gas, water, and telephone, telegraph, and cable television services. About half of Florida's municipalities levy the tax at the full 10 percent rate. In 1981–82, this tax brought $287 million to Florida municipalities. Its burden falls almost entirely on consumers; it is somewhat regressive; it is likely to yield revenues that correspond reasonably well with trends in inflation and population growth. When the tax rate approaches the 10 percent maximum, it will encourage inefficiencies in economic activity that in turn will magnify the tax burden.

Changes in Florida's Tax System

Overall, Florida's tax system compares favorably with the tax systems of other states. Florida has succeeded better than most in minimizing the total tax burden on its lower-income citizens, at the same time avoiding unnecessary tax barriers to new industry and economic development. The major problem of taxation that Florida faces is that tax revenues are not growing as fast as inflation and population.

Unless state programs were to be cut back, which few leaders advocated, Florida had to find changes in current tax rules or new tax sources to create the additional revenue needed in the 1980s. In the process, it is desirable that the new taxes and amended rules should take into account the continuing adequacy of revenues generated by specific taxes. The changes recommended in this chapter to improve the revenue adequacy of current tax rules would also, for the most part, improve the fairness of those taxes and their impact on economic efficiency. Both alcoholic beverages and motor fuels could be taxed according to their selling price, and in 1983 the motor fuels tax was partially switched to an ad valorem basis. The sales tax base could be broadened to include more consumer services. But unfortunately none of these changes would yield the increase in revenue that Florida needed to meet increased costs due to inflation and population growth—to say nothing of the added costs of new programs. The inadequacy of revenue from the current tax system was especially severe as the state government undertook to pay the larger share of the costs of local governmental services in order to permit a reduction in the property tax.

The most obvious way to raise more tax revenues for the state is to raise the sales tax rate, and it was done in 1982, from 4 to 5 percent. In 1983, alcoholic beverage taxes were increased significantly, and the corporation income tax was amended to include a worldwide unitary system for apportioning income.

Two other major changes might be considered. First, Florida might replace the current sales tax structure entirely with a *retail gross revenues tax*. Such a tax would be imposed upon all retail (consumer) sales, on tangible goods and intangible services without distinction. If basic necessities such as food and medicine were still exempt from this tax, it would be superior to the current sales tax in its fairness, revenue adequacy, and economic efficiency. A retail gross revenue tax would probably be shifted to nonresidents in about the same proportion as the sales tax now is. Second, Florida might introduce a *personal income tax*. Such a tax could be made mildly progressive and could contribute significantly to revenue adequacy. But there are two major drawbacks to implementing a personal income tax: little or none of its burden could be shifted to non-Florida residents, and a vote of the people to amend the state constitution would be required, which might be impossible to achieve.

Florida's Tax System

A constitutional amendment proposed for the November 1984 general election ballot will, if passed, impose severe revenue limits on all levels of government in Florida. In 1983, the amendment was being attacked in court because it may relate to more than one subject. The proposed amendment would restict all levels of government to spending at 1980–81 levels, plus no more than a 5 percent annual increase in budget levels except that, in the case of the real property tax, new construction would be assessed. Any further increase in the budget would require specific prior voter referendum approval on the item or items increased. No allowance was made for the fact that in the seventies and early eighties some cities and counties increased in population by more than 100 percent, placing great local burdens on roads, sewerage, and schools, and on state-supported law enforcement, prisons, and state roads and bridges.

In a state where population increases are the fourth highest in the nation (3 percent annually) and high inflation is likely throughout the eighties, the impact on the quality of government services will be disastrous if the amendment passes. The amendment would force official state revenues to be reduced by 22.6 percent in 1985, the first year of implementation. This reduction amounts to $2.4 billion and is seven times as large as the severe revenue shortfall of 1982–83 which resulted from prolonged recession and brought significant reductions in quality of government services. This deterioration in services would continue each year thereafter. By 1990, the level of government services per capita provided by state, county, and municipal governments would be only 50 percent of current levels.

It is unlikely, of course, that Florida's citizens would allow things to go that far, and the amendment, if passed, would probably be repealed or greatly amended before 1990. Even so, this amendment could bring Florida a decade of traumatic and unstable politics and government.

Selected References

Elebash, Clarence C. "Analysis of Florida General Revenues, Fiscal Year 1972–73 to Present." *Business and Economic Dimensions* (Spring 1978).

Florida Legislature. *Analysis of Selected Florida Tax Sources, 1977–78*. Tallahassee, 1977.

Florida Senate, Committee on Finance, Taxation, and Claims. *Florida Tax Handbook, 1983*. Tallahassee, 1983.

Qualls, LeRoy L. "Florida's Tax System: An Analysis and Evaluation." *Business and Economic Dimensions* (Spring 1978).

State of Florida, Office of the Comptroller. *Annual Report of the Comptroller.* Tallahassee, 1983.

Thompson, Ralph B., ed. *Florida Statistical Abstract 1978*. Gainesville: University Presses of Florida 1978.

Florida's Extractive Industries: Agriculture and Forestry

18A

by H. B. Clark

UNIVERSITY OF FLORIDA

Food production—agriculture—is one of Florida's most important industries. It generates new wealth and is relatively free from business-cycle influences. It is highly competitive with food production elsewhere in the United States and abroad. The total annual production in Florida for all industries in 1978 was $69 billion; 2.7 percent of this amount, $1.8 billion, was farm income; another $7 billion was value added by the processing and marketing of farm and forest products. (These figures exclude forest and fisheries income and are compatible with University of Florida Bureau of Business and Economic Research figures which have a different basis from USDA figures found in tables 18.2 and 18.3.)

The agriculture industry presents a unique combination of economic characteristics. Farming is subject to great uncertainties of yields and prices and to rigidities of production processes. Most farming requires larger and larger investments of capital, which are financed mostly by loans. Farmers, therefore, are operating in a higher-risk environment than ever before. As costs of inputs (fertilizers and insecticides, fuels, and labor, for example) increase, the prices received by farmers tend not to increase enough to yield a positive long-run net return. This is called the "cost-price squeeze."

Younger farmers are especially sensitive to this squeeze. Many able young farmers have failed in recent years, in part because of forces beyond their control, and others are alarmed. These were the reasons behind the dramatic American Agricultural Movement of 1978. The tractor-cades of 1978 and 1979 were organized by younger farmers who insisted that some of the risks of farming be shared by society at large.

If the risks of farming are not shared more equitably, food production will gradually decrease. As supply decreases, food prices will increase, and the remaining farmers will be able to compete for capital with other sectors of the economy. If the number of farmers were to be reduced in this way, it is seriously questionable that the private sector would provide adequate food reserves for unusual circumstances. And consumers would not willingly accept the wide variation in food prices—as well as the high level of prices—that would result from a totally free market system.

In recent years, agricultural exports have been extremely important in U.S. foreign exchange. The nonagricultural sector has had a negative balance of payments every year since 1970, but the agricultural sector has shown a positive balance: In 1977 and 1978 the former was down $40 billion and $43 billion, respectively; the latter sector was up $10 billion and $13 billion (USDA, 1978).

Our food production system—in which a very small number of primary producers supply an amazing variety of foods in unparalleled abundance to an industrialized urban population of consumers—is surely an important asset of our society. It is also an economically fragile one. Its characteristics must be understood if sound public policies are to be implemented to ensure adequate food supplies not only for ourselves but for much of the rest of the world as well.

Characteristics of Agriculture

Before we examine the current condition of agriculture in Florida, its prospects, and the role of government in agricultural industries, it will be helpful to consider some aspects of farming and food marketing.

(1) Capital turnover in agriculture is relatively slow compared to the turnover in most other industries. A grocery store will turn over its capital investment 11 times per year, whereas an Iowa farm turns its capital over only once every 13 years and a citrus grower every 15 years. This slow turnover places farmers in a precarious financial position, for it requires that they have access to long-term credit. (In the public utilities industry, capital turnover is also slow; but because the services of public utility companies are critically necessary, they have come under public control and enjoy a guaranteed profit.)

(2) Because farmers depend upon biological processes, they cannot quickly adjust supply to demand. For some products (tree crops, for example) the production process takes ten years or more.

(3) Many resources used in agriculture—land, labor, building, equipment, and livestock—have few alternative uses. Thus farming is inflexible with respect to resource use; farmers cannot easily shift to other businesses in response to changing demands. They do well in good times but poorly in bad times.

(4) As technology changes ever more rapidly, farmers are under pressure to stay abreast of technological advances. To do so usually demands the investment of more capital in larger-scale production to enlarge output. Nearly all technological innovations tend to increase output and to demand more capital, usually substituting capital for labor. Techonological innovations, therefore, increase the farmer's need for credit.

(5) Variations in both quality and quantity of yield due to weather are always present. The seasonal nature of agriculture production causes highs and lows in resource use. In some parts of the country, school schedules are adjusted to make student labor available in seasons of high demand. The uncertainty of yield is a fact of the farmer's life, and the longer the production process the greater the uncertainty. A citrus grove will not begin to yield a commercial crop before about seven years; mature beef cattle take five years; corn takes four months, radishes one month.

(6) Supply and demand will change much less over any given interval than will prices. (Economists say that the elasticity of supply and the elasticity of demand are low with respect to price.) Therefore, the prices of farm products fluctuate greatly. These wide price changes are beyond the farmer's control unless special actions are taken to control supply through marketing orders or to reduce the price variations through monopolistic practices or government controls.

(7) The system of holding or owning land in the United States in the past has usually required generation-to-generation financing. It has been a system of inheritance in which the assets of the deceased are divided among his or her heirs. Successful farming operations have thus been divided in each generation. But the pressures of today's world of capital-intensive farming are focused in just the opposite direction and dictate keeping the large-scale farm operation intact and expanding its output. For society at large, as well as for the individual farm operator, it has become important to pass to the next generation an ongoing farming operation unreduced in size. One means of ensuring the integrity of large farming operations over generations has been to incorporate them. For the benefit of the consumer it is crucial that we find ways to maintain and enlarge the size of farms across generations.

The attitudes of farmers, their expectations of government, and their demands of the larger society can only be understood in the context of this unique combination of characteristics of the agriculture industry.

Historical Background

European agriculture in the United States began in Florida. The place was the presidio of St. Augustine; the time was the late sixteenth century. Pedro Mendez Canzo, eighth governor of the presidio, wanted his civilians and soldiers to take up farming. The allowance of cash and food, the *situado*, expected from Mexico was frequently late, so he tried to make the presidio self-sufficient. To encourage food production Mendez allocated land to the few Spaniards living there, set up the first farmers' market in North America, and even devised a system of weights and measures, important for marketing.

While Americans have learned much about farming since then, and while we are able to produce many food items in sufficient quantities to feed our citizens and much of the rest of the world, nationally we have not reached Mendez's goal of self-sufficiency desirable in today's world, in which exchange of goods and services is accomplished through a complex marketing system. For agriculture, that system involves scores of people, from a long time before a crop is planted till long after it is harvested and becomes available to the consumer in a store or market.

Our complex food delivery system revolves around each of the many individuals participating in it. Each is earning a living, adding on the cost of his or her services to enjoy a sufficient personal income. The specialization and interdependence of our food delivery system make for efficiency and a higher standard of living, but they require that the system be finely tuned. Only if each person in the system does what is expected of him or her will the system provide us with food; the alternative, not far off if the system should collapse, is starvation.

This division of labor by specialization is called the "principle of comparative advantage." It is present in any cultural setting, but it manifests itself more strongly as technologies of production and communications improve. Jesse Fish, who lived in St. Augustine from 1736 to 1790, shipped a few oranges by water to cities along the Atlantic shore; but the citrus industry did not amount to much for decades because the market was restricted to an area within a few miles of the producing area, except in instances of crude transportation by boat. Fruit and vegetable production predated the coming of railroads; but production was always in close proximity to transportation by water, which was basically too slow for perishable products. Farming was organized largely for subsistence; surpluses went to people nearby or were fed to livestock. It is reported that in 1876, J. "Pig" Brown of New River (Bradford County) raised peppers and other crops just for his hogs. And in 1881, Hamilton Disston bailed the State of Florida out of economic crisis by purchasing 4 million acres in central Florida from the state for 25 cents per acre, thus opening up much of Florida's peninsula for development. The farming efforts of Disston failed because he gambled on transportation by water rather than by railroad to reach the markets.

Commercial farming in Florida never amounted to much until the railroads opened up markets for the pioneer farmers. But the building of the railroads stimulated crop and livestock production. The first cross-state railroad (the Florida Railroad, 1860) linked Fernandina to Cedar Key. A branch line south from Waldo was extended to Ocala in 1881; it skirted Orange and Lochloosa

Mechanized cultivation of row crops on Florida's muck soil. Photo courtesy IFAS.

lakes. The fertile hammock land in south Alachua and north Marion counties was thus opened for rapid expansion of crops, especially vegetables.

Another railroad called the Jacksonville, Gainesville, and Gulf (later called the Tampa-to-Jacksonville) was built in 1887 and opened up more land for farming. A major landmark was the completion of the Florida East Coast Railroad to Dade County. When the first passengers began arriving by railroad in Fort Lauderdale in 1896, farmers moved into the neighborhood; shortly thereafter winter vegetables were going by rail to northern markets. The pattern of farm production areas was thus determined by transportation developments. In 1880 there were estimated to be 10,000 acres in vegetables, potatoes, strawberries, and melons; by 1910 the acreage had increased to 54,000 and by 1970 to 408,650. There was a large increase in vegetable production during World War I, when demand for food for the war effort increased dramatically and prices were high.

Cotton and tobacco were important crops in Florida, especially in the northern part of the state. These crops were tied to the economies of Alabama and Georgia. As cotton production has waned in the southeastern U.S., it has disappeared even faster in Florida. Being nonperishable, cotton and tobacco could be compressed into bales with high intrinsic value. St. Marks and Cedar Key were important ports for shipment of cotton before 1875. Transportation of cotton and tobacco was a problem, of course, but much less so than for perishable fruits, vegetables, and even grain crops. Similarly, livestock were driven on foot to market. But since markets for Florida's livestock were small and far away, cattle drives in Florida were insignificant in size compared to those of the American West, though Florida's predated the western drives by about a century. Today, virtually no cotton is grown in Florida. Tobacco production is substantial in a few northern counties around Alachua, Live Oak, and Lake City.

The livestock industry in Florida has a long and colorful history, beginning on the Spanish *ranchos* in the late 1600s. The Indians raised cattle, as did the early settlers. Cattle roamed the state freely until a fence law was passed in 1950. Open ranges led to rustling and much violent behavior. The Brahman bull was brought into Florida in the 1850s, initiating a long and concerted effort to improve the quality of livestock. Today the screw worm and the Texas tick have been eradicated, cattle are fenced, and the livestock industry is modern; Florida ranks tenth in the nation in numbers of beef cattle.

Similarly, a rich and colorful folklore has grown up around the timber and forest products industry in Florida. The virgin timber was mostly cut out between 1900 and 1930. Since that time, "domestication" of tree farming has taken place, and the pulp and paper industry has been added to lumber, pole, and furniture manufacturing. Today Florida ranks third in pulpwood production. About half of the state's 35 million acres is in commerical forest, but parts of these forest acres are also used as pasture for livestock.

In sum, agricultural production in Florida has been closely related to access to markets. As transportation and refrigeration improved, the market area for Florida products increased; today it is worldwide. As the population of Florida increased, the market outlets within the state grew; they now support mostly Florida's dairy and poultry industries. Just what the dynamics of the law of comparative advantage hold for the future is hard to say. Mexico and Brazil are competing strongly today in vegetable and citrus production, respectively. In January 1979 the United States was importing Mexican tomatoes grown under fewer restrictions than are imposed on Florida growers. It was believed that President Carter allowed these imports as a trade-off for assurances of Mexican natural gas sales to warm U.S. homes and run U.S. factories. When Cuba returns to the American market scene, there will be added competition. Farmers and food processors in Florida will be affected by economic pressures to a greater degree than ever before, and those economic pressures will be colored by domestic and world politics.

Governmental Agencies: State

Department of Agriculture and Consumer Service.—Florida's Department of Agriculture and Consumer Services is headed by the state commissioner of agriculture who is elected to a four-year term by the voters. The commissioner is also a member of the cabinet of the State of Florida.

The department began with the adoption of the constitution of 1885. Before then the commissioner of immigration had been empowered to attract settlers to Florida; in 1871 the constitution was amended, consolidating the offices of surveyor general and commissioner of immigration under a new commissioner of lands and immigration. The new state constitution became effective 1 January 1887, and it renamed the commissioner of lands and immigration the commissioner of agriculture and gave him supervision of state prisons in addition to his other duties.

Over the years the legislature added many responsibilities for inspection and regulation to the Florida Department of Agriculture. The supervision of state prisons was removed from the office in 1957 and given to a new Division of Corrections. That reorganization became effective in January 1961.

In 1967 the Florida legislature created the Office of Consumer Services and placed it under the commissioner of agriculture. In 1969 a new state constitution was adopted, and that office became the Division of Consumer Services. The department was renamed the Florida Department of Agriculture and Consumer Services, and the Florida Forestry Service became a division in it.

The Department of Agriculture is charged with the responsibility of enforcing regulatory laws designed to protect the safety and welfare of consumers and producers. To carry out this responsibility the department is organized into ten divisions with specific powers and duties of regulation. An eleventh, the Division of Administration, has the function of overall coordination of programs within the department (see fig. 18.1). A growing activity of the department is consumer protection: for example, for years weights and measures in stores and gas stations have been checked for accuracy. More recently, consumers have had recourse to the department when they feel that they have been mistreated.

The department owns and operates fifteen farmers' markets scattered over the state from Bonifay to south Dade County. Most of these sheds have refrigerated rooms. Space in the sheds is rented to farm groups or brokers either for a fixed rent or on a volume basis. Equipment in the sheds is furnished by the renter. The total cost of operating the system of farmers' markets is paid from the rental income they generate. In addition the department has nine agricultural education pavilions used by the youth of the state.

Institute of Food and Agricultural Sciences (IFAS).—The land grant college system, later established in Florida as the Institute of Food and Agricultural Sciences, dates from 1862 when the Morrill Act was passed by Congress. Under the act a grant of land was made to each state. The income received from the sale of this land was to be used as seed money for the building of an agricultural and mechanical college in the state. In Florida, 30,000 acres were given for each of Florida's two senators and one congressman, a total of 90,000 acres. This land (or, rather, the script for it) was sold to an Ohio bank. The money from this sale was invested, and the interest earned was used to support a land grant college in the amount of about $72,000 a year in the early years.

Florida's land grant college was established in Lake City in 1884; in 1905, under the Buckman Act (1903), the institution was moved from Lake City to Gainesville and together with five other schools was merged into the University of Florida. The primary purpose of the college was to provide residential instruction to college-age youth.

The second institution in the land grant college system was the experiment stations established under the Hatch Act of 1887. The land grant colleges were running out of new ideas and new findings in the agricultural sciences. (The author's instructor in farm management, for example, had earned a master of science degree in agriculture around 1895 by writing about the economies of milk buckets and milking stools and how to milk a cow by hand.) Academic and farm leaders brought pressure to create a research component in order to make study at the agricultural colleges more instructive.

The experiment stations established under the Hatch Act began to make significant discoveries. A method was needed to communicate these discoveries to farmers, both former students and those who had never gone to college. Hence, in 1914, with the passage of the Smith-Sever Act, the third agency of the educational system was established, the agricultural extension service. With that service came the county agents and county home agents to carry to the farmers the findings of the research conducted by the experiment stations.

Thus, at the beginning of World War I, the land grant college system was functioning and the nation was in fair shape for increasing its agricultural production. In Florida the state university system is the center around which most of the experimental and educational extension work is done and controlled. Having all these services tied to the university system has tended to reduce political pressure and probably has increased the quality of the work. (In less de-

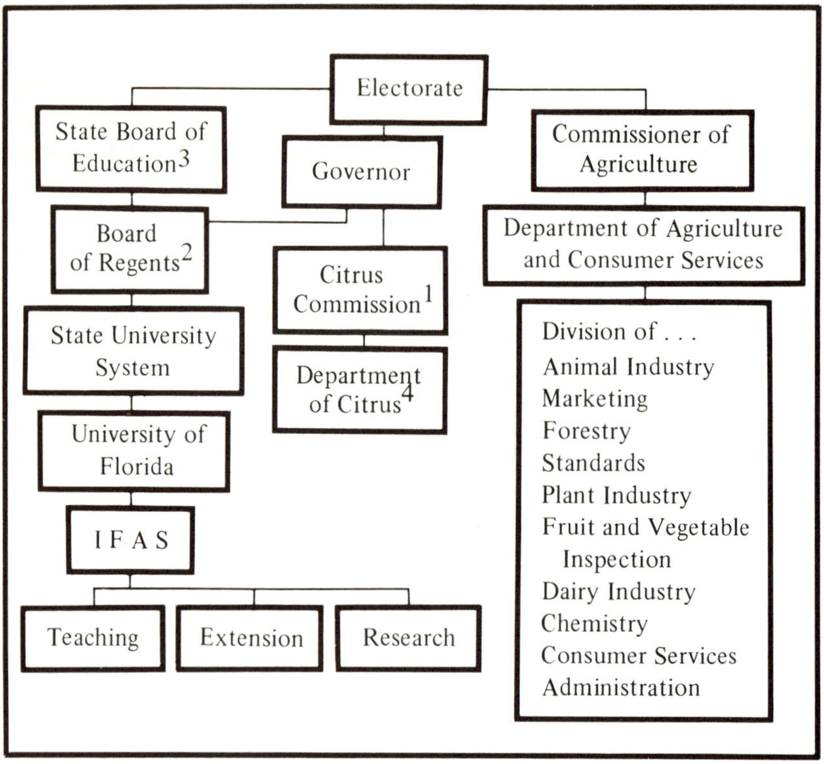

Fig. 18.1. Agricultural Services, Education, and Regulation in Florida.

1. Members of the Citrus Commission are appointed by the governor with the approval of the senate.

2. Members of the Board of Regents are appointed by the governor with the approval of the senate. The regents report to the State Board of Education.

3. When the governor and the cabinet sit as the State Board of Education, they are the final authority for education at all levels in the state.

4. The Department of Citrus is made up of employees who carry out policies set by the Citrus Commission.

veloped countries agricultural research and educational extension are frequently separated from the agricultural colleges, and in those cases politics and bureaucratic jealousies have hurt the system.)

The Institute of Food and Agricultural Sciences (IFAS) is a part of the University of Florida, which is part of the state's system of higher education, administered by the governor and the Board of Education and by the Board of Regents appointed by the governor. The institute employs about a thousand academic and professional staff members working in Gainesville, at the branch stations, and in every county. At the university there are twenty-two departments, each responsible for teaching, research, and extension activities on campus and at the branch research centers. The county extension staff, in cooperation with the county governments, serves local needs as determined by local advisory committees. County extension staff is supported by specialists from the Gainesville campus or the research centers. There are twenty-two research centers scattered throughout the state from near Pensacola in the west to the Everglades in the south. These stations adapt plant and animal research to the local soils and climate.

One of the primary aims of IFAS today is to ensure that both urban and rural people are served. In addition to traditional research on plant and animal production, much emphasis is being given to land and water use, rural development, food science and nutrition, protection of the environment, marine fisheries, and international activities concerned with world food problems.

The School of Forest Resources and Conservation is part of IFAS. Its activities include teaching, research, and educational extension work in all aspects of tree farming, wood processing, wildlife ecology, range management, and resource conservation.

Another institutional arrangement, the vocational agriculture program, was established by the Smith-Hughes Act of 1916. This act provided for teaching agriculture and home economics in the public schools. Federal funds supplement state funds to give an extra dimension of teaching and demonstration to the public school programs. The Vo-Ag program is administered by the state Department of Education.

In addition to the adult education work of the county extension staff, there is a special youth program called 4-H (head, heart, hands, and health), which uses special projects for training young people in the business of farming, homemaking, recreation, and citizenship.

Florida Citrus Commission.—Created by an act of the legislature in 1935, the Florida Citrus Commission was redesigned under the new state constitution in 1968 as the Florida Department of Citrus. Those portions of the Florida Statutes relating to citrus are known as the Florida Citrus Code.

The Florida Department of Citrus is a state-operated organization charged with regulating the Florida citrus industry and with assisting it in the profitable marketing of citrus fruits and products. To this end the Department of Citrus plans and conducts campaigns and special programs for commodity advertising, publicity, and sales promotion designed to increase the demand for and the consumption of Florida citrus. It also pays the salaries of those conducting research on citrus culture, product processing, and marketing.

The governing body of the Department of Citrus is a commission composed of twelve citrus industry representatives appointed by the governor of Florida for three-year terms (four members are appointed each year). Seven members must be growers, each representing one of the industry's grower districts; three must be engaged in processing and two in the shipping of fruit.

Governmental Agencies: Federal

Finally, a number of federal agencies directly affect agriculture in Florida. They administer marketing orders, market news and information, and grading and inspection services. The Agricultural Stabilization and Conservation Service has responsibility for price support programs and for payments for conservation practices. The U.S. Forest Service, in conjunction with the state Division of Forestry, oversees conservation of forests in the state and administers the national forests in Florida. A third, the Soil Conservation Service, in cooperation with state conservation agencies has completed soil maps of the entire state; it also makes recommendations regarding land use. A fourth, which will be discussed under the topic of agricultural finance, is the Farmers Home Administration.

Citrus

Florida's citrus industry, highly important to the state's economy, is one of the most interesting agricultural industries anywhere. Most fruit is grown, processed, and sold under participation, or cooperation, agreements; that is, most fruit goes into some sort of nonprice plan. The processor receives, processes, and sells the fruit, deducts the costs of processing, selling, and a reasonable profit, and returns the residual to the growers. This mode of operation is common to Minute Maid and Pasco Packing Co. and to all cooperatives, such as Golden Gem, Plymouth Citrus Growers, and Florida Citrus World. Many of Florida's citrus groves are cared for under a service arrangement.

Grove-care companies may be either cooperatives or private organizations operating for profit. The trees are sprayed, pruned, and fertilized; the fruit is picked, hauled, and processed; and in many cases the owner of the grove never sees the fruit and may not even know the difference between a grapefruit and an orange. Indeed, owning a citrus grove in Florida can be about as carefree as owning stocks and bonds. In many cases even state and local tax payments are made by the cooperative grove-care agency.

Grove owners can, of course, do all their own work and sell their fruit as they wish. But it is usually more economical to have the work done by well-equipped grove-care organizations, and a participation agreement reduces risks by ensuring a market for fruit (in years of large crops, marketing facilities can sometimes handle no more fruit than that supplied by participating growers).

The number of citrus industry associations in Florida suggests the significance of group action in our economic and political system. To secure favorable legislation or administrative rulings at federal, state, and local levels of government, group action is increasingly important. Farmers, especially citrus growers, have continually had to resort to group action to improve their bargaining position in the marketplace. For the individual producer of perishable fruits and vegetables, the timely availability of transportation facilities (trucks and railroad cars) is a recurring problem because of the extreme concentrations of seasonal production. Group efforts by growers help to alleviate this problem.

The fourteen citrus industry organizations in Florida are listed in table 18.1. These associations are involved in economic, political, and educational activities for the benefit of members—except for the Growers Administrative Committee and Shippers Advisory Committee and the Indian River Grapefruit Committee, which were formed to implement federal marketing orders (FMOs). The FMO, which legalizes monopolistic control of the supply of citrus shipped out of state, permits producers of perishable or nonstorable commodities to cooperate to control supply, thereby stabilizing prices.

TABLE 18.1. Florida's 14 Citrus Organizations

Organization	Established	Location
Seald Sweet Growers, Inc.	1909	Tampa
Growers and Shippers League of Florida	1923	Orlando
Florida Canners Association	1931	Winter Haven
Indian River Citrus League	1931	Orlando
Florida Citrus Production Managers Association	1937	Waverly
United Growers and Shippers Association	1937	Orlando
Growers Administrative Committee and Shippers Advisory Committee	1937	Lakeland
Florida Grapefruit Shippers Association	1946	Orlando
Florida Citrus Mutual	1948	Lakeland
Florida Tangerine Cooperative	1951	Lakeland
Florida Citrus Packers Association	1960	Lakeland
Indian River Grapefruit Committee	1962	Lakeland
Citrus Central	1965	Apopka
Indian River Shippers Association	1974	Vero Beach

All of Florida's citrus industry associations provide important services, but only a few can be discussed here. Seald Sweet Growers, Inc., was founded in 1909 as the Florida Citrus Exchange. It was a supercooperative sales association selling fresh fruit for about forty fresh-fruit packinghouses scattered throughout the citrus belt. Through the years the Seald Sweet brand has been firmly established and now is also used for processed citrus products.

Florida Citrus Mutual is a cooperative of grove owners with affiliated members who are citrus dealers and handlers. Its primary aim is to protect citrus growers through political and educational means. It records statistical information and advises growers about citrus fruit prices at any given time.

Florida Canners Association is a trade association that oversees the interests of citrus processors. It has been especially important in improving the quality of citrus products and improving the efficiency of product processing.

Growers and Shippers League of Florida deals with all matters pertaining to transportation. The association is especially active in matters of rates, rules, charges, and services. It has been the official transportation agency of the Florida Department of Citrus since 1939 and for the Canners Association since 1945.

Citrus Central is a supercooperative designed to provide a means for member cooperatives to engage in joint marketing and product development, joint manufacturing of supplies such as containers, and other activities, such as advertising, that cannot be done economically by members acting alone. The economies effected by Citrus Central are especially important in this era of large-scale marketing, when a steady stream of uniform quality is demanded by food retailers.

Other Agricultural Associations

The *Florida Fruits and Vegetables Association* (FFVA) in Orlando has played an important role in Florida agriculture since the beginning of World War II. The organization was formed for two purposes. The first purpose was to represent Florida growers in Washington when various price ceilings were being placed on food products. The price rollbacks frequently resulted in distortions of normal price relationships, and to get redress required an organized effort, for which FFVA was formed. The second purpose was to import or sponsor offshore labor from the Bahamas and Jamaica to help harvest farm products in Florida when labor was in short supply. From these beginnings FFVA grew, and its activities have expanded into those of a trade association handling all types of problems common to fruit and vegetable growers.

The *Florida Cattlemen's Association,* headquartered in Kissimmee, is another organization important to Florida. The association was founded in the early 1930s to promote and protect the best interests of cattlemen. In addition to political matters, the association is heavily involved in research and education in cooperation with IFAS and the federal Department of Agriculture.

Three associations embrace the nursery and garden supply industries in Florida: the *Florida Seedsmen and Garden Supply Association* (Orlando), the *Florida Nurserymen and Growers Association* (Tampa), and the *Florida Foliage Association* (Apopka). These are typical trade associations supported by membership dues; their mission is to promote trade associations of members in political, economic, and social matters.

Another organization, the *Florida Sugar Cane League* (Clewiston), was organized in 1964. The rapid expansion of sugarcane production after the Cuban crisis brought with it the need for a trade association to look after industrywide political and economic problems. It is a nonprofit organization financed by membership dues.

The *Florida Forestry Association* (FFA), located in Tallahassee, was founded in 1923 to promote Florida's forest industry through educational, political, and social means. The association speaks for the members, who pay annual dues, and like the other trade associations FFA is nonprofit. It solicits grants to finance special educational projects such as fire protection, one of its continuing efforts. Most legislation related to the forest industry is the result of the FFA's efforts.

There are three other organizations, more general in nature, to be considered.

The *Florida Farm Bureau Federation* (FFBF) is the largest general farm organization in Florida. Organized in the fall of 1941 when there was widespread dissatisfaction with the marketing of citrus, it has 80,000 member families including both associate and active members. Its primary mission continues to be educational and political. In recent years it has also made available to members a rather complete insurance program and has offered tires, batteries, and auto and truck accessories for sale. It is now marketing farm products for Florida's farmers and is importing products from other states through sister federations.

A very important activity of the FFBF is to influence legislation at all levels of government. Its educational efforts, secondary in importance, include programs for women and young farmers and for experienced farmers as well. Special attention is being given to safety, crime prevention, estate planning, and communications.

The word *federation* is noteworthy. The American FBF is a union of state associations, and the Florida FBF is a union of county associations. This structure encourages local autonomy as far as is feasible. It strives to solve problems of farmers at the lowest political level, to encourage independence, and to promote decentralization.

The *Florida Horticultural Society* (FHS) has been and remains the most important educational and research-oriented organization in Florida agriculture. Researchers, farmers, manufacturers, and agribusinesses came together in 1888 to advance the development of plant culture. The society provides a means for research needs to influence the studies undertaken and for research results to be applied in production refinements. Its meetings today are more important than ever.

Finally, the *Florida Agricultural Council*, incorporated in the 1940s, is a group of dedicated agricultural leaders representing every facet of Florida's agriculture. It is composed of two representatives from each of the thirty-five major commodity and agribusiness organizations in the state. The primary business of the council is conducted by an executive committee, elected annually. Because the council has no professional staff workers, the executive committee members, especially the president and the secretary-treasurer, are pivotal to the execution of the programs of the council.

The primary purpose of the council is to support the adequate funding, through private or public sources, of the agricultural teaching, research, and extension programs of the Institute of Food and Agricultural Sciences of the University of Florida. It also supports the agricultural regulatory programs of the state whenever a coordinated effort between these regulatory programs and the research and educational programs of IFAS is needed to meet a critical problem of the industry. Over the years, the council has served effectively in legislative matters and has become an all-important sounding board in the development of new programs for research and education. Its effectiveness has been due to its broad representation of Florida's diverse agriculture, the unselfish service of its membership, its flexibility, and its dedication to the progress of all of Florida's agriculture.

There are many more organizations related to Florida agriculture than can be discussed here. For instance, dairymen are highly organized, as are producers of swine, honey, peaches, and poultry. It takes well-managed group action to protect one's interests under our form of government and in our type of economic system, and to that end Florida agriculture is well organized.

Marketing Orders in Florida

A marketing order provides price stability for farmers producing perishable, nonstorable products, similar to the stability that price supports and acreage control provide to producers of storable crops like corn, wheat, rice, cotton, tobacco, and peanuts. By controlling the quantity that flows through the marketing channels to consumers, it is possible to influence the market price. For marketing orders to be effective, all or nearly all producers must comply. The marketing order thus creates a form of legalized monopoly.

This legalizing of monopolistic behavior is provided for under the federal Marketing Order and Agreements Act of 1937. (Some states, notably California, have state marketing orders that supplement federal orders.) Marketing orders are especially designed for Florida agricultural products like citrus, tomatoes, celery, limes, avocados, milk, and sometimes shade tobacco (grown in the Quincy area). These orders permit the secretary of agriculture to sanction recommendations of the growers when they feel that price stabilization is needed in the interest of the consumers at large. Citrus orders take the form of setting a minimum standard for quality and of controlling the flow to market at certain critical times of the year, especially during the Christmas period.

During certain weeks of the year Florida is the primary source of celery in the U.S. Supply is controlled during these weeks under the celery marketing order, implemented by a celery exchange, to ensure that a glut does not occur, causing disastrously lower prices. The price of celery is set weekly, and the quantity harvested is based upon the quantity that will sell at that price.

The tomato industry is the largest single commodity of Florida fruits and vegetables (after citrus and sugarcane). It also dominates U.S. supply at certain times of the year. The demand for tomatoes, like that for celery and many other agricultural products, is relatively inelastic—which means that if too many tomatoes go to the market the price will drop to very low levels. Control of supply is therefore effective.

A similar order is designed to control the supply of limes and avocados going to market in any given time, and informal efforts are made to control the supply of pole beans and sweet corn.

Milk, unlike any other product, is produced under a market order system whereby the price is established by an economic formula. This method evolved because milk producers needed protection against slumps in prices in order to maintain expensive production units—very large investments in land, buildings, milk cows, and equipment. Indeed, milk has almost become a public utility, something that is critically needed, that requires very large initial capital investment, and that competition cannot be relied on to supply adequately over a period of time.

Marketing orders for milk would not have been instituted had not dairy farmers been highly organized into cooperative groups. Today, the three area dairy cooperatives—Miami, Tampa, and upper Florida—are federated in Dairy Farmers, Inc. These associations work aggressively for the interests of milk producers and monitor compliance with the marketing orders in effect for milk.

Marketing orders are thus common in Florida and have been reasonably effective in stabilizing prices to the benefit of both producers and consumers. The consumers' welfare, after all, is the responsibility of the secretary of agriculture, without whose approval marketing orders cannot be used.

Agricultural Finance

Credit has been a continuing problem for farmers in the United States. As farmers have become more commercial and more dependent upon markets for the sale of most of their output, the problem has become more acute. And as new technologies have developed, making it prudent for farmers to purchase more of the inputs to their production processes, credit has become even more necessary. During World War I, credit became very critical because farmers were prospering. Reasoning that they could afford to adopt new technology, many of them went into debt to buy more land or new equipment. After World War I, farm prices dropped drastically, especially in the fall of 1921. This weakened the financial position of many farmers, with respect to both their cash flow and their net worth.

Pressures on the federal government to improve the availability of farm credit resulted in what is known today as the Farm Credit System (FCS), a cooperative credit system owned by borrowers but enabled under acts of Congress. The FCS is the dominant source of credit for U.S. farmers. Government loans to farmers are made by the Farmers Home Administration and to a minor degree by the Small Business Administration. Other sources of credit are commercial banks, insurance companies, and individuals under private arrangements.

Although established under acts of Congress and incorporated accordingly, FCS is not a federal agency. Originally the money required to capitalize the banks came from appropriated funds of the federal government, but all government funds have long since been repaid. The FCS is completely borrower-owned, so borrowers have to invest in the banks in order to provide the capital base.

There are three banks in this system: one for production loans of one to seven years to individuals, one for long-term loans to individuals to buy real estate, and one to provide credit to farmers' cooperatives. Individuals wishing to borrow money for short or long terms will find a Production Credit Association or a Land Bank Association in their home county or a nearby county; these two associations are often merged in a Farm Credit Service, and all loans are handled by one person in one office. Farmers' cooperatives wishing to borrow money apply directly to the district headquarters (for Florida, the district headquarters of the Farm Credit System is in Columbia, South Carolina). Because many commercial banks in Florida have not been interested in making agricultural loans, the FCS associations make the majority of the loans to farmers in Florida. The cooperatives in Florida, which are common in fruit, vegetables, milk, poultry, and sugar marketing, use the Columbia Bank for Cooperatives to a substantial degree. Some commercial banks in Florida make a special effort to finance farmers. In addition, certain life insurance companies are active in making loans, especially long-term real estate loans; but in general the life insurance companies are quite selective and only make loans for large amounts.

Loans by individuals are quite common in the sale and purchase of land. This is advantageous to the seller under the current income tax system, whereby, if the seller takes less than 30 percent as a down payment and stretches out the payments over a period of years, he or she pays an income tax only on that portion of the payment received each year. Consequently, many people who have farm land to sell will finance the buyer, which helps both parties.

The formal and informal sources of agricultural credit have thus gone through many changes over the years and today are very important for the success of food producers. People who succeed in growing food and fiber products must be as adept at financial management as they are at producing plant or animal products.

PIK Program

Under the 1981 Agriculture Marketing Act, the USDA initiated a Payment-in-Kind (PIK) program for farmers. In Florida, staple crops coming under the program are corn, grain, sorghum, rice, upland cotton, and wheat; all but wheat will be eliminated in 1984. Participating farmers sign agreements to cut acreage and in return receive surplus produce, which they may sell. In Florida, 4,279 such agreements were signed in 1983. The program rids the government of costly storage and at the same time controls production. One problem arises when farmers cultivate more intensively so that in good crop years there will still be a market surplus.

Agricultural Subsidies

In 1983, the total annual cost of federal subsidies to farmers was $21 billion, including PIK programs. Such subsidies had been only $3 billion in 1971 but by the end of the 1970s had reached $6 billion. But under the Reagan administration, the 1981 agricultural act pushed subsidies up over six times the annual rate at the beginning of the 1970s, greatly increasing the federal debt. The drought of 1983 avoided, at least temporarily, adding to carryover agricultural surpluses. However, there have been an increasing number of bankruptcies among small farms and an increase in the proportion of production by large farms, many of which are corporately owned.

Florida's Agriculture Today

Florida contains 35 million acres; about 16 million acres are in farms. Of this 16 million only 2.3 million acres are used for crops; the remaining 13.7 million acres are about equally divided between permanent pasture and forest and woodlands. Much of the woodlands is grazed. Florida's agriculture is big and highly competitive with farming elsewhere in the United States and abroad. The state's total receipts from primary marketing of farm, forest, and fishery products were over $2.75 billion in 1977 (see table 18.2). The value added as the products move to consumers is another $7 billion. Florida ranks between twelfth and fourteenth among the fifty states in value of farm products. Florida's agriculture grew faster in both volume and value between 1965 and 1975 than that of any other state. About one-fourth of the jobs in Florida—in farm machinery sales and maintenance, farm chemicals, farm labor, farm produce transportation and marketing, and food purveyors and restaurateurs—are related to agriculture and the food industry.

Florida's rank in food production does not show that the state is almost the only supplier of vegetables at certain seasons of the year and supplies nearly all of the processed citrus juice in the nation. The state is also a key supplier of foliages, flowers, and other ornamentals. The more common agricultural enterprises such as beef, dairy, and poultry production are rather unusual in Florida in that they are highly concentrated into a few large producing units. Sugarcane, avocados, mangoes, and limes are special to Florida and a very few other states. Table 18.3 shows farm receipts by commodities.

Livestock and livestock products.—Cash receipts from livestock and related products totaled about $746 million in 1977 (see tables 18.2 and 18.3).

Beef cattle are found all over the state, especially in large ranches in central and southern Florida where drainage, soil, and weather make crop production unprofitable. There are smaller ranches in the northern part of the peninsula and the Panhandle. Many general farmers in this area raise some beef cattle along with swine, poultry, and row crops. Most operations in Florida are of the cow-calf type, which means that Florida produces a very large number of calves; these calves are shipped out of the state after weaning, at a weight of around 400 pounds, to eat high-quality grasses and clovers in states such as Alabama and Mississippi, thence to the feedlot where they add the final 300 to 400 pounds. About 75 percent of what a beef cattle animal eats in its life is forage, most of which can be utilized only by a ruminant animal. (Persons who argue that eating meat is wrong because the grain fed to cattle can be eaten by man fail to understand that most beef comes from animals that have never had any grain at all. Moreover, most grains fed to livestock are not suitable for human consumption.) Improvements in breeding stock have resulted in much-improved meat quality from their offspring. The numbers of cattle raised in Florida are expected to increase by one-third between 1974 and 1985.

Historically *dairy farms* were located near cities and towns because milk could be transported only a few miles when technology was crude. Dairies were therefore small, serving only the people in the immediate area. Today, milk can be shipped hundreds of miles and has a shelf life of over two weeks. Hence, dairies are getting large, especially in Florida, which has the largest dairy herds in the United States. There are about 400 dairy farms in Florida today. Even though Florida dairies produce more than 90 percent of the total needs of consumers in Florida, fluctuations in the number of tourists cause times of large deficits and other times of small surpluses. In general, milk production keeps pace with consumption needs. One of the primary purposes of milk marketing orders, which set milk prices, is to assure a supply of milk that matches the needs of consumers. In the early 1980s an annual surplus of milk and cheese products was stimulated by federal subsidies and finally resulted in some curtailment of federal price supports for dairy farmers.

Swine production is confined largely to North Florida and the Panhandle, where feed grains are grown. In this area production of feeder pigs (50–100 lbs.) is common. These pigs are finished by feedlots especially equipped to produce slaughter hogs. Some farmers who breed sows and farrow pigs feed them until they reach slaughter weights, but this is becoming less common. There are

TABLE 18.2. Value of Florida's Agricultural Products, 1977

Product	Cash Receipts from Primary Marketing (millions of $)	Farmers' Share (%)	Retail Value Wherever Sold (millions of $)
Livestock and products	746	57.9	1,288
Fruits and nuts	717	25.6	2,800
Vegetables, truck	568	36.0	1,578
Field crops	294	32.0	919
Forest products			
small farmer	13[a]	4.0	325
corporate holdings	77[a]	4.0	1,925
Fishery products			
dock value	90	32.5	277
Ornamentals	249	50.0	498
Total	2,754		9,610

Source: Data are from U.S. Department of Agriculture, with farm share value estimated by agricultural economists from the University of Florida.

a. Forest products value is stumpage value.

TABLE 18.3. Florida Cash Farm Receipts from Marketing, by Commodities (in thousands of dollars)

	Five-year Averages							Annual		
	1940–44	1945–49	1950–54	1955–59	1960–64	1965–69	1970–74	1975	1976	1977
Field crops:										
Corn	744	1,094	1,081	2,451	5,044	9,696	13,169	30,916	43,011	21,983
Cotton	1,564	1,855	5,184	2,574	2,785	1,373	1,712	899	2,753	1,667
Peanuts	3,197	4,971	4,813	5,113	6,520	9,118	21,852	35,081	33,838	35,189
Sugarcane	4,422	7,971	11,001	10,398	25,463	52,379	113,408	307,308	188,412	142,354
Sweet potatoes	647	994	1,084	312	331	a	a	a	a	a
Soybeans	b	b	b	b	b	7,037	21,052	25,793	46,490	42,853
Tobacco, all types	6,263	15,568	21,609	21,000	26,977	29,355	30,064	28,671	36,351	30,698
Other crops[c]	255	392	1,046	3,537	5,472	4,114	6,544	12,256	15,007	19,476
Truck crops:										
Potatoes, Irish	5,356	8,807	13,854	17,911	16,336	22,287	23,212	23,911	39,736	44,295
Strawberries	1,884	2,675	2,854	1,941	4,756	6.054	6,135	8,375	8,862	8,653
Truck crops[d]	60,479	94,182	126,217	146,830	169,713	238,029	312,868	467,051	498,863	515,455
Fruit and tree nuts:										
Oranges and tangerines	67,909	96,428	141,003	213,876	273,669	275,179	381,978	519,815	508,365	544,267
Grapefruit	25,877	30,135	36,964	40,599	49,508	65,258	117,958	121,958	107,682	124,863
Limes	655	733	1,286	1,181	1,519	2,790	4,885	11,034	10,816	8,800
Avocados	338	549	948	1,074	1,360	2,367	5,164	10,427	9,400	8,634
Pecans	650	755	909	1,338	843	1,102	1,529	1,615	1,494	2,597
Other fruits and nuts[e]	455	1,832	2,385	2,527	6,062	9,975	20,208	30,819	23,705	27,390

TABLE 18.3—*continued*

Other products:										
Forest	1,354	3,038	5,756	8,582	8,789	4,413	8,020	8,952	12,796	13,165
Greenhouse & nursery	5,405	13,290	23,946	33,292	56.600	79,289	111,317	222,540	241,213	249,389
Total crops	187,484	285,269	401,940	514,536	661 746	819,805	1,201,075	1,867,875	1,828,794	1,841,728
Livestock & Livestock Products:										
Cattle & calves	7,456	22,165	35,269	56,246	67,269	10,357	173,335	185,640	208,877	276,873
Dairy products	14,280	28,487	42,326	71,056	86,844	107,068	160,217	222,833	240,150	239,211
Hogs	8,465	16,916	15,827	13,646	11,344	115,523	21,248	26,339	21,480	27,362
Eggs	4,318	2,703	15,561	23,648	37,701	60,811	80,409	102,375	121,723	111,394
Chickens & broilers	5,412	10,477	11,467	8,415	6,968	15,146	36,630	66,073	69,012	72,811
Others[f]	1,451	3,073	4,392	5,376	4,777	6,855	13,196	19,990	21,979	18,052
Total livestock & livestock products	41,382	83,821	124,842	178,387	214,903	315,760	485,036	623,250	683,211	745,703
Total Crops, livestock, & livestock products	228,866	374,090	526,782	692,923	875,649	1,135,565	1,686,111	2,491,125	2,512,015	2,587,431
Governments payments	4,413	4,356	3,452	5,531	10,346	18,500	15,941	12,875	5,440	20,750
Grand totals	233,279	378,446	530,234	698,454	886,995	1,154,065	1,702,052	2,504,000	2,517,455	2,608,181

Source: USDA, ERS, *The Farm Income Situation and Farm Income, State Estimates*.
[a]Included in truck crops or not reported.
[b]Included in other crops.
[c]Includes wheat, oats, hay, sorghum grain, grass, clover and lupine seed, Austrian winter peas, ramie for fiber, and field crops.
[d]Includes watermelons and cantaloupes.
[e]Includes lemons, pears, persimmons, pineapple, plums, other berries, coconuts, bananas, guavas, loquats, mangoes, papayas, kumquats, tangelos, and tung nuts.
[f]Includes sheep and lambs, turkeys, turkey eggs, other poultry, beeswax, honey, wool, horses and mules, other livestock.

about 500 registered garbage feeders clustered around the large cities (Miami, Orlando, Tampa, and the like), who process garbage according to health standards and feed it to about 30,000 hogs at any one time. Small-scale hog farmers usually sell their hogs through the local auction markets. Large producers sell directly to the meat-packing companies. There is some tendency for hogs to be produced under contracts similar to those for broiler chickens.

Horse production is centered in Marion County and is one of the fastest growing enterprises today. The common breeds of horses are quarter horses and thoroughbreds. The thoroughbreds are grown in and around Marion County, where the grasses and clovers are of high quality because the parent rock for the soil is limerock with phosphate. Quarter horses are the most numerous and are produced all over the state in small units. Larger-scale quarter horse farms are usually close to the thoroughbred-producing areas.

Poultry farms are scattered over the state. Eggs, somewhat like milk, tend to be produced close to populated areas. Hence there are large laying flocks in Central Florida near Tampa and around Jacksonville. Florida ranks seventh in egg production in the United States and exports about 35 percent of its egg production. Broilers are produced in North Florida (Jacksonville to Live Oak) and around De Funiak Springs in the Panhandle. Florida ranks thirteenth in the nation in broiler production and exports over 50 percent of its production. Both eggs and broilers are produced largely in integrated units where the inputs and outputs are controlled by the integrator and the farmers produce under contract. Financing of production is largely furnished by the integrator. Goldkist cooperative with headquarters in Atlanta is one of the large firms serving Florida.

Fruits and nuts.—Fruits and tree nuts produced cash receipts of $716.5 million in 1977 (see tables 18.2 and 18.3).

Citrus dominates this group, as can be seen in table 18.3. Historically, there are two production areas: an interior area from Alachua and Putnam counties in the north down to Highlands and De Soto counties in the south; and the Indian River area from Brevard County to Broward County along the east coast. Most of the citrus along the west coast, north and south from Tampa Bay, has been replaced by urban development.

Total acreage of citrus has been reduced slightly in recent years. In the calendar years 1976 and 1977 approximately 50,000 acres were taken out of production and only 28,000 acres of new trees were planted. Most of the new plantings are in the southern parts of the two major production areas, and most of the acres going out of production are in older producing areas where urban encroachment is taking place. It is estimated that total citrus acreage will not change much during the next decade, but shifts in growing areas will continue.

There have been many improvements in citrus culture. Improved rootstock, the use of mineral elements as soil supplements, and water control are major contributors to production. Big strides have been made in citrus processing;

frozen concentrate is the major new product, but citrus powder may prove to be important in the future. Picking citrus fruit is the industry's major problem today. Finding harvesting labor for any crop is difficult, and for this reason mechanical harvesting of all sorts of farm products is being developed intensively. Many mechanical picking methods for citrus are being tried. More and more fruit will be mechanically harvested each year from now on, and by 1990 nearly all citrus and other agricultural products will be so harvested.

Vegetables and truck crops.—Truck crops are a close third behind livestock and citrus in sales, with cash receipts of $568.4 million in 1977 (see tables 18.2 and 18.3). Nine major growing areas and their principal crops are listed in table 18.4. Other vegetables are grown in these areas, of course. Also, other areas of

TABLE 18.4. Florida's Truck Crop Areas

Area	Major Crops
Homestead	Tomatoes, potatoes, beans, Cuban vegetables
Delray Beach	Peppers, squash, eggplant, tomatoes
Belle Glade	Celery, sweet corn, radishes, leafy greens
Immokalee	Watermelons, tomatoes, peppers, cucumbers, squash
Manatee-Ruskin	Tomatoes, squash, peppers, strawberries
Zellwood	Sweet corn, carrots, leafy greens, radishes
Sanford	Cabbage, celery, cucumbers
Hastings	Potatoes, cabbage
Plant City	Strawberries, squash, peppers

the state are also important growing areas. For example, Sumter, Marion, and Alachua counties produce significant amounts of vegetables and in recent years, vegetables have caught on in Gadsden County. Watermelons are grown commercially in over thirty-three counties. Programs of assistance to small-scale farmers in the Panhandle feature truck crops. Special attention is also being given again to growing food by individuals for home use. Generally, vegetable crops promise to increase in importance in Florida.

Field crops.—Grown largely in North Florida, field crops had receipts of $294 million in 1977 (see tables 18.2 and 18.3). Sugarcane, the major exception, is grown south of Lake Okeechobee. Most field crops are grown on a large number of relatively small family farms; large farming operations have not been successful. Moreover, two important crops, tobacco and peanuts, are grown under the government allotment program, which allocates production among farmers.

Greenhouse and nursery.—Showing rapid growth in recent decades, greenhouse and nursery production is now worth about $250 million annually. It is centered around Palm Beach–Miami, around Apopka, and to a lesser extent around Sarasota. The future is bright for this maturing industry, but the competition is very keen today because profits were good up until 1975. Unskillful nursery owners have been forced out of business in recent years.

Forest and wood products.—Most forest lands are owned by large timber companies (see table 18.2). Because of the integrated nature of the industry—owners of trees being also the processors of lumber, poles, plywood, and paper pulp—the value of forest products becomes very great. This industry provides jobs for thousands of Floridians; for example, the state Division of Forestry estimated that in 1976 there were 1,621 wood products firms, employing 37,000 workers with a payroll of $420 million. Besides the economic benefits, forests provide important recreational benefits to all citizens as well as the conservation of animal and plant life.

Migrant Labor

The facts and issues regarding migrant labor in Florida have been admirably summarized in *Farm Labor in Florida,* a 1977 study by Leo Polopolus, from which most of the following details are taken.

Most farm workers work on family-size farms; only 17 percent of the overall labor payroll is paid by large corporation-type farms. Interstate migrant workers represent about 29 percent of farm laborers in Florida, and the trend is downward. The large farms hire most of this migratory labor.

Farming in Florida, large or small, is less profitable than most alternative businesses, and there is great variation in profits. As costs of farming have increased, it has been more and more difficult to attract capital from alternative investments.

All laborers, migrant or not, are protected by social legislation, both federal and state. In addition to Social Security the federal government has provided for health and safety of workers, and the state has new regulations regarding housing, sanitation, and the education of children. Private church agencies also have projects.

Farm labor wage rates in Florida are among the highest in the country. In 1977, the average farm wage rate was $3.31 an hour. Piece rate workers average $3.85 an hour. Farm wage rates in Florida are shown in the data published by the Florida Crop and Livestock Reporting Service for January 1979 (table 18.5).

Farm workers, migrant or not, are not exploited by farm employers any more than the workers exploit themselves. Rather, they are exploited by the system. Wages are paid indirectly from prices paid by consumers. It has been national policy to have relatively cheap food prices. (The percent of disposable income spent for food in the United States has been less than 20 percent for decades, and the same has been true for Canada and some Western European countries. Most countries in the world spend over half their income for food.) Any increase in farm labor wage rates without increases in prices paid by consumers would mean fewer farmers, less food production, higher wholesale food prices, and much less employment in agriculture. Hence, persons who feel that farm laborers should be paid more must realize that all consumers would have to be willing to pay higher food prices.

Migrant laborers are in a precarious position also because farm production is subject to weather hazards. A freeze may mean that there are no jobs at all. The farmer cannot afford to guarantee jobs if weather eliminates the need for workers.

TABLE 18.5. Farm Wages Rates in Florida
(dollars per hour)

		Type of Worker		
State	All Hired	Field Livestock	Machine Operator	Supervisor
Florida	3.31	3.07	3.25	4.94
Alabama	2.50	2.25	2.98	n.a.
Arizona	2.87	2.60	2.79	4.50
California	3.41	3.11	3.32	5.02
Georgia	2.62	2.42	2.75	4.24
Texas	2.74	2.38	2.62	4.52
U.S.	2.96	2.68	3.04	4.78

Source: Polopolus, *Farm Labor in Florida*.
n.a.: Not available.

Data on annual earnings of farm workers are scanty and unreliable, since payment is frequently in cash and few records are kept. It was reported in a study made in 1970–71 that full-time farm workers earned $4,178 per annum and that part-time farm workers (averaging 35.5 hours per week) earned $2,571 per annum (Polopolus and Emerson, 1975).

The tension between increasing farm wage rates while continuing to provide jobs is serious. Since agriculture serves to employ many persons who have virtually no alternative employment opportunity, programs that increase farm labor costs cause unemployment among workers presumably "helped" by the programs. The competition for Florida's farming products within and outside the United States is so great that wage increases force a gradual substitution of machines for labor. As machines are substituted for labor, only the more skilled workers will retain their jobs. The unskilled will be on welfare or in retraining programs. If farms are forced to shut down, all jobs are lost.

Moreover, many migrant workers, lacking educational opportunities or the experience necessary to cope with our complex political economy, have living habits that are self-defeating. No matter what the migrants' current conditions, the problems of all disadvantaged persons must be solved by getting at their basic cause, a task for society in general and beyond the means or ability of the farmer or the migrant laborer alone to solve.

Florida's Farm Labor Situation, 1978–79

Of the 29,000 interstate migrant workers, 8,000 are in a special category of "offshore" workers (Bahamians, Jamaicans), imported to cut sugarcane (see table 18.6). They come without family, cut cane for a few months, and return home. Housing, food, and medical and other services are provided by the employer. This program is closely supervised by federal and state officials in order to ensure that it has no adverse effect upon employment for domestic workers.

The composition of interstate migrants is changing and the number is diminishing. Twenty years ago, workers from the southeastern U.S. dominated this group; most were blacks. Today, Mexican-Americans are dominant, a minority of them illegal aliens. These workers bring their families and, being family-oriented, resist working far away from home. Therefore, besides working seasonally in agriculture, they tend to find local jobs outside agriculture. It is reported that about 40 percent of migrant workers have supplementary nonfarm income. In the future, the growing resistance of people to move around, their ability to find other employment locally, and the substitution of capital for labor will reduce the need for migrant labor.

As the number of migrants diminishes and as they tend to reside in one place, participation in the political processes will grow. There is little such participation by migrants at this time. Most of the politicizing is done by nonfarm persons wishing to help. Nevertheless, there are many programs in effect today to improve the levels of income, housing, health care, and education of migrants.

In 1979 the United Farm Workers, led by Cesar Chavez, had one contract in Florida—with Minute Maid (Coca Cola, Inc.), which employs about 1,200 farm workers. Because Florida has a "right to work" law, membership in a union is voluntary.

Two other unions active in Florida are bargaining agents for farm workers. The Retail/Wholesale Department Store Workers Union has organized Yoder Brothers, Inc. (Ft. Myers), which produces flowers and employs about 550 persons. The International Association of Machinists has contracts that include farm workers as well as mill workers with Okeelanta, Talisman, and Osceola sugar companies in the Lake Okeechobee area. Most workers in this union are mill workers. Several citrus-processing plants are unionized, but no farm workers are included in these contracts.

Organizing farm workers in Florida is progressing very slowly. No more than 2,000 farm workers are covered by unions today. There is much talk today about increasing the effort. If unions do succeed in organizing farm workers, thereby increasing farm labor costs, the rate at which machines will replace labor will increase. Moreover, some farm employers who want to remain free from a labor union will increase wages and fringe benefits to stall or delay union organization. In any event, the result is the same: higher labor costs will reduce farm employment. Farmers who cannot pass along to consumers the increases in production costs will cease farming or shift to farm enterprises that require little labor.

TABLE 18.6. Florida's Farm Laborers, 1979

Year-round hired farm workers	33,000
Seasonal workers who live at home and prefer seasonal work	33,000
Migrant workers, intrastate	4,000
Migrant workers, interstate	29,000
Total hired farm workers	99,000

SOURCE: Author's estimates made from interviews with persons in hiring, supervision, and regulatory farm labor programs. The U.S. Employment Service records only interstate movement.

There is no question that migrant labor is needed in the U.S. food production system, from Florida to Maine to California. Although many outsiders view migrant laborers as disadvantaged, they are working under better conditions than ever before. Employers are generally humane and want to improve wages and working conditions because they need workers. Unless farmers are able to pass along more of their increasing costs to consumers in the future, farm output will diminish until increased prices for farm products permit the remaining farmers to make a profit comparable to that of other industries. Farmers, for years caught in a cost-price squeeze, have adopted new technologies to cut costs. These efforts will continue, but success will be harder to achieve. To blame the farmer or to invite action against the farmer, corporate or not, at critical times of the growing season is really to miss the point. If carried to the extreme, farming would become a public utility under government controls, with administered prices and guaranteed returns on investment based upon mediocre productivity.

Environment, Energy, and Florida's Agriculture

As we enter an age of relative resource scarcity, Florida's agriculture has been forced increasingly to compete for its resources as society struggles to achieve multiple goals of environmental quality, energy independence, and continued abundance of low-cost food and fiber for consumers.

This situation manifests itself in several ways. For example, of Florida's 35 million acres of land, nearly three-fourths are devoted to agriculture. Ironically, the most intensive agricultural production occurs in urban counties. Yet it is in these counties that agricultural land has disappeared most rapidly in the face of urban development. Difficult policy questions concerning how much agricultural land to preserve, and in which locations, are issues requiring more emphasis than ever before on identifying and achieving a fair balance between private rights and the public interest.

Competition for resources also occurs, as population growth in urban areas, growth in phosphate mining, and growth in agricultural use of irrigation systems all draw upon Florida's supply of fresh water. As water management districts establish their authority for requiring consumptive use permits, Florida agriculturalists increasingly are forced to document and justify their need for irrigation water. Another problem relating to agriculture and water supply occurs when fertilizers and cattle manure run off into streams and then into lakes. Over time this runoff can cause eutrophication of shallow lakes, which gradually die and become weed- or slime-filled swamps.

Implementation of environmental programs of pesticide regulation and water quality regulation will continue to have effects on the availability of inputs into agricultural production processes and on production practices of agricultural and forestry enterprises. Cancellation by the Environmental Protection Agency of registration of pesticides for which substitutes are not available could result in decreased productivity or increased production costs. Regulations which inhibit new pesticide development will have similar effects. The net results could be lower crop yields, higher food prices, and more extensive use of land, labor, and management inputs.

As energy supplies become increasingly costly and unreliable, Florida agriculture faces the challenge of developing an increasingly energy-efficient operation. It will also face pressures to divert resources from the production of food and fiber to the production of biomass for alcohol production.

In sum, agricultural productivity in Florida and the United States has been outstanding. But it has had its undesirable costs. One of them is destructive exploitation of people, land, water, energy, and air. The costs of reducing undue exploitation must be shared by all in a reasonably equitable way. Much of the strain and stress expressed in the politics of agriculture throughout our country today arises from disagreements about how to distribute those costs. Solutions will come by treating causes rather than symptoms. We are fortunate so far to be concerned by these more abstract matters rather than by critical shortages of bread, rice, or beans.

References

Akerman, Joe A., Jr. *Florida Cowman: A History of Florida Cattle Raising*. Kissimmee: Florida Cattlemen's Association, 1976.

Cooper, J. Francis. *Dimensions in History*. Gainesville: University of Florida, 1976.

Department of Community Affairs, Division of Community Services. "Farmworker Programs in Florida." Tallahassee, 1977.

———. *Florida Migrant Labor Problems*. Tallahassee, 1977.

Florida Citrus Showcase. *Florida Citrus Festival '74*. Winter Haven, 1974.

Hopkins, James T. *50 Years of Citrus*. Gainesville: University of Florida Press, 1960.

Institute of Food and Agricultural Sciences. *Agricultural Growth in an Urban Age*. Gainesville: University of Florida, 1975.

Polopolus, Leo. *Farm Labor in Florida*. Institute for Social Policy Studies, Special Report. Tallahassee, 1977.

Polopolus, Leo, and Emerson, Robert. *Agricultural Labor and Unemployment Insurance*. Bulletin 767. Gainesville: Florida Agricultural Experiment Station, 1975.

Rose, Norman G. *Economic Reports* 48, 64, 69, 74, 85. Historical (Vegetables) Series. Gainesville; University of Florida, 1974–77.

Shofner, Jerrell H. *History of Jefferson County*. Tallahassee: Sentry, 1976.

Swanson, Henry F. *Countdown for Agriculture in Orange County*. Orlando, 1975.

U.S. Department of Agriculture, Economic Research Service. *The Farm Income Situation and Farm Income, State Estimates*. Supplement to Statistical Bulletin 557. Washington, 1977.

U.S. Department of Agriculture, Economics, Statistics, and Cooperative Service. *U.S. Foreign Agricultural Trade Statistical Report, Calendar Year 1978*. Washington, 1978.

Florida's Extractive Industries: Marine Products

18B

by James C. Cato

UNIVERSITY OF FLORIDA

Because of unique geographic, economic, and environmental factors, Florida has a diverse marine and aquatic products industry. Florida's general coastline is 1,250 statute miles long, with a tidal coastline of 8,426 miles. The river and stream shorelines of the state extend for 23,752 miles. Of Florida's total shoreline, 55 percent is beach, 36 percent is marshland, and the remaining 9 percent is mangrove shoreline.

The population is highly concentrated near the coasts. This particular mix of a large coastal population and a shoreline covered with bays and estuaries—areas important in the life cycle of most fish and shellfish—necessitates careful use, wise planning, and farsighted management of marine resources.

Management of Fisheries

Management of Florida's marine resources within the territorial sea resides with the Marine Fisheries Commission, its seven members appointed by the governor subject to confirmation by the senate. Its creation in 1983 represented a major change in the way marine fisheries are managed in Florida. Whereas the legislature had previously enacted state fishery laws, the Marine Fisheries Commission has full rule-making authority over marine life, with the exception of endangered species. Its rulings are subject to final approval by the cabinet and governor sitting as the head of the Department of Natural Resources, which enforces the commission rules.

The U.S. Congress passed in 1976 the Magnuson Fishery Conservation and Management Act, creating a new management for marine resources in the fishery conservation zone encompassing the area from a state's territorial water outward to 200 miles. Eight federal fishery management councils were established, charged with administering management plans for each fishery, including determination of how each is to be utilized and whether foreign countries are to be allowed access to it. Two of these councils are important to Florida: the Gulf of Mexico Fishery Management Council, located in Tampa, governs the conservation zone from Texas through Florida's west coast, and the South Atlantic Fishery Management Council, located in Charleston, S.C., controls the zone from North Carolina south through Florida's east coast.

The U.S. Department of Commerce is the federal agency dealing with fishery resources. Most activities important to seafood producers are run by the department's National Oceanic and Atmospheric Administration (NOAA). Within that agency, the National Marine Fisheries Service and the National Sea

Grant Office run research, management, enforcement, and extension programs. The sea grant program, administered in Florida through the State University System, focuses on the sea in much the same way that the land grant program focuses on food producers through land grant colleges.

Florida belongs to the Marine Fisheries Compacts for the Gulf states and Atlantic states. Representing various states, the commissions created by these compacts promote better use of states' fisheries by developing joint programs for their protection and promotion and for the prevention of waste.

A number of industrial associations, some existing in Florida, play a major role in fisheries utilization. The Southeastern Fisheries Association, the Organized Fishermen of Florida, and the Florida League of Anglers are the major statewide groups.

The Common Property Resource

Marine fisheries represent a stock resource. Under proper management the fisheries are "harvested" each season so that the remaining stock can reproduce and rebuild to allow for the same harvest level the following season. The discussion in the rest of this section is taken partially from Smith (1975).

In industries where all resources (land and labor) are privately owned, high profit levels entice new firms to enter the market. But total profits eventually decline as the industry expands, and competition forces up the cost of resources.

These economic forces are at work in the fishing industry, as in any other, but with one main difference: fishery resources are generally considered to be property of all the people in common, and no individual has private property rights in them. (There are some exceptions, such as private oyster leases.) Only after harvesting are the resources privately owned. Since the primary resource—the fish—is not private property, its cost does not increase as more people compete for its use. Costs rise in proportion with the effort required to catch the fish. If the total industry fishes beyond acceptable conservation levels, this effort is the result of rational decisions by many individuals, and the effort of one fisherman imposes an unanticipated cost on all the other fishermen. The dominant economic characteristics of the fishing industry are very high or very low profits and a considerable degree of instability.

Expansion beyond the most efficient use of capital and labor often occurs in fishing, and sometimes expansion will occur beyond the biological limits required to support the fishery or the ecological system. Management programs attempt to curb such expansion by making the fishermen's efforts less efficient (gear restrictions, size limits, closed areas) or by actually limiting the entry of boats and fishermen. Such restrictions mean that those who are working in a limited fishery enjoy a higher return on their capital and labor and thereby avoid the worst levels of instability.

Fish swimming free are owned by all the people, commercial seafood producers and recreational fishermen alike, but these two groups are often at odds. Recreational fishermen feel that seafood producers catch too many fish and infringe on their rights. Seafood producers maintain that consumers who do not fish recreationally are deprived of the opportunity to consume seafood products. Constant planning and management are needed to reconcile the different goals and objectives of these two groups and to contain conflict.

Today's Catch

U.S. commercial finfish and shellfish landings in 1981 came to 6 billion pounds, worth $2.4 billion at the dock (fishermen's value). Florida's contribution to the total was 215 million pounds, valued at $173 million. Florida ranked ninth among states in pounds landed but sixth in their value, since a large portion of Florida's seafood products are higher-valued species. Shellfish landings account for about two-thirds of total value but only about one-third of the pounds landed. About 70 percent of Florida's production comes from the Gulf of Mexico, the remainder from the Atlantic Ocean.

Commercial marine landings occur in all coastal counties in Florida except Flagler and Jefferson, and in several inland counties located on rivers. St. Lucie, Pinellas, Monroe, Hillsborough, Lee, Duval, Escambia, Franklin, Dade, Bay, and Brevard counties are the most productive and jointly contribute about 80 percent of the total value of landings. Monroe (in the Florida Keys) is the most productive.

About 80 different species of finfish and shellfish were recorded commercially in 1981. Ten species of finfish were valued at $1 million or more at dockside: in order of importance, grouper, swordfish, mullet, king mackeral, red snapper, pompano, spotted sea trout, Spanish mackeral, tilefish, and yellowtail snapper. Seven species of shellfish were valued at over $1 million or more at dockside: shrimp, spiny lobster, calico scallops, oysters, stone crabs, blue crabs, and bait shrimp. These 17 species account for 93 percent of the value and 75 percent of the pounds of all marine products landed in Florida.

About 12,000 identified commercial fishermen harvest seafood using 6,200 boats and vessels (although about 25,000 boats are registered commercially in Florida). The predominant gear types are shrimp otter trawls, hoop nets, crab and lobster traps, gill and trammel nets, hand and troll lines, and oyster tongs. Since October 1, 1983, a license is required to sell fish commercially in Florida, a change that will produce better statistics in the future regarding the actual number of people selling fish commercially in the state.

Diversity in production is likewise reflected in the various types and levels of seafood processing. In 1980, Florida had 473 seafood processing and wholesale plants employing 7,345 people on a seasonal average and 6,185 on a yearly average. About 88 percent of the employment occurred in the 184 processing plants, which include some of the world's largest shrimp-processing plants, a variety of fish processors, and specialized processing for oysters, blue crabs, calico scallops, and so on. The degree of sophistication varies from the larger automated shrimp firms working 24 hours a day packaging numerous products for over 100 private labels to the small cottage-size firm packaging the same raw material but depending on hand labor and pulse production.

Other commercial ventures in Florida are aquaculture (or mariculture, in saltwater) and the tropical fish industry. Pond, cage, and raceway production of catfish is not as important in Florida as in other southeastern states because of competition from the native catch and poor soil for holding water, although about 7 million pounds of catfish worth $2.7 million were commercially harvested from the wild in 1981. Other species on which there has been some aquaculture or mariculture work are shrimp, freshwater shrimp, pompano, turtle, clams, oysters, and marine worms.

Florida produces over 95 percent of the tropical or "ornamental" fish and plants raised in the United States. While it is somewhat difficult to separate the fraction that can be identified as "aquaculture" in the literal sense, it is clear that the total 1981 annual value of Florida's tropical fish industry ($75 million) is significantly greater than that of the total catfish ($31 million), trout ($24 million), or oyster ($37 million) aquaculture industries for the entire country. Florida is thus easily the leading aquaculture state in the country economically, followed by Mississippi's catfish ($18.8 million) and Idaho's trout ($18 million) industries. Florida's domestic production of tropical fish is $26 million. The remaining value is from imported fish shipped through Florida dealers. Tropical fish farms are concentrated near Lakeland, Tampa, and Miami to utilize nearby airports, freshwater supplies, and mild climates.

In 1980–82, resident and tourist anglers spent 58.6 million angler days in Florida saltwater fishing (Bell, 1982), with an estimated $1.871 billion in direct expenditures and $3.187 billion in indirect expenditures. The average resident tourist is forty-one years of age, 75 percent are male, 89 percent are Caucasian, and their mean household income is $19,000. Tourist anglers average forty-nine years of age, 93 percent are male, 93 percent are Caucasian, and they have an average household income of $25,000.

The tourists come from 39 states and 9 countries. The states that led in numbers of residents who were marine fishers in Florida and their percentages were Georgia (16), New York (9), Ohio (8), Pennsylvania (7), Alabama (6), and Michigan (5). Canada provided 2 percent. The main regions of fishing effort can be grouped into five coastal areas separated along county boundaries: 9 percent of the fishing took place from Escambia through Wakulla, 21 percent from Taylor through Hillsborough, and 12 percent from Sarasota through Collier. On the Atlantic side, Nassau through Brevard had 22 percent and Indian River through Monroe 36 percent of the statewide total. Over three-fourths of all recreational angling effort occurs within the territorial sea.

The participation rate in marine recreational angling is higher in Florida than in any other state along the Gulf of Mexico. There is a participant for every 4.5 persons in Florida, the high number due partly to the tourist anglers but also to the nearness of all residents to the coasts. At the same time, Florida has more persons per license than any other state because no saltwater sportfishing license is required.

Some idea of freshwater recreational fishing activity can be determined from license sales. Based on the number of licenses sold per 1,000 residents, the inland counties, particularly near Lake Okeechobee and in North Florida, show the highest rates of participation.

Concern for the Future

Some kinds of Florida's traditional seafood have reached, or soon will reach, steady state yield. For example, red snapper production has ranged between three million and five million pounds since 1970, and no biological or ecological indications suggest any substantial increase in production. Similar trends are apparent for spiny lobsters, shrimp, grouper, mackerel, and blue crab. Pertinent federal and state management schemes are in the process of setting harvest levels at optimum yields to assure continued production. Technological advances to assist harvest of traditional species may provide more efficient production, but average total annual production is not expected to increase. New technology must always be examined to see if more efficient harvests would mean fewer fishermen employed in specific fisheries. Excessive increases in production could overfish natural stocks and, for certain species, decrease profits per unit of fishing effort (overcapitalization). These concerns do not eliminate the need for fuel-efficient means of harvest, and fishing efficiency versus fishermen employment must be considered on a species basis.

Fortunately, the warm, extensive Florida coast provides access to a large variety of new or nontraditional seafood resources. Currently available and underutilized species include a vast array of pelagic and ground fishes, certain mollusks, and deep-sea crustaceans. Estimates for the Gulf and South Atlantic region show an annual stock of nonused species in excess of 9 billion pounds. Assuming its participation in developing unused fishery resources at the same level as traditional production in the Southeast, Florida has potential access to over 2.5 billion pounds annually of new seafood resources. These nontraditional resources offer the greatest opportunity for increasing production and value in the Florida seafood industry.

Concern with the productivity of estuaries is especially high in Florida. Ninety-four percent of the value of the Gulf of Mexico commercial catch (98 percent in 1970) consisted of estuarine-dependent species (McHugh, 1976), only the Chesapeake Bay region having a higher percentage. Most economists agree that biological research has not adequately defined the quantitative relationship of fishing output response to availability of marsh. Since no marsh probably means no fish, most biologists estimate the value of the marsh to be high. At this point there may still be sufficient marsh to maintain adequate fishery production, but the problem needs attention as people continue to build in the coastal zones.

Many believe that Florida fisheries are declining: between 21 and 50 percent of polled sports fishermen in Florida thought there were declines in stocks of snappers, sea trout, grouper, king mackerel, dolphin, and catfish (Bell, 1982), with water pollution and habitat destruction seen as the main reasons.

The basic problem will become one of political and economic allocation. Like many common property resources, fisheries can be used without cost. No user has the exclusive right to the resource, nor can others be excluded from its use. When the resources become limited and the users compete for available fish, no market exists to allocate them and the political system must solve the problem. Not only is this true for the competition between the fishermen themselves but also for that between the fishermen and coastal developers.

User groups often want to use economic impact estimates as a tool in allocation. Extreme care must be taken in using this kind of estimate. Optimum allocation of resources should result in a position where the last unit allocated to each group brings identical benefits, so that one group's having a larger economic impact does not mean that it should receive a larger allocation. For example, in a highly developed fishery, the economic impact of reallocation could occur by taking incremental amounts of the fishery from the recreational sector and giving them to the commercial. Recreational fishermen may still participate (assuming the incremental change is small), and the "new" fish in the commercial sector create value as they are traded in the market.

There are other uses of our resources that are related to fisheries and habitat. In 1981, Florida ranked first nationally in the dollar value of boat and motor sales. The number of recreational boats registered in the state increased by 360,000 (298 percent), to 480,864, from 1964 to 1981. Florida's market accounted for 10.5 percent of national retail sales of boats, motors, trailers, and marine accessories in 1980. Retail sales for marine recreation in Florida were

$845 million in 1981. Approximately 55 percent of the registered boats in Florida are under 16 feet; only 5 percent are over 26 feet.

In 1981 there were 482 private and 27 public marinas in Florida, representing 24,000 wetslips and 20,000 dry storage spaces. An undetermined number of additional berthing facilities exist in the form of private homeowner docks and docks for boats associated with condominiums, motels, hotels, and private clubs. Studies indicate almost total utilization with pressures expected to grow.

Conclusions

Marine products represent an important part of Florida's economy in several ways. The industry there contributes to the national food supply. Its producers have extensive investments in boats and equipment, thus boosting those industries, and they themselves employ a considerable number of people. Marine products are important to the tourist industry and to recreational activities. To protect and accommodate these functions requires coordination of federal and state policies through various federally sponsored councils and through still other governmental organizations.

References

Bell, F. *The Economic Impact and Valuation of Saltwater Recreational Fisheries in Florida*. Sea Grant Report no. 47. Gainesville, 1982.

Centaur Management Consultants. *Economic Activity Associated with Marine Recreational Fishing*. Washington, 1977.

Florida Department of Commerce. *Florida 1977 Tourist Study.* Tallahassee, 1977.

McHugh, J. L. "Estuarine Fisheries: Are They Doomed?" In *Estuarine Processes,* 1:15–27. New York: Academic Press, 1976.

Prochaska, F. J., and Cato, J. C. *An Economic Profile of Florida Commercial Fishing Firms: Fishermen, Commercial Activities and Financial Consideration*. Sea Grant Report no. 19. Gainesville, 1977.

Smith, F. S. *The Fisherman's Business Guide*. Camden, Maine: International Marine Publishing Company, 1975.

Florida's Extractive Industries: Mining

18C

by Manning J. Dauer

UNIVERSITY OF FLORIDA

Income from mining in Florida totaled $1.9 billion in 1981. Mining falls low on the scale of contribution by industry to Florida's annual income, considerably lower than tourism, agriculture, manufacturing, real estate and banking, construction, transportation, and governmental services. But the value of Florida's mineral production increased greatly in the seventies.

Oil and natural gas production account for an annual income of $870 million. The severance tax on oil and gas contributes $50 million annually to state income, and the total severance tax on all minerals (including oil and gas) comes to $80 million a year. While the dollar value of oil production in Florida looms large in the state's mineral production, it is not large in relation to national oil output. Discoveries of oil in Florida have centered in two areas. Plans have been projected for possible offshore drilling both in the Gulf of Mexico and in the Atlantic Ocean, and exploration of possible drilling sites has been made in national forests, such as the Ocala National Forest. These plans present conservation and pollution problems, but so far none has become serious.

Next in contribution to state income is the production of phosphates, an important component of fertilizer. Florida is the leading phosphate producer in the United States and one of the leaders in world production. A 1972–74 agreement between Armand Hammer, representing Occidental Petroleum Corporation, and the USSR launched a major exporting business to supply Russia with phosphoric acid for fertilizer. In return, American farmers will receive equal value in ammonia and other fertilizer components from the USSR. In 1980, following the USSR's invasion of Afghanistan, President Jimmy Carter placed an embargo on the shipment of Florida's phosphates and phosphoric acid to the USSR. This embargo was lifted by President Reagan.

Other important minerals produced in Florida are limerock (among other things, an important component in the manufacture of Portland cement in Florida, itself a $100 million annual enterprise), certain rare clays and earths, and building rock, sand, and gravel.

Problems exist in these areas of Florida's economy, principally that of a limited amount of minerals. Unlike agricultural products, mineral deposits will ultimately be exhausted. Moreover, the discovery of minerals in Florida at the close of the last century produced mining practices that left the land scarred with open pits. Phosphate and limerock mining in Florida involve stripping the topsoil and then extracting the rock, which is found some feet below the surface. Massive craters are thus produced. However, limerock and phosphate companies, under pressures in the 1960s, have since spent millions of dollars in reclaiming mine areas and in recontouring the land, and returning it to agricultural, recreational, or developmental use. Further, in 1971 a severance tax of 5 percent on pit value of mined phosphate was enacted by the legislature. Half or more of this tax is rebated to the company for satisfactory land reclamation practices. In 1980 the governor proposed legislation to require submission of advance plans for recontouring before strip-mining operations may begin.

There exist other types of problems from phosphate production: extensive use of large amounts of water, emission of toxic fumes such as fluorides and particulates, both causing air pollution, and the production of waste products, slime and sludge, which contaminate nearby land areas, rivers, and streams. All of these problems have led to intense political battles.

As Florida's population increases, competition for water resources arises among city populations, agricultural enterprises, and the mining industries. To help resolve these problems, the legislature passed the Florida Land and Water Management Act in 1972, dividing the state into five water management districts that allocate water quantity among competing users, and the phosphate industry is cleaning and returning for reuse a considerable amount of the water it uses.

Air pollution problems, especially from fluoride emissions, created a long-running battle in the 1950s and 1960s between environmentalists and industrialists. Seeking resolutions, the Florida Department of Health and Rehabilitative Services, and later the Department of Environmental Regulation, developed air pollution regulations and began to monitor air quality. In turn, phosphate companies have spent millions of dollars to install many types of air pollution control devices.

The problem of output of slime and sludge was alleviated by the enactment of state standards for the holding dams that impound such waste, to prevent runoff into neighboring land, rivers, and swamps. Companies are fined and are required to pay for cleanup work if these dams break.

New problems involving Florida mining emerged in the 1970s. For example, some of the land reclamation projects—although eliminating unsightly pits and craters and even contributing to new housing areas—have created one problem while solving another. Phosphate rock has some radioactivity, and the uncovering and mining of deposits leaves the land area emitting certain amounts of radon gas. The amounts emitted in the open air are probably not harmful. But if a formerly mined area is made into a real estate project and Florida-style residences are erected, with a concrete slab on the ground, the inhabitants of the residences are then exposed to some radon gas. While the level is not high, continual exposure over a period of years raises the possibility of cancer. New

Phosphate dragline. This excavator deposits the ore in a pit, where it is broken up by high pressure water and liquefied. The slurry is then pumped by pipeline to a plant where the phosphate is separated from sand and clay in the ore. The water is recycled and reused. State law requires that land from which phosphates have been mined must be reclaimed. Florida's phosphate mining and processing account for one-third of the world's production and are the third largest industry in Florida.

standards will probably be developed to wrap such concrete slabs in impenetrable plastic to prevent contamination. The extent of the problem is under investigation.

Another newly discovered problem is that of diseases developed by workers in phosphate mining. In September 1979 eighteen phosphate companies underwrote a three-year, comprehensive study under the auspices of the University of North Carolina, to survey workers in various phases of phosphate operations, report on any increase in diseases, and make recommendations for corrective action.

The pumping of water for extraction of minerals and other uses has produced problems because the water table is lowered and part of the surface then collapses (portions of the Florida land surface cover limestone caves, some of which were formerly filled with water). When the surface gives way in this manner, it creates what is known as a sinkhole. However, this phenomenon is not a major threat and has rarely caused serious damage.

Starting in the 1960s, conservation programs of the phosphate industry became sophisticated. Forecasting future uses of mine sites, actual excavation areas for draglines now anticipate later plans for reclamation; for example, the deepest part of a pit can be planned so that when the mining operation is over, it can be transformed into a lake surrounded by a golf course. Also, to avoid air pollution, stacks as high as 400 feet and scrubbers have been installed in phosphate-processing plants.

Florida is the leading source of phosphate for American fertilizers and, as a leading exporter, contributes heavily to food production not only in Florida but also in the nation and in foreign countries. High development of technology in the field does not make phosphate and other Florida mining a labor-intensive industry, and for labor there are some health hazards, which are now under scrutiny. However, Florida's mining industry makes a positive contribution not only to the state's economy but also to the agricultural industry of the United States.

There is a controversy developing over the amount of phosphate reserves. The U.S. Bureau of Mines estimates only 3.5 billion additional tons in proven reserves, which could be as little as a 20-year supply of fertilizer for U.S. agriculture. The phosphate industry estimates a 12 billion ton reserve, probably counting lower quality ores. But even this means a limited supply. What then of American export policy? Could we develop a shortage to match that in our oil supplies, one that affects our food supply? Should our exports be controlled?

Summary

Mining in Florida makes an increasing contribution to the state's economy. The modest level of oil production is important. Limerock and cement production contribute significantly to cement manufacture for industry and for road building. Phosphate plays an important role in American agriculture. Deposits, particularly of the nonmetallic minerals, are sufficiently great that these industries may be expected to continue indefinitely. At the same time, to accommodate such industries calls for considerable planning by the government and by industry to protect the environment.

References

Blakely, A. Fredric. *The Florida Phosphate Industry*. Cambridge: Wertheim Committee, Harvard University, 1973.

Considine, Bob. *The Remarkable Life of Dr. Armand Hammer*. New York: Harper and Row, 1975.

Mineral Yearbook. Washington: U.S. Government Printing Office, annual.

Yon, J. William, and Oglesby, W. R. "Florida Mining Industry." In *Florida Handbook*.

Government and Education

by Ralph Kimbrough, Kern Alexander,
and James Wattenbarger

UNIVERSITY OF FLORIDA

19

Education is primarily a development process of the capabilities of each individual. Much of this development is generated by the individual. The family also makes contributions. But in an increasingly complex society the role of the school has become extremely significant.

Moreover, the individual may be deprived if his or her capabilities are not developed. Part of this deprivation will affect employment and the making of a living. In addition, if an appreciation of reading and other cultural areas is not developed, the individual cannot enjoy as broad a range of experience nor lead as rich a life as he or she might have. Individuals who develop their capacities fully can better participate in society and in government.

In the United States, providing strong and effective programs of public education has for many years been a high-priority function of state government. The continuity, even the very survival, of a free democratic society is dependent on an educational program that is consistent with the democratic values it teaches. Because our society relies heavily on our schools to transmit our civic values (as well as other kinds of values) to every younger generation, with the control of education goes the power to lead the people.

Democratic values, however, are not the inevitable fruits of education. Within this century the world has seen the use of the power of education by totalitarian regimes to further their antidemocratic goals. Adolf Hitler first demonstrated how a regimented state public school system may be used to further extreme reactionary ideas. Stalin used the Soviet school system to indoctrinate the young to accept a brutal dictatorship. One of the highest priorities of the Castro regime in Cuba has been to establish a strong public educational program dedicated to furthering Communism.

In addition to their essential contributions to transmitting the values of our democratic society, the public schools, colleges, and universities in the United States contribute enormously to the general welfare of the people. Without an educated citizenry our complex industrial, urban society would eventually collapse. Community leaders interested in economic and industrial development soon realize how a strong public school system and a strong college and university system contribute to meeting their objectives. In concert with other institutions of our society, our schools and colleges contribute significantly to the "good life," a fact well recognized by many Americans.

Yet citizens sometimes overlook the fact that the schools are in interaction with the society generally. What the educational leadership seeks to accomplish through its institutions is heavily conditioned by the very society those institutions serve. When the schools seek to maintain high levels of training for the young or to advance knowledge through research, their interest is the common well-being of our society, not the aggrandizement of their institutions.

It is not surprising to find that the ills of society are quickly reflected in our schools. A community whose system of governance is ailing is very likely to have an inadequate school system. The schools can seldom surpass the expectations of the citizens they serve if those expectations are poorly reflected in the larger system of civic institutions and governance of which the schools are but a part. How the schools, colleges, and universities of Florida are organized and governed to respond to the needs and expectations of Florida's citizens is the subject of this chapter.

The Development of Elementary and Secondary Education in Florida

As it has been in other states, educational progress in Florida has been marked by sharp ups and downs, by significant, unique events that have reshaped subsequent arrangements for public education. These watersheds in the development of public education are to a great extent responses to the political, economic, and certain social conditions of their times — whenever education is perceived as the mechanism through which social needs are properly addressed and satisfied.

Public education in Florida was born out of a political response to the transfer of sovereignty from Spain to the United States in 1821. The requirement was made that public lands be set aside to endow public education even though Florida was still a territory. Economic conditions were such by 1845, the year of statehood, that Florida could not support the public schools centrally, and as a result the legislature authorized the state's first local property taxes.

As the great fever of the Civil War and its aftermath swept the nation from the mid-1850s to the late 1870s, public education in Florida was virtually ignored. The new state constitution of 1885 marked the beginning of a period of importance for public education in Florida; it provided for the election of a state superintendent of public instruction. By the turn of the century, the school system had progressed rapidly under the positive leadership of the state superintendent's office. During this period the principle of compulsory education was established, and some uniformity of curriculum and of textbooks was attained. The movement toward uniformity led to the conference in Gainesville in 1918 that produced the first general course of study for elementary and secondary schools. In spite of this progress, however, the schools suffered greatly from the economic and political conditions that produced the depression of the 1930s and World War II.

In Florida, as in most states, a new surge of interest in education came about immediately after the war. In 1945, with the approval of the legislature, the governor appointed a Citizens' Committee on Education to make an intensive two-year study of education in the state. The resulting report laid bare the poor and even desperate condition of the schools. To alleviate the pervasive undernourishment of education, immediate and significant steps were taken. Under the political leadership of Governor Millard F. Caldwell and state Senator LeRoy Collins, Professors R. L. Johns and Edgar L. Morphet devised the Minimum Foundation Program, which, when enacted into law in 1947, provided a high standard of educational adequacy and equality for nearly three decades. This law established a mechanism whereby the state determined realistically the educational needs of local school districts and provided a reasonable level of funding to all schoolchildren regardless of whether the schools they attended were in rich or poor school districts. The 1947 legislation signaled a new era of education in Florida that continues today.

No single event in the history of education in Florida or the nation as a whole has equaled the impact of the decision of the U. S. Supreme Court in 1954 in *Brown* v. *Board of Education,* a great landmark in the history of federalism. The effects of the ruling — which rejected the doctrine of "separate but equal" facilities or programs — on public education and on social conditions of the country generally will resound for many generations. Slowly and not without further struggles, American blacks have used the opportunities opened to them by the Court's decision to move into the mainstream of American life. As previous discriminatory practices in public education were outlawed, an expanding interest in other areas of denial of civil rights, such as housing and labor, has further affected the schools. Before *Brown* a child's attendance at the public school was thought of as a privilege and not as a right. This attitude has changed, and equal protection and due process of law now thoroughly protect the child's educational interests. This case set off a great movement, which extended beyond matters of race and brought about a judicial concern for social justice (though possibly, in some cases, overreaction has occurred) and which has led to an entirely new environment for the interactions of students, parents, teachers, school administrators, and lawmakers. In the vast area of legislation and judge-made law, at least four areas of important changes may be identified: desegregation, procedural due process for students, teachers' rights, and changes in methods of financing education.

The Desegregation Movement

A hundred years after the Civil War, America's blacks were still denied civic equality. The history of repression of blacks by whites was similar all across the American South, including Florida. The state's educational system progressed little during Reconstruction. With the reemergence of educational progress in the 1880s and 1890s came the notorious Jim Crow laws. The great debate over legal segregation of public facilities was etched into stone in 1896 by the U. S. Supreme Court in *Plessy* v. *Ferguson,* wherein the court embraced the Massachusetts principle of separate-but-equal and sanctified it as the law of the land.

After this decision, Florida's school systems settled into a dual pattern of education. By the school year 1926–27 this pattern had produced marked discrimination. The average monthly salary for white male teachers that year was $176, but the black male teacher earned only $88. The average length of that school year was 160 days for white children but only 123 days for black children. Some counties had even greater disparities: in Gilchrist County white children attended school 157 days per year but black children only 30 days per year. By the time of the *Brown* decision in 1954, discrimination, though less severe than in the 1920s, still offered the black student schooling that was inferior in quantity and quality.

From *Brown* emerged frantic efforts to provide more equal but still separate facilities. The implementation decision in this case, *Brown II* (1955), produced the standard of "with all deliberate speed," which became a watchword for delay. However, as the state moved into the 1960s, delusions of separatism soon passed. The Civil Rights Act of 1964 clearly expressed the position of the U. S. Congress, and by the end of the decade the Supreme Court in a resounding decision in *Alexander* v. *Holmes* removed all possibility of further delay by declaring that Florida and all other southern states must become desegregated "immediately." The deadline of 1 February 1970 was set for every school district in the state to redistribute children among the schools in such a manner as to remove all vestiges of past *de jure* segregation. By resorting primarily to busing, all school districts redistributed their pupils in accordance with the Supreme Court's mandate. Although some disputes continued thereafter in a few school districts, the public school system in Florida was formally and legally desegregated.

Procedural Due Process for Students

Most people agree that the individual is entitled to rudimentary fair play when dealing with the government. Fundamental fairness is not a new idea; philosophers have discussed it for over 2,000 years. For the English-speaking world, the Magna Charta in 1215 first set forth the principle of fairness as a restraint on government. Since that time, considerations of the rights of man, natural justice, and the right of the individual to be heard against his or her government have ennobled Western letters.

Yet it was not until 1961 that to be entitled to a hearing was considered a fundamental right of children in public schools. Procedural due process guaranteed by the Fourteenth Amendment was not extended to administrative hearings in education until the landmark case of *Dixon* v. *Alabama* (1961). Here for the first time the federal courts held that a student must be given the opportunity to have a hearing before his or her suspension or expulsion from a public educational institution. In 1963 a Florida court adopted this rule for the public education system of Florida; it held that before dismissal from school a student must be given adequate notice and the opportunity for a fair and impartial hearing.

These cases had a far-reaching impact on the conduct of the schools. Suddenly students were viewed as having rights rather than privileges; teachers and school administrators were forced to observe certain procedural rules when they took action against a student that could result in a significant detriment to the student's educational progress. Recent court decisions have further guaranteed these rights of students by holding that a school official or administrator who fails to use fair procedures may be personally liable for damages.

Recognition of Teachers' Rights

Teachers' rights have not gone unnoticed by the courts. To the contrary, their interests and liberties have been expanded substantially beyond the academic freedoms that have always been inherent in classroom instruction. Gone are the days when Florida school board members could require that a newly hired female teacher remain single, refrain from wearing powder or eye make-up, or remain publicly silent on the civic issues raised in a school board election. It was not until 1968 that the Supreme Court laid down rules that allow a teacher to express openly his or her personal political beliefs. No longer do teachers shed their constitutional rights when they enter the school building; they possess all the rights and immunities of other citizens in or outside public employment. Teachers may comment editorially in newspapers on current political issues without fear of reprisal from offended board members or powerful citizens.

The new era of teacher independence and assertiveness has seen the advance of the collective bargaining movement. In 1968, the same year in which the Supreme Court assured teachers of their basic political rights in the landmark case of *Pickering* v. *Board of Education,* Florida teachers launched a statewide strike that involved over 35,000 public schoolteachers. This was the first such statewide teachers' strike in the nation, and the repercussions from this episode still echo throughout the state. The collective bargaining movement has probably had as profound an effect on the conduct of the public schools as has any other single event — except desegregation — in Florida public school history.

A single strike, however, does not establish a movement of such crucial consequences without important contributing circumstances. Florida's new constitution of 1968 stated that "The right of employees, by and through a labor organization, to bargain collectively shall not be abridged." Even though this same section of the new constitution specifically forbade public employees from striking, it opened the door for lawful labor organization and collective bargaining in the public sector. Subsequent Florida Supreme Court action interpreted the new constitutional provision to guarantee a public employee "the right to bargain as a member of a union or labor organization. . . ." Later, the court further identified the right of public schoolteachers to bargain collectively with the right of nongovernmental employees to do so, except that governmental employees could not lawfully strike. This court decision compelled the legislature to enact a collective bargaining law for public employees.

Shortly after the collective bargaining law was enacted, teachers across the state, following statutory procedure, organized and elected their bargaining agents, opening a new era for the public schools of Florida. The relationship between schoolteachers and school administrators, previously seen as cooperative, became an adversary one: lines were carefully drawn between manager and employee in contracts negotiated by labor unions on behalf of teachers. The precise effect of this change on education is still uncertain, but collective bargaining is going to play a pervasive role in the future development of public schools.

Recent Developments in Financing Public Schools

The great movement for equality initiated by the *Brown* decision has continued to expand; it has touched nearly every aspect of the educational program. Monetary resources to implement changes were essential, so it was natural that school funding should come under careful scrutiny. In the milestone year 1968, several cases were launched in the nation's courts to bring about more equal funding among school districts. Complainants in all cases alleged violations of the Fourteenth Amendment and of various provisions for equal educational opportunity in state constitutions. Although in Florida suits the plaintiffs did not win, in other states the courts did hold that methods of school funding then in use were defective under state constitutions. The most famous, a California case (*Serrano* v. *Priest,* 1971), found that the state's entire system of school financing was unconstitutional. Ultimately, the Supreme Court was to hold that differentials in available educational resources among school districts were not discriminatory in a way that would make the equal protection clause apply to state methods of school funding. By this time, however, the controversy had caused most legislatures to reexamine their formulas for state aid to local schools; Florida was no exception.

During the early seventies, the Florida Department of Education and the Florida legislature authorized two major studies of the state's system of educational finance. One study was undertaken by the National Educational Finance Project, University of Florida, and the other by the Schultz Commission. Both reports recommended changes that more adequately identified educational needs and increased fiscal equalization among school districts. Each study built on the framework of the 1947 Minimum Foundation Program. The result, in 1973, was a new law, the Florida Education Finance Program (FEFP). Instead of basing state aid on the number of classrooms or teachers to establish the minimum educational program, a new method was devised that gave weight to the number of pupils. Students are counted (in terms of full-time equivalents, or FTEs), and differential costs are assigned to different types of instructional programs. The amount of state aid to local systems is then based on the difference between the sum needed and the sum collected locally through property taxes.

An important effect of the new formula was increased fiscal equalization that resulted from requiring a 7-mill minimum for local property taxes. Fiscal equalization was further enhanced in 1974 by setting the maximum at 8 mills and the minimum at about 6.4 mills.

The new formula of local taxing plus equalizing state assistance based on measured needs created greater uniformity of educational funding among all school districts. The quality of a child's education thus depended less on the property values or tax assessment philosophies of the local school district. Under this new program, Florida had one of the most nearly equalized educational systems in the country. Other states looked to Florida's new system of funding equalization as an example; its effects were widely studied, discussed, and in some cases emulated.

The equalization effect of the FEFP can be illustrated by observing its effects on two school districts, one wealthy and one very poor. In 1979 Glades County had over $100,000 of assessed valuation of property per full-time equivalent pupil, whereas Gadsden had only about $17,000. The state finance program corrects for this disparity in local wealth by providing over $800 per full-time equivalent pupil to Gadsden County while providing only about $300 to the more affluent Glades. While the inherent differential in wealth between the two counties is about 7 to 1, the available school dollars from state and local sources combined differ only by about 1.3 to 1.

The attractiveness of the new financing structure was somewhat obscured by the economic recession of 1974, which cut into available funding. Any good fiscal system must be judged according to at least three criteria: accommodation of differing educational needs, fiscal equalization, and adequacy of funding. Structurally, the new system provided for the first two criteria very well, but as the state's economy cooled, projected increases in the state's general fund did not materialize and the entire educational system was left seriously underfunded. So acute was the problem that by 1978 the state's school system had not recovered from the lack of fiscal resources. The rollback in the local school levy from 10 to 8 mills and the failure of the state general fund to perform as expected left the public schools in a financial straitjacket. Various studies of the day indicated that in 1978 Florida's tax effort for education was one of the lowest in the nation. Depending on the particular measures used, the state ranked between forty-fifth and fiftieth in tax effort to support elementary and secondary schools.

In 1979 the Florida legislature further increased state control over both content and funding of public schools. It appropriated some additional funds but required that they be used for kindergartens and for basic education in grades one through three. The 1980 increase of the homestead exemption to $25,000 gravely compounded schools' and local governments' fiscal problems. The resulting increased millage assessments on remaining taxable property have stimulated demand for an added one cent sales tax to replace lost local revenue. The amendment that increased the homestead exemption for school tax purposes only also extended the exemption to renters who are permanent residents. The legislature is empowered to raise the exemption to partially offset inflation. Annual local budget increases may not be greater than 5 percent, exclusive of income from new construction on the tax rolls. The overall effect is to further reduce local tax revenue sources.

Distressingly, Florida did not perform much better in supporting its higher-education system. After an analysis of comparative financial statistics among the states, Ralph B. Thompson in *The Financial Status of the State University System,* concluded that in 1978 Florida ranked forty-second among the states in its efforts to support higher education.

While the Florida legislature has retained a commitment to free public schools, in higher education it has moved to increase the amount of tuition charged to the college student. In Florida, state university tuition has reached the highest level of any southeastern state. A rationale is that poorer students can borrow money or may receive scholarships. However, the net result is to create debt problems for many young adults who then must repay loans. The original Jeffersonian idea of the state university as being free for those with ability who could not pay is being altered, and this ultimately can be expected to make social mobility more difficult. Ironically, the Western European and Scandinavian democracies have moved in the opposite direction since World War II; for example, in the 1970s German universities abolished all tuition fees.

Changing Politics and the Control of Education in Florida

Consistent with the national pattern, the Florida system for administering education in kindergarten through twelfth grade is decentralized. Federal influence is present in a variety of programs funded by Congress. Even though education is a state function, there are thus federal, state, and local controls over public education. Because Florida's structure for the administration of public education is very different from the general administrative pattern elsewhere in the United States, there is debate about it and whether it should be changed.

During the 1960s there was a transformation of the political process for control of education in Florida. The system, particularly in financial support, has not fared well following these political changes. Before this political transformation the control of education at the state level was what one observer (Iannaccone, 1967) referred to as a statewide monolithic system.

The Florida legislature was dominated by representatives from rural areas, the so-called pork chop gang. Rural dominance was not unique to Florida; most state legislative positions were not equitably apportioned before the one-person–one-vote ruling by the Supreme Court (see chapter 6). Educational leaders tended to interact directly with the legislative leaders in the development and passage of educational legislation. Leaders of the educational establishment, particularly those concerned with legislation for the public schools (grades K through 12), were largely drawn from prominent figures in the teachers' association, school superintendents, the state Department of Education, and a few leading university people. Within this monolithic legislative establishment there was, of course, conflict and competition, but such pressures were conveniently controlled.

During the early 1960s pressures were building. Competition between urban and rural interests was noticeable. Teachers were becoming more militant and were moving toward unionization. Several events during the 1967–70 period resulted in a final break in the bonds that held the old order together and produced a transformation that survives today. Among these events were legislative reapportionment, constitutional revision, governmental reorganization, the rise of a two-party system, the increased effectiveness of black voters, the statewide teachers' strike in 1968, a tremendous increase in federal education programs passed by Congress, and court action on racial desegregation. The failure of the teachers' strike served to fragment educational groups, a process that had been building for several years before 1968.

In the breakup of the old order, power over education was "up for grabs." The legislature came out the winner. Although there was an attempt to strengthen the office of the governor through the 1969 reorganization act, the legislature clearly thrust itself forward as the primary policy maker in Florida education. This was accomplished in part by a rather dramatic shift toward year-round committee operation coupled with annual meetings and sizable increases in salaries. The most powerful control, however, came through the employment of many full- and part-time staff specialists in major fields of government. Impressive numbers of people were employed to assist in the study, development, and preparation of educational bills. This burst of activity meant increased loads on state Department of Education personnel to furnish information for legislative committee work. As a consequence, the legislature, using its own extensive advisory staff system, relied less frequently on educational specialists outside its own system for major legislation. Those interested in influencing educational legislation found that lobbying the educational staff of the legislature was as important as lobbying the legislators themselves.

This growth of legislative power was accompanied by an alarming loss of power among other leaders interested in educational improvement, whose concerns became divided. For example, in 1979 there was intense conflict between two teachers' associations, affiliates of the National Education Association and of the American Federation of Teachers. School administrators have formed an umbrella group, the Florida Association of School Administrators, to represent their interests. Other groups interested in educational legislation, such as the Florida School Boards Association and parents' groups, no longer identify closely with teachers' interests. As a result of this fragmentation, educators have had little influence over educational legislation during the period 1970–83. As discussed earlier, Florida's level of financial support for education has not kept pace with that of many other states.

The State Board of Education and the Commissioner of Education

The state control of school administration resides in a somewhat unusual ex officio Board of Education (see fig. 19.1). Only one other state in the nation (Mississippi) places the educational system under an ex officio board, although one or two officials may serve as ex officio members in a number of states. In Florida the governor and members of the elected cabinet (secretary of state, attorney general, treasurer and insurance commissioner, comptroller, commissioner of agriculture, commissioner of education) serve as the state Board of

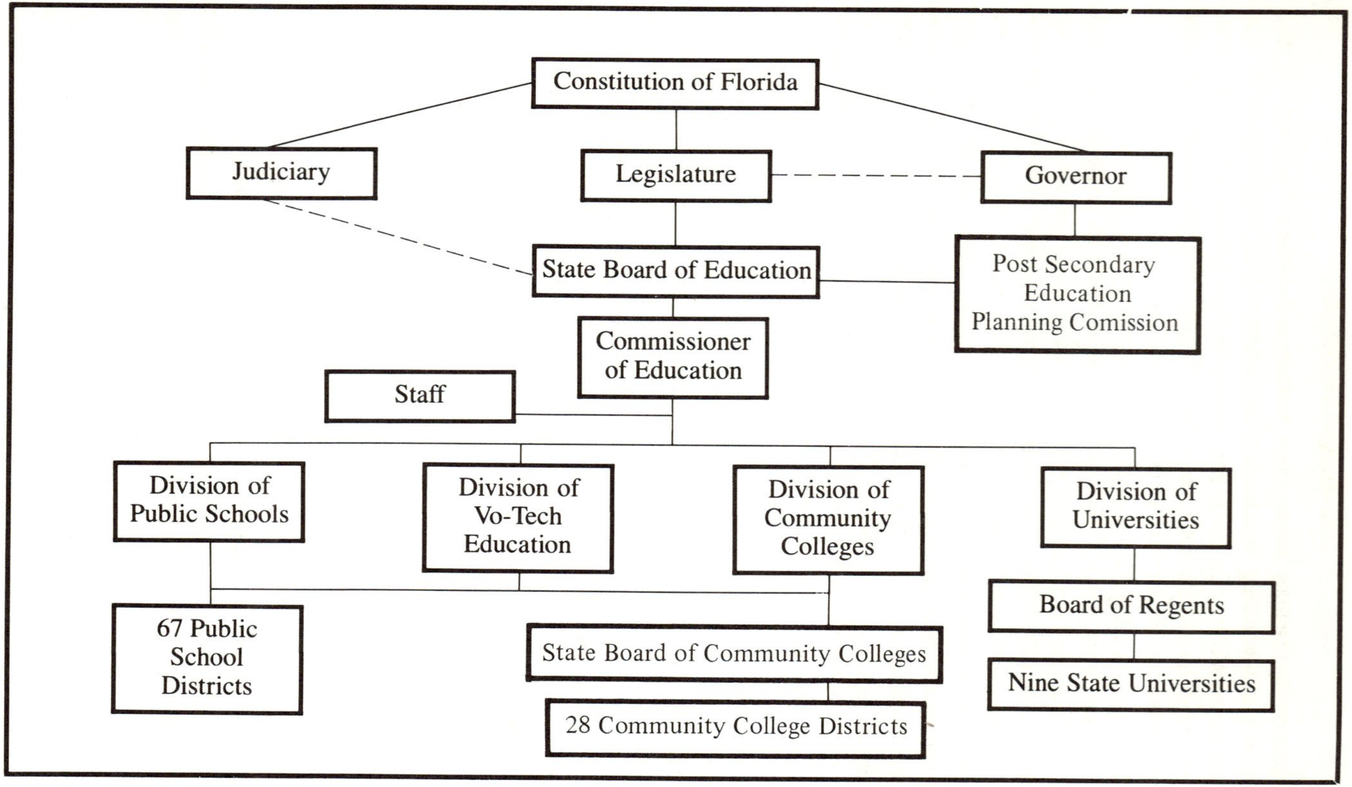

Fig. 19.1. State Control of Education in Florida.

Education by virtue of their offices. In most states (thirty-two in 1972) members of the state Board of Education are appointed by the governor; in fifteen other states they are elected. In these states the boards serve the sole function of controlling the state educational system, whereas the Florida cabinet serves many governmental functions.

Since the Florida board is so unusual, it is reasonable to ask how well it functions. Florida's educational governance was analyzed by Frank DePalma in the Educational Governance Project, parallel studies of twelve states conducted by Ohio State University personnel. His findings on the function of the ex officio board were not complimentary.

To understand the nature of the cabinet system in Florida, one must realize that the members are chosen in statewide elections and that they provide administrative services in such areas as agriculture, banking and finance, education, and insurance. The cabinet sits as ten different boards with ten different agendas. In practice the cabinet members responsible for specific board functions (e.g., education) prepare the agenda for that board. DePalma found the board meetings to be perfunctory and routine. Each member has special interests in obtaining positive action on agenda items; thus a kind of "I'll scratch your back if you'll scratch mine" practice prevails. Each member is given a great deal of autonomy in the governmental area he or she administers. Consequently, educational items on the agenda are heavily influenced by the commissioner of education. Practically all of the commissioner's recommendations are approved. Moreover, the large volume of cabinet business means that very little time may be devoted to items making up the agenda, resulting in superficial examination of important educational proposals. With the exception of the commissioner of education, cabinet members generally avoid participating in educational matters.

This unusual system also means that the commissioner of education sits on many other boards and participates in many decisions completely outside the field of education. The power of the commissioner of education to sit as a voting member of the state Board of Education is a source of much political control over the administration of education in Florida. Since the commissioner must run for office, he or she must build a strong statewide political organization; this becomes another source of political power. The commissioner of education also heads the state bureau for administering the state educational program, the Department of Education. Since the administrative process involves significant decisions, this is an additional source of influence because the commissioner dominates the politics of the bureaucracy.

The Department of Education is the administrative agency for the state program as established by the legislature and the state Board of Education. Within the department are specialists in every area of education (e.g., curriculum and instruction, finance and business services, school plant facilities, personnel, student services, and many others). Thus the department is charged with the administration of many large and complex educational programs in Florida, and it is of necessity a very large and complex organization.

Some Reflections on the State System

Much has been written about the wisdom of retaining the state's present system of education. Various changes have been proposed, but few significant changes have been acceptable. In the November 1978 election, proposals to amend the constitution and make important changes in the system were overwhelmingly defeated. Among these proposals were a separate Board of Education, appointment of the cabinet, and appointment of the commissioner of education. These changes faced the voters as part of a long, complicated list of constitutional amendments, including a controversial referendum on casino gambling. Political analysts feel that the electorate, confused and alienated by the long list of amendments, turned them all down, regardless of merit.

Most authorities in educational management feel that the Florida system is in need of reorganization and change. As indicated previously, the cabinet Board of Education does not really consider educational policy in depth, leaving this function largely to the discretion of the commissioner of education. The fact that the commissioner doubles as a policy maker and executive violates the principle of separation between policy making and administration. When the people vote for the cabinet, they are not voting for a Board of Education; they are selecting a secretary of state, an attorney general, a treasurer and insurance commissioner, a comptroller, a commissioner of agriculture, a commissioner of education, and a governor. Thus direct participation of the people in electing representatives to set state educational policies is difficult except insofar as that responsibility is fixed on the commissioner of education.

Many authorities insist that a separate lay state Board of Education should be selected through appointment or popular election. There is some difference of opinion on whether board members should be elected or appointed; the method used in most states is appointment by the governor. This allows more time for lay citizen participation in analysis and study of educational needs and policies. The primary function of the state board should be to formulate and adopt policies and to select the chief state school officer (the commissioner of education in Florida) to administer the policies.

Some philosophical and practical problems are associated with making state boards of education function well. Within the past decade the state legislature has subsumed much political power in establishing educational policies. Thus, one of the fundamental problems of the state governance of education is how to increase lay participation and control over state education policies through increasing the power of the state Board of Education or the governor or both. In this regard the dominance of the state legislature becomes a fundamental issue for future attempts at governmental reorganization.

A further addition to the educational system was made by Governor Graham in 1980, the Postsecondary Education Planning Commission (PEPC), which was charged with developing methods of coordinating various elements of higher education. This lay board has a small professional staff. At the same time, staffs of the House and Senate Education Committees work with other education agency staffs. The outcome is that much of the legislation affecting both higher education and public schools and appropriations for both are worked on by the house staff, the senate staff, the governor's education staff, and the presiding officers of the house and senate. This procedure lessens the influence of the state Department of Education, which had been dominant in the 1960s and 1970s. In 1981 the legislature established the governor's PEPC by statute. The 1983 legislature assigned it a number of special studies related to coordinating and controlling higher education and to coordinating adult education, vocational education, community colleges, and universities.

Local Control of Education

The great increase in state and federal participation in the administration of education leaves many citizens concerned about how much power local boards of education have over school policies. Although there are reasons for this concern and there probably has been a reduction in local autonomy over the public schools, much decision-making authority still remains with local school boards.

Florida is one of only four states whose school districts follow county lines exclusively. The county is the local school district in Florida. Some other southern states that have county districts also have city and special school districts. Because it uses the county unit, Florida has only 67 school districts; a large state using the common school district may have over 1,000 districts. Most authorities believe that Florida's districting is administratively superior to that of states with many small districts.

The lay county Board of Education in Florida is elected to oversee the operation of the public schools for each district. The members of most of the districts are chosen in partisan elections for staggered terms. Special legislative acts, however, have resulted in different practices for electing board members and differences in the size of the boards. Most school districts have five-member boards; several of the urban districts have seven-member boards. Although school boards in Florida are fiscally independent (as recommended by authorities), their ability to set taxes is controlled by a limitation (ceiling) on millage.

In most of the school districts of Florida the superintendent of schools is elected, a practice long abandoned elsewhere except in the most rural districts of a few southern states. In eighteen of Florida's largest school districts, most of them urban, the county school superintendents are appointed by the county Board of Education.

The practice of electing board members and school superintendents by partisan ballots is considered archaic by most authorities. A majority of citizens and educators in the United States agree that an elected board of education should appoint the superintendent of schools. Although the so-called county school superintendents in states outside the South are elected, they do not actually operate the schools as Florida superintendents do. They are, for the most part, intermediate officials who perform clerical duties.

Charles D. Mould reported the results of a rather intensive study of the differences between elected and appointed school superintendents for seven school systems in Florida that had changed to the appointive method after 1968. He found that an overwhelming number of citizens, board members, teachers, and other administrators felt that the appointive administrations were superior to elected administrations in those districts. Resulting administrative changes were considered desirable by most authorities. Citizens interviewed felt that the appointed superintendents were as responsive to citizen opinion as were elected superintendents.

The Central Office and School Centers

The school superintendent in Florida serves as the chief executive officer of the Board of Education and heads the central office staff to administer the school program consistent with board policies, state regulations, and statutes. The larger and more complex the school district, the more complex the central administrative and supervisory unit. In large, complex central offices, there may be as many as five or more levels of supervisors and administrators (e.g., assistant superintendents, area superintendents, supervisors, directors, coordinators, and the like).

Below the central office staff are the school centers, or individual schools headed by principals. Some very large school systems (i.e., Dade County) also have area superintendents who are responsible for all public schools in a particular part of the district. The school centers serve geographic portions of the district called attendance zones. Traditionally, these attendance zones were based on the neighborhood school concept or were geographically compact attendance areas near the school. However, the two *Brown* decisions by the Supreme Court led to a variety of practices — open enrollment, pairing, and clustering to facilitate racial desegregation of the schools — that superseded the neighborhood school concept in many schools. These changes precipitated a prolonged controversy involving Florida's schools. Unfortunately, no one has accurately estimated the effects of this latest controversy on the state's schools, nor has anyone foretold the long-term consequences.

For many years, especially during the movement to consolidate the schools in the 1940s and 1950s, the state policy was to establish the "6-3-3" or "K-6-3-3" plan for the organizational pattern of school centers. That is, the aim was to establish a system of kindergarten through sixth grade in elementary schools, seventh through ninth grade in junior high schools, and tenth through twelfth grade in senior high schools. Beginning in the mid-1960s, interest grew in variations on the elementary, middle school, and high school organizations. Consequently, many school districts have adopted the concept of the middle school (sixth through eighth grades) to replace the earlier junior-high approach. In addition, a variety of vocational-technical centers, adult education centers, and alternative schools serve school district clients. In 1977 there were approximately 1.6 million children and youth enrolled in the elementary and secondary schools of Florida. Of this number approximately 137,000 were in exceptional student programs and almost 572,000 were in vocational programs. In addition to these K through 12 programs, the public schools offer a wide variety of post-secondary programs of adult and continuing education.

Recent Legislation Affecting Public Education

As part of the political transformation of the 1960s, the Florida legislature assumed considerable interest in the nature of education. Much of the resulting legislation involved the concept of accountability. For example, the legislature passed a statute in 1969 requiring that all universities be placed on a "planning-programming-budgeting" system within twelve months — an ill-advised piece of legislation that was impossible to comply with. Such legislation was appealing as a symbol of the legislature's demand for accountability of public agencies.

The interest in accountability may be seen in the passage in 1973 of the Florida Education Finance Program, which has been admired across the United States. The full-time equivalent student feature of this legislation was seen by some legislators and educators as facilitating the possibility of greater autonomy for school principals. Through school-based management, more autonomous school principals could be held more directly accountable. The legislation further directed that principals were responsible for annual written reports to parents concerning the progress of the school. A citizens' school advisory council was also required, but the legislature relented to some degree and stipulated that this could be satisfied by a districtwide advisory council. The clear expression was, however, to establish for each school a school advisory council, thus making each school accountable not only to district and state authorities but also to its local constituency as well. A recent law extends accountability to universities and colleges, requiring prospective teachers to take a state examination and measuring results in regard to the institutions from which they graduated.

Product-based accountability required the establishment of standards for productivity. The first such legislation required a passing score on a "functional literacy examination" for graduation from high school. The examination tested basic arithmetical and mathematical knowledge and English language and composition skills. The name of this examination was later changed to State Student Assessment Test, Part II (SSTE-II). An achievement test in reading, writing, and mathematics, known as State Student Assessment Test, Part I (SSAT-I), is administered to students in grades 3, 5, 8, and 10. To receive a high school diploma, students must reach designated standards on this test and on the minimum competency examination (SSAT-II). Remedial instruction is provided, and students have five opportunities to achieve minimum standards. Thus the primary thrust of Florida legislation has been toward a products-based accountability, which some critics feel is more useful for assembly-line production than for human service professions. For example, standard treatment-based (process) accountability (i.e., generally accepted accounting principles) is the basis of accountability in medicine and the accounting profession.

During the two years following its initial use, the SSTE-II became a controversial issue in Florida. Those favoring the use of the test insisted that it would result in improved education in Florida and that it would reorient schools toward the basics and away from trivial programs. Remedial courses helped many students improve their standing on the basic subject tests. Proponents also argued that the test requirement would hold the educational system accountable.

Opponents of the test, on the other hand, argued that it was never properly validated; consequently, they claimed, no one knew whether it was really measuring functional literacy. Strong opposition arose because of the belief that the test was racially biased. In 1978 and 1979, from the time of the initial test, remedial programs for those first failing reduced the number not passing from over 20,000 to around 4,000. Several lawsuits were filed during these years to prevent the use of the test and to allow the 4,000 seniors who had not passed the test to graduate with a diploma.

In response to a suit, a federal district judge upheld the validity of the test as not racially biased. However, because black graduating seniors had started in schools that were still segregated in the first several grades, the same suit found that these students remain the victims of earlier discrimination. Consequently the court ordered the immediate granting of high school diplomas to the 4,000 students who did not pass the test in 1979 and ruled that the withholding of diplomas could only begin with those graduating from high school in 1983 and thereafter. This 1979 decision was reaffirmed by the court in 1983, and passing the State Student Assessment Test is required for graduation. Florida has moved deeper into testing as a means to improve the level of scholarship in its educational programs. However, beginning with the 1983 legislative session, testing was coupled with the establishment of specific state curriculum standards for high school graduation.

The testing program was extended to colleges and universities through the College Level Academic Skills Test (CLAST) for college sophomores. Since August 1, 1983, college students at the sophomore level have had to score satisfactorily on the test before admission to the junior level. There has been considerable controversy over cutoff scores, some estimating that 28 percent would fail the test. Concern was expressed that a disproportionate percentage of black students might not pass it.

Based on the identification of twenty-three competencies for success as a teacher, the Florida Teacher Certification Examination was tested in 1980–82. Since July 1, 1982, all teacher education program graduates must pass this examination to be certified to teach in Florida. State law further specified that approval of individual programs at each institution is contingent upon at least 80 percent of its graduates passing the test.

In 1983 the legislature coupled this testing strategy with some stringent statewide academic requirements for high school graduation. The RAISE (Raise Achievement in Secondary Education) bill requires that by the 1986–87 school year, Florida high school students must earn a minimum of 24 credits for graduation, including four credits in English, with major concentration in composition and literature, three in mathematics, three in science, one in American history, one in world history, one-half credit each in economics, American government, vocational education, fine arts, life management skills, and physical education, and nine in electives. The far-reaching legislation contained numerous other requirements to upgrade basic instruction. For example, each school district was required to establish performance standards for each academic program in grades 9 through 12. Students graduating must have a 1.5 cumulative grade-point average on a 4.0 scale in all courses for graduation, and those participating in interscholastic extracurricular activities must maintain a 1.5 grade-point average for the semester preceding their participation.

The 1983 legislature also added provisions for the education and payment of teachers. The RAISE bill provided that at least 30 semester hours of upper division courses should be in the subject area of specialization. Some funds were appropriated for the preparation of teachers for critical areas (e.g., mathematics, science) and for in-service education in these areas. The legislature also tilted toward the concept of merit pay for teachers, a controversial proposal. A 15-member Florida Quality Instruction Incentives Council was created to assist, among various duties, in the development of a statewide merit pay plan for teachers, which, if approved, will go into effect during the 1984–85 school year.

Passage of the reform-oriented RAISE bill and accompanying legislation may have been helped by national concern for the quality of educational programs, which was stimulated by a 1983 report of the National Commission on Excellence in Education, *A Nation at Risk: The Imperative for Educational Reform*.

Higher Education

The needs of Florida's citizens relative to postsecondary education are met by two kinds of public institutions, community colleges and universities. Baccalaureate degrees and graduate study are provided through a system of universities under the operational and coordinative control of the Board of Regents. In 1984 there were nine universities; six are four-year institutions offering graduate and professional degrees in addition to the baccalaureate degree, and three offer only upper-division and limited graduate and professional study. These three, however, have been authorized to present a plan for admission of freshman and sophomore students as soon as they are ready to do so. There are 28 community colleges located in all areas of the state, providing vocational-technical or occupational education, associate degrees, and a variety of continuing education courses. They are operated by local boards of trustees, which are coordinated by the state Board of Education. The 1983 legislature created a State Board of Community Colleges which has assumed the position of director of these colleges. Almost three-fourths of the freshmen in Florida colleges begin their college work at a community college.

In addition to these collegiate institutions, many local school districts provide courses and programs for adults through vocational schools, community school programs, and adult education programs. There are also a number of proprietary schools that provide technical and business-oriented training to adults, located for the most part in urban areas. Privately supported colleges and universities complete the available educational opportunity in Florida and serve a relatively sizable group of out-of-state students as well as Florida residents.

Altogether these facilities serve a large number of persons each year; over 350,000 students were enrolled in the fall term of 1982 in the public institutions alone.

State Structure for Public Community Colleges

The state Board of Education is the top-level agency responsible for education in Florida. All four of the divisions operating under its supervision are concerned to some extent with postsecondary education. However, the Division of Community Colleges and the Division of Universities are the state agencies with major responsibility for this level of education.

The Division of Community Colleges is under the direction of a State Board of Community Colleges established by the legislature in 1983. It is comprised of eleven lay citizens appointed for five-year terms by the governor and approved by four members of the state Board of Education with confirmation by the senate in regular session. In addition the commissioner of education is an ex officio member as is one student who is registered in a public community college, who serves a one-year term.

The State Board of Community Colleges is responsible for establishing and developing rules and policies that will assure the operation and maintenance of a State Community College System subject to the approval of the State Board of Education. It appoints an executive director of the Community College System who is in charge of the board's office. The executive director and the staff are responsible for conducting systemwide program reviews and preparing a proposed legislative budget, including a three-year priority list for fixed capital outlay projects. The role of the staff of the Division of Community Colleges is to provide leadership for the 28 institutions. Other staff in the Department of Education may also work with the community colleges in special areas such as buildings, vocational and technical education, and special services.

The twenty-eight colleges are located in accord with an overall plan developed by the Community College Council in 1955–57. The plan provided for a college within commuting distance of 99 percent of the state's population and was implemented in a step-by-step fashion during the years 1957–68 by legislative authorizations. Each college district includes at least one county and in a number of instances up to four or five counties. The college is operated by a Board of Trustees with members appointed by the governor. The employment of personnel, development of the college budget, and general day-to-day operations are the responsibility of this local Board of Trustees.

The colleges are responsible for providing the first two years of a four-year baccalaureate program, and about 25 to 35 percent of entering enrollees follow this kind of program. Community colleges are also responsible for providing an increasing number of technical and vocational courses and programs. Semiprofessional and technical programs emphasize health-related occupations (nursing, dental hygiene), engineering-related occupations (civil engineering technician, chemical technician), business-related positions (data processing, midmanagement), and public service occupations (police science, fire technology). In addition many community colleges provide skills training in construction, electricity, automotive mechanics, and related areas. A third major area of curriculum concern is the great variety of courses for adult and continuing education, including courses for personal, occupational, and recreational development. Each college emphasizes the education that is considered to meet the specific and peculiar needs of the area it serves. Therefore, the program in Miami is different from that in Lake City, the common thread being basic general education and liberal arts.

The typical community college student is twenty-nine years old and is a resident of the community where the college is located. Dormitories are not provided on campus, except at one college in a rural area of the state serving statewide forestry education needs. Students who have not performed well in their previous education will find help in improving reading and mathematics skills, a major concern of the community colleges. A particularly strong emphasis is placed upon counseling by the college authorities.

The state plan has been fully implemented and will not in all likelihood be changed in the future except in minor ways. No more community colleges are envisioned. However, since accessibility is a primary consideration in community college philosophy, the multi-location college has evolved, having two or three campuses and using a number of facilities for centers all over the area served. High-school buildings, churches, shopping centers, mobile units, leased quarters of various sorts — all are used by the colleges for extending educational courses and programs. Such programs are not limited to late afternoon and evening, although the major offerings are at those times. Community groups of various interests find the colleges interested in their educational needs and willing to provide related programs.

The growth of these institutions has been rapid during the 1960s and 1970s. Full-time enrollment has tended to slow down and even decrease, however, during the late seventies. Part-time enrollment has become a predominant mode, with more part-time students than full-time students in every category.

The State University System

The Division of Universities is under the direction of the Board of Regents. The board numbers ten members who are appointed by the governor and approved by the senate. Nine regents are appointed to six-year terms; the tenth, a student member, is appointed to a one-year term. The commissioner of education is also an ex officio but participating member. The regents employ a chancellor as the chief executive officer of the State University System (SUS). Each of the nine universities is under the immediate leadership of a president, also appointed by the Board of Regents.

The staff of the regents serves in a consultative role to the operational activities of the nine universities, which in turn operate under the Board of Regents' policies and state Board of Education regulations, as well as statutes. The law is generally far more explicit in referring to the universities than it is for the community colleges.

These nine institutions include three (University of Florida, Gainesville; Florida State University, Tallahassee; and Florida A&M University, Tallahassee) that have been in operation since the mid-nineteenth century and six newly established institutions (University of South Florida, Tampa; Florida Atlantic University, Boca Raton; University of Central Florida, Orlando; University of West Florida, Pensacola; University of North Florida, Jacksonville; and Florida International University, Miami). All maintain a number of campus centers in order to extend education beyond their campuses to serve appropriately the educational needs of the entire state.

The largest institution is the University of Florida, which in the fall of 1982 enrolled more than 34,000 students. The smallest is the University of North Florida, an upper-division university and one of the newest, with 4,000 students. Fall enrollment for 1982 in the SUS was almost 135,000 students.

Baccalaureate degree programs in a variety of areas are available in each institution. Master's degree programs in limited areas are available at the new universities and in more areas at the older institutions. Doctoral degree programs are available at the University of Florida and Florida State University in a large number of fields, and in a limited number of fields at the University of South Florida, Florida Atlantic University, and the University of Central Florida. Professional degrees in law, medicine and related health areas, and other professional areas are available in one or more of the older universities. The greatest growth in adding these new opportunities occurred during the early 1960s but has slowed down in great measure since 1970.

The expansion of Florida's state university system was guided by several long-range studies, the first of which was completed in 1957. Each new unit added to the university system has been established under a plan approved by the Board of Regents and implemented by the state legislature. The extension into urban areas of university-level opportunities for training, the development of upper-division universities, and the selection of specific roles for each institution have been matters of continuing, heated discussion, sometimes over a period of more than thirty years. The most recent statement on the role and scope of the university system was adopted by the Board of Regents in 1978.

Florida's university system through its institutional research and through a number of outstanding professors has contributed directly as well as indirectly to the state's economic, political, social, and educational development. Many products (for example, frozen orange juice concentrate), human resource development, and constitutional and legal revisions (such as legislative reapportionment) have originated through the services of individuals who are members of the faculty of one of the SUS institutions.

The state university and community college systems are both under the general supervision of the state Board of Education, and they are therefore subject to the same overall policies. The emphasis from the state legislature in reflecting the general public's attitude has been placed upon accountability and the larger focus of society on job competency and personal growth. The development of role-and-scope assignments of responsibility for each university in the SUS and for the community college system is recognized as a major responsibility of the state-level leadership. This leadership in both systems has worked closely with the public in developing understanding of these roles, although not always with admirable success.

Consideration of the needs and problems of students who are moving from high school to community college to university has been formally recognized in an articulation agreement designed to assure uniform policies for transfer among the institutions and in special emphasis on the College Level Equivalency Program (CLEP), advanced placement, and other measures for encouraging progress and more rapid individual student development. The attempt to alleviate potential transfer problems has been a major effort of the professional leadership in the higher education system of Florida.

As discussed, in 1983 a College Level Academic Skills Program resulted in the develoment of a test which is administered to all college sophomores in the public community colleges and universities. This test is still in the experimental stages, although it is envisioned that a cutoff score will be established to be used as a basis for receiving the associate in arts degree and for admission to the junior level of the university system. Until this score is established, the test may be considered experimental.

Some Problems in Higher Education

There are several problems that hamper the postsecondary institutions in their assigned roles. The greatest problem is finance. During a period when national expenditures for higher education increased by 32 percent, Florida's expenditures per student decreased by 22 percent. While there are several special factors that affect the attitude in Florida toward financial support for education — such as the large in-migration of a diverse population in which a large number of persons are over sixty years of age and have grown children in other states —

negative national attitudes toward higher education during the 1970s have also had their effect in this state. The continued undersupport for Florida's university system and community colleges can result in only one outcome — the deterioration of the systems. Other state services have also needed increased resources, but the long-range results of underfinancing higher education may have more lasting influence on Florida's future economic and resource development than it would in any other area.

Another, somewhat related problem is the duplication and rivalry that often develops between local school districts and community college districts. This duplication is expensive to the state and is caused by local high schools and community colleges offering educational programs for persons past the age of eighteen in vocational, technical, and other adult education areas. Several regions of the state have held this to a minimum level through management by local councils; other areas have been able to do very little in reducing the rival, duplicated programs. The 1983 Legislature provided for strengthening the Regional Coordinating Councils with greatly increased responsibilities for coordination and with at least half of their members to be from the lay community.

Another potential duplicative area is the increasing rivalry between the community colleges and some of the universities for enrollment of freshman and sophomore students. The creation of upper-division universities and the high level of admission requirements for other institutions, along with the ceilings placed on freshman enrollment by the Board of Regents, has kept this rivalry at a minimum or almost nonexistent level. However, unless role and scope agreements among institutions are observed, the rivalry could increase. The authorization for the upper division universities to add freshmen and sophomores will undoubtedly increase the rivalry.

A fourth problem is concerned with the improvement of the quality of available education. While there is little agreement on defining specifically those factors which constitute quality, most agree that faculty who are respected experts would constitute a major quality force. Florida has lost some of its capable faculty to other states at both university and community college levels. Florida has also cut back funds for new positions to an extent that prevents employment of an adequate number of new faculty each year. Limited faculty expansion has created problems of a static milieu for college development and improvement as well as causing in some instances the unadvisable overuse of part-time and adjunct faculty because they are less expensive. A number of institutions have found themselves spending over 85 percent of the budget on salaries, leaving little for other expenses.

A final problem is diminished public support for higher education. The enthusiasm and excitement of a rapidly expanding system is no longer a potent force. As a result, Florida's business and political leaders have not recently demonstrated the kind of support that was typical during the 1950s and 1960s. Decreasing numbers of graduating high-school seniors yield decreasing numbers of freshmen attending colleges. An uneasy attitude toward higher education has appeared nationwide and has been present in Florida to a similar degree, especially since 1970.

These problems are correctable. Florida has planned and built one of the finest community college systems in the nation, one which serves the entire state. At the same time, Florida has expanded its university system from three to nine institutions, making university-level instruction available throughout the state. These two systems complement each other. With popular support for quality education, they can produce a program of higher education unsurpassed by that of any other state in the nation.

Selected References

Alexander, Kern, and Jordan, K. Forbis. *Constitutional Reform of Public School Finance*. Gainesville: National Educational Finance Project, University of Florida, 1972.

Alexander, Kern; Johns, R. L.; and Jordan, K. Forbis. *Financing the Public Schools of Florida*. 2 vols. Gainesville: National Educational Finance Project, University of Florida, 1973.

Campbell, Roland F., and Mazzoni, Tim L., Jr., eds. *State Governance Models for the Public Schools*. Columbus: Educational Governance Project, Ohio State University, 1974.

DePalma, Frank. "The Governance of Education in Florida." Columbus: Educational Governance Project, Ohio State University, 1973.

Governor's Citizens' Committee on Education. *Improving Education in Florida*. Tallahassee, 1973.

Iannaccone, Laurence. *Politics in Education*. New York: Center for Applied Research in Education, 1967.

Johns, R. L. *The Evaluation of the Equalization of Educational Opportunity in Florida, 1926 to 1967*. Gainesville: National Educational Finance Project, University of Florida, 1976.

Kimbrough, R. B., and Nunnery, M. Y. *Educational Administration: An Introduction*, 2d ed. New York: Macmillan, 1983.

Mould, Charles D. "A Survey of Perceived Differences in Administration under Elected and Appointed School Superintendents in Florida." Ph.D. dissertation, University of Florida, 1975.

Thompson, Ralph B. *The Financial Status of the State University System*. Economic Leaflets, 38, no. 1. Gainesville: Bureau of Economic and Business Research, College of Business Administration, University of Florida, January 1979.

Wattenbarger, James L., and Cage, Bob N. *More Money for More Opportunity*. San Francisco: Jossey-Bass Publishers, 1974.

Health and Social Services

20

by Lewis Bowman and Philip L. Smith

UNIVERSITY OF SOUTH FLORIDA

The State of Florida provides a broad range of health and social services to its citizens and oversees the spending of millions of dollars a year for these services. The Florida Department of Health and Rehabilitative Services (DHRS), the state government's largest agency, provides by far the largest portion of these services. It currently serves over a million clients a year, employs over 34,000 persons, and had an annual operating budget of $2.2 billion in FY 1982–83. We will describe current health and social service operations in Florida with emphasis on the structure and functions of DHRS and the impact of national trends.

The terms "services" and "service programs" refer here to the organized provision of any service or good (tax-supported) offered to individual citizens as their right (based on need or eligibility criteria such as age, income level, disability, residency, etc.) for the purpose of maintaining, improving, or restoring any aspect of personal functioning (physical, emotional, social, financial, etc.).

The Florida DHRS offers a range of preventative, habilitative, and rehabilitative public health programs in conjunction with local governments. It also offers social and economic services to low-income families and individuals; child welfare services (including foster care, adoptions, and protective services in the event of child abuse); social and economic services to the elderly, the mentally and physically handicapped, youthful offenders, and retarded citizens; and special medical services to children.

Other units of state government in Florida engage actively in the delivery of health and social services. For example, in conjunction with local school districts, the Florida Department of Education coordinates programs of services to students including guidance and counseling, psychological services, and visiting teacher/school social work. These programs, offered at both the primary and secondary levels, are logically considered to be social services rather than instruction, since they focus on problems (or prevention of problems) of individual functioning and self-development.

The Florida Department of Corrections (until 1975 the Division of Corrections within the Florida DHRS) also provides social service programs. Though the major focus of any adult correctional system is the protection of the larger society (the social control function), such a system is also responsible, at least secondarily, for providing some rehabilitative services such as counseling, therapy, family support, and discharge planning, as well as a range of services associated with probation and parole.

Florida offers numerous other service programs to individuals through other state departments—consumer protection through the Office of the Attorney General, community development programs through the Department of Community Affairs, unemployment compensation through the Division of Employment Security and workmen's compensation through the Bureau of Workmen's Compensation, both in the Department of Labor and Employment Security—to mention only several. Some federally administered health and social service programs also operate in Florida: the Veterans' Administration (VA hospitals), the Social Security Administration (Old Age Survivors, Disability Insurance, Medicare, and Supplemental Security Income), the Bureau of Indian Affairs, the U.S. Department of the Interior (health and social service programs for American Indians), and the U.S. Public Health Service. But a large number of health and social service programs are within the jurisdiction of the state's DHRS.

Historical Perspectives

The Florida Department of Health and Rehabilitative Services was created as an umbrella health and social service agency by a legislative act in 1969 and reorganized extensively in 1975.

The various program offices comprising DHRS were previously independent, existed as part of other state agencies, or were essentially nonexistent. Their consolidation into one comprehensive agency was reflective of the national trend in the mid- to late sixties. By 1974 thirty-three states had established some type (either confederated, consolidated, or integrated) of combined human services agencies (Council of State Governments, 1977).

In order to understand this complex health and social service organization and its programs, it is helpful to have historical perspective concerning the events that brought into existence the era of the American welfare state (see Vasey, 1958; Wilensky and Lebeaux, 1965; Prigmore and Atherton, 1979; Morris, 1979; Axiun and Levin, 1982; Dinitto and Dye, 1983; Bell, 1983).

In Western civilization, governmental responsibility for the preservation or restoration of the welfare of the populace dates to the ancient societies of Greece and Rome. These states had such programs as orphanages for the children of slain soldiers and grain distribution centers for the poor. Later, with the emergence of Christianity and the Judeo-Christian beliefs expressed in the Old and New Testaments, the church in unity with the state assumed virtually total responsibility for the provision of social welfare services.

The contemporary institution of social welfare in America traces its roots to Elizabethan England. A number of social, economic, and political events in England—especially the emergence of mercantilism—brought about the dissolution of feudalism and with it the displacement of large numbers of serfs from the land. The wandering of displaced serfs, the migration of the poor to the cities, and the resultant debilitating poverty provoked the passage of the Elizabethan Poor Law of 1601. This legislation established three principles readily visible in our current social welfare system. First, it recognized the responsibility of the crown to provide for the common welfare of its subjects, thus setting forth the principle of governmental intervention. Second, it defined "categorical poverty," giving rise to distinctions between "deserving" and "undeserving" poor. Third, it formed the principle of "local relief" by mandating parish or county relief programs. All these principles have been dramatically reflected in the development of American social welfare.

The Protestant Reformation and the growing strength of various Protestant denominations had considerable impact on emerging social welfare systems in Western Europe in the seventeenth, eighteenth, and nineteenth centuries. The Judeo-Christian beliefs in the sanctity of poverty and the noble act of charity were countered by the Protestant work ethic. The rigid and highly moralistic tone of Protestantism fit quite nicely with the precepts of the emerging school of classical economic theory, which provided the theoretical and ideological bases for laissez-faire capitalism. The poor came to be viewed as a lazy, indolent work force to be manipulated by the industrialists and to be chastised for their lack of productivity by the Protestants. These ingredients combined with the Social Darwinism of the nineteenth century and the rugged individualism nourished by the American frontier to produce a political system that was practiced variously in American democracy as elitism, classism, racism, sexism, and ageism. These practices, although not transplanted in a monolithic political cultural pattern, help form the backdrop of social welfare policy and program development in America (Elazar and Zikmund, 1975, chap. 1).

Social welfare programs in colonial America were largely extensions of the English poor law system, emphasizing local relief and making clear distinctions between the "deserving" and the "undeserving" poor. Almost all forms of social problems—disability, mental illness, orphanage, retardation, and so forth—were ultimately viewed as poverty since these problems were manifested in individuals as economic dependency. Services were delivered mostly through such facilities as hospitals for the poor, almshouses, orphanages, and other forms of institutional relief. Some limited assistance was provided outside the context of the institution—for example, legally binding the able-bodied to employers or placing children in apprenticeships (essentially creating an early form of work subsidy programs).

The rapid growth of population in America in the nineteenth century, the liberalizing of ideology concerning the poor and minorities, and the necessity of dealing with large dependent populations, such as former slaves and defeated American Indian tribes, led to an increased use of noninstitutional programs ("outdoor relief"). These programs took the form of actual cash payments (though this practice was not widespread), the provision of products such as food and clothing, and the improvement of housing conditions. Such provisions were generally made available under the auspices of local governmental units or private philanthropic societies. Most notable among the latter was the Charity Organization Society, which developed in New York in the late nineteenth century. The formation of this organization marked the beginning of organized charities in America. Federal intervention on behalf of citizens' welfare was limited in this period to legislation directed at specific populations with special problems (for example, the creation of the Freedmen's Bureau and the Bureau of Indian Affairs) or to addressing some of the problems of emerging industrialism in America (workmen's compensation, child labor laws, etc.).

Concurrently many states were beginning to set up programs to deal with recognized social problems. Among these were programs for preventative, habilitative, and rehabilitative public health, responsibility for the care of the indigent mentally ill, and responsibility for the care of dependent children. Programs for children received considerable attention in the late nineteenth and early twentieth centuries, leading to the establishment of the Children's Bureau in the U.S. Department of Labor in 1912.

Social welfare programs in America prior to the Great Depression were characterized by their lack of comprehensiveness. They dealt with individual aspects of the problems of poverty, mental and physical illness, poor or unsafe housing, poor or unsafe working conditions, and dependency. The bulk of these programs were operated by private philanthropic organizations, although by 1930 a number of state and local governmental agencies had established service programs in these areas. Federal intervention was still limited primarily to the special problems of large dependent populations and to the problems of emerging industrialism.

The stock market crash of 1929 and the resulting depression provoked a new era of governmental responsibility for the general welfare, the emergence of the welfare state. Economically, the Great Depression illustrated the problems of unregulated, laissez-faire capitalism—that in a modern, technologically advanced nation some form of governmental regulation of the economic situation was mandatory to prevent the ravages of inflation and recession.

The Great Depression also forced critical reexamination of our beliefs in Social Darwinism, liberalizing American thought regarding the nature of poverty and dependency. Many persons held in high esteem by society were devastated by economic conditions totally beyond their control. The public began to recognize and give credence to environmental deficiency rather than personal deficiency as the causal factor in poverty.

Much federal legislation important to the advancement of social welfare programming in America was passed during Roosevelt's New Deal. By far the most important was the Social Security Act of 1935. Initially, two programs were created, Old Age and Survivors Insurance (or Social Security) and a federal-state system of unemployment insurance. These two tax-supported social insurance programs exist today in modified form along with numerous other such programs created through a series of amendments to the original Social Security Act of 1935. This act also established a federal grant-in-aid program to the states to help them provide financial assistance to dependent children, the aged, the blind, and, later, the disabled.

The programs that were established by the 1935 Social Security Act, or subsequently grew out of it, are the basis for both federal social insurance programs and state-administered federal grant-in-aid programs. At the federal level, the U.S. Department of Health and Human Services (HHS), formerly Health, Education, and Welfare, regulates those programs established by the Social Security Act or its amendments. As other programs were amended, the number of state-administered, federally regulated programs grew. Through subsequent legislative additions, programs were established to aid the physically handicapped to secure training and employment (vocational rehabilitation), to provide protection from financial need as a result of rising medical care cost (Medicare and Medicaid, Titles XVIII and XIX), and to deal with the special problems and needs of children and the elderly.

In the 1960s many critical changes and innovative developments occurred in the health and social services fields. Among programs enacted under Kennedy's New Frontier and, subsequently, Johnson's Great Society, were

> the *Work Incentive Program,* to provide job training and job placement for Aid to Families with Dependent Children (AFDC) recipients;
>
> the *Food Stamp Program,* a joint Department of Health, Education, and Welfare — Department of Agriculture program to improve nutrition by increasing the food-purchasing power of low-income families;
>
> the *Mental Retardation and Community Mental Health Centers Construction Act,* to provide aid to local areas in developing community programs for the treatment of retardation and mental illness;
>
> the *Economic Opportunity Act,* which designated a federal agency responsible for mobilizing the War on Poverty;
>
> the *Appalachia Regional Development Act,* to provide economic relief to the depressed areas of the southern Appalachians;
>
> the *Model Cities Program,* to bring comprehensive community development and economic and social services to deteriorating inner-city areas.

These programs had dramatic impact at both state and local levels because many provided direct federal funding to units of state and local government or to private nonprofit corporations for program development and/or expansion.

The programs of the 1960s represented the most comprehensive federal effort ever attempted to deal with a broad range of social and economic problems. These programs needed considerable cooperation and interagency coordination at the federal level. This need was particularly evident in programs like Model Cities, which had "cross-funding" from as many as four separate federal agencies. Many comprehensive local programs were funded simultaneously from the Department of Health, Education, and Welfare (DHEW), the Department of Housing and Urban Development (DHUD), the Department of Labor (DOL), and the Office of Economic Opportunity (OEO). Many of these programs were directly or indirectly administered through the state counterpart to the federal agency — for example, departments of public welfare, public health, vocational rehabilitation, and employment security, housing authorities, economic opportunity agencies, and so forth. A resulting trend toward consolidation developed at the state level, with federal encouragement.

Following the inauguration of Richard Nixon in 1969, a trend toward consolidation of social welfare programs at the state level was given further impetus by the Nixon administration's emphasis on management efficiency in social programs. Although the comprehensive health, social, and economic service programs of the 1960s were receiving less emphasis at this time — and, in fact, many were ultimately phased out — many states moved to consolidate diverse health, social, and economic programs into single, large, comprehensive, centralized, state departments. There was a programmatic thrust toward comprehensiveness, integration of service delivery, and cost-benefit efficiency.

Following the election of Jimmy Carter in 1976 there was modest discussion of welfare reform at the federal level with a new system of "workfare" suggested to replace several existing federally financed programs. This change did not transpire as crises developed in other domestic policy areas (for example, energy) and in foreign relations.

The election of Ronald Reagan in 1980 heralded a new approach to social welfare policy issues—or, as some analysts have suggested, a return to pre-"New Deal" strategies. As part of its "new federalism," the Reagan administration has sought to divest the federal government of as much responsibility and control as possible for health and social service programs and to return responsibility and control to the states. Currently this policy is being implemented in some program areas through the block grant strategy established by the Omnibus Budget Reconciliation Act of 1981 (an act of Congress which consolidated 57 health, education, and community development categorical grants into nine new block grants). Through the block grant mechanism, funds are provided directly to the states, generally at levels lower than previous federal expenditures, to support specified programs. Federal deregulation may accompany this transfer of responsibility. The ultimate impact of this defederalization at the state level has not been fully determined. However, there is a growing recognition that the funds provided to the states in aggregate are less than those previously allocated to support the same programs separately, thus forcing states to reduce expenditures, selectively or across-the-board, or to increase the percentage of state dollars available. The latter strategy would have an impact on taxpayers via increased state taxes.

Organization and Operations in Florida

Much of the current health and social services policy and organization in Florida is rooted in changes wrought by demographic, legal, and subsequent political changes in the 1950s, 1960s, and 1970s. In state government, demographic changes in the fifties and sixties, such as rapid immigration to urban areas and some legislative reapportionment, facilitated challenges to the traditional pork choppers (Dauer, 1972, pp. 92 ff.). By 1966 liberal urban and suburban legislators were able to initiate a constitutional revision commission, whose work culminated in the adoption of a new state constitution by the voters in 1968. A federal court of appeals decision in 1967, which ordered special districting and elections, also had a dramatic impact on the make-up of the state legislature. In resulting special elections, the voters selected a disproportionate number of urban and suburban legislators (Lynn, 1976), who were more favorable than the pork choppers to increased involvement in the provision of health and social services. During the seventies and eighties, this change of attitude was to have considerable impact on the services offered and on organization for planning and service delivery.

The new constitution provided for reorganization of the state executive agencies by 1 July 1969. Over 200 executive agencies, councils, and programs were to be reduced to no more than 25. The Governmental Reorganization Act of 1969 subsumed the myriad executive agencies, councils, and programs into 21 departments.

Florida's DHRS was created in the 1969 reorganization. Sixteen agencies, councils, and programs were consolidated into seven line divisions to constitute the department: Corrections, Family Services, Youth Services, Retardation, Mental Health, Vocational Rehabilitation, and Health (National Academy of Public Administration [NAPA], 1977). Three staff offices—Administrative Services, Planning and Evaluation, and Drug Abuse—were created to complete the structure at that time. In 1973 two additional line divisions, Aging Services and Children's Medical Services, were added (see fig. 20.1).

The DHRS was to be an umbrella agency to serve the state's health, social services, and rehabilitation needs. A study of the integration of human services noted the changes in Florida: "the goal of the super-agency was to develop a unified organizational structure from the previously separate departments, a de-

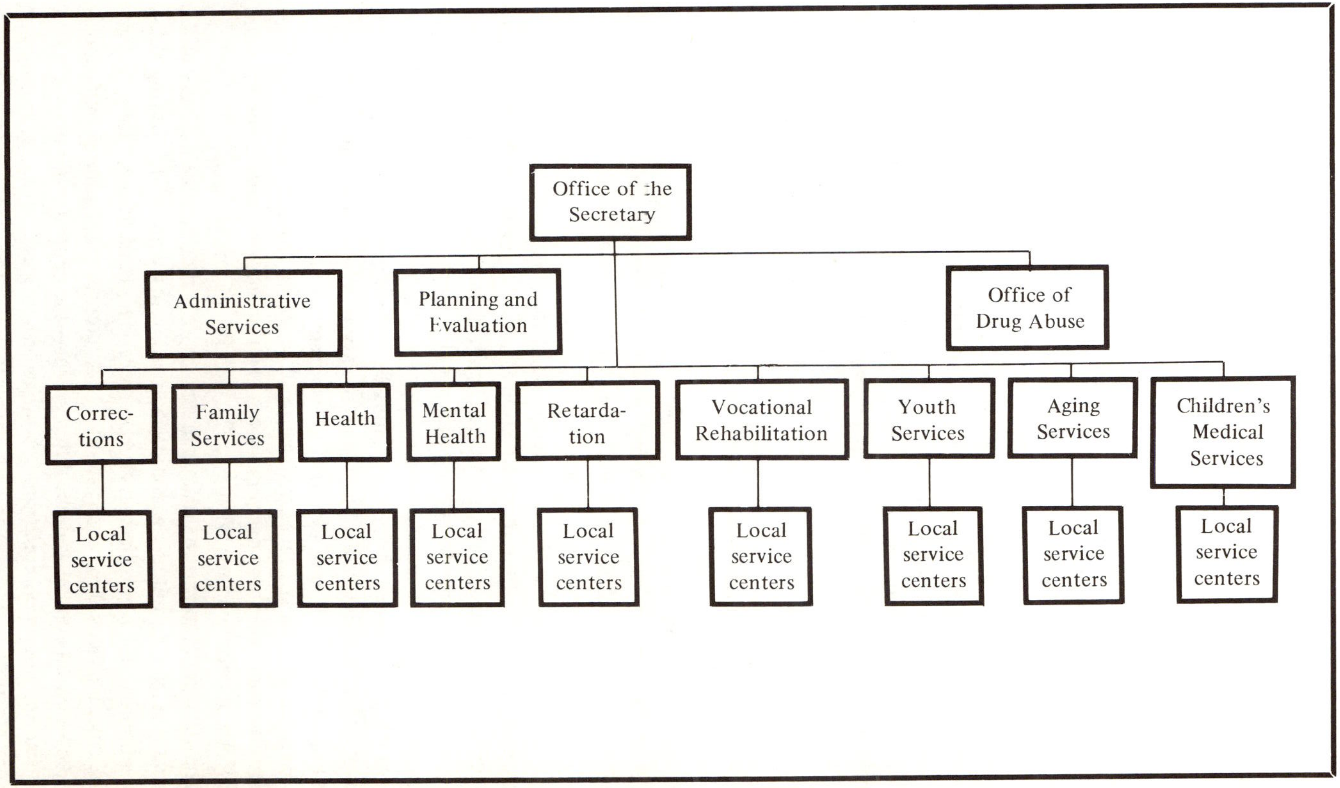

Fig. 20.1. State of Florida Department of Health and Rehabilitative Services, 1973.

partmental program budgeting system, and a strong planning and evaluation capacity as a means to weld together a cohesive state service delivery system'' (Gans and Horton, 1975, p. 153). The new arrangement was supposed to coordinate and integrate services to facilitate the handling of casework and the delivery of services. Prescriptive and empirical questions, some as yet unanswered, were raised about the "proper" approach to organizing state facilities. These questions were not unique to Florida because the debate over centralization that began in Florida in the late 1960s was also occurring in other states.

Successful reorganization of governmental units entails much more than merely shifting units on an organizational chart. Professional identities have to be considered, long-standing institutional loyalties have to be adapted, organizational norms have to be breached, and bureaucrats have to make lateral career moves. The reorganization of DHRS did not escape these problems of transition. It became clear that not all of the philosophical arguments over reorgnization had been resolved. Some wanted to establish the umbrella agency at the state level but to continue decentralized service delivery mechanisms, by program and county-by-county. Others wanted a comprehensive department at the state level with regionalized service delivery. Another group wanted three separate departments—corrections, social services, and health.

Related problems were unresolved. The responsibility for appointing division directors, for example, initially rested with the governor. This arrangement proved problematic, so in 1973 the legislature reassigned these responsibilities to the DHRS secretary. The controversial retention in DHRS of the Divisions of Corrections, Health, and Vocational Rehabilitation produced continuing criticism of the reorganization efforts. For example, the vocational rehabilitation establishment (the U. S. Department of Health, Education, and Welfare and many private agency personnel) campaigned nationally for the consolidation of state social services into a single umbrella department to increase integrated services delivery. But when Florida moved to a regionalized delivery system to implement this goal, the vocational rehabilitation establishment opposed the "loss of identity" of its programs. This situation emerged as an example of "picket fence federalism," wherein federal, state, and local agency personnel develop barriers to protect individual programs from intrusion by efforts at coordination (Wright, 1978, pp. 58–65 and passim).

The 1969 reorganization created an agency in which service delivery at the district level was essentially accomplished program by program. No single district administrator controlled service delivery. The Palm Beach Project (Comprehensive Services Delivery System — CSDS) represented a compromise position between no control and absolute control—the central CSDS person was a *coordinator,* not an *administrator.* A major lesson was learned: a coordinator who must cajole, persuade, and beg rather than command loses administrative effectiveness. This circumstance was noted as a major failure of the CSDS project and was responsible, in part, for the single administrator model pursued in the 1975 reorganization.

The battle between specialist and generalist is ever present in administrative and personnel decisions. The general unwillingness of specialists among the professionals manning the agencies to coordinate planning and delivery across program boundaries (and the lack of license given the coordinator to *command* coordination) was at the root of the problems in the Palm Beach County demonstration. This lack of coordination was multiplied statewide. The CSDS in Palm Beach County utilized a single local manager who had to be, by definition, a generalist. This person's responsibilities included developing an administrative structure which consolidated all programs and delivery of services for clients acquired through common (central) intake. This produced considerable redefinition of specialists' jobs in various programs subsumed under a generalist in a central location.

The Florida legislature was very much interested in the CSDS "experiment," the progress of which was monitored closely by the House Health and Rehabilitative Services Committee. The chairman of this committee noted that the lack of an effective single intake and referral system and competent intake counselors in the demonstration project in Palm Beach County was clear evidence that the entire 1969 reorganization had failed. He said, "A Comprehensive Services Delivery System project, pilot tested in Palm Beach County, failed to achieve hoped-for goals because local administration could not overcome jealously guarded program identities in specialized service fields. . . . Skills of the intake counselors were not great enough to keep control of client management. Thus, coordination of service delivery to the needy was lost" (Hodes, 1976).

Overall, the unresolved argument was whether the 1969 reorganization was adequate to fulfill the goals of consolidation of administrative decision making at the state level and the integration of comprehensive services for delivery at the local level throughout the state. In reality, the reorganization had produced a loose federal arrangement in which the divisions were the basic units. The NAPA study noted that, according to accounts of legislators and administrators, little effective unification had occurred (NAPA, 1977, pp. 5–7). In addition to the lack of development of an integrated intake system to facilitate comprehensive services delivery, reorganization failed to integrate the number of separate programs organizationally subsumed under DHRS (DHRS divisions simply retained program control at the district level) and had generally failed to resolve the many policy questions that had prompted reorganization in the first place. When problems affecting large numbers of persons — clients, agency personnel, and politicians — are unresolved, innocuous tinkering with administrative structures is not the way to resolve them. Binding policy decisions are made in political arenas.

The nature of the organization to deliver social and health services continued to be a volatile political issue in Florida in the 1970s. It produced severe political conflict between Governor Reubin Askew and Florida Senator Dempsey Barron, between various members of the legislature and DHRS Secretary O. J. Keller, between various program specialists and the generalists who were appointed to coordinate and integrate programs, and between political liberals and conservatives in the state. In 1975 another Governmental Reorganization Act was passed, and DHRS was reorganized again (Florida Statutes, 1975, Chap. 20.19).

The second reorganization of DHRS, which occurred in 1975, integrated the management and decentralized the delivery of services at the same time. It converted the loose federation of categorical programs (divisions) into a more tightly centralized structure at state headquarters and at the regional level. The Division of Corrections was separated from DHRS, combined with the Probation and Parole Commission, and given departmental status as the Department of Offender Rehabilitation. But attempts to include the Division of Youth Services with Corrections were resisted, and Youth Services remained in DHRS. Similarly, despite continuing controversy, the Division of Health was retained in DHRS.

Three positions for assistant secretaries were created to provide more centralized management at the state level. These persons are appointed by the secretary of DHRS, to serve at the secretary's pleasure and to report directly to the secretary. The assistant secretary for operations was in charge of all departmental employees who provided services to clients or provided support services. The staff functions of the eight program offices (formerly divisions) and the planning and evaluation functions (formerly a division) of DHRS were the responsibility of the assistant secretary for program planning and development. The assistant secretary for administrative services directed state level personnel, financial management and budget, procurement, civil rights, and related functions.

The secretary of DHRS was given the authority to appoint a deputy assistant secretary for program planning and a deputy assistant secretary for health planning and development. These persons were responsible to the assistant secretary for program planning and development.

Each of the eight program offices was headed by a program staff director, appointed by the secretary of DHRS, who served at the secretary's pleasure and reported to the assistant secretary for program planning and development. The program officers served in a staff capacity but had no line capacity.

Under the 1975 reorganization 11 districts were created to accomplish the decentralization of service delivery on a regional basis throughout the state. Geographical, demographic, and other considerations resulted in districts that varied widely in population and size, from less than a half million to over 1.5 million residents and from 1,081 to 11,684 square miles.

Each district was headed by a generalist district administrator with full line authority over all operations in the district, whose duties were to

> ensure that all programs conform with statewide policies;
>
> direct and coordinate all personnel, facilities, and programs of DHRS located in the district;
>
> apply standard procedures as established by the secretary;
>
> centralize as much as possible all administrative functions within the district necessary for the provision of client services;
>
> be responsible for the delivery of all department-provided and -purchased services in the district (Florida DHRS, District VI, 1978, p. 12).

Even state facilities having wider regional or statewide functions were assigned to the jurisdiction of the district administrator in whose district the facility was physically located. For example, all state hospital administrators report to the district administrator in their respective districts. The Florida Mental Health Institute in Tampa, which has a statewide mission of research, training, and service to clients, was geographically in District VI, and its director reported to the District VI administrator.

Each district had eight program offices analogous to those at the state level. It was in these district program offices that service-related operational decisions were made. Service delivery was coordinated through a program manager, with actual delivery of services to clients occurring within two or more networks.

A service network's main purpose was to operate DHRS programs in its subarea of a district. Each network had a manager and a client support services supervisor plus client contact personnel to deliver services. Each district had between two and five service networks, a total of 40 statewide. Program and administrative support personnel were not assigned to the networks but rather were retained at the district level, thus enabling network managers to coordinate and deliver services in their areas.

The reorganization act of 1975 also provided an advisory council of 12 members for each district, to assist the coordination (case management) and integration (service delivery) of DHRS operations with those of other private and public institutions. These councils, with mobilization, information, and legislative functions, were to incorporate the citizenry in DHRS activities.

Human Rights Advocacy Committees at the state and district levels were another provision of the 1975 reorganization. The eight members of the statewide

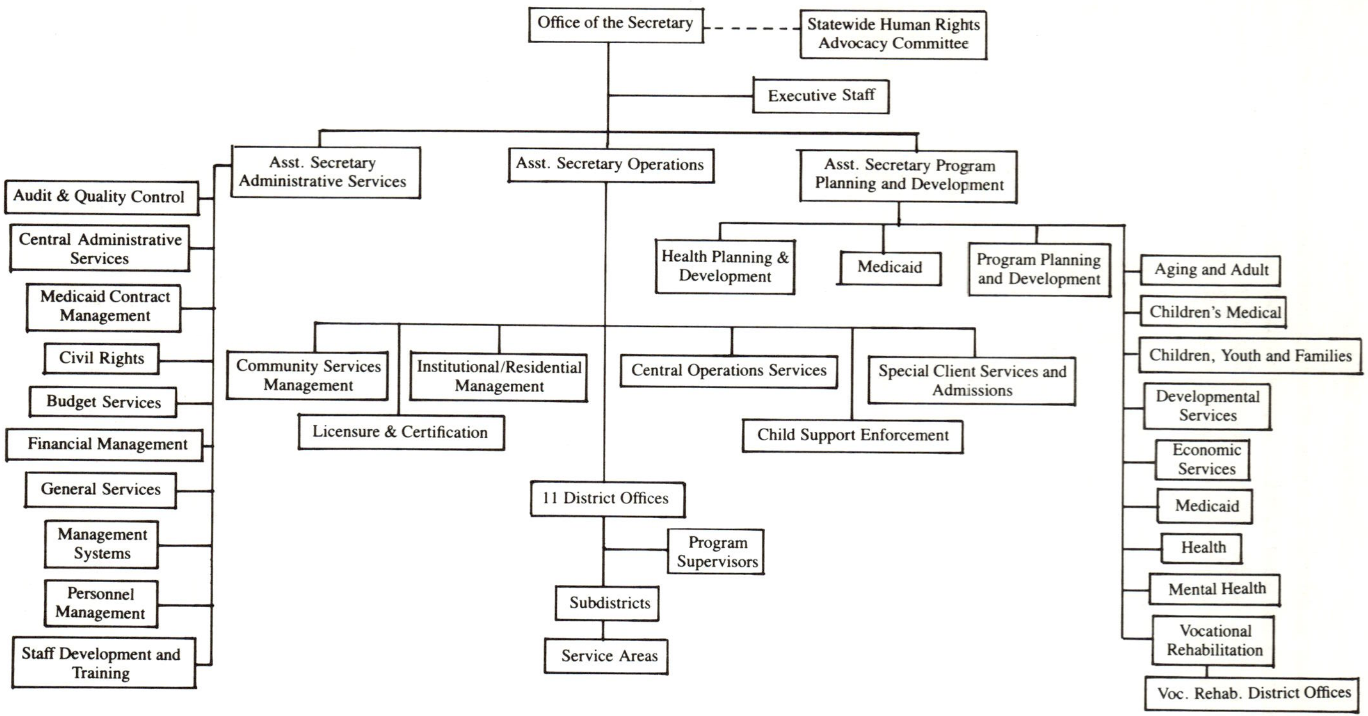

Fig. 20.2. State of Florida Department of Health and Rehabilitative Services, 1983.

committee are appointed by the governor and must include two elected public officials (including one county commissioner), two representatives of nonfederal agencies or civic organizations, two representatives from health and social service consumer organizations (which have received service from DHRS within two years), and two state residents representing none of the other groups. The statewide committee is a third party to protect the rights of DHRS consumers by reviewing individual complaints and programs. District committees have up to 11 members and must include at least two consumers, two providers, two representatives of professional organizations, and one medical or osteopathic physician. The district committees have the same functions as the statewide committees: they try to resolve difficulties for clients within the district. When they are unsuccessful, the matter may be appealed to the statewide Human Rights Advocacy Committee for action.

Since the 1975 changes were implemented, several more have been made in the DHRS organization (see fig. 20.2). At the state level, a Medicaid Office has been added to Program Planning and Development, and a Medicaid Program Office has been added, raising the number of program offices from nine to ten. Several programs' responsibilities have changed. A number of the social programs have been moved from Economic Services (formerly Social and Economic Services) to Children, Youth, and Family Services (formerly Youth Services). The former Retardation Program has been expanded to cover additional problems and is named Developmental Services. At the service delivery level, the networks have become "areas" and client support services supervisors have assumed greater managerial responsibility.

The question of whether the 1975 reorganization and subsequent changes have worked cannot be definitively answered at this time. The reorganization had three goals: to integrate services and to provide comprehensive services for all clients, including those needing multiple services; to implement administrative decentralization, from state to district levels; and to consolidate the delivery of services on a districtwide basis under a single management structure headed by a generalist administrator. Both the NAPA study and an internal study on the status of services integration indicated partial realization of these goals by the end of 1978. By that time the basic reorganizational structure was in place, and some services were being delivered on an integrated basis (DHRS, 1978b; NAPA, 1977).

There are three major components to services integration: the capacity to cut across independent programs for a comprehensive approach to a client's problem; an information and referral network for clients whose needs go beyond the capacities of a single agency; and an organizational structure capable of supporting and implementing policy (see Agranoff, 1977, p. 528). Each of these components had been debated during reorganization of human services delivery in Florida.

Several mechanisms have been utilized in varying degrees to implement the goal of integrated services delivery in the state: collocation of DHRS service delivery units, development of a common intake mechanism, a case management system (CAMS) for multiproblem clients, information and referral systems, and cross-program staff meetings, training, and staffing (Florida DHRS, 1978b, pp. 12–25). As shown in table 20.1, none of these mechanisms was fully operational at the end of 1978. Even when they were operative, their form or emphasis often varied in different districts.

Collocation of service units was the most widely implemented of the mechanisms for services delivery. The NAPA study was extremely laudatory: "The collocation and redistribution of services has been a distinct success, matched nowhere else in the country. The potential is demonstrated in Broward County where each of the three networks has established at least one comprehensive center providing all major services as well as one or two community centers offering several services. Formerly no two services were collocated and some were available at only one site in the county. The collocation has made DHRS staff better informed about and more ready to refer clients to other DHRS programs. Staff . . . are discovering common clients, using common resources, and developing a cooperative outlook" (NAPA, 1977, p. 92). The internal study of DHRS showed that, statewide, DHRS leases were reduced from over 600 in 1975 to fewer than 350 near the end of 1978 (Florida DHRS, 1978b, p. 12). Except for the health program, this change was significant in each of its programs. The difference was attributed to the continuing involvement of Florida's county governments in furnishing space for public health services delivery (ibid., p. 13). By 1983, the collocation of DHRS units was as fully operative as feasible.

TABLE 20.1. The Status of Selected DHRS Services Integration Mechanisms in Florida, 1978–83

	Fully Operative		Significantly Operative		Partially Operative		Little Progress		Not Operative	
	'78	'83	'78	'83	'78	'83	'78	'83	'78	'83
Collocation of DHRS service units		X	X							
Common intake system							X	X		
Case management system for multiproblem clients							X			X[a]
Information and referral system				X[b]	X					
Cross-program staff meeting					X	X				
Cross-program training		X			X					
Cross-program staffing				X	X					

Source: Derived from information in Florida DHRS, 1978b, pp. 12–25; 1983 figures from DHRS, Office of Inspector General, Evaluation Section.

a. Not funded.

b. Subcontracted.

A common intake system has not developed. Considerable controversy still surrounds the need for and feasibility of this mechanism in Florida's efforts to integrate service delivery. This debate is not surprising because implementation of such a system threatens the regular functional programs and personnel more profoundly than does the implementation of other integrating mechanisms. In setting up a common intake mechanism, one usually assumes that agencies will go beyond mere coordination of service delivery and lose part or all of their identification as the provider of a single service. Client-contact workers (intake counselors, for example) employed in one program, such as vocational rehabilitation, would be expected to have adequate knowledge of *all* programs to counsel *any* incoming client. Even when this extreme integration is not actually made operational, under a common intake system workers would be funded in one program area but would have somewhat diversified responsibilities. Such a situation is so threatening to workers in every level of a program that it is easy to understand the difficulty in implementing the practice, notwithstanding its alleged efficiency in fund utilization, accountability, and comprehensive, unified services to clients (Agranoff, 1977, chap. 16).

The difficulties associated with collocation, common intake, and some of the other mechanisms for services delivery might cause one to expect significant progress in developing the *case management system* (CAMS) in Florida. Such a system avoids some of the problems caused by geographic and functional changes associated with the other mechanisms. The case manager works out a plan for a client, then monitors other services following the progress of the client. This approach assumes that the client is lost in the flow of many others unless the case is handled by someone especially trained for serving as a case manager. But recent research indicates that client contact personnel were found to be effective in coordinating services for clients with multiple problems (Agranoff et al., 1977, pp. 80–81). Florida shares the difficulties of many states and localities that have tried to implement this full operation, and it has not been implemented statewide even though it was mandated in 1975 (Florida DHRS, 1978b, p. 17). Earlier, DHRS maintained that even though no formal case assignment and management system was operating in any district, the philosophy of such a system underlies the approach to working with multiproblem clients (ibid., p. 18). The DHRS also believed that the CAMS mechanism was functionally operative in some areas, on an informal basis, through the total changes occurring in service delivery—not the least being that client contact personnel were perceiving themselves as case managers and thereby assumed that role. However, continuing lack of funds doomed the CAMS efforts.

The remaining service delivery mechanisms are operative at some level (see table 20.1). The continuing development of adequate *information and referral systems* and *cross-program staffing and training* may facilitate services integration more quickly and more effectively than other highly touted mechanisms:

they are less threatening because they can be implemented on a piecemeal basis and pose less radical shifts in job perception and performance.

The 1975 reorganization took the first steps toward the goal of administrative decentralization, from state to district level, through the initiation of the mandated district structure. Florida's unusual centralization of statewide administrative authority in the Department of Administration and Department of General Services probably has impeded this process in DHRS. Nevertheless, substantial decentralization has occurred from state to district level and then to the service areas (ibid., p. 27).

Generalist managers have been installed as district administrators, program managers, and direct service supervisors. Several of these persons were hurriedly extracted from specialized program positions because of the tight schedule the legislature had mandated for reorganization, notwithstanding that their new generalist duties cut across program areas; many had to learn about other programs on the job. Program-specific personnel seem to have resisted this development somewhat, as would be expected (ibid., pp. 34–39). The shift to generalist managers has been less marked in the areas of health, mental health, and vocational rehabilitation than in other areas.

Given the massive tasks of reorganizing, it is not surprising that many problems remain. The distinction between the roles of staff and line personnel has been unclear in policy and operational matters. Similarly, definitions of roles and relationships on the state and district levels are ambiguous, particularly in the relationship between the personnel of the program offices and the personnel who operate the programs in the field.

One critical development has threatened the entire reorganization effort. Florida's 1975 reorganization has been the most extreme effort in the nation to decentralize decision-making and to produce integrated services delivery simultaneously. The mandated reorganization brought the state into direct conflict with some federal legislation passed in 1973, which requires that vocational rehabilitation services be provided by a state agency, or division of a state agency, whose primary concern and direction is the administration of that program. The state-level Division of Vocational Rehabilitation with line authority was converted to the Vocational Rehabilitation Program Office with only a staff function. The U. S. Department of Health, Education, and Welfare was strongly considering a waiver for Florida because of its innovative efforts to solve some of the problems of services integration. However, several interest groups, including the National Rehabilitation Association, the National Association of the Deaf, and the American Foundation for the Blind, opposed any waiver. This controversy received national attention (Pierce, 1978; Oestreich, Schreiber, and Apple, 1978). The attempt to get a waiver was defeated in the courts, and DHRS had to abide by the federal guidelines in the Vocational Rehabilitation program. This problem was resolved when DHRS established direct program control from the Vocational Rehabilitation Program Office.

A similar controversy arose when the Social and Rehabilitation Service of the U. S. Department of Health, Education, and Welfare raised much the same question about administrative responsibility for federal grant-in-aid funds utilized for Florida's public welfare programs. The State of Florida maintained that DHRS should be considered the state welfare agency, while DHEW maintained that only the Division of Family Services (now Social and Economic Services) could be so considered. After considerable negotiation the state prevailed; however, these incidents dramatically illustrate inherent problems in the umbrella agency approach to administration and fiscal responsibility involving federal/state intergovernmental relations.

Health and mental health are two other program areas where there is controversy about structural arrangements. The Florida Medical Association, the Florida Psychiatric Association, and some other groups have pressed strongly for medical rather than generalist professionals to direct operations as well as staff functions in health and mental health programs. In 1978 the Florida State Constitution Revision Commission proposed a change in the executive branch — a Department of Health to be headed by a physician. The voters defeated this proposed revision, but controversy about the issue continues. The previously referenced DHRS internal study called "the relatively independent status of the county health units and district mental health boards" (Florida DHRS, 1978b, p. 41) a significant inhibition to reducing program autonomy in these policy areas. Outside evaluators have also warned against removing health and mental health from under the DHRS umbrella (NAPA, 1977, pp. 95–96). Funding and organizational problems in public health in the pre- and post-reorganization period and options for their resolution were studied by DHRS in considering the future of public health in Florida (Florida DHRS, 1978a). This report contains many critical problems and options and recognizes the probability of continued controversy in the area of public health.

Program Offices: Responsibilities and Services

Florida's DHRS has been continually changing since its inception in 1969, which makes it difficult to formulate a definitive statement about the functions and responsibilities of each program area at any particular time. It also reduces the possibility of exact comparisons for trend analyses on a program-by-program basis. The program offices plan and develop a wide array of statewide services (Florida DHRS, District VI, 1983, pp. 34–71). Each office has a relatively clearly delineated set of responsibilities. These offices are located at DHRS state headquarters, where their personnel interpret state and federal statutes and regulations, set standards, and administer directly to clients in the 11 districts.

Even though one of the goals of the 1975 reorganization was to develop integrated services delivery, programs are still organized and funded on an individual basis. And even though the secretary, the assistant secretary for operations, and the district administrator are responsible for the delivery of all services, each program still has its own set of services and requirements for eligibility (Florida DHRS, District VI, 1978).

Aging and Adult Services. — For Floridians over sixty years of age and for disabled adults in each of the 11 DHRS districts, the Aging and Adult Services programs come directly through staff involvement or indirectly through contractual or grant arrangements between DHRS and local agencies or organizations. The program assesses the needs of the elderly or disabled and plans the provision of services on a continuing basis. Specialized services for elderly and disabled adults who cannot be self-sufficient or live independently aid in the reduction of unnecessary institutionalization. Aging and Adult Services also licenses adult congregate living facilities and adult foster homes and monitors their compliance with standards of safety, nutrition, and sanitation. Generally, all elderly and mentally or physically impaired adults with limited financial resources are eligible to receive services rendered under this program. One aspect of the program, Protective Services, is available to persons over eighteen years of age who need protection from abuse, neglect, or exploitation.

Children's Medical Services. — Diagnosis, treatment, and prevention of chronic, handicapping conditions in children are the primary functions of Children's Medical Services clinics in each of the 11 DHRS districts in Florida. These clinics are staffed with medical, social service, and nursing personnel who consult with specialists to provide comprehensive evaluations of patients' symptoms. Any child up to age 21 with a condition which will impair growth and development is eligible for diagnostic evaluation in the clinic. However, acceptance into the Children's Medical Service program for actual treatment of the condition is determined by financial indigency.

Health. — The DHRS is responsible for public health services in Florida, but public health programs are administered locally in each of the 67 counties. Basically, the county health departments or units are cooperative ventures supported by funds from DHRS, the counties in which they are located, fees for services when appropriate, contracts for services to community groups, and other federal and state sources. Preventive services offered include adult screening for glaucoma, diabetes, hypertension, cardiovascular illnesses, and cervical cancer, immunization, physical exams, counseling, nutritional education, referral and dental care, chronic disease drugs, and environmental engineering. Others include epidemiological services, family planning, financial counseling, health education, blood testing, maternal care, Medicaid screening, medical clinics, nursing consultation, pregnancy testing, prenatal services, venereal disease services, vital statistics, and a supplemental food program for women, infants, and children under four years of age.

Mental health.—The objectives of the DHRS mental health service delivery system are the prevention, early detection, treatment, and follow-up care of people with mental, emotional, and behavioral disorders, including drug and alcohol problems. Six facilities (four hospitals, one institute, and one forensic center) provide psychiatric and rehabilitative treatment to full-time residential clients. Community mental health facilities provide partial hospitalization, consultation, and education for drug abusers, alcoholics, the elderly, children, and others. Comprehensive alcoholism and drug programs offer specialized intensive treatment. Utilization of community support systems as an alternative to institutionalization of mentally disabled clients is the proposed trend in Florida's mental health program (Slater, Gordon, Patterson, and Bowman, 1978). Eligibility is based on need; fees are charged according to ability to pay.

Developmental services.—Each DHRS district provides services for retardation, cerebral palsy, epilepsy, and autism in the form of community and institutional programs. Community services are designed to avoid institutionalization of persons presently living in the community and to ensure, through follow-up care and therapy, that persons formerly in institutions will not have to return. The degree of community retardation services rendered a client is determined by diagnosis and evaluation, after which therapy, education, medical and dental services, or placement in a community group home, foster home, or residential treatment center may be prescribed. The program's goal is for the person to live as independently and normally as possible. Social service workers offer supportive guidance to the client and the client's family.

State institutional services for a retarded citizen are prescribed in a habilitation plan, updated annually to note progress in the client's rehabilitation. There are state facilities (Sunland Training Centers) to which retarded clients are sent. Social service workers are an integral part of the habilitation plan because they aid the family in developing a stable residential environment to which the client should eventually return. Emphasis is on training the client to become self-sufficient; hence, specialized therapy is utilized.

Eligibility for services from the Office of Developmental Services must be determined through diagnosis and evaluation. The disability, except for epilepsy, must have occurred before the age of eighteen.

Economic services.—Programs in Social and Economic Services (SES) are funded by state and federal funds. As of 1983, services offered included Aid to Families with Dependent Children (AFDC); Refugee Assistance Program (RAP); AFDC–Foster Care (AFDC–FC); Adult Payments Program; Food Stamps (FS); Overpayment, Fraud, and Recoupment (OFR); Child Support Enforcement (CSE); Win Demonstration Project (WIN); State Employment Service (FSES); and the Low Income Home Energy Assistance Program (LIHEAP).

Eligibility to receive these services or financial support is based on varied state and federal guidelines relating to income and other resources or on membership in a specified population.

Vocational Rehabilitation.—The Vocational Rehabilitation program serves clients who are at least fourteen years of age, have a physical or mental handicap interfering with their ability to earn a living, and have a reasonably good prospect for eventual employment. Available services include evaluation, counseling, treatment, training, transportation, maintenance, tools, and placement. Except for some counseling, these services are puchased from local vendors.

Children, Youth, and Family Services.—The Children, Youth,and Family Services program has responsibility for juvenile deliquency services, juvenile dependency services, services to low-income families, and mental health services to children and families. Included are residential treatment services and community nonresidential services to youths who need help to avoid becoming delinquents or who are delinquents and need treatment services. Thus the Youth Services Program Office is responsible for planning, developing, and coordinating programs to prevent, control, and treat juvenile delinquency.

The residential treatment services include secure detention to provide a setting for temporary observation, recreation, education, and medical care; community-based treatment centers, including halfway houses and START centers (short-term adolescent residential treatment); group treatment homes; and training schools.

The community nonresidential services include probation and aftercare, TRY centers (for training and rehabilitation of youth with school difficulties), training in marine institutes, family group homes, Eckerd Wilderness Camps in Districts I and III, intensive counseling, and nonsecure detention.

Children under 18 years of age who have violated the law and have been referred are eligible for services.

Medicaid.—Florida does not provide services to all medically needy individuals but rather limits participation in the Medicaid program to recipients of public assistance to help them defray the costs of medical care. So persons in Florida who do not qualify for public assistance are ineligible for medical services funded through Medicaid. The services are funded by federal and state governments with some county assistance in hospital and nursing home care. The state began providing the mandatory services under Title XIX of the Social Security Act in 1970 and has added selected optional services.

Funding

In FY 1982–83, the operating budget of DHRS was $2.2 billion, approximately 20 percent of the state's budget. A little over half of the operating budget came from federal sources. Florida has usually funded health and social services at levels below national and regional averages, according to various measures that show that utilization of state and local funds and the capacity or willingness to utilize federal funds have been below these averages. In 1970, for example, Florida was among the states responding least actively in providing necessary medical services under Medicaid (Davidson, 1978, pp. 54–70).

In the late 1970s, Florida ranked last among the 11 southern states on several state government expenditure indicators (*Florida Statistical Abstract,* 1978). Whether the measure is expenditures per capita or general expenditures per $1,000 of personal income, Florida's expenditures are considerably below the national average. In expenditures for major public welfare programs and hospitals, Florida spends less than the other southern states and below the national average. It also has one of the lowest tax rates in the United States.

Current Trends and Issues

Programmatic trends in health and social services—whether in Florida, in other states, or nationally—can be discussed in three broad contexts. The first is program structure and administration; trends in this area relate to the organization's structure with regard to service delivery and patterns of program administration. In the second dimension—service delivery strategies—the trends relate to ways in which services are brought to bear. The third dimension is program configuration, and in this context trends relate to the form and nature of specific programs. As we examine health and social services in Florida, it becomes evident how each of these dimensions has been influenced by major social and political events of the sixties and seventies (see fig. 20.3).

The 1960s: the Kennedy-Johnson era.—The 1960s represented a period of dramatic activity in social welfare. As one sorts through the social and political developments of the decade in an attempt to understand better the guiding principles of the Great Society, certain themes emerge.

The decade of the sixties was a period of great *social activism*. With the formation, or attempted formation, of new political coalitions, several large segments of society—disenfranchised groups—began to play a critical role in decision making at the federal level. "Action" was the cry of these groups—the poor, the minorities, student activists, and others.

Another major theme of the times was *human rights*. A logical extension of civil rights, human rights evolved as the civil rights movement broadened to encompass other populations—especially the poor. The benefits available through various federal, state, and local government programs were being seen as benefits available by virtue of entitlement of human right rather than as the charitable offerings of a wealthy society to its poorer members. Some writers view the sixties as a change from the "welfare state" phase of social welfare development in America to a "welfare society." This transition is marked by a shift from highly selective and somewhat stigmatized charitable programs to programs due citizens as their right, delivered without stigma. This is a distinction made by a number of writers on social welfare in their references to institutional development (in the sense of "social institution") compared to residual programming (see Romanyshyn, 1971, pp. 5–15; Wilensky and Lebeaux, 1965, p. 138). It should be noted that events of the 1970s and 1980s have represented a turnaround in our movement toward the concept of a "welfare society." Clear distinctions are again being drawn between "good" and "bad" programs determined by the nature of the clientele and the form of provision offered. A concern for human rights does continue, however, in commitments toward the protection of client-patient rights.

The third theme of the 1960s is a manifestation of human rights and social action through *citizen participation,* which emerged in the Great Society as an ideological base for involving the recipients or consumers of social welfare services in the planning and delivery of those services. Citizen participation became the rallying cry of the Office of Economic Opportunity and in fact was a requisite condition for establishing many OEO and Model Cities programs.

The 1970s: the Nixon-Ford-Carter era.—By 1970 most of the programs of the Great Society had been terminated, modified, or reduced to such an extent that they were unrecognizable. Human rights and social action had given way to law and order and social control. Citizen participation in the development and delivery of social welfare programs was no longer considered mandatory but, in fact, of rather questionable desirability. Manifestations of these themes did carry over into the seventies and will continue to be evident in the eighties; however, the agenda for the Nixon-Ford-Carter era pointed toward management efficiency, benign neglect, and social control in public programming.

The watchword of the seventies in social welfare programming was *management efficiency.* Acronyms like MBO (management by objectives) and PPBS (planning-programming-budgeting system) crept into the language of social welfare professionals. Numerous private sector manpower utilization, planning, management, and budgeting technologies were adapted for the public sector. To many, cost-benefit analysis became a more important indicator than did estimates of social effectiveness in programming.

Another major theme in social welfare programming in the seventies might be described as "a return to normalcy," or, as it came to be called, *benign neglect* (a phrase coined by Moynihan describing the Nixon administration's strategy of downplaying the activist civil rights position of the sixties). The return to normalcy was actually the return of control of the social welfare system to the bureaucrats and the reestablishment of a more conservative base, both fiscally and administratively, for program operation.

The theme of *social control* emerged in social welfare programming partly as a backlash of the rather radical events of the sixties and partly as a consequence of the reactionary nature of the Nixon administration.

The 1980s: the Reagan era and beyond.—The election of Ronald Reagan in 1980 brought new revisionist strategies to the broad arena of social welfare policy. As part of his "new federalism," a primary theme in welfare programming in the 1980s is *defederalization*. It is a stated posture of the Reagan administration to phase out federal responsibility and control in a number of selected social welfare program areas and to return responsibility and control to the states. The first step toward this goal was the creation of the block grant program (described earlier in this chapter).

As selected programs were defederalized, federal expenditures on social welfare were reduced. States were then faced with reducing expenditures in health and social services or raising revenues to offset the decreases in federal expenditures. The proponents of defederalization and reduced federal spending argue that clients of health and social services programs need not suffer, necessarily, as a result of decreased expenditures nor will it be imperative for states to generate additional revenues. Their argument is based on a projected reduction in administrative costs and an increased reliance on volunteers for the provision of many social welfare services. Hence, *volunteerism* is the second emerging theme of the 1980s.

Program structure and administration.—Several key issues and trends emerge as the current program structure and administration of DHRS in Florida are examined. Since its organization in 1969, and with each subsequent total or partial reorganization, there has been a trend toward centralization of authority. The trend has been evident at both state and district levels—e.g., the relationship of the office of the secretary to the program offices at the state level and the relationship of the district administrator to the program offices at the local level. The impact of decentralization from state to district level has been felt in program administration. *Decentralization for operations has occurred, but centralization of authority is clearly apparent and is clearly a reflection of the management efficiency theme of the seventies.* Likewise, the increased emphasis in DHRS on the utilization of management techniques in planning, budgeting, administration, and evaluation reflects the same approach.

One manifestation of this phenomenon was the trend in the late sixties and throughout the seventies toward including a broad range of health and social service programs under the canopy of a centralized human service department. Among the states in the region, Florida is not only in the forefront of this trend toward program centralization (Council of State Governments, 1977b, p. 385)

FIG. 20.3. Impact of Social and Political Themes of the 1960s and 1970s on Structures, Strategies, and Programs in Health and Social Services

The 1960s: The Kennedy-Johnson Era	Program Structure/ Administration	Service Delivery Strategies	Program Configuration
Human rights	Emphasis on deprofessionalization	Least restrictive alternative; community based programming; deinstitutionalization	Emphasis on extensive array (breadth) of programs
Citizen participation	Recognition of client/patient rights (consumerism)	Emphasis on information and referral strategies	Emphasis on income redistribution alternatives (work training and job placement programs)
Social action	Sensitivity to and protection from liability Presence of formal grievance procedures for consumers Adversarial relationships between adm/staff agency/clientele	Emphasis on creation of specialized access structures (centralized multiprogram intake)	Emphasis on restoration of functioning programs (health, mental health, retardation, vocational rehabilitation)

Fig. 20.3—*continued*

The 1970s: The Nixon-Ford-Carter Era			
Management efficiency	Emphasis on centralization of authority	Emphasis on decentralization for operations	Emphasis on programs dealing with offender populations — felons, drug abusers, alcohol abusers
Benign neglect (return to normalcy	Emphasis on use of mangement techniques in planning/budgeting/ administration/evaluation	Emphasis on coordination integration	Emphasis on "at risk" or populations in need of protection — abused children, the elderly, crime victims
Social control	Emphasis on cost = effective vs. social = effective approaches for program development	Emphasis on case management techniques Emphasis on use of management information systems Emphasis on purchase of service (private vendors)	

Note: The themes listed as representative of the 1960s and 1970s and their relationships to social programming should be viewed in aggregate, as each impact across the three dimensions is examined. There is not necessarily a one-to-one relationship betwee the individual themes and any given impact in any of the three dimensions. Also it should be noted that the statements of impact across the three dimensions are reflective of *current* conditions. The manifestations of the various themes at the time of their occurrence were many and varied—for example, community control of programming in the 1960s. These have not been treated here since they have passed with time. Only those remaining manifestations that are relevant to current trends and issues are identified.

The two major themes that have emerged in the 1980s are *defederalization* (of programs) and *volunteerism* (increased reliance on the voluntary sector for provision of services). Experience has been insufficient to confirm the strength of these themes in relation to their persistence through the decade or their ultimate impact on program structure and administration, service delivery strategies, and program configuration. Certainly the most significant impact to date has been in the area of program administration as the states have assumed new program responsibilities.

but has gone even further: it has decentralized operations through development of district administration of all program operations on a day-to-day basis. *In essence, Florida has centralized the administrative structure for policy making, while decentralizing operations for service delivery.*

One can also view the legacy of the sixties in current administrative patterns in DHRS. The emphasis on declassification of the personnel system ("deprofessionalization") reflects the citizens' participation trend of the sixties. The utilization of indigenous personnel in service delivery fostered the paraprofessionalism movement (Pearl and Reissman, 1965). Similarly, the recognition and establishment of an appropriate administrative mechanism for the protection of clients' and patients' rights and redress of grievances is reflective of the human rights issue of the sixties.

Administratively, DHRS must be viewed as operating essentially from a private-sector model. This model places emphasis on cost-benefit approaches and program and case management based on an "objectives" model with the goal of more sophisticated fiscal planning.

Defederalization of selected programs and the block grant strategy have not yet significantly altered the administrative structure of Florida's DHRS and may not in the future. However, certain administrative procedures have been altered in reference to funding mechanisms (for example, increased state control of community mental health programs through disbursement of funds).

Service delivery strategies.—In viewing the development of DHRS over the last several years, one can observe trends in delivery strategies that are a product of both the innovative social themes of the sixties and the more conservative management themes of the seventies. For example, the emphasis on human rights has been translated into clients' and patients' rights. The movement away from institution-based programs toward community-based programs came about partly because of recognition of the desirability of maintaining patients in their communities.

The trend toward community-based programming was given added social and legal impetus by the patients' rights movement. Not only has there been a growing recognition over the last several years in the professional community of the right of individuals to have delivery of services which would maximize their freedom of choice, but several critical court decisions have established the principle of "least restrictive alternative" for client populations like the mentally ill, the retarded, the elderly, and others. As a result of this movement, DHRS is currently moving toward a massive deinstitutionalization program in Florida (Slater, Gordon, Patterson, and Bowman, 1978). The goal of this program is to depopulate the state's mental hospitals, retardation centers, and other institutions serving the state's citizens. The implications of this movement as an extension of community-based programming should be obvious. New demands will be placed on existing networks of community services, both public and private, to provide critical community support services for deinstitutionalized populations. Another outcome will be the rapid development of small congregate living facilities to serve deinstitutionalized populations in need of continuing care. In this area, state programmers are likely to clash with local authorities over the location of these facilities because local land-use zoning ordinances undoubtedly will be called into question.

Other trends in DHRS service delivery strategies can be traced to the Great Society. These include the emphasis on the provision of information and referral as a basic service delivery strategy and the creation of specialized access structures (centralized multiprogram intake units) within each DHRS district office. These trends reflect the rapid program development that occurred in the sixties and the difficulties encountered in getting people to the appropriate service. Both these trends represent an attempt by DHRS to reduce fragmentation and to provide more comprehensive services to a broader population. The initiation of a 24-hour protective service hotline for reporting child abuse also reflects these trends.

The emphasis on management efficiency inherited from the seventies is visible in current DHRS operations. For example, centralization of administration and decentralization of operations reflects the management efficiency model. Emphasis on coordination and integration of services, on case management techniques, and on the use of management information systems for program monitoring and review purposes also reflects the desire for efficiency.

Another trend of interest is the purchase of service (purchasing specific services for a client population by contractual arrangements with private vendors). Such purchases were made possible by passage in 1974 of Title XX (amendment to the Social Security Act). States may provide specified services directly to specific populations or enter into contractual arrangements for the provision of those services. Federal funds continue to be available on a matching basis for certain specified services, while other services are now covered under block grants. Such an arrangement allows DHRS considerable flexibility in service provision. A major argument set forth in support of this service delivery strategy is that the state can not only provide a broader array of services to target groups but can purchase such services as they exist in a community on a cost-saving basis, since it is unnecessary and wasteful to replicate services at the state level which are available through local government programs or from private vendors. The development of purchase-of-service provisions has also returned or diverted to the private sector much of the business of health and social service provision.

The impact of the strategies emerging early in the 1980s will probably continue and reinforce the trend toward the private vendorship of services both in terms of purchase-of-service and an increased emphasis on volunteerism. The block grant strategy does stand to have a potential turnaround impact, however, on the trend toward deinstitutionalization. As fewer dollars are available across-the-board for health and social service programs, expenditure reductions in the mental health area may have a negative impact on the availability of community-based mental health programs, thus limiting the number of persons that may have access to such services as an alternative to institutionalization.

Program configuration. — The actual thrust of social welfare programs relative to target population and to the nature and the intention of the services provided (maintenance, habilitation, social control, etc.) represents the final area where issues and trends may be identified. Several important trends can be observed in DHRS relative to program configuration over the last several years which are a legacy of the sixties. With the impetus provided by the proliferation of programs and extension of private vendor services, one of the observable trends in current programming is the emphasis placed on multiple services to broad populations.

Carrying over from the sixties, a number of programs are proposing income maintenance alternatives. Work training and job placement programs are two examples. Beyond the Work Incentive Program, in operation for over a decade, emphasis is being placed on job-related programs through information and referral. Welfare reform proposals early in the Carter administration called for phasing out programs created by the Comprehensive Employment Training Act (CETA), but the suggested replacement was a new federal system of "workfare." While this reform measure was not realized programmatically, the concept remains in place. These kinds of programs are seen in the aftermath of the system-threatening years of the sixties as highly preferred and relatively noncontroversial alternatives to basic income redistribution strategies such as major tax revision.

Another trend in DHRS representing the legacies of the sixties is the emphasis on "restoration of functioning" programs, such as health, mental health, retardation, and vocational rehabilitation. The Florida Mental Health Institute was established at Tampa to serve as a demonstration and training site for the development of better methods of treatment for the mentally handicapped. The subsequent conveyance of this facility to the University of South Florida by the legislature did not necessarily reflect a change in attitude toward the treatment of the mentally handicapped but rather transpired as a result of disagreements at the state level about specific administrative arrangements and functions. Public health programs have received considerable attention and have expanded into new areas such as family planning. Programs for retarded citizens and other handicapped groups are receiving similar attention; the major moves are toward community-based treatment and small group-care facilities.

The Nixon era marked a shift in program configuration. In keeping with the "law and order" theme of the Nixon administration, considerably more emphasis was placed on programs dealing with so-called offender populations. In Florida, for example, increased attention to correctional programs helped in making the Department of Offender Rehabilitation a separate and independent department of state government in 1975. This department (now the Department of Corrections) represents the consolidation of two state agencies, the Division of Corrections from DHRS and the State Probation and Parole Commission. A similar effort was made to remove juvenile corrections from DHRS, to become a part of the new Department of Offender Rehabilitation. But this move was successfully opposed with strong arguments that juvenile corrections must reflect a social services approach rather than the more punitive approach of social control. Other offender populations receiving specific attention through DHRS are drug and alcohol abusers. A special Office of Drug Abuse was established in the office of the secretary, and alcoholism received considerable attention through a specialized institute established at Avon Park. These programs are now in Mental Health.

An even more dramatic illustration of emphasis on specific populations resulting from a desire to achieve law and order and social control can be seen in programs designed to deal with "at-risk" populations, those in need of some form of special protection—abused children, the elderly, and victims of violent crimes. Within DHRS, development of programs to serve these populations has been evident. There has been renewed interest in the protection of children and the preservation of children's rights, with increased attention to child welfare programs. A program office (earlier a division) of Aging and Adult Services in DHRS has directed considerable attention to the problems of the elderly, especially their vulnerability as crime victims. Following passage of the Crimes Compensation Act by the legislature in 1978, DHRS helped plan and develop statewide programs to aid victims of violent crimes.

Emerging social welfare strategies suggest the utilization of mechanisms outside the structure of social welfare services, both public and private. For example, one strategy of the Reagan administration is to meet the needs of groups that may be marginal recipients of social welfare services by creating economic advantages for them through revisions to the tax structure and stimulation of the marketplace (Heatherly, 1981).

Conclusions

As new social and political themes develop in the eighties, variations in program structure and administration, service delivery strategies, and overall program configuration for health and social services in Florida undoubtedly will occur.

We have examined some probabilities in these areas, but the ultimate impact in Florida and other states has yet to be determined. One ominous note for health and social services in Florida is the proposed state tax revision embodied in Proposition One (an initiative constitutional amendment to roll back taxes to the 1980 level with a 5 percent possible increase; it will be voted on in 1984 unless a court challenge intervenes). If this referendum passes, its impact on state health and social services will be disastrous. If funding cutbacks for state agencies are borne equally, the projected reduction in expenditures for DHRS for 1985–86 would be approximately 23 percent, with additional reductions every year thereafter. This possibility, coupled with reduction of federal expenditures, does not encourage an optimistic outlook.

References

Agranoff, Robert. 1977. "Services Integration." In *Managing Human Services,* edited by Wayne F. Anderson, Bernard J. Frieden, and Michael J. Murphy. Washington: International City Management Association.

______, et al. 1977. "Research on Administrative Change in Human Services: Some Organization and Non-Organization Issues." In *Human Resources Administration: Papers from the 1977 ASPA Conference,* edited by Alex Pattakos. Washingon: American Society for Public Administration.

Axinn, June, and Levin, Herman. 1982. *Social Welfare—History of American Response to Need.* New York: Harper and Row, Publishers.

Bell, Winifred. 1983. *Contemporary Social Welfare.* New York: Macmillan.

Council of State Governments. 1977a. *Human Services Integration: State Functions in Implementation.* Lexington, Ky.: Council of State Governments.

______, 1977b. *Book of the States.* Lexington, Ky.: Council of State Governments.

Dauer, Manning J. 1972. "Florida: The Different State." In *The Changing Politics of the South,* edited by William C. Havard. Baton Rouge: Louisiana State University Press.

______. 1978. "Proposed 1978 Florida Constitutional Revision and Proposal on Casino Gambling." Gainesville: Public Administration Clearing Service, University of Florida, Civic Information Series No. 61.

Davidson, Stephen M. 1978. "Variations in State Medicaid Programs." *Journal of Health Politics, Policy, and Law* 3 (Spring): 54–70.

de la Parte, Louis, Jr. 1976. "Response to a Public Policy Process." *Evaluation* 3:79–80.

Dinitto, Diana M., and Dye, Thomas R. 1983. *Social Welfare: Politics and Public Policy.* Englewood Cliffs, N.J.: Prentice-Hall, Inc.

Elazar, Daniel J., and Zikmund, Joseph, II, eds. 1975. *The Ecology of American Political Culture*. 2d ed. New York: Thomas Y. Crowell Co.

Florida. Department of Health and Rehabilitative Services. 1978a. "The Future Role and Mission of Public Health in Florida: Meeting the Challenges of the 1980s and Beyond." Report by the Strategic Planning Group for Public Health Services. Tallahassee: DHRS.

______. 1978b. "The Status of Services Integration: Preliminary Findings and Conclusions of a Department Self-Appraisal." Tallahassee: DHRS.

______. n.d. *Proposed Comprehensive Annual Services Program Plan for Social Security Act Title xx, July 1, 1978–June 30, 1979*. Tallahassee: DHRS.

______, District VI. 1978. *District VI: Organization and Operation*. Tampa: DHRS.

______. 1983. *District VI: Organization and Operation*. Tampa: DHRS.

Florida Statistical Abstract, 1978. Gainesville: University of Florida.

Gans, Sheldon P., and Horton, Gerald T. 1975. *Integration of Human Services*. New York: Prager Publications.

Heatherly, Charles L., ed. 1981. *Mandate for Leadership—Policy Management in a Conservative Administration*. Washington: Heritage Foundation.

Hodes, Richard S. 1976. "Response to a Public Policy Process." *Evaluation* 3:82.

Linn, Margaret W. 1976. "Response to a Public Policy Process." *Evaluation* 3:85.

Lynn, Lawrence E., Jr. 1976. "A Study of the Public Policy Process." *Evaluation* 3:59–78.

Macaroo, David. 1978. *The Design of Social Welfare*. New York: Holt, Rinehart and Winston.

Morris, Robert. 1979. *Social Policy of the American Welfare State*. New York: Harper and Row.

National Academy of Public Administration. 1977. *Reorganization in Florida: How Is Service Integration Doing?* Washington: Report of a Panel of the National Academy of Public Administration.

Oestreich, Richard; Schreiber, F. C.; and Apple, L. E. 1978. "Reorganizing—or Homogenizing?—Government." *Washington Post,* April 15.

Pearl, Arthur, and Reissman, Frank. 1965. *New Careers for the Poor: The Non-Professional in Human Service*. New York: The Free Press.

Pierce, Neal R. 1978. "A Counterattack on Florida's Bureaucracy War." *Washington Post,* February 20.

Prigmore, Charles A., and Atherton, Charles P. 1979. *Social Welfare Policy Analysis and Formulation*. Lexington, Mass.: D.C. Heath and Co.

Romanyshyn, John. 1971. *Social Welfare: Charity to Justice*. New York: Random House and the Council on Social Work Education.

Slater, Arthur L.; Gordon, Katherine K.; Patterson, Roger L.; and Bowman, Lewis. 1978. *Deinstitutionalizing the Elderly in Florida's State Mental Hospitals: Assessing the Problems*. Tampa: Human Resources Institute, University of South Florida, Monograph Series No. 2.

Vasey, Wayne. 1958. *Government and Social Welfare*. New York: Henry Holt & Co.

Wilensky, Harold L., and Lebeaux, Charles N. 1965. *Industrial Society and Social Welfare*. New York: The Free Press.

Wright, Deil S. 1978. *Understanding Intergovernmental Relations*. North Scituate, Mass.: Duxbury Press.

Part Four

Summary

21

Summary and Conclusion

by Manning J. Dauer

UNIVERSITY OF FLORIDA

The three parts of this book cover an introduction to Florida and its government today. The first part contains the state's background, history, demography, social structure, and politics. In the second part we examine the structure of Florida's government — the legislative, executive, and judicial branches of state government and regional, county, city, and metropolitan levels of local government. In the third we explore government functions as they relate to citizens in particular areas — taxation and public finance, the environment, education, business, labor, agriculture, minorities, and social services. At the same time, we consider how the three levels of government—federal, state, and local—interact in these policy areas.

In this summary we analyze further the question of whether Florida politics is most accurately described as a pluralist or elitist version of democracy. This issue is raised in chapter 1 and is considered in many of the later chapters.

The information in this book about politics in America, and especially in Florida, is examined to see whether it supports the concept that an elite controls government decisions or whether such decisions result from input from a number of sources, with the result that Florida's political processes can be called pluralist.

Next we look at the finding that Florida is a moderately conservative state and how this trend affects party structure and voting patterns, and we study how the remarkable growth in the state has caused innovation in government structure and changes in party and voting statistics. We survey many problems caused by this growth in such areas as the environment, social services, education, taxation, and interest groups.

The third section of this chapter contains a series of vignettes of political leaders of Florida, old and new, and how some styles of leadership cause ethical problems, how positions of leadership are attained, and how different styles of leadership have affected government in Florida. The information in this section reinforces the argument that Florida's government is pluralist.

We move last to a consideration of the causes of the major problems that face Floridians and how the factors that brought on some of these problems relate to governmental processes. The major problems, of course, are energy shortages and inflation. There are others, though all are affected in some degree by these two major ones. One example of such cause and effect is the influx of the aged into the state and the resulting heavy demands on the health and social services structures.

Elitism v. Pluralism

A central issue of the introductory chapter is whether representative government in the United States is elitist or pluralist. We conclude from available material that pluralism best describes the functioning of America's and of Florida's politics.

There is evidence for this conclusion in the impact of lobbies and campaign contributions (chapter 4). Lobbyists influence the process of legislation as well as the work of executive agencies. Special interest lobbies often offset each other in their impact. For example, representatives of labor disagree with many of the policies supported by business, but they often compromise, as, for example, in the revision of the workmen's compensation law. On issues like ERA there are opposing alliances, each representing groups of women. Public interest lobbies like Common Cause and the League of Women Voters have an impact on many issues. On others, citizens' groups such as the Audubon Society influence environmental decisions (chapter 14). Are these examples evidence of a division among elites? Or do they indicate that the citizen, when he organizes with others, has an impact on policy decisions?

The history of adoption of the fiscal disclosure amendment to the Florida Constitution is recounted in chapter 6. Three sessions of the Florida legislature refused to enact a stringent fiscal disclosure law. Thereupon citizens' groups, led by Governor Reubin Askew, circulated an initiative petition to add to the constitution a section requiring fiscal disclosure for public officials. When the necessary number of signatures had been secured, the section was placed on the ballot and was adopted with a favorable majority of over 70 percent of the voters in the 1976 general election. We have here an excellent example of direct impact by organized voters. This illustration is unusual, but there is other evidence of the impact of different groups of citizens in elections (chapter 5). It is argued that the Florida legislature, the state's executive officials, Florida's delegation to Congress, and Florida's presidential election results are all consonant with the moderate-conservative orientation of the state. The weight of the material thus corroborates the argument that representative government is pluralist, not elitist.

At the same time every citizen does not have equal impact on government. Some argue that democracy should assure such equality, but this argument is not supportable. Our argument is rather that citizens may form in groups which together may influence policy. Often some groups combine in a coalition behind a candidate, and through this representative in government they may influence policy. On another issue such a coalition will divide, and other coalitions will form.

In elitist theory the elite make the decisions and manipulate their followers. In pluralist theory, there is a proper role for leadership; followers and leaders interact, each influencing the other. If a leader departs too far from his supporters, he can always be stopped in a subsequent election, and other leaders are brought in. The effective leader can often influence his followers by explaining and advocating or opposing policies and by forming effective coalitions. Some leaders are officers of government. Others have influence on voters because of what they write, how they act as spokesmen for various groups, or how they use media presentation.

In observing the influence of groups, interesting patterns of pluralism develop. In local government there are many examples of neighborhood associations and citizen input (chapters 11–13). The chapter on local government contains data showing the degree to which our society is pluralistic, based on the input of citizens' groups, but it also shows increasing control by professionals at the local level (city managers and planners), thus supporting the presence of some measure of elitism.

In the discussion on minorities there are examples of elder citizens' groups, black organizations, and others which have influenced governmental policies (chapter 15). Similar examples may be found in the chapters on business and labor (16) and on agriculture (18). The advisory councils called for by federal legislation in many sectors not only have a direct impact on the federal government but also play a role in local and state governments. The earliest of these councils is found in agriculture. Since the 1930s, the federal law has called for farmers of particular commodities to enter into acreage and marketing agreements. Participants then have the advantage of guaranteed minimum prices for their crops. These groups in turn can have impact on state policy and on local government issues. Today this pattern has been extended to include local citizens' advisory councils required under federal law for urban housing and renewal programs and for federal health, education, and welfare programs. The same requirement is made for cities or other units of government which take federal funds and then must have affirmative action programs with councils representing minorities. Thus federal grants often have an impact beyond a specific grant program.

Voting Patterns and Party Structure

Florida is moderately conservative, as shown in the chapter on social and political factors in twentieth-century Florida (3) and Florida's electoral politics (5). Since World War II the state has gone Democratic in three presidential elections (for Truman in 1948, Johnson in 1964, and Carter in 1976). The remaining six presidential elections were carried by Republicans, Eisenhower twice, Nixon three times, and Reagan once. In Florida's delegation to the House of Representatives, Republicans average one-third of the seats, conservative or moderate Democrats hold seven or eight seats (about 55 percent), and liberal Democrats hold two or three seats (15 to 20 percent).

But in state politics, Republicans have held only 35 percent of the seats in the legislature, and this figure had fallen to just under 30 percent of the total at the beginning of the eighties. Only one Republican governor has been elected in the years since World War II. The Republican party in Florida has simply not strengthened its party organization in proportion to the strength it has shown in presidential politics. Florida's party structures are weak partly because of the long use of the primary for nominating candidates. Republicans simply do not contest county and local offices in most counties; correspondingly their party committes in most counties are weak. Democrats, building on a long tradition of one-party dominion, have stronger party organizations at the state and county levels and offer candidates in local elections in almost all counties.

Our evidence is that Florida's politics is highly individualistic, bringing about a factionated political structure and weak party discipline. Relationships between the governor and the legislature depend much on the individual qualities of the governor and little on party structure.

Structural Change in Florida's Government

One can speculate that, given the moderate/conservative orientation of Florida's citizens, there would be little change if there were little growth. But growth is rapid and probably will continue so. The 1980 census shows a population of 9.74 million, ranking the state as the seventh most populous. Continued growth makes the projected population for 1990 such as to rank the state fourth in the country. While there is a comparatively low level of taxation and of support for social services and public education, there is considerable experimentation at all levels of state government.

There has been a sharp remodeling of legislative procedures. Annual sessions of the legislature were mandated by the 1968 constitution, and for a decade there were annual budgets. But as executive agencies of the state needed more assurance for planning use of funds, there was a return to biennial budgets at the time the 1979 legislature met. After World War II a professional staff was organized under a Legislative Reference Service. But after 1968 a further step was taken: establishing permanent staff for legislative committees, with committees and staff functioning year-round. Thus the Legislative Reference Service was superseded. Innovative changes in state government departments were mandated by the legislature, for example, the decentralization of social services out of Tallahassee and into 11 Health and Rehabilitative Service regions. There were a number of innovations in local government (chapters 11–13), including the establishment of planning regions and water districts and two types of innovative systems of metropolitan government.

In environmental politics, legislation was adopted in 1972 to protect environmentally endangered lands and citizens voted bond issues to provide for land purchases. The 1968 constitution has a section in Article II admonishing the legislature to protect clean air and access to beaches.

There has been extensive reorganization in both the executive and the judicial branches. Administrative departments have been consolidated into fewer than 25 agencies. The cabinet system has been retained, but the governor has greatly increased his power of management, especially in regard to preparation and administration of the budget. Judicial nominating commissions have been added to the constitution, to recommend candidates for judicial appointments. Courts have been consolidated into four levels. Justices and judges of the highest courts — the state Supreme Court and the District Courts of Appeals — have been placed under the merit retention system known as the Missouri Plan. Trial levels of courts — circuit and county courts — have moved to nonpartisan opposed elections of judges. The Florida Supreme Court ordered a one-year experiment in telecasting court proceedings, including trials. At the close of that experiment 75 percent of the Florida Bar voted against permitting such telecasts. But in 1979 the court pronounced the experiment successful, and such proceedings are now open to TV broadcasts, under supervision of the presiding judge.

Florida has pioneered in developing a Government in the Sunshine Law, which requires that all meetings of public officials, except for judges' conferences in chambers and grand jury proceedings, be announced in advance and be held in public. The same rules apply to public documents, except for certain disciplinary processes, the work of grand juries, and some individual personnel records. Fiscal disclosure requirements are discussed in chapter 6 on the Florida Constitution.

Many of these structural changes, as well as some substantive ones, have been made possible because of reapportionment. For example, the votes for changes in women's rights (shown in chapter 15 on minorities) were made possible because of South Florida's votes in the legislature from districts added by the 1967 and 1971 reapportionments. The same is true of the pattern whereby planning and environmental legislation was adopted in 1972–75. The impact of reapportionment is greater than earlier studies of the effects of reapportionment had indicated.

Leadership

There are a variety of ways in which effective leadership is attained and conducted. The several types of leadership presented will demonstrate some of the ways in which leaders form coalitions and how they present issues. (Governors and their leadership capabilities are discussed in chapter 7.)

Few individuals are in politics to make money, but some are actually corrupt and perhaps a larger number take advantage of knowledge gained in office to make effective investments or to get sales for products with which they are connected. The first three portraits are of Florida politicians who presented the state with different kinds of ethical problems.

The political demagogue. — Sidney J. Catts is easily the best example of the demagogue in Florida politics. Governor from 1917 to 1921, Catts came to the state from Alabama as a Baptist minister and for a time headed a large church in Defuniak Springs, in West Florida.

He later turned to farming, then toured the state as a salesman and preached guest sermons on Sundays in his eloquent tub-thumping speaking style. He entered the Democratic primary for the governorship in 1916 and wound up in close competition with a regular democrat, State Treasurer W. V. Knott. The primary results were disputed; the state supreme court declared Knott to be the party's nominee. Catts declared that he had been counted out illegally and filed as a candidate on the Prohibition ticket in the general election of 1916. He won the election and was inaugurated governor in 1917.

Catts was campaigning at a time marked by anti-Catholicism, American nativism, and anti-black sentiment in the nation, but this was also a period of late populism and progressivism and emphasis on trustbusting on behalf of small businesses. Catts played on these prejudices to form his coalition of backers.

Once in office, Catts began to appoint cronies to state positions, declaring "it's a poor cat that won't look out for its own kittens." He called for legislation outlawing monasteries and nunneries in the state. He sponsored some legislation favorable to labor unions and sought to improve public education. He pardoned many criminals and was charged, but not convicted, of selling pardons. He ran for the U. S. Senate but was defeated. Thereafter, in the 1920s he returned to farming and also founded Catts Patent Medicine business, offering medicine to cure the ills of both humans and horses. He formed a real estate firm which advertised land in the Florida Everglades. His brochure stated that the topsoil on this land was so rich that it could be sold as fertilizer. He stood trial in federal court on charges of holding blacks in peonage but was not convicted. Later he was charged in a counterfeiting case but again was not convicted. In the middle of all this he ran for the governorship again but was not reelected. He stands easily as the biggest scoundrel in Florida politics.

While Catts sought money from public office, he was primarily playing on prejudice to create a political coalition of white farmers, laborers, and religious fundamentals who would support what he sought to present as a cause for the common man.

Corruption in politics. — Thomas David O'Malley was elected state treasurer of Florida in 1970 and reelected in 1974. The state treasurer of Florida also serves as insurance commissioner and regulates that industry. In this capacity he licenses insurance companies and sets rates.

O'Malley was a colorful campaigner, emphasizing his independence from big business. Shortly after his reelection in 1974, a number of charges were filed against him relative to his work as insurance commissioner. These charges included pressuring companies to buy paintings from exhibits he and his family were sponsoring and not reporting on income tax receipts from these and other sources. Nine articles of impeachment were voted by the Florida House of Representatives, and in July 1975 he resigned rather than face impeachment charges in the senate. His health had collapsed, but by 1978–79 he had recovered sufficiently to face trials and appeals on criminal charges.

Political favoritism. — Haydon Burns was governor of Florida from 1965 to 1967; before that he was mayor of Jacksonville. As mayor he had used political followers, dressed as "Burns's Blitzers," to stage campaign parades. The Blitzers, including many public employees given time off from work and those given city contracts, were also used in his campaign for the governorship. After election to office he issued written directives accompanied by written lists of campaign contributors to the effect that state credit cards be used and other purchases be made from those people listed. He proposed a large state bond issue for building state roads and sponsored the campaign with potential contractors' funds to pay for advertisements urging voter approval of the bond issue. But the electorate defeated it. Burns ran for reelection but was defeated in the democratic primary and retired from public office after a two-year term.

Effective public service but attention to private benefit. — Two examples will be given of good and effective public service but with questionable attention to private business benefits.

Robert L. F. Sikes was a member of the U. S. House of Representatives from the First Congressional District in West Florida from 1941 to 1979. During this period he was prominent as a member of the Armed Services Committee and the Arms Services Appropriations Subcommittee. During the attention to building up defense before World War II, he was instrumental in expansion of the U. S. Naval Air Station at Pensacola and in the establishment of Eglin and Tyndall fields in West Florida. He also supported agricultural legislation quite beneficial to West and North Florida growers of staple crops such as tobacco. He supported much New Deal legislation in the Roosevelt and Truman administrations and was active in support of Presidents Franklin Roosevelt, Harry Truman, John F. Kennedy, and Lyndon Johnson and the candidacy of Adlai Stevenson. Sikes sponsored many civic enterprises, and public centers in his district are sometimes named for him. He was dubbed the "he-coon" of Florida politics. In the 1970s the U. S. House of Representatives passed fiscal disclosure regulations, and investigations showed that some of Sikes's investments in stocks of defense companies were not reported. He also was involved in beach property purchases and in the installation of a private bank on the Pensacola

Left, Haydon Burns, governor, 1965 – 67. Below, Millard Caldwell, governor, 1945 – 49. Photos courtesy State Photographic Archives, Tallahassee.

naval base. As a consequence he had to resign important committee assignments or face being stripped of them by the Democratic Caucus. In the House there was a vote of reprimand but not of censure.

His case is an example of a person with ability and a significant service record who saw financial opportunities and engaged in activities not illegal at the time but contrary to later rules for members of the U. S. House of Representatives.

County Commissioner X is a farmer with fairly extensive agricultural holdings who also has a sand and gravel business from deposits on his land. This sand and gravel business is the only one in the county. During several terms on the county commission, the county road department purchased sand and gravel from him, paying only the standard rate. Because of possible conflict of interest, this commissioner did not vote on road contracts. It was public knowledge that he owned the sand and gravel business. To require the road departments to purchase outside the county would have meant paying higher costs for delivery.

During his terms on the commission, a county road was constructed which bordered his land. For the right of way the county paid him the appraised price of the land on which the road itself was to be built. He received the standard price set for other appraised or condemned land for right-of-way.

Having knowledge of this new road and believing that it would increase the value of certain adjacent properties, he bought some of this acreage from other owners and held it in anticipation of a rise in value after the road was announced.

There was nothing illegal in his doing business with the road department or in selling land for the road. In using knowledge from his official position and purchasing land from a neighbor he did nothing illegal, but was he acting unethically?

Styles and types of effective leadership. — Turning from examples of ethics and types of issues that may arise in politics, we now look at examples of styles of leadership and coalition building which illustrate different kinds of voter appeal.

Millard F. Caldwell was governor of Florida from 1945 to 1949. Emphasizing his administrative ability in the 1944 Democratic primary, he defeated a populist type of candidate. As governor at the close of World War II, he launched a strong drive for the Minimum Foundation Program for public schools, stressing that Florida could not grow unless the quality of public schools was improved. On this basis he enlisted strong support from civic clubs, chambers of commerce, PTAs, and the general citizenry, and he succeeded in securing this program from the legislature. With a surplus in the state treasury from funds accumulated during the war, he also launched a program to upgrade state roads. To secure better management of state government departments he introduced the first central state budget under the governor and cabinet. He was an effective, no-nonsense administrator who fulfilled his campaign promise that he would be an efficient administrator.

Fuller Warren, one of the most effective and entertaining speakers in Florida politics, followed Caldwell as governor. He waged a populist campaign, promising to modernize the state by upgrading laws affecting citrus crops, to prevent shipment of fruit before it was ripe. He also proposed legislation to increase auto tourism by improving roads and requiring that farmers with livestock have fenced pastures. (As late as 1948 cattle and hogs could graze on the road right-of-ways; if a motorist hit one, he was responsible for injury to the cow or other livestock.) Warren also pledged that there would not be a state sales tax.

The Green Fruit Law and the requirement that livestock be fenced were immediately passed by the legislature, but the wartime fiscal surplus was exhausted and new taxes had to be enacted. Finally a sales tax was passed, but before he would sign it the governor insisted it not be levied on food and medicine.

As an administrator Warren was out of his depth. He found administrative work distasteful, had little understanding of how to coordinate governmental matters, and had so many friends whom he wished to appoint that he often could not decide on who should fill an office. He left office without funds but continued to be in much demand as a public speaker.

Claude D. Pepper was elected to the U. S. Senate in 1936 and served until 1950, when he was defeated for reelection. During those 14 years he strongly supported the Roosevelt New Deal and the Truman programs that followed. He had put together a farmer-labor coalition with support from small business. He assumed national leadership; he was, along with Hugo Black, the most liberal of southern senators and one who ranked with any of the Democratic liberals nationally. As long as farmers needed price supports and orange growers needed purchases from federal school lunch funds, his base in Florida held firm. But by 1950, with prosperity and full employment returning to the state, Florida's voters had moved in a moderate-conservative direction. Pepper had stood in the 1940s as a leading advocate of national health insurance, but by 1950 the state as a whole had moved away from such programs. He also had advocated a moderate stance in regard to the U.S.S.R. which caused him, in the McCarthy period, to be dubbed by his opposition as "pink Pepper" or "red Pepper." So although an excellent speaker and an indefatigable campaigner, Pepper was defeated for the Democratic renomination. After his defeat, he tried again for the senate but again was unsuccessful. Meanwhile he resumed the practice of law and opened an office in Miami in addition to one in Tallahassee. In 1962 he returned to politics, this time from the more liberal constituency of Miami and Miami Beach. Since then he has been an effective member of the U.S. House of Representatives Rules Committee and chairman of the Subcommittee on Aging. In this latter capacity he resumed national leadership of legislation affecting the aged and legislation on health. President Johnson gave him one of the pens with which he had signed the bill establishing Medicare and Medicaid.

Pepper is an example of a political leader who, during his period in the senate, maintained a reasonably consistent position but whose political coalition disintegrated — not because of failure of political capacity but because of changes in social and economic base. He found a new political base in the smaller geographic confines of a U. S. House of Representatives congressional district. But once back on the national scene, his leadership qualities were again in evidence.

Another type of effective leadership is demonstrated by persons who have subject matter expertise in a particular field, thus having leadership qualities in a specific area of legislation. There are four good examples of such leaders in Florida.

Steven Pajcic, Duval County, has been an important member of the Florida House of Representatives. His mastery of taxation and public finance has given him great influence, and he has been chairman of the House Committee on Taxation. He and his staff have developed a knowledge of the yield of each form of taxes and of what is called the incidence of taxation—who ultimately pays each tax, how the burden falls on different income levels of citizens, different practices in other states, and how Florida's taxes compare with those levied elsewhere. Such information commands the respect of other legislators and gives him powerful influence when tax legislation is being prepared and enacted.

Claude Pepper, senator, 1936 – 50; congressman, 1962 –. Photo courtesy State Photographic Archives, Tallahassee.

Another example of such expertise bringing a leadership role is *Maxine Baker* of Dade County, who served in the Florida House of Representatives from 1963 to 1972. She made a special study of welfare legislation and of state institutions which treat the mentally ill in Florida and throughout the country. She influenced much legislation in these areas and brought about the enactment of what is called the Baker Act. This act not only provides for standards of treatment but also requires periodic reexamination and appraisal of inmates to avoid "warehousing" those originally placed in institutions for treatment.

Representative *Perry Murray* was a citrus farmer from Polk County. Elected speaker of the house in 1949, he already had an impressive career of leadership in the years after World War II. He sponsored state budget reform legislation; then as speaker he gave leadership to developing tax sources to meet the governmental problems attendant upon the growth of the state after the war. His career was cut short by an accident but not before he had won much respect and contributed greatly to the development of new procedures in government, education, and taxation.

The last example of this group is Representative *Gwendolyn Cherry*, who served in the House of Representatives from 1970 to her death in an accident in 1979. The first black in the legislature, a teacher and a lawyer, she had impact on legislation affecting both education and minorities. Her knowledge on such topics was a source of influence on committees and on legislative action, especially that affecting blacks and minorities.

All four of these examples illustrate the role of experience and the influence leaders may have based on their mastery of certain fields.

Leadership in the legal field. — Three individuals will be cited to illustrate leadership in the legal field and in the courts.

Richard W. Ervin was attorney general of Florida from 1949 to 1964 and then a justice of the Florida Supreme Court, which he served as chief justice from 1969 to 1971. During his second term in the elective office of attorney general, the U. S. Supreme Court in 1954 called for briefs from the states to the case of *Brown* v. *Board of Education*. Over the opposition of the governor, Attorney General Ervin filed a brief. This act of filing acknowledged that the Supreme Court could determine the matter of integration and issue an order to a state. The Florida brief was the only one filed by a southern state. Ervin presented evidence of Florida's citizens' attitudes on compliance and requested action that would provide gradual integration, starting in those sections of the state with greatest acceptance, then extending to the remainder of the state. In this way, he predicted, there would be peaceful compliance. This plan was the one ultimately adopted by the Court. Despite this unpopular stand on integration, Ervin was reelected attorney general and then to the state supreme court.

Chesterfield (H.) Smith is a lawyer with offices in Bartow and Lakeland, Florida. He has been president of the Florida Bar and also of the American Bar Association. In 1965 he was appointed chairman of the State Constitution Revision Commission. Under his guidance, the members of this commission studied the Florida Constitution and presented a draft to the legislature. Thus was the Florida Constitution and the structure of Florida government modernized. The proposals were modified somewhat by the legislature before being presented to the voters; they approved them in 1968 as the present state constitution. In 1973–74, as president-elect and then president of the American Bar Association, Smith spoke out against President Nixon's actions and called for appropriate investigation and impeachment. He aroused much controversy, but he felt public confidence would be restored after the rule of law was upheld.

Justice *Joseph W. Hatchett* was appointed by Governor Askew to the Florida Supreme Court in 1975, the first black justice on that court. Subsequently he was elected by the voters to a full term and in 1979 was nominated by President Carter (and subsequently confirmed by the senate) as a judge of the U. S. Fifth Circuit Court of Appeals. Those screening for the latter appointment found that his decisions were well reasoned and that he maintained a high reputation both for knowledge of the law and for fairness.

Left, Ruth Bryan Owen, congresswoman, 1929 – 33. Photo courtesy State Photographic Archives, Tallahassee. Below, Representative Steve Pajcic, 22d District of Florida. Photo courtesy Florida House of Representatives.

Other categories of leadership. — There are other varied qualities which account for the emergence of individuals as leaders. Some have personal qualities that attract voters and also have administrative capability. Others have administrative capability but lack appeal to voters. We will compare five who show various combinations of qualities.

Ruth Bryan Owen became one of the first women in the U. S. House of Representatives when she was elected from Miami in 1928 and reelected in 1932. She was selected by President Franklin Roosevelt as minister to Denmark, and later, under President Harry Truman, she was appointed an alternate delegate to the U. N. General Assembly. In addition to national and state political leadership, she made contributions to international policies.

Jack Eckerd came to Florida as a druggist and businessman and built up the Eckerd drugstore chain to become a multimillionaire. Desirous of performing public service in the 1970s he headed a group of businessmen who, at the request of Governor Askew, studied state government practices in all areas of management of state executive department affairs. They devoted much time to this service, and their findings were of great financial benefit to the state. He was then appointed by President Ford to head the U. S. General Services Administration. He returned to Florida and in 1978 won the Republican nomination for the governorship but lost the general election.

As a political candidate, Eckerd was not well informed on state issues in areas outside management. He was also not an effective speaker. But he showed leadership capacity in improving governmental administration. He is an example of a very effective business individual who can aid government in certain aspects but may not be able to attract votes and himself win public office.

Nelson Poynter came to Florida from Indiana when his family took over the *St. Petersburg Times* in the 1920s. He inherited ownership of the newspaper and built it into a regionwide circulating metropolitan daily. Serving a conservative area of the state, the paper developed in-depth reporting about governmental problems, local, state, and national. At the same time, the paper had good coverage of each locality and features such as sports, arts and leisure, church news, and real estate and business developments, with the result that it became a model of effective journalistic endeavor. Poynter found a need in Washington for a periodical which would present analysis of national issues. He founded the *Congressional Quarterly* and the *Congressional Quarterly Almanac*. These journals summarized the work of government agencies, ran leading articles on government issues, and charted the votes of congressmen. Their accuracy and penetration made them virtual necessities for journalists, business leaders, and students of government.

When Poynter died in 1978, he left his enterprises to a foundation which has pledged to continue these programs and to use part of the profits to study and assess newspapers, radio, and television and their impact on the public. Part of such study includes conferences among media representatives, government officials, and students of both the media and government.

Poynter showed great courage in probing critical issues of public concern and in publishing articles showing more than a stereotyped view of local, state, national, and international issues.

Reubin O'D. Askew, a member of the legislature from Pensacola, was elected governor of Florida for two four-year terms (1971–79). In his race in

1970 he broke from the pack of candidates by advocating a corporate income tax to distribute more equitably the burden of state taxation and to provide additional needed state revenue. A constitutional amendment to provide such taxes was proposed by the legislature, and Askew led the successful campaign for voter approval in 1972. Next he led another successful campaign to expand Florida's Government in the Sunshine Law to require fiscal disclosure by public officers. When the legislature refused to approve such legislation, he sponsored a drive to place this measure on the ballot through initiative petition. It was subsequently approved as a constitutional amendment. He regarded this law as a way of helping restore public confidence in the integrity of elected officials. He also sponsored important environmental legislation, state planning legislation, and a bond issue for the purchase of environmentally endangered lands. At the end of his administration, he led opposition to another petition amendment proposed to the state constitution, which would have legalized casino gambling on Miami Beach and in southern Broward County. In addition to the moral issue, he urged rejection because of prospective damage to law enforcement and to the reputation of the state as a desirable place for family tourism.

Reubin Askew, governor, 1971 – 79. Photo courtesy Office of Special Representative for Trade Negotiations, Washington.

Askew provided needed leadership in appointing women and blacks to public office. When vacancies occurred, he appointed a number of women as judges of the state's county and circuit courts. For a vacancy on the state supreme court he appointed a black justice, Joseph W. Hatchett. When the incumbent secretary of state resigned to run for another office, he appointed another black, Jesse J. McCrary, who thus became the first black state cabinet member to serve in the twentieth century. Askew defended busing to promote integration at a time when he was running for reelection and an anti-busing proposal was on the ballot. Interestingly, he carried the election overwhelmingly at the same time the public was voting strongly against busing.

Askew did not win all his battles. He failed to secure senate confirmation of an important appointee. He was not able to persuade the legislature to enact fiscal disclosure. He then turned to the use of initiative petition to amend the constitution; he succeeded, but he never secured full implementing legislation. He campaigned in 1978 for a constitution revision proposal that would abolish the cabinet as elected individuals and permit the governor to appoint them, but he failed to secure voter approval. He endorsed the Equal Rights Amendment, but the legislature did not approve it. He did not show special concern for either higher education or public education so far as proposing programs or increasing financial support. He did sponsor improvements for state prisons and state hospitals.

In Askew we have another example of the role of leadership in focusing timely public attention and providing proposed solutions on many emergent issues. The reputation that Askew gained as governor became national in scope. In 1972 he was offered the Democratic vice-presidential nomination, but he refused it. There was movement in several states for campaigns to nominate him as the Democratic presidential candidate in 1976, but he would not endorse such campaigns. Upon leaving the governorship he resumed the practice of law, this time in Miami, and accepted some assignments in a consulting capacity to the president. In 1979 he was appointed by the president as ambassador in charge of trade negotiations, and he moved to Washington. In 1983, he launched an unsuccessful campaign for the Democratic presidential nomination.

Leroy Collins was a member of the state legislature from Leon County (Tallahassee) from 1934 to 1954 and rose to a position of leadership in that body. Following the death of Governor Dan McCarty in 1953, Senate President Charley Johns became governor until a special election could be held in 1954 to fill the remaining two years of the unexpired term. Thereupon Collins and Johns ran for the two-year term, which Collins won. After that term, the state supreme court ruled that Collins could run for the succeeding four-year term, which he also won.

Collins was an effective governor. Holding office during the period of integration, he assumed a moderate position. He argued at first that integration should not be forced; but once court decisions were made, he complied and provided protection for integration of local schools as well as integration of the state universities. He successfully led the movement for construction of the Sunshine State Parkway. He sought unsuccessfully to promote reapportionment and to stimulate state constitutional revision, but the rural-dominated legislature thwarted him in both efforts.

By the end of his administration he had risen to national stature and was chosen as chairman of the National Governors Conference and as keynote speaker and presiding chairman of the Democratic National Convention of 1960. Leaving the governorship, he became chairman of the National Association of

Broadcasters. Following the election of Lyndon Johnson, he became director of Community Affairs, with the principal duty of improving race relations in troubled communities. Returning to Florida, he ran for the U. S. Senate in 1968; he was dubbed "ultra-liberal" and was defeated by the Republican candidate, Edward Gurney. He then practiced law in Tallahassee, served as a hard-working member of the State Constitutional Revision Commission of 1977–78, and spoke out against capital punishment.

Our leaders summarized. — These vignettes of leaders in Florida politics show a variety of ways in which leadership may be attained and exercised. The first group illustrates a number of problems related to corruption. The next group was involved with ethical issues which do not fall under the legal definition of corruption. The different styles of leadership presented illustrate that there is no single model of a leader. This factor demonstrates that representative government functions are best defined as pluralistic, that is, with interaction between leaders and followers.

Energy

The problems of energy shortages are having and will continue to have a strong effect on the state of Florida. In 1973–74 the Arab oil embargo brought about a sharp recession. Subsequently, until 1979, the situation improved, as did the national and state economies. Despite the seriousness of current problems, polls show that a majority of citizens do not accept the idea that energy is limited; they think that there is a conspiracy of the oil companies and that once prices of gasoline and diesel oil go above a particular amount shortages will disappear.

The evidence is decidedly to the contrary, and the impact on the U. S. and on Florida will cause extensive readjustment, at both levels, in people's life styles, and in government policies. Here we are primarily concerned with the effects of energy problems on government policies and what alternative policies are available regarding use of finite fossil fuels.

Americans have built their lives on the expectation of cheap and plentiful energy. The U. S. has 5 percent of the world's population but was responsible for 29.9 percent of the world consumption of energy in 1976. Earlier, when we were consuming our own resources, one might have defended our consumption, although our supplies of oil had peaked because of such use; today we import annually about half of the oil we use.

Our basic assumption is that cheap energy from whatever source is at an end, and we have not a temporary shortage but a permanent situation. What kind of drastic changes and readjustments might be expected?

Fortunately America is still rich in some other fossil fuels which can replace oil, principally coal. Before we turned to oil because it was cheaper, coal was the major source of energy in the U. S. There are still plentiful deposits. It costs more to mine coal than to obtain oil, and coal supplies are not sufficiently great that it can be expected to replace all oil as a gasoline source. Such use would lead to exhaustion of coal supplies and would push the cost of coal to prohibitive levels. But to provide heat, power, and electricity at a cost higher than that of using oil is well within present technology.

Other partial substitutes for oil can be found in shale deposits and in heavy oil-like deposits called tarsoils. These can be extracted to provide fuel and gasoline but at a much higher cost than that of presently used fuels or of coal. The processing of shale oil and tarsoils demands access to extensive supplies of energy and the use of large quantities of water. The water needed is in areas of the West where there is already competition for water use by agriculture, by metropolitan areas, and by existing industries. In addition, the processing would cause considerable ecological damage and problems of disposal of large supplies of crushed rocks and other spoil materials.

Electric power can be provided by nuclear power plants, but these present a number of problems. The cost of building such plants has increased vastly, and there are problems of the disposal of nuclear waste and of safety.

Solar energy offers a virtually inexhaustible source. A Harvard Business School study in 1979 estimated that this source of energy is more promising than any other and that after ten years it could account for up to 20 percent of America's energy use. Of lesser importance are such possible sources of energy as wind power or alcohol from grains. Hydroelectric power is capable of only small additional development.

Of the important changes that are to come, the primary one will be a turning away from the motor vehicle for long-distance transportation. The 1979 trucking strike over the cost of diesel fuel was symptomatic of more than a temporary stringency. The efficiency ratio of freight trains to trucks is one to four; that is, a freight train is four times as efficient in hauling tonnage as a truck, according to studies by the National Science Foundation and by the Batelle Institute. This fact has been obscured temporarily because of tax-supported highways, especially the interstate highway systems, in combination with low fuel costs. We may expect an end to long-distance trucking and the rejuvenation of rail transport.

By the same token there will be greater use of public transportation by individuals. Airline, bus, and train travel is already increasing, and there is less intercity transportation by automobile. A rejuvenation of passenger train service to match that existing in most Western countries and in Japan will bring even further increases in train travel.

Within localities, public transportation in the form of bus and ultimately in city surface or subway transport may be expected to increase. One effect of such an increase will be the limiting of the spread of cities. More people will walk to public transportation stations, and real estate may develop accordingly, pointing to a likely redevelopment of the central city.

To meet heating and ventilation needs homes will be smaller and better insulated, and natural ventilation may replace so much dependence on air conditioning. Cluster housing, apartments, and condominiums may be expected to increase in proportion to single houses, each with a lot.

Many people are expected to continue to move to Florida because of the higher cost of fuel in colder climates. There will have to be serious readjustments in the state, but there also will be new attractions for a different type of Florida living. For example, Florida's tourist attractions could be clustered, and visitors could reach them by public transportation, then move from one attraction to another on foot or by public transport. In the long run, some manufacturing may move to Florida, thus giving the state a more balanced economy. Some of these projections are speculative, but many are based on studies of energy supplies and projected energy demands that would have to be met if Americans' life styles were to continue. It was projected that Florida's electric consumption will double or triple in the next several decades and that U. S. consumption would likewise increase greatly. But with available energy sources, these consumption demands cannot be met. Consequently, what we have done is to project decreased energy sources and then to consider adaptations accordingly. America made a bad error when the interstate highway system was projected in the 1950s and completed in the following 20 years. Other countries more realistically maintained local rapid transit systems and improved passenger and freight capacity by rail.

In the fuel crisis of 1974 the State of Florida developed a small Office of Energy, placed in the Department of Administration. In 1979 this office was moved to the Office of the Governor, and the governor himself has devoted considerable time to energy problems. In the long run, however, federal energy policies will determine state policies. At the time of World War II the government was highly successful in developing artificial rubber; the government supplied capital for plant construction but ultimately sold the plants to private producers without monetary loss. The same process took place under government auspices in aluminum production. Nuclear energy too developed under government auspices; the government continued production of nuclear fuel but licensed private electric generating plants.

In the 1930s, without tax expenditure or government borrowing, the Tennessee Valley Authority was created as a federally chartered corporation; it offered bonds for sale but did not use federal tax monies. It vastly increased electric productivity, as did rural electrification cooperatives, which, also as federally chartered corporations, developed both generating plants and distribution lines in much of rural America. Prior to that time rural electrification had not been carried successfully by private enterprise alone; extensive government stimulation was needed, and it worked. Again, under current conditions, we can wait decades for possible private development of alternative energy sources. But even though we are often critical of government intervention, we observe that one of the important roles of government is that of facilitator and stimulator. At present, U. S. dependence on energy sources abroad makes us extremely vulnerable in foreign policy and contributes to inflation. Consequently, there is every reason to expect forthcoming federal government action. At the same time, such government stimulation can take place without a great centralized operating program. As it did in rubber and aluminum production and rural electrification, the government can act as stimulator, but the operating agency is a decentralized government-chartered corporation or private enterprise.

States and localities must give careful attention to planning proper locations for closer living clusters, access to public beaches and parks, and, above all, improved public transportation. All of these plans will require coordination by federal, state, and local governmental agencies. There is a state Department of Transportation, but building some public transportation may be on contract and not all of it need be planned and built by government.

Inflation

Inflation, affecting all U. S. citizens, is a problem of the national economy. It is also in part a derivative of the energy shortage, and both of these matters are affected by federal policies. For state and local governments inflation has important effects. If government wages are to keep up with inflation and if supplies are to be purchased, then budgeted amounts must be increased. Citizens still in their earning and working years may expect to have earning increases. Some retirement and some Social Security beneficiaries receive payments at least partially geared to the rate of inflation. But many retirees who are on fixed incomes, such as those dependent on fixed interest payments from bonds or on fixed pensions, find that the checks they receive have decreasing purchasing power. Consequently their ability to pay taxes lessens. In such cases an increasing tension develops between the price levels and tax rates.

If government services are to be maintained in a period of inflation, increasing revenue becomes necessary. Several of the principal sources of Florida's tax revenue do go up with inflation. The chief state revenue source is the sales tax, 5 percent on all items purchased except food and drugs; these exceptions give some relief to citizens on fixed incomes. For years Florida's gasoline tax, the primary source of road and bridge funds, was fixed at 8 cents per gallon. When road funds became increasingly inadequate because of inflation, the 1983 legislature changed the formula to increase state and local road funds. The primary revenue source for local governments is the property tax. Florida law requires periodic reassessment of real property values.

The unionization of teachers and other government employees intensifies wage demands in annual collective bargaining sessions. Elective officials ultimately set annual pay raises. Possibly to decrease these pressures, some Florida governmental units contract out for certain services, such as trash and garbage collection. In any event bargaining on public employees' salaries has become an area of increasing stress.

Other Problems

Health. — Rising medical and hospital costs are another matter of increasing public concern. Health costs have increased more rapidly over the last decade than any other part of an individual's expenditures. Florida's increasing number of senior citizens make this general problem a most pressing one for the state. If a more comprehensive plan of national health service or insurance is provided, the state and local government role may not be so great. But the Florida legislature has a requirement for the reporting of hospital costs, and there will be increasing pressure for some limitation on such costs. Also, it may be expected that either under national auspices or through citizens' movements there will be increasing adoption of health maintenance organizations (HMOs). Such organizations are most extensive in California and Minnesota but are well known elsewhere. Under an HMO, an individual or a family pays a fixed annual rate, which entitles those covered to medical examination and to whatever treatment is necessary throughout the year. The HMO charges may also include hospital care, home nursing, rest home payments, and drugs, in which case the annual rate is increased. Provisions of an HMO apply to sizable groups, and payments are usually made through payroll deductions covering all those employed in a large enterprise or in a particular type of work. In some places in Florida such systems exist, for example, in Tampa for over 70 years. A group of doctors or a clinic is necessary for such a contract, with a result that the individual patient cannot specify a particular doctor. Medical circles object to the limitation on the patient-doctor relationship and to the fact that the doctor or surgeon is on a fixed fee or salary.

Because of the increasing number of aged in Florida, the caliber of service provided by nursing homes is an increasing problem. For some time state inspection and licensing have been required, but they will receive increasing attention.

Social services. — Florida's level of payments to those on welfare is low compared with the national average (chapter 20), and this low rate is expected to continue. The Florida Legislature shows concern for maintenance of standards in public institutions and rest homes; it also is concerned with having more weeks of unemployment coverage when the unemployment rate is high, but the payment rate to an individual is not high. In this respect, the legislature responds to the moderate-conservative pattern of the state voters. There is also concern that a higher rate of welfare payments might attract welfare migrants from other states. Consequently, it is difficult to predict any substantial rise in the rate of social service payments.

Housing. — The rapid rise of interest rates in combination with inflation and with the growth of Florida's population has brought great pressure on housing

Seminary Lane, a low-income housing development built under the auspices of the Gainesville Housing Authority. Photo courtesy Michael Dunlap.

construction, slowing down the rate of home and apartment building by Florida's extensive construction industry. As a consequence, multifamily units such as condominiums and mobile home communities have appeared in every part of Florida. There has been great pressure for low-cost housing, but shortages also exist at all levels. Many apartments are being converted to condominiums: in 1979, 10,000 apartment units in Dade County (Miami) and 7,000 in Broward County (Ft. Lauderdale) were converted, and renters were required either to purchase or to be displaced. There is pressure for local or state moratoriums on such conversions in some parts of the state. Housing presents yet another problem which impacts on government policies at state and local levels.

Some general problems. — America and Florida have increasing numbers of citizens over 65, who will form a larger proportion of the population. To achieve a desirable life style for this part of the population, there will have to be new departures in social and medical services. Increased population density means a greater need for government to protect the quality of air and the environment. Steps were taken in this direction with the passage of the Environmentally Endangered Lands Act in 1972, but continual vigilance on the part of citizens is necessary. There is increasing public concern over both public school and higher education, including research (chapter 19). A statewide testing program instituted by the legislature requires students to pass examinations in English and mathematics before receiving high school diplomas. Other requirements have been introduced for admission of students to colleges of education and for competency tests before college graduates are certified to teach. The 1983 legislature provided an additional $230 million to upgrade schools, and a part of the program will require a system of merit pay for teachers beginning in 1984. Blacks and more recently arrived minorities continue to face many problems (chapter 15). The issue of criminal justice shows Florida's particular involvement with the courts and the law (chapter 10B). Increased leisure time provided by our society has provoked government action in the arts and recreation. Citizens are increasingly concerned with tax issues (chapter 17), producing much antigovernment feeling.

Thus there is a dilemma caused by public pressure to provide services and the necessity of finding revenue to pay for those services. Florida has tried considerable experimentation in providing such services efficiently and in the restructuring of government agencies at all levels for more efficient use of time, money, and personnel. This acceptance of change will continue to be necessary as new problems arise and as the density of population brings about added complexities.

Revenue Sharing and Tax Problems

At the end of the first year of the Reagan administration, Florida faced increased problems in maintaining service programs. Federal revenue-sharing sources in categorical and block grants suffered a reduction of half a billion dollars, a figure that may double. These reductions threaten Medicare, Medicaid, health programs, clean air programs, and the upgrading of sanitary sewer and water pollution programs, among others. Compounding the loss of federal revenue, the increase of the homestead exemption in 1980 from $5,000 to an eventual $25,000 resulted in a fiscal crisis affecting especially cities, counties, and schools; thus the pressure on the 1982 legislature for an additional one cent state sales tax and other tax adjustments.

Conclusions

Florida today stands as a southern state, but except in the northern tier of counties this southern background is not a dominant factor in state politics. Rather, like the other rapid growth states of the nation — California, Arizona, Nevada, and, to a degree, Texas — Florida is entering another period of change. The problems discussed here all have impact on the political process. The moderate-conservative social and economic basis of most of the state is not likely to be modified, but the energy issue, inflation, growth, and the changing age of the population all present sharp challenges to governmental institutions. There is no sign that the number or intensity of these problems will decrease. Under these circumstances the citizen is best advised to give serious attention to elections and to the political process. Such citizen impact is vital in the democratic process.

Appendix 1

Florida Cabinet

Governor: D. Robert Graham
*Lieutenant Governor: Wayne Mixson
Secretary of State: George Firestone
Comptroller and Banking Commissioner: Gerald Lewis
Treasurer and Insurance Commissioner: William Gunter
Attorney General: Jim Smith
Commissioner of Agriculture: Doyle Connor
Commissioner of Education: Ralph D. Turlington

*Not a cabinet member.
Office address of each is State Capitol, Tallahassee, Florida.
Terms from the first Tuesday after the first Monday in January 1983 to first Tuesday after first Monday in January 1987.

Supreme Court Justices

Chief Justice: James E. Alderman
Justices: James Adkins, Jr
Joseph Boyd
Raymond Ehrlich
Ben Overton
Parker Lee McDonald
Leander J. Shaw, Jr.
Staff: Sid S. White, Clerk
Tony Similgin, Marshal
Brian Polley, Librarian

The Supreme Court is located just west of the State Capitol in Tallahassee, Florida.

Governors of Florida

Territorial

Andrew Jackson	1821–22 (Florida Territories)
William Duval	1822–34 (first territorial governor)
John H. Eaton	1834–36
Richard K. Call	1836–39
Robert Raymond Reed	1839–41
Richard K. Call	1841–44
John Branch	1844–45

State

William D. Moseley	1845–49
Thomas Brown	1849–53
James E. Broome	1853–57
Madison S. Perry	1857–61
John Milton	1861–65
William Marvin	1865–66
David S. Walker	1866–68
Harrison Reed	1868–73
Samuel T. Day	1872 (acting governor during impeachment proceedings against Governor Reed)
Ossian B. Hart	1873–74
Marcellus L. Stearns	1873 (acting governor, June–November)
Marcellus L. Stearns	1874–77
George F. Drew	1877–81
William D. Bloxham	1881–85
Edward A. Perry	1885–89
Francis P. Fleming	1889–93
Henry L. Mitchell	1893–97
William D. Bloxham	1897–1901
William S. Jennings	1901–5
Napoleon Bonaparte Broward	1905–9
Albert W. Gilchrist	1909–13
Park Trammell	1913–17
Sidney J. Catts	1917–21
Cary A. Hardee	1921–25
John W. Martin	1925–29
Doyle E. Carlton	1929–33
David Scholtz	1933–37
Fred P. Cone	1937–41
Spessard L. Holland	1941–45
Millard F. Caldwell	1945–49
Fuller Warren	1949–53
Dan T. McCarty	1953 (died September 1953)
Charley E. Johns	1953–55 (acting governor)
LeRoy Collins	1955–61
Farris Bryant	1961–65
Haydon Burns	1965–67
Claude Kirk, Jr.	1967–71

Reubin Askew	1971–79
D. Robert Graham	1979–

Appendix 2

Executive Documents

Governor. — The governor delivers a message which is printed in the legislative *Journal*. His other speeches appear in mimeograph form as press releases. His most important printed document is his budget, issued to the legislature with his recommendations for specific expenditures for the coming year. He also recommends taxes to bring in income to balance the expenditures in the budget. The budget is a long and detailed document; it is the basis for legislative hearings by the appropriate fiscal committees, and it becomes the basis for the Appropriations Act.

Other executive departments. — Executive documents are printed by each department of the state government. The secretary of state prints many important series of state documents, including *Election Laws of the State of Florida* and *Primary and General Election Returns by County*. The latter includes returns only for state offices; election returns for county and city offices are not printed. The student interested in local elections must secure county and precinct returns from the local elections officer. It should be observed that under the Florida Sunshine Law all single copies of printed documents are a matter of public record. Thus office records can be examined unless they relate to personal records of individuals who are not seeking public election or appointment. Such noncandidate records are open to the supervisor and to the individual concerned, but not to third parties.

Other cabinet officers, in addition to the secretary of state, issue annual reports of the work of their offices. The attorney general issues an important printed series entitled *Opinions of the Attorney General*. These interpret Florida laws and questions referred to the attorney general by state and local officials for his ruling. They are binding unless a different interpretation is given on such a matter in a court case.

Other Florida departments of government issue many reports and rulings which are binding on employees and on citizens. For such a ruling to be given, a hearing must be held under the Florida Administrative Procedures Act. Such rulings concern matters not covered in detail in statutes passed by the legislature, and they are binding unless changed by the legislature itself or by a later administrative ruling. For example, administrative rulings may cover the detail of how hunting licenses are issued or revoked, motor vehicle registration hours, rules governing public employees, public school regulations, university requirements for degrees, and so on.

Judicial Documents

All court decisions are, of course, public documents and are available through the clerk of the court. Florida Supreme Court reports are printed and are found in the *Southern Reporter.* Court reports interpret the constitution and the law, and higher court decisions may overrule lower court decisions. There are numerous indexes to court decisions by case and topic. Federal court decisions are also printed, starting at the top with *United States Supreme Court Reports*.

Local Government Documents

City charters, and amendments thereto, are printed, although the amendments may be in typewritten form until there is a periodic updating. They are found at the office of the city clerk and usually at the city attorney's office. Except for the annual fiscal report, other city documents are not usually printed. The record of the journal of a city or county commission is found in the office of the appropriate clerk. The city building code is usually printed and is public, in any event. Records of other city departments are public except for employee personnel files. City or county ordinances are also kept in the office of the appropriate clerk.

Election returns for local units of government are found in the files of the appropriate supervisor of elections or clerk.

Special Districts

Reports of special districts or special bodies, such as regional planning councils and special drainage and fire districts, are found in offices of such districts. An exception exists when a county commission acts as a special urban service district, in which case the records are kept by the county.

Other Special Data Services

The *County and City Data Book* is published by the U.S. Bureau of the Census. It contains many data on population and financial matters concerning local units of government. The same is true of the state volumes of the decennial U.S. Census for each state. Likewise, much demographic and fiscal data is issued by the U.S. Bureau of the Census on computer tapes. These can be used to analyze distribution of income, business data, etc., for each unit of government, city or county, and for smaller units within each county known as census tracts or census enumeration districts. The student of the social sciences will find this material of great use in analyzing social problems, and it is also of value to the business community and to government officials and planners.

A Note on Florida State Documents

Legislative documents.—Unlike the federal government, Florida has no state printing office. State documents are contracted to private printers, a procedure followed by other states. Since Florida was admitted to the union in 1845, its two principal documents have been the *Journal of the Florida House* and the *Journal of the Florida Senate*. These are printed daily while the legislature is in regular or special session. Copies appear on members' desks each morning, containing the events of the previous day's session. Unlike the *Congressional Record* printed by the U.S. Government Printing Office for the Congress, speeches and remarks of members are not printed in these journals. They contain simply the list of bills introduced, the record of the committees to which these are referred, and the records of the work on the floor of the house and senate. These journals record passage of the bill on first, second, or third reading, text of amendments adopted, a summary of the vote for or against the bill on each reading, and, if enough members request it, a list of the roll-call vote with all pro and con votes by name on each amendment on passage and a further record of the disposition of the bill after veto. At the end of the session, the *Journal* is bound, with an index of bills by number and topic.

Each bill introduced is given a number, for example, HB1, SB1. Joint resolutions, such as proposals for constitutional amendments, are given a separate number sequence, such as HJR1 or SJR1.

The clerks of the house and senate each print as separate documents a list of house and senate members with brief biographical sketches. They also print booklets containing the rules of each body and a list of each body's committees and committee members.

A calendar is printed by the clerk and the secretary containing the scheduled time and place of committee hearings. This record is maintained on a computer, and there is a computer listing in each office of the status of each bill in terms of place before committee, place on calendar, etc. Proceedings of committees are available from committee staff but are rarely printed. The governor's message at the start of a session is usually printed in the *Journal*.

Copies of bills as introduced are printed and sent to each member. The official sequence is kept by the clerk of the house and secretary of the senate. When the bills are reported out to the floor of house or senate, proposed amendments are printed.

All laws remain in force unless repealed, except for the annual or biennial appropriations act. This act, which remains in force for only one or two years, authorizes expenditure of state funds and is not a permanent part of the statutes or laws of the state.

Parties, Organizations, and Lobbies

Republican Party

Executive Director
103 E. Call St.
Tallahassee, FL 32302

301 1st St., S.E.
Washington, DC 20003

Democratic Party

State Headquarters
P.O. Box 1758
Tallahassee, FL 32302

1625 Massachusetts Ave., N.W.
Washington, DC 20036

Florida Chamber of Commerce

P.O. Box 5497
Tallahassee, FL 32301

Florida Bar Association

Tallahassee, FL 32301

Common Cause

222 W. Pensacola St., Room 126
Tallahassee, FL 32301

2030 M St., N.W.
Washington, DC 20036

League of Women Voters

2119 Carroll Garden Lane
Tampa, FL 33617

1730 M St., N.W.
Washington, DC 20036

NAACP

1790 Broadway
New York, NY 10019

AFL–CIO

2972 Waller St.
Jacksonville, FL 32205

815 16th St., N.W.
Washington, DC 20006

Index